John Senior.

ELECTRONIC COMMUNICATIONS

Second Edition

Electronic Communications

Second Edition

DENNIS RODDY
JOHN COOLEN

Lakehead University
Thunder Bay, Ontario
Canada

Reston Publishing Company, Inc.
Reston, Virginia
A Prentice-Hall Company

Library of Congress Cataloging in Publication Data
Roddy, Dennis
  Electronic communications.
  Includes index.
  1. Telecommunication. 2. Electronics.
I. Coolen, John, joint author. II Title.
TK5101.R56   1980   621.38   80-13291
ISBN 0-8359-1631-6

© 1981 by
Reston Publishing Company, Inc.
A Prentice-Hall Company
Reston, Virginia

10 9 8 7 6 5 4

Printed in the United States of America

Contents

Preface

This book is intended for use in the final year of a technology program in telecommunications. The level of treatment presupposes a detailed knowledge of electronics, mathematics, and basic electric circuits, such as form part of most telecommunications technology programs at community colleges and technical institutes.

Some repetition of basic material is included for the sake of completeness, but the applications and illustrative examples are all directed towards the field of telecommunications. The text covers in considerable detail communications fundamentals, circuits, modulation, transmission and radiation, and systems, including data transmission and line communications.

Our thanks go to the reviewers who at an early stage in the writing suggested the five sections into which the chapters are now grouped, and who provided much helpful detailed criticism. Our thanks also go to the many people and organizations who provided information such as drawings and data sheets, and to Sherry Goldbecker and the staff of Reston Publishing Company who made the book possible.

Dennis Roddy
John Coolen
Lakehead University
Thunder Bay, Ontario

PREFACE TO SECOND EDITION

In this second edition the material has been reorganized along lines suggested by reviewers and users. The opportunity has also been taken to include up-to-date material on integrated circuits and special transistor packages specifically intended for communications circuits, and a new chapter has been included on Digital Communications.

To make room for these additions the chapters on Untuned Amplifiers, and Power Supplies have been dropped, as most of this material can be found in Electronics Texts; only topics of particular applicability to communications have been retained and incorporated in the relevant chapter sections relating to area of application. The opportunity has also been taken to correct those errors which have been drawn to the attention of the authors.

As with the first edition, our thanks go to those companies which supplied an abundance of useful data and information on their products. Progress in analog microcircuits is as impressive as that in the digital field, and unfortunately it was not possible to include descriptions of all the many new circuits and applications available. The reader is referred to the excellent Application Notes and Data Handbooks provided by manufacturers, a partial listing of these being: G.E. Transistor Manual, Motorola Application Notes, National Semiconductor Linear Applications Handbook, RCA Linear Integrated Circuits Handbook SSD-240, and Signetics Analog Data Manual.

Dennis Roddy
John Coolen
Lakehead University
Thunder Bay, Ontario

Part One
Communications Fundamentals

Chapter 1
Analysis of
Passive Circuits

1.1 INTRODUCTION

Passive circuits are those which contain only resistance, inductance, and capacitance (or their equivalents, as in the case of certain types of filters described in Section 1.15). Many such circuits are encountered in electronic communication systems, and some of the more usual ones will be examined in this chapter. It is assumed that the student is familiar with the basic circuit concepts and laws (as found, for example, in B. Zeines, *Electric Circuit Analysis*, Reston Publishing Company, Inc., Reston, Va., 1972); some of the more important results are summarized in Sections 1.3 and 1.5.

1.2 SOURCE REPRESENTATION

The voltage or current source supplying a circuit may also be represented by circuit components, but should be separately identifiable from the circuit itself. The two idealized source representations most commonly used are the *constant–voltage equivalent circuit*, Fig. 1.1(a) and the *constant–current equivalent circuit*, Fig. 1.1(b). In both cases, R_s represents the internal resistance of the source. For the voltage circuit, E represents the generated EMF, there being zero resistance within the E circle. E is constant, that is, it is independent of the loading applied to the terminals; it may, of course, be time–varying. For the current circuit, I is the generated current, the resistance of the generator branch being infinite. I is constant, i.e., independent of external loading; but also, of course, it may be time–varying.

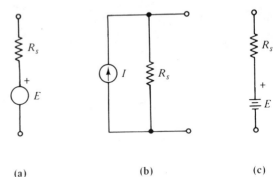

FIGURE 1.1. Source representations: (a) Voltage; (b) Current; (c) Battery.

(a) (b) (c)

      A given source may be represented by either one of these circuits; that is, they are alternative ways of looking at the same source. The choice of which equivalent circuit to use is often a matter of personal preference, although the physical source may suggest the most appropriate one; a good example of this is the battery, represented as shown in Fig. 1.1(c).

1.3 SUMMARY OF BASIC RESULTS FOR RESISTIVE NETWORKS

      A voltage V (which may be time-varying) applied to a constant resistance R results in a current I given by Ohm's law:

$$V = I \cdot R \qquad (1.1)$$

Conventionally, the voltage and current are represented by arrows, as shown in Fig. 1.2(a); the current arrow shows the direction of conventional current flow (which may be real positive–charge movement in the direction of the arrow, or electron movement in the opposite direction), while the voltage arrow points to the more positive of the two terminals. Keeping in mind that conventional current flows from the more positive to the less positive terminal, it will be seen that the two arrows convey the same information, but this little bit of redundancy turns out to be useful in circuit analysis. In some texts the voltage arrow is replaced by a + sign, as shown in Fig. 1.2(b). Again it is well to keep in mind that this is not a direct–current

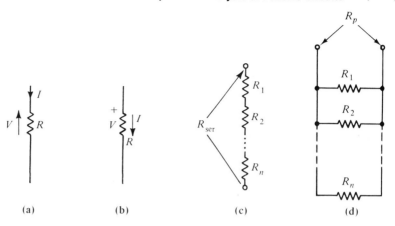

(a)   (b)   (c)   (d)

FIGURE 1.2. Symbols for Voltage, Current and Resistance: (a) Conventional Symbols for Voltage and Current; (b) Alternative Symbols for Voltage and Current; (c) Total Resistance of a Series group; (d) Total Resistance of a Parallel group.

symbol, as the voltage may be time-varying. The current may also be indicated by an arrow alongside the component symbol, Fig. 1.2(b).

The effective series resistance R_{ser} of the chain of resistors shown in Fig. 1.2(c) is given by

$$R_{ser} = R_1 + R_2 + \cdots + R_n \qquad (1.2)$$

The effective parallel resistance R_p of the network shown in Fig. 1.2(c) is obtained from

$$\frac{1}{R_p} = \frac{1}{R_1} + \frac{1}{R_2} + \cdots + \frac{1}{R_n} \qquad (1.3)$$

In terms of conductance G, this can be written as

$$G_p = G_1 + G_2 + \cdots + G_n \qquad (1.4)$$

Where only two resistors are involved, Eq. (1.3) may be rearranged to give

$$R_p = \frac{R_1 \cdot R_2}{R_1 + R_2} \qquad (1.5)$$

As a check on calculations, it is worth noting that the effective series resistance will always be greater than the greatest single resistance in the chain, while the effective parallel resistance will always be less than the least single resistance in the parallel network.

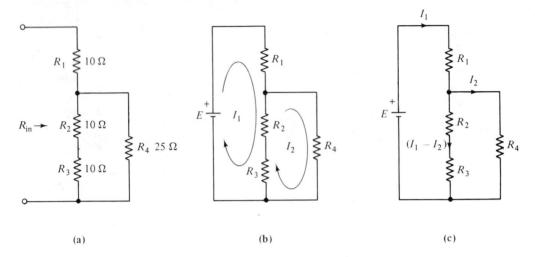

FIGURE 1.3. (a) A series–parallel circuit. The circuit currents: (b) Mesh; (c) Branch.

1.4 ANALYSIS OF RESISTIVE CIRCUITS

A *series–parallel circuit* is shown in Fig. 1.3(a). Note that the three 10-Ω resistors are *not* in series because they do not carry the same current. To find the effective input resistance of this circuit, i.e., the resistance between the terminals, first combine R_2 and R_3 in series to give

$$(R_2 + R_3) = 10 + 10 = 20 \ \Omega$$

Next combine R_4 in parallel with $(R_2 + R_3)$:

$$= \frac{25 \times 20}{20 + 20} = 11.1 \ \Omega$$

Finally, add this value to R_1 in series, so that the effective input resistance R_{in} is

$$R_{in} = 10 + 11.1 = 21.1 \ \Omega$$

Proper application of Kirchhoff's loop (or mesh) equations can considerably simplify circuit analysis; although their use may not be justified in such a simple circuit as shown in Fig. 1.3(a), this will be used to illustrate the principle. This circuit is redrawn in Fig. 1.3(b), with a battery source E applied. The input resistance R_{in} is

$$R_{in} = \frac{E}{I_1} \qquad (1.6)$$

Current I_1 is imagined to circulate around the loop consisting of E, R_1, R_2, and R_3, and current I_2 around loop R_2, R_3, and R_4. The actual currents would be as shown in Fig. 1.3(c), but it will be seen that for both circuits the current carried by R_2 and R_3 is the same, $I_1 - I_2$. The advantage of the first method is that the Kirchhoff's loop equations can be written down systematically; thus, from Fig. 1.3(b), following the circulating currents clockwise around each loop,

$$E = I_1(R_1 + R_2 + R_3) - I_2(R_2 + R_3)$$
$$0 = -I_1(R_2 + R_3) + I_2(R_2 + R_3 + R_4)$$

Solving these by the use of determinants,

$$I_1 = \frac{\begin{vmatrix} E & -(R_2 + R_3) \\ 0 & R_2 + R_3 + R_4 \end{vmatrix}}{\begin{vmatrix} R_1 + R_2 + R_3 & -(R_2 + R_3) \\ -(R_2 + R_3) & R_2 + R_3 + R_4 \end{vmatrix}}$$

$$= \frac{E(R_2 + R_3 + R_4)}{(R_1 + R_2 + R_3)(R_2 + R_3 + R_4) - (R_2 + R_3)^2}$$

Therefore, $\quad R_{in} = \dfrac{E}{I_1} = \dfrac{(R_1 + R_2 + R_3)(R_2 + R_3 + R_4) - (R_2 + R_3)^2}{R_2 + R_3 + R_4}$

$$= R_1 + R_2 + R_3 - \frac{(R_2 + R_3)^2}{R_2 + R_3 + R_4}$$

Using the values given in the example,

$$R_{in} = 10 + 10 + 10 - \frac{(10 + 10)^2}{10 + 10 + 25}$$

$$= 30 - \frac{400}{45}$$

$$= 21.1 \ \Omega$$

1.4.1 Simple Potentiometer

The *potentiometer* (or *potential divider*) consists of a resistor which has a variable tapping point, as shown in Fig. 1.4(a). Assume constant input voltage E, and let the potentiometer tap be set at some fraction a of the total resistance R. It is required to find the output voltage V_L in terms of the other quantities. Applying Kirchhoff's voltage laws to the loops containing I_1 and I_2,

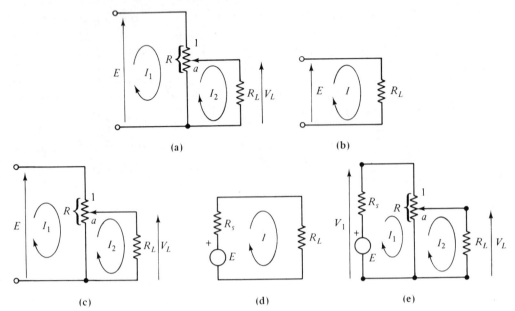

FIGURE 1.4. (a) Resistive potentiometer; (b) and (c) Used to determine insertion loss I_2/I. (d) and (e) Used to determine insertion loss I_2/I taking into account source resistance.

$$E = I_1 R - I_2 aR$$

$$0 = -I_1 aR + I_2(aR + R_L)$$

Solve for I_2:

$$I_2 = \frac{\begin{vmatrix} R & E \\ -aR & 0 \end{vmatrix}}{\begin{vmatrix} R & -aR \\ -aR & (aR + R_L) \end{vmatrix}}$$

$$= \frac{EaR}{R(aR + R_L) - (aR)^2}$$

$$= \frac{Ea}{R_L + a(1 - a)R}$$

The output voltage V_L is given by

$$V_L = I_2 R_L$$

$$= \frac{EaR_L}{R_L + a(1 - a)R} \tag{1.7}$$

$$= \frac{Ea}{1 + a(1 - a)(R/R_L)} \tag{1.8}$$

The potentiometer ratio is

$$\frac{V_L}{E} = \frac{a}{1 + a(1 - a)(R/R_L)} \qquad (1.9)$$

For $R_L \gg R$, the ratio becomes

$$\frac{V_L}{E} \approx a \qquad (1.10)$$

The ratio V_L/E is also known as the *voltage transfer function*. Another important parameter is the *insertion loss*, which is defined as the ratio of load currents with, and without, the network. From Fig. 1.4(b) and (c), the insertion loss is I_2/I:

$$I = \frac{E}{R_L} \qquad \text{[Fig. 1.4(b)]}$$

$$I_2 = \frac{Ea}{R_L + a(1 - a)R} \qquad \text{(as before)} \qquad \text{[Fig. 1.4(c)]}$$

Therefore, insertion loss $= \dfrac{I_2}{I}$

$$= \frac{a}{1 + a(1 - a)(R/R_L)} \qquad (1.11)$$

This is seen to be the same as the voltage transfer function, but this is only true where the source resistance can be neglected. Where the source resistance has to be taken into account, Fig. 1.4(d) and (e),

$$I = \frac{E}{R_s + R_L} \qquad \text{[Fig. 1.4(d)]}$$

$$E = I_1(R + R_s) - I_2 aR$$

$$\qquad \text{[Fig. 1.4(e)]}$$

$$0 = -I_1 aR + I_2(aR + R_L)$$

Therefore, $I_2 = \dfrac{EaR}{(R + R_s)(aR + R_L) - (aR)^2}$

and insertion loss $= \dfrac{I_2}{I}$

$$= \frac{aR(R_s + R_L)}{(R + R_s)(aR + R_L) - (aR)^2} \qquad (1.12)$$

The voltage transfer function is defined generally as

$$\frac{\text{voltage output from network}}{\text{voltage input to network}} \qquad (1.13)$$

From Fig. 1.4(e), this is seen to be V_L/V_1, and a little thought will show that this is equal to the ratio V_L/E already established for Fig. 1.4(c).

1.4.2 Attenuator Pads

An *attenuator pad* is a resistive network that is used to introduce a fixed amount of attenuation between a source and a load. One commonly used circuit is the T attenuator, shown in Fig. 1.5(b). The insertion loss also gives the attentuation, usually expressed in decibels.

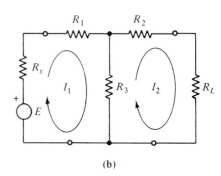

FIGURE 1.5. (a) Circuit without attenuator; (b) A T attenuator inserted in circuit (a).

(a)　　　　(b)

From Fig. 1.5(a): $\quad I = \dfrac{E}{R_s + R_L}$ $\qquad (1.14)$

From Fig. 1.5(b): $\quad E = I_1(R_s + R_1 + R_3) - I_2 R_3$

$$0 = -I_1 R_3 + I_2(R_2 + R_3 + R_L)$$

$$\therefore \quad I_2 = \frac{\begin{vmatrix} R_s + R_1 + R_3 & E \\ -R_3 & 0 \end{vmatrix}}{\begin{vmatrix} R_s + R_1 + R_3 & -R_3 \\ -R_3 & R_2 + R_3 + R_L \end{vmatrix}}$$

$$= \frac{E R_3}{(R_s + R_1 + R_3)(R_2 + R_3 + R_L) - R_3^2}$$

$$\text{insertion loss} = \frac{I_2}{I}$$

$$= \frac{R_3(R_s + R_L)}{(R_s + R_1 + R_3)(R_2 + R_3 + R_L) - R_3^2} \qquad (1.15)$$

and insertion loss in decibels $= -20 \log_{10}\left(\frac{I_2}{I}\right)$ (1.16)

The negative sign is to show that attenuation occurs; that is, the insertion loss will come out as a positive number of decibels.

Example 1.1   Calculate the attenuation in decibels for a T pad for which $R_1 = R_2 = 31 \ \Omega$; $R_3 = 25 \ \Omega$. The pad connects a 50-Ω generator to a 50-Ω load.

Solution

$$\frac{I_2}{I} = \frac{25(50 + 50)}{(50 + 31 + 25)(31 + 25 + 50) - (25)^2}$$

$$= \frac{2500}{(106)^2 - (25)^2}$$

$$= 0.236$$

$$-20 \log_{10}\frac{I_2}{I} = 12.56 \ \text{dB}$$

The attenuator will usually maintain matched conditions, as described in the next paragraph, and as illustrated by Problem 4, Section 1.16.

A simpler type of pad is the one for which the circuit is shown in Fig. 1.6. This is frequently used to match a source to a load; that is, when it is inserted between source and load, the effective resistance seen by the source is equal to the source impedance in value, and the effective source impedance, as seen by the load, is equal in value to the load impedance. From the circuit of Fig. 1.6(a),

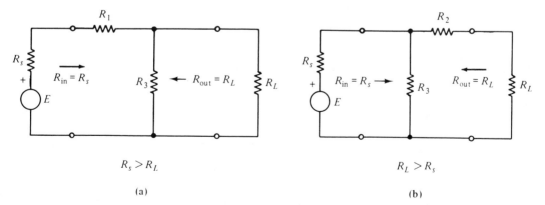

$R_s > R_L$

(a)

$R_L > R_s$

(b)

FIGURE 1.6.   (a) L attenuator $R_S > R_L$; (b) L attenuator $R_S < R_L$.

$$R_s = R_{\text{in}} = R_1 + \frac{R_3 R_L}{R_3 + R_L}$$

$$\therefore R_s - R_1 = \frac{R_3 R_L}{R_3 + R_L}$$

$$\therefore \frac{1}{R_s - R_1} = \frac{1}{R_3} + \frac{1}{R_L} \qquad (1.17)$$

And
$$R_L = R_{\text{out}} = \frac{R_3(R_1 + R_s)}{R_3 + R_1 + R_s}$$

or
$$\frac{1}{R_L} = \frac{1}{R_3} + \frac{1}{R_1 + R_s} \qquad (1.18)$$

The term $1/R_3$ can be eliminated from Eqs. (1.17) and (1.18), giving

$$\frac{1}{R_s - R_1} - \frac{1}{R_L} = \frac{1}{R_L} - \frac{1}{R_s + R_1}$$

$$\therefore \quad \frac{1}{R_s - R_1} + \frac{1}{R_s + R_1} = \frac{2}{R_L}$$

$$\therefore \quad \frac{2R_s}{R_s^2 - R_1^2} = \frac{2}{R_L}$$

$$\therefore \quad R_1^2 = R_s^2 - R_s R_L$$

$$\therefore \quad R_1 = \sqrt{R_s(R_s - R_L)} \qquad (1.19)$$

The term R_3 can then be determined from Eq. (1.17) by substituting for R_1 from Eq. (1.19). For this result to be valid, $R_L < R_s$; otherwise, R_1 becomes an imaginary quantity. If $R_L > R_s$, the circuit of Fig. 1.6(b) must be used, and the equation becomes

$$R_2 = \sqrt{R_L(R_L - R_s)} \qquad (1.20)$$

Example 1.2   An L network is used to match a 75-Ω generator to a 50-Ω load. Determine the values of the network resistors.

Solution   The circuit of Fig. 1.6(a) must be used:

$$R_1 = \sqrt{75(75 - 50)}$$

$$= 43.3\ \Omega$$

and
$$\frac{1}{R_s - R_1} = \frac{1}{R_3} + \frac{1}{R_L}$$

Therefore,
$$\frac{1}{75 - 43.3} = \frac{1}{R_3} + \frac{1}{50}$$

$$\frac{1}{31.7} - \frac{1}{50} = \frac{1}{R_3}$$

$$R_3 = \frac{31.7 \times 50}{50 - 31.7}$$

$$= 86.6 \ \Omega$$

Example 1.3   Repeat Example 1.2 but with $R_s = 10 \ \Omega$ and $R_L = 50 \ \Omega$.

Solution   The circuit of Fig. 1.6(b) must be used:

$$R_2 = \sqrt{R_L(R_L - R_s)}$$

$$= \sqrt{50(50 - 10)}$$

$$= 44.72 \ \Omega$$

and analogous
to Eq. (1.17):
$$\frac{1}{R_L - R_2} = \frac{1}{R_3} + \frac{1}{R_s}$$

Therefore,
$$\frac{1}{50 - 44.72} = \frac{1}{R_3} + \frac{1}{10}$$

$$\frac{1}{5.28} - \frac{1}{10} = \frac{1}{R_3}$$

$$R_3 = \frac{10 \times 5.28}{10 - 5.28}$$

$$= 11.19 \ \Omega$$

1.5   IMPEDANCE AND REACTANCE

Ohm's law and Kirchhoff's laws can be extended to alternating–current circuits provided that the two additional circuit properties of inductance and capacitance are taken into account. With sinusoidal (or cosinusoidal) currents, these properties are accounted for in terms of impedance. The concepts of impedance and phasors, and the complex number representation of these will be found in any good textbook on electric circuit analysis; see for example, B. Zeines, *Electric Circuit Analysis*, Reston Publishing Company, Reston, Va, (1972). A summary of the more important results is given here.

The impedance Z of a circuit is defined as the ratio of phasor voltage V across the circuit to the phasor current I through the circuit:

$$Z = \frac{V}{I} = R + jX \qquad (1.21)$$

where $j = \sqrt{-1}$.

By definition, the real part R, of the impedance is the *resistance* of the circuit, and the imaginary part X, the *reactance*. The circuit may physically consist of a resistance R connected in series with a reactance X, which may be an inductance, or capacitance, or a combination of these; or, it is also possible for Eq. (1.21) to represent the equivalent impedance of a more complex network. One important equivalence representation is covered in section 1.7.

FIGURE 1.7. Impedance representation of (a) an R-C circuit, (b) an R-L circuit. Admittance representation of (c) an R-C circuit, (d) an R-L circuit.

For the circuit shown in Fig. 1.7(a):

$$\begin{aligned} Z &= R + jX_C \\ &= R + j(-1/\omega C) \\ &= R - j/\omega C \end{aligned} \qquad (1.22)$$

i.e. by definition, capacitive reactance is:

$$X_C = -1/\omega C \qquad (1.23)$$

ω is the angular frequency of the sinusoidal voltage or current.
For the circuit of Fig. 1.7(b):

$$\begin{aligned} Z &= R + jX_L \\ &= R + j\omega L \end{aligned} \qquad (1.24)$$

i.e., inductive reactance is defined as:

$$X_L = \omega L \qquad (1.25)$$

As shown in Fig. 1.7, the sign convention for voltage drop across a reactive element is the same as that for resistance.

Excluding for the moment, mutual–inductive coupling (this is considered in Section 1.11), the effective reactance of a series network X_{ser} is

$$X_{\text{ser}} = X_1 + X_2 + \cdots + X_n \qquad (1.26)$$

Where the individual reactances are all inductive, the equivalent series inductance is obtained from Eqs. (1.26) and (1.25) as

$$L_{\text{ser}} = L_1 + L_2 + \cdots + L_n \qquad (1.27)$$

Where they are all capacitive, the equivalent series capacitance C_{ser} may be obtained from Eqs. (1.23) and (1.26) in the form

$$\frac{1}{C_{\text{ser}}} = \frac{1}{C_1} + \frac{1}{C_2} \cdots + \frac{1}{C_n} \qquad (1.28)$$

The effective reactance of a parallel network of reactances is given by

$$\frac{1}{X_p} = \frac{1}{X_1} + \frac{1}{X_2} + \cdots + \frac{1}{X_n} \qquad (1.29)$$

Where the individual reactances are all inductive, this leads to an expression for the equivalent parallel inductance (excluding mutual inductance) of

$$\frac{1}{L_p} = \frac{1}{L_1} + \frac{1}{L_2} + \cdots + \frac{1}{L_n} \qquad (1.30)$$

Where the individual reactances are all capacitive, the equivalent parallel capacitance is obtained as

$$C_p = C_1 + C_2 + \cdots + C_n \qquad (1.31)$$

As a check on calculations, it may be noted that L_{ser} should be greater than the largest single inductor in the series network, while L_p should be smaller than the smallest single inductor in the parallel network; for capacitors, C_{ser} should be smaller than the smallest capacitor in the series network while C_p should be greater than the greatest capacitor in the parallel network.

Example 1.4   Calculate the impedance of (a) a $5\,\Omega$ resistor in a series with a $1.0\ \mu\text{H}$ inductor, and (b) a $5\,\Omega$ resistor in series with a $0.02533\ \mu\text{F}$ capacitor, at a frequency of $1.0\ \text{MHz}$.

Solution   **(a)**
$$Z = 5 + j\,2\pi \times 10^6 \times 10^{-6}$$
$$= 5 + j\,6.28 \ \Omega$$

(b)
$$Z = 5 - j/2\,\pi \times 10^6 \times 0.02533 \times 10^{-6}$$
$$= 5 - j\,6.28 \ \Omega$$

1.6   ADMITTANCE AND SUSCEPTANCE

The admittance Y of a circuit is defined as the ratio of the phasor current through the circuit to the phasor voltage across the circuit. Thus:

$$Y = \frac{I}{V} = G + j\,B \tag{1.32}$$

It will be seen that admittance is therefore the reciprocal of impedance:

$$Y = 1/Z \tag{1.33}$$

By definition, the real part G, of admittance is the *conductance* of the circuit, and the imaginary part B, the *susceptance*. For a circuit consisting of an idealized resistance R in parallel with an idealized capacitance C, Fig 1.7 (c), the admittance is:

$$Y = G + j\,B_C$$
$$= \frac{1}{R} + j\,\omega C \tag{1.34}$$

Thus, the conductance is: $G = 1/R$ (1.35)

and the capacitive susceptance is $B_C = \omega C$ (1.36)

For a circuit consisting of an idealized resistor R in parallel with an idealized inductor L, Fig 1.7 (d), the admittance is:

$$Y = G + j\,B_L$$
$$= G + j(-1/\omega L)$$
$$= G - j/\omega L \tag{1.37}$$

Thus, the inductive susceptance is $B_L = -1/\omega L$ (1.38)

In practice it may not be permissible to assume idealized components. This is especially true for inductors, for which the series resistance is usually significant. The admittance of this type of component is treated in section 1.7.

Example 1.5   Calculate, for a frequency of 1.0 MHz, the admittance of (a) a 1 kΩ resistor in parallel with a 200 pF capacitor, and (b) a 1 kΩ resistor in parallel with a 126.6 μH inductor.

Solution   (a)

$$Y = \frac{1}{10^3} + j\,2\pi \times 10^6 \times 200 \times 10^{-12}$$

$$= 10^{-3} + j\,12.57 \times 10^{-4} \qquad \text{Siemens (S)}$$

$$= 1 + j\,1.257 \text{ mS}$$

(b)

$$Y = 10^{-3} - j/(2\pi \times 10^6 \times 126.6 \times 10^{-6})$$

$$= 1 - j\,1.257 \text{ mS}$$

1.7   SERIES AND PARALLEL EQUIVALENCE

Impedance is the more convenient quantity to use when dealing with series circuits, and admittance when dealing with parallel circuits, although the final value of admittance is usually converted to parallel resistance and reactance (rather than leaving it in the form of conductance and susceptance). A very useful equivalence can be established between series and parallel circuits, *at a given frequency.*

Consider first a circuit which can be represented as a resistance R in series with a reactance X.

$$Z = R + j\,X$$

The equivalent admittance is:

$$Y = 1/Z$$

or,

$$G + jB = \frac{1}{R + jX}$$

$$= \frac{R}{R^2 + X^2} - j\,\frac{X}{R^2 + X^2}$$

Therefore, the equivalent conductance is:

$$G = \frac{R}{R^2 + X^2} \qquad\qquad (1.39)$$

And, the equivalent susceptance is:

$$B = -\frac{X}{R^2 + X^2} \qquad (1.40)$$

Example 1.6

A 100-pF capacitor has a series lead resistance of 1Ω. Determine the equivalent parallel circuit at a frequency of 15.9 MHz.

Solution

$$X_C = \frac{-1}{2\pi \times 15.9 \times 10^6 \times 100 \times 10^{-12}}$$

$$= -100 \ \Omega$$

From Eq. (1.39),

$$G = \frac{1}{1^2 + 100^2}$$

$$\cong 10^{-4} \ \text{S}$$

Therefore the equivalent parallel resistance of the circuit is $10^4 \ \Omega$, or $10 \ \text{k}\Omega$.

From Eq. (1.40),

$$B = \frac{-(-100)}{1^2 + 100^2}$$

$$\cong 0.01 \quad \text{S}$$

The equivalent parallel capacitance is found from application of Eq. (1.36) as:

$$B = \omega C_{eq} = 0.01$$

$$\therefore C_{eq} = 100 \ \text{pF}.$$

The equivalent circuits are shown in Fig 1.8 (a) and (b). It is important to realize that the *values* shown are good only for a frequency of 15.9 MHz. Changing the frequency will change the values of the equivalent components, as illustrated in the next example.

Example 1.7

An inductor can be represented as a 15.92 μH inductance in series with a 10Ω resistance. Determine the equivalent parallel circuit for a frequency of (a) 10 MHz, and (b) 20 MHz, assuming the series component values remain constant.

Solution

(a)

$$X_L = 2\pi \times 10^7 \times 15.92 \times 10^{-6}$$

$$= 1000\Omega$$

FIGURE 1.8. (a) Series and (b) parallel equivalent circuits for Example 1.6.

From Eq. (1.39)

$$G = \frac{10}{10^2 + 1000^2}$$

$$\cong 10^{-5} \quad S$$

and

$$R_p = \frac{1}{G} = \underline{\underline{100\,k\Omega}}$$

From Eq. (1.40), the equivalent susceptance is:

$$B = -\frac{1000}{10^2 + 1000^2}$$

$$\cong \underline{\underline{-1.0 \quad mS}}$$

The equivalent parallel inductance is found from application of Eq. (1.38) as:

$$B_L = -1/\omega L_{eq} = -10^{-3}$$

Therefore at a frequency of 10 MHz, $L_{eq} = 1/2\pi \times 10^7 \times 10^{-3}$

$$= \underline{\underline{15.92\,\mu H}}$$

(b) Increasing the frequency to 20 MHz increases X_L to 2000Ω. Applying Eqs. (1.39) and (1.40) as before gives:

$$G = \frac{10}{10^2 + 2000^2}$$

$$\cong \frac{10^{-5}}{4}$$

and therefore $\qquad\qquad R_p = \dfrac{1}{G} = 400 \text{ k}\Omega.$

From Eq. (1.40) $\qquad\qquad B = -\dfrac{2000}{10^2 + 2000^2}$

$$\cong -1.0 \text{ mS}$$

Therefore the equivalent parallel inductance is $15.92\ \mu\text{H}$ as before. It will be seen in this particular example, that whereas there is negligible change in the value of equivalent parallel inductance, and indeed this is approximately equal to the series inductance value, the equivalent parallel resistance value increases approximately in proportion to the frequency squared.

Clearly a similar procedure can be followed to obtain an equivalent series circuit from a given parallel circuit. Consider a conductance G in parallel with a susceptance B, so that:

$$Y = G + jB$$

The equivalent impedance is $\quad Z = 1/Y$

Hence $\qquad\qquad R + jX = \dfrac{1}{G + jB}$

or $\qquad\qquad R + jX = \dfrac{G}{G^2 + B^2} - j\,\dfrac{B}{G^2 + B^2}$

Therefore the equivalent series resistance is:

$$R = \dfrac{G}{G^2 + B^2} \qquad\qquad (1.41)$$

and the equivalent series reactance is:

$$X = -\dfrac{B}{G^2 + B^2} \qquad\qquad (1.42)$$

Example 1.8   A capacitor can be represented by a capacitance of 50 pF in parallel with a dielectric loss resistance of 10 MΩ. For a frequency of 1.0 MHz, determine the equivalent series circuit.

Solution $\qquad\qquad\qquad\quad G = 10^{-7}\ \text{S}$

and, $\qquad\qquad\qquad\quad B = 2\pi \times 10^6 \times 50 \times 10^{-12}$

$$= 314.2\ \mu\text{S}$$

From Eq. (1.41) $R = \dfrac{10^{-7}}{10^{-14}+(314.2)^2 \times 10^{-12}}$

$\cong 1.013\Omega$

and from Eq. (1.42) $X = \dfrac{-314.2 \times 10^{-6}}{10^{-14} + (314.2)^2 \times 10^{-12}} \cong -\dfrac{1}{314.2 \times 10^{-6}}\Omega$

Thus, since $X \cong -1/B$, the equivalent series capacitance does not differ significantly from the parallel value.

1.8 SERIES RLC CIRCUIT

The total impedance for the series RLC circuit is

$$Z = R + j(X_L + X_C) \qquad (1.43)$$

$$= R + j(\omega L - 1/\omega C) \qquad (1.44)$$

This is the series impedance in complex form, Fig. 1.9(a). The complex form contains sufficient information to determine Z completely, since

(a)

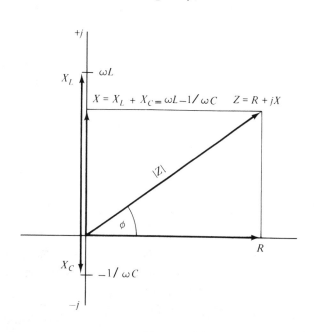

(b)

FIGURE 1.9.   (a) A series RLC circuit; (b) Its impedance diagram.

$$|Z| = \sqrt{R^2 + X^2} \qquad\qquad (1.45)$$

and
$$\phi = \tan^{-1}\left(\frac{X}{R}\right) \qquad\qquad (1.46)$$

Here,
$$X = X_L + X_C = \omega L - \frac{1}{\omega C} \qquad\qquad \text{Fig. 1.9 (b).}$$

1.8.1   Series Resonance and Q Factor

The series RLC circuit is resonant when the phase angle ϕ is equal to zero. This means that X must be zero since $\phi = \tan^{-1}(X/R)$:

$$\therefore \quad X = X_L + X_C = 0$$

or
$$X_L = -X_C \qquad\qquad (1.47)$$

Denoting this condition by the subscript 0:

$$\omega_0 L = -(-1/\omega_0 C)$$

or
$$\omega_0 L = \frac{1}{\omega_0 C}$$

$$\therefore \quad \omega_0 = \frac{1}{\sqrt{LC}} \qquad\qquad (1.48)$$

and
$$f_0 = \frac{1}{2\pi\sqrt{LC}} \qquad\qquad (1.49)$$

This simple but very important equation defines the *resonant frequency* of the series circuit. Clearly, at f_0 the impedance of the circuit is minimum and purely resistive, since

$$Z_0 = R + j\left(\omega_0 L - \frac{1}{\omega_0 C}\right)$$

$$= R + j0 \qquad\qquad (1.50)$$

The L or C of the circuit can be adjusted to bring the circuit into resonance with the applied frequency, a process known as *tuning*. The circuit is also referred to as a *series tuned circuit*. At frequencies below resonance the circuit impedance appears capacitive since the j coefficient is negative, and inductive at frequencies above resonance since the j coefficient is positive.

The widest application of the tuned circuit is as a frequency selective filter, illustrated in its simplest form in Fig. 1.10(a). The input to the system

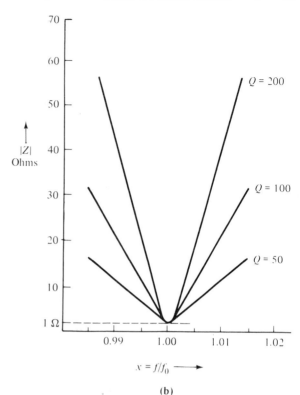

FIGURE 1.10. (a) The series tuned filter; (b) Selectivity curves for various Q factors for a series RLC circuit.

consists of two sinusoidal signals f and f_0 $(f \neq f_0)$, while the output current in the load R_L will consist almost entirely of a signal at f, providing $R_L \gg R$, the signal at f_0 being filtered out by the series tuned circuit across the line. The effect that the series tuned circuit has on the signal f depends on how close f is to f_0 and on an important characteristic of the circuit termed the *selectivity*. The selectivity, in turn, is a function of the Q *factor* (*Quality factor*) of the circuit. The Q factor of a series tuned circuit can be defined as the ratio of inductive voltage to resistive voltage at resonance:

$$Q = \frac{V_L}{V_R}$$

$$= \frac{\omega_0 L}{R} \tag{1.51}$$

Note that the *resonant frequency* is used in the definition of Q for a resonant circuit. Also, at resonance, $\omega_0 L = 1/\omega_0 C$; therefore

$$Q = \frac{1}{\omega_0 CR} \tag{1.52}$$

The equation for series impedance may be written in terms of Q:

$$Z = R + j\left(\omega L - \frac{1}{\omega C}\right)$$

$$= R\left[1 + j\left(\frac{\omega L}{R} - \frac{1}{\omega CR}\right)\right]$$

$$= R\left[1 + j\left(\frac{\omega}{\omega_0}\frac{\omega_0 L}{R} - \frac{\omega_0}{\omega}\frac{1}{\omega_0 CR}\right)\right]$$

$$= R\left[1 + j\left(\frac{\omega}{\omega_0} - \frac{\omega_0}{\omega}\right)Q\right] \qquad (1.53)$$

$$= R(1 + jyQ) \text{ where } y = \frac{\omega}{\omega_0} - \frac{\omega_0}{\omega} \qquad (1.54)$$

The impedance modulus is

$$|Z| = R\sqrt{1 + y^2 Q^2} \qquad (1.55)$$

The curve of $|Z|$ against frequency f/f_0 is sketched in Fig. 1.10(b). Obviously, the narrower the curve, the more selective the circuit is, and, as will now be shown, a high Q factor results in better selectivity.

The selectivity is measured in terms of the bandwidth, B_{3dB}, Fig. 1.11. This is referred to as the "3–dB bandwidth" because the $\sqrt{2}$ impedance levels correspond to a 3–dB drop in current from its resonant value, for a constant voltage input. Almost any impedance level could have been chosen

FIGURE 1.11. The 3–dB bandwidth for a series RLC circuit.

for defining bandwidth, but the $\sqrt{2}$ level has the advantage of simplifying the arithmetic. The specific values of y_3 corresponding to the 3–dB bandwidth points f_1 and f_2 are found by equating

$$R\sqrt{1 + y_3^2 Q^2} = R\sqrt{2}$$

$$\therefore \quad 1 + y_3^2 Q^2 = 2$$

or

$$y_3 = \frac{1}{Q} \tag{1.56}$$

Note, $y_3 = \dfrac{1}{Q}$ must be positive.

At limit f_2:

(Note: $f_2 > f_0$ and y_3 is positive.)

$$y_3 = \frac{f_2}{f_0} - \frac{f_0}{f_2} = \frac{1}{Q}$$

$$\therefore f_2^2 - \frac{f_0 f_2}{Q} - f_0^2 = 0$$

$$\therefore f_2 = \frac{f_0}{2Q} \pm \sqrt{\left(\frac{f_0}{2Q}\right)^2 + f_0^2} \tag{1.57}$$

At limit f_1:

(Note: $f_1 < f_0$ and y_3 is positive.)

$$y_3 = \frac{f_0}{f_1} - \frac{f_1}{f_0} = \frac{1}{Q}$$

$$\therefore f_0^2 - \frac{f_1 f_0}{Q} - f_1^2 = 0$$

$$\therefore f_1 = -\frac{f_0}{2Q} \pm \sqrt{\left(\frac{f_0}{2Q}\right)^2 + f_0^2} \tag{1.58}$$

The 3–dB bandwidth is obtained from (1.57) and (1.58) as

$$B_{3\,\mathrm{dB}} = f_2 - f_1 \tag{1.59}$$

$$= \frac{f_0}{Q} \tag{1.60}$$

This shows the importance of the Q factor in determining selectivity, a high Q resulting in a narrow 3–dB bandwidth. For series tuned circuits the Q factor typically ranges from about 10 to 300. The effect of increasing Q on selectivity is shown in Fig. 1.10(b); R is assumed to remain constant and Q varied by varying L/C, since

$$Q = \frac{\omega_0 L}{R} = \frac{1}{R}\sqrt{\frac{L}{C}}$$

1.9 PARALLEL TUNED CIRCUIT

The parallel circuit is as shown in Fig. 1.12(a), the capacitance assumed to have negligible resistance. The admittance of the circuit can therefore be written as

$$Y = \frac{1}{R + j\omega L} + j\omega C \tag{1.61}$$

$$= \frac{R - j\omega L}{R^2 + \omega^2 L^2} + j\omega C$$

$$= \frac{R}{R^2 + \omega^2 L^2} + j\left(\omega C - \frac{\omega L}{R^2 + \omega^2 L^2}\right) \tag{1.62}$$

(a)

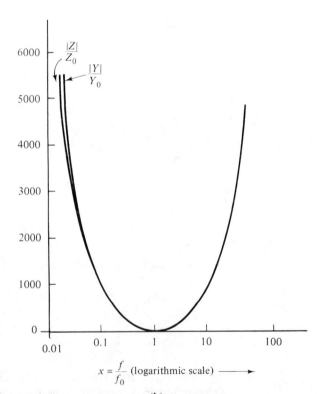

$x = \dfrac{f}{f_0}$ (logarithmic scale) $\longrightarrow$

(b)

FIGURE 1.12. (a) Parallel tuned circuit; (b) Generalized selectivity curves for parallel and series tuned circuits.

At resonance the admittance is real (i.e., the j coefficients equate to zero):

$$\therefore \omega_0 C = \frac{\omega_0 L}{R^2 + \omega_0^2 L^2}$$

or,
$$R^2 + \omega_0^2 L^2 = \frac{L}{C} \tag{1.63}$$

$$\therefore \omega_0^2 = \frac{1}{LC} - \frac{R^2}{L^2}$$

or,
$$\omega_0 = \sqrt{\frac{1}{LC} - \frac{R^2}{L^2}} \tag{1.64}$$

This shows that the parallel resonant frequency depends on the circuit resistance, a situation that does not occur for the series circuit. In practice it is usually the case that $(R/L)^2 \ll 1/LC$, and then the same equation applies for both series and parallel resonance.

The admittance at resonance is purely conductive and is

$$Y_0 = \frac{R}{R^2 + \omega_0^2 L^2} \tag{1.65}$$

From Eq. (1.63), $R^2 + \omega_0^2 L^2 = L/C$; therefore,

$$Y_0 = \frac{CR}{L} \tag{1.66}$$

The impedance at resonance is purely resistive and is denoted by R_D to signify a *dynamic resistance*:

$$R_D = \frac{1}{Y_0} = \frac{L}{CR} \tag{1.67}$$

This is close to, but does not quite equal, the maximum impedance modulus obtainable. Where the approximate form of resonant frequency equation can be used, the maximum impedance coincides with the impedance at resonance.

The ratio Y/Y_0 shows how admittance varies with frequency relative to the resonant value. Usually, $\omega^2 L^2 \gg R^2$ so that Eq. (1.62) for Y can be simplified, and using Eq. (1.66) for Y_0 gives:

$$\frac{Y}{Y_0} \cong \frac{L}{CR} \left[\frac{R}{\omega^2 L^2} + j\left(\omega C - 1/\omega L\right) \right]$$

$$= \frac{1}{\omega^2 LC} + j\left(\frac{\omega L}{R} - \frac{1}{\omega CR}\right)$$

$$= \frac{\omega_0^2}{\omega^2} + j y Q \tag{1.68}$$

Where yQ is as given in Eq. (1.54), and $LC = \omega_0^{-2}$.

$$\therefore |Y| = Y_0 \sqrt{\left(\frac{\omega_0}{\omega}\right)^4 + (yQ)^2} \qquad (1.69)$$

The curve of $|Y|$ versus f/f_0 is similar to that for $|Z|$ versus f/f_0 for the series circuit, as shown in Fig. 1.12(b). Only at the low–frequency end do the curves differ, and the frequency has been plotted on a logarithmic scale to bring this out. It follows, therefore, that the 3–dB bandwidth for the parallel circuit is also given by

$$B_{3\,dB} = \frac{f_0}{Q} \qquad (1.70)$$

The parallel tuned circuit may also be used as a filter, because it presents a high impedance to signals at resonant frequency, as shown in Example 1.9. It should be noted that the dynamic impedance R_D applies only at resonant frequency. Direct currents, for example would encounter a resistance of R only, the d.c. resistance of the coil. Before working example 1.9, it may be noted that useful alternative expressions for Eq. (1.67) for R_D may be derived utilizing Eqs. (1.51) and (1.52) for the Q factor of a circuit. Thus:

$$R_D = \frac{L}{CR} \qquad (1.67)$$

$$= \omega_0 L Q \qquad (1.71)$$

$$= \frac{Q}{\omega_0 C} \qquad (1.72)$$

$$= Q^2 R \qquad (1.73)$$

Example 1.9

A parallel tuned circuit has a Q factor of 200 when tuned to resonance at 10 MHz. The value of tuning capacitance is 10pF. Calculate (a) the dynamic impedance, and (b) the d.c. resistance, assuming this does not change with frequency.

Solution

(a) Applying Eq. (1.72):

$$R_D = \frac{200}{2\pi \times 10^7 \times 10 \times 10^{-12}}$$

$$= 318\,k\Omega$$

(b) From Eq. (1.73) $\quad R = \frac{R_D}{Q^2} = \frac{318 \times 10^3}{(200)^2} = 7.96\Omega$

At frequencies below resonance, the circuit *impedance* appears inductive and above resonance, capacitive. This is most easily remembered by noting that near zero frequency, the inductance will be a near short–circuit; therefore, all the current will be inductive. And as frequency approaches infinity, the capacitive reactance approaches a short–circuit, making the total current capacitive.

1.9.1   Self Resonance of a Coil

A real inductor has, in addition to self–inductance and resistance, a self–capacitance which is distributed throughout the coil. Because of its distributed nature, a real inductor cannot be represented exactly by any circuit, but can be approximated as shown in Fig. 1.13(a), in which the distributed properties of resistance, inductance, and capacitance are represented by lumped components R, L, and C_0. Clearly, then, the real inductor will behave like a parallel tuned circuit; that is, it will appear as an inductance below its self–resonant frequency and as a capacitance above its self–resonant frequency. The admittance expression, Eq. (1.62), for the parallel circuit may therefore be used to represent the *coil*; making use of the approximation $\omega^2 L^2 \gg R^2$, Eq. (1.62) simplifies to:

$$Y \cong \frac{R}{\omega^2 L^2} + j\left(\omega C_0 - \frac{1}{\omega L}\right)$$

$$= \frac{R}{\omega^2 L^2} - j\left(\frac{1 - \omega^2 L C_0}{\omega L}\right) \qquad (1.74)$$

This allows the coil to be represented by the parallel circuit of Fig. 1.13(b), *which only applies for frequencies below the self–resonant frequency of the coil.*

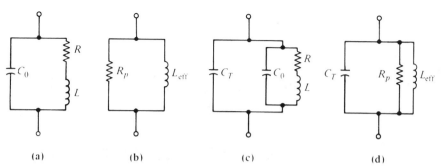

(a)   (b)   (c)   (d)

FIGURE 1.13.   (a) The approximate circuit for an inductor including self–capacitance; (b) Its parallel equivalence at frequencies below self–resonance; (c) A parallel tuned circuit; and (d) Its equivalent circuit, taking into account C_0.

The effective parallel resistance R_p is seen to be obtained from

$$\frac{1}{R_p} = \frac{R}{\omega^2 L^2}$$

or

$$R_p = \frac{\omega^2 L^2}{R} \qquad (1.75)$$

and the effective parallel inductance of the coil, L_{eff}, from

$$\frac{1}{\omega L_{\text{eff}}} = \frac{1 - \omega^2 L C_0}{\omega L}$$

or

$$L_{\text{eff}} = \frac{L}{1 - \omega^2 L C_0} = \frac{L}{1 - (\omega/\omega_0)^2} \qquad (1.76)$$

Suppose that this coil is used in a tuned circuit, Fig. 1.13(c), which has a resonant frequency, ω_T, well below the self–resonance, ω_0, of the coil (i.e., the external tuning capacity $C_T \gg C_0$). At circuit resonance, ω_T, the dynamic impedance of the circuit is, from Eq. (1.71)

$$R_D = Q\omega_T L \qquad (1.77)$$

Now, the equivalent circuit of Fig. 1.13(d) will appear to have an effective Q factor, Q_{eff}, which can be used in Eq. (1.71) along with L_{eff} to give:

$$R_D = Q_{\text{eff}}\omega_T L_{\text{eff}} \qquad (1.78)$$

But since the circuits of Fig. 1.13(c) and (d) are equivalent then:

$$Q\omega_T L = Q_{\text{eff}}\omega_T L_{\text{eff}}$$

$$\therefore \quad Q_{\text{eff}} = Q\frac{L}{L_{\text{eff}}} \qquad (1.79)$$

Substituting from Eq. (1.77) into Eq. (1.79) gives

$$Q_{\text{eff}} = Q(1 - \omega^2 L C_0) = Q\left[1 - \left(\frac{\omega}{\omega_0}\right)^2\right] \qquad (1.80)$$

where $Q = \omega_T L/R$ is the Q factor as previously defined, neglecting self–capacitance. Over a wide range of frequencies Q is approximately constant because, although ωL increases with frequency, R also increases with frequency, owing to the skin effect, and the ratio $\omega L/R$ remains approximately constant. It will be seen, however, that the effective Q factor, Q_{eff}, taking into account self–capacitance, decreases with increasing frequency.

Care must be exercised as to how Q_{eff} is used. For a parallel tuned circuit, Fig. 1.13(c) or (d), the dynamic resistance can be calculated from either of the expressions, Eqs. (1.77) or (1.78), i.e., either QL, or $Q_{eff}\ L_{eff}$ is used in the calculation. Alternatively, Eq. (1.72) can be used providing either $Q/(C_T + C_0)$, or Q_{eff}/C_T is substituted in this.

In calculating the bandwidth for a *parallel* tuned circuit from Eq. (1.70), Q, and not Q_{eff} must be used:

$$\text{Bandwidth} = \frac{f_T}{Q} \qquad (1.81)$$

This is because, for a specified resonant frequency, C_T will be adjusted to absorb C_o, (since C_T and C_o are in parallel). In the case of a series tuned circuit, C_T is no longer in parallel with C_o. Effectively C_T resonates with L_{eff} to give a circuit Q-factor of Q_{eff}, so that the bandwidth is, from Eq. (1.60):

Series Circuit: $$\text{Bandwidth} = \frac{f_T}{Q_{eff}} \qquad (1.82)$$

It should be noted that for most Q-meters the test circuit is series tuned so that the meter indicates Q_{eff}, and not Q.

1.10 SKIN EFFECT

The self–induced EMF in a conductor resulting from the rate of change of flux linkages opposes the current flow which gives rise to the flux (Lenz's law). Normally it is assumed that all the flux links with all the conductor. However, the actual flux linkages increase toward the core of the conductor, since the magnetic flux within the conductor only links with the inner section; in Fig. 1.14(a), for example, flux line ϕ_1 links with the complete conductor, while flux line ϕ_2 links only with the section of radius a. The self-induced EMF is greatest at the center of the conductor, which experiences greatest flux linkages and becomes less toward the outer circumference. This results in the current density being least at the center, and increasing toward the outer circumference, since the induced EMF opposes the current flow (Lenz's law). Of course, the lower current density at the center results in lower magnetic flux there, which tends to offset the effect producing the nonuniform distribution, and in this way, equilibrium conditions are established. The overall effect, however, is that the current tends to flow near the surface of the conductor, this being referred to as the *skin effect*. Because the current is confined to a smaller cross section of conductor, the apparent resistance of the conductor increases. The increase is more noticeable for thick conductors and at high frequencies (where the rate of change of flux linkages is high). Equally important is the fact that the resistance becomes dependent on frequency.

(a)

FIGURE 1.14. (a) Magnetic flux linkage in a conductor; (b) Litzendraht wire.

(b)

With coils, a special type of wire is often used to reduce skin effect, this being known as *Litzendraht wire (Litz wire,* for short). This is made up of strands insulated from each other and wound in such a way that each strand changes position between center and outer edge, over the length of the wire, Fig. 1.14(b). In this manner, each strand on average has equal induced EMF²s, so that over the complete cross section (made up of the many cross sections of the individual strands), the current density tends to be uniform.

1.11 MUTUAL INDUCTANCE

Reaction between inductive circuits that are physically isolated can occur as a result of common magnetic flux linkage. This effect can be taken into account by means of a mutual inductance M. For a harmonically varying current I_1, in an inductance L_1 which is magnetically coupled to an inductance L_2, the induced EMF in L_2 is given by

$$E_2 = \pm j\omega M \cdot I_1 \qquad (1.83)$$

The sign to be used depends on the physical disposition of the coils, and is illustrated in Fig. 1.15(a) and (b). Note that M cannot be identified with a

FIGURE 1.15. Mutual inductance coupling showing possible polarities (a) and (b); (c) The ac equivalent circuit.

physical winding in the sense that L_1, and L_2 can, and it has to be determined by measurement. In practice, it may prove easier to determine what is termed the coefficient of coupling k, where

$$M = k \sqrt{L_1 \cdot L_2} \qquad (1.84)$$

k ranges between 0 and 1.

A useful equivalent circuit for mutual–inductive coupling is shown in Fig. 1.15(c), for the $+j\omega M$ situation; the terminals 1-1 and 2-2 are to be identified with the corresponding terminals in Fig. 1.15(a). Note that the equivalent circuit is only valid for ac conditions; it shows a dc path where none may exist in the actual circuit.

Where mutual inductance is present between two inductors connected in series, the effective series inductance is given by

$$L_s = L_1 + L_2 \pm 2M \qquad (1.85)$$

Where they are connected in parallel, the effective parallel inductance is given by

$$L_p = \frac{L_1 L_2 - M^2}{L_1 + L_2 \mp 2M} \qquad (1.86)$$

It can be seen that Eqs. (1.85) and (1.86) reduce to Eqs. (1.27) and (1.31) when M is zero. By utilizing mutual inductance between two coils, the effective inductance can be altered in steps, by making the appropriate connections, from a minimum L_{min} to a maximum L_{max}, where

$$L_{min} = \frac{L_1 \cdot L_2 - M^2}{L_1 + L_2 + 2M} \qquad (1.87)$$

$$L_{max} = L_1 + L_2 + 2M \qquad (1.88)$$

Furthermore, by making M variable, for example, through physically altering the spacing between the coils, a continuously variable inductance is obtained.

1.12   COUPLING CIRCUITS

Signal transfer from one circuit to another often requires some form of coupling circuit other than a direct connection. Transformer coupling, which utilizes the mutual–inductance effect, is widely used, and can be considered separately in two broad areas: low frequencies (e.g., power and audio frequencies); and high frequencies (e.g., radio frequencies). Although both methods rely on mutual–inductance coupling, the practical details of the circuits are sufficiently different to warrant different methods of analysis.

1.12.1   Low–Frequency Transformers

In the ideal low–frequency transformer, all of the magnetic flux ϕ set up by the primary ampere-turns links with the secondary winding (or secondary windings, as there may be more than one). Also in the ideal case, the voltage drops in the primary and secondary windings can be neglected, as can the power loss in the magnetic core.

Under these conditions, the applied primary voltage, V_p, is equal to the back EMF induced in the primary winding of N_p turns, which by Faraday's law of magnetic induction gives

$$V_p = N_p \cdot \frac{d\phi}{dt} \qquad (1.89)$$

Likewise, ignoring the voltage drop in the secondary winding, the EMF induced in the secondary E_s, will be equal to the secondary terminal voltage, V_s, so

$$V_s \cong E_s = N_s \cdot \frac{d\phi}{dt} \qquad (1.90)$$

It follows, therefore, that

$$\frac{V_p}{V_s} = \frac{N_p}{N_s}$$

$$= n \qquad (1.91)$$

where $n = N_p/N_s$ is the turns ratio.

When the secondary is loaded such that it draws a current I_s, the secondary ampere–turns $N_s I_s$ must balance the primary ampere–turns $N_p I_p$ (otherwise, the unbalance would result in a change in induced current in such a direction to restore balance). It follows, therefore, that

$$\frac{I_p}{I_s} = \frac{N_s}{N_p}$$

$$= \frac{1}{n} \qquad (1.92)$$

Clearly, from Eqs. (1.91) and (1.92) $V_p \cdot I_p = V_s \cdot I_s$ which is to be expected for an ideal transformer.

The load Z_L connected to the secondary may be referred to the primary as Z_L' in the following way. The secondary load, Fig. 1.16(a), is

$$Z_L = \frac{V_s}{I_s} \qquad (1.93)$$

The load, as seen from the primary terminals, is

$$Z_L' = \frac{V_p}{I_p} \qquad (1.94)$$

Substituting for V_p and I_p from Eqs. (1.91) and (1.92), and using the relationship in Eq. (1.93), Eq. (1.94) for Z_L' may be transformed [Fig. 1.16(b)] to

$$Z_L' = n^2 \cdot Z_L \qquad (1.95)$$

Although based on the ideal transformer, this relationship is usually sufficiently accurate for practical calculations and proves to be very useful in such.

By similar arguments, a voltage generator source of EMF E and internal resistance R_s may be transferred to the secondary so that the load appears to be fed from a source of EMF E/n, and internal resistance R_s/n^2, Fig. 1.16(c).

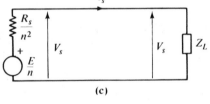

FIGURE 1.16. The ideal low–frequency transformer (a) Circuit; (b) Circuit referred to primary; (c) Circuit referred to secondary.

The low–frequency circuit model for a practical transformer is shown in Fig. 1.17(a). In the practical transformer, a small primary current is required to set up the magnetic flux in the core; this can be accounted for by showing an inductance L_c in parallel with the ideal primary. There will also be eddy–current and hysteresis power losses in the core. These losses are dependent on the primary voltage and independent of current and can be represented by a resistance R_c in parallel with the ideal primary. Each winding will have ohmic resistance, this being represented by R_p for the primary and R_s for the secondary. Each winding that carries current will produce a certain amount of magnetic flux which does not link with other windings; this is known as *leakage flux* and its effect is represented by the inductances L_p and L_s.

The equivalent circuit of Fig. 1.17(a) may be redrawn with all components referred to either primary or secondary side, as already discussed. The circuit referred to primary is shown in Fig. 1.17(b).

At the high–frequency end of the range it may be necessary to take into account the self-capacities of the windings and the mutual capacitance

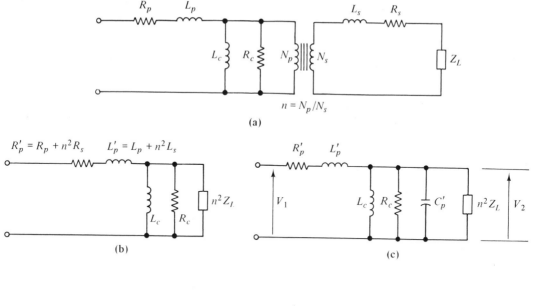

$$n = N_p/N_s$$

(a)

$R'_p = R_p + n^2 R_s$ $L'_p = L_p + n^2 L_s$

(b)

(c)

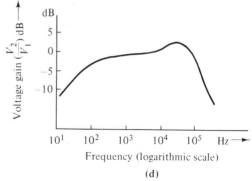

FIGURE 1.17. (a) The practical transformer equivalent circuit; (b) Referred to primary; (c) Referred to primary and taking capacitance into account; (d) The frequency response.

(d)

between these. The equivalent circuit referred to the primary is shown in Fig. 1.17(c), in which C'_p takes into account all the capacitive effects. The voltage gain/frequency response for the transformer is shown in Fig. 1.17(d). At low frequencies, gain falloff occurs because of L_c. At midfrequencies, L_c and C'_p exhibit a broad parallel resonance (low–Q) response, while the effect of L'_p is negligible, so the response curve is reasonably flat in the midband range. At the higher frequencies L'_p and C'_p exhibit series resonance, resulting in a peak in the response curve. Beyond this, the shunting effect of C'_p causes gain falloff.

It must be kept in mind that the equivalent circuits discussed are valid only for the ac signal, and cannot be used, for example, for analysis of dc conditions.

1.12.2 High-Frequency Transformers

In the radio–frequency range the parameters L_1, L_2, and k are readily measured. Therefore, it is more convenient to represent the circuit in terms of these parameters. If a magnetic core is used for tuning, for example, its losses can be taken into account by a reduced Q factor, which can also be measured.

The basic circuit is shown in Fig. 1.18(a). Z_L may be a load resistor or it may be a tuning capacitor for the secondary. The equivalent circuit is shown in Fig. 1.18(b), in which

$$Z_p = R_p + j\omega L_p \qquad (1.96)$$

$$Z_s = R_s + j\omega L_s \qquad (1.97)$$

$$Z_m = j\omega M \qquad (1.98)$$

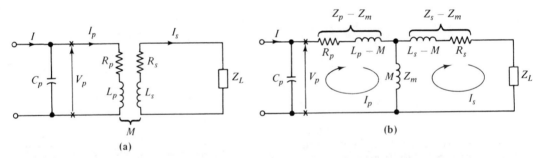

FIGURE 1.18. (a) The high–frequency transformer circuit; (b) The equivalent circuit.

Analyzing the circuit from points X-X by applying Kirchhoff's voltage law to the two loops (note that C_p, the primary tuning capacitor, does not enter into the equations at this point):

$$V_p = I_p Z_p - I_s Z_m \qquad (1.99)$$

$$0 = -I_p Z_m + I_s (Z_s + Z_L) \qquad (1.100)$$

Solving these for I_p yields

$$I_p = \frac{V_p (Z_s + Z_L)}{Z_p(Z_s + Z_L) - Z_m^2} \qquad (1.101)$$

The effective primary impedance, seen to the right of points X-X, Fig. 1.18(b), is

$$Z_p' = \frac{V_p}{I_p}$$

$$= Z_p - \frac{Z_m^2}{Z_s + Z_L} \qquad (1.102)$$

For the case where Z_L is a load resistor R_L and Z_s is a small coupling loop, such that $|Z_L| \gg |Z_s|$, the effective primary impedance becomes

$$Z_p' = Z_p - \frac{Z_m^2}{R_L}$$

$$= R_p + j\omega L_p + \frac{\omega^2 M^2}{R_L}$$

$$= R_p \left(1 + \frac{\omega^2 M^2}{R_p R_L} \right) + j\omega L_p \qquad (1.103)$$

Thus the effective series resistance of the primary is seen to be increased, and is given by

$$R_p' = R_p \left(1 + \frac{\omega^2 M^2}{R_p R_L} \right) \qquad (1.104)$$

Defining the Q factor of the primary circuit *by itself* as

$$Q_p = \frac{\omega_0 L_p}{R_p} \qquad (1.105)$$

and of the secondary as

$$Q_s = \frac{\omega_0 L_s}{R_L} \qquad (1.106)$$

and recalling that $M = k \sqrt{L_p L_s}$, Eq. (1.104) for R_p' can be written

$$R_p' = R_p(1 + k^2 Q_p Q_s x^2) \quad \text{where } x = \frac{\omega}{\omega_0} \qquad (1.107)$$

at resonance, $x = 1$ and R_p' becomes

$$R_{p0}' = R_p(1 + k^2 Q_p Q_s) \qquad (1.108)$$

The effective dynamic impedance of the circuit, from Eq. (1.67) is

$$R'_D = \frac{L_p}{C_p R'_{po}}$$

$$= \frac{R_D}{1 + k^2 Q_p Q_s} \qquad (1.109)$$

Example 1.10   A tuned primary has an undamped Q factor of 100 and is tuned to resonate at 1MHz by a 200-pF capacitor. The primary is mutually inductive coupled by means of a secondary coil of self-inductance 0.13 mH to a load of 5 $k\Omega$, the coefficient of coupling being $k = 0.2$. Determine the effective load referred to the primary at resonance.

Solution

$$R_D = \frac{Q_p}{\omega_0 C_p}$$

$$= \frac{100}{2\pi \times 10^6 \times 200 \times 10^{-12}}$$

$$= 79.6 k\Omega$$

$$Q_s = \frac{\omega_0 L_s}{R_L}$$

$$= \frac{2\pi \times 10^6 \times 0.13 \times 10^{-3}}{5 \times 10^3}$$

$$= 0.163$$

Therefore,

$$R'_D = \frac{79.6}{1 + (0.2)^2 \times 100 \times 0.163}$$

$$= 48 \, k\Omega$$

The effective Q factor of the primary is seen to be

$$Q'_p = \frac{Q_p}{1 + k^2 Q_p Q_s x^2} \qquad (1.110)$$

Equation (1.110) follows, since

$$\frac{Q'_p}{Q_p} = \frac{R_p}{R'_p}$$

Although the effective Q factor is a function of frequency, (i.e., of x), at frequencies within about $\pm 10\%$ of resonance, the variation may be ignored, and the frequency response of the circuit as a whole is given by the equation for a parallel tuned circuit, Eq. (1.68). It is left as an exercise for the student to show that, for a constant–current signal source I, the primary voltage V_p is given approximately by

$$V_p = \frac{I \cdot R_D'}{(1 + jyQ_p')} \qquad (1.111)$$

and the load voltage by

$$V_L = V_p k \sqrt{\frac{L_s}{L_p}} \qquad (1.112)$$

Another common arrangement is where Z_L is a secondary tuning capacitor C_s. When the circuits are tuned to the same resonant frequency, this is known as a synchronously tuned transformer; $L_p C_p = L_s C_s = (\omega_0)^{-2}$. Analysis may be carried out in a manner similar to that for the equivalent circuit of Fig. 1.18(b), although this is much more lengthy and involved. For the case where the circuits are identical (that is, $Q_p = Q_s = Q$; $C_p = C_s = C$), the expression for the output voltage V_2 is

$$V_2 = \frac{-jIR_D kQ}{x[(1 + (xkQ)^2 - y^2Q^2) + j2yQ]} \qquad (1.113)$$

At resonance, $\omega = \omega_0$ and therefore $x = 1$ and $y = 0$. Let V_{2o} represent the output voltage at resonance; then

$$V_{2o} = \frac{-jIR_D Q}{1 + k^2Q^2} \qquad (1.114)$$

The $-j$ shows that V_{2o} lags I by $90°$, an important result in the theory of phase discriminators.

The modulus of V_{2o} is a maximum when $kQ = 1$, as can be proved by differentiation. For $kQ = 1$, the transformer is said to be *critically coupled*; for $kQ < 1$, it is *undercoupled*; and for $kQ > 1$, it is *overcoupled*. This is illustrated in Fig. 1.19, where the modulus is plotted against x for $kQ = 0.5$, 1.0, and 1.5. A value of $IR_D = 1$ V was used as reference, and $Q = 100$.

The 3–dB bandwidth of the critically coupled circuit can be shown to be

$$B_{3\,dB} = \sqrt{2}\frac{f_0}{Q} \qquad (1.115)$$

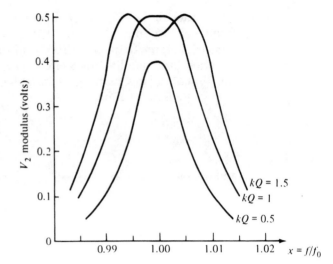

FIGURE 1.19. Frequency response curves for coupled circuits.

(i.e., it is $\sqrt{2}$ times that of a single tuned circuit). At the same time it can be shown that the 60–dB bandwidth is *reduced* by a factor of about $\sqrt{10^3}$ from the single tuned circuit bandwidth, which of course is indicative of the steep sides on the response curve of the critically coupled circuit.

The double–humped curve of Fig. 1.19 is a feature of the overcoupled circuit. This is often combined with critically coupled circuits (or slightly undercoupled) to obtain a composite response which is flat along the top and which has sides that are falling away sharply. Figure 1.20 illustrates the

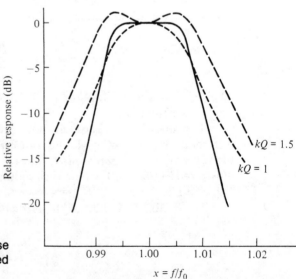

FIGURE 1.20. Composite response
curve for combined critically coupled
and overcoupled circuits.

composite response of a $kQ = 1$ and a $kQ = 1.5$ combination of trans-formers. The curves are plotted in decibels relative to the resonant (or mid-frequency) response, against the frequency variable $x = \omega/\omega_0$. It should be noted that the overall, or composite, curve is obtained simply by *adding* the decibel response of the individual circuit curves.

1.12.3 Tapped Inductor

The *tapped inductor*, Fig. 1.21(a), provides a form of mutual inductive coupling for which the coupling coefficient k (between the two sections of the coil) may be assumed to be unity. Often, the coil forms the tuning induc-tor of a resonant circuit as shown in Fig. 1.21(a), but this of course is not necessarily always the case. The coil can be treated as a transformer of turns ratio $n = N/N_1$, and the equivalent circuit of Fig. 1.21(b) drawn. Note that the coil L remains in the circuit, as this corresponds to the magnetizing coil L_c in Fig. 1.17(b).

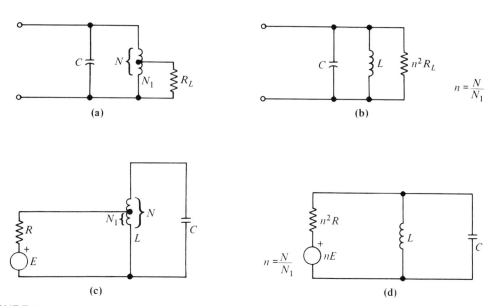

FIGURE 1.21. (a) The tapped inductor as a transformer; (b) Referred to pri-mary; (c) Tapped on primary side; (d) Is (c) referred to secondary.

The circuit is often used to reduce the loading effect of R_L on the Q factor of the tuned circuit. An example will illustrate this.

Example 1.11   A tuned circuit has an undamped Q factor of 200 and an undamped dynamic impedance of $1M\Omega$. A load of $5k\Omega$ is tapped into the coil in the ratio 1:10. Find the equivalent Q factor of the circuit.

$$n^2 R_L = (10)^2 \times 5 \times 10^3$$

$$= 0.5 \, M\Omega$$

The effective dynamic impedance is the undamped R_D in parallel with the effective load $n^2 R_L$.

$$R_D' = \frac{0.5 \times 1}{0.5 + 1}$$

$$= 0.333 \, M\Omega$$

Assuming that C remains unchanged, the Q factor will be reduced in the ratio R_D' / R_D:

$$Q' = 200 \times \frac{0.333}{1}$$

$$= 67$$

This is low, but had the load of $5k\Omega$ been connected directly across the tuned circuit, the effective Q factor would have been

$$Q' = 200 \times \frac{0.005}{1}$$

$$= 1.0$$

Note that, although the voltage gain of the circuit is reduced by a factor $1/n$, because of the effect of the step–down transformer if the circuit forms the load of a voltage amplifier, the voltage gain will be approximately proportional to $n^2 R_L$, which is n^2 times what it would have been had R_L been connected directly; the overall effect on voltage gain therefore is to give a step up in voltage of approximately n times.

Where the loading effect of the source on a circuit has to be reduced, the tapping point is placed on the input side, as shown in Fig. 1.21(c). Of course, both input and load may be tapped down on the coil. From the point of view of the circuit, the source resistance R is stepped up in the ratio n^2, and the source voltage is stepped up by the voltage step–up ratio n. The equivalent circuit *referred to the secondary* is therefore as shown in Fig. 1.21(d).

1.12.4 Capacitive Tap

The arrangements of Fig. 1.22(a) is often used to couple a load resistance R_L to a tuned circuit while reducing the damping effect of R_L on

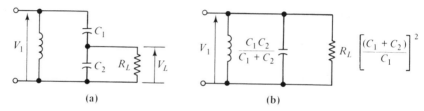

FIGURE 1.22.   (a) Capacitive tap; (b) Referred to input.

the tuned circuit. The easiest method of analyzing this circuit is to find the admittance presented by the C_1, C_2, R_L branch.

$$Y = \frac{j\omega C_1(G_L + j\omega C_2)}{j\omega C_1 + G_L + j\omega C_2}$$

$$= \frac{G_L(\omega C_1)^2}{G_L^2 + \omega^2(C_1 + C_2)^2} + j\frac{\omega C_1(G_L^2 + \omega^2 C_2(C_1 + C_2))}{G_L^2 + \omega^2(C_1 + C_2)^2} \quad (1.116)$$

where $G_L = 1/R_L$. Note how the admittance of G_L and C_2 in parallel (Y_p) is simply the sum of the conductance and susceptance, while the admittance of C_1 in series with the parallel circuit of C_2 and G_L requires use of the formula $Y_1Y_p/(Y_1 + Y_p)$ where $Y_1 = j\omega C_1$.

For the tap to be effective in practice, it must be arranged that $\omega C_2 \gg G_L$ so that the expression for Y becomes

$$Y \cong \left(\frac{C_1}{C_1 + C_2}\right)^2 G_L + j\omega\frac{C_1 C_2}{C_1 + C_2} \quad (1.117)$$

From this, the equivalent circuit of Fig. 1.22(b) can be drawn. Clearly, the effective tuning capacity is C_1 in series with C_2, and the effective resistance across the circuit is R_L increased by the factor $[(C_1 + C_2)/C_1]^2$.

The output voltage V_L across R_L is, for $\omega C_2 \gg G_L$, from Fig. 1.22(a)

$$V_L \approx V_1 \cdot \left(\frac{C_1}{C_1 + C_2}\right) \quad (1.118)$$

This reduction in voltage is the price paid for the reduced damping on the tuned circuit.

Many other coupling arrangements are possible and the general principles of analysis described in the previous sections can be applied. Usually there will be restrictions and approximations permissible for a given practical situation which simplify the analysis. An attempt should be made to simplify algebraic expressions and to collect terms together for comparison before these are evaluated; obviously, algebraic manipulation is useful only where it results in simplification or it brings out the significance of certain terms.

1.13 THÉVENIN'S THEOREM

Thévenin's theorem states that any two–terminal linear network of sources and impedances can be replaced by a voltage–generator equivalent circuit, the EMF E' of which is equal to the open–circuit voltage appearing between the terminals, and the internal impedance Z' of which is equal to the impedance appearing between the terminals when all sources are replaced by their internal impedances. As a specific example, consider the circuit of Fig. 1.23(a) for which it is desired to reduce the signal source and the 100-Ω input resistance to an equivalent voltage source. Looking to the left of the terminals 1–1, the open–circuit voltage [i.e., with the amplifier load removed, Fig. 1.23(b)] is

$$E' = \frac{3 \times 100}{50 + 100}$$

$$= 2\,\mu V$$

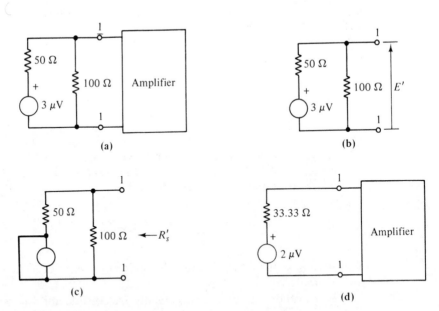

(a) (b) (c) (d)

FIGURE 1.23. (a) Circuit example used to illustrate Thevenin's theorem; (b) Load removed; (c) Internal source short–circuited; (d) Thevenin equivalent circuit.

The internal impedance seen when the source EMF is short–circuited, Fig. 1.23(c), is

$$R_s' = \frac{50 \times 100}{50 + 100}$$

$$= 33.33 \ \Omega$$

The equivalent circuit is therefore as shown in Fig. 1.23(d).

Thevenin's theorem offers a powerful means of simplifying circuits for the purpose of analysis.

1.14 MAXIMUM POWER TRANSFER

Where a signal source is required to deliver power to a load, the power transfer should be a maximum. The average power delivered to the load Z_L, Fig. 1.24(a) is

$$P_L = V_R \cdot I$$

$$= \frac{ER_L}{\sqrt{(R_s + R_L)^2 + (X_s + X_L)^2}} \cdot \frac{E}{\sqrt{(R_s + R_L)^2 + (X_s + X_L)^2}}$$

$$= \frac{E^2 R_L}{(R_s + R_L)^2 + (X_s + X_L)^2} \qquad (1.119)$$

(a)

(b)

FIGURE 1.24. (a) Signal source delivering power to load; (b) Power as a function of load impedance.

Looking first at the effect of X_L on P_L, it will be seen that by making $X_L = -X_s$, P_L will be at a maximum given by

$$P_L = \frac{E^2 R_L}{(R_s + R_L)^2} \qquad (1.120)$$

R_L can now be varied to maximize this expression and the best value is obtained by equating the differential coefficient of P_L with respect to R_L to zero:

$$\frac{dP_L}{dR_L} = \frac{E^2[(R_s + R_L) - 2R_L]}{(R_s + R_L)^3} = 0$$

from which $\qquad R_s = R_L \qquad (1.121)$

Combining this with the condition on X_L, it is seen that for maximum power transfer, the load impedance must be the complex conjugate of the source impedance, or

$$R_L + jX_L = R_s - jX_s \qquad (1.122)$$

This is known as a *conjugate match*, and although it results in maximum power transfer, it is good at only one frequency (i.e., that which makes $jX_L = -jX_s$).

Substituting $R_L = R_s$ in Eq. (1.120) gives the maximum available power:

$$P_L = \frac{E^2 R_s}{(R_s + R_s)^2}$$

$$= \frac{E^2}{4R_s} \qquad (1.123)$$

Alternatively, if the constant–current generator representation of a source is used, Fig. 1.1(b), then:

$$P_L = \frac{(IR_s)^2}{4R_s}$$

$$= \frac{I^2 R_s}{4} \qquad (1.124)$$

Equation (1.124) gives the maximum available power in terms of the constant current I and internal resistance R_s. This presentation is used, for example, in Eq. (4.51), which is used in the determination of noise factor.

Equation (1.124) may be written in terms of source conductance $G_s = 1/R_s$:

$$P_L = \frac{I^2}{4G_s} \qquad (1.125)$$

When compared with Eq. (1.123) the duality of the voltage and current representations becomes apparent.

Where operation is required over a range of frequencies, the best value for Z_L is that which produces a true *reflectionless match*, which is

$$Z_L = Z_s \qquad (1.126)$$

or
$$R_L + jX_L = R_s + jX_s$$

Reflectionless matching is not as efficient as conjugate matching, as illustrated in Fig. 1.24(b). However, it does give a fairly broad maximum, and there are other considerations which make it the usual choice when signal transmission over lines is required, as described in Chapter 12.

1.15 FILTERS

1.15.1 LC Filters

LC filters made up of several cascaded L, T, or II sections are frequently used for bandpass purposes in telephony and radio work. Such filters are very similar to transmission lines, and in some instances transmission lines are used as filters. The analysis of *LC* filters is very similar to that of transmission lines, which are dealt with in detail in Chapter 12.

The L section forms the basic component of these filters, as shown in Fig. 1.25(a). It is comprised of a series element which has half the value of a full series standard element, and a shunt element which has twice the value of a full shunt element. If the series element is a capacitance and the shunt element is an inductance, a high–pass filter is formed. If the series element is an inductance and the shunt–element a capacitance, a low–pass filter is formed.

Two basic L sections may be joined with their shunt elements in parallel to form the basic T section, which is comprised of two series half-elements and a shunt full element, as shown in Fig. 1.25(b). Also, two L sections may be joined with their series elements connected to form a basic II section comprised of a full series element and two double shunt elements, as in Fig. 1.25(c). The equivalent T and II sections have identical transmission

FIGURE 1.25. LC filters: (a) General filter half- (or L-) section; (b) Two half-sections combined to form a T section; (c) Two half-sections combined to form a Π section; (d) Simple high-pass half-section; (e) Simple low-pass half-section.

characteristics but differ in their characteristics impedances. The characteristic impedances of the T and Π sections are given by

$$Z_{0T}^2 = Z_1 Z_2 (1 + Z_1/4Z_2) \qquad (1.127)$$

$$Z_{0\Pi}^2 = \frac{Z_1 Z_2}{(1 + Z_1/4Z_2)} \qquad (1.128)$$

The characteristic impedances of the T and Π sections are related by

$$Z_{0T} Z_{0\Pi} = Z_1 Z_2 \qquad (1.129)$$

When the impedance Z_1 in Fig. 1.25(a) is made a capacitance and Z_2 is made an inductance, a high-pass filter section is formed, as shown in Fig. 1.25(d). When Z_1 is made an inductance and Z_2 is made a capacitance, then a low-pass filter is formed, as shown in Fig. 1.25(e).

The frequency response characteristics of several filter sections are shown in Fig. 1.26. Figure 1.26(a) shows a plot of the attenuation and phase shift between the input and output signals for a simple low-pass T- or Π-section filter. For frequencies below the cutoff value, the filter ideally has zero attenuation. For frequencies above the cutoff value, the attenuation rises sharply with frequency. However, within the passband, (below f_c) the phase shift varies from 0° at dc to 180° at cutoff. This type of filter must be followed by a phase compensation network, or serious distortion of the transmitted signal will result.

Figure 1.26(b) shows the type of frequency response characteristic produced by a more complex filter, the m-derived filter. The main difference between this filter and the simple one already presented is that the shunt element is a series-tuned circuit. It is tuned to a frequency slightly above the cutoff frequency, and at that frequency the attenuation rises to infinity (zero transmission throught the filter). This creates a much sharper cutoff of signals at frequencies above cutoff. A sudden reversal of the phase shift also occurs at the zero frequency f_0 as well, but since this is outside the useful bandpass of the filter, it does not cause any problems.

Figure 1.26(c) shows the frequency response for a simple high-pass filter T or Π section. Again, there is zero attenuation within the passband (above f_c) and rapidly rising attenuation for frequencies below f_c. The phase shift again varies in the passband, but is 180° for all frequencies below f_c. Figure 1.26(d) shows what happens when a signal is passed through a simple low-pass filter section in tandem with a simple high-pass section. The result is a bandpass filter, providing the cutoff frequency of the high-pass section is lower than that of the low-pass section. Within the bandpass, there is zero attenuation, with attenuation rising rapidly outside the band. Again, the phase varies within the passband, and is constant ± 180° outside the passband (not shown).

1.15.2 Piezoelectric Crystal Filters

Piezoelectric crystals exhibit the property that when an electric potential is applied across the faces of the crystal, it physically bends or deforms. Conversely, when the same crystal is mechanically deformed by pressure, an electric potential is developed between the crystal faces. The crystal also exhibits the phenomenon of mechanical resonance when it is excited with an

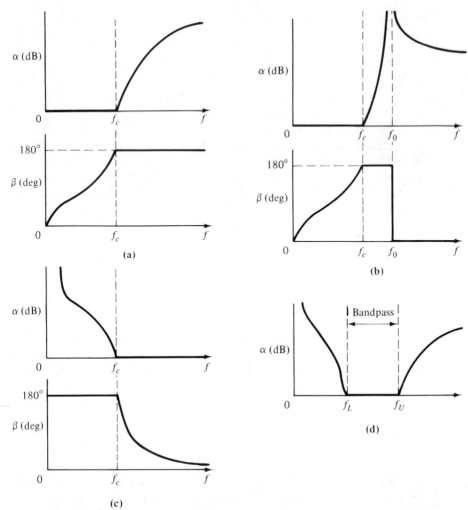

FIGURE 1.26. Frequency response characteristics of some LC filters: (a) Attenuation and phase shift response for a simple low–pass T- or ⊓ –section filter; (b) Response for a more complex (*m*–derived) low–pass filter section; (c) Response for a simple high–pass filter T or ⊓ section; (d) Response for a bandpass filter made up of a simple high–pass section in tandem with a simple low–pass section.

alternating potential of the correct frequency. The frequency of mechanical resonance is determined by the size and shape of the crystal sample in question and can be controlled over several orders of magnitude, from about 20 kHz to about 50 MHz, with considerable precision. In form, the packaged crystal is a slice of crystal cut in such a way as to give the desired mechanical resonant frequency, with isolated electrodes deposited on opposite sides so that a capacitive device is made.

Electrically the mechanical resonance of this device makes the crystal look like a very high-Q series resonant circuit, with a capacitor in parallel with it. This capacitor causes a second parallel resonance, which occurs at a frequency that is very close to the mechanical resonant point. The reactance of a quartz crystal is plotted in Fig. 1.27, and shows that for low frequencies up to the series mechanical resonance, the crystal is capacitive. For frequencies between the series resonant and parallel resonant points, the reactance is inductive; and for frequencies above the parallel resonance, the reactance is again capacitive. At series resonance $X_{Ls} = X_{Cs}$ and the reactance is zero, and at parallel resonance $X_{Ls} = (X_{Cs}$ ser. $X_{Cp})$ and the reactance is infinite. The resonant frequencies of the crystal are very well defined and very stable, provided that the operating temperature is kept constant, making it very well suited as the high-Q resonant circuit which controls the operating frequency of oscillator circuits. This use of the crystal is discussed in Chapter 6.

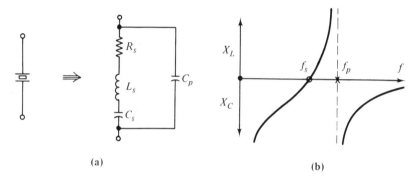

(a)   (b)

FIGURE 1.27. The quartz piezoelectric crystal: (a) The graphic symbol and the equivalent circuit of a quartz crystal; (b) Variation of crystal terminal reactance with frequency.

The reactance characteristic of the quartz crystal is changed radically by placing an inductance in parallel with it. The series resonant frequency remains unchanged, but the parallel resonant frequency is moved higher, so the separation between the two is greater than is the case for the crystal by itself.

Placing an inductor in series with the crystal has similar drastic effects on the reactance characteristic. In this case, however, the parallel resonant frequency remains unchanged while the series resonant frequency is caused to move lower and a second series resonant frequency is created.

The frequency separation between the series and parallel resonant frequencies of the crystal itself is small, of the order of a few hundred hertz at most for a 1-MHz crystal. Frequency spreading by means of series or parallel inductors can increase this separation to a few thousand hertz, making it possible to use the crystals as bandpass filter elements for IF amplifiers and for sideband separation.

The crystal gate shown in Fig. 1.28(a), is a narrow–band sharp-cutoff filter circuit which makes use of the reactance characteristic of the crystal itself. It has been used for separating the sidebands in SSB circuits. When the capacitance of C_2 is relative large, as high-pass sharp-cutoff filter with the characteristics of Fig. 1.28(b) is formed. At the frequency f_∞, the reactance of the crystal is capacitive and equal in magnitude to that of the capacitor C_2, so the signal fed to the output through the crystal is equal in magnitude and opposite in phase to that fed through C_2, causing a complete cancellation at the output. At frequency f_0 the reactances are again equal in magnitude, but this time the crystal is inductive. The signal through the crystal is shifted by 90° while that through the capacitor is shifted by $-90°$, so both arrive at the output in phase with each other. For frequencies above f_0 up to f_1, just below the parallel resonant frequency of the crystal, the attenuation remains low as the signal is propagated through the capacitor C_2. Severe phase–shift distortion occurs near f_p, so the usable passband is only between f_0 and f_1. The cutoff beyond f_1 is quite gentle, but f_0 and f_∞ are only separated by a few hundred hertz, providing a sharp lower cutoff. Frequency shifting by a series inductor can be used to increase the passband to usable widths.

When the reactance of C_2 is made considerably higher, a low–pass filter with the characteristic of Fig. 1.28(c) results. Again at f_0 the crystal reac-

(a)

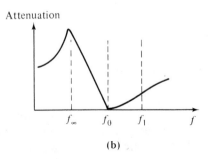

(b)

FIGURE 1.28. The crystal gate: (a) The circuit; (b) A plot of attenuation versus frequency for the case where X_{C2} is small, giving a high–pass characteristic; (c) A plot of attenuation versus frequency for the case where X_{C2} is large, giving a low–pass characteristic.

(c)

tance is equal to that of the capacitor, and inductive, so the signals arrive at the output in phase with each other. At f_∞ the crystal reactance is equal to that of the capacitor and capacitive, resulting in complete signal cancellation, this time at a frequency higher than f_0 (and f_p). For frequencies below f_0 down to f_1 near f_s, the attenuation is low, determined by X_{C2}. Phase-shift distortion near f_s prevents use of frequencies below this, and again the usable bandpass can be increased by using a series inductor.

The crystal gate is inexpensive to build and uncritical in its adjustment, making it attractive, but it suffers from the disadvantage of providing a very narrow usable passband width. The crystal lattice filter is a more complicated circuit, but it provides bandwidths of a few hundred hertz to several tens of kHz and essentially flat response characteristics within the passband. Further, sharp cutoff can be provided on both the upper and lower edges of the passband.

Figure 1.29(a) shows the circuit of a full–lattice filter and Fig. 1.29(b) shows a half–lattice filter. The attenuation characteristics of both are the same, and are shown in Fig. 1.29(c). The crystals used in the lattice are matched pairs, so that crystals CR_1 and CR_2 are identical, and CR_3 and CR_4 are identical to each other but different from CR_1 and CR_2. The crystals are chosen so that the series resonant frequency of CR_3 and CR_4 coincides with the parallel resonant frequency of CR_1 and CR_2. The inductances of the coils in the input and output circuits are effectively in parallel with the crystals and act to space out the separation between series and parallel resonance and provide the second parallel resonance of each crystal.

At $f_{\infty 1}$ the reactances of X_1 and X_3 are both inductive and equal, so the in–phase and antiphase signals fed to the output cancel, providing infinite attenuation. This is very near the parallel resonant frequency of X_1 and just past this frequency f_{01} occurs where again the crystal reactances are equal, but X_1 is capacitive and X_3 is inductive, so the signals arrive at the output in phase with each other. $f_{\infty 1}$ and f_{01} delineate the lower cutoff frequency of the filter.

At $f_{\infty 2}$ the reactances X_1 and X_3 are equal but capacitive, so that cancellation again takes place. This occurs just above and very near the upper parallel resonant frequency of X_3. Just below $f_{\infty 2}$, the reactances are again equal, but opposite, so that the signals are again in phase, at f_{05}. These frequencies delineate the upper cutoff frequency of the filter.

At f_{03} the reactances X_1 and X_3 are again equal and opposite, so the signals arrive in phase. At frequency f_{02}, crystal 1 has zero reactance, shorting the input to the output. At frequency f_{03}, crystal 3 has zero reactance and again the output is connected directly to the input. Between these frequencies, the signal is fed to the output with very low attenuation values, providing the bandpass of the filter. Outside the band, attenuation is relatively high, and can be improved by providing additional gradual cutoff filtering in tandem, such as with a normal IF amplifier filter.

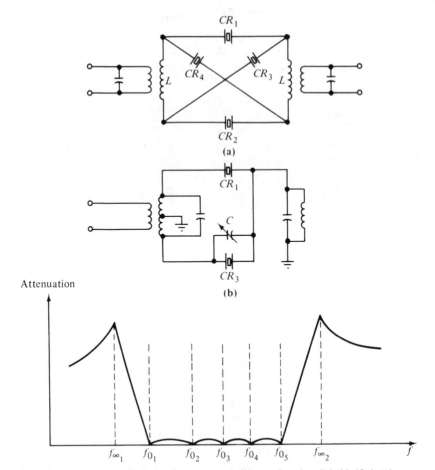

FIGURE 1.29. (a) Full–lattice crystal filter circuit; (b) Half–lattice crystal circuit; (c) Attenuation versus frequency for lattice filters.

1.15.3 Electromechanical Filters

A metal disk which is mechanically driven with an axially applied oscillating force will exhibit a resonant mode which is analogous to parallel resonance in an electrical circuit. Similarly, an axially driven rod will exhibit series resonance. When a series of disks and rods are interconnected to form a ladder network, and the resonances of the various components are carefully chosen, a bandpass filter with sharp–cutoff characteristics results. Collins Radio has developed a mechanical filter of this type for use as sideband filters in communications receivers. These filters are electrically driven through magnetostrictive couplers and generally operate in the 100–kHz region. Bandwidths up to 5 kHz with very sharp cutoff characteristics are available. The unit is packaged in containers that are about 2 inches long and ½ inch square, and are arranged for printed–circuit–board mounting. The mechanical filter is pretuned at the factory, and no further adjustment is necessary or permitted, making it a very convenient component for receiver manufacture.

The ceramic filter is also a type of mechanical filter, but in this case the resonant components are in the form of disks of a piezoelectric ceramic such as barium titanate, arranged in a ladder configuration. The piezoelectric ceramic disks provide their own electromechanical conversion, and separate transducers are not necessary. In this respect the ceramic filter is more akin to the quartz crystal filter.

The ceramic filter is smaller than the mechanical filter, by about half, and has characteristics which are more nearly those of a complex crystal filter. They are also less complex and easier to manufacture than the mechanical filter and thus somewhat cheaper, which makes them very attractive for use in receivers. Ceramic filters are currently available in frequencies around 500 kHz and bandwidths ranging from 2 to 50 kHz.

1.15.4   The Complex Transfer Function of a Filter

The *complex transfer function* is analogous to the voltage transfer function introduced by Eq. (1.10), but takes into account the amplitude and phase–shift dependence on frequency. It is usually denoted by $H(\omega)$ where

$$H(\omega) = \frac{V_{out}}{V_{in}} \qquad (1.130)$$

The complex transfer function consists of two parts, a modulus, $|H(\omega)|$, and a phase–shift, $\underline{/\Theta(\omega)}$, so

$$H(\omega) = |H(\omega)| \cdot \underline{/\Theta(\omega)} \qquad (1.131)$$

The use of the complex transfer function will be found, for example, in Sections 2.3 and 4.2.3.

1.16   PROBLEMS

1.   A battery has an internal resistance of 0.01 Ω and an EMF of 2 V. Derive an equivalent constant–current generator circuit to represent the battery.

2.   A 10-Ω and 15-Ω resistor are connected in series. Find the equivalent conductance.

3.   Explain what is meant by the voltage transfer function of a circuit. Determine the voltage transfer function of the circuit shown in Fig. 1.5(b), where each resistor is 10.0 Ω.

4.   For the T attenuator of Example 1.1, show that the generator sees an effective load of 50 Ω and that the load is fed by a generator of equivalent internal resistance of 50 Ω.

5.   For the L network of Example 1.2, determine the insertion loss, in decibels.

6.   For the L network of Example 1.3, determine the insertion loss, in decibels.

7.   A 1.0–mH inductor has series resistance of 50 kΩ. Determine the impedance at a frequency of 15.9 MHz. Draw the phasor diagram for the circuit, showing the component voltages and the total voltage when a 15.9 MHz sinusoidal current of 1 mA peak flows through the inductor.

8.   A 0.1–μF capacitor has an effective parallel resistance of 100 kΩ, which may be assumed constant. Determine the modulus and phase angle of the impedance at a frequency of 60 Hz.

9.   A 2–μH inductor has a series resistance of 10 Ω. Determine the equivalent parallel circuit which represents the inductor at a frequency of 100 MHz. Does the inductance value change? Is the equivalent parallel resistance a function of frequency?

10.   A capacitor can be represented by the parallel combination of 20 pF and 100 kΩ, these values being constant. Determine the equivalent series representation at a frequency of 100 MHz. Do the series components vary with frequency?

11.   Calculate the minimum and the maximum capacitance values obtainable using three 0.01–μF capacitors.

12.   Two windings are arranged such that the coefficient of coupling between them is 0.01. The self–inductances of the windings are 10mH and 5 mH. Calculate the maximum and minimum inductance values obtainable from the combination.

13.   Explain what is meant by "series resonance of a tuned circuit." A 2–μH inductor has a series resistance of 2 Ω. Calculate the capacitance value required for series resonance at 50 MHz. A 1-V rms sinusoidal signal at the resonant frequency is applied across the series circuit. Calculate the voltage appearing across the inductor and across the capacitor.

14.   Show that the variable y introduced in Eq. (1.54) is given by $y \cong \pm 2\Delta f/f_0$, where $\Delta f = |f - f_0|$, at frequencies close to resonance. Using this, plot the modulus and phase angle of the series impedance of an LRC circuit as a function of $\pm 2\Delta f/B_3$, where B_3 is the bandwidth and $R = 1$ Ω.

15. The inductor and capacitor in Problem 13 are connected in parallel. Find the parallel resonant frequency. Does this differ significantly from the series value?

16. A parallel tuned circuit is resonant at 50 MHz when the tuning capacitor is 50 pF. The Q factor of the circuit is 150. Calculate the dynamic impedance of the circuit. A sinusoidal signal of 2 V rms at the resonant frequency is applied across the circuit. Calculate: (a) the total circuit current; (b) the current in each branch. State any approximations made.

17. A coil is self–resonant at 20 MHz and has a Q factor of 200 (neglecting self–capacitance), which may be assumed constant. Calculate the effective Q factor at frequencies of 5 MHz and 10 MHz.

18. Explain briefly what is meant by skin effect and why it is undesirable. What steps may be taken to reduce skin effect in inductors?

19. To function properly, a circuit has to be connected to a 600–Ω signal source. The actual source is a 50–Ω microphone. Calculate the turns ratio of the matching transformer required. State any assumptions made.

20. A parallel tuned circuit is resonant at 10.7 MHz with a tuning capacity of 200 pF. The Q factor is 150. The circuit is loosely coupled to a 50–Ω resistive load through an untuned mutual-inductive coupling loop of self-inductance $0.1\,\mu$H and $k = 0.1$. Determine: (a) the dynamic impedance of the circuit at resonance; (b) the 3-dB bandwidth.

21. Explain briefly why an overcoupled tuned transformer should show two peaks. How can the response curves of tuned transformers be combined to produce a flat–topped response with sharply falling sides?

22. A signal source of EMF E and 1–kΩ internal resistance is tapped midway along an inductor which is tuned to parallel resonance. A 1–kΩ resistive load is also connected to the tapping point. Assuming that the resistance of the tuned circuit is negligible, show that the voltage across the tuned circuit is E.

23. Two 10–pF capacitors are connected in series to form the tuning capacitor of a 100–MHz parallel resonant circuit. The dynamic impedance of the circuit is 1 MΩ. A 10–kΩ load is connected across one of the capacitors. Determine: (a) the effective dynamic impedance of the loaded circuit; (b) the effective tuning capacity.

24. State Thevenin's theorem. Use it to show that the T attenuator and source in Example 1.1 can be replaced by an equivalent voltage generator of internal resistance 50.1 Ω and EMF $0.24E$, where E is the original source EMF.

25. Explain what is meant by a conjugate match. A signal source can be represented by an equivalent voltage generator of internal series impe-

dance $(50 + j10)$ Ω at 200 MHz. Calculate the series RC values of load required for conjugate matching. The internal EMF of the source is 3 μ V. Determine the maximum average power delivered to the load.

26.   A signal source can be represented by an equivalent constant-current generator the internal impedance of which is a 600-Ω resistance in parallel with a 10-pF capacitance. Determine the parallel load required for conjugate match at 300 MHz.

27.   Explain how the crystal lattice filter acts to provide bandpass filtering.

Chapter 2
Waveform Spectra

2.1 INTRODUCTION

Signals are characterized by an amplitude/time variation of some physical quantity; for example, the ear detects the air pressure/time variation in a sound wave. When transmitted through a telecommunications channel, at some point the signal is converted to analogous voltage- and current–time variations, which for brevity will be referred to as the *signal waveform*. A fact of fundamental importance in communications is that the time waveform of a signal can be represented by a series of sine and/or cosine waves. Such a representation is termed the *spectrum* of the signal. The reason the sine (or cosine) wave is chosen as the basic waveform type is because the response of a channel to this type of wave is easily determined mathematically and by measurement, and the results can be extended to the wave represented by the series of sine or cosine waves.

A sinusoidal waveform is shown in Fig. 2.1(a), which is described by the equation

$$v = V_{max} \sin 2\pi ft \qquad (2.1)$$

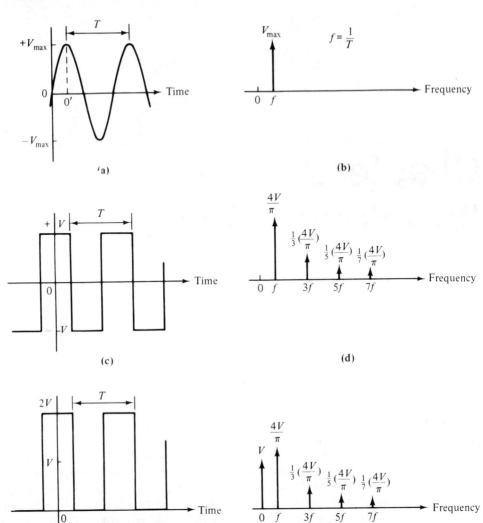

FIGURE 2.1. (a) A sinusoidal voltage waveform; (b) Spectrum of a sinusoidal waveform; (c) A square voltage waveform; (d) Frequency spectrum of a square wave; (e) A square wave with a positive dc component; (f) Frequency spectrum.

Alternatively, if the zero–time origin is started at 0′ instead of 0, the wave can be described by

$$v = V_{max} \cos 2\pi ft \qquad (2.2)$$

Since the choice of time origin is arbitrary, the choice of representing the wave by sine or cosine will usually be unimportant. Again, it should be noted that Eq. (2.1) can be expressed as

$$v = V_{max} \cos \left(2\pi ft - \frac{\pi}{2}\right) \tag{2.3}$$

The spectrum of the sinusoidal wave is simply a straight line of height V_{max}, positioned at f on the frequency axis, as shown in Fig. 2.1(b). The amplitude spectrum takes no account of whether the wave is represented by sine or cosine. A separate phase angle/frequency graph may be shown if this information is required.

2.2 COMPLEX REPETITIVE WAVES

Any waveform, other than the sine or cosine wave, which repeats itself at regular intervals is termed a *complex repetitive wave*. The period T over which the waveform repeats is termed the *periodic time*. The spectrum for any complex repetitive wave can be found by means of a mathematical method known as *Fourier analysis*, but only the results of Fourier analysis for some common types of repetitive waveforms will be used here.

The rectangular wave shown in Fig. 2.1(c) can be represented by the Fourier series

$$v = \frac{4V}{\pi}(\cos \omega t - 1/3\cos 3\omega t + 1/5\cos 5\omega t - 1/7\cos 7\omega t + \cdots)$$

where $\omega = \dfrac{2\pi}{T} \quad = 2\pi f \tag{2.4}$

Note that the symmetry of the square wave about the axes is similar to a cosine wave and as a result the series (2.4) contains only cosine terms.

The series has an infinite number of terms, but it can be seen that the amplitude of each term decreases as $1/n$. It will also be seen that the series contains only odd harmonics (i.e., components at frequencies f, $3f$, $5f$, etc.). The spectrum for the rectangular wave is shown in Fig. 2.1(d).

It must be clearly understood that the spectrum is more than just an alternative mathematical way of representing the wave. The component cosine waves for example, in the series for the rectangular wave, are as physically real as the original time waveform, and could be tuned out by means of frequency–selective filters. The first three components of the rectangular wave spectrum are shown in Fig. 2.2. Adding these produces the resultant waveform shown dotted, and it will be seen that this approaches the rectangular wave shape.

By shifting the rectangular wave up on the voltage axis, Fig. 2.1(e), a zero–frequency component is added to the spectrum, Fig. 2.1(f). This zero-

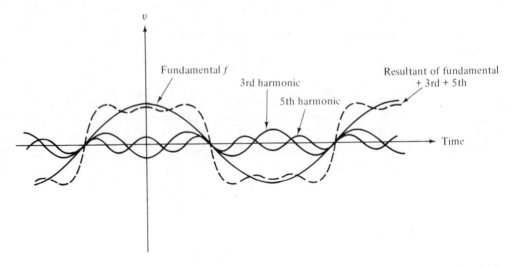

FIGURE 2.2. An illustration of how the three sinusoidal components add to approximate a square wave.

frequency component is just the average, or "dc," value of the waveform, and is the value that would be read on an average–reading voltmeter, such as a moving–coil meter. *Any waveform that is not symmetrical in area about the time axis will have a zero-frequency component.*

The series for the square wave of Fig. 2.1(e) is

$$v = V + \frac{4V}{\pi} (\cos \omega t - 1/3\cos 3\omega t + 1/5\cos 5\omega t - \cdots) \qquad (2.5)$$

thus showing the zero–frequency or "dc" component to be V.

The train of rectangular pulses, Fig. 2.3(a), has the spectrum shown in Fig. 2.3(b). This has a zero-frequency component and contains both odd and even harmonics (i.e., components at frequencies f, $2f$, $3f$, $4f$, etc., where $f = 1/T$). The amplitude of the spectrum components depends on the ratio of "on" time to periodic time, τ/T, the series being given by

$$v = \frac{V\tau}{T} + \frac{2V\tau}{T} \left(\frac{\sin x}{x}\cos \omega t + \frac{\sin 2x}{2x}\cos 2\omega t + \frac{\sin 3x}{3x}\cos 3\omega t + \cdots \right) \qquad (2.6)$$

where $x = \pi\tau/T$. The series is written this way because the function (sin nx)/nx is a well–known mathematical function and is readily available in tabular form. The amplitude of the "nth" harmonic is seen to be

$$V_n = \frac{2V\tau}{T} \frac{\sin (nx)}{nx} \qquad (2.7)$$

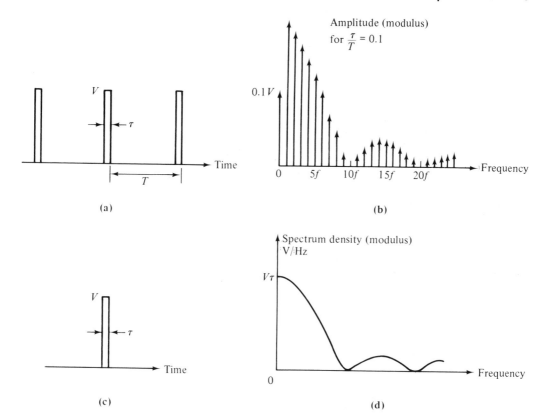

FIGURE 2.3.   (a) A train of positive–going rectangular voltage pulses; (b) Frequency spectrum; (c) A single positive–going rectangular voltage pulse; (d) Spectrum density function of a single pulse.

By letting T approach infinity, the train of rectangular pulses approaches a single pulse, Fig. 2.3(c). Also, as $T \rightarrow \infty$, $f \rightarrow 0$, and the spacing between the harmonic components shrinks to zero so that the spectrum becomes *continuous*, Fig. 2.3(d). By continuous is meant that there are no discrete harmonic frequencies, and only the envelope of the spectrum can be determined. This is given by

$$V(f) = V\tau \frac{\sin \pi f \tau}{\pi f \tau} \tag{2.8}$$

$V(f)$ in this case represents the *spectrum density* and has the units volts/frequency, V/Hz. The single pulse is an example of a nonrepetitive wave and is included here because its properties follow easily from those of the repetitive pulse waveform.

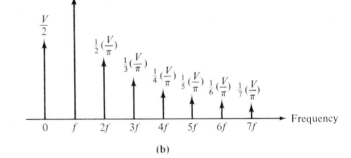

FIGURE 2.4. (a) A rising–ramp
triangular voltage waveform;
(b) Frequency spectrum.

Another function frequently encountered in practice is the sawtooth
wave, shown in Fig. 2.4(a). The Fourier series for this is

$$v = \frac{V}{2} - \frac{V}{\pi}(\sin \omega t + \tfrac{1}{2}\sin 2\omega t + \tfrac{1}{3}\sin 3\omega t + \cdots) \qquad (2.9)$$

The spectrum is shown in Fig. 2.4(b).

2.3 EFFECT OF FILTERING ON COMPLEX SIGNALS

As mentioned in Section 1.15.4, the complex transfer function of a filter
can be expressed in two parts, the modulus $|H(\omega)|$ and phase shift $\Theta(\omega)$.
The *modulus* affects the *amplitude* of the component waves of a spectrum,
this appearing on the spectrum graph as a change in the height of the arrows
representing the component amplitudes. The *phase shift* affects the *phase* of
the component waves, and although this does not show up on the spectrum
graph, it will be apparent on the output waveform. These results can be
shown mathematically. Let the Fourier representation of the input wave be

$$v_i(t) = V_1 \sin \omega_0 t + V_2 \sin 2\omega_0 t + \cdots + V_n \sin n\omega_0 t \qquad (2.10)$$

After passing through a filter that has a transfer function $H(\omega)$, the output wave will be

$$v_0(t,\omega) = H(\omega)v_i(t,\omega) \tag{2.11}$$

$$v_o(t) = |H(\omega_0)|\, V_1\sin(\omega_0 t + \Theta(\omega_0)) + |H(2\omega_0)|\, V_2\sin(2\omega_0 t + \Theta(2\omega_0))$$
$$+ \cdots + |H(n\omega_0)|\, V_n\, \sin(n\omega_0 t + \Theta(n\omega_0)) \tag{2.12}$$

This shows that the amplitude of the nth component of the output is

$$|H(n\omega_0)|\, V_n \tag{2.13}$$

where V_n is the amplitude of the nth component of input and the phase shift of the output component relative to the input component is

$$\Theta(n\omega_0) \tag{2.14}$$

When a signal passes through a network, amplitude and phase distortion may therefore both be introduced in the transfer process. Figure 2.5 shows the transfer function of a hypothetical network and its effect on an input signal consisting of a fundamental and a second harmonic. The input spectrum is shown in Fig. 2.5(b) and the modulus and phase shift of the transfer function as functions of frequency in Fig. 2.5(c) and (d). Since the modulus is constant at unity, the output spectrum is identical to the input, as shown in Fig. 2.5(e). The phase shift of this hypothetical network is shown as being zero at the fundamental frequency and π radians at the second harmonic. The second harmonic therefore undergoes a 180° phase shift. Figure 2.5(f) shows the input waveform, the component waves being shown dotted, and Fig. 2.5(g) shows the output waveform. In each case, the resultant wave can be obtained by graphically adding the component waves. The output wave is seen to differ from the input wave, and therefore distortion (in this case, phase distortion) has occurred. Mathematically the result may be shown as

$$\text{Input:} \quad v_i(t) = \sin\omega_0 t + \tfrac{1}{2}\sin 2\omega_0 t \tag{2.15}$$

$$\text{Output:} \quad v_o(t) = \sin\omega_0 t + \tfrac{1}{2}\sin(2\omega_0 t + \pi)$$
$$= \sin\omega_0 t - \tfrac{1}{2}\sin 2\omega_0 t \tag{2.16}$$

This is an example of phase–shift distortion.

As a second example, consider another hypothetical network, the modulus and phase shift as functions of frequency being shown in Fig. 2.6(c) and (d). Assuming the same input as in the previous example, the output spectrum will be as shown in Fig. 2.6(e), where the fundamental component

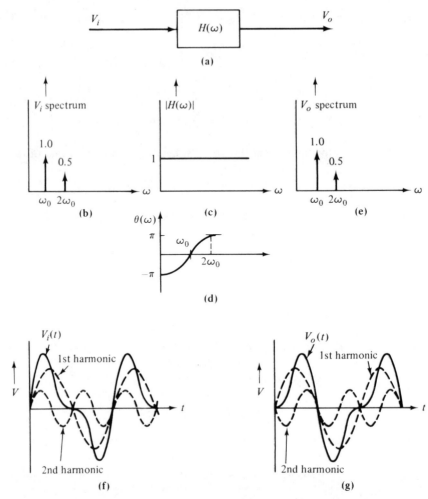

FIGURE 2.5.   A network with a transfer function with constant amplitude but with varying phase shift causing phase distortion: (a) The network; (b) Input signal frequency spectrum; (c) Transfer function amplitude plot; (d) Transfer function phase plot; (e) Output signal frequency spectrum; (f) Input signal waveform; (g) Output signal waveform.

is seen to be attenuated by half. Figure 2.6(d) shows that no phase shift occurs. The resultant output wave (along with the component waves shown dotted) will be as shown in Fig. 2.6(g). For comparison, the input wave is shown in Fig. 2.6(f). For the input wave as given by Eq. (2.15), the output wave in this case is given by

$$v_o(t) = \tfrac{1}{2}\sin \omega_0 t \ + \ \tfrac{1}{2}\sin 2\omega_0 t \tag{2.17}$$

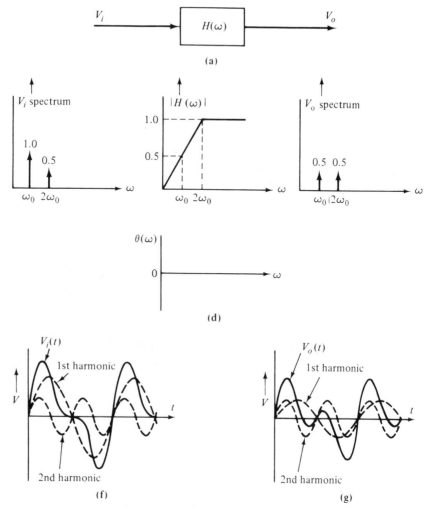

FIGURE 2.6. A network with a transfer function with a constant phase shift but varying amplitude causing amplitude distortion: (a) The network; (b) Input signal frequency spectrum; (c) Transfer function amplitude plot; (d) Transfer function phase plot; (e) Output signal frequency spectrum; (f) Input signal waveform; (g) Output signal waveform.

This is an example of amplitude distortion.

The modulus and phase–shift parts of the complex transfer function are not independent; that is, given one as a function of frequency, the frequency dependence of the other is then also determined. Although in principle the output wave can be reconstructed from the spectrum and phase information, this is seldom a practical approach, and special mathematical techniques are utilized to determine the shape of the output wave. However, it is important to know what components are present in the output spectrum, and a few illustrative examples follow.

2.3.1 High-Pass Filter

A *high–pass filter* (HPF) is one that passes the high–frequency components of a spectrum with negligible distortion of amplitude and phase. A simple example is the dc blocking capacitor, Fig. 2.7(a). In this circuit, R represents the input resistance of the following stage. Suppose that a square wave, Fig. 2.7(f), is applied to the input, and let the time constant CR of the filter be very much greater than the periodic time T of the wave. This is equivalent to making the resistance R very much greater than $|X_c|$ at the fundamental frequency.

The input spectrum of the square wave is shown in Fig. 2.7(b). The modulus and phase shift of the transfer function as functions of frequency are shown in Fig. 2.7(c) and (d). As can be seen, there will be negligible distortion of amplitude or phase, and so the output spectrum will be, for the ac components, unchanged. However, the filter does eliminate the dc component, which results in the output square wave being symmetrical about the time axis (i.e., the average value is zero).

Now, consider a similar filter but with the time constant very much less than the periodic time of the wave, Fig. 2.8. The modulus and phase shift as functions of frequency are shown in Fig. 2.8(c) and (d), where, for definiteness, $T = 440CR$ (this makes $|X_c| = 10R$ at the seventh harmonic). In addition to eliminating the dc component, the other components, as far as the seventh, are reduced to approximately equal amplitudes; they are also phase–shifted by approximately $90°$. Elimination of the dc component again means that the output wave will be symmetrical about the time axis. The attenuation and phase shift of the other components results in a sharply peaked wave, as shown in Fig. 2.8(g). Although this wave could, in principle, be reconstructed from the spectrum and phase information, it is easier to consider the circuit as a differentiator in order to obtain an idea of the shape of the output wave. This is justified, since, for $T \gg CR$ (or $|X_c| \gg R$) the voltage v_c across C is very much greater than the voltage v_o across R. Hence

$$v_c \gg v_o$$

Therefore,
$$v_i \cong v_c$$

$$\frac{dv_i}{dt} \cong \frac{dv_c}{dt}$$

$$= \frac{1}{C}\frac{dq}{dt}$$

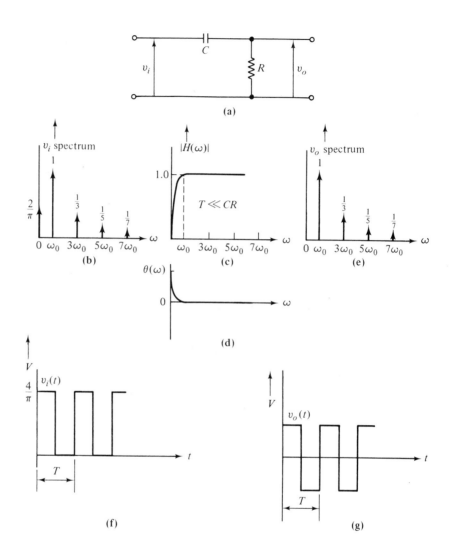

FIGURE 2.7.   A high–pass filter: (a) The network; (b) Input signal frequency spectrum; (c) Transfer function amplitude plot; (d) Transfer function phase plot; (e) Output signal frequency spectrum; (f) Input signal waveform; (g) Output signal waveform.

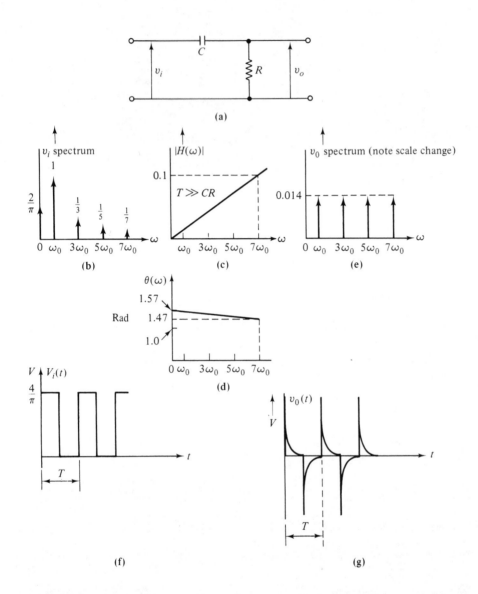

FIGURE 2.8. A differentiating network: (a) The network; (b) Input signal frequency spectrum; (c) Transfer function amplitude plot; (d) Transfer function phase plot; (e) Output signal frequency spectrum; (f) Input signal waveform; (g) Output signal waveform.

$$= \frac{i}{C}$$

$$\therefore \qquad i = C\frac{dv_i}{dt}$$

and
$$v_0 = iR$$
$$= RC\frac{dv_i}{dt} \qquad (2.18)$$

Thus the output voltage is proportional to the rate of change of the input signal, provided that v_o is small relative to v_i. The rate of change of the rise and fall sides of v_i are positive- and negative-going impulses, Fig. 2.8(g), while the rate of change of the flat top and bottom is zero. Practical limitations will introduce an exponential approach from the impulses to the zero level as shown in Fig. 2.8(g).

2.3.2 Bandpass Filter

A simple example of a *bandpass filter* (BPF) is the parallel resonant circuit shown in Fig. 2.9(a). Here, the transfer function has to be expressed in terms of the currents, since the voltage across the circuit is common to input and output. Thus

$$H(\omega) = \frac{i_o}{i_i} \qquad (2.19)$$

The modulus and phase shift as functions of frequency are sketched in Fig. 2.9(c) and (d). For a square-wave input current, Fig. 2.9(f), the input spectrum will be as shown in Fig. 2.9(b), and the output spectrum, when the circuit is resonant at the third harmonic, will be as shown in Fig. 2.9(e). Here again, the dc component is eliminated since the inductance L (assumed to be resistanceless) will short-circuit any dc away from the output load R_L. The phase shift is zero at the resonant frequency (the third harmonic of input). The output current and voltage (which is also the voltage across the tuned circuit) are sinusoidal at frequency $3f_0$, where $f_0 = 1/T$. This principle is used in certain types of frequency multipliers; in this example, the frequency of the signal has been tripled on passing through the filter.

2.3.3 Low-Pass Filter

As a final example, the effect of a simple *low-pass filter* (LPF) on a square-wave input will be examined. The LPF circuit is shown in Fig.

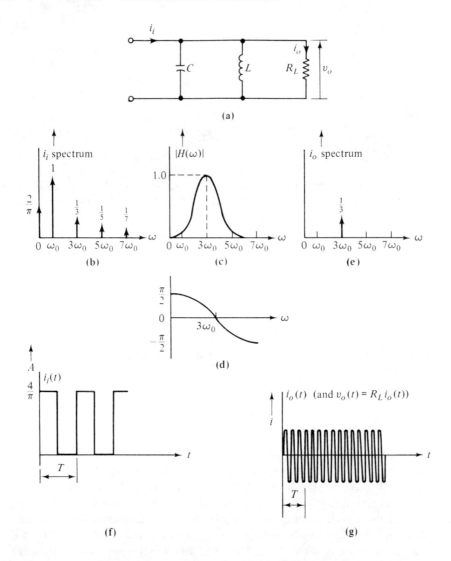

FIGURE 2.9. A bandpass filter: (a) The network; (b) Input signal frequency spectrum; (c) Transfer function amplitude plot; (d) Transfer function phase plot; (e) Output signal frequency spectrum; (f) Input signal waveform; (g) Output signal waveform.

2.10(a), and the modulus and phase shift as functions of frequency in Fig. 2.10(b) to (e). Two curves are shown in each case, one for $CR \ll T$ and one for $CR \gg T$. Clearly, the dc component is transmitted by this filter.

For the condition $CR \ll T$, the square wave is transmitted practically unchanged, as shown by the sequence of graphs Fig. 2.10(b), (d), (f), and

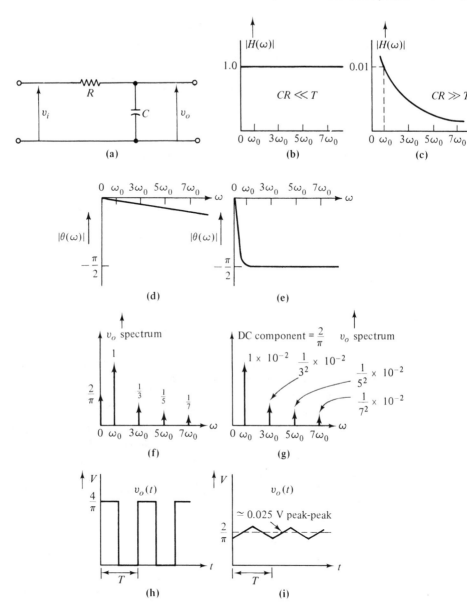

FIGURE 2.10.   A low-pass filter: (a) The network; (b) Transfer function amplitude plot for CR ≪ T; (c) Transfer function amplitude plot for CR ≫ T; (d) Transfer function phase plot for CR ≪ T; (e) Transfer function phase plot for CR ≫ T; (f) Output signal frequency spectrum for CR ≪ T (same as the input signal frequency spectrum); (g) Output signal frequency spectrum for CR ≫ T; (h) Output signal waveform for CR ≪ T (same as the input signal waveform); (i) Output signal waveform for CR ≫ T.

(h). For $CR \gg T$, the circuit integrates the square wave about the mean level. Mathematically this can be justified—as, for $CR \gg T$, the voltage across R, v_R, is very much greater than v_o, the voltage across C, since $R \gg |X_c|$. In the example shown in Fig. 2.10(c) and (e), $CR = 100T/2\pi$, which makes $R = |100X_c|$ at the fundamental frequency. Hence

$$v_R \gg v_c$$

and therefore,
$$i \cong \frac{v_i}{R}$$

$$\frac{dq}{dt} = \frac{v_i}{R}$$

$$\therefore \qquad C\frac{dv_c}{dt} = \frac{v_i}{R}$$

and since $v_c = v_o$, it follows that

$$v_o = \frac{1}{RC} \int v_i \, dt \qquad (2.20)$$

The low–pass filter under these conditions acts as an "integrator" circuit; its action should be compared to the high–pass filter used as a "differentiator."

Note that the capacitor charges up to the mean voltage level. The spectrum of the output in this case is shown in Fig. 2.10(g) and the output waveshape is sketched in Fig. 2.10(i). Reference to a table of Fourier series [see, for example, entries 23.7 and 23.8 in Murray R. Spiegel, *Mathematical Handbook of Formulas and Tables* (Schaum's Outline Series), McGraw–Hill Book Company, New York] shows that the triangular wave has a spectrum in which the components decrease as the square of the component number and are shifted by $\frac{1}{2}\pi$ radians compared to the corresponding square–wave components. The low–pass filter with $CR \gg T$ alters the spectrum in just this way. Note that the wave is significantly modified.

2.4   PROBLEMS

1.   The Fourier series for a square wave of 1V amplitude is

$$v(t) = \frac{4}{\pi} \left(\sin \omega t + \frac{\sin 3\omega t}{3} + \frac{\sin 5\omega t}{5} + \dots \right)$$

By comparing this with the Fourier series for Fig. 2.1(c), sketch the square wave correctly relative to the voltage/time axes.

2. The Fourier series for a half-wave-rectified sinusoidal current wave of 1A amplitude is

$$i(t) = \frac{1}{\pi} + \frac{1}{2}\sin \omega t - \frac{2}{\pi}\left(\frac{\cos 2\omega t}{1 \times 3} + \frac{\cos 4\omega t}{3 \times 5} + \frac{\cos 6\omega t}{5 \times 7} + \cdots \right)$$

Draw accurately to scale the spectrum up to the eighth harmonic. What is the value of the dc component?

3. The wave of Problem 1 is passed through a high-pass filter, Fig. 2.8(a), for which $|X_c| = 10R$ at the seventh harmonic. Calculate the harmonic amplitudes up to the seventh.

4. A square wave voltage is applied to the input of the crystal lattice filter of Fig. 1.29(a). The fundamental frequency of the square wave is at $f_{\infty 1}$ and the thirteenth harmonic at $f_{\infty 2}$. *Sketch* the output spectrum. What type of filtering action is involved?

5. The rectified current of Problem 2 is passed through a low-pass filter, Fig. 2.10(a), for which $R = 100|X_c|$ at the fundamental. Calculate the ratio of peak fundamental voltage to steady voltage at the output if the output load is equal to $\frac{1}{2}R$.

Chapter 3
Audio Signals

3.1 INTRODUCTION

Audio waves can be analyzed by Fourier methods similar to those described in Chapter 2. For example, one complete cycle of the sound waveform *e* as in *e*at is shown in Fig. 3.1(a), and the corresponding spectrum is shown in Fig. 3.1(b). Fourier analysis for sound waves is useful in that it indicates the basic structure of the wave, but it would be impossible to carry out the analysis for every sound. For example, raising the fundamental frequency of the sound *e* increases considerably the number of harmonics in its spectrum. Also, no two voices are exactly the same, the *timbre* or quality of a speaking voice depending on the number of harmonics and their relative amplitudes. The frequency range required for speech is determined by listening tests involving large numbers of people, which also avoids the need for analyzing individual sounds.

3.2 FREQUENCY RANGE REQUIRED FOR SPEECH

Two factors determine the frequency range required for satisfactory speech transmission; the intelligibility/frequency distribution, and the

78

(a)   (b)

(mN/m² = millinewtons per square meter. 1 mN = 100 Dynes.)

FIGURE 3.1. (a) Pressure versus time waveform of the sound *e*; (b) Frequency spectrum of the same waveform.

energy/frequency distribution. Special listening tests have been devised to measure intelligibility, these being known as *articulation tests.* In one form of articulation test, a group of listeners is asked to record syllables as they hear them announced over a loudspeaker as the frequency range of the transmission is reduced in steps. The number of correctly recorded syllables as a percentage of the total number transmitted at each step is termed the *articulation efficiency.* The syllables are unrelated to one another (i.e., they are "nonsense syllables"). In this way, results due to good guesswork are reduced. It is found in practice that an articulation efficiency of 80% corresponds to about 100% intelligibility for normal speech.

Curves of articulation efficiency against frequency are shown in Fig. 3.2(a) and (b). Figure 3.2(a) shows the effect of suppressing the high frequencies in speech. It is seen that to maintain a high articulation efficiency, frequencies up to at least 2.5 kHz must not be suppressed. Figure 3.2(b) shows the effect of suppressing the low frequencies. It is seen that all frequencies below 1.5 kHz can be suppressed without drastically reducing the intelligibility. The conclusion is, therefore, that the intelligibility is contained in the high–frequency components (1.5 to 2.5 kHz) of speech.

Looking now at the energy distribution, Fig. 3.2(c) shows the percentage of total energy transmitted to the listeners as the high frequencies are suppressed. As much as 80% is transmitted, even though all frequencies above 1 kHz are suppressed. Figure 3.2(d) shows that suppressing all frequencies below 1 kHz reduces the energy transmitted to 15%. The conclusion is, therefore, that the energy in speech sounds is contained in the low frequencies. The frequency limits adopted internationally on the basis of such tests are 300 to 3400 Hz. This range passes about 60% of the total

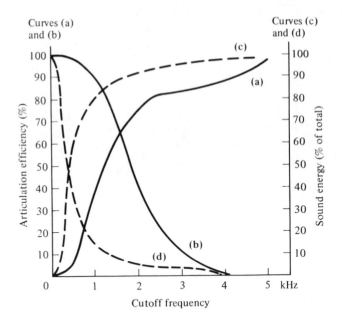

FIGURE 3.2. (a) Articulation efficiency as a function of upper cutoff frequency; (b) Articulation efficiency as a function of lower cutoff frequency; (c) Sound energy as a function of upper cutoff frequency; (d) Sound energy as a function of lower cutoff frequency.

energy and allows about 85% articulation efficiency. Since the type of tests involved cannot fix the frequency limits precisely, these may be different for specific applications. For example, speech transmission for entertainment purposes may require 80 to 8000 Hz in order to capture the "naturalness" of the speaker's voice.

3.3 FREQUENCY RANGE REQUIRED FOR MUSIC

Direct *frequency analysis* of the output of a large orchestra shows that the sound energy covers the frequency range 15 to 20,000 Hz. However, listening tests with a large audience, including professional musicians, have shown that a very much smaller frequency range, 160 to 8000 Hz, is preferred for *monaural* reproduction. Monaural systems do not bring out the diffuse nature of an orchestra and tend to unnaturalize the performance. The criterion "naturalness of reproduction" or "true fidelity" therefore has little meaning for monaural systems. It should be noted that any system may be called a "high–fidelity" system provided that it meets certain minimum requirements, such as minimum bandwidth, minimum amplitude versus frequency distortion, minimum harmonic distortion, or minimum dynamic range, while still not producing "true" fidelity.

Separate tests, in which the sound passed directly from an orchestra to an audience through an "acoustical frequency filter," showed that the audience had a distinct preference for the full frequency range. In view of the conflicting evidence, and with the introduction of stereophonic systems, a frequency range of 50 to 15,000 Hz is accepted as satisfactory for reproducing music.

The various frequency–range requirements are summarized in Fig. 3.3.

FIGURE 3.3.   Frequency–range requirements for various types of audio signals.

3.4   SOUND PRESSURE LEVELS

Sound is produced by variations in air pressure around the average steady-state barometric pressure, caused by the physical movement of objects and surfaces in the air. The frequency of these variations ranges from below 1 Hz to several hundred kHz, but only those within the range from about 16 Hz to 16 kHz are audible to, or can be detected by the human ear.

The alternating variations of pressure at a sound source cause sound waves to radiate out from the source in the same manner as waves are caused in water by a dropped stone. The waves travel with a certain velocity of propagation, which depends on the medium through which they are traveling (air, water, metal, etc.), and they transmit energy at a certain rate (expressed in watts), as discussed in Section 3.5.

Sound pressure levels may be stated in terms of peak values of pressure variations, or they may be stated in terms of average pressure variations about the barometric level. These pressure levels are stated in microbars (μ bars) or in newtons per square meter, where 1μ bar $= 0.1$ N/m^2. When sound pressure levels are stated, they are usually quoted in decibels (see Appendix A) above the average threshold of hearing level, which is accepted as $p_0 = 2 \times 10^{-4} \mu$ bar of pressure variation average (0 dB), and

$$\text{SPL} = 20 \log_{10} \left(\frac{p}{p_0} \right) \tag{3.1}$$

Sound pressure levels range from the threshold of hearing at 2×10^{-4} μ bar to well above the threshold of pain at 120 dB (corresponding to 200 μ bars). Since the power transmitted by a sound wave is proportional to the square of the pressure, the sound–intensity ratio in decibels, as stated in Section 3.5, coincides with the sound pressure level in decibels. A chart of sound pressure levels given in μ bars, compared to the corresponding decibel level and the corresponding intensity level at the average ear is presented in Fig. 3.4. On this chart the levels of some typical sounds are shown.

The sound power generated by a large orchestra ranges from a few microwatts at the softest passages to many watts at the loudest passages. Speech powers range from a few microwatts when whispering to a few milliwatts when shouting. However, it is the sound intensity at the listener which determines the loudness, and this depends on the acoustical properties of the room as well as on the position of the listener in the room. Therefore, a reproducing system does not necessarily have to produce sound powers of the same magnitude as the original sound. Usually considerably less power is needed. For instance, in a telephone conversation, the earpiece of the handset is held close to the ear. What is important is that the reproducing system should be capable of handling the same power ratio as in the original sound. If, for example, in the original sound, power ranged from 1 mW to 10 W, the reproducing system should be capable of handling a 10^4:1 power ratio, although the power output from it may be only 10 μ W to 100 mW. It is also important that peak values of power are used when assessing the power output of a system.

3.5   SOUND INTENSITY

Sound intensity is defined as the average rate of transmission of sound energy in a given direction through a cross–sectional area of 1 m² at right angles to the direction. It is expressed in watts per square meter and is proportional to the square of the sound pressure (in newtons/square meter). Sound intensity expressed in watts/square meter is convenient for use in communications engineering, since it is expressed in the same units as electrical power.

The ear is extremely sensitive. It can detect sound intensities of the order of 10^{-13} W/m². This corresponds to a movement of the eardrum of 10^{-12}m, a distance equal to one hundredth the diameter of a hydrogen molecule. Hearing is not equally sensitive at all frequencies. The minimum sound intensity that can be heard is termed the *threshold of hearing*. Figure 3.5 shows how this varies with frequency. Sound intensity is usually expressed in decibels above the threshold of hearing because loudness is approximately proportional to the logarithm of intensity (see Section 3.7). A logarithmic frequency scale is also used. Decibel and logarithmic units and scales are discussed in Appendix A.

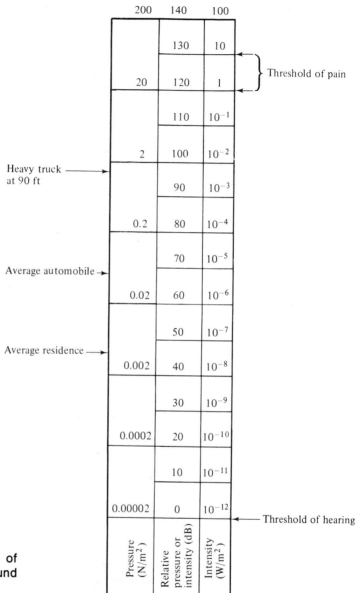

FIGURE 3.4. Comparison of sound pressure level and sound intensity level scales.

The upper limit of hearing is determined by the separation of the linkage between the outer and inner ear. This limit is felt, rather than heard, and is therefore termed the *threshold of feeling* (or threshold of pain). Figure 3.5 also shows how the threshold of feeling varies with frequency.

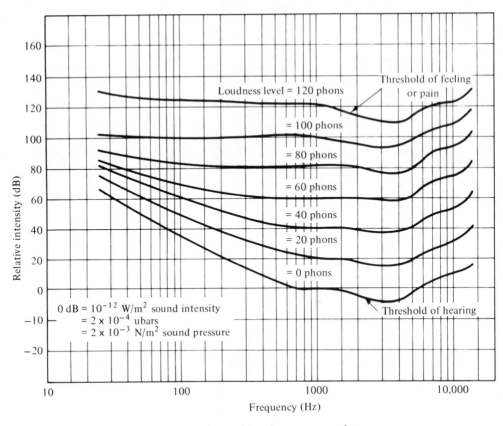

FIGURE 3.5.   Fletcher—Munson curves of equal loudness versus frequency.

The power ratio between maximum and minimum intensities is 10^{12}, or 1 million million—hence the need for the decibel scale to accommodate this enormous range. The decibel zero reference for sound intensities is standardized at 10^{-12} W/m² at 1000 Hz (i.e., the threshold of hearing at 1000 Hz). The threshold levels shown in Fig. 3.5 are "averaged" results, that is, they are arrived at from the results of many tests involving many people. Although intensity can be measured, threshold level cannot. The latter depends on the opinion of the listener, or subject, and is termed a *subjective measurement*.

3.6   LOUDNESS LEVEL

Loudness is also a subjective quantity. Loudness cannot be measured in the same way that intensity can. Although two tones of different frequencies may have the same relative intensity, they will not seem equally loud. The threshold curves of Figure 3.5 represent particular *equal loudness levels.* It is possible to have varying degrees of loudness between these limits. To enable sounds at different frequencies to be compared for loudness, the intensities of tones at 1000 Hz are adopted as standard levels of loudness. To "measure" the loudness of a tone, the intensity of a 1000-Hz tone is adjusted until it is judged to have the same loudness as the unknown. The relative intensity of the 1000-Hz tone is then said to be the equivalent loudness of the unknown. A new unit, the *phon,* is introduced for loudness levels measured in this way. The relative intensity in decibels for the 1000-Hz tone is equal to the equivalent loudness level in phons.

The threshold–of–hearing curve represents a loudness level of 0 phons. The threshold–of–feeling curve represents a loudness level of 120 phons, since the relative intensity at 1000 Hz is 120 dB above the threshold of hearing. Other equal loudness curves are plotted in Fig. 3.5. These are known as *Fletcher-Munson curves,* after the engineers who first obtained them experimentally at Bell Telephone Laboratories. The curves show that at low frequencies a smaller change in relative intensity is required for a given change in loudness, compared to the high frequencies. As shown in previous sections, many sounds cover a frequency spectrum. A volume control that reduces the relative intensities by the same amount will alter the character of a sound, since it will alter the loudness of the components by unequal amounts.

The phon is a unit of *equal loudness level* but not a unit of loudness. For example, a 2:1 increase in loudness is not a 2:1 increase in the number of phons. The usefulness of the unit is that it allows sounds of the *same* loudness sensation to be compared; but it provides no connection between one loudness level and another.

3.7   LOUDNESS

The most common way of measuring loudness is to ask the listener to judge when a 2:1 increase in loudness sensation appears to occur, when the intensity is increased. It is obvious that some initial standard is needed, and this is simply provided by defining one. The agreed standard is the loudness sensation produced by a 1000–Hz sine wave 40 dB above the *listener's* threshold of hearing. This loudness is defined as 1 *sone.* A loudness judged by the listener to be *n* times this is *n* sones. Thus 500 millisones is half the loudness sensation of the standard. At any other frequency, a loudness level of 40 phons will produce the same loudness sensation as the standard; hence the definition of the loudness standard can be extended to mean that *a pure tone of loudness 40 phons produces a loudness sensation of 1 sone.*

The relationship between loudness level and loudness is not of the straight–line form (i.e., loudness is not proportional to loudness level). The relationship has been established experimentally and is published in graphical form by the American National Standards Institute as Z24.2–1942. A useful result from this graph is that above loudness of 1 sone, a 10–phon increase is required for a 2:1 increase in sones.

There will also be a minimum change in intensity which is just discernible as a change in loudness. Again, this must be established experimentally, and the figure is about 1 dB for normal speech and music. For pure tones and careful experimental procedure, values as low as 0.1 dB have been recorded. These values apply over a limited range of frequencies and intensities, which include the normal speech range. Because the change is a fixed number of decibels, the response of the ear to intensity is logarithmic over the ranges involved. This means that the minimum change required is a fixed percentage of the existing intensity.

3.8 PITCH AND FREQUENCY

Pitch, like loudness, is a subjective quantity. It is determined mainly by the frequency of the sound, where this is a pure tone. Changes of pitch can occur due to changes in intensity, even though the frequency is maintained constant. In engineering practice, the definition of pitch is designed to take into account its subjective nature and also the fact that it may vary with intensity. The *mel* is the unit of pitch, and by definition a pure tone of 1000 Hz of loudness 1 sone produces a pitch of 1000 mels.

The relationship between pitch and frequency is nonlinear. By definition, a frequency of 1000 Hz establishes a pitch of 1000 mels, but a frequency of 2000 Hz corresponds to a pitch of about 1500 mels, and a frequency of 400 Hz to about 500 mels.

The ear can judge a given frequency *ratio* but not a given frequency difference. For example, a change from 1000 Hz to 3000 Hz is recognized as being the same as 3000 Hz to 9000 Hz, a ratio of 3:1. It is not recognized as being the same as the change from 3000 Hz to 5000 Hz, although this is the same frequency difference. This property of the ear can be verified in a practical way, by playing a recording of a melody at the wrong speed. The melody will be recognizable because the frequency ratios have not altered.

3.9 INTERVALS AND OCTAVES

The ratio of two frequencies is termed their *interval*. Thus, the interval between 1000 Hz and 100 Hz is 10:1. An interval of 2:1 is termed an *octave*, and in the example above there are approximately 3.32 octaves.

Sometimes, frequency—or more loosely, pitch—is expressed in octaves. For such purposes, the reference frequency is usually 1000 Hz.

In terms of octaves, a frequency ratio f_1/f_2 may be expressed as

$$\frac{f_1}{f_2} = 2^{\text{octaves}} \tag{3.2}$$

Hence

$$\text{octaves} = \log_2\left(\frac{f_1}{f_2}\right) = \frac{\log_{10}\left(\dfrac{f_1}{f_2}\right)}{\log_{10}2} \tag{3.3}$$

3.10   SOUND DISTORTION

If the variation of amplitude with time of a sound wave is altered in any way from the original, *distortion* is said to occur. Nearly all serious distortion is caused by the equipment in the transmission channel, and is (1) nonlinear (i.e., harmonic distortion), caused primarily by tubes and transistors, and (2) linear (i.e., amplitude/frequency and phase/frequency distortion), caused by inductance and capacitance. The ear itself can introduce two effects which are similar to these forms of distortion. These are (1) generation of combinations tones, and (2) masking.

Two frequencies, f_1 and f_2, can combine to produce new frequencies, $f_1 + f_2$ and $f_1 - f_2$. These are known as the *summation tone* and the *difference tone*, respectively. They may be produced outside the ear, when they are known as *objective* combination tones, or they may be generated inside the ear, when they are termed *subjective* combination tones. Since new frequencies are introduced, the effect is similar to nonlinear distortion. It does not, however, have the unpleasantness of nonlinear distortion. It can work to advantage by generating low–frequency fundamental tones which many loudspeakers and earphones cannot reproduce.

Masking is an effect that occurs in the ear where a louder sound can reduce, or even stop, the nerve voltage generated by a weaker sound. Thus a noisy location can result in a reduction or even loss of a signal due to masking. Furthermore, high frequencies are more easily masked than low frequencies, and the effect is similar to amplitude/frequency distortion.

3.11   ROOM ACOUSTICS

The performance of an otherwise well–designed communications system can be completely ruined by a room that has poor acoustical properties. Hard, smooth surfaces reflect sound. If a room is large, echoes are created that can make speech unintelligible or result in a blurring of musical phrasing. Soft furnishings absorb sound, which results in a deadening effect.

This can rob music of much of its purpose, but it is not troublesome with speech, provided sufficient energy is available to make up for that absorbed.

The best measure of the acoustic properties of a room is *reverberation time*. This is defined as the time taken for the density of sound energy in the room to drop to one millionth of its initial value. This is equivalent to the relative intensity dropping by 60 dB. The reverberation time depends on (1) the room volume, (2) the total surface area, and (3) the total absorption in the room. The materials used in the construction and the furnishings of the room will in general absorb different amounts of sound energy. The *absorption coefficient* of a material is the fraction of the total received sound energy that is absorbed by it. Thus,

$$\text{absorption coefficient} = \frac{\text{energy absorbed by surface}}{\text{total energy received by surface}}$$

The absorption coefficient not only varies with the type of material, but for a given material it varies with the frequency of the sound. Table 3.1 gives values that have been determined for various materials. It will be seen, for example, that unpainted brickwork absorbs about twice the amount of sound energy as painted brickwork. It will also be seen that special material, such as acoustic plaster, has a comparatively high absorption coefficient. This material is specially made to reduce the reverberation time of rooms. It is used in lecture theatres, telephone exchanges, and so on, where clarity of speech is essential and extraneous sounds, such as noise and echoes, must be deadened.

TABLE 3.1. ABSORPTION COEFFICIENTS FOR SOME COMMON MATERIALS

MATERIAL	500 Hz	1000 Hz
Brick, unpainted	0.03	0.04
Brick, painted	0.016	0.02
Carpet, felt, on solid floor	0.3	0.4
½-inch insulation board on studs	0.3	0.3
½-inch perforated insulation board on solid backing	0.55	0.65
Acoustic plaster	0.25	0.3

Note: The values in the table are intended to give some idea of the order of the absorption coefficient for various materials. The quality of the material will affect the absorption coefficient; for example, poor-quality carpet is likely to have a lower value than the value listed.

Consider a room that has surfaces, S_1, S_2, S_3, ... square feet, each surface having its own absorption coefficient a_1, a_2, a_3,.... Let the volume of the room be V cubic feet. The reverberation time T of such a room is given approximately by

$$T = \frac{0.05V}{a_1S_1 + a_2S_2 + a_3S_3 + ...} \text{ seconds} \qquad (3.4)$$

The denominator of this expression is termed the absorption of the room. The unit of absorption is named the *sabine*, after W. C. Sabine, who laid the foundations of acoustic theory of buildings. It will be seen that each area has an individual absorption of $(a \times S)$ sabines. The advantage of the sabine unit is that it allows the absorption of objects, such as people, to be readily stated. Thus Sabine found that the average absorption for a person was 4.7 units or, in the present nomenclature, 4.7 sabines.

The following example will show how the reverberation time of a room is calculated.

Example 3.1   Calculate the reverberation time of a living room 8 ft high × 13 ft wide × 20 ft long; volume, 2080 ft³.

Solution

	AREA (ft²)	ABSOLUTE COEFFICIENT AT 1 kHz	ABSORPTION (SABINES)
End walls, insulation board	196	0.3	58.8
Sidewalls, plaster on brick	212	0.03	6.4
Windows	36	0.075	2.7
Doors	24	0.1	2.4
Ceiling, plaster on lathes	260	0.025	6.5
Carpet	200	0.4	80
Tile floor	60	0.015	0.9
Curtains			2.0
Settee and easy chairs			16
Hard furniture			5
Total absorption			180.7

$$\text{reverberation time at 1 kHz} = \frac{0.05 \times 2080}{180.7} \text{ s}$$

$$= 0.57 \text{ s}$$

With four persons present in the room, the total absorption would increase by $4.7 \times 4 = 18.8$ sabines. The total absorption would then be approximately 200 sabines, and

$$\text{reverberation time} \cong 0.57 \times \frac{181}{200}$$

$$= 0.55 \text{ s}$$

This would be ideal for speech, but it is on the low side for music. By sacrificing some comfort, as for example removing the carpet, the quality of music reproduction would be improved. Preference no doubt lies with less quality and more comfort.

Generally speaking, less energy is absorbed at low frequencies and so may give rise to too great a reverberation time. Special methods are adopted to reduce this, one being the use of mechanical resonators. This may consist of a diaphragm of fibrous felt material (roofing felt has been used), the size of which is adjusted so that it is most easily set into vibration at the frequency at which it is desired to reduce the reverberation time. The energy that produces the vibration is extracted from the sound wave, and in this manner the reverberation time is reduced.

In the acoustic design of rooms the following points should be observed:

1. Concave surfaces must be avoided since they result in undesirable "focusing" of the sound.

2. Large, unbroken wall areas should be avoided; some irregularity is desirable in order to diffuse the sound.

3. Where special sound–absorbent material is used, it should be randomly distributed throughout the available wall area, not concentrated in one region.

3.12 ELECTROACOUSTIC TRANSDUCERS

Electroacoustic transducers convert sound waves to electrical signals, and vice versa. At the sending end, the sound wave is converted to an electrical signal by means of a microphone, of which there are a large variety in use; only a few of these will be described here. At the receiving end, the commonly available transducers for converting the electrical signal into a sound wave are telephone receivers, headsets, and loudspeakers.

3.12.1 Microphones

Microphones are electromechanical transducers that convert changes in air pressure into corresponding changes in electrical signal. Several varieties exist, which may be classified according to five basic principles of operation. These are variable resistance, variable reluctance, moving-coil induction, variable capacitance, and piezoelectric.

Three parameters are used to describe the quality of a microphone. The first is output level, which can be described either as an absolute output level in watts when a reference level of sound pressure signal at 1000 Hz is applied to the microphone, or it can be described in decibels referred to a standard power output level under similar input conditions. The power output level so measured gives a measure of the sensitivity of the microphone.

Frequency response is measured as a plot of the output level in decibels referred to some convenient level as in Fig. 3.6(a), and with the input signal held constant in amplitude for all frequencies, plotted against the log of frequency. The ideal microphone has a flat frequency response over the entire audio range from 16 Hz to 20 kHz, with no response at all outside this range. Practical microphones deviate widely from this ideal.

Most microphones also exhibit a directional response in their pickup characteristic. This directivity is considered in much the same manner as directivity in antennas is treated, and polar plots of the response are provided for each unit. These polar plots are usually measured in the horizontal plane but are sometimes also provided in the vertical plane for special-purpose microphones. Figure 3.6(a) shows the frequency responses for several types of microphones, showing the different sensitivities, while Fig. 3.6(b) shows the polar directivity plot for a cardioid-type microphone.

The *carbon microphone*, used as the transmitter in telephone handsets, is a variable-resistance unit. It is characterized by a limited frequency response, as shown in Fig. 3.6(a), by a relatively low source resistance of about 100 Ω, and very rugged construction. Figure 3.7(a) shows the cross section of a carbon microphone. It is constructed with a metal diaphragm across one end of a metal case which is cylindrical in shape. A plungerlike metal contact is attached to the diaphragm so that movement of the diaphragm is transmitted through the plunger into the bed of carbon granules within the microphone. An insulated fixed contact is also embedded in the carbon granules to form the second electrode. When a compressing sound wave strikes the diaphragm, it pushes on the plunger and compacts the carbon granules, lowering the contact resistance between them. When the pressure is released, the resistance rises. A bias current is passed through an external load resistor from a battery to provide the electrical conversion, since varying the resistance causes similar variations in the current.

This type of microphone suffers from an inherent distortion. The variation in microphone resistance can be made to be almost directly proportional to the variation in air pressure on the diaphragm, but the current is an inverse function of the resistance, making the output signal voltage across the load resistor inversely proportional to the change of sound pressure.

The microphone resistance is made up of two components, R_0, which is the resistance of the microphone with no sound pressure signal present, and

(a) Carbon microphone
(b) Moving-coil microphone
(c) Crystal microphone (sound cell type)

(a)

Source: Dennis Roddy, *Radio and Line Transmission*, Vol. 1 (Elmsford, N.Y.: Pergamon Press, 1972)

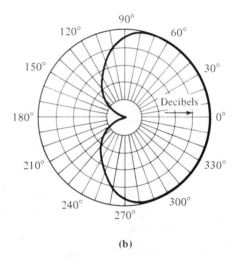

FIGURE 3.6. (a) Frequency-response characteristics of several types of microphones; (b) Polar directional response of a cardioid–type microphone.

(b)

r, which is the variation of the microphone resistance about R_0 due to the varying sound pressure. Figure 3.7(b) shows the equivalent circuit of the microphone connected in its bias circuit. The output voltage is

$$v_{\text{out}} = iR_L = E \frac{R_L}{R_L + R_0 + r} = \frac{ER_L}{R_L + R_0} \left(1 + \frac{r}{R_L + R_0}\right)^{-1} \qquad (3.5)$$

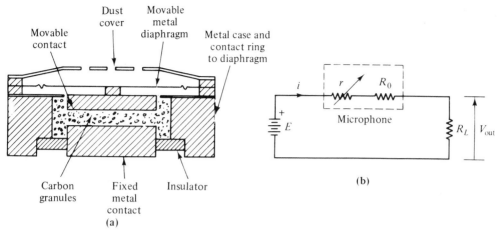

FIGURE 3.7. (a) Cross section of a carbon microphone; (b) Electrical equivalent circuit of a carbon microphone.

The binomial expansion of this expression is

$$v_{out} = \frac{ER_L}{R_L + R_0} \left[1 - \frac{r}{R_L + R_0} + \left(\frac{r}{R_L + R_0} \right)^2 - \dots \right] \quad (3.6)$$

If r is made much smaller than $R_L + R_0$, then

$$v_{out} \cong \frac{ER_L}{R_L + R_0} \left(1 - \frac{r}{R_L + R_0} \right) \quad (3.7)$$

If the sound wave is sinusoidal, then v_{out} is also sinusoidal:

$$v_{out} \cong \frac{ER_L}{R_L + R_0} \left(1 - \frac{r \sin \omega t}{R_L + R_0} \right) \quad (3.8)$$

Unless the resistance variation is made to be a small percentage of the total circuit resistance, severe harmonic distortion occurs. A second disadvantage of this type of microphone is that bias current from a battery must be provided before the electrical output can be obtained.

The carbon microphone is small, cheap, very rugged, and produces a relatively high output signal level, so that it finds its chief applications in telephone systems and in portable radio systems.

The *variable–reluctance microphone* shown in Fig. 3.8(a) is one of two basic types of magnetic microphones. Both of these microphones have the advantage that they do not require bias current for their operation, but the signal output levels are correspondingly low. The variable–reluctance microphone is made with a moving diaphragm of magnetic material such as silicon steel suspended above the pole pieces of a permanent magnet. Induction coils are wound on the pole pieces and connected in series aiding. When air pressure increases on the diaphragm, the air gap in the magnetic circuit is reduced, reducing the reluctance and causing the magnetic flux to concentrate within the magnetic structure. As the flux lines move in, they cut the coil turns and induce an EMF in them. When the diaphragm moves away from the pole pieces, the air gap widens, increasing the reluctance, and the flux lines move away from the pole pieces, inducing an EMF of the opposite polarity in the coil.

This type of microphone is not often used because the diaphragm must be made of a magnetic material, and it is difficult to construct one that is not too rigid or does not have interfering mechanical resonances. The source impedance of such a microphone is high, about 5 to 10 kΩ, but its output is comparatively low, in the microvolt region.

The *moving-coil microphone* shown in Fig. 3.8(b) has basically the same structure as a moving-coil loudspeaker. An induction coil is wound on a nonmagnetic cylinder attached to the diaphragm and mounted in the cylindrical air gap of a permanent magnet. The diaphragm can be made nonmetallic and the electrical contact wires to the coil can be glued to the surface of the diaphragm. When a sound wave strikes the diaphragm, it causes the coil to move back and forth in the magnetic field, and an EMF is induced in the coil which is directly proportional to the velocity with which the coil is moving.

The light diaphragm makes it possible to construct a moving-coil

FIGURE 3.8. Magnetic microphones: (1) Variable-reluctance microphone; (b) Moving-coil microphone.

microphone with very linear frequency response within the audio band, and this type is often used for music recording or broadcasting applications. As mentioned, no bias is required, but the source impedance tends to be low, typically about 20 Ω, and the generated signal levels are also low, typically a few hundred microvolts. The diaphragm structure must be delicate if good frequency response is to be obtained, so this type of microphone is seldom used for telephony work.

The *capacitor microphone* shown in Figure 3.9(a) is made up of a metal diaphragm suspended above a fixed metal backplate and insulated from it. A constant dc voltage, usually several hundred volts, is applied through a load resistor between the diaphragm and the backplate. When the diaphragm is moved by the sound wave, its capacitance varies with the changing spacing between the diaphragm and the backplate. The charge on the capacitance tends to remain constant, so the voltage across it varies directly with the sound pressure wave. Capacitor microphones with excellent frequency response have been made, and they are frequently used as "standard" microphones against which others are calibrated. They are delicate because of the narrow separation between the diaphragm and backplate and the thin diaphragm needed, and a high-voltage supply and signal amplifier must be located very close in use. As a result, they are not used for run-of-the-mill communications applications.

The *piezoelectric microphone* shown in Fig. 3.9(b) is a self–generator that does not need a bias supply. Rochelle salts and certain types of piezoelectric ceramics are used as the active crystals in these microphones. A crystal of such material cut along certain planes to form a slice, and with foil electrodes attached to the two surfaces, exhibits piezoelectric characteristics. When pressure is applied to the crystal, it deforms, and a momentary displacement of charge within the structure creates a difference of potential

FIGURE 3.9.   Other microphones: (a) Capacitor microphone; (b) Piezoelectric crystal microphone.

between the two foil plates. Conversely, if an electric potential is applied between the two faces of the crystal, the crystal physically bends or deforms. This phenomenon is the same one which allows the use of quartz crystals to control oscillator frequency.

Figure 3.9(b) shows a sketch of a bimorphic crystal (really two crystals connected back to back and acting in push–pull) coupled to a diaphragm. The output of such a unit is quite high, typically about 100 mV. The crystal may also be exposed directly to the sound wave instead of being coupled with a diaphragm, giving much better frequency response, but with a much lower output level, typically less than 1 mV. These microphones can be made quite rugged and provide reasonably good frequency response. They are used for a wide variety of applications from radiotelephony and broadcasting to general–purpose recording systems.

3.12.2   Telephone Receivers and Handsets

Telephone receivers are electromagnetic transducers which convert the electrical telephone signals into sound pressure waves. They are made compact and of very rugged construction to withstand the abuse of telephone usage. The original telephone receiver was a large horseshoe–shaped permanent magnet with a coil wrapped around it. A diaphragm made of magnetic material such as soft iron was suspended over the open pole pieces to complete the magnetic path and was held in place by the magnetic force of attraction. When an alternating current passed through the coil, it alternately aided or opposed the field of the permanent magnet, and the force exerted on the diaphragm was reinforced or lessened. The diaphragm vibrated in time with the varying force of the magnetic field and produced sound waves.

Figure 3.10 shows a more compact version of the same type of receiver which was in use from the early 1920s until the late 1950s in North America. Two small but very strong permanent bar magnets provide the magnetic bias field. This field is channeled to the diaphragm through the two formed soft–iron pole pieces on which the coils are mounted, as shown in Fig. 3.10(b). The whole magnetic structure is fastened to an aluminum frame which also supports the magnetic diaphragm, a perforated cover, and a dust–cover membrane held in place by a formed aluminum collar. A fiberboard cover fastened to the back of the magnetic structure carries a contact button and a contact ring through which the electrical connections are made from spring contacts in the handset.

The magnetic bias field is necessary because if it were not present, the diaphragm would vibrate at twice the frequency of the applied signal current. A magnetic diaphragm suspended above the poles of an electromagnet with no permanent magnetic field would experience no attracting force when the current through the coils was zero. The diaphragm would experience maximum attraction force when the current reached maximum

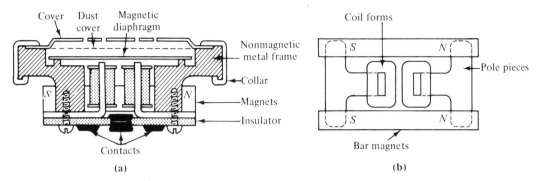

FIGURE 3.10. Magnetic diaphragm–type telephone receiver: (a) Cross section; (b) Magnetic structure.

value of either polarity. Thus the diaphragm would be pulled in twice during each cycle of the applied signal current. With a permanent magnetic field component present, the diaphragm always experiences a positive attracting force. With maximum positive signal, the force would be twice the zero-signal force, and with maximum negative signal the force would approach a zero value. The diaphragm would thus oscillate around its bias position at the same frequency as the signal current.

The receiver described above has been almost entirely replaced by a different version, called a ring–armature receiver, which was introduced in the 1950s. Figure 3.11 shows a cross section of such a receiver unit. In this unit the heavy magnetic diaphragm is replaced by a very lightweight dome-

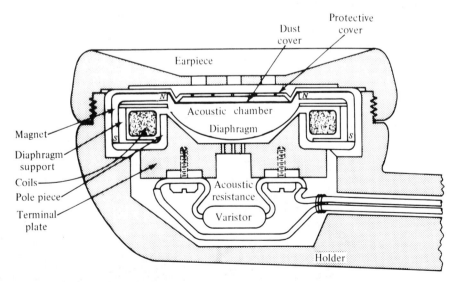

FIGURE 3.11. Cross section of a ring–armature telephone receiver.

shaped diaphragm made of aluminum which is fastened to a ring–shaped disk of magnetic material which forms the armature. The magnetic structure is formed by a cylindrical permanent magnet with an L–shaped cross section and an L–shaped cylindrical soft iron pole piece attached to it. The driving coil is wound inside this magnetic structure, and the ring–shaped armature is suspended in the gap between the magnet and the pole piece, supported by a nonmagnetic support ring. A Bakelite backplate provides support for the screw terminals to the coil, and also provides an acoustical resistance chamber to damp oscillations of the diaphragm. In service, a bilateral varistor diode is connected between the terminals to clip off or limit high–amplitude noise pulses which may be generated by switching equipment. The acoustical chambers in front of and behind the diaphragm are carefully designed so that the mechanical resistance encountered by the diaphragm closely matches the electrical impedance of the telephone circuit. A perforated protection cover and a dust membrane are crimped around the top of the unit and the whole unit is mounted inside the earpiece of a handset. Typical terminal impedances range from 100 to 2000 Ω.

3.12.3 Loudspeakers

In applications where individual privacy of communication is not necessary, such as with broadcast receivers and certain types of telephone circuits, loudspeakers are used to convert the electrical voice signals back into sound waves. The most commonly used type of loudspeaker is the *cone–type moving–coil loudspeaker*. A cross section of such a speaker is shown in Fig. 3.12(a). Voice–frequency electrical currents pass through the coil of wire (voice coil), which is wound on a cylindrical form held in the annular air gap of the magnetic structure. This magnetic structure is made up of a soft iron frame, which forms one pole piece, and a very strong cylindrical permanent magnet. When a positive current is passed through the coil, a force is generated between the coil and the permanent magnet which causes the coil to move axially out of the pole structure. It is restrained lightly by the spring action of the corrugated spider mounting, which keeps the coil centered. When the current reverses, the direction of the magnetic force also reverses, and the coil is pulled back into the pole structure. When alternating current is applied to the coil, the coil moves in and out in time with the alternating current. When the coil moves, the attached paper cone also moves, and alternately compresses and expands the air in front of the speaker. The air pressure resistance presented to the cone and coil is reflected into the electrical circuit as an equivalent load resistance.

Figure 3.12(b) shows an equivalent circuit of the moving-coil loudspeaker. In this circuit, R_s represents the dc coil resistance and L_s represents the effective series inductance of the coil. R_L is the electrical equivalent of the acoustical load resistance encountered by the cone, and L_p is the electri-

FIGURE 3.12. Loudspeakers: (a)
Cone–type moving–coil loudspeaker;
(b) Equivalent circuit of a loudspeaker;
(c) Horn–type loudspeaker.

cal equivalent inductance representing the mechanical springiness of the coil structure. At very low frequencies, X_{Lp} will be very much smaller than the effective acoustical load R_L, and acoustical output will be reduced. At midband frequencies, X_{Lp} will be larger than R_L but X_{Ls} will be smaller than R_L, so most of the input power will be delivered to the acoustical load. At higher frequencies, X_{Ls} will predominate and reduce delivery of current to the load, again reducing the acoustical output.

The ac load impedance of the voice coil as measured at the terminals is a function of the magnetic field force, the coil size, and the efficiency of the acoustical coupling of the cone. Typical values are low, ranging from 1 Ω to about 300 Ω with 4, 8, and 16 Ω being commonly used values. Power ratings are usually stated in terms of the maximum input power that the speaker will handle without being physically damaged. Power ratings range from a few milliwatts in the case of the small 1–inch–diameter speakers used for portable receivers to several hundred watts in the case of large public address system speakers used in auditoriums or outdoors.

The cone of the speaker is used to improve the efficiency of coupling between the coil motion and the surrounding air. Much greater efficiency is obtained when the output from a speaker unit is fed into the throat of an acoustical horn. The horn is used as an impedance transformer, and also as a radiator in much the same manner as horn antennas are used to radiate radio waves. Figure 3.12(c) shows the structure of a typical *horn–type loud-speaker*. The driver unit is of the same type of structure as the cone–type speaker except that the cone is omitted. A shell–like dome attached to the coil couples to the air in the throat chamber of the horn. Although entirely unnecessary from an acoustical point of view, the horn structure is folded back on itself. This is done to conserve physical space, since an unfolded horn might be as much as 2 m in length, and 1 m across the mouth. Such units have power–handling capabilities of more than 100 W, operating at a 16–Ω input impedance.

3.13   PROBLEMS

1.   What part does resonance play in shaping speech sounds? Explain briefly why any spoken word cannot be represented by a single sine wave.

2.   Would you expect a singing voice to generate more, less, or about the same number of harmonic waves as a speaking voice? Which voice would contain the highest frequency components? Given reasons for your answers.

3.   Explain how the frequency limits are determined for speech communications circuits. How would you expect the limits to differ between commercial use and entertainment use?

4.   State the upper– and lower–frequency limits generated by a large orchestra. What is the single most important factor which determines satisfactory limits for music reproduced by electrical means?

5.   Write a short essay, "High-Fidelity Listening," either approving or disapproving of high-fidelity systems.

6.   In reproducing sounds electrically, is it important that the original power levels be reproduced? Give reasons for your answers.

7.   Define and explain the term "sound intensity," and state the units in which this is commonly measured.

8.   Define and explain: (a) loudness level; (b) loudness. Explain carefully the difference between them and state the units in which each is measured.

9.   Three pure tones of frequencies 100 Hz, 500 Hz, and 1000 Hz are separately adjusted to produce for each a loudness level of 100 phons. The tones are combined as a composite sound and passed through a transmission

system which reduces all intensities equally by 50 dB. With reference to Figure 3.5, describe the effect to be expected on the balance of the composite sound.

10. A 1000-Hz tone has its loudness level increased from 60 phons to 80 phons. What will be the approximate increase in loudness sensation? With reference to Figure 3.5, estimate the increase in loudness sensation of a 100-Hz tone which has the same loudness level and undergoes the same change in relative intensity.

11. Explain what is meant by the pitch of a sound, and state the factors on which this depends.

12. Discuss the difference between "concert pitch" and the "mel" as a unit of pitch.

13. The pitch of a pure tone is stated to be 2000 mels. State its most likely frequency, in hertz. How many octaves is it above 1000 Hz?

14. Concert pitch is defined as a pure tone of 440 Hz. With reference to 1000 Hz, state this in: (a) mels; (b) octaves. Why can (a) be stated only as a "most likely" value?

15. Explain what is meant by "summation difference tones." In what way can these be of advantage?

16. Describe briefly one phenomenon which makes it difficult to listen to speech in the presence of a noisy background.

17. Define and explain the term "reverberation time." Explain why this is an important factor in the overall design of a communication link.

18. It is planned to record a talk given in a theater, the reverberation time of which is 1.2 s, when the audience is present. Is the result likely to be satisfactory? Give reasons for your answers. Suggest how this value may be modified to give better results.

19. A public telephone is to be installed in one corner of a large common room, for which it is not possible to provide a closed cubicle. Describe briefly how the effects of noise and echo would be reduced.

20. Explain how the carbon button microphone works and why it is used for telephony.

21. Explain how the ring-armature receiver works and point out the major differences between it and the magnetic diaphragm receiver.

22. In terms of power rating and physical size, what type of loud-speaker would you provide for: (a) a communications receiver placed in the communications room of a police station; (b) an FM broadcast receiver placed in your living room; (c) a public address system for an army parade square?

23. Measurements on a loudspeaker show that it has a dc resistance of 0.5 Ω, a series inductance of 0.4 mH, a parallel inductance of 0.5 H, and an

acoustical load resistance of 15.5 Ω. Find the upper and lower cutoff frequencies of the speaker if it is driven from a 16-Ω source.

24. Express the following ratios in decibels: (a) voltage ratios: 5:1, 10:1, 10^6:1; (b) current ratios: 0.1:1, 1:1, 10^{-10}:1 (c) power ratios: 1:1, 50:1, 1:60.

25. The voltage gain of an amplifier is given as 100 dB, this being the ratio of output to input voltage expressed in decibels. Calculate output voltage given that the input voltage is 1μV. Can the power gain be determined from the information given?

Chapter 4
Noise

4.1 INTRODUCTION

Reception of a signal in a telecommunication system may be marred by noise, which can originate from a variety of sources. One obvious source, for example, could be faulty connections in equipment, a source that, in principle anyway, could be eliminated.

Noise also occurs where electrical connections that carry current are made and broken, as, for example, in the ignition system of automobiles or at the brushes of an electrical machine. Again, in principle, noise from these sources can be effectively suppressed at the source.

Natural phenomena that gives rise to noise include electric storms, solar flares, and certain belts of radiation in space. The only effective means of reducing such noise is to reposition the receiving antenna where possible to minimize noise reception while ensuring that the received signal is not also seriously reduced.

There are also natural, or fundamental, sources of noise within electronic equipment; these sources are termed *fundamental* because they are an inescapable part of the physical nature of the materials used in making electronic components. Such noise is found to obey certain physical laws, and an understanding of these enables equipment to be designed in which the effects of noise is minimized.

As commonly understood, noise is audible, although in a wider sense it also covers visual disturbances such as those that occur in television reception or in chart recording of data. In the telecommunications context, *noise* will also be used to refer to the *electrical* disturbance that gives rise to the audible or visual noise, and to errors in data transmission.

4.2 THERMAL NOISE

The free electrons within a conductor are in random motion as a result of receiving thermal energy. Thus, at any given instant of time an excess of electrons may appear at one or other end of the conductor, and although the average voltage resulting from this is zero, the average power available is not zero (just as an average signal power output can be obtained from a sinusoidal voltage of zero average).

Because the noise power results from thermal energy, it is known as *thermal noise* (or sometimes *Johnson noise*, after its discoverer). It would be expected that thermal noise power would be related to the temperature of the conductor, and it is found that the average power is proportional to the absolute temperature of the conductor. It is also found that the average noise power is proportional to the frequency bandwidth, or spectrum, of the thermal noise; this will be explained in more detail later.

The law relating available noise power (average) to temperature and bandwidth is

$$P_n = kTB \text{ watts} \tag{4.1}$$

where

P_n = available average noise power, watts

T = temperature of conductor, kelvins

B = bandwidth of noise spectrum, hertz

k = Boltzmann's constant

   = 1.38×10^{-23} joule/kelvin

This is a particularly simple but powerful law which can be justified on physical grounds. It means that a conductor can be considered as a generator of electrical energy by virtue of its being at a finite temperature. The instantaneous voltage/time waveform would be typically as shown in Fig. 4.1(a). In Chapter 2 it is explained that every voltage/time waveform has a frequency spectrum, and in the case of thermal noise voltage, it is the power spectrum density that is significant. The power spectrum density is the aver-

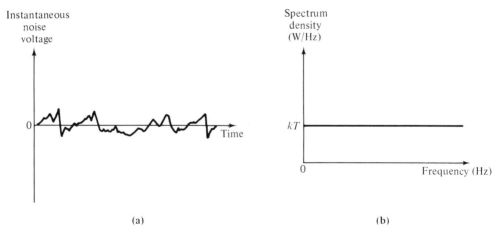

FIGURE 4.1. (a) The voltage/time variation for noise voltage; (b) The noise power spectrum density for thermal noise.

age noise power per hertz of bandwidth, and from Eq. (4.1) this is simply

$$S_n = kT \qquad \text{watts/hertz} \tag{4.2}$$

Thus the spectrum density graph for thermal noise is as shown in Fig. 4.1(b). At room temperature ($T = 290$ K), the spectrum density is

$$S_n = 1.38 \times 10^{-23} \times 290$$
$$= 4 \times 10^{-21} \text{ W/Hz}$$

For a bandwidth of 1 MHz, the available noise power is

$$P_n = S_n \cdot B \tag{4.3}$$
$$= 4 \times 10^{-21} \times 10^6$$
$$= 4 \times 10^{-15} \text{ W}$$

This may be thought a small amount of power, but it has to be compared with available signal power to be seen in correct perspective. The signal may be of the order of $1.0 \, \mu$ V EMF in a 50–Ω source, which results in an available signal power [see Eq. (1.121)] of

$$P_s = \frac{(1.0 \times 10^{-6})^2}{4 \times 50}$$
$$= 5.0 \times 10^{-15} \text{ W}$$

The signal and noise powers are seen to be of the same order of magnitude, and any subsequent amplification will not improve the signal-to-noise ratio.

Since the conductor is a generator of electrical power (albeit noise power), it has an equivalent voltage, or an equivalent current, generator circuit representing the noise source. Consider first the voltage equivalent circuit. The average power delivered by a voltage generator of internal rms voltage E_s, and internal resistance R_s, to a load R_L, Fig. 4.2(a), when matched $(R_s = R_L)$ is a maximum, is given by Eq. (1.121) as

$$P_{L\max} = \frac{E_s^2}{4R_s} \tag{4.4}$$

(a)   (b)   (c)

FIGURE 4.2. (a) A voltage generator of internal rms voltage E_s and internal resistance R_s, connected to a load resistance R_L; (b) The voltage–generator equivalent circuit for a noise source; (c) The current–generator equivalent circuit for a noise source.

Applying this reasoning to a conductor of resistance R, considered as a noise generator of rms noise voltage E_n, gives

$$kTB = \frac{E_n^2}{4R}$$

$$E_n^2 = 4RkTB \tag{4.5}$$

This equation shows that the thermal noise properties of a conductor may be represented by the equivalent circuit of Fig. 4.2(b). This is one of the most useful representations of noise and is widely used in calculations of noise performance of equipment. When using it, it is best to work in terms of E_n^2 rather than E_n, for reasons that will be explained later.

The current generator equivalent circuit for thermal noise is shown in Fig. 4.2(c), which can be derived following similar reasoning for that of the voltage circuit. The mean–square noise current [from Eq. (1.123) on substituting kTB for P_L] is

$$I_n^2 = 4GkTB \quad \text{where } G = \text{conductance} \quad \left(= \frac{1}{R} \right) \tag{4.6}$$

If a conductor of resistance R delivers thermal noise power to a load resistance R_L, it follows that the load resistance R_L must also deliver thermal noise power to the conductor, and in thermal equilibrium, the net exchange of power is zero. If, however, the load is an output indicator (i.e., loudspeaker), the noise output will be that resulting from both R_L and R.

4.2.1 Resistors in Series

The noise voltage equivalent circuit is shown in Fig. 4.3(a). Since two resistors in series can be replaced by a single resistor $R_s = R_1 + R_2$, the circuit can be redrawn as Fig. 4.3(b). It follows from this that

$$E_n^2 = 4R_s kTB \tag{4.7}$$

$$= 4(R_1 + R_2)kTB$$

$$= E_{n1}^2 + E_{n2}^2 \tag{4.8}$$

This shows that the resultant noise voltage *squared* is equal to the sum of the *squares* of the individual noise voltages or, alternatively,

$$E_n = \sqrt{E_{n1}^2 + E_{n2}^2} \tag{4.9}$$

Note that just summing the noise voltages $(E_{n1} + E_{n2})$ would have given the wrong result; for this reason it is best to work in terms of noise voltage squared.

The argument can clearly be extended to any number of resistors in series, giving for the resultant noise voltage:

$$E_n^2 = 4(R_1 + R_2 + R_3 + \cdots)kTB \tag{4.10}$$

4.2.2 Resistors in Parallel

For two resistors in parallel, the equivalent noise circuit is as shown in Fig. 4.3(c). Here, it is easiest to work in terms of conductance G and the current–generator equivalent circuit. Since two conductances in parallel can be replaced by a single conductance $G_p = G_1 + G_2$, the circuit can be redrawn as Fig. 4.3(d). From this,

$$I_n^2 = 4G_p kTB \tag{4.11}$$

$$= 4(G_1 + G_2)kTB$$

$$= I_{n1}^2 + I_{n2}^2 \tag{4.12}$$

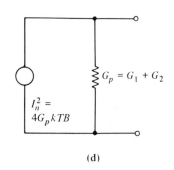

FIGURE 4.3. (a) Two noise sources connected in series; (b) The voltage–generator
equivalent circuit for the series connection;
(c) Two noise sources connected in parallel;
(d) The current–generator equivalent circuit for
(c); (e) The voltage–generator equivalent circuit for (c).

The argument can be extended to any number of resistors in parallel, to give

$$I_n^2 = 4(G_1 + G_2 + G_3 + \cdots)kTB \qquad (4.13)$$

If it is desired to obtain the voltage–generator equivalent circuit for resistors in parallel, the equivalent parallel resistance R_p is used as shown in Fig. 4.3(e), where

$$\frac{1}{R_p} = \frac{1}{R_1} + \frac{1}{R_2} + \frac{1}{R_3} + \cdots$$

and $\quad E_n^2 = 4R_p kTB$ \hfill (4.14)

Example 4.1 Two resistors, 20 kΩ and 50 kΩ, are at room temperature (290 K). Calculate, for a bandwidth of 100 kHz, the thermal noise voltage: (a) for each resistor; (b) for the two resistors in series; (c) for the two resistors in parallel.

Solution $\quad\quad\quad\quad\quad\quad kT = 4 \times 10^{-21}$ W/Hz at room temperature.

(a) For the 20–kΩ resistor:

$$E_n^2 = 4 \times (20 \times 10^3) \times (4 \times 10^{-21}) \times (100 \times 10^3)$$
$$= 32 \times 10^{-12} \text{V}^2$$
$$E_n = 5.66 \mu \text{V}$$

For the 50–kΩ resistor:

$$E_n = 5.66 \times \sqrt{\frac{50}{20}}$$

$$= 8.95 \mu \text{V}$$

(Note the use of proportionality here.)

(b) In series, $\quad\quad\quad\quad R_s = 20 + 50$
$$= 70 \text{ k}\Omega$$

Therefore, $\quad\quad\quad\quad E_n = 5.66 \times \sqrt{\frac{70}{20}}$

$$= 10.59 \mu \text{V}$$

(c) In parallel, $\quad\quad\quad\quad R_p = \frac{20 \times 50}{20 + 50}$

$$= \frac{100}{7} \text{ k}\Omega$$

Therefore, $$E_n = 5.66 \times \sqrt{\frac{100}{7 \times 20}}$$

$$= 4.78 \mu V$$

4.2.3 Reactance and Equivalent Noise Bandwidth

Inductive and capacitive reactances do not generate thermal noise. This follows from the fact that reactance cannot dissipate power. Consider a reactance connected to a resistor, Fig. 4.4. Assume that the reactance delivers noise power P_1 to the resistor, and that the resistor delivers noise power P_2 to the reactance. For thermal equilibrium the power received by the reactance must equal the power delivered by it, but since the received power (i.e., the power dissipated by the reactance) is zero, the power delivered by it must also be zero.

FIGURE 4.4. The power exchange between a reactance and a resistance is $P_1 = P_2 = 0$.

The effect of reactance on the noise spectrum must, however, be taken into account. It can be shown that, when noise passes through a passive filter which has a complex transfer function $H(\omega)$ (see Section 1.15.4), the noise output spectrum density S_{no}, for an input density of $S_n = kT$ [see Eq. (4.2)] is

$$S_{no} = |H(\omega)|^2 kT \qquad (4.15)$$

Two important cases will be analyzed. The first is where a resistor is shunted by a capacitor (which may be the self–capacitance of R), Fig. 4.5(a). The RC network forms a low–pass filter for which E_n is the input and V_n the output. The modulus of the transfer function for this filter is easily determined from normal ac circuit theory to be

$$|H(\omega)| = \frac{1}{\sqrt{1 + (\omega CR)^2}} \qquad (4.16)$$

Hence $$S_{no} = \frac{kT}{(1 + (\omega CR)^2)} \qquad (4.17)$$

The output spectrum is seen to decrease as ω increases. The total noise power available at the output is obtained by integrating (i.e., summing) S_{no} over the complete frequency spectrum, from zero to infinity. The details of the integration are quite straightforward and will be omitted here. The result is that the total noise power available at the output, P_{no}, is

$$P_{no} = \frac{kT}{4RC} \tag{4.18}$$

FIGURE 4.5.   (a) Noise voltage acting around an RC circuit; (b) The equivalent voltage–generator circuit for (a) using the effective bandwidth; (c) Noise voltage acting around a tuned circuit; (d) The equivalent voltage–generator circuit for (c).

Comparing Eq. (4.18) with Eq. (4.1), an *effective* noise bandwidth B_{eff} may be defined where

$$B_{\text{eff}} = \frac{1}{4RC} \tag{4.19}$$

This allows the equivalent circuit of Fig. 4.5(b) to be drawn. For this, the noise spectrum, instead of trailing off to infinity, is level at kT up to a bandwidth B_{eff}, at which it cuts abruptly off.

It will be seen that V_n can be simplified to

$$V_n^2 = 4RkT\frac{1}{4RC}$$

$$= \frac{kT}{C} \tag{4.20}$$

This again emphasizes the point that although C does not contribute to the noise, it limits the mean square value.

The second example is the tuned circuit of Fig. 4.5(c) in which the capacitor is assumed lossless, the only noise generating component being the series resistance of the coil. Consider first the situation where the circuit is resonant, and the noise bandwidth is restricted to a small value Δf around the resonant frequency. From the definition of Q factor, Section 1.8, the output mean square voltage is

$$V_n^2 = Q^2 E_n^2$$
$$= 4Q^2 rkT \Delta f \qquad (4.21)$$

But $Q^2 r$ is equal to R_D, the dynamic impedance of the circuit (see Section 1.9), and therefore

$$V_n^2 = 4R_D kT \cdot \Delta f \qquad (4.22)$$

This result by itself is important, as often the bandwidth is limited physically to some small percentage of f_0 about f_0. An example will illustrate this.

Example 4.2

The parallel tuned circuit at the input of a radio receiver is tuned to resonate at 120 MHz by a capacitance of 25 pF. The Q factor of the circuit is 30. The channel bandwidth of the receiver is limited to 10 kHz by the low frequency sections. Calculate, at room temperature, the effective noise voltage of the tuned circuit, as limited by the l.f. bandwidth.

Solution

$$R_d = \frac{Q}{\omega_0 C}$$

$$= \frac{30 \times 10^{12}}{2 \times \pi \times 120 \times 10^6 \times 25}$$

$$= 1.59 \, \text{k}\Omega$$

$$\Delta f = 10^4 \, \text{Hz}$$

$$(V_n)^2 = 4 \times 1.59 \times 10^3 \times 4 \times 10^{-21} \times 10^4$$

$$= 0.254 \times 10^{-12}$$

$$V_n = 0.50 \, \mu\text{V}$$

Where the bandwidth is unrestricted, the total noise spectrum must be taken into account using Eq. (4.15). For the circuit of Fig. 4.5(c), again considering E_n as the input and V_n as the output, the modulus of the transfer function is easily seen to be

$$|H(\omega)| = \frac{|X_c|}{|Z_s|} \qquad (4.23)$$

where Z_s is the series impedance of the circuit and X_c is the reactance of C. S_{no} is found by substituting Eq. (4.23) in Eq. (4.15), and the total available power at the output is found by integrating S_{no} over the complete frequency spectrum as before. This is a more difficult integral than the previous one, but the result is that

$$P_{no} = \frac{kT}{4R_D C} \qquad (4.24)$$

and thus

$$B_{\text{eff}} = \frac{1}{4R_D C} \qquad (4.25)$$

The equivalent noise–generator circuit for the tuned circuit is as shown in Fig. 4.5(d).

A relationship between B_{eff} and the 3–dB bandwidth of the circuit can be found. Referring to Section 1.9, substituting Eq. (1.70) in Eq. (1.73) gives

$$R_D = \frac{1}{2\pi B_{3\,\text{dB}} \cdot C} \qquad (4.26)$$

and substituting this in Eq. (4.25) gives

$$B_{\text{eff}} = \frac{\pi}{2} B_{3\,\text{dB}} \qquad (4.27)$$

In the foregoing it was assumed that the Q factor remained constant, independent of frequency; this is necessary to simplify the analysis but is not fully justifiable. However, the result obtained gives a good indication of the noise expected.

The idea of an equivalent noise bandwidth B_{eff} can be extended to cover the case of an amplifier or radio receiver. Suppose that the relative power–gain, or relative voltage–gain–squared, response curve is as shown in Fig. 4.6(a). B_{eff} is given directly by the area under the response curve (since, to a different scale, the relative power, or voltage–gain–squared response curve has the same shape as the power spectrum density curve). A relative response curve simply means that the ordinate values are scaled relative to the maximum value, and thus the maximum value of the relative curve is unity.

For a radio receiver, the noise is generated almost entirely at the front end (RF sections), while the effective bandwidth is determined by the low-frequency sections. For a single–sideband receiver (see Section 9.1) B_{eff} is determined by the area, as already described. For a double-sideband receiver (see Section 8.2.1), the effective noise bandwidth is doubled, as both sidebands contribute independently to the noise. Thus the effective noise bandwidth, B'_{eff}, Fig. 4.6(b), is

$$B'_{\text{eff}} = 2B_{\text{eff}} \qquad (4.28)$$

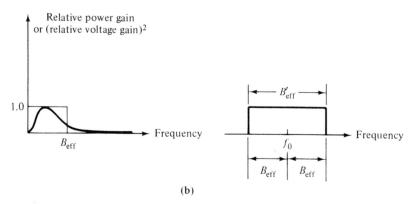

FIGURE 4.6.   (a) Effective noise bandwidth as defined by the relative power-gain response curve of an amplifier; (b) Effective noise bandwidth for a double-sideband receiver.

4.3 SHOT NOISE

A second fundamental source of noise, the term *shot noise*, was originally used to describe the plate current noise resulting from random fluctuations in electron emission from cathodes in vacuum tubes; the analogy was made with the effect of lead shot from a gun striking a target. Shot noise also occurs in semiconductor devices where carriers are liberated into potential barrier regions, such as occur at *pn* junctions.

Shot noise is found to have a uniform spectrum density like thermal noise, and the mean-square noise current depends directly on the direct component of current. Shot noise is also a function of the operating conditions of the device, and a number of special cases have been analyzed; only two of these will be considered here, the temperature–limited diode, and the *pn*–junction diode.

A *temperature-limited diode* is a vacuum–tube diode in which the emission from the cathode is limited only by its temperature; for example, increasing the heater current will increase the temperature, and hence the shot noise current. The mean–square shot noise current is found to be given by

$$I_n^2 = 2I_{dc}\, q_e\, B \qquad \text{amperes}^2 \qquad (4.29)$$

where I_n = noise component of current, amperes

I_{dc} = direct component of current, amperes

q_e = magnitude of electron charge

  = $1.6 \times 10^{-19} C$

B = effective noise bandwidth, hertz

The importance of Eq. (4.29) is that it shows that the noise current is known in terms of an easily measured direct current, and this is used as the basis of one type of noise-measuring method (described in Section 4.10.4).

A similar equation applies for the semiconductor *pn-junction diode:*

$$I_n^2 = 2(I + 2I_0)q_e\, B \qquad \text{amperes}^2 \qquad (4.30)$$

where I is the direct current across the junction, amperes, and I_0 the reverse saturation current, amperes.

Equation (4.30) only applies at low frequencies and for low injection [this is somewhat analogous to the temperature limitation of the vacuum-tube diode, Eq. (4.29)].

4.4 PARTITION NOISE

Partition noise occurs wherever current has to divide between two or more paths, and results from the random fluctuations in the division. It would be expected, therefore, that a diode would be less noisy than a transistor (all other factors being equal) if the third electrode draws current (i.e., the base current). It is for this reason that the inputs of microwave receivers are often taken directly to diode mixers. The spectrum for partition noise is flat.

In older, vacuum-tube-type receivers and amplifiers, partition noise in pentodes was sufficiently great to make the triode the preferred tube for high-frequency amplification.

4.5 LOW-FREQUENCY, OR FLICKER, NOISE

Below frequencies of a few kilohertz, a component of noise appears, the spectrum density of which increases as the frequency decreases. This is known as *flicker noise* (sometimes it is referred to as $1/f$ noise). In vacuum tubes, the main causes of flicker noise are slow changes which take place in the oxide structure of oxide–coated cathodes, and migration of impurity ions through the oxide.

In semiconductors, flicker noise results from fluctuations in carrier density, and it is much more troublesome in the semiconductor amplifying device compared to the vacuum-tube counterpart, at low frequencies. The fluctuations in carrier density cause fluctuations in the conductivity of the material; this, in turn, produces a fluctuating voltage drop when a direct current flows, which is the flicker-noise voltage. It follows that the mean-square value of this is proportional to the square of the direct current flowing.

4.6 HIGH–FREQUENCY, OR TRANSIT–TIME, NOISE

In semiconducting devices, when the transit time of carriers crossing a junction is comparable with the periodic time of the signal, some of the carriers may diffuse back to the source, or emitter. It can be shown that this gives rise to an input admittance in which the conductance component increases with frequency. This conductance has associated with it a noise current generator similar to that shown in Fig. 4.2(c), and since the conductance increases with frequency, so also does the spectrum density. A similar effect occurs in vacuum tubes when the transit time of electrons from cathode to control grid is comparable to the periodic time of the signal.

4.7 GENERATION–RECOMBINATION NOISE

In semiconductor devices, some impurity centers will be ionized on a random basis, being energized thermally; thus a random generation of carriers occurs in the device. Also, the carriers can recombine with ionized impurity centers on a random basis either directly or through trapping centers. The overall result is that the conductivity of the semiconductor has a randomly fluctuating component which gives rise to a noise current when direct current flows through the semiconductor. The spectrum density of this type of noise has not been fully established.

4.8 EQUIVALENT NOISE RESISTANCE

It is sometimes convenient to represent the noise which originates in a device (active or passive) by means of a *fictitious* resistance R_n, assumed to generate the noise at *room temperature*, the actual device then being assumed noiseless. The noise resistance should be part of the manufacturer's data for the device, given for specified operating conditions. Clearly, it is important than any deviation from the specified operating conditions be taken into account in applying the concept of noise resistance.

An amplifier may have a specified noise resistance R_n and an actual input resistance R_i, Fig. 4.7(a). The equivalent mean-square noise voltage appearing at the input terminals is

$$V_n^2 = 4(R_i + R_n)kTB \qquad (4.31)$$

In effect, the amplifier noise is referred to the input circuit so that the amplifier may be assumed noiseless, Fig. 4.7(b). The main advantage in using R_n is that it enables the amplifier–noise contribution to be compared directly with the input-circuit contribution. It is essential to grasp the idea that R_n is a fictitious resistance which does not affect the real resistance at the input. In the previous example, Fig. 4.7(b), the input resistance remains at R_i even though the effective resistance from the point of view of noise generation is $(R_i + R_n)$.

Example 4.3

For the circuit of Fig. 4.7(a), calculate the signal voltage and the equivalent noise voltage appearing at the input terminals for an effective noise bandwidth of 10 kHz and at room temperature (290K), where $R_n = 400\Omega$, $R_i = 600\Omega$, $R_s = 50\Omega$, and $E_s = 1.0\mu V$.

Solution

The easiest method of solving this problem is to apply Thevenin's theorem (See Section 1.13) to reduce the input circuit to that shown in Fig. 4.7(c). Note that R_n does not affect this. From Fig. 4.7(c) the terminal signal voltage V_s' is

$$V_s' = V_s = 0.923\mu V$$

The noise voltage V_n is obtained from

$$
\begin{aligned}
V_n^2 &= 4(R_p + R_n)kTB \\
&= 4(46.15 + 400)kTB \\
&= 4 \times 446 \times 4 \times 10^{-21} \times 10^4 \\
&= 1.6 \times 4.46 \times 10^{-14}\,\text{volt}^2 \\
V_n &= 0.267\mu V
\end{aligned}
$$

Note that this contains the noise contributions from R_s and R_i in parallel, R_n effectively being a noise source in series with R_p.

(a)

(b)

FIGURE 4.7. (a) An amplifier with input resistance R_i and equivalent noise resistance R_n; (b) The noise circuit representation for (a); (c) An amplifier of input resistance 600 Ω and noise resistance 400 Ω, fed by a source of internal resistance 50 Ω and internal EMF 1 μ V—the Thevenin equivalent circuit for signal input.

(c)

4.9 SIGNAL-TO-NOISE RATIO

In a telecommunications system the noise power in comparison with the signal power is important and the best measure of this is the *signal-to-noise power ratio* (S/N).

Example 4.4　For the system of Fig 4.7, the signal-to-noise power ratio is

$$S/N = \frac{V_s^2}{V_n^2} \quad \text{(since power is proportional to voltage squared)}$$

$$= \left(\frac{0.923}{0.267} \right)^2$$

$$= 11.95$$

In decibels, this is

$$(S/N)_{dB} = 10 \log_{10} 11.95$$

$$= 10.77 \text{ dB}$$

More generally, suppose that the input signal source and input resistance can be represented by the Thévenin equivalent circuit of V_s in series with R_p and that the amplifier has an equivalent noise resistance R_n, Fig. 4.7(c); then the S/N ratio of the system is

$$S/N = \frac{V_s^2}{4(R_p + R_n)kTB} \tag{4.32}$$

4.9.1 Effect of Amplification on S/N Ratio

Mixer stages in receivers have notoriously high values of equivalent noise resistance. Therefore, a large signal is required to maintain an acceptable S/N ratio, as shown by Eq. (4.32). Weak signals have to be amplified before being applied to the mixer stage and of course the amplifier must not contribute excessive noise; otherwise, no improvement in signal-to-noise ratio results. In order to see the effect of the amplifier, it is best to transfer all noise sources to the input, that is, an equivalent source is postulated at the input which results in exactly the same output as the actual source. Figure 4.8(a) illustrates a mixer with noise resistance R_{nm} preceded by an amplifier of voltage gain A and noise resistance R_{na}. The mixer noise voltage generator V_{nm}^2 can be replaced by a noise voltage generator V_{nm}^2/A^2 at the input to the amplifier; this follows, since on going through the amplifier the mean-square noise voltage is amplified by A^2, resulting in a mixer component of noise V_{nm}^2 at the input to the mixer, as was originally the case. The equivalent circuit is shown in Fig. 4.8(b).

The total noise voltage referred to the amplifier input is then

$$V_n^2 = V_{na}^2 + \frac{V_{nm}^2}{A^2}$$

$$= 4 \left(R_{na} + \frac{R_{nm}}{A^2} \right) kTB \tag{4.33}$$

FIGURE 4.8. (a) An amplifier of voltage gain A and equivalent noise resistance R_{na}, connected between a mixer of noise resistance R_{nm} and a source of effective internal reistance R_p and EMF V_s; (b) The euivalent circuit for (a) showing all noise sources referred to the input of the amplifier.

The S/N ratio with the amplifier connected is

$$S/N = \frac{V_s^2}{4(R_p + R_{na} + R_{nm}/A^2)kTB} \qquad (4.34)$$

whereas that obtainable with the signal source fed directly into the mixer would be

$$(S/N)_{mixer} = \frac{V_s^2}{4(R_p + R_{nm})kTB} \qquad (4.35]$$

It follows that for the amplifier to result in an improvement in S/N:

$$R_{na} + \frac{R_{nm}}{A^2} < R_{nm}$$

For really worthwhile improvement, $R_{nm}/A^2 \ll R_{na}$, so the S/N ratio becomes that of the amplifier alone.

Example 4.5 With $R_{nm} = 200$ kΩ, $R_{na} = 1$ kΩ, and $A = 100$; then

$$\frac{R_{nm}}{A^2} = 20\Omega$$

The mixer noise is, therefore, negligible (20 Ω compared with 1000 Ω) compared to the amplifier noise. The *improvement* in signal-to-noise ratio depends, or course, on the source resistance R_p also, and is in the ratio

$$\frac{R_p + R_{nm}}{R_p + R_{na} + R_{nm}/A^2}$$

Assuming a typical value of $R_p = 50$ Ω, the improvement ratio becomes

$$\frac{50 + 200 \times 10^3}{50 + 1000 + 20} = 187{:}1$$

In decibels, this is a **22.7-dB** improvement in the S/N ratio. Effectively, it means that the system is 187 times more sensitive in power detection or $\sqrt{187} = 13.67$ times more sensitive in voltage detection. Note that it is not 100 times more sensitive in voltage detection even though the voltage gain is 100. Why? For a voltage gain $A = 10$, and the other parameters as before, $R_{nm}/A^2 = 2$kΩ and the mixer noise is not negligible, although an overall improvement in S/N is still obtained. The improvement in this case is

$$\frac{50 + 200 \times 10^3}{50 + 1000 + 2000} = 65.6{:}1 \qquad \text{(in power)}$$

This is an **18.2-dB** improvement in S/N ratio, which is certainly significant.

4.9.2 Tandem Connection

Where a number of telecommunications links operate in *tandem* (i.e., one following the other), the overall S/N ratio will be less than that of any one of the links. Let M be the number of links in tandem transmitting a signal P_s. The noise powers P_{n1}, P_{n2}, ..., P_{nM}, will add so that the overall S/N ratio at the output will be

$$(S/N)_{\text{dB}} = 10 \log_{10} \left(\frac{P_s}{P_{n1} + P_{n2} + \cdots + P_{nM}} \right) \qquad (4.36)$$

Where the links are identical such that $P_{n1} = P_{n2} = \cdots = P_{nM} = P_n$, the overall S/N ratio becomes

$$(S/N)_{dB} = 10 \log_{10}\left(\frac{P_s}{MP_n}\right) \tag{4.37}$$

$$= 10 \log_{10}\left(\frac{P_s}{P_n}\right) - 10 \log_{10}M$$

$$= (S/N)'_{dB} - M_{dB} \tag{4.38}$$

where $(S/N)'_{dB}$ is the signal-to-noise ratio of any one link, and M_{dB} is the number of links expressed in *decilogs* (i.e., M is treated as a power ratio and the decibel value taken).

Example 4.6 Let the number of links be three, each having an S/N ratio of 60 dB. The overall S/N ratio is

$$(S/N)_{dB} = 60 - 10 \log_{10}3$$

$$= 55.23 \text{ dB}$$

If the S/N ratio of one link is much worse than any of the others, that link will determine the overall S/N ratio. Considering the previous example again, for a given P_s let the S/N ratio for two of the links each be 60 dB, and let the third link have an S/N ratio of 40 dB. The various noise powers will be

$$P_{n1} = P_{n2} = P_s \times 10^{-6}$$

$$P_{n3} = P_s \times 10^{-4}$$

The total noise power is

$$P_{nt} = P_{n1} + P_{n2} + P_{n3}$$

$$= P_s(2 \times 10^{-6} + 10^{-4})$$

$$\cong P_s \times 10^{-4}$$

The overall S/N ratio is, therefore,

$$(S/N)_{dB} \cong 10 \log_{10}\left(\frac{P_s}{P_s \times 10^{-4}}\right)$$

$$= 40 \text{ dB}$$

This is the S/N of the worst link. Signal-to-noise ratio is discussed further in relation to modulation methods in Sections 9.7 and 10.6.

4.10 NOISE FACTOR

The *noise factor* F of an amplifier (or any network) may be defined in terms of the signal-to-noise ratio as follows:

$$F = \frac{\text{available } S/N \text{ power ratio at input}}{\text{available } S/N \text{ power ratio at output}}$$

$$= \frac{P_{si}}{P_{ni}} \times \frac{P_{no}}{P_{so}} \tag{4.39}$$

Here, P_{si} is the signal power available at the input, P_{ni} the noise power available at the input, P_{so} the signal power available at the output, and P_{no} the noise power available at the output. The temperature of the input source is defined as room temperature.

The S/N available at the output will always be less than that at the input, since any amplifier or network will add noise. Therefore, the noise factor is a measure of the amount of noise added (i.e., it is the factor by which the amplifier degrades the available signal-to-noise ratio at the input) and F will always be greater than unity.

F is frequency-dependent in many cases, and where it is determined at one frequency it is known as the *spot noise factor*. Clearly, the frequency must be stated along with the noise factor. An average value of F can also be found over the frequency range of interest, this being known as the *average noise factor*, F_{av}. In this chapter only the spot noise factor will be discussed, so it may be assumed that the frequency is known.

Available powers are used in the definition, as these can be defined unambiguously. The available power from a source is the maximum average power a source can deliver [as given by Eq. (1.123)] and is obtained under matched conditions. The available input powers (signal and noise) may not actually be delivered to the input of the amplifier because of mismatch, but the available output powers depend on the *actual* input powers and, therefore, any mismatch is taken into account.

The available power gain G is

$$G = \frac{P_{so}}{P_{si}} \tag{4.40}$$

(Do not confuse with conductance.) Therefore, from Eq. (4.39),

$$F = \frac{P_{no}}{GP_{ni}} \tag{4.41}$$

or
$$P_{no} = FGP_{ni} \tag{4.42}$$

As already stated in Eq. (4.1), $P_{ni} = kTB$, and for noise factor, temperature T is defined as T_o :

$$\therefore P_{no} = FGkT_o B \qquad (4.43)$$

This shows that the output noise power is increased by a factor F over what it would have been if the amplifier had been noiseless.

4.10.1   Noise Factor F in Terms of R_n

The output S/N is given by Eq. (4.32), since both signal and noise will be amplified by the same amount and the noise of the amplifier is taken into account by R_n. The available input signal-to-noise ratio is

$$(S/N)_{in} = \frac{V_s^2}{4R_p kT_o B} \qquad (4.44)$$

Therefore,
$$F = \frac{(S/N)_{in}}{(S/N)_{out}}$$
$$= \frac{R_p + R_n}{R_p} \qquad (4.45)$$

Note that the input resistance R_i of the amplifier is included in the effective source resistance R_p, and that if R_n were zero, F (noise *factor*) would be equal to unity.

Sometimes the noise factor is expressed in decibels, in which case it is customary to refer to it as the *noise figure:*

$$\text{noise figure} = F_{dB} = 10 \log_{10} F \qquad (4.46)$$

Thus, in the case where $R_n = 0$, the noise *figure* would be zero.

4.10.2   Amplifier Input Noise in Terms of F

The total noise referred to the input can be represented by P_{no}/G, and it follows from Eq. (4.43) that this is

$$P_{ni(total)} = FkT_o B \qquad (4.47)$$

The source contributes $kT_o B$ of this; therefore, the amplifier must contribute the amount P_{na}, where

$$P_{na} = FkT_o B - kT_o B.$$
$$= (F - 1)kT_o B \qquad (4.48)$$

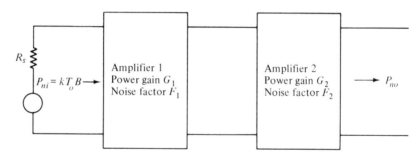

FIGURE 4.9. For two amplifiers in cascade, the overall noise factor is $F = F_1 + (F_2 - 1)/G_1$.

4.10.3 Amplifiers in Cascade

This is similar to the problem of an amplifier and mixer in cascade, which was solved in terms of R_n. In this case, available noise powers are used, since F is defined in terms of these. Referring to fig. 4.9, the noise input to amplifier 1 is $F_1 k T_o B$ [from Eq. (4.47)], and therefore the noise input to amplifier 2 is G_1 times this plus the contribution from amplifier 2 itself, which is given by Eq. (4.48):

$$\text{noise input to amplifier 2} = G_1 F_1 k T_o B + (F_2 - 1) k T_o B$$

The output noise power, which is that from amplifier 2, is G_2 times the input noise power to amplifier 2:

$$P_{no} = G_2 G_1 F_1 k T_o B + G_2 (F_2 - 1) k T_o B$$

The overall gain is $G = G_1 G_2$, so the overall noise factor, from Eq. (4.41), is

$$F = \frac{P_{no}}{G_2 G_1 P_{ni}}$$

$$= \frac{G_2 G_1 F_1 k T_o B + G_2 (F_2 - 1) k T_o B}{G_2 G_1 k T_o B}$$

$$= F_1 + \frac{F_2 - 1}{G_1} \tag{4.49}$$

The argument is easily extended for additional amplifiers, to give

$$F = F_1 + \frac{F_2 - 1}{G_1} + \frac{F_3 - 1}{G_2 G_1} + \ldots \qquad (4.50)$$

This is known as *Friiss' formula*.

Example 4.7 A mixer stage has a noise figure of 20 dB and this is preceded by an amplifier that has a noise figure of 9dB and an available power gain of 15 dB. Calculate the overall noise figure referred to the input.

Solution

$$F_2 = 20 \text{ dB} = 100{:}1 \text{ power ratio}$$

$$F_1 = 9 \text{ dB} = 7.94{:}1 \text{ power ratio}$$

$$G_1 = 15 \text{ dB} = 31.62{:}1 \text{ power ratio}$$

Using Friiss' formula

$$F = F_1 + \frac{F_2 - 1}{G_1}$$

$$= 7.94 + \frac{100 - 1}{31.62}$$

$$= 11.07$$

This is the overall noise factor. The overall noise figure is

$$F_{dB} = 10 \log_{10} 11.07$$

$$= \mathbf{10.44 \text{ dB}}$$

Note that the noise figures must be converted to noise factors, and the gain converted to a power ratio, before Friiss' formula can be used.

4.10.4 Measurement of Noise Factor

The most common method is to use the shot noise as produced in a diode to determine the noise factor of an amplifier. The diode may be a temperature-limited vacuum-tube type, or it may be a semiconductor type; in either case, the shot-noise current is given by an equation of the form of Eq. (4.29):

$$I_n^2 = 2 I_{dc} q_e B \qquad (4.29)$$

The equivalent circuit for the noise-generating diode is shown in Fig. 4.10, in which resistance R is the load resistance. This is usually chosen to match the input to the amplifier under test, and for the input to radio receivers, for example, may be 50Ω.

FIGURE 4.10. The equivalent circuit for a
noise-generating diode.

With the noise generator connected to the input of the amplifier under
test and the direct current I_{dc} set to zero, the noise output from the amplifier
is

$$P_{no} = FGkT_o B \qquad (4.43)$$

With the direct current now adjusted to some value I_{dc}, the available
additional noise power at the input is

$$P_{n\,add} = \frac{I_n^2}{4} R \qquad (4.51)$$

[This follows an application of the maximum power transfer equation as
developed in Section 1.14, Eq. (1.123)].
    The additional noise power observed at the output will be

$$GP_{n\,add} = G \cdot \frac{I_n^2}{4} \cdot R$$

$$= \frac{G(2I_{dc}q_e B)R}{4}$$

$$= \tfrac{1}{2} GI_{dc}q_e BR \qquad (4.52)$$

The total noise output therefore becomes

$$P'_{no} = P_{no} + \tfrac{1}{2} GI_{dc}q_e BR \qquad (4.53)$$

But the new noise power output can also be considered as an increase in
the original noise output by some factor X:

$$P'_{no} = XP_{no} \qquad (4.54)$$

It follows, on equating Eqs. (4.53) and (4.54), that

$$XP_{no} = P_{no} + \tfrac{1}{2} GI_{dc}q_e BR$$

or $$X(FGkT_o B) = FGkT_o B + \tfrac{1}{2} GI_{dc}q_e BR \qquad (4.55)$$

on substituting for P_{no} from Eq. (4.43). Equation (4.55) can be rearranged to give

$$F = \frac{I_{dc} q_e R}{2(X - 1)kT_o} \qquad (4.56)$$

In normal measurements, the direct current is increased from zero until the noise power output is doubled (i.e., $X = 2$); the measurements are also made at room temperature, for which $kT_o = 4 \times 10^{-21}$J; the value for electron charge is $q_e = 1.6 \times 10^{-19}$C. Substituting these values into Eq. (4.56) gives

$$F = 20 I_{dc} R \qquad (4.57)$$

Thus the noise factor F is determined directly in terms of the direct current of the diode I_{dc}. For the particular case when $R = 50\Omega$, Eq. (4.57) becomes

$$F = I_{dc} \qquad \text{where } I_{dc} \text{ is measured in mA} \qquad (4.58)$$

that is, the noise factor is *numerically* equal to the direct current in mA for the conditions stated.

4.11 NOISE TEMPERATURE

Yet another way of representing noise is by means of *equivalent noise temperature*. Care must be taken because the equivalent noise temperature is used in two somewhat different ways.

4.11.1 Equivalent Noise Temperature T_e of Amplifier Input

Here it is postulated that the noise associated with the amplifier input, $(F - 1)kT_o B$, as given by Eq. (4.48), can alternatively be represented by some hypothetical temperature T_e such that

$$kT_e B = (F - 1)kT_o B \qquad (4.59)$$

$$\therefore \qquad T_e = (F - 1)T_o \qquad (4.60)$$

This shows that T_e is just an alternative measure for F.

Friiss' formula can be rewritten in terms of an overall noise temperature. Friiss' formula, Eq. (4.50), is

$$F = F_1 + \frac{F_2 - 1}{G_1} + \frac{F_3 - 1}{G_2 G_1} + \cdots$$

Subtracting 1 from both sides,

$$F - 1 = (F_1 - 1) + \frac{F_2 - 1}{G_1} + \frac{F_3 - 1}{G_2 G_1} + \dots \quad (4.61)$$

Substituting for the various $(F - 1)$ from Eq. (4.60):

$$\frac{T_e}{T_0} = \frac{T_{e1}}{T_0} + \frac{T_{e2}/T_0}{G_1} + \frac{T_{e3}/T_0}{G_2 G_1} + \dots$$

or
$$T_e = T_{e1} + \frac{T_{e2}}{G_1} + \frac{T_{e3}}{G_2 G_1} + \dots \quad (4.62)$$

4.11.2 Equivalent Noise Temperature of Antenna

The available noise power from an antenna, as from any source, is

$$P_n = kTB \quad (4.1)$$

The mean-square noise voltage is as given by Eq. (4.5), which for an antenna becomes

$$E_n^2 = 4R_{rad} kTB \quad (4.63)$$

where R_{rad} is the radiation resistance of the antenna (see Section 15.8). The radiation resistance is not the physical resistance of the antenna wire, which may be assumed negligible; it is a fictitious resistance derived from the radiating properties of the antenna. The fact that it can be used in a receiving situation is a result of what is known as the *reciprocity theorem* for antennas.

The problem then arises: What temperature must be used for an antenna? It is found that the temperature to be used depends on the thermal radiation received by the antenna. In fact, it is possible to take into account man-made noise received by the antenna, as well as naturally occurring noise, in the definition of antenna noise temperature by defining this in terms of the total available noise power delivered by the antenna:

$$P_{n_{ant}} = kT_{ant}B \quad (4.64)$$

That is,
$$T_{ant} = \frac{P_{n_{ant}}}{kB} \quad (4.65)$$

In terms of the noise power spectral density $S_n(f) = P_{n_{ant}}/B$

$$T_{ant} = \frac{S_n(f)}{k} \quad (4.66)$$

The noise power spectral density decreases with increasing frequency so that the noise temperature of the antenna varies with frequency as shown in Fig. 4.11 (man-made noise excluded). Thus, a satellite with its antenna pointed toward earth would "see" an effective noise temperature of about 290K, while the earth station, with its antenna pointed toward the satellite in space, would "see" an effective noise temperature of about 3.5 K except when it points toward the sun, when the noise increases considerably. This is not shown in Fig. 4.11. Losses in the antenna feeder will also contribute noise, as will man-made sources, so that the antenna noise temperature for an earth station in a satellite communications system is in the range 20 to 30 K, while the satellite antenna noise temperature will be of the order of 300 K. For microwave links on the surface of the earth, where the antennas are not pointed directly at the earth, the noise temperature is of the order of 150 K.

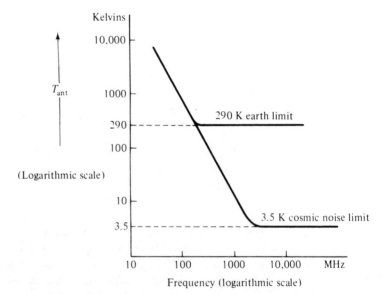

FIGURE 4.11. Variation with frequency of the effective noise temperature of an antenna.

The available noise power $P_{n_{ant}} = kT_{ant}B$ is independent of the gain of the antenna (if man-made noise received as "signals" is excluded), so that increasing the gain of the antenna will increase the signal and therefore improve the signal-to-noise ratio.

Knowing the antenna noise temperature and the equivalent noise temperature of the input, the total noise temperature is simply

$$T = T_{ant} + T_e \qquad (4.67)$$

and the total noise power at the input is

$$P_n = kTB$$
$$= k(T_{ant} + T_e)B \qquad (4.68)$$

Example 4.8   An antenna that has an effective noise temperature of 15 K is fed into a microwave amplifier that has an effective noise temperature of 20 K. Calculate the available noise power per unit bandwidth $S_n(f)$, at the input for this particular antenna temperature.

Solution

$$P_n = k(T_{ant} + T_e)B$$

and
$$S_n(f) = \frac{P_n}{B}$$

$$= 1.38 \times 10^{-23} \times (15 + 20)$$

$$= 48.3 \times 10^{-23} \text{W/Hz}$$

As an additional example, for a noise bandwidth of 4 MHz, the available noise power would be

$$P_n = 48.3 \times 10^{-23} \times 4 \times 10^6$$

$$= 193 \times 10^{-17} \text{ W}$$

This is an exceedingly small amount of power, but it is of the same order of power received at the earth station in a satellite communications system.

4.12   APPLICATIONS

Equivalent noise resistance R_n, noise factor F, and equivalent noise temperature T_e are merely different ways of expressing the same information. Each method has its advantages, generally associated with the type of circuitry involved. Equivalent noise resistance is often quoted for vacuum tubes, while spot noise factor at a frequency of 1 kHz is the preferred method for transistors. Table 4.1 lists values that are typical for vacuum tubes, and Fig. 4.12 shows how transistor noise factor varies with frequency. The increase in noise factor at low frequencies results from the inverse frequency noise discussed in Section 4.5. Transistor noise factor also increases with increase in emitter current. This is because much of the noise in transistors comes from fluctuations in conductivity of the semiconductor material as discussed in Section 4.7, so that the noise voltage, which is the product of direct current times resistance fluctuation, is dependent on the direct current. Figure 4.12 is only intended to show the range of values expected at low frequencies. At high frequencies, F will increase again.

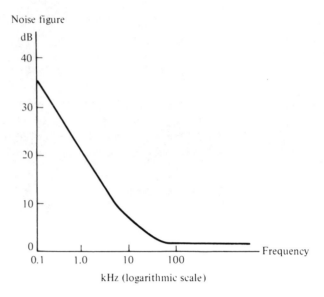

FIGURE 4.12. Variation with frequency of the noise figure of a transistor.

TABLE 4.1. Typical Values (in kΩ) for Vacuum-Tube Noise Resistance

Triode amplifier	0.3
Triode mixer	6.5
Pentode amplifier	1.5
Pentode mixer	10
Multigrid mixer	250

In the VHF and UHF range of frequencies, noise factor is the preferred method of specifying the noise performance of amplifiers and receivers. In the microwave range, noise temperature is preferred, since the noise temperature of the antenna will be known and a direct comparison can easily be made among the various noise contributions.

Example 4.9   Figure 4.13 shows the first few stages of a microwave receiver intended for space-satellite communications. Calculate the signal power needed at the antenna to produce a signal-to-noise ratio of 20 dB at the output of the IF stage.

FIGURE 4.13.   The input stages of a low-noise microwave receiver, used for Example 4.9.

Solution

$$F_3 = 12 \text{ dB} = 15.85{:}1 \text{ power ratio}$$

$$T_{03} = (15.85 - 1) \times 290$$

$$= 4306 \text{ K}$$

$$F_2 = 6 \text{ dB} = 3.98{:}1 \text{ power ratio}$$

$$T_{e2} = (3.98 - 1) \times 290$$

$$= 864 \text{ K}$$

and

$$G_2 = 20 \text{ dB} = 100{:}1 \text{ power ratio}$$

$$G_1 = 25 \text{ dB} = 316{:}1 \text{ power ratio}$$

Applying Friiss' formula, Eq. (4.62),

$$T_e = 20 + \frac{864}{316} + \frac{4307}{316 \times 100}$$

$$= 20 + 2.73 + 0.136$$

$$= 22.87 \text{ K}$$

Applying Eq. (4.68), the total noise at the input is

$$P_n = 1.38 \times 10^{-23} \times (28 + 22.87) \times 5 \times 10^6$$

$$= 351 \times 10^{-17} \text{ W}$$

It is assumed here that the effective noise bandwidth is limited by the bandwidth of the output stage. Given that

$$\frac{P_s}{P_n} = 20 \text{ dB} = 100{:}1 \text{ power ratio}$$

$$P_n = 100 \times 351 \times 10^{-17} \text{ W}$$

$$= 0.351 \text{ pW}$$

4.13 PROBLEMS

1. Explain how thermal noise power varies: (a) with temperature; (b) with frequency bandwidth. Thermal noise from a resistor is measured as 4×10^{-17} W for a given bandwidth and at a temperature of 20°C. What will the noise power be when the temperature is changed to 50°C? to 77 K?

2. Calculate the rms noise voltage appearing across a 10-kΩ resistor at room temperature and for an effective noise bandwidth of 10 kHz.

3. Three 5-kΩ resistors are connected in series. For room temperature ($kT = 4 \times 10^{-21}$ J) and an effective noise bandwidth of 1 MHz determine: (a) the noise voltage appearing across each resistor; (b) the noise voltage appearing across the series combination. (c) What is the rms noise voltage which appears across the same three resistors connected in parallel under the same conditions?

4. The noise generated by a 1000-Ω resistor can be represented by a rms current source of 4.0 nA in parallel with the 1000-Ω resistor. Show that this is equivalent to having the noise represented by a root-mean-square noise voltage source of $4\,\mu$V in series with the resistor.

5. Explain what is meant by effective noise bandwidth. A signal-measuring circuit is equivalent to a parallel combination of 1000-Ω resistance and $0.5\text{-}\mu$F capacitance. Calculate the effective noise bandwidth.

6. Explain why inductance and capacitance do not generate noise. Explain also how they control the noise in a circuit. A parallel tuned circuit is resonant at a frequency of 1 MHz and has a Q factor of 50. The tuning capacitor is 200 pF. Calculate the effective noise bandwidth of the circuit. Also calculate, at room temperature, the rms noise voltage appearing across the circuit.

7. The tuned circuit of Problem 6 is placed at the input of a double-sideband AM receiver and as a result the Q factor is reduced effectively to 25. The receiver has an audio bandwidth (i.e., the audio signal bandwidth of the audio stages) of 3 kHz. Calculate, at room temperature, the rms noise voltage at the tuned circuit that will be effective in producing an audio output.

8. Write brief notes on the sources of noise other than thermal, which arise in electronic equipment. In particular, describe how the power spectrum density varies with frequency for the various sources.

9. An amplifier has an actual input resistance of 5000-Ω and an equivalent noise resistance of 1000Ω referred to the input. What is the total effective input resistance of the amplifier? What is the rms noise voltage, at room temperature, at the input of the amplifier for a noise bandwidth of 1 kHz?

10. In Problem 9 a signal source of 50 Ω internal resistance is connected to the input of the amplifier via a 10:1 step-up matching transformer (which

may be assumed lossless). What is the rms noise voltage at the input under these conditions, assuming room temperature?

11. A signal generator of internal resistance 50 Ω, and internal EMF 10μ V is connected to the input of an amplifier that has an effective noise resistance of 1200 Ω and an input resistance of 75 Ω. Calculate the S/N ratio at the input, for a noise bandwidth of 1 kHz, and at room temperature.

12. In Problem 10, what will be the S/N ratio at the input when the signal source has an internal EMF of 1.0μ V?

13. In a rather cheap short-wave receiver, the antenna circuit is fed directly into the mixer circuit. The input coupling is such that the antenna is matched to the 10-kΩ input resistance of the mixer. The mixer has an equivalent noise resistance of 100 kΩ. Calculate the antenna EMF necessary to produce a S/N power ratio of 20 dB, if the input transformer has a step-up ratio of 10:1 and the effective noise bandwidth is 10 kHz. Room temperature may be assumed.

14. The short-wave receiver in Problem 13 is improved by inclusion of a voltage amplifier between antenna circuit and mixer. The amplifier has a voltage gain of 15:1, an equivalent noise resistance of 1000 Ω and an input resistance of 10 kΩ, to which the antenna is matched as before. Calculate the new antenna EMF required for the 20-dB S/N ratio.

15. Three telephone circuits, each having a S/N ratio of 44 dB, are connected in tandem. What is the overall S/N ratio? A fourth circuit is now added, which has a S/N ratio of 34 dB. What is the overall S/N in this case?

16. The noise factor of a radio receiver is 15:1. What is its noise figure? If the input S/N ratio is 35 dB, what will be the output S/N ratio?

17. Given that the noise figure of an amplifier is 11 dB, what is the fraction of the total available noise, at the input, contributed by the amplifier?

18. A mixer circuit having a noise figure of 16 dB is preceded by an amplifier having a noise figure of 9 dB and an available power gain of 25 dB. What is the overall noise figure of the combination?

19. Explain what is meant by: (a) the equivalent noise temperature of an amplifier input; (b) the equivalent noise temperature of an antenna. Given that the equivalent noise temperature of an amplifier is 25 K, what is its noise factor?

20. An antenna has an equivalent noise temperature of 50 K and is connected to a microwave receiver that has an equivalent noise temperature, referred to the input, of 60 K. Calculate the available noise power referred to the input for a bandwidth of 10 MHz.

21. The mixer stage of a microwave receiver has a noise figure of 11 dB and is preceded by a low-noise amplifier having an available power gain of 20 dB and an equivalent noise temperature of 33 K. Calculate the effective

noise temperature of the combination referred to the input of the amplifier. Calculate the signal power required at the input in order that the S/N ratio be 40 dB, for a bandwidth of 5 MHz, and an antenna noise temperature of 50 K.

Part Two
Electronic
Communications
Circuits

Chapter 5
RF and Broadband Amplifiers

5.1 TUNED RF AMPLIFIERS

Tuned RF amplifiers are commonly used to provide the front end selectivity and amplification in radio receivers to separate incoming signals from the antenna, to provide the precise bandpass filtering required in the intermediate frequency (IF) amplifiers of receivers, and to provide the harmonic removal filtering needed in transmitting circuits. At the higher frequencies, stability becomes a severe problem, and those types of amplifiers that have very low internal feedback, such as the common-base amplifier and the cascode amplifier, are favored. Even with this, it is often still necessary to provide special compensation or neutralization to maintain stability under operating conditions.

The bandpass filter characteristics are generated by one or more tuned circuits within the amplifier circuit. Usually voltage amplification is desired, and as a result the parallel tuned circuit is the favored one. Since the bandwidth of a tuned circuit's response is depedent on its Q, which is, in turn, dependent on the amount of resistance within or attached to the tuned circuit, special care in providing proper impedance matching to the tuned circuit is necessary to maintain the desired characteristics. This is especially true of transmitter power circuits where very low impedance circuits must be connected to the tuned circuits without lowering the Q too much.

5.1.1 Single-Tuned Class A Amplifier (Transformer Coupled with Tuner Primary)

Figure 5.1(a) shows a transformer-coupled circuit. The tuned circuit is the primary of the transformer, and the transformer acts as a load isolator. Radio-frequency transformers usually have coefficients of coupling which are much less than unity, and, as a result, the load impedance of the secondary has little effect on the primary. If the transformer were tightly coupled, the load impedance would be coupled into the primary. The real part would load the Q down and cause a widening of the bandwidth, while any reactance would detune the circuit. Similarly, the complex output admittance of the amplifier can cause detuning and loading of the primary. The detuning

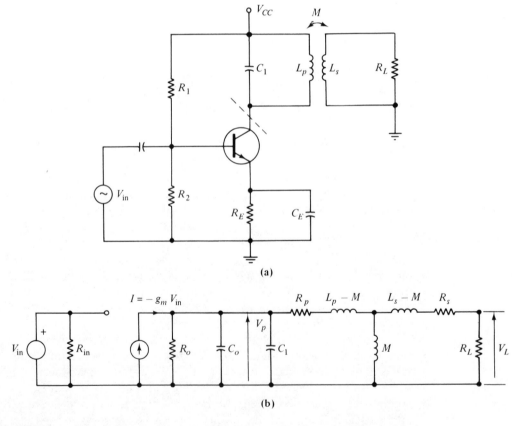

FIGURE 5.1. Single-tuned class A amplifier: (a) Transformer-coupled circuit; (b) Equivalent circuit.

effects can be accounted for by making either the capacitor or the inductor adjustable over a small range. However, any loading effects must either be made negligible by efficient coupling methods or be accounted for in the desired bandwidth calculations. In some critical cases, it may be possible to adjust the shunt resistance to provide the desired bandwidth.

Impedance transformation using either tapped transformer coils or tapped capacitors, both on the primary and on the secondary of the transformer, is necessary with bipolar transistors because of their generally low impedance levels. To obtain sufficiently high Q's, especially at higher frequencies, dynamic impedance, R_D, values ranging from 10 kΩ to 1 MΩ are needed, while the bipolar transistor only gives resistances of 1 to 10 kΩ. The impedance transformation also serves to reduce the effect of parasitic reactances on the resonant frequency. The process of impedance transformation is discussed in Chapter 1.

The equivalent circuit is shown in Fig. 5.1(b) where use is made of the equivalent mutual inductance circuit of Fig. 1.18(b). Analysis follows the methods given in Section 1.12.2, as illustrated in the following example.

Example 5.1   The amplifier shown in Fig. 5.1(a) uses a transistor CE amplifier which has a transconductance of 30 mS at the resonant frequency, and an output conductance comprised of 100 kΩ in parallel with 5 pF of capacity. The transformer has a primary inductance of 75 μH, secondary inductance of 100 μH, coefficient of coupling of 0.01, primary resistance of 10 Ω, secondary resistance of 10 Ω. The primary is tuned with a 50-pF capacitor and the secondary is loaded by a 4 kΩ resistance. Find: (a) the resonant frequency; (b) the effective Q of the tuned circuit; (c) the 3-dB bandwidth; (d) the small signal voltage gain at resonance, (e) the dB rejection of a signal 150 kHz above the resonant frequency.

Solution   (a)   The effective tuning capacity is C_o in parallel with C_1:

$$C_p = 50 + 5 = 55 \text{ pF}$$

A calculation check will show that $1/(L_p C_p) \gg (R_p/L_p)^2$ so that the approximate form of resonant frequency, Eq. (1.48), may be used. A calculation check will also show that $R_s \gg |X_s|$; hence, from Eq. (1.103), the secondary does not detune the primary. Therefore:

$$f_o = \frac{1}{2\pi \sqrt{L_p C_p}}$$

$$= \frac{1}{2\pi \times \sqrt{75 \times 10^{-6} \times 55 \times 10^{-12}}}$$

$$= 2.48 \text{ MHz}$$

(b) The undamped Q of the primary, Eq. (1.105), is:

$$Q_p = \frac{w_o L_p}{R_p}$$

$$= \frac{2\pi \times 2.48 \times 10^6 \times 75 \times 10^{-6}}{10}$$

$$= 117$$

And for the secondary, Eq. (1.106):

$$Q_s = \frac{w_o L_s}{R_L}$$

$$= 117 \times \frac{10}{75} \times \frac{100}{4000}$$

$$= 0.39 \qquad \text{(Note the use of proportionality to ease calculations.)}$$

The factor $(1 + k^2 Q_p Q_s)$ for $x = 1$ (see Section 1.12.2) is equal to

$$(1 + k^2 Q_p Q_s) = (1 + 0.01^2 \times 117 \times 0.39)$$

$$= 1.005$$

Hence Q_p', from Eq. (1.108), is

$$Q_p' = \frac{117}{1.005} = 116$$

This shows that the secondary loading is negligible; however, the loading of the transistor output resistance will be considerable and is accounted for as follows. The dynamic impedance, Eq. (1.72), including the secondary load, but not the transistor loading, is

$$R_D' = \frac{Q_p'}{w_o C_p}$$

$$= \frac{116}{2\pi \times 2.48 \times 10^6 \times 55 \times 10^{-12}}$$

$$= 135 \text{ k}\Omega$$

And taking R_o, Fig. 5.1(b), into account:

$$R_D'' = \frac{135 \times 100}{135 + 100}$$

$$= 57.4 \text{ k}\Omega$$

The effective Q-factor, therefore, is:

$$Q_p'' = Q_p' \times \frac{R_D''}{R_D'}$$

$$= 116 \times \frac{57.4}{135}$$

$$= 49$$

(c) The 3-dB bandwidth [see Eq. (1.70)] is

$$B_{3\text{dB}} = \frac{f_o}{Q_p''}$$

$$= \frac{2.48}{49} \text{ MHz}$$

$$= 50.6 \text{ kHz}$$

(d) The small signal voltage gain is $A_v = (V_L / V_{in})$. Using Eqs. (1.111) and (1.112), and substituting $-g_m V_{in}$ for I

$$\therefore \quad A_v = -\frac{g_m R_D'' k}{(1 + jy Q_p)} \sqrt{\frac{L_s}{L_p}}$$

Note that R_D'' and Q_p'' and not R_D' and Q_p' are used.
At resonance, $y = 0$

$$\therefore \quad A_{vo} = -g_m R_D'' k \sqrt{\frac{L_s}{L_p}}$$

$$= 30 \times 10^{-3} \times 57.4 \times 10^3 \times 0.01 \times \sqrt{\frac{100}{75}}$$

$$= -19.9 \text{ V/V}$$

(e) The gain modulus, relative to the resonant value, is

$$A_r = \frac{|A_v|}{|A_{vo}|}$$

$$= \frac{1}{\sqrt{1 + (y Q_p'')^2}} \quad \text{[Using Eq. (1.69) with } \omega \approx \omega_o.\text{]}$$

At 150 kHz off-tune,

$$y \cong \frac{2 \times 0.150}{2.48} \text{ (See Problem 14 in Section 1.16)}$$

$$= 0.121$$

$$\therefore \quad A_r = \frac{1}{\sqrt{1 + (0.121 \times 49)^2}}$$

$$= \frac{1}{6}$$

$$= -15.6 \text{ dB}$$

5.1.2 Single-Tuned Class A Amplifier (Transformer Coupled with Tuned Secondary)

Figure 5.2 shows the circuit of a single-tuned class A amplifier. The chief difference between this circuit and the one presented in the previous section is that the resonant circuit is series-tuned instead of parallel-tuned. Also, since the primary of the transformer is not tuned, the amplifier is feeding an untuned reactive load formed by the parallel combination of the amplifier output capacitance and the primary inductance, resulting in a net phase shift in the output voltage other than 180°.

Again, analysis follows the general methods described in Chapter 1, as illustrated by the following example.

Example 5.2

The amplifier of Fig. 5.2(a) uses a transistor with a transconductance of 10 mS, an output resistance of 2 kΩ, and an output capacity of 5 pF. The other parasitic capacities are small enough to be ignored. The other circuit components have the values given below.

$$L_p = 10\,\mu\text{H} \qquad L_s = 20\,\mu\text{H} \qquad \text{Coupling } k = 0.01$$
$$R_p = 1\,\Omega \qquad R_s = 0.5\,\Omega \qquad R_L = 100\,\text{k}\Omega \qquad C_s = 20\,\text{pF}$$

Find the gain and bandwidth of the amplifier.

Solution

The equivalent circuit for the amplifier, using the mutual inductance equivalent circuit of Fig. 1.18(b), is shown in Fig. 5.2(b). The resonant frequency of the secondary will be used, but the effect of primary loading on the phase and gain-bandwidth will be shown. Using the methods described in Chapter

(a)

$Y_o = G_o + j\omega_o C_o$ (b)

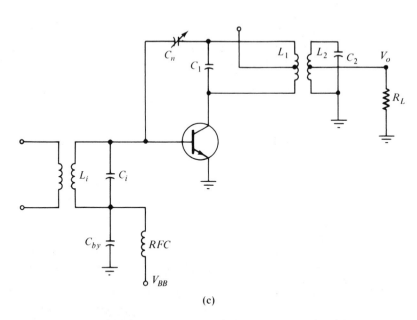

(c)

FIGURE 5.2. (a) Circuit for a transformer-coupled class A amplifier with tuned secondary; (b) Equivalent circuit for (a); (c) Double-tuned transformer-coupled amplifier circuit.

1, the resonant frequency and the impedances and admittances of Fig. 5.2(b) may be evaluated as

$$w_o = 5 \times 10^7 \text{ rad/s}$$

$$Z_m = j\sqrt{50}\,\Omega \qquad [\text{Eq. (1.98)}]$$

$$Z_p = 1 + j500 \ \Omega \qquad [\text{Eq. (1.96)}]$$

$$Z_s = 0.5 + j1000 \ \Omega \qquad [\text{Eq. (1.97)}]$$

$$Z_L = 10 - j1000 \ \Omega$$

(The equivalent series impedance of $R_L \parallel C_s$, [see Eqns. (1.41 and 1.42)])
$$Y_o = (0.5 + j0.25) \times 10^{-3}\text{S}$$

The total impedance of the secondary at resonance is $Z_s + Z_L = 10.5 \ \Omega$ (resistive). The effective primary impedance can be evaluated, using Eq. (1.102), as

$$Z_p' = 1 + j500 + \frac{50}{10.5}$$

$$\cong j500 \ \Omega$$

This shows that only the reactance of L_p is significant, the primary resistance and the resistance reflected from the secondary being negligible by comparison. The primary voltage [see Fig. 5.2(b)] is

$$V_p = \frac{I}{Y_o + (1/Z_p')} = \frac{-g_m V_{in}}{Y_o + (1/Z_p')} = \frac{-g_m V_{in} Z_p'}{1 + Y_o Z_p'} \qquad (5.1)$$

This would have been $-g_m V_{in} Z_p'$ had Y_o been zero. From Eqs. (1.99) and (1.100), the secondary current may be evaluated as

$$I_s = \frac{V_p Z_m}{Z_p(Z_s + Z_L) - Z_m^2} \qquad (5.2)$$

and clearly
$$V_L = I_s Z_L \qquad (5.3)$$

Collecting Eqs. (5.1), (5.2), and (5.3) and substituting numerical values gives

$$A_v = \frac{V_L}{V_{in}} = -6.73(1.06 - j0.302)$$

Had Y_o been zero, the gain would have been -6.73. The actual gain modulus is 7.39, or 17.4 dB. This slight increase over the 6.73 value results from the partial tuning effect of C_o in parallel with L_p.

The bandwidth is controlled by the secondary Q factor:

$$Q_s = \frac{w_o L_s}{R_s'}$$

$$\text{BW} = \frac{f_o}{Q_s} = \frac{w_o}{2\pi Q_s} = \frac{R_s'}{2\pi L_s}$$

$$= \frac{10.5}{2\pi \times 20 \times 10^{-6}}$$

$$= 83.6 \text{ kHz}$$

5.1.3 Double-Tuned Transformer-Coupled Amplifier

The *double-tuned transformer-coupled amplifier* circuit is formed by resonating both the primary and the secondary circuits of the output coupling transformer, as shown in Fig. 5.2(c). The transfer function of the double-tuned transformer was given in Section 1.12.2, where it is seen that if the transformer coupling is greater than a critical value, the amplitude-versus-frequency plot will exhibit a double-humped shape with steep outside skirts (Fig. 1.19). The bandwidth of the result is primarily determined by the effective Q of the primary and secondary tuned circuits, which must be the same to maintain symmetry in the response. Impedance transformation is accomplished on both sides usually by tapping the feed points down on the inductors (capacitive transformation is used in some cases).

5.2 NEUTRALIZATION

When an amplifying device is operated at frequencies near its upper cutoff frequency, a parasitic capacity between the output and input provides a path for feedback. If both the input and output circuits are tuned, then a circuit identical to the tuned input/tuned output oscillator is formed, and unless some measures are taken to stabilize the circuit, it will oscillate. Even if the input and output circuits are tuned, the feedback path may introduce sufficient phase shift to allow oscillation to occur.

Several schemes for neutralizing this feedback path are available, and three of them will be discussed here: the Hazeltine circuit, the Rice circuit, and a method for neutralizing an amplifier with common circuit feedback.

Figure 5.3(a) shows the Hazeltine neutralization scheme for tuned input/tuned output amplifiers. The output coil is center-tapped and the tap used as the power supply feedpoint of the amplifier. The other end of the coil, point N, is connected through a small capacitor back to the input. The portion of the circuit formed by the amplifier output voltage, the two halves of the coil, the feedback capacitance, and the neutralizing capacitance form

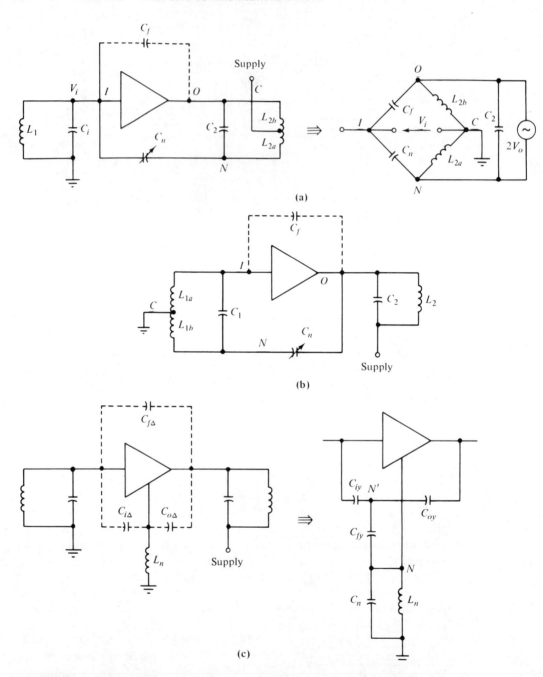

FIGURE 5.3. (a) Hazeltine neutralization system and equivalent bridge circuit; (b) Rice neutralization system; (c) Neutralization of common circuit feedback—circuit showing parasitic elements and the equivalent circuit.

a bridge to the input, as shown in Fig. 5.3(a). For the bridge to null, producing zero voltage across the amplifier input, it is only necessary for the impedance cross products to be equal, so that at the frequency of operation,

$$X_{Cf} X_{L2a} = X_{c_n} X_{L2b} \qquad (5.4)$$

and

$$C_n = C_f \cdot \frac{L_{2b}}{L_{2a}} \qquad (5.5)$$

Figure 5.3(b) shows the circuit for the Rice scheme of neutralization. In this case, the input coil is center-tapped so that $L_{1a} = L_{1b}$, and the neutralization capacitance equal to the feedback capacitance is connected between the other end of L_1 (point N) to the output of the amplifier.

A voltage appearing at the output drives a phase-shifted current through C_f and L_{1a}, producing a voltage at the amplifier input. However, the same output drives an identical-valued current in the opposite direction through C_n and L_{1b}. The currents in L_{1a} will be equal and opposing, so that the feedback voltage appearing at the amplifier input will be zero. Null will occur when

$$X_{cf} = X_{c_n} \qquad (5.6)$$

so that

$$C_f = C_n \qquad (5.7)$$

Both of these circuits are used for amplifiers into the VHF and UHF range, as long as no appreciable reactance appears in the amplifier common circuit. The method of adjusting both amplifiers is basically the same.

1. Turn off the amplifier power supply, but maintain input drive signal.
2. Adjust C_n.
3. Vary the output tank tuning capacitor C_2 and observe any change in input bias current.
4. Repeat steps 2 and 3 until no change occurs in the bias current when the output tank tuning is varied, indicating correct neutralization.

Figure 5.3(c) shows an amplifier that has common circuit reactance L_n, causing feedback which may be positive. This will occur at extremely high frequencies (UHF and microwave), when the inductance of the wiring must be accounted for. The parasitic capacitances of the amplifier form a delta configuration around the three terminals. Figure 5.3(c) shows the equivalent circuit resulting when the delta capacitances are replaced by their equivalent Y capacitances. The transformation is accomplished by

$$C_{xy} = \frac{Ci\,\Delta Co\,\Delta + Co\,\Delta Cf\,\Delta + Cf\,\Delta Ci\,\Delta}{Cx\,\Delta} \qquad (5.8)$$

where $x = i, o,$ or f.

Now if the network formed by C_{fy}, C_n, and L_n is made series resonant, then a virtual short to ground will exist at the series resonant frequency from the point N', preventing any of the output signal from reaching the input circuit. Resonance is established when

$$X_{C_{fy}} = X_{C_n} \| X_{L_n} \qquad (5.9)$$

If the input and output circuits are tuned, the adjustment procedure is the same as that stated above.

5.3 SPECIAL RF AMPLIFIERS

5.3.1 Common-Base Amplifier

The common-base amplifier is used frequently in RF amplifiers for two reasons. First, it provides usable voltage gain to a much higher upper cut-off frequency than the common-emitter stage, and second, the feedback capacity between the output and input is very much lower than that for the common-emitter stage. The same arguments are true for the triode vacuum tube operated in the common grid mode and the field-effect transistor operating in the common gate mode.

Two things limit the frequency response of an amplifier gain. The first of these is the shunting effect which occurs because of the parasitic capacitances between the input terminals of the amplifier, and the second is the cutoff frequency at which the amplifying device gain begins to fall. The first of these can be designed around by making the ratio of source resistance to input resistance of the amplifier sufficiently low that the break frequency formed by the net source resistance and the input capacity is considerably higher than the gain cutoff frequency. If this is done, the overall response is limited by the gain cutoff frequency of the amplifying device, and this is a function entirely of the geometry and the material used in making the device, and can only be modified by choosing a transistor with a higher cut-off frequency.

The bipolar transistor suffers from two major parasitic capacitances, the junction capacitance between base and emitter, and the junction capacitance between base and collector. The first is a function of the bias current, and the second is the reverse-biased junction capacity of the collector-base junction, which is independent of current but dependent on collector potential. Although these two capacitances predominate, three other very small ones exist, which are simply the interelectrode capacities between the leads of the device. At the extreme frequencies the lead inductances also have some effect, but generally these lead capacitances and inductances will not have an effect until a frequency well above that dictated by the two main capacitances is reached, and they can be ignored. In any event, their effects can be canceled by neutralization if necessary. Figure 5.4(a) shows the parasitic capacitances in the common-base model of the bipolar transistor.

When the transistor is used in the common-emitter mode, the common-base output capacitance C_{ob} is connected between the input and output. This capacitance is reflected into the input circuit multiplied by the voltage gain (the Miller effect), and reacts with the source resistance to produce a very low cutoff frequency, well below the gain cutoff frequency unless the source resistance is very low. This puts a limitation on the usefulness of the amplifier. C_{ob} also provides a feedback path between the collector and

FIGURE 5.4. Common-base amplifier: (a) Circuit model showing parasitic reactances; (b) Plot of current gain versus log frequency for CE and CB amplifiers.

emitter, which at higher frequencies can make the transistor unstable (it will oscillate) and will have to be neutralized if it is to be used.

When the same transistor is used in the common-base mode, the feedback capacitance is the collector-to-emitter capacitance. But this is made up of the two capacitances C_{ob} and C_e in series, and since the intermediate base point is grounded, any feedback signal through this path is prevented from reaching the input. The two capacitances are merely connected between the input terminals and between the output terminals and can be canceled if the amplifier is tuned. The only remaining feedback capacity is that between the leads, and this usually can be kept sufficiently small as to be ignored, or can be neutralized, as mentioned in Section 5.2.1.

The current gain of the common-base amplifier is simply the h_{fb} value of the transistor up to the alpha cutoff frequency. Above this value it falls off at -20 dB per decade. The frequency-dependent value of current gain is given as

$$A_{i(f)CB} = \frac{-h_{fb}}{1 + j(f/f_\alpha)} \qquad \text{(for CB amp)} \qquad (5.10)$$

This compared to the value for the common-emitter amplifier, which is

$$A_{i(f)CE} = \frac{-h_{fe}}{1 + j(f/f_\beta)} \qquad \text{(for CE amp)} \qquad (5.11)$$

The two cutoff frequencies are related approximately by the following:

$$f_\beta = \frac{f_T}{h_{fe}} \qquad (5.12)$$

where f_T is the frequency at which the CE current gain h_{fe} goes to unity.

$$f_\alpha \cong \frac{f_T}{n} \qquad \text{where } n = 1 \text{ to } 2 \qquad (5.13)$$

These facts are illustrated in Fig. 5.4(b) and point out that the cutoff frequency of the CB amp is about h_{fe} times the cutoff frequency of the CE amp, unless it is limited by the input-circuit time constant to less than these values.

The voltage gain of the CE amp and that of the CB amp at low frequency is virtually the same and is given by

$$A_{v_{CB}} = A_i \frac{R_L}{R_i} \cong \frac{R_L}{h_{ib}} \qquad (5.14)$$

Since A_i is a function of frequency in each case and the cutoff frequency is different in each case,

$$A_{v(f)} \cong -h_{fe}\frac{R_L}{h_{ie}}\frac{1}{1 + j(f/f_\beta)} \qquad \text{(for CE amp)} \qquad (5.15)$$

and
$$A_{v(f)} = \frac{R_L}{h_{ib}}\frac{1}{1 + j(f/f_\alpha)} \qquad \text{(for CB amp)} \qquad (5.16)$$

It should also be noted that the input impedance is a function of frequency as well, and will begin to change radically at the frequency determined by the input circuit time constant. Since this frequency can be controlled to some extent it is usually possible to maintain constant input impedance to frequencies beyond the gain cutoff point.

The following example will illustrate the summary presented here.

Example 5.3
A transistor has the following characteristics:

$C_{ob} = 10\,\text{pF}$ $I_E = 0.26\,\text{mA}$ $V_T = 26\,\text{mV}$ $h_{oe} = h_{re} = 0$

$h_{fe} = 89$

$f_T = 300\,\text{MHz}\ f_T = 2f_\alpha$ $R_L = 2\,\text{k}\Omega$ $R_s = 100\Omega$

Calculate and compare the input circuit cutoff frequency and the gain cutoff frequency for the CB and CE modes of operation of the transistor. Also calculate and compare the current gains, voltage gains, and input resistances for the two modes.

Solution
$$h_{ib} = \frac{V_T}{I_E} = \frac{0.026}{0.26} = 0.10\,\text{k}\Omega = \frac{1}{g_m}$$

$$h_{ie} = (h_{fe} + 1)h_{ib} = 90 \times 0.1 = 9\,\text{k}\Omega$$

$$C_e = \frac{g_m}{2\pi f_T} = \frac{1}{2\pi h_{ib}f_T} = \frac{1}{2\pi \times 100 \times 300\,\text{MHz}} = 5.3\,\text{pF}$$

(a) For the CE mode,

$$C_{in} = C_e + C_{ob}(1 + g_m R_L) = 5.3 + 10 \times [1 + (10 \times 2)] = 215\,\text{pF}$$

$$R_s' = R_s \parallel h_{ie} = 100 \parallel 9000 \cong 100\Omega$$

The input-circuit cutoff frequency is

$$f_{\text{in}} = \frac{1}{2\pi C_{\text{in}} R_s'} = \frac{1}{2\pi \times 215 \text{ pF} \times 100} = 7.40 \text{ MHz}$$

$$A_{v(lf)} = \frac{-R_L}{h_{ib}} = \frac{-2}{0.1} = -20$$

$$A_{i(lf)} \cong -h_{fe} = -89$$

The gain cutoff is

$$f_\beta = \frac{f_T}{h_{fe}} = \frac{300}{89} = 3.37 \text{ MHz}$$

(b) For the CB mode,

$$C_{\text{in}} = C_e = 5.3 \text{ pF}$$

$$R_s' = R_s \| h_{ib} = 100 \| 100 = 50 \ \Omega$$

The cutoff frequency of the input circuit is

$$f_{\text{in}} = \frac{1}{2\pi C_{\text{in}} R_s'} = \frac{1}{2\pi \times 5.3 \text{ pF} \times 50} = 600 \text{ MHz}$$

$$A_{v(lf)} = 20 \qquad A_{i(lf)} = -h_{fb} \cong 1$$

The gain cutoff is

$$f_\alpha = f_T \div 2 = 300 \div 2 = 150 \text{ MHz}$$

In comparison, the CE amp is limited to an upper cutoff frequency corresponding to its β cutoff frequency. The input cutoff frequency is above that and has no immediate effect. The CB amp, similarly, is limited by its gain cutoff and not by the input circuit. The CB amp has a limit of 150 MHz as compared to the limit of 3.37 MHz for the CE amp. The voltage and current gains in the two cases are identical, except for the different cutoff frequencies. The input impedance of the CB amp is much lower than that of the CE amp and is more resistive than capacitive. If stray capacitances in leads are ignored, the feedback capacitance in the CB amp is negligible as compared to a value of 10 pF for the CE amp. Therefore, the CB amplifier is preferred for high-frequency operation.

5.3.2 Cascode Amplifier

The *cascode amplifier* is a composite amplifier pair which is frequently used for RF applications. It consists of a common-emitter stage followed by a common-based stage, directly coupled to each other, and combines some features of both types of amplifiers. The input resistance is essentially that of the common-emitter amplifier, the current gain essentially that of the CE amplifier, the voltage gain essentially that of the CB amplifier, but the reverse feedback coefficient is the product of h_{re} and h_{rb} which is extremely small. The result is extremely good isolation between input and output. The feedback between input and output is about the same as for the CB amplifier, so that neutralization is rarely needed.

Figure 5.5(a) shows the schematic of a tuned cascode amplifier. The input is connected between base and emitter of the first transistor operating with the correct current level. The collector of the first transistor is connected directly to the emitter of the second transistor, whose base is ac-grounded through a bypass capacitor. Another external bias supply keeps the second transistor operating at the same current level. The second collector feeds the load.

(a) (b)

FIGURE 5.5. Cascode amplifier: (a) Circuit; (b) Equivalent circuit at low frequencies.

Figure 5.5(b) shows the equivalent circuit at low frequencies for the amplifier. From this circuit it can be shown that

$$R_i = h_{ie_1} \qquad (5.17)$$

$$R_o = \frac{1}{h_{ob_2}} \qquad (5.18)$$

$$A_i = h_{fe_1} h_{fb_2} \cong h_{fe_1} \qquad (5.19)$$

$$A_v = A_{v_1} A_{v_2} = \left(\frac{h_{fe_1} h_{ib_2}}{h_{ie_1}} \right) \left(\frac{h_{fb_2} R_L}{h_{ib_2}} \right) \cong \frac{R_L}{h_{ib_2}} \qquad (5.20)$$

where $h_{ib_1} = h_{ib_2}$ and $h_{fb_2} = 1$ and $h_{ie_1} = h_{ib_1} (1 + h_{fe_1})$

The effective voltage gain of the first stage is seen to be approximately unity. Thus near the cutoff frequency the collector-base capacity of the first stage C_{cb1} is multiplied only by a Miller factor of two times, to give a net input capacity of $C_i \cong C_{be1} + 2 C_{cb1}$, which is much smaller than that usually associated with a CE amplifier, and its cutoff frequency is therefore much higher. The output capacity is simply the collector-base capacity of the second stage C_{cb2}.

The main advantage of this circuit is its good isolation between input and output. When it is used as a tuned amplifier little or no neutralization is needed to maintain stability.

5.3.3 Dual Gate MOSFETs.

Compared to bipolar transistors the insulated gate field effect transistor offers a number of advantages when used for RF amplification. The main advantages are: higher input impedance and therefore less circuit damping, ability to handle a greater dynamic range of input signal, less distortion resulting in lower cross modulation (cross modulation is when modulation from one carrier is transferred to another as a result of nonlinearity of the amplifying device).

Insulated gate field effect transistors are usually referred to as MOS-FETs, this standing for Metal-Oxide-Semiconductor-Field-Effect-Transistors. One disadvantage of the MOSFET is the ease with which gate insulator breakdown can occur as a result of electrostatic potentials (e.g. such as can be generated by synthetic clothing). To circumvent this most units are now fabricated with protective diodes built in as part of the gate structure, see Fig. 5.6.

Dual gate MOSFETs are used in RF amplifiers as they offer certain advantages over the single gate type. The additional gate allows automatic gain control (AGC, see section 8.8) bias to be easily applied to the amplifier independent of the signal input, and the device is readily connected in the cascode configuration by grounding the AGC gate to signal frequencies.

(a)

(b)   92CM-25751

FIGURE 5.6. Dual-gate-pro-
tected n-channel depletion-type
MOS field-effect-transistor: (a)
sideview cross section; (b) schematic symbol; (c) used as an RF
amplifier. (Courtesy RCA Solid
State Division)

(c)   92CS-26114

Fig. 5.6(a) shows in cross-section the constructional features of a dual
gate MOSFET, and Fig. 5.6(b) shows the circuit symbol. The protective
diodes are readily identified in these diagrams. Fig. 5.6(c) shows how the
unit may be connected as a cascode RF amplifier with AGC bias. The signal
is applied at the 75Ω input, the block labelled Traps consisting of tuned
circuit filters. Fixed bias is applied to the signal gate through the 820 kΩ and

120 kΩ potentiometer network with the input capacitor providing a dc block. The input resistance of the device and biasing network is essentially the 820 kΩ in parallel with the 120 kΩ, as the transistor itself will have an input resistance of many Megohms.

The second gate is grounded to signal frequencies through the 1000 pF AGC line filter capacitor. The RF output is obtained by mutual inductive coupling into the drain circuit. The 270 Ω source resistance bypassed with the 1000 pF capacitor provides additional dc bias between source and gate.

The dual gate MOSFET can also be used as a mixer and this application is described in section 5.4.3.

5.4 FREQUENCY CONVERSION AND MIXERS

Frequency conversion is the changing of the frequency of a carrier with its modulation from one frequency to another. This occurs when the signal is mixed with a second signal such as the output of an oscillator in such a manner that the output contains products of the two signals. One of these products will contain the sum and the difference frequencies of the two input signals. Other components are present as well, but all components except the desired one may be removed by bandpass filtering. Two general methods can be used to accomplish the mixing function, additive mixing, and muliplicative mixing. The output frequency is termed the intermediate frequency (IF).

The input to a mixer is the input signal voltage, which has a magnitude of V_s at a frequency of f_s. The output is usually a current component at the IF frequency $(f_o - f_s)$ which will have a magnitude that will be proportional to V_s. A constant of proportionality can be defined which is called *conversion transconductance*. The conversion transconductance is thus given by

$$g_c = \frac{I_{IF}}{V_s} \tag{5.22}$$

where I_{IF} is the magnitude of that component of the output current at the IF, and V_s is the magnitude of the input signal voltage at f_s.

5.4.1 Additive Mixing

Additive mixing occurs when the input signal is simply added to the output of a local oscillator and then passed through a device with a non-linear transfer function such as a diode. Diodes with essentially square-law response are usually used because this yields under certain conditions an almost proportional relationship between the input signal and the output signal. The output from the mixer contains many signal components, including the difference frequency and the sum frequency and several harmonics of each. Generally this output is passed directly to an IF amplifier which acts as a bandpass filter just wide enough to pass modulation sidebands around the IF, and providing whatever gain is required to boost the signal to the final detection level. Figure 5.7(a) shows the block diagram of an additive mixing system.

The input signal V_s at frequency f_s containing the modulation sidebands is added directly to the output from the local oscillator V_o at frequency f_o. A buffer amplifier is often used to provide isolation between the oscillator and the input circuit to prevent mutual detuning. The magnitude of V_o is usually made very much larger than V_s for a reason that will be discussed below. The added signals are then passed through a device such as a diode whose output contains a component that is proportional to the square of its input. The diode may be either a separate device from the adder, or as is more often the case, it can be the base-emitter junction of the amplifier transistor.

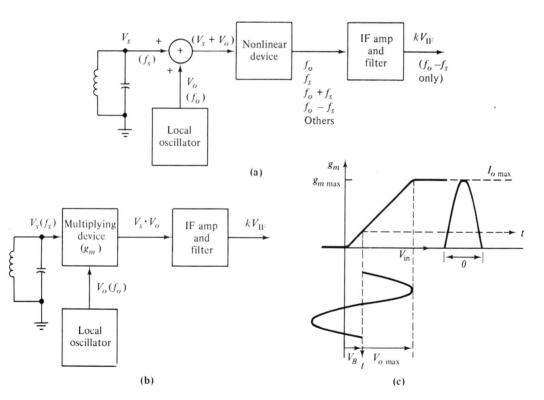

(a)

(b)

(c)

FIGURE 5.7.   Superheterodyne frequency converter or mixer systems: (a) Additive mixing; (b) Multiplicative mixing; (c) Transconductance variation in a multiplicative mixer.

The circuit action may be analyzed in this manner. The output of the summing device produces the sum of the two signals, where

$$v_s = V_s \sin \omega_s t$$

$$v_o = V_o \sin \omega_o t$$

$$V_o \gg V_s \quad \text{and} \quad \omega_o > \omega_s$$

so that $\quad v_t = v_s + v_o = (V_s \sin \omega_s t) + (V_o \sin \omega_o t) \quad$ (5.23)

If a diode with a square-law characteristic is used, then the diode characteristics may be stated as a power series of terms as

$$i_d = i_o + av_t + bv_t^2 + \cdots \tag{5.24}$$

The squared term component of current is

$$i_2 = bv_t^2$$

$$= b(v_o + v_s)^2$$

$$= b(v_o^2 + v_s^2 + 2v_o v_s)$$

$$= b(V_o^2 \sin^2 \omega_o t + V_s^2 \sin^2 \omega_s t + 2 V_o V_s \sin \omega_o t \sin \omega_s t] \tag{5.25}$$

The product $\sin \omega_o t \sin \omega_s t$ can be expanded by the use of trigonometric identities to give

$$\sin \omega_o t \sin \omega_s t = \tfrac{1}{2} \cos(\omega_o - \omega_s)t - \tfrac{1}{2} \cos(\omega_o + \omega_s)t$$

so that the current contains a term at the intermediate frequency, IF, which is

$$i_{(IF)} = bV_o V_s \cos(\omega_o - \omega_s)t \tag{5.26}$$

The magnitude of $i_{(IF)}$ is

$$|i_{(IF)}| = bV_o V_s = g_c V_s \tag{5.27}$$

from which the conversion transconductance g_c given by Eqn. (5.22) is seen to be:

$$g_c = bV_o \tag{5.28}$$

The magnitude of the local oscillator voltage is made large, so that a large transconductance can be obtained. The output is then proportional to the input in amplitude but has a carrier frequency of $(f_o - f_s)$. The sidebands are also reproduced around the new carrier frequency without either amplitude or phase distortion.

5.4.2 Multiplicative Mixing

Multiplicative mixing occurs when the transconductance of the mixer circuit is caused to vary with the local oscillator voltage, so that the output current becomes a function of the product of v_o and v_s. Figure 5.7(b) shows the block diagram of a multiplicative mixer. The analysis of this circuit is as follows: Again the input voltages are

$$v_s = V_s \cos \omega_s t \tag{5.29}$$

$$v_o = V_o \cos \omega_o t \qquad \text{where } V_o \gg V_s \tag{5.30}$$

The cosine functions are used to agree with the Fourier series given below. The mixer output current is given by

$$i_m = g_m v_s \tag{5.31}$$

but g_m is a function of the oscillator voltage v_o. A device is chosen whose transconductance is directly proportional to the applied bias voltage magnitude, up to a saturating maximum g_{max} occuring at $V_{b\,max}$, as shown in Figure 5.7(c). The bias is made to vary around a fixed bias point with v_o so that the positive peaks of v_o drive the device just to saturation, and the negative peaks drive it a considerable way into cutoff (class AB). The transconductance function becomes a clipped sinusoid as shown in Figure 5.7(c), whose value may be stated in terms of a Fourier series as

$$g_m = \frac{g_{max}}{V_{b\,max}} \cdot V_o\,(a_o + a_1 \cos \omega_o t + \cdots) \tag{5.32}$$

where the Fourier coefficient a_1 is of particular interest and is also a function of the clipping angle Θ shown in Figure 5.7(c). Ignoring all but the fundamental component of the g_m function, the mixer output current becomes

$$i_m = g_m v_s = \frac{g_{max} a_1 V_o}{V_{b\,max}} \cos \omega_o t \cdot V_s \cos \omega_s t \tag{5.33}$$

$$= \frac{g_{max} a_1 V_o V_s}{2 V_{b\,max}} [\cos(\omega_o - \omega_s)t + \cos(\omega_o + \omega_s)t] \tag{5.34}$$

and $\qquad i_{IF} = g_c V_s \tag{5.35}$

where $\qquad g_c = \dfrac{g_{max} a_1 V_o}{2 V_{b\,max}}$ and the bias $V_B = V_o \cos\left(\dfrac{\pi - \Theta}{2}\right) \tag{5.36}$

$$\text{and } V_{b\,max} = V_B + V_o$$

The value of the coefficient a_1 is a maximum when the clipping angle ($\Theta/2$) is 0.68π rad (about 122°), and has a maximum value of $1.68 \div \pi$. For this value, the g_c has a maximum value of

$$g_{c_{\max}} = \frac{1.68 \, g_{\max}}{\pi} = 0.27 \, g_{\max} \tag{5.37}$$

5.4.3   Mixer Circuits

Many circuit combinations are possible that will work as mixers. Diodes are sometimes used as the mixing nonlinear device, but more often a transistor or a vacuum tube is used because of the additional gain that may be realized from it.

Figure 5.8(a) shows a bipolar transistor used to mix the input signal with the signal from a separate local oscillator circuit. This circuit is basically an additive circuit, because the total base-emitter signal voltage is the sum of the signal voltage and the local oscillator output voltage. The base-emitter junction serves to produce the necessary squared components. The oscillator input is made much larger than the signal input, but is kept low enough so that clipping does not occur. This produces a large value of g_m while preventing the overproduction of harmonics. The output current from the transistor containing the IF component drives the primary of a double-tuned IF transformer connected to the IF amplifier input stage. The signal may be coupled into the base tank circuit by mutual coupling from a previous RF stage or from an antenna, or the tank may be a ferrite rod antenna. The bias on the transistor is adjusted by the values of R_1 and R_2 so that the transistor is in conduction, near the cutoff point, and the maximum curvature of the base-emitter characteristic is near the operating point. The oscillator voltage drives the bias through this region of maximum curvature. Higher values of transconductance may be obtained by bypassing the emitter resistor R_E with a series resonant circuit tuned to the signal frequency, but the result will be to allow interaction between the signal tank and the local oscillator circuit. Impedance matching taps are shown on all tank circuits.

Figure 5.8(b) shows the circuit of a multiplicative mixer which uses a dual-gate field effect transistor as the multiplying device. Figure 5.8(c) shows the effect that variation of the bias voltage on gate 2 has on the transconductance through gate 1. It is almost linear and can be approximated by a straight line. The input signal is fed to gate 1, which is biased into the active region. The oscillator output is applied to gate 2. The bias on gate 2 is such that without oscillator signal a slightly positive bias is applied, keeping it up on the g_m curve near the axis, Figure 5.8(c). Sufficient oscillator signal is applied to drive the operating point just up to the saturation level on the positive peaks, and somewhat into cutoff on the negative peaks, which should give nearly maximum conversion transconduc-

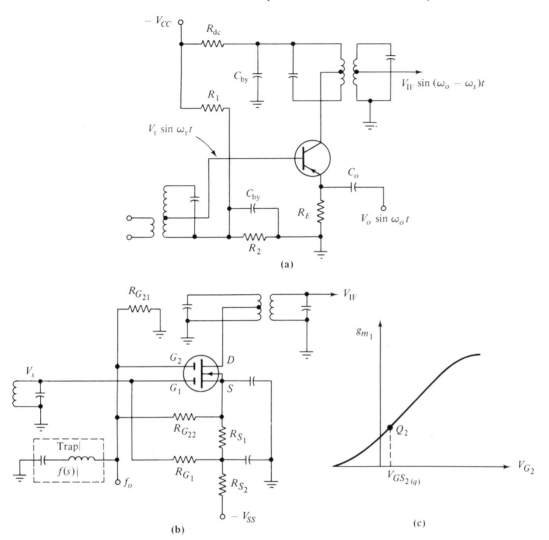

FIGURE 5.8. (a) Bipolar transistor additive mixer; (b) Mulitplicative mixer using a double-gate FET; (c) Variation of signal gate transconductance as a function of the oscillator gate voltage.

tance. A trap (series resonant circuit) is connected between G_2 and ground to shunt any signal voltage that might be fed to this gate. It is tuned to the signal frequency.

Again the output current feeds the input of a double-tuned IF transformer. An example follows which illustrates the calculation of the conversion transconductance of such a circuit.

Example 5.4   A dual-gate FET has the following characteristics:

Gate 1: $g_{1_{max}}$ = 1.5 mS

g_{1o} = 1.0 mS (at V_2) = 0)

$V_{po\,2}$ = -3.0 V

Gate 2: $g_{2_{max}}$ = 0.8 mS

g_{2o} = 0.6 mS (at V_1 = 0)

$V_{po\,1}$ = -2.5V

The circuit is arranged so that gate 2 is biased to cutoff, and is driven just to saturation by the oscillator voltage. Gate 1 is biased to zero volts. It is assumed that the g-V curves are linear.

(a) Plot the g-V curves on the same axes.
(b) Find the straight-line equations for the curves.
(c) Find $V_{1_{max}}$ and $V_{2_{max}}$.
(d) Find the peak oscillator voltage.
(e) Find g_c.

Solution   (a) See Figure 5.9 for the g-V curves for the FET

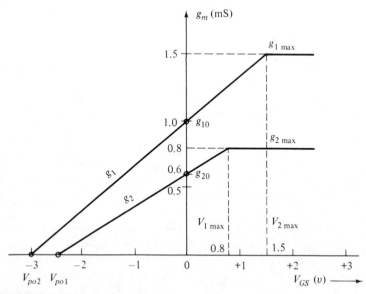

FIGURE 5.9. Transconductance versus voltage curves for a dual-gate field effect transistor.

(b)   Slope of g_1 curve $= \dfrac{g_{1o}}{-V_{po2}} = \dfrac{1.0}{3.0} = 0.333$

Slope of g_2 curve $= \dfrac{g_{2o}}{-V_{po1}} = \dfrac{0.6}{2.5} = 0.24$

The curve equations are

$$g_1 = 1.0 + 0.33\,V_2$$

$$g_2 = 0.6 + 0.24\,V_1$$

(c) $V_{2\,max} = \dfrac{g_{1\,max} - 1.0}{0.333} = \dfrac{1.5 - 1.0}{0.333} = 1.50\text{ V}$

$V_{1\,max} = \dfrac{g_{2\,max} - 0.6}{0.24} = \dfrac{0.8 - 0.6}{0.24} = 0.833\text{ V}$

(d) $V_{op} = V_{2\,max} - V_{po2} = 1.5 - (-3.0) = 4.5\text{ V}$

(e) $g_c = \frac{1}{2} a_1 g_{1\,max}$

$g_c = \frac{1}{2} \times \frac{1}{2} \times 1.5 = \mathbf{0.375}$ **mS**

[the mixer responds to the positive half-cycle of the oscillator voltage, so $a_1 = \frac{1}{2}$ (the Fourier coefficient of the first harmonic of a half-wave rectified sine wave).]

5.5   IF AMPLIFIERS

The IF amplifiers used in receiver systems are special fixed-tuned units usually with two or more cascaded stages. They incorporate a number of features: voltage gain to raise the signal level at the output of the converter to that needed by the detector; bandpass filtering action to allow only the wanted signal to pass to the detector; automatic gain control to prevent overloading of the detector; and, in the case of FM systems, signal amplitude limiting to prevent amplitude variations from interfering with detector operations.

The gain requirements of IF amplifiers are somewhat similar, regardless of the particular type of receiver. As a rule, sufficient gain is included in the RF and mixer stages ahead of the IF so that the signal level presented to the IF input is of the order of 1 mV. Most detectors, AM, FM, or PM, require signal levels of about 1 V to perform adequately. This means that IF circuits must provide a signal voltage gain of about 1000, or 60 dB. Two or three cascaded stages usually provide the required gain. This may vary from as little as 40 dB for cheap AM broadcast receivers to as much as 80 dB for special communications receivers, but usually the 60-dB figure is adequate. This gain is the overall required, and any gain included to compensate for loss in filters and coupling circuits must be provided above this figure.

The filter bandpass characteristic of the IF amplifier depends on the type of signal that it is to handle. If ordinary AM broadcast signals are to be received, the ideal IF filter would have a bandpass of just less than 10 kHz. The usual AM IF frequency used is 455 kHz, so the filtering characteristic can be accomplished with tuned circuits with a Q of about 100, which is quite practical. When AM SSB signals are being received, initial filtering is still done with the 10-kHz bandwidth, but this is followed by a very sharp cutoff sideband pass filter which usually has a bandpass of about 3 kHz total. This filter is either mechanical, ceramic, or crystal lattice. Double conversion is often used in such systems, with a first IF at about 2 MHz, with a 10-kHz bandwidth, followed by a second IF at either 455 kHz or perhaps a lower one between 100 and 300 kHz. The sideband filters are included in the second IF, and the total gain, including both IF strips and the second converter gain, is as before, that is, 50 to 80 dB. FM signals are usually received at VHF or higher frequencies, with a total bandwidth of about 200 kHz for broadcast, and about 30 kHz for narrow-band voice communications. The IF in these cases is usually 10.7 MHz, although others have been used. Again, the Q required is about 100, which is realizable with tuned circuits. Television and microwave communications require bandwidths in the order of 6 to 12 MHz, and usually the IF for these is chosen in the range of 40 to 100 MHz. At these frequencies discrete-component tuned circuits are still usable, along with transistor amplifiers.

Stagger tuning is a technique often used to obtain the bandpass filter characteristic of the IF amplifier. Figure 5.10(a) shows the circuit layout for a stagger tuned IF amplifier that might be used for an AM receiver. It consists of two amplifier stages which provide enough gain to make up for the losses in the transformers and to provide the overall net gain requirement, and three interstage transformers. The amplifiers are basically two class A small-signal amplifiers with tuned input and tuned output. As such, either individual-stage neutralization or overall neutralization must be provided to maintain stability.

The three transformers are all undercritically coupled so that no double humping occurs in their response. This means that each of the tuned circuits is effectively isolated from all the others and acts independently. Each has a Q which results in a much narrower bandwidth than is required overall. The first and last circuit are tuned to the center IF frequency, circuits 2 and 3 are tuned to about 2 kHz either side of center frequency, and circuits 4 and 5 are tunded about 4 kHz either side of center. The individual tuned circuit responses are sketched in Figure 5.10(b). Because the tuned circuits are isolated and do not react with one another, their responses (in dB) add

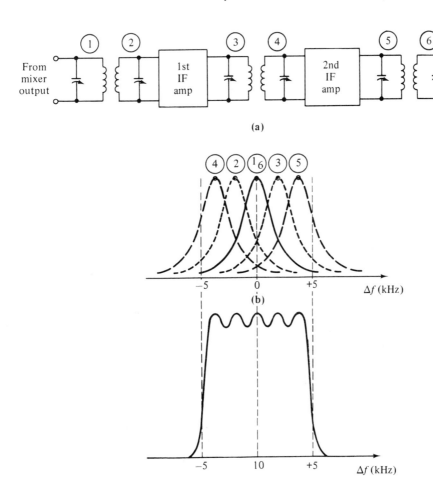

FIGURE 5.10. A stagger tuned IF amplifier: (a) Circuit; (b) Frequency responses of each tank taken independently; (c) The overall IF circuit response.

directly to give an overall response similar to Figure 5.10(c). The ripple across the top can usually be kept within 1 dB, and skirt steepness can cause the response to drop as much as 60 dB between 4 and 6 kHz offcenter. The form of this response is similar to a Chebyshev filter, and quite often such filters are used in place of the tuned transformers.

It has already been noted that in the case of SSB systems it is necessary to include a special sideband filter with about a 3-kHz bandwidth and extremely steep skirts. This usually takes the form of a mechanical or a crystal or ceramic lattice filter. With the increasing availability of operational amplifiers designed to operate at IF frequencies and to provide as much as 100 dB of gain in a single unit, the use of such filters as the only IF filtering is becoming commonplace. Circuit design becomes very much simpler if one can simply pick an amplifier with sufficient gain and a filter with the required bandpass off the shelf.

Automatic gain control (AGC) is usually included in the first stage of the IF amplifier if it is to be used for AM signals. This is necessary especially if there is no RF stage to prevent strong signals from overloading the detector circuit and causing distortion.

In the FM systems, amplitude variations in the signal level presented to the detector are undesirable, because they cause distortions in the output. Amplitude limiting is provided in one stage of the IF amplifier of such receivers. These circuits provide maximum gain until the output signal level reaches a predetermined threshold. For any signal level above this, the output remains constant at the value of the threshold. One scheme for accomplishing this limiting function is to make one stage (usually the last one) of the IF amplifier a class B or class C amplifier with fixed bias, followed by a tuned circuit. As the input signal amplitude increases, the tube or transistor is driven farther and farther into conduction until saturation occurs. For signal levels higher than that necessary to saturate the amplifier, no further increase in the current amplitude can occur, and the output signal remains at constant amplitude. Another method, used with IC amplifiers, is to use a delayed AGC-type negative feedback system. The amplifier is left with maximum gain for signal levels lower than threshold, but lowered for higher levels. The response of this limiting AGC must be fast enough to correct for changes at frequencies up to the maximum modulation frequency.

Figure 5.11(a) shows the schematic for a typical AM transistor IF amplifier. Two *PNP* transistors provide the gain, both of them operating in the class A mode. Three stagger-tuned transformers provide the coupling. The input and output of each transformer is tapped down to provide the necessary impedance matching because the input and output resistances of the amplifiers is too low to provide the required Q. Bias for the second stage is fixed while that for the first stage is derived from an AGC signal from the detector. Neutralizing capacitors are provided on each stage to stabilize them. The tapped transformer coils make neutralization very easy. Decoupling of the power supply leads to each stage is necessary if stability is to be maintained. The transistors must have a beta cutoff frequency at least as high as the IF if their full gain is to be realized.

Figure 5.11(b) shows an FM IF strip made with integrated circuit amplifiers. The first IC is an MFC 4010, which is limiting amplifier designed specifically for 10.7-MHz IF circuits. It provides up to 60 dB of gain, and limiting at an output of about 200 mV. The second IC is an MC 1357 circuit which includes further limiting gain and a complete quadrature detector circuit. Selectivity is provided by the tuned input transformer and a ceramic

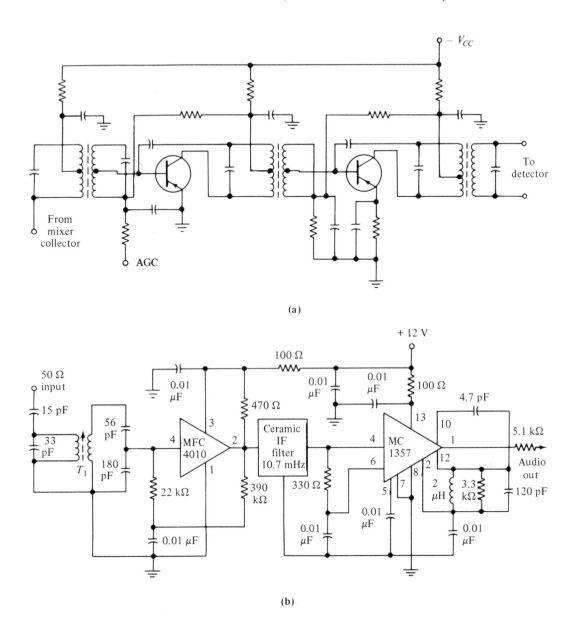

(a)

(b)

T_1 Miller No. 8851 A
Filter Vernitron FM-4 ceramic filter

FIGURE 5.11. (a) A transistorized AM IF strip; (b) An integrated circuit FM IF amplifier including detector. (Extracted from Motorola Application Note AN543). (Courtesy of Motorola, Inc.)

IF filter. The only other tuned circuit required is the simple parallel-tuned network in the detector to provide the necessary phase shift. All the other components are capacitive bypass or coupling, or resistive bias networks. These chips were specifically designed for use in inexpensive FM receivers, and their cost is very low. The whole strip can be assembled on a printed circuit card about 5×10 cm in size.

5.6   BROADBAND VIDEO AMPLIFIERS

Amplifiers used to amplify the video signals in television systems require flat amplitude response and linear phase response from 10 Hz to about 6 MHz. To allow such operation, several things must be accomplished in the design of the amplifier. The first of these is to choose an amplifying device with a sufficient gain-bandwidth product so that the transistor limitation on frequency response falls above the required upper cutoff frequency. For instance, if a bipolar transistor were chosen, and if it were to be operated without feedback, its beta cutoff frequency would have to be above the upper cutoff frequency. If the midband gain were reduced, either by loading or applying negative feedback, the gain cutoff point would move upward and would be roughly given by the gain-bandwidth equation.

$$G \cdot \text{BW} = A_v f = A_{v \max} f_u \qquad (5.38)$$

where $A_{v\max}$ is the voltage gain for frequencies below the upper cutoff frequency f_u, and A_v is the voltage gain at some frequency f above f_u. RC coupling is used in such amplifiers, and the coupling circuits used also limit the frequency response. The size of the series coupling capacitors used between stages limits the lower cutoff frequency. There are three ways to handle this problem: use a larger capacitor, or provide a low-frequency compensation network or d.c. couple the amplifier.

Increasing the size of the capacitor is easier as far as low frequencies are concerned, but if this capacitor is increased too much, its physical size will make the shunt stray capacitance too large, spoiling the high-frequency response. It may be necessary to use the more complicated compensation networks shown in Figure 5.12(b). Figure 5.12(a) shows the uncompensated amplifier and its approximate equivalent circuit. In this circuit, if the frequency is lower than that given by the RC time constant, and the corner frequency is

$$\omega = \frac{1}{C_2(R_i + R_L)} \qquad (5.39)$$

the gain drops off at the rate of -20dB/decade of frequency. Increasing the

FIGURE 5.12. Low-frequency compensation of *RC*-coupled amplifiers: (a) Uncompensated amplifier with its equivalent circuit; (b) Compensated amplifier with its equivalent circuit; (c) Bode plot approximations for both the uncompensated and the compensated amplifiers.

value of C_2 lowers the value of the corner frequency by the inverse ratio. The response of both amplitude and phase vs. frequency is sketched as the solid lines in Figure 5.12(c).

The compensation network of Figure 5.12(b) uses a split-load resistor. An additional resistor R_2 shunted by the capacitor C_1 is added in series. At midband frequencies, C_1 shunts out R_2, and only the normal load resistance R_L has effect. For frequencies lower than the original corner frequency, the capacitance C_2 allows more and more of the resistor R_2 to have effect, causing the gain of the amplifier to rise, canceling out the loss due to C_2. The overall gain function is given approximately where $R_2 \gg \dfrac{1}{\omega C_1}$ by

$$A_v(\omega) \cong A_{v\,mid} \frac{\left(1 - j\dfrac{1}{\omega C_1 R_L}\right)}{\left(1 - j\dfrac{1}{\omega C_1 R_2}\right)\left(1 - j\dfrac{1}{\omega \dfrac{C_1 C_2}{C_1 + C_2}(R_i + R_L)}\right)}$$

By making the time constant $C_1 R_L$ equal to $C_2 R_i$, the gain function reduces to

$$A_v(\omega) = \frac{A_{v\,mid}}{\left(1 - j\dfrac{1}{\omega C_1 R_2}\right)} \tag{5.41}$$

and the lower cutoff frequency is now controlled by the time constant $C_1 R_2$, much lower than that of the uncompensated amplifier. The results of the compensation are illustrated in Figure 5.12(c). Both the amplitude and phase-cutoff frequencies are lowered.

At the high-frequency end, cutoff is usually caused by the effects of shunt capacity between the signal circuit and ground. This is due to input capacity in the following amplifier, to output capacity in the amplifier in question, and to wire stray capacitance. The upper cutoff frequency of this amplifier can be raised by including a small inductor in series with the load resistor, as shown in Figure 5.13(a). Assuming that the natural cutoff frequency of the amplifying device is much higher than that caused by the shunt capacity, and that both the amplifier output resistance and the following-amplifier input resistance are much larger than the load resistance, the equivalent circuit of the uncompensated amplifier becomes that of Figure 5.13(b), where C_t is the sum of the output capacitance C_o, the input capacitance C_i, and the stray capacitances C_s. The cutoff frequency is given by

$$\omega = \frac{1}{C_t R_L} \qquad \text{where } C_t = C_o + C_i + C_s \tag{5.42}$$

When the coil is included with the load resistor, the equivalent circuit

FIGURE 5.13. The shunt peaked compensated FET amplifier: (a) Circuit showing compensating inductor; (b) Equivalent circuit without compensation; (d) Series-compensated amplifier.

becomes a very heavily damped, parallel-resonant circuit, as shown in Figure 5.13(c). The resonant frequency of this circuit is given by

$$\omega = \frac{1}{\sqrt{LC_t}} \tag{5.43}$$

It can be proved that for this circuit to provide "maximally flat" frequency response,

$$L = 0.360 R_L^2 C_t \tag{5.44}$$

Since the values of C_t and R_L are already fixed, it is only necessary to calculate the required value of L from Eq. 5.44. Generally, this will give an improvement in the cutoff frequency of about two times, as illustrated by the following example.

Example 5.5   An *RC*-coupled amplifier has an output capacity of 10 pF and a load resistance of 2 kΩ. It is coupled to another amplifier with an input capacitance of 25 pF, and the net stray-wiring capacitance adds another 5 pF. Both the output and input resistances are much larger than R_L and can be ignored. Find the uncompensated upper cutoff frequency, the value of inductance necessary to compensate for maximally flat response, and the new upper cutoff frequency.

Solution   Uncompensated,

$$C_t = C_o + C_s + C_i = 10 + 25 + 5 = 40 \, \text{pF}$$

$$\omega = \frac{1}{C_t R_L} = \frac{1}{40 \, \text{pF} \times 2 \, \text{k}\Omega} = 12.5 \, \text{Mrad/s}$$

$$f = \frac{\omega}{2\pi} = 2.0 \, \text{MHz}$$

Compensated maximally flat,

$$L = 0.36 \times 2^2 \times 10^6 \times 40 \times 10^{-12} = 57.6 \, \mu\text{H}$$

$$f_{\text{comp}} = \frac{1}{2\pi \sqrt{LC_t}} = 3.32 \, \text{MHz}$$

This is the frequency at which the peaking circuit resonates, and the actual 3-dB cutoff frequency will be slightly higher.

Figure 5.13(d) shows a different way of compensating such an amplifier. In this case, a small inductor is included in series with the coupling capacitor, and the process is known as *series compensation*. Although the calculations involved in such a compensation are quite complex, somewhat better results can be obtained than with the shunt-compensation technique. However, unless the application is critical, the extra effort involved is not worth it, and the shunt-peaking circuit is more often used. Extra care in choosing the amplifying devices and operating modes to minimize input and output capacitances is more profitable. Stray capacitances can be reduced by careful layout, keeping all signal lines as short as possible.

5.7   CLASS C AND LINEAR AMPLIFIERS

5.7.1   Class C Amplifier

A class C amplifier is any amplifier that conducts over less than one half of its input drive cycle. With tuned class C amplifiers, the output is forced to be a sine wave because of the resonant action of the output tank circuit. If the output tank is tuned to the fundamental of the driving frequency, the amplifier current pulses the tank once every cycle. If it is tuned to the second harmonic, the tank is pulsed every other cycle. Since current is flowing in the amplifying device only during short current pulses, very high efficiencies can be realized. Theoretical maximum efficiencies for fundamental operation range to over 90%, and for this reason class C amplifiers are used as power output stages and modulators of transmitters.

Very high power transmitters in all frequency ranges still make use of vacuum power tubes operating in the class C mode, but for the frequencies up to 1 GHz at moderate power levels, transistors are becoming popular. A good analysis of a tube-type class C amplifier has been given by B. Zeines in *Electronic Communication Systems* (Prentice-Hall, Inc., Englewood Cliffs, N.J., 1970).

Figure 5.14(a) shows the circuit of a transistorized fixed-bias class C amplifier. The input signal is inductively coupled to the input tank circuit, which is tuned to the fundamental frequency. Fixed bias is provided through a decoupling network consisting of an RF choke and a bypass capacitor, through the input tank to the base, from a dc source. This dc bias keeps the base circuit biased well beyond cutoff, and no base current can be drawn until the input signal voltage exceeds the cutoff threshold voltage. Base current then flows only during the positive peaks of the input voltage, and is limited in magnitude by the transistor input resistance.

Figure 5.14(b) shows the approximate base voltage and current waveform that result. Conduction begins when the input voltage v_s exceeds the threshold voltage which is the sum of the bias voltage and the base-emitter cut-in voltage.

$$|V_{s_{thresh}}| = |V_{BB}| + |V_{BE}| \qquad (5.45)$$

The *conduction angle* is the portion of the input angle during which conduction takes place [Fig. 5.14(b)]. The is given approximately by

$$\Theta_b = 2 \cdot \cos^{-1}\left(\frac{|V_{s\,thresh}|}{V_{sp}}\right) \qquad (5.46)$$

The collector current will be approximately the same shape as the base current pulse *provided* that the transistor does not saturate. Maximum drive conditions are those which provide just enough base current so that the collector voltage is driven just to zero at its negative peak. Under these conditions, maximum power output will occur. If the collector is driven into saturation, harmonic distortion (clipping) in the load voltage will result, and signals will be transmitted at one or more of the higher harmonics, a situation that is usually undesirable.

It must be emphasized that the collector current waveform will be a

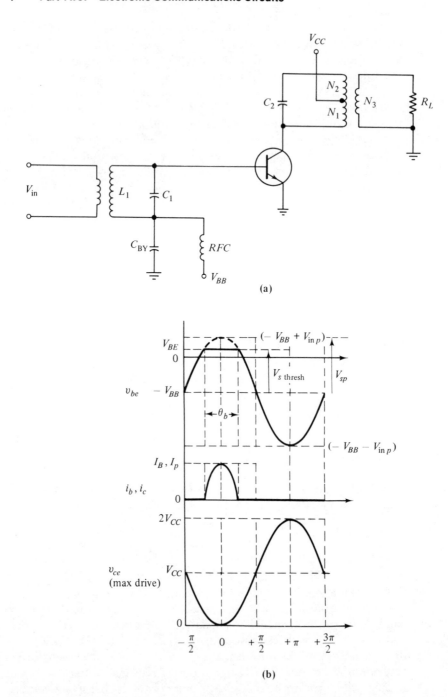

FIGURE 5.14. Class C amplifier: (a) A typical circuit using fixed bias; (b) Waveforms for full-drive conditions.

clipped sinusoid only if the transistor is perfect. However, it is not, since the base-emitter junction at high frequencies does not behave as a perfect rectifier due to its nonlinear reactive component, and the current gain of the transistor varies with the current level. As a result, the actual current pulse in the collector will be narrower and sharper than the expected sinusoid, and will contain more harmonics.

An analysis of the transistor gain functions will yield only grossly approximate results unless complicated nonlinear models are used, so this analysis is not attempted here.

A Fourier analysis of the ideal current pulse in the collector circuit, however, indicates how much of the current pulse contributes to the signal. The ideal current pulse is assumed to be a truncated cosine pulse (i.e., a cosine wave that has had the bottom sliced off it). The Fourier analysis of the ideal pulse shows that for a given conduction angle and a peak pulse amplitude, I_p, the total current is given by

$$\begin{aligned} i_p &= I_{dc} + i_{fund} + i_{2nd} + i_{3rd} + i_{4th} + \cdots \\ &= I_p \cdot n_{dc} + I_p \cdot n_1 \cdot \cos \omega t + I_p \cdot n_2 \cdot \cos 2\omega t + \cdots \end{aligned} \qquad (5.47)$$

Figure 5.15 shows plots of n_{dc}, n_1, n_2, n_3, and n_4 versus the conduction angle Θ_b for $0 < \Theta_b < 180°$. These plots show that the fundamental and dc components rise steadily with increasing conduction angle, but that the second, third and fourth harmonics peak out between 60° and 120°. Thus this is the best range of operation for frequency multiplication operation. The ratio of the fundamental component to the dc component, which determines the collector efficiency, peaks in the same range. In practice the bias or drive is adjusted to yield peak output for minimum dc current.

When the output tank circuit is tuned to the fundamental frequency, its parallel reactance becomes infinite, leaving only the dynamic load resistance R_L'' in the collector circuit, at fundamental frequency. At higher frequencies, the tank circuit is capacitive, and shorts most of the higher harmonic current to ground. The collector signal voltage is given as

$$v_{ce} = V_{CC} - i_c Z_{tank} \cong V_{CC} - n_1 I_p R_L'' \sin \omega_o t \qquad (5.48)$$

where n_1 in this case is the value of the coefficient of the fundamental for the real collector current waveform under operating conditions.

From Eq. (5.48) the peak fundamental voltage is $n_1 I_p R_L''$. At full drive, the magnitude of the peak fundamental voltage is equal to the supply voltage V_{CC}.

The signal power output at maximum drive may now be calculated as

$$P_{o_{max}} = \frac{(I_p n_1)^2 R_L''}{2} = \frac{V_{CC}^2}{2 R_L''} = \frac{V_{CC} I_p n_1}{2} \qquad (5.49)$$

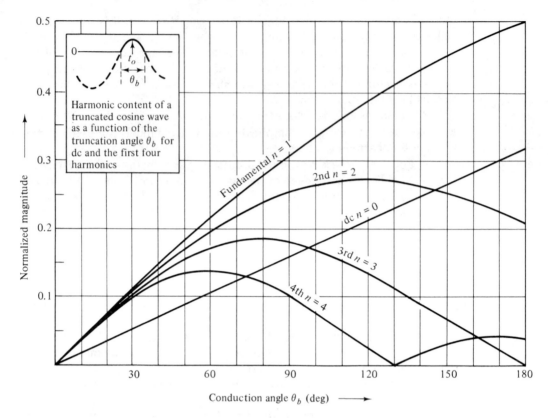

FIGURE 5.15. A plot of the Fourier coefficients of a class C current wave-form as a function of the conduction angle θ_b.

The dc power input to the collector circuit is

$$P_{dc} = V_{CC} I_C = V_{CC} n_{dc} I_{pp} \tag{5.50}$$

and the collector efficiency is calculated from these powers as

$$\eta_c = \frac{P_o}{P_{indc}} = \frac{n_1}{2n_o} \times 100\% \tag{5.51}$$

This shows that the circuit need only be adjusted to give maximum RF power output at a minimum dc input current to assure best efficiency.

If the output tank circuit is tuned to a higher harmonic, n_x, all the other harmonics are shorted, and wherever n_1 appears in the power equations, n_x is substituted. Lower efficiencies result, but the circuit will act as a frequency multiplier.

Power is also dissipated in the base circuit, and a certain amount of signal power must be applied to drive the amplifier to maximum output.

Under maximum drive conditions the circuit power gain can be calculated as

$$A_p = \frac{P_o}{P_{\text{in}}} \tag{5.52}$$

Drive signal conditions are usually monitored in operation by providing a dc milliammeter to measure the dc base current, and a peak-reading RF voltmeter to measure the base signal voltage. A second dc ammeter is provided in the collector circuit, which is used to indicate correct output tank tuning. When there is sufficient drive on the base circuit, and the output tank is tuned through resonance, the collector current will dip to a minimum value when the tank is tuned to the drive frequency. At other frequencies a higher value of current will flow because of the shunting effect of the tank reactances. The circuit is adjusted to give maximum power output (just at saturation) without producing undue harmonic output.

In the above analysis the base bias was provided by an external source. This is often inconvenient, and self-bias is used instead. The preferred form of self bias is to place a parallel R-C combination in the emitter lead of the transistor. The capacitor is then charged by the dc component of the collector current to provide a DC voltage for biasing the base which is proportional to the input signal level. As a result the circuit will automatically adjust itself to small variations in input signal level. The time constant RC of the emitter circuit is made relatively much longer than the fundamental frequency period.

5.7.2 Push-Pull Class C Amplifier

The class C amplifier injects energy into the output tuned circuit only during the short time at the peak of the input cycle during which the amplifier goes into conduction. It relies on storing sufficient energy in the tuned circuit during this short period to maintain the output oscillation during the remainder of the cycle, similar to a flywheel or pendulum effect in mechanical systems. A large improvement in the efficiency of energy transfer and output waveform linearity can be obtained by operating two class C amplifiers in push-pull into the same tuned output circuit, with one amplifier supplying the positive peaks and the other supplying the negative peaks.

A push-pull class C amplifier is shown in Figure 5.16. It uses two triode vacuum-tube amplifiers, and their operation in each case is identical to that discussed in the previous section.

The input circuit is a transformer whose secondary is tuned by a split-stator capacitor with the rotor grounded. (The net tuning capacitance is the series equivalent of the capacities of the two sections.) The grid of the first tube is fed from the top of the input tank circuit and the grid of the second tube is fed 180° out of phase with the first from the bottom of the input tank circuit. The bias circuit acts in conjunction with the grid-cathode diodes to

FIGURE 5.16.   Push-pull class C power amplifier using triode vacuum tubes.

provide a bias voltage which is proportional to the average of the driving signal amplitude, with the tubes being driven toward cutoff as the signal increases. A small fixed bias is supplied from V_{CC} as well, to limit the plate current during no-signal conditions to a safe level. This fixed bias can be switched out after the circuit has been adjusted and proper drive signal levels obtained, allowing higher grid currents to flow.

The plates of the two tubes are connected to opposite ends of the output tank circuit, which is also tuned with a split-stator capacitor that has a grounded rotor. The plate supply current is introduced through a center tap on the output transformer primary, through an RF choke coil and a dc ammeter. The load is coupled through the secondary of the transformer, which provides the proper impedance matching.

The Miller capacitance in each tube provides a feedback path which makes each tube look like a tuned input/tuned output oscillator. Neutralizing capacitors are included which connect each grid to the opposite plate. Since the plate signals are 180° out of phase with each other and also 180° out of phase with their inputs, the signals fed back by the neutralizing capacitors are of the correct phase to cancel out the Miller capacitance feedback signals. These capacitors are adjusted to give stable operation under full output conditions.

Push-pull amplifiers help to reduce harmonic distortion in the output waveform by cancellation. It can be shown that, providing the circuit is exactly balanced, all the even-numbered harmonics are canceled out when the two opposing signals are added in the output transformer primary. The second harmonic is usually the largest of these, and the hardest to suppress, so that class C push-pull aids in the suppression of the second harmonic.

5.7.3 Linear Power Amplifier

The class C power amplifier provides the best amplifying efficiency, and its use in the output stages of transmitters is desirable from that point of view. However, its transfer function is not linear. That is, its voltage gain is not the same at all input signal amplitudes. This occurs because the bias is derived from the input signal and is made proportional to it. As a result, as signal increases, bias voltage increases and the gain drops. This is not serious if the waveform being amplified has a constant amplitude, as is the case for angle modulation or for interrupted carrier telegraph.

However, when an amplitude-modulated signal is passed through a class C amplifier, the envelope waveform of the modulation becomes distorted because of the changing bias at different signal levels. This distortion in the modulation is unacceptable, and as a result the class C amplifier cannot be used for this application and a linear amplifier must be used. The most commonly used linear amplifier is the class B amplifier, either single-ended or push-pull. Figure 5.17(a) shows the circuit of a cross-neutralized push-pull class B amplifier. Triode tubes are used, although bipolar power transistors may be used for lower power output levels.

Bias for the tubes is provided from a fixed supply and no grid leak is provided. The input tank circuit is coupled directly to the grids. The bias level is set so that with no input signal present both tubes are just cut off, or they may be operated with a very small amount of plate current to counteract crossover distortion in the same way as with the class B audio amplifier. The rest of the circuit is exactly the same as for the push-pull class C amplifier of Section 5.7.2.

The transconductance curve for the triode, as shown in Figure 5.17(b), is almost linear over most of the range from cutoff to grid saturation, except for a small kink near the axis. This kink is responsible for the crossover distortion problem. The sketch shows the amplitude-modulated signal applied to the grid. The maximum and minimum points of the modulation envelope fall between zero bias and cutoff, and the carrier signal varies around the V_{CC} bias supply level. The zero-modulation carrier level is halfway between these extremes. The resulting plate current wave carries a modulation envelope waveform that is very nearly the same as the input modulation waveform, indicating a minimum of distortion.

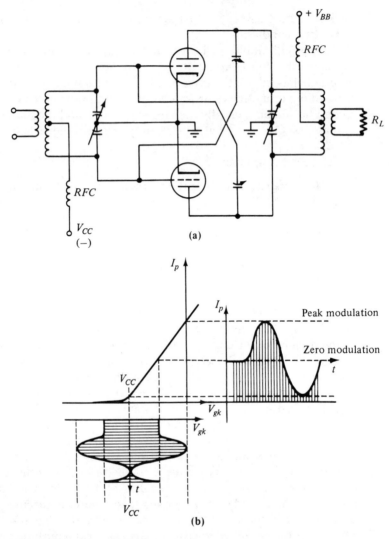

FIGURE 5.17. Class B push-pull linear amplifier: (a) Circuit; (b) Transconductance curve for one tube showing the relation between grid voltage and plate current for varying modulation conditions.

Power-conversion efficiency is much lower than with the corresponding class C amplifier. The ideal class B push-pull plate circuit efficiency is 78 %, while that for the class C amplifier can be as high as 90 %. Linearity is gained at the expense of efficiency and the fact that larger tubes or transistors are needed for the same signal power output because of the greater heat dissipation.

One way around the problem of using class C for amplitude-modulated signals is to use a class C final amplifier and modulate it at high level, using plate modulation. With careful design and the use of negative feedback, it is possible to modulate the class C amplifier in a linear manner. It is done at the expense of very high power modulating amplifiers and large modulation transformers. At microwave frequencies, amplifying devices with sufficient gain for the linear mode of operation are difficult to obtain, and one reason why frequency modulation is preferred to amplitude modulation at microwaves is that class C amplifiers can be used.

5.8   TRANSMITTER AND AMPLIFIER MATCHING

5.8.1   Transmitter Matching Networks

Transmitter matching networks have two basic functions. First, they form the final tuned circuit in the transmitter chain, and must provide sufficient Q so that the harmonics produced by the final amplifier are prevented from reaching the antenna. Second, they must provide the impedance matching that is necessary between the final amplifier and the load if the desired power transfer is to be obtained. Inherent in the first function is that if the load has any reactive component at the point of connection, this reactive component must be canceled by the matching network *before* the impedance matching function can be performed. Usually the transmitter will feed the antenna through a transmission line, which requires a second matching network at the antenna end so that no standing waves appear on the line itself. The impedance of the terminated line at the feed end is purely resistive if this match is properly made.

Several types of LC circuits can be used for the impedance-matching function. These include the single-tuned tranformer, the L-match and the Π-match. At microwave and VHF frequencies, stub matching and quarter-wave transformer sections of line are used to accomplish the same functions. An analysis of these three circuits follows.

Transformer match.   The circuit, shown in Figure 5.18(a), is seen to be similar to that of Figure 5.1(a). Applying the analysis of Section 1.12.2 (and bearing in mind the approximations involved), the load impedance at resonance, as seen by the transmitter, is R_D' as given by Eq. 1.109, and when matched for maximum power transfer $R_s = R_D'$. The circuit Q is Q_p' as given by Eq. 1.110, but matching reduces this by a factor of two, so that the overall Q factor, including the effect of R_s, when matched, is:

$$Q_{\text{eff}} = \tfrac{1}{2} Q_p' \qquad (5.53)$$

L-Match   This circuit is often used for transmitter output matching

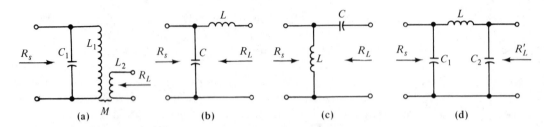

FIGURE 5.18. Transmitter matching networks: (a) Transformer match; (b) L-match with series L; (c) L-match with series C; (d) Π-match.

because of its simplicity, and either of the forms shown in Figure 5.18(b) and (c) may be used. For either network, let the input branch be represented by $Z_1 = jX_1$, and the series branch containing the load R_L by $Z_2 = R_L + jX_2$ (i.e., the network elements are assumed lossless). The admittance of either network, as seen by the transmitter, is (using the results of Section 1.7)

$$Y = -j\frac{1}{X_1} + \frac{R_L}{R_L^2 + X_2^2} - j\frac{X_2}{R_L^2 + X_2^2} \tag{5.54}$$

At resonance the j-coefficients equate to zero to give

$$-\frac{1}{X_1} = \frac{X_2}{R_L^2 + X_2^2} \tag{5.55}$$

or

$$R_L^2 + X_2^2 = -X_1 X_2 \tag{5.56}$$

The admittance at resonance then becomes

$$Y_{res} = \frac{R_L}{R_L^2 + X_2^2} \tag{5.57}$$

$$= -\frac{R_L}{X_1 X_2} \tag{5.58}$$

Hence, the dynamic impedance [see Eq. (1.67)] is

$$R_D = -\frac{X_1 X_2}{R_L} \tag{5.59}$$

For either network, this reduces to

$$R_D = \frac{L}{C \cdot R_L} \tag{5.60}$$

The effective Q-factor of the network is simply the Q of the branch containing R_L:

$$Q = \frac{X_2}{R_L} \qquad (5.61)$$

When matched, $R_o = R_D$, and this reduces the Q by a factor of two, so that the overall Q-factor including the effect of R_o when matched, is

$$Q_{\text{eff}} = \tfrac{1}{2} Q \qquad (5.62)$$

The resonant condition, Eq. 5.56, can be expressed as

$$R_L^2 + X_2^2 = \frac{L}{C}$$

$$\therefore X_2^2 = \frac{L}{C} - R_L^2$$

For $X_2 = \omega L$, the resonant frequency may be evaluated as

$$\omega_o^2 = \frac{1}{LC} - \frac{R_L^2}{L^2} \qquad (5.63)$$

which is the condition expressed by Eq. (1.64). Equation 5.63 can be rearranged as

$$\omega_o^2 = \frac{1}{LC} \left(1 - \frac{CR_L^2}{L} \right)$$

$$= \frac{1}{LC} \left[1 - \left(\frac{R_L}{R_D} \right)^2 \right] \qquad (5.64)$$

and when matched, R_s can be substituted for R_D. It also follows from Eq. 5.64 that the equivalent inductance is

$$L_{\text{eff}} = \frac{L}{1 - \left(\dfrac{R_L}{R_s} \right)^2} \qquad (5.65)$$

For $X_2 = -1/\omega C$, a similar analysis yields

$$\omega_o^{-2} = LC \left[1 - \left(\frac{R_L}{R_s} \right)^2 \right] \qquad (5.66)$$

and

$$C_{\text{eff}} = C \left[1 - \left(\frac{R_L}{R_s} \right)^2 \right] \qquad (5.67)$$

In practice, both X_2 and X_1 are made adjustable. X_2 is adjusted to give the necessary value of Q to provide the proper impedance ratio, and then X_1 is adjusted to tune out the reactance. The tuning of the transmitter proceeds by observing (for a class C amplifier) the plate (or collector) current meter. X_2 is progressively adjusted to increase the value of plate current, and after each change, X_1 is adjusted to the point of minimum plate current, or the bottom of the "dip," indicating resonance. Adjustment continues until the plate (collector) current at the bottom of the resonant dip is a maximum, indicating that power match has been obtained and the circuit is in resonance.

The Π-Match The circuit is shown in Figure 5.18(d). The parallel combination of R_L' and C_2 can be converted, by the method of Section 1.7, to an equivalent series impedance Z_L where

$$Z_L = \frac{R_L'}{1 + Q_L^2} - j\frac{R_L' Q_L}{1 + Q_L^2} \tag{5.68}$$

$$= R_L - jR_L Q_L \tag{5.69}$$

where
$$Q_L = \omega_o C_2 R_L' \tag{5.70}$$

The circuit can now be reduced to that of Figure 5.18(b) and the previous analysis applied, but with

$$R_L = \frac{R_L'}{1 + Q_L^2} \qquad X_2 = \omega L - R_L Q_L$$

Defining $Q_1 = (R_s/X_1)$ and since, when matched, $R_s = R_D$, Eq. 5.59 now yields $X_2 = -Q_1 R_L$. Substituting this in the resonant condition [Eq. (5.56)] gives, after some manipulation,

$$\frac{R_L'}{R_s} = \frac{1 + Q_L^2}{1 + Q_1^2} \tag{5.73}$$

The effective dynamic impedance of the circuit when matched is $R_s \parallel R_D = \frac{1}{2} R_s$. The effective circuit Q factor is

$$Q_{\text{eff}} = \frac{1}{2} Q_1 = \frac{R_s \omega_o C_1}{2} \qquad \text{when matched} \tag{5.74}$$

The resonant frequency will be determined to a good approximation by L, C_1, C_2' in series, where $C_2' = C_2/(1 + Q_L^{-2})$.

Circuit adjustment is accomplished by changing C_2 to adjust the impedance ratio, and changing C_1 to maintain resonance, with basically the same "dipping" method already outlined. An example follows to illustrate the calculations.

Example 5.6

A Π match is to be used to match a transmitter with a 4-kΩ output impedance into a 75-Ω coaxial cable to be matched antenna. The frequency of operation is 12 MHz and the desired effective Q is 20. Find the values of C_1, C_2, and L when tuned and matched for maximum power transfer.

Solution

Find C_1 from Eq. 5.74

$$-X_{C1} = \frac{R_s}{2Q_{eff}} = \frac{4000}{2 \times 20} = 100 \ \Omega$$

$$\omega_o = 2\pi f_o = 2\pi \times 12 \text{ MHz} = 75.4 \text{ Mrad/s}$$

$$C_1 = -\frac{1}{\omega_o X_{c_1}} = \frac{-1}{-100 \times 75.4 \text{ Mrad}} = 133 \text{ pF}$$

To find the value of C_2:

$$Q_1 = 2Q_{eff} = 40$$

From Eq. 5.73

$$Q_L^2 = \left[\frac{R_L'}{R_s}(1 + Q_1^2) \right] - 1 = \left[\frac{75}{4000}(1 + 40^2) \right] - 1 = (5.39)^2$$

From Eq. 5.70

$$\omega_o C_2 = \frac{Q_L}{R_L} = \frac{5.39}{75} = 0.0072 \text{ S}$$

$$C_2 = \frac{0.072}{75.4 \times 10^6} = 955 \text{ pF}$$

Find the equivalent series capacitances.

$$C_1' \cong C_1 = 133 \text{ pF}$$

$$C_2' = C\frac{Q_L^2}{Q_L^2 + 1} = 955 \times \frac{5.39^2}{5.39^2 + 1} = 923 \text{ pF}$$

Find the inductance.

$$C_{eff} = C_1' \text{ser. } C_2' = \frac{133 \times 923}{133 + 923} = 116 \text{ pF}$$

$$L = \frac{1}{\omega^2 C_{eff}} = \frac{1}{(75.4 \text{ Mrad})^2 \times 116 \text{ pF}} = 1.52 \ \mu \text{ H}$$

5.8.2 Line Matching of Amplifiers

At UHF and higher frequencies it is impossible to build discrete components of the small size required to form the impedance matching and tuning networks needed for amplifiers. Resonant cavities and shorted sections of transmission line are used to form these networks at the higher frequencies, above about 300 MHz, and occasionally at lower VHF frequencies as well. Wavelengths for this band of frequencies range from 10 cm to 1 cm, so that shorted stubs can be made easily to act as inductors, capacitors, and tuned circuits, and short sections of line can be used as transformers for impedance matching.

At VHF frequencies, sections of coaxial line and occasionally resonant cavities are used for the purpose. For the higher frequencies, waveguide sections are used instead. Microstrip and stripline printed-circuit versions of wave guides are popular for low-power UHF circuits, where all the components necessary for an amplifier except the transistor can be realized in printed-circuit form. Figure 5.19 illustrates the method. Suppose the output admittance at the collector is $G_o + jB_o$ (assumed capacitive for the purposes of illustration). Short-circuited stub 1 is inductive in accordance with Section 12.11(i), and parallel resonates with jB_o to leave G_o. Length l of the transforming section is selected in accordance with the general impedance equation [Eq. (12.82), the reciprocal relationship actually being used for admittance] to transfer G_o to an admittance $(1/100) + jB$ (assumed inductive for illustration). Stub 2 is also selected in accordance with Section 12.11(i) to parallel resonate with $+jB$, leaving an output admittance of $1/100$, or resistance of 100 Ω. In practice, the calculations would most likely

FIGURE 5.19.   A common-base amplifier with line matching.

be carried out with the aid of a Smith chart. Note that stub 1 will be less than $\frac{1}{4}\lambda$ long whereas stub 2 will be greater than $\frac{1}{4}\lambda$ long, since both are short-circuited stubs. Stub 2 could have been made an open-circuited stub with a length less than $\frac{1}{4}\lambda$, but generally open-circuited stubs should be avoided [see Section 12.11(ii)].

5.9 PROBLEMS

1. The circuit of Figure (a) uses a vacuum triode with an output resistance of 2000 Ω and an output capacitance of 10 pF. It is to amplify signals of 25 MHz. The transformer has a primary inductance of 1μH and a series resistance of 1 Ω. If the secondary is loose-coupled so that the secondary load has negligible effect on the primary Q, to find the size of capacitor needed to tune the amplifier, and the effective Q and bandwidth of the circuit.

2. The circuit of Figure 5.2(a) uses a tranformer with $L_s = 500\ \mu$H and $k = 0.01$. The coil resistances are small enough to be ignored. If the amplifier has an output resistance of 500 Ω and the circuit is to have a bandwidth of 10 kHz at an operating frequency of 250 kHz, find: (a) value of primary inductance needed to match the amplifier; (b) secondary tuning capacitance; (c) secondary load resistance if no appreciable coupling from the primary exists.

3. An amplifier has an internal feedback capacitance of 10 pF, which has to be neutralized. It operates at 5 MHz, and the output transformer is connected with a tapped primary at $N_a : N_b = 1{:}3$. Its primary inductance is $5\ \mu$H. If Hazeltine neutralization is to be used, calculate the size of neutralizing capacitor needed.

4. If the input transformer is tapped with the same ratio as in Problem 4, calculate the size of neutralizing capacitor for Rice neutralization of the same amplifier.

5. An amplifier has an input capacity of 50 pF, an output capacity of 5 pF, and a feedback capacity of 10 pF. Calculate the size of inductor needed to common-circuit-neutralize this amplifier at 50 MHz.

6. Calculate the conversion transconductance of a multiplicative mixer circuit for which g_{max} is 2 mS at $V_{B_{max}} = 2$ V. The bias level is adjusted so that the Fourier coefficient a_1 is 0.25 and the local oscillator generates a peak-to-peak voltage of 1 V.

7. An additive mixer uses a diode whose characteristic can be approximated by equation $I_d = 0.002\ V_d + 0.0005\ V_d^2$. Find the conversion transconductance if the oscillator voltage produced is 0.5 V peak to peak.

8. Explain the principle of stagger tuning of transformer-coupled IF amplifiers.

9. Why is stagger tuning preferable to in-line tuning?

10. Calculate the lengths of tuning stubs and transformer sections needed if an amplifier with an output resistance of 1500 Ω is to be matched to a 600-Ω line, at 50 MHz. The line has a velocity factor $(1/\sqrt{\epsilon_r})$ of 0.8, and the same type of line is to be used for the sections.

11. Why is the common-base amplifier preferred for many RF amplifier applications?

12. The uncompensated amplifier of Figure 5.1(a) has a first-stage load resistance of 5 Kohms, a coupling capacitance of 1.0 uF and an input resistance to the second stage of 10 Kohms. (a) Find the uncompensated lower cutoff frequency. (b) Find the values of C_1, R_2 needed to extend the lower cutoff frequency to 1 Hz.

13. The FET amplifier of Figure 5.13(a) has $R_c = 5$ K, $C = 10$ uF, $C_o = 2$ pF, $C_i = 15$ pF, $C_s = 1$ pF. (a) Find the uncompensated upper cutoff frequency. (b) Find the value of compensating inductor to give maximally flat compensation. (c) Find the compensated value of the upper cutoff frequency.

14. A transmitter output amplifier is matched to the load by a tuned transformer. The output resistance of the amplifier is 10 Kohms, the load resistance is 600 Ohms and the frequency is 1 MHz. (a) What turns ratio is required for the transformer, assuming a coupling coefficient of unity. (b) If the effective Q is to be 20, determine the values of L_1 and C_1.

15. A 10 MHz transmitter with an output resistance of 5 ohms is to be matched to a 50 ohm transmission line using an L-match network. (a) Which circuit configuration [Figure 5.18(b) or (c)] should be used? Why? (b) Find the values of L and C required. (c) What is the effective Q of the network?

16. The transmitter of Problem 15 is to be matched using a Pi-network with an effective Q of 25. Find the values of C_1, C_2 and L required.

Chapter 6:
Oscillators

6.1 INTRODUCTION

Electronic communications systems could not operate without sources of sinusoidal electrical waves. Many types of oscillator circuits are used to produce these sinusoids, and a few of the more commonly used ones are presented on the following pages.

Feedback oscillators, RC and tuned LC types, are discussed first. These circuits are applicable to frequencies from the audio range up to the VHF range, and may use any convenient three-terminal amplifying device. Discussion here is limited to the bipolar transistor and the field-effect transistor. The crystal-controlled oscillator is included as a tuned LC type, and a discussion of the factors affecting the frequency stability of oscillators is included.

The principles of negative resistance oscillators using two-terminal negative resistance devices is presented.

Although it is not an oscillator in its own right, the frequency synthesizer is included here because it promises to revolutionize the frequency-control scene in communications in the near future, making possible complex systems which until now have just not been economically feasible.

6.2　POSITIVE FEEDBACK OSCILLATOR

Positive feedback forms the basis for many of the more commonly used oscillator circuits. Figure 6.1 shows the general form of the feedback amplifier circuit. Under certain conditions, positive feedback can be created, and oscillations will build up in the circuit.

Barkhausen stated the conditions necessary for a feedback circuit to oscillate. Simply stated, the *Barkhausen criterion* says that, if a feedback circuit is to *maintain* oscillation: (1) the net gain around the feedback loop must be ≥ 1, and (2) the net phase shift around the loop must be a positive integer multiple of 2π radians or 360°:

$$\text{Loop Gain} = |GH|\ \underline{/\Theta} \tag{6.1}$$

where $n = 0, 1, 2,\ldots$, $\Theta = n \cdot 360°$, and $|GH| \geq 1$.

Most electronic amplifiers are of the sort which create a phase inversion or a phase shift of 180° and some value of gain greater than unity. In oscillator circuits, an amplifier of this sort is included in the forward part of the loop (G in Figure 6.1) and a passive phase shifting network of some type is used in the feedback part of the loop (H in Figure 6.1). From Figure 6.1, the total loop gain can be stated as the product of the two complex numbers, G and H. The overall gain with feedback is expressed as

$$A_v = \frac{G}{1 - GH} \tag{6.2}$$

where　A_v　= overall circuit complex gain (magnitude and phase angle)
　　　　G　= forward-portion complex gain
　　　　H　= feedback-portion complex gain
　　　　GH = loop complex gain

In many oscillators, G and H each have a phase shift of 180° or are negative. If the magnitude of $|GH|$ is unity, the overall gain with feedback is ∞,

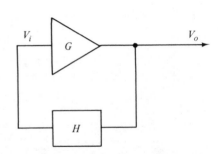

FIGURE 6.1.　The oscillator as a positive feedback amplifier.

indicating that oscillations will take place. If the magnitude $|GH|$ is greater than unity, oscillations will grow. In practical oscillators, these oscillations continue to grow until amplifier nonlinearities such as saturation limit the gain $|GH|$ to unity. After that, the magnitude adjusts itself automatically to maintain unity gain, or a "stable" condition of oscillations.

Frequency of oscillations is determined by components in H which create the additional 180° phase shift. These components are chosen carefully so that the 180° phase shift occurs at only one frequency, and the circuit oscillates at that frequency.

6.3 RC PHASE-SHIFT OSCILLATOR

The RC phase-shift oscillator is a direct application of the theory of feedback as expressed by the Barkhausen criterion. Figure 6.2 shows the arrangement of the circuit. Virtually any RC network that will provide the required phase shift can be used. The one shown uses three RC lead sections in cascade, each with the same time constant (i.e., equal R's and equal C's). At the frequency of oscillation, each section provides about one third of the total phase shift of 180° required. The amplifier provides a further 180° phase shift and the necessary gain to compensate for the losses of the shifting network.

$$
\begin{aligned}
g_m &= 4.0 \text{ mSie} \\
r_d &= 18 \text{ k}\Omega \\
C &= 0.001 \text{ }\mu\text{F} \\
R &= 100 \text{ k}\Omega \\
R_D &= 18 \text{ k}\Omega
\end{aligned}
$$

FIGURE 6.2. The RC phase-shift oscillator.

The analysis of the phase-shift network shows that at the frequency for which the phase shift of the network is 180°, the losses of the network reduce the output voltage to 1/29 of the input voltage, and the frequency at which this occurs is given by

$$f_{180} = \frac{1}{2\pi\sqrt{6}RC} \quad \text{and} \quad \left|\frac{V_o}{V_i}\right|_{180} = \frac{1}{29} \tag{6.3}$$

The amplifier must provide a minimum gain of 29 in order to maintain oscillations. In practice, a gain of about 10 dB larger than this would be provided to guarantee that oscillations will start.

Since the output of the phase-shift network is connected to the input of the amplifier, the input resistance of the amplifier will load the phase-shift network sufficiently to change its characteristics. It is therefore desirable for the amplifier to have an input resistance much higher than the value of R used in the phase-shift network, or some isolating network must be provided so that the network is undisturbed by the connection of the amplifier.

The amplitude of oscillations is controlled by the fact that as amplitude increases, the amplifier drives into a nonlinear portion of its characteristics, and its effective gain is reduced, to the value 1/29. The output can be maintained more nearly sinusoidal if the gain of the amplifier is maintained nearer to the value 29, so that the peaks do not drive so far into the nonlinear region. An amplifier with automatic gain control can be used to provide an almost pure sinusoidal output.

The phase-shift oscillator is most often used to generate low-frequency sinusoidal signals for testing purposes. The variation of the values of C or R or both allow adjustment of the frequency of oscillation over very wide ranges, from a few hertz to several megahertz. Ganged capacitors are used to allow for frequency adjustment.

Example 6.1   The oscillator of Figure 6.2 uses a FET which is biased to give a transconductance $g_m = +4.0$ mS with a dynamic drain resistance $r_d = 18$ kΩ. Its interelectrode capacities can be ignored, and the loading of the amplifier output by the shifting network can be ignored. Find:

(a) The frequency of oscillation

(b) Whether or not it will oscillate.

Solution   (a) The frequency of oscillation is

$$f_o = \frac{1}{2\pi\sqrt{6}RC} = \frac{1}{6.28 \times 2.45 \times 0.001\mu F \times 0.1M\Omega} = 650 \text{ Hz}$$

(b) The complex input impedance of the phase-shift network works out to about $83 - j270$ kΩ; in parallel with the 18-kΩ drain resistor, its loading effect is negligible. (It causes about a 3° error in the phase-shift calculation.) Thus the load of the amplifier may be taken as 18 kΩ. The voltage gain is calculated as

$$A_v = -g_m\,(r_d\,\|R_D\,) = -4.0 \times (18\,\|\,18) = -36$$

This gain is sufficient to maintain oscillations.

6.4 TUNED LC OSCILLATOR

The tuned LC oscillator is another example of the feedback type of oscillator. This equivalent circuit is valid only in determining the startup gain of the circuit. The circuit is shown in Figure 6.3(a), with its equivalent circuit in Figure 6.3(b). The gain in this case is provided by a common-emitter amplifier, although any amplifier that provides sufficient inverting gain will suffice. The load of the amplifier is comprised of the parallel-tuned LC tank circuit, in parallel with the amplifier output resistance, and the amplifier input resistance reflected back through the transformer. The transformer provides a convenient coupling medium to the input, and serves primarily to provide the 180° phase shift necessary to provide positive feedback. The coupling capacitor, base resistor, and the base-emitter junction provide a clamping circuit which biases the transistor toward cutoff as the signal level rises. This causes a reduction in the amplifier gain, until the loop gain falls to unity, just sufficient to maintain oscillations.

At the parallel resonant frequency of the tank circuit made up of the transformer primary inductance and the capacitor, the net susceptance of the tank is zero, and the tank circuit looks like a pure resistance. Under these conditions, the phase shift in the amplifier is 180° and the transformer provides a further 180° shift, yielding a net shift of 0° (or 360°) for the loop. If the frequency should drop below the resonant value, the tank looks like an inductance and causes the voltage gain to lead the 180° value by a small amount. If the frequency is high, the tank is capacitive, and the output voltage lags. Oscillation can only take place at the frequency for which the loop phase shift is zero, that is, at the parallel resonant frequency of the tank circuit.

The amplifier must only make up for the circuit losses and the turns ratio of the transformer. Since the transformer can provide a turns ratio greater than unity, it is possible to make an oscillator of this type using an amplifier with a voltage gain less than unity!

Resistive loading of the tank circuit does two things. It causes a slight shift of the resonant frequency, and it causes the frequency determination to

(a)

(b)

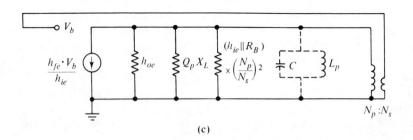

(c)

FIGURE 6.3.   The tuned *LC* oscillator: (a) Circuit; (b) ac equivalent circuit; (c) Simplified ac equivalent circuit.

be less stable. Thus it is desirable to use a tank circuit with a high Q, especially at the higher frequencies. The resonant frequency of the oscillator is given by Eq. (6.4) along with the gain required of the amplifier:

$$f_o = \frac{1}{2\pi\sqrt{LC}} \text{ and } |A_v|_{(amp)} \geqq \frac{L_p}{M} \qquad (6.4)$$

assuming amplifier output resistance has negligible effect.

The base resistors provide the initial bias conditions to allow oscillations to start. The transistor is biased to the middle of its active region, where it provides the greatest gain. After the oscillations start to buildup, each successive positive peak drives the base into conduction and charges the coupling capacitor up more negatively. This puts a bias on the base of the transistor during the rest of each cycle which cuts the transistor off. The mode of operation of the transistor after this is as a class C amplifier. The magnitude of oscillations will continue to build up until the circuit nonlinearities or self-bias reduces the loop gain to unity.

Output can be obtained from the circuit either by capacitive coupling from the collector or by another secondary winding on the transformer. Usually, a buffer amplifier with a constant high value of input impedance will follow to prevent load changes from affecting the oscillator stability.

Example 6.2

The circuit of Figure 6.3 uses a transistor with an $h_{fe} = 100$, $h_{ie} = 5\,k\Omega$, $h_{oe} = 1/50\,k\Omega$. The transformer has a mutual inductance of $25\,\mu H$ and a primary inductance of $100\,\mu H$ and a Q of 100 at the resonant frequency. The tuning capacitor is $100\,pF$. Secondary circuit loading is negligible. Find:

(a) The frequency of oscillation

(b) Whether it will oscillate or not

Solution

(a) The frequency of oscillation is

$$f_o = \frac{1}{2\pi\sqrt{LC}} = \frac{1}{6.28 \times \sqrt{100\,\mu H \times 100\,pF}} = 1.59\,\text{MHz}$$

(b) The amplifier load resistance is

$$R'_L = \frac{1}{h_{oe}} \,\|\, Q_p X_L$$

$$= 50\,k\Omega \,\|\, (100 \times 2\pi \times 1.59\,\text{MHz} \times 100\,\mu H)$$

$$= 33.3\,k\Omega$$

The amplifier gain is

$$A_v = -\frac{1 + h_{fe}}{h_{ie}} \cdot R_L'$$

$$= -\frac{1 + 100}{5} \times 33.3$$

$$= -673$$

$$\frac{L_p}{M} = \frac{100}{25} = 4 \ll |A_v|$$

This is more than sufficient to guarantee oscillations.

6.5 TUNED CIRCUIT OSCILLATORS

6.5.1 General Oscillator Form

The general form of a tuned circuit oscillator is shown in Figure 6.4. An inverting amplifier provides the necessary gain, and a delta network of three complex impedances forms the phase-shifting network between the input and output of the amplifier. The circuit oscillates at the frequency for which the loop phase shift is $0°$, and the loop gain is equal to or greater than unity. The amplitude of oscillations is limited by the amplifier being driven into its nonlinear region, where its gain is reduced.

The circuit can be analyzed by breaking the circuit at the amplifier input and calculating the loop gain from V_i to V_i'. If the amplifier input

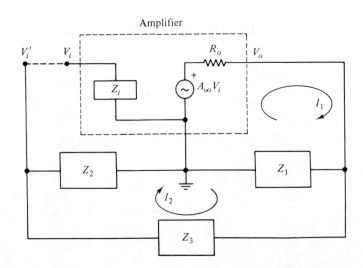

FIGURE 6.4. The general oscillator circuit. Z_1, Z_2, and Z_3 form a series-resonant circuit.

impedance is large enough to be ignored, two loop equations can be written as follows:

$$A_{vo} V_i = +I_1(R_o + Z_1) \quad -I_2(Z_1)$$
$$0 = -I_1(Z_1) \quad +I_2(Z_1 + Z_2 + Z_3)$$

Also,

$$I_2 = \frac{V_i'}{Z_2}$$

and

$$Z_i \cong \infty$$

Solving these equations gives

$$A_{v(\text{loop})} = \frac{V_i'}{V_i}$$

$$= -A_{vo} \frac{Z_1 Z_2}{Z_1^2 - (Z_1 + Z_2 + Z_3)(R_o + Z_2)} \tag{6.5}$$

But at resonance, $(Z_1 + Z_2 + Z_3)$ forms a high-Q series resonant circuit, the loop resistances of which are small enough to be ignored, and the sum of the three reactances is zero, so that

$$Z_1 + Z_2 + Z_3 = (X_1 + X_2 + X_3) = 0 \tag{6.6}$$

and the loop gain reduces to

$$A_{v(\text{loop})} = -A_{vo} \frac{X_2}{X_1} \geq 1 \tag{6.7}$$

A number of commonly used resonant circuit oscillators can be analyzed using this procedure. Some of these are summarized in Table 6.1

TABLE 6.1. Resonant-Circuit Feedback Oscillators

Circuit	Z_1	Z_2	Z_3
Hartley oscillator	L	L	C
Colpitts oscillator	C	C	L
Clapp oscillator	C	C	Ser. LC (net L)
Tuned in/tuned out oscillator	Par. LC (net L)	Par. LC (net L)	C
Pierce crystal oscillator	C	C	Crystal (net L)

according to the reactance types used for the three impedances, and include the familiar Hartley and Colpitts circuits.

6.5.2 Colpitts Oscillator

A field-effect-transistor Colpitts oscillator is shown in Figure 6.5(a). Z_1 and Z_2 are capacitors, and Z_3 is an inductor. The RF choke provides a low-resistance dc path for the collector current while blocking the signal. The coupling capacitor C_c and the base resistor R_g act to bias the transistor into the class C mode once oscillations have started.

$$C_c = 0.001 \ \mu F$$
$$R_g = 100 \ k\Omega$$
$$C_1 = 50 \ pF$$
$$C_2 = 500 \ pF$$
$$L_3 = 75 \ \mu H$$

(a)

(b)

FIGURE 6.5. (a) Colpitts oscillator; (b) Clapp oscillator; (c) Hartley oscillator.

(c)

The resonant frequency, as determined from Eq. (6.6), is

$$f_o = \frac{1}{2\pi \sqrt{L_3 C_{eq}}} \tag{6.8}$$

where $C_{eq} = C_1 C_2 / (C_1 + C_2)$, the value of C_1 in series with C_2. The minimum gain required of the amplifier to maintain oscillation is derived from Eq. (6.7), for $A_{v(loop)} \geq 1$

$$|A_{vo}| \geq \frac{X_1}{X_2} = \frac{C_2}{C_1} \qquad (6.9)$$

Example 6.3

The Colpitts oscillator of Figure 6.5(a) uses an n-channel juntion FET biased to give an initial $g_m = 2$ mS and an $r_d = 10$ kΩ. Find the frequency of oscillation, and whether or not oscillations will start.

Solution

The frequency of oscillation will be

$$C_{eq} = \frac{C_1 C_2}{C_1 + C_2} = \frac{500 \times 50}{500 + 50} = 45.5 \text{ pF}$$

$$f_o = \frac{1}{2\pi \sqrt{L_3 C_{eq}}}$$

$$= \frac{1}{2\pi \sqrt{75 \times 10^{-6} \times 45.5 \times 10^{-12}}}$$

$$= 2.72 \text{ MHz}$$

The open-circuit gain of the amplifier is

$$A_{vo} = -g_m \, r_d = -2 \text{ mS} \times 10 \text{ kΩ} = -20$$

The total loop gain [from Eq. (6.7)] is

$$A_{v(loop)} = -A_{vo} \left(\frac{C_1}{C_2} \right) = +20 \times \frac{50}{500} = +2 (> 1)$$

Therefore, oscillations will start.

6.5.3 Clapp Oscillator

The *Clapp oscillator* is a particular version of the Colpitts circuit. The difference between the two is that X_3 is comprised of an inductor and capacitor in series, such that the net reactance at resonance is inductive. The capacitors used for X_1 and X_2 are much larger than the one used in X_3, so the series resonant frequency is controlled mainly by C_3. As a result, changes in the input impedance of the amplifier, which appear in parallel with C_1, do not have as much effect on the resonant frequency as they do in the Colpitts circuit, and the result is a much more stable oscillator circuit. The Clapp oscillator is shown in Figure 6.5(b).

The resonant frequency is determined by L_3 in series with an equivalent capacitance made up of the series combination of C_1, C_2, and C_3, as given by Eq. (6.8), where

$$C_{eq} = C_1 \text{ ser. } C_2 \text{ ser. } C_3 = \frac{1}{\dfrac{1}{C_1} + \dfrac{1}{C_2} + \dfrac{1}{C_3}} \qquad (6.10)$$

Equation (6.9) gives the gain requirement for self-starting oscillations.

6.5.4 Hartley Oscillator

The *Hartley circuit* is one of the most frequently used of the resonant oscillators. It fits the general form of the oscillator presented in Eq. (6.4) but uses two inductances for X_1 and X_2 and a capacitance for X_3. Three distinct types arise, depending on whether the two coils are uncoupled, are two independent coils with mutual coupling, or are two parts of a single tapped coil. The latter configuration is nearly always used in practice, and is analyzed here.

The circuit utilizing an *n*-channel enhancement-mode insulated-gate FET is shown in Figure 6.5(c). The biasing for this takes advantage of the special characteristics of the transistor and is particularly simple, no resistors being required. The tapped coil forms a mutually inductive coupled circuit for which the coefficient of coupling k is unity (see Section 1.12.3), and the impedances Z_1 and Z_2 must take account of this. Detailed analysis gives

$$\frac{Z_2}{Z_1} = \frac{X_2}{X_1} = \frac{L_2 + M}{L_1 + M} \qquad \text{(assuming coil resistance is zero)}$$

$$= \frac{N_2}{N_1} \qquad (6.11)$$

(*Note* this is not $(N_2/N_1)^2$ as might have been expected with $L \propto N^2$.)
The resonant frequency is given by

$$f_o = \frac{1}{2\pi \sqrt{L_t C_3}} \qquad (6.12)$$

where $L_t = L_1 + L_2 + 2M$, and L_1 and L_2 are the inductances of sections N_1 and N_2 excluding mutual inductance, and $M = \sqrt{L_1 L_2}$. Substituting Eq. (6.11) in Eq. (6.7), the maintenance condition becomes

$$A_{v(loop)} = -A_{vo} \frac{N_2}{N_1} \geq 1 \qquad (6.13)$$

Example 6.4   The Hartley oscillator shown in Figure 6.5(c) is biased to give $g_m = 1.5$ mS, and a drain resistance of 10 kΩ. The coil is tapped to give a turns ratio $(N_1/N_2) = 3$, with $L_t = 64\,\mu H$ and $C_3 = 39$ pF. Calculate the frequency of oscillation, and determine whether oscillation will self-start.

Solution   From Eq. (6.12)

$$f_o = \frac{1}{2\pi\sqrt{64\,H\mu \times 39\,pF}} = 3.19\,MHz$$

From Eq. (6.13)

$$A_{v(loop)} = -(-1.5 \times 10) \times \tfrac{1}{3} = 5 (> 1)$$

Therefore oscillation will be self-starting.

6.6   CRYSTAL OSCILLATORS

The characteristics of quartz peizoelectric crystals were discussed in Section 1.15.2 on filters. Their use as the frequency control elements in oscillator circuits is discussed here. Crystals can be used to control any of the tuned LC oscillators which were discussed previously, by appropriate connections. The crystal may be used to replace an entire LC tank circuit, or it may be used to replace one of the reactances in a tank circuit. The Pierce crystal oscillator circuit illustrates the method.

The Pierce oscillator, like the Clapp oscillator, is basically a Colpitts oscillator in which the inductor is replaced by the crystal. The circuit is shown in Figure 6.6(a), with an equivalent circuit shown in Figure 6.6(b) in

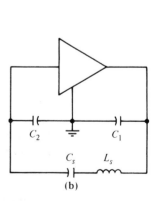

(a)   (b)

FIGURE 6.6. The Pierce crystal oscillator: (a) Circuit; (b) Equivalent circuit.

which the crystal has been replaced by its equivalent circuit. The resonant frequency of the circuit is determined by the series resonance of the circuit made up of C_1, C_2, C_s, and L_s. C_1 and C_2 are both very much larger than C_s, so the resonant frequency is almost entirely dependent on the value of C_s. The input capacity of the amplifier and C_1, C_2, are effectively swamped out by C_s, and the resonant frequency is almost the series value of the crystal itself. The feedback ratio is the ratio of X_{C2}/X_{C1} [from Eq. (6.7)], and the required loop gain is determined in the same manner.

Any energy withdrawn from the circuit to drive successive amplifier stages is the equivalent of spoiling the Q of the crystal, and special coupling circuits must be used to minimize the loading effect. In practice, a parallel-tuned tank circuit tuned to the desired frequency is placed in the collector circuit and the next stage transformer coupled through this tank. The load impedance presented to the amplifier can thus be increased to the point of were it does not greatly affect the crystal Q.

Example 6.5   The circuit of Figure 6.6 uses a 5-MHz quartz crystal, and a transistor with $h_{ie} = 5\,\text{k}\Omega$, $h_{fe} = 99$, $h_{oe} = 0.02\,\text{mS}$, $C_2 = 5000\,\text{pF}$. Find the value of C_1 necessary to give a 20-dB guarantee that oscillations will be self-starting.

Solution

$$A_{vo} = -\frac{1 + h_{fe}}{h_{oe} \cdot h_{ie}} = -\left(\frac{1 + 99}{0.02 \times 5}\right) = -1000$$

$$A_{v(loop)} = \frac{-A_{vo}\,C_1}{C_2} = +10 \qquad \text{(from the 20 dB requirement)}$$

$$C_1 = \frac{10\,C_2}{|A_{vo}|} = \frac{10 \times 5000}{1000} = 50\,\text{pF}$$

6.7 STABILITY

The stability of oscillator operation can be discussed from a number of points of view. First, will the oscillator produce the desired frequency? Will the oscillator start up by itself and maintain oscillations under all normal load conditions? Will it maintain oscillations at the desired level under all load conditions? Will it produce a sinusoidal output, or will it contain harmonics? These topics will each be discussed in turn.

6.7.1 Frequency Stability

Practically all the components in an oscillator will have some effect in determining the frequency of oscillation. The frequency of the tuned oscillator, for example, is dependent on the series *impedance* of $Z_1 + Z_2 + Z_3$. The analysis given above assumed that these were all ideal isolated reactances (negligible resistance) which is not quite the truth. Amplifier output and input resistances and circuit resistances spoil the Q and broaden out the impedance curve near resonance. Also, the parasitic capacities in the amplifier appear directly in parallel with Z_1 and Z_2. These parasitics can vary over a wide range, depending on the amplifier supply voltage, temperature, and loading, and unless some effort is made to isolate these changing elements from the tank circuit, they will cause changes to occur in the resonant frequency.

The amount of change occurring in the amplifier parameters can be reduced by providing its power from a voltage-regulated source and by using a buffer amplifier with a high input impedance to isolate the oscillator from successive stages. Temperature effects can be minimized by operating the oscillator at low power levels, and providing thermal isolation against ambient temperature variations (the whole oscillator circuit may be mounted in a temperature-regulating crystal oven, for instance).

Isolation of the tank circuit from the amplifier parasitics can be improved by means of impedance transformation. In the Hartley oscillator this may be accomplished by providing a second tap point on the coil L_2 so that the amplifier input capacity only appears in parallel with a fraction of L_2. Further, the ratio L/C can be increased (within limits) so that the reactance of the coil L_2 is very much larger than the parasitic reactance, and its detuning effect will not be so pronounced. For the Colpitts circuit, the ratio C/L can be increased so as to swamp the parasitic capacity, but the degree of improvement is limited by the small size of coil that may result.

The Clapp circuit provides a greater degree of stability, because the oscillating frequency is almost entirely due to the series reactance of Z_3, and any convenient values of L_3 and C_3 may be used to yield the correct frequency. Isolation from the amplifier may be improved by several orders of magnitude. The price that must be paid for this improvement, however, is that more gain is required from the amplifier to maintain oscillations.

The tuned circuit itself may experience changes of parameters which will cause a change of oscillator frequency. Temperature changes can cause significant changes of parameters. These temperature changes may be partially compensated by choosing elements whose temperature coefficients cancel out in the circuit, and the whole circuit may be placed in a temperature-controlled environment. Each component in the tank circuit must be a rigid entity and must be protected from mechanical vibrations. Even very small distortions of a coil will cause a shift of the oscillating frequency. Microphonics or changes of the tank-circuit parameters by sound waves or mechanical vibrations cause frequency modulation of the oscillator and is a common and serious problem. Acoustic shielding and shock mounting are a must for the oscillator.

A low Q in the tank circuit (because of coil resistance or loading) results in a broadening of the notch which appears in the impedance versus frequency curve for the tank circuit. The result is that the frequency of oscillation can shift a considerable amount near the true oscillation frequency. The higher the Q becomes, the less this shift is allowed to become. Circuit Q's from 10 to 1000 are practical in ordinary LC circuits and, with careful design, yield frequency stabilities to about 1 part in 10^4. For stabilities greater than this, crystals must be used. A quartz crystal run at ambient temperature can give stabilities of about 1 in 10^5 while a temperature-controlled oscillator can give about 1 in 10^6.

6.7.2 Self-starting

Self-starting is ensured by guaranteeing that the amplifier is biased to a point before oscillation where its gain provides several dB more than the minimum according to the Barkhausen criterion. If self-starting is to be guaranteed under all operating conditions, it is necessary to make sure that the amplifier is unaffected by temperature and supply variations, as mentioned above.

6.7.3 Amplitude Stability

The amplitude of oscillations is determined by the factors which reduce the amplifier gain to the point where the loop gain is unity. These factors may be the inherent nonlinearity of the amplifying device, such as the onset of saturation, self bias, or externally provided amplitude clipper. In any case, the amplitude is subject to variation with load, operating conditions, and supply variations.

A more stable mode of operation can be obtained by using an amplifier whose gain can be controlled by the application of an external bias voltage. An amplitude detector is used to provide a bias voltage which increases with increasing signal amplitude, and this increasing bias is used to decrease the gain of the amplifier (automatic gain control). Very good amplitude stability can be obtained by this means, even under varying load conditions.

6.7.4 Linearity

Some harmonic distortion will result in the output waveform of any oscillator which relies on the amplifier nonlinearity to limit oscillation amplitude. The larger the signal amplitude is allowed to become, the more pronounced is the nonlinearity of operation, and the more harmonic content that will be produced.

Linear operation with a minimum of harmonic generation can be obtained by operating the oscillator at signal levels well below the total range of the amplifier used. The degree to which this can be done is limited by the amount of gain margin necessary to start and maintain oscillations, because the reduced amplitude is obtained by reducing the loop gain. A more reasonable way to do this is to use an amplifier that does operate linearly over a wide range of amplitudes, and to use an error feedback system to limit the amplitude of oscillations to well within the linear region of operation. Practically pure sinusoidal output can be obtained by this latter method.

6.8 NEGATIVE RESISTANCE OSCILLATORS

Certain two-terminal devices exhibit the property of negative resistance over some portion of their characteristics; that is, over some portion of their operating range, an increase of terminal voltage causes a decrease of terminal current. The dynamic resistance which is the inverse slope of the I-V curve of the device is a negative quantity in this range. If such a device is connected in series or in parallel with a tuned LC tank circuit and biased to a stable operating point within the negative resistance portion of its characteristics, so that the magnitude of its negative dynamic resistance is greater than the damping or loading resistance in the tuned circuit, the circuit will oscillate. In other words, the negative resistance device acts as an energy source which replaces the tank energy dissipated in its internal resistance and the load.

Two basic configurations are possible. The tank circuit may be series-resonant and the negative resistance made part of the series loop; or it may be parallel-resonant and the negative resistance placed in shunt with it. The parallel-resonant circuit is more properly called a negative conductance oscillator. Figure 6.7 illustrates these two circuits. The series impedance of the series-resonant circuit is given by

$$Z_s = R_s + j\left(\omega L_s - \frac{1}{\omega C_s}\right) \qquad (6.14)$$

If the resistance r has a value equal in magnitude to R_s, and negative, the real portion of the impedance expression disappears, and the circuit will maintain oscillations. If the negative impedance has a larger magnitude than R_s, then oscillations will grow in magnitude until some nonlinearity decreases the negative resistance to the critical value. The circuit will oscillate at the frequency for which the series reactance is zero. The conditions are given by

$$|r| \geq |R_s| \qquad \text{to guarantee oscillation} \qquad (6.15)$$

$$f = \frac{1}{2\pi\sqrt{L_s C_s}} \qquad \text{gives the frequency of oscillation} \qquad (6.16)$$

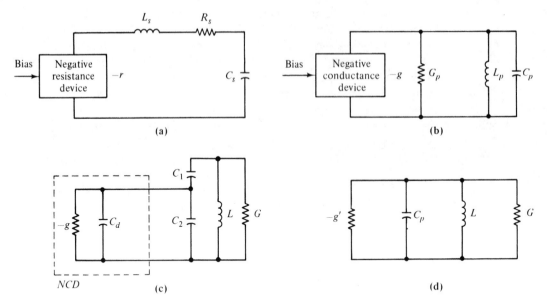

FIGURE 6.7. (a) Negative resistance series-resonant oscillator; (b) Negative conductance parallel-resonant oscillator; (c) Loosely coupled negative conductance oscillator circuit; (d) Equivalent circuit.

The parallel circuit shown in Figure 6.7(b) is the dual of the series circuit. The admittance expression for the parallel circuit is

$$Y_p = G_p + j\left(\omega C_p - \frac{1}{\omega L_p}\right) + g \qquad (6.17)$$

where $\qquad |g| \geq |G_p| \qquad$ to guarantee oscillation $\qquad (6.18)$

and $\qquad f = \dfrac{1}{2\pi \sqrt{L_p C_p}} \qquad$ gives the frequency of oscillation $\qquad (6.19)$

Again, as the amplitude of oscillation increases, the nonlinearity of the negative conductance limits the amplitude by reducing the magnitude of g at the extreme excursions.

Practical negative resistance devices such as tunnel diodes also have a reactive component present in their characteristics. For the tunnel diode, this reactive component is the junction capacity of the diode, and since its value is dependent on diode voltage and temperature, it can cause undesired shifts in the resonant frequency of the oscillator, especially at higher frequencies, where the tank capacity is quite small. Greater stability is usually accomplished by using an impedance transformation between the negative resistance device and the tank circuit. Capacitive coupling is preferred because the resulting circuit is less prone to parasitic oscillation. Figure 6.7(c) shows how the coupling is accomplished for a parallel-resonant circuit. The effective negative conductance g' felt by the tank circuit is obtained from Eq. (1.117) as

$$|g'| \cong |g| \left(\frac{C_1}{C_1 + C_2} \right)^2 \tag{6.20}$$

The reactive component of the negative resistance device is in parallel with C_2, and if C_2 is very much larger than C_1, the detuning effect will be small. However, the ratio C_2/C_1 cannot be made too large or it will become impossible to maintain oscillations because the condition of Eq. (6.21) cannot be met.

$$|g'| \cong |G_p| \tag{6.21}$$

6.9 FREQUENCY SYNTHESIZERS

The frequency synthesizer is not a frequency generator in the same sense as an oscillator but is a frequency converter, which uses a phase-locked loop and digital counters in a phase-error feedback system to keep the output running in a fixed phase relation to the reference signal. Output frequency stabilities are determined by the stability of the reference oscillator, which is typically a crystal-controlled oscillator circuit.

The principles of the frequency synthesizer were developed about 1930, but only found application in very sophisticated equipment because of the cost of the components. Microcircuit chips designed especially for this application are available now at very low cost, and frequency synthesizers are finding increasing application for channel selection in communication equipment.

6.9.1 Phase-Locked Loop

The heart of the frequency synthesizer is the phase-locked loop. A simple phase-locked loop is illustrated in Figure 6.8, and its operation may be described as follows. A stable oscillator produces a square-wave reference frequency f_r which provides one of the inputs to the phase-detector circuit. This reference frequency may be any convenient value but is usually chosen so that a crystal oscillator circuit may be used. A voltage-controlled oscillator (VCO) generates the final output frequency f_o, and is designed so that it will tune over the whole range from the minimum frequency to the maximum frequency desired. Its output is fed directly to the load, and also is

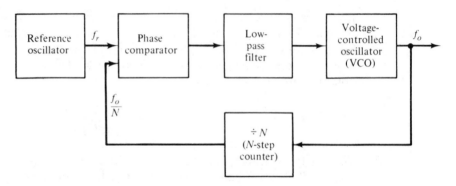

FIGURE 6.8. Basic phase-locked loop frequency synthesizer.

used to drive a programmable binary counter which provides the function of frequency division ($\div N$, where N is the number programmed into the counter). The output of the counter is a square wave at the reference frequency which provides the second input to the phase-comparator circuit.

The phase comparator is a logic circuit which produces a dc signal whose amplitude is proportional to the phase difference between the reference signal f_r and the counter output f_o/N. This dc signal is filtered to smooth out noise and slow the response of the circuit to prevent overshoot or oscillations and is applied as the control input to the VCO. When the phase difference between the two signals f_r and f_o/N is zero, the dc output from the phase comparator is just exactly that needed to tune the VCO to the frequency $f_r \cdot N$. If a phase difference exists between the two, the bias applied to the VCO will change in a direction to raise or lower the frequency f_o just sufficiently so that the phase difference will disappear. Once the VCO output reaches the value $N \cdot f_r$, it will "lock onto" that frequency, and the feedback loop will prevent it from drifting.

The output frequency f_o is adjusted to a new value by changing the number by which the counter divides. This is accomplished by means of thumbwheel switches or by means of a register into which a new number for N can be entered to control the set point of the counter. The number N is the number of pulses which the counter will count before it recycles, coded in binary.

6.9.2 Prescaling

The simple frequency synthesizer described above will only produce output frequencies which are integer multiplies of the reference frequency f_r. If other frequencies intermediate between these values are desired, prescaling must be used. Another reason for the use of prescaling is because at high frequencies (above 100 MHz) programmable counters are not available. Fixed-modulus prescale counters are used to count down to a frequency below the 100-MHz limit, and then the prescaler output can drive a low-frequency programmable counter, which is readily available.

Figure 6.9 shows how a prescaler circuit can be used to allow division by a noninteger number (a number that contains a fractional part). The prescaler circuit is a two-modulus counter; that is, in one mode, it produces an output for every P input pulses, and in the other mode, an output for every $P + 1$ pulses. Two low-frequency programmable counters count the output pulses from the prescaler circuit, the main counter counting B pulses and the second counter counting A pulses.

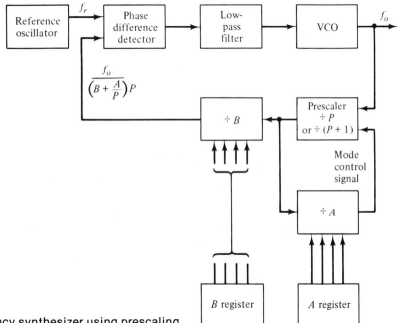

FIGURE 6.9. Frequency synthesizer using prescaling.

At the beginning of a cycle, both counters are set to their programmed numbers (i.e., B and A). As long as the A counter countains a nonzero number, the prescaler will be conditioned to count in the $P + 1$ mode, so the counter chain will count down for $(P + 1) \cdot A$ pulses, until the A counter goes to zero. At this point, the prescaler circuit will be forced to count in the P mode, and also the input to the A counter will be turned off so that the A counter will remain in the zero state until the B counter completes its count. At the point where the A counter has reached the zero state, the B counter will contain the number $(B - A)$ and will then proceed to count down from $(B - A)$ on every Pth pulse from the output. When the B counter reaches zero, both counters reset to their programmed numbers and the cycle begins again.

The result of this prescaling procedure is shown in Eq. (6.22), which relates the output frequency to the reference frequency in terms of the three-counter moduli.

$$f_o = N \cdot f_r$$
$$= \left(B + \frac{A}{P}\right) \cdot P \cdot f_r$$
$$= [(B - A) \cdot (P) + (A) \cdot (P + 1)]f_r \qquad (6.22)$$

Since any fractional number may be stated to a very near approximation as the ratio of two integers, the number of precise frequencies which may be "dialed up" on this frequency synthesizer is very much expanded. A further advantage is that only the prescaler circuit need operate at very high frequencies, and the programmable counters can be made from readily available low-frequency components.

6.9.3 Applications

The most obvious application of the frequency synthesizer is as a digitally programmed (manual or remote) signal generator which may be used for testing purposes, frequency measuring at radio-monitoring stations, or in laboratory frequency-measuring apparatus. Because of the ease of remote setting of the digital numbers to select the output frequency, the synthesizer is increasingly being used in computer-controlled testing stations and other computer-controlled apparatus.

The frequency synthesizer is also being used in multichannel communication link transceivers, where it is necessary to frequently switch from one channel to another. The frequency synthesizer generates the local oscillator frequency for the receiver mixer and also the primary frequency source for the transmitter. The switching is usually done manually, but may also be done automatically, as would be the case in a frequency-diversion system. Since the output frequency will have a stability comparable to that of the reference which may be a crystal oscillator, the flexibility of a variable-frequency oscillator is obtained with the stability of the crystal oscillator. Since most of the components used are inexpensive microcircuits, the result is high-quality but inexpensive communication equipment.

6.10 PROBLEMS

1. A phase-shift oscillator is to be designed for a frequency of 10 kHz, using a special transistor (Darlington pair) with a h_{ie} of 100 kΩ, a h_{fe} of

2000. Base-bias resistors give a parallel combination of 100 kΩ. The third resistor in the phase-shift network is replaced by the amplifier input resistance, and the other two resistors are to have the same value. Calculate the values of R and C, and the value of R_c if the amplifier is to have 6 dB more gain than the minimum needed to maintain oscillations. Check that the input impedance of the phaseshift network does not load the amplifier.

2.   For the LC tuned oscillator of Figure 6.3, calculate the frequency of oscillation and the decibel amount by which the gain exceeds the minimum required to maintain oscillations, when the following circuit conditions exist:

turns ratio	= 3:1	R_1	= 22 kΩ
L_p	= 10 mH	R_2	= 1 kΩ
R_p (coil resistance)	= 20 Ω	h_{ie}	= 8 kΩ
C	= 1 μF	h_{fe}	= 65
C_c	= 1 μF		

3.   A Colpitts oscillator has a coil with an inductance of 50 μH and is tuned by a capacitor of 300 pF across the amplifier input and 100 pF capacity across the output. Find the frequency of oscillation and the minimum gain which the amplifier must provide to maintain oscillations.

4.   A Clapp oscillator is used to tune a radio receiver. For the circuit of Figure 6.5(b), $C_1 = 1000$ pF, $C_2 = 10,000$ pF, $L_3 = 50 \mu H$, and C_3 is a 5- to 150-pF variable capacitor. (a) Find the tuning frequency range of the oscillator. (b) If the amplifier uses a bipolar transistor with a h_{ie} of 2 kΩ and h_{oe} of 0.1 mS, find the minimum h_{fe} the transistor must have to guarantee oscillations.

5.   The Hartley oscillator of Figure 6.5(c) uses a FET with a g_m of 2 mS and a r_d of 20 kΩ. The total coil inductance is 20 μH with a turns ratio N_1/N_2 of 10. It is tuned with a 10-pF capacitor. Find the frequency of oscillation and the amplifier gain margin in decibels (amount by which the gain exceeds the minimum required to maintain oscillations).

6.   A crystal oscillator has the crystal connected between the amplifier input terminals, and a parallel-resonant tank circuit between the amplifier output terminals. A small capacitor provides the feedback path between the input and output. The crystal is series-resonant at 1.50000 and parallel-resonant at 1.50001 MHz. (a) What frequency must the output tank circuit be tuned to guarantee oscillations? What will the frequency of oscillation be? How stable is this parts per million? (b) If the tank circuit were tuned to the second harmonic, would the circuit still oscillate? (c) What frequency would the crystal vibrate at under these conditions?

7.   A negative conductance oscillator uses a coil with $L = 10 \mu H$ and $Q_o = 100$, in parallel with a capacitor of 50 pF. Find the minimum value of

conductance that the negative conductance device must generate, and the frequency of oscillation.

8.   The frequency synthesizer in Figure 6.9 is run from a 1.0000-MHz crystal reference oscillator to produce an output of 180 MHz. The main counter will only work up to 80 MHz, and a prescaler P which divides by 4 is used. Find the values of B and A which are appropriate to these conditions.

Chapter 7
Receivers

7.1 INTRODUCTION

Radio receivers perform the following functions. They serve to separate a wanted radio signal from all other radio signals which may be picked up by the antenna, and to reject all the others. They amplify the separated signal to a usable level. Finally, they separate the intelligence signal from the radio carrier and pass it to the user.

This chapter will examine the operating principles of some of the more commonly used radio receivers, treating them mostly on a block-diagram basis and referring to previous chapters for the individual detailed circuits.

7.2 SUPERHETERODYNE RECEIVERS

Early receivers used for the reception of amplitude-modulated signals or interrupted-carrier telegraph signals used the tuned radio frequency or TRF principle. They were simply a chain of amplifiers, each tuned to the same frequency and followed by a detector circuit. These receivers suffered from poor adjacent signal selectivity, especially when required to tune over wide frequency ranges because the Q of tuned circuits changes with frequency.

The superheterodyne receiver was developed to improve this adjacent channel selectivity by placing most of the frequency selectivity in the *intermediate frequency* (IF) stages after the first frequency conversion. Obtaining this selectivity at the IF is much easier because the circuits remain fixed-tuned at the IF, and do not vary as different stations are selected. The *superheterodyne principle* is such that when two sinusoidal signals of different frequencies are mixed together, either so that they multiply, (or add and are passed through a circuit with a nonlinear transfer function), the output signal will contain signal components at the sum, the difference, and each of the two original frequencies. There will also be mixtures of the harmonics of these signals, but if the two base frequencies are carefully chosen, these will not interfere.

This principle forms the basis of amplitude modulation and all frequency-conversion operations—for example, the frequency multiplexing of telephone channels. The superheterodyne broadcast receiver was the original application of this principle, and is still one of the largest. The name "superheterodyne" is a contraction of "supersonic heterodyne," or the production of beat frequencies above the range of hearing.

The basic superheterodyne receiver is illustrated in Figure 7.1. The first stage is a tuned RF amplifier, the main purpose of which is to improve signal-to-noise ratio (see Section 4.9.1). It also gives some improvement in RF selectivity and a reduction of oscillator re-radiation. However, it is usually omitted in cheaper receivers. The output from the tuned RF stage is fed to the signal input of an oscillator-mixer circuit in which the heterodyning takes place. The oscillator circuit is usually tuned by capacitance tuning, and the three tuning capacitors are mechanically ganged to a single control knob. The oscillator and mixer may be separate circuits, or they may be combined as in the autodyne mixer circuit.

The mixer output (the difference frequency for down-conversion in the receiver) is fed to two tuned IF amplifiers, which are fixed-tuned and provided with sufficient selectivity to reject adjacent channel signals. The output from the IF amplifier is fed to the detector, where the audio signal is extracted, or demodulated. The detector also provides signals for automatic gain control (AGC) in AM receivers, or automatic frequency control (AFC) in FM receivers. The automatic gain control signal is applied to one or more of the IF and RF amplifiers, while the AFC signal is used to correct the local oscillator frequency. The audio output is passed through a volume control to an audio amplifier, which usually consists of one low-level voltage amplifier followed by a power amplifier, and finally is coupled to a speaker.

(a)

(b)

FIGURE 7.1. (a) A superheterodyne receiver circuit. (b) Signal spectra in the superheterodyne receiver.

7.3 CHOICE OF INTERMEDIATE AND OSCILLATOR FREQUENCIES

The intermediate frequency (IF) is generally chosen to be lower than the lowest signal frequency to be converted, although in some special cases an up-conversion may be used. The actual frequency chosen is a compromise. The lower the IF, the easier it is to obtain the selectivity needed to reject adjacent channel signals. However, the rejection of image signals (see Section 7.4) is improved by going higher in frequency. If the IF is too high, and falls inside the signal frequency range, direct feed-through may occur.

The choice of oscillator frequency range is mostly determined by the tuning capacitor tuning range, stated as a ratio,

$$\text{range} = \frac{C_{\max}}{C_{\min}} = \left(\frac{f_{\max}}{f_{\min}}\right)^2 \qquad (7.1)$$

The oscillator frequency f_o may be made either less than the signal frequency f_s or greater than the signal frequency. If it is made less, then

$$\text{IF} = f_s - f_o \qquad (7.2a)$$

If it is made greater, then

$$\text{IF} = f_o - f_s \qquad (7.2b)$$

If the oscillator frequency is made lower than the signal frequency, the range over which the oscillator must tune will be larger than if the oscillator frequency is chosen to be higher. If a high value of IF is also chosen, the tuning range of the oscillator capacitor will become excessive. This problem is less critical at higher signal frequencies but is severe in the MF band, as illustrated in the following example.

Example 7.1

Find the tuning range necessary for the oscillator capacitor in an MF superheterodyne receiver which tunes over the range of signals from 500 kHz to 1600 kHz, and uses an IF of 465 kHz, if the oscillator is:

(a) Higher than the signal frequency

(b) Lower than the signal frequency.

Solution

The frequency range of the signal frequency is 500 to 1600 kHz, which gives a frequency ratio of

$$\frac{f_{s\max}}{f_{s\min}} = \frac{1600}{500} = 3.2$$

Since the capacitance necessary to tune the circuit varies as the inverse square of the frequency, the ratio of capacitance needed becomes

$$\frac{C_{smax}}{C_{smin}} = \left(\frac{f_{smax}}{f_{smin}}\right)^2 = 3.2^2 = 10.24$$

(a) For $f_o > f_s$, the range of f_o is

$$465 + (500 \text{ to } 1600) = (965 \text{ to } 2065)\,\text{kHz}$$

This gives a frequency ratio for the oscillator of

$$\frac{f_{omax}}{f_{omin}} = \frac{2065}{965} = 2.14$$

and a capacitance ratio for the oscillator capacitor of

$$\frac{C_{omax}}{C_{omin}} = 2.14^2 = 4.58$$

(b) For $f_o > f_s$, the range of f_o is

$$-465 + (500 \text{ to } 1600) = 35 \text{ to } 1135 \text{ kHz}$$

The corresponding ratios are

$$\frac{f_{omax}}{f_{omin}} = \frac{1135}{35} = 32.4 \quad \text{and} \frac{C_{omax}}{C_{omin}} = 32.4^2 = 1052 \quad \text{(Impractical!)}$$

The upper oscillator range must be used. This combination of IF and oscillator frequencies is typical of nearly all AM broadcast receivers for the MF band intended for the domestic market.

7.4 IMAGE REJECTION

The superheterodyne mixer circuit produces signal components at the IF frequency which are the difference between the oscillator frequency and the signal frequency. Equation (7.2) shows that the signal can be either above or below the oscillator frequency and still produce an IF signal. If the front end (RF stage) of the receiver does not have very selective tuning, which would be the case if only a single tuned circuit were used, the RF stage when tuned to a signal frequency at f_o − IF will also respond to a signal at f_o + IF. This other signal is referred to as the image frequency f_i, which is given by

$$f_i = f_s \pm 2\mathrm{IF} \tag{7.3}$$

where the plus sign is used for the case when $f_o > f_s$ and the minus sign when $f_o < f_s$. The image frequency can only be rejected by the selectivity of tuned circuits placed *before* the mixer. Once the image frequency has been converted to the IF, it cannot be separated from the desired signal.

Figure 7.2 shows the response of a single tuned circuit plotted against frequency. Peak response occurs at the signal f_s, with only a slight drop in response at the limits of the IF bandpass, which is also shown. The oscillator f_o is shown at f_s + IF and the image is shown at f_s + 2IF. The image-rejection ability is the amount in decibels by which the tuned circuit response is down from its resonant response, and can be readily calculated for the single-circuit case. The following example illustrates the problem.

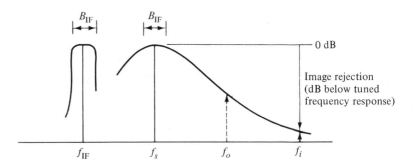

FIGURE 7.2. Image frequency rejection.

Example 7.2   An AM broadcast receiver has an IF of 465 kHz and tunes to 500 kHz with a Q of 50 at that frequency. Calculate the image rejection in dB.

Solution   From Eq. (1.55), the relative response is

$$A_r = \frac{1}{\sqrt{1 + y^2 Q^2}}$$

For this example

$$yQ = \left(\frac{1430}{500} - \frac{500}{1430} \right) 50$$

$$= 126$$

and $$A_r \cong \frac{1}{126} \quad (\text{or } -42 \text{ dB})$$

Thus, if a station with the same signal strength as the desired signal is received at the image of 1430 kHz, it will appear in the output attenuated by -42 dB. If a tuned RF amplifier were included, then the selectivity would be doubled, and the image rejection would become -84 dB—more than enough.

A phenomenon similar to image reception which occurs at higher frequencies is that of *double spotting.* This occurs for exactly the same reason as does image response, and happens in the following way. As the local oscillator is tuned down the spectrum, a signal f_s is received, at the frequency $f_o - $ IF. As the local oscillator frequency is reduced further, the same signal is again received, this time with the local oscillator tuned below the signal so that f_s (now the image frequency) is now $f_o + $ IF. It will be reduced in amplitude, depending on how good the image rejection of the RF amplifier is. The effect of double spotting is that the same station appears to be received for two different settings of the tuning dial.

One solution to both image response and double spotting is to improve the sharpness of selectivity of the RF amplifier, or to increase the IF so that the image lies outside the response of the amplifier, or a combination of both.

Another solution to the problem of image response is to choose a first IF frequency which lies above the maximum frequency to be tuned, with the local oscillator tuning the range above that frequency. The image frequencies for such a system lie even higher, above the oscillator frequencies and can easily be removed in the RF stage by a low-pass filter with a cutoff below the first IF. The system has been somewhat impractical until recently because IF filters with a narrow-enough bandpass at the higher frequencies were not available. Recent advances in crystal and ceramic filters have provided a range of narrow band IF filters for frequencies in the VHF range, and the system is now quite practical.

7.5 ADJACENT CHANNEL SELECTIVITY

The selectivity of the RF stages of a receiver are a function of frequency, being best at low frequencies and getting poorer as frequency increases. Also, it is difficult to get several high-Q tuned circuits to track properly when they are tuned. For this reason, the selectivity of the RF stages of most receivers is purposely left much wider than is necessary for single-channel operation, and the final selectivity is obtained in the IF amplifier.

Channel assignments in an increasingly crowded spectrum are made as close together as possible, with 10-kHz spacing being typical of AM stations in the MF and HF bands. Wider spacing is used for FM stations, and even wider for television and microwave systems. It should be possible for two stations to occupy adjacent channels with minimum spacing between them, and the receiver should be able to separate them. The ideal IF channel bandpass characteristic is illustrated in Figure 7.3(a). It has a flat-topped response within the band, is centered on the channel frequency f_1, has vertically straight skirts, and has uniform rejection ideally infinite outside of the band.

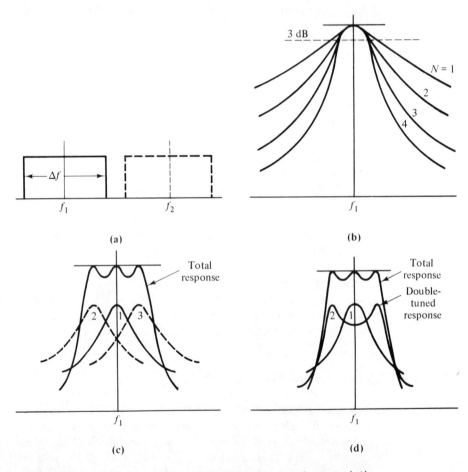

FIGURE 7.3. Adjacent channel selectivity: (a) Ideal bandpass characteristic showing an adjacent channel; (b) Response of cascaded single-tuned circuits; (c) Response of stagger-tuned circuits; (d) Response of overcoupled double-tuned circuits.

Under these ideal conditions, no signal from the band around the adjacent channel frequency f_2 will interfere with the signal of f_1. Practical filters are far from ideal, however, and more or less of the adjacent channel signal will be allowed through. A good receiver should provide 60- to 80-dB rejection of adjacent channels, perhaps more for high-quality broadcast. Typically IF selectivity has in the past been obtained by using several cascaded high-Q tuned circuits in different combinations. The most straightforward system simply uses an IF amplifier consisting of two or more amplifiers, and several undercoupled transformers—all tuned to the IF. Each contributes a single resonance curve, and the total IF response is simply the product of all the IF curves. The Q's are chosen so that the overall response has a 3-dB bandwidth of the required bandpass, and steeper skirts are obtained for each additional tuned circuit in the chain. This system suffers somewhat from both amplitude and phase distortion over the channel bandwidth, although reasonable adjacent channel selectivity can be obtained with five circuits. The response of this system is illustrated in Figure 7.3(b).

Better in-band distortion characteristics can be obtained with the single-tuned system without undue sacrifice of selectivity by stagger tuning. An odd number of tuned circuits is required, and these are tuned so that one is on the center frequency, and each successive pair is tuned to a pair of frequencies equidistant and successively further from the center frequency, as illustrated in Figure 7.3(c). The overall response is again the product of the individual responses, but this time it has several peaks, forming a ripple across the top of the bandpass. This ripple can be "smoothed" by adding more tuned circuits tuned closer together. The steepness of the skirts of the response is dependent on the number of tuned circuits as well.

The overcoupled double-tuned transformer offers a unique variation to the stagger-tuning problem. When two circuits are tuned to the same frequency and then tightly coupled, the overall response will have a double hump, as shown in Figure 1.19. The frequency deviation of the humps from center is dependent on the degree of overcoupling, and the steepness of the skirts is dependent on the circuit Q. Two or more of these transformers are cascaded to make the total IF filter. This system has the advantage over the stagger-tuned system that isolating amplifiers need only be placed between pairs of tuned circuits instead of between individual circuits, thus reducing the total number of amplifiers needed. A typical IF amplifier using the overcoupled transformers would consist of three transformers and two amplifiers. The first transformer would be undercoupled, and each of the others double-tuned and overcoupled, providing a bandpass with five-hump ripple. The ripple amplitude is easily kept to less than 1 dB, and phase distortion is not a serious problem. The analysis of amplifiers of this type is presented in Chapter 5.

IF bandpass in more expensive communications receivers and in special-purpose receivers of recent vintage commonly use one or more integrated circuit amplifiers and special filters such as the crystal lattice filters or mechanical resonator filters discussed in Section 1.15.

High-frequency operational amplifiers have become available in integrated-circuit form, making it possible to build active filters with a wide variety of bandpass characteristics without using inductors. This allows a large reduction in the physical size of receivers. Entire IF amplifiers can now be built in single chips and entire receivers built with the use of two or three such chips. This topic is discussed in more detail in the Section 5.5.1.

7.6 SPURIOUS RESPONSES

The section on image rejection pointed out that a careful choice of IF and good tracking of high-Q coils in the RF stage would effectively suppress the image frequency. Spurious responses are another matter. These will result when a second received signal near the desired signal in frequency passes through the RF tuned circuits and enters the mixer. Since the mixer is inherently a nonlinear device, harmonics of the oscillator frequency, and of the desired signal, and the undesired signal will all be produced and mixed in the mixer. When the sum or difference of any of these products falls within the passband of the IF, it will interfere with the desired IF component as a spurious response.

Generally, an IF will be produced if either of the following equations are satisfied.

$$\text{IF} = \pm nf_o \mp mf_u \qquad (7.4)$$

where f_o = oscillator frequency

f_u = undesired signal

n, m = 1, 2, 3, ... (harmonic numbers)

Rearranging these two equations gives equations which yield all the possible undesired frequencies that could cause interference in terms of the oscillator frequency,

$$f_u = \frac{n}{m} f_o \pm \frac{\text{IF}}{m} \qquad (7.5)$$

A spurious response chart may be made by plotting f_u versus f_o for all the different combinations of n and m up to, say, the fourth harmonic (giving 26 lines, including the desired signal and the image), on linear paper over the tuning range. Figure 7.4 illustrates the chart plotted for up to the

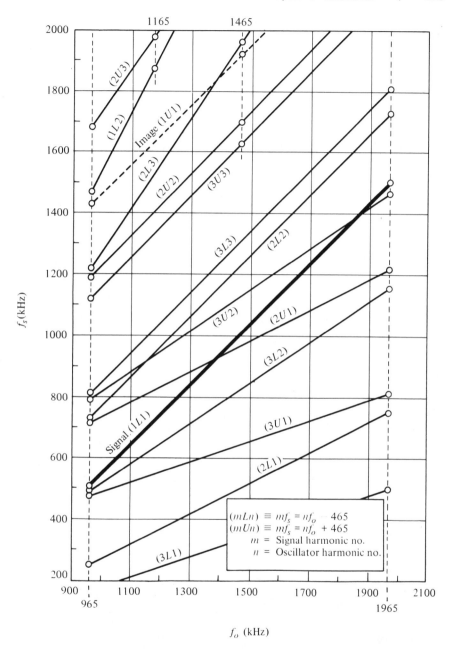

FIGURE 7.4. Spurious response chart for a receiver with a 465-kHz IF.

second harmonic of the signal and the third harmonic of the oscillator. The following example shows how the chart can be used.

Example 7.3   An AM broadcast receiver uses a 465-kHz IF to tune the range from 500 to 1600 kHz. Identify the spurious responses that may occur when the receiver is tuned to 1100 kHz.

Solution   At 1100 kHz, the oscillator is tuned to $1100 + 465 = 1565$ kHz. On the spurious response chart of Figure 7.5 the 1565-kHz oscillator frequency line intersects the desired signal line at 1100 kHz. It also intersects the spurious line $(2f_u - f_o)$ at approximately 1020 kHz. On calculation, the exact spurious frequency would be 1015 kHz, and a strong signal at that frequency would create interference.

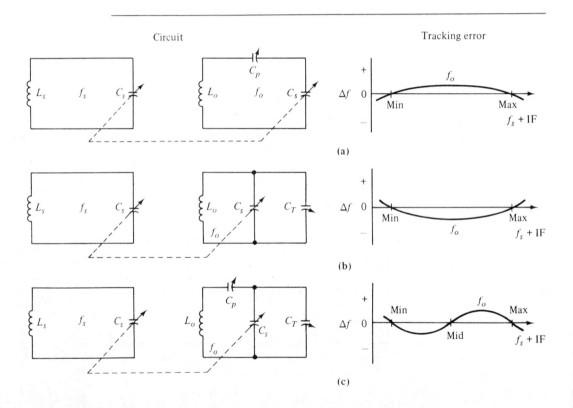

FIGURE 7.5. Superheterodyne receiver tracking methods: (a) Padder tracking; (b) Trimmer tracking) (c) Combination or three-point tracking. In each case both sections of the tuning capacitor have the same value, and the resulting tracking error is shown.

The reduction of the spurious responses requires a number of things. First, the front end must be carefully designed so that no more bandwidth than is absolutely necessary is provided, to reduce the strength of the interfering signals. Next, the oscillator must be carefully designed so that it puts out as little harmonic content as possible. And finally, the mixer should be designed and adjusted so as to produce as few harmonics and at as low an amplitude as possible. Any effort to reduce the spurious responses must, of course, take place before the mixing process if it is to be successful. The undesired signals cannot be removed once mixing has taken place.

7.7 TRACKING

The oscillator tuning of a superheterodyne receiver should follow or track the signal circuit tuning so that for all settings of the dial, the difference between the two is precisely the IF. It was shown in example 7.1 that for the MF band, a capacitance tuning range of 10.24:1 is required in the signal circuit and a range of 4.58 is required in the oscillator circuit. A capacitance considerably smaller than that for the RF stage is required for the oscillator section if proper tracking is to be obtained.

This different capacitance may be obtained in a number of ways. For single-band receivers, a special tuning capacitor can be used which is designed to track over the proper range for that band. In this case the rotor of the oscillator section can be made with a smaller number of plates, giving a lower total capacitance, and one of the plates can be segmented so that small adjustments can be made throughout the tuning range, giving almost perfect tracking.

When a receiver is made to tune more than one band, however, specially made capacitors cannot be used, and ganged capacitors with identical sections must be used. A different value of inductance and special extra capacitors called *trimmers* and *padders* are used to adjust the capacitance of the oscillator to the proper range. The circuit may be made to adjust with only a small padder capacitor in series with the tuning capacitor. Or the circuit may be adjusted with a single trimmer capacitor in parallel with the tuning capacitor, or a combination of both may be used. Figure 7.5 illustrates the methods of connecting the tuned circuits, when equal-ganged capacitors are used. Either trimmer or padder adjustment allows the oscillator to match the desired frequency at either end of the band, but not in the middle, while more or less tracking error is created in midband. For the padder circuit, the oscillator tunes below the frequency it should in midband, so the IF created is higher than it should be and a positive error is created. The trimmer circuit causes the oscillator to tune high, and a negative error is produced. Also, a much larger error is produced by the padder circuit. The combination circuit is such that it can be adjusted to give zero error at three points across the band, at each end and at the middle.

The value of padder capacitor required for the circuit of Figure 7.5(a) is found as follows:

1. Find the minimum and maximum oscillator frequencies and the required oscillator capacitance ratio.
2. Obtain the capacitance ratio and maximum value of the signal circuit tuning capacitance.
3. The oscillator tuning capacitance is given by

$$C_o = C_s \text{ ser } C_p = \frac{C_s C_p}{C_s + C_p} \qquad (7.6)$$

and will have exactly the correct values at $f_{o_{max}}$ and $f_{o_{min}}$. Therefore using ratios,

$$\frac{C_{o_{max}}}{C_{o_{min}}} = \frac{C_{s_{max}} \text{ ser } C_p}{C_{s_{min}} \text{ ser } C_p} = \frac{C_{s_{max}}}{C_{s_{min}}} \cdot \frac{(C_{s_{min}} + C_p)}{(C_{s_{max}} + C_p)} \qquad (7.7)$$

and this equation can be solved directly for C_p.

4. The oscillator coil value is then found as

$$L_o = \frac{1}{(2\pi f_{o_{min}})^2 \cdot C_{o_{max}}} = \frac{1}{(2\pi f_{o_{max}})^2 \cdot C_{o_{min}}} \qquad (7.8)$$

The value of trimmer capacitor required in Figure 7.5(b) is found in the same way except that, in step 3,

$$C_o = C_s \text{ par } C_t = C_s + C_T \qquad (7.9)$$

Example 7.4
Find the value of padder capacitor and oscillator inductor to give two-point tracking for the receiver of Example 7.1, assuming the value of $C_{s_{max}}$ to be 350 pF. Also find the error in oscillator tracking frequency for a signal frequency of 1 MHz.

Solution
(a) From example 7.1(a),

$$\frac{C_{o_{max}}}{C_{o_{min}}} = 4.58 \qquad \frac{C_{s_{max}}}{C_{s_{min}}} = 10.24 \qquad \begin{array}{l} f_{o_{max}} = 2065 \text{ KHz} \\ f_{o_{min}} = 965 \text{ KHz} \end{array}$$

Now, $C_{s_{min}} = \dfrac{350}{10.24} = 34.2 \text{ pF}.$

and from equation (7.7)

$$4.58 \ = \ 10.24 \cdot \frac{(34.2 + C_p)}{(350 + C_p)}$$

giving $C_p = 221.3\,\mathrm{pF}$

(b) $C_{o_{\max}} = \dfrac{350 \times 221.3}{350 + 221.3} = 135.6\,\mathrm{pF}$

$C_{o_{\min}} = \dfrac{34.2 \times 221.3}{34.2 + 221.3} = \ 29.6\,\mathrm{pF.}$

giving $\dfrac{135.6}{29.6} = 4.58$ as required.

then $L_o \ = \ \dfrac{1}{(2\pi \times .965\,\mathrm{MHz})^2 \times 135.6\,\mathrm{pF}} = 201.5\,\mu\mathrm{H}$

(c) At 1 MHz, $\dfrac{C_{s_{\max}}}{C_{s_{\mathrm{mid}}}} = \left(\dfrac{f_{\mathrm{mid}}}{f_{\min}}\right)^2 = \left(\dfrac{1000}{500}\right)^2 = 4$

then $C_{s_{\mathrm{mid}}} \ = \ \dfrac{350}{4} = 87.5\,\mathrm{pF}$

and $C_{o_{\mathrm{mid}}} = \dfrac{87.5 \times 221.3}{87.5 + 221.3} = 62.7\,\mathrm{pF.}$

giving an actual value of

$$f'_{o_{\mathrm{mid}}} \ = \ \frac{1}{2\pi \sqrt{L_o \cdot C_{o_{\mathrm{mid}}}}} = \frac{1}{2\pi \times \sqrt{201.5\,\mu\mathrm{H} \times 62.7\,\mathrm{pF}}}$$

$$= 1418\,\mathrm{KHz.}$$

The desired value is

$$f_o = 1000 + 465 = 1465\,\mathrm{KHz}$$

giving a tracking error of

$$\mathrm{err} \ = \ 1418 - 1465 = -47\,\mathrm{KHz}$$

The oscillator frequency is lower than it should be, so the station will appear at a point higher on the dial than marked, and the signal tuning circuit will be tuned 47 KHz high.

For three point tracking, Fig. 7.5(c), two equations in terms of C_p and C_T must be set up.

7.8   AUTOMATIC GAIN CONTROL

When a receiver without automatic gain control (AGC) is tuned to a strong station, the signal may overload the later IF and AF stages, causing severe distortion and a disturbing blast of sound. This can be prevented by using a manual gain control on the first RF stage, but usually some form of AGC is provided. The AGC derives a varying bias signal which is proportional to the average received signal strength and uses this bias to vary the gain of one or more IF and/or RF stages. When the average signal level increases, the size of the AGC bias increases, and the gain of the controlled stages decreases. When there is no signal, there is a minimum AGC bias, and the amplifiers produce maximum gain.

Simple AGC is used in most domestic receivers and many cheaper communications receivers. In simple AGC receivers the AGC bias starts to increase as soon as the received signal level exceeds the background noise level, and the receiver immediately becomes less sensitive. The AM detector used in these receivers is a simple half-wave rectifier which produces a dc level that is proportional to the average signal level. This dc level is put through an RC lowpass filter to remove the audio signal and then applied to bias the base of the RF and/or IF stage amplifier transistor. The time constant of the filter must be such that it is at least 10 times longer than the period of the lowest modulation frequency received, which is usually around 50 Hz, or about 0.2 s. If the time constant is made longer, it will give better filtering, but it will cause an annoying delay in the application of the AGC control when tuning from one signal to another. The circuit of Figure 7.6(a) uses a time constant of about ¼s.

The circuit shown uses the main signal detector diode for two purposes, detection and the provision of AGC bias. Some compromise in the performance of each is necessary, and in better receivers a second detector is used especially for the AGC. Also, signals may be picked off earlier in the IF and fed to a separate IF amplifier to supply the AGC, thus reducing loading on the IF circuits.

Better response can be obtained by including more gain in the feedback loop. This is accomplished by providing a dc amplifier stage after the filter section. This amplifier produces enough source resistance so that several RF/IF stages may be easily driven from the same AGC line.

(a)

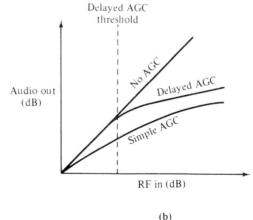

(b)

FIGURE 7.6. Automatic gain control: (a) Simple AGC applied to an IF amplifier; (b) Response of a receiver with either simple or delayed AGC compared to one without AGC.

Connection to the RF stage in transformer-coupled circuits is easily accomplished. The lower end of the input transformer secondary is isolated from ground with a bypass capacitor and connected directly to the AGC line. A resistance back to the collector supply provides the bias current to the base necessary to maintain full class A gain when very low or no signal is present. When several stages operating at the same frequency are connected to the same AGC line, decoupling between them must be used to prevent instability. This can be easily done by feeding the AGC to the earlier stage through a second filter section with the same time constant, and providing good local bypassing at each stage input point.

Delayed AGC is used in most of the better communications receivers. Delayed AGC is obtained when the generation of the AGC bias is prevented until the signal level exceeds a preset threshold, and then increases proportionally after that. The threshold may be fixed by the circuit design, or may be adjustable, and is usually adjusted to start taking effect when the signal has risen nearly to the level which produces the receiver maximum output under maximum sensitivity conditions (full gain). A delayed AGC response characteristic is illustrated in Figure 7.6(b), where it is compared with responses for no AGC and simple AGC.

Delayed AGC is easiest to achieve when an AGC amplifier is included in the circuit. In this case, the amplifier is biased well beyond cutoff by a fixed bias source from which the AGC bias is subtracted. The AGC level then must overcome the fixed bias before any bias is passed on to the controlled amplifiers.

AGC is not usually supplied in the less expensive FM receivers, because these have sufficient amplifier gain so that the last stage operates in saturation for most signals anyway to obtain the necessary amplitude limiting for good detection. AGC may be provided on some FM receivers to prevent overloading the RF stage, and in this case it is used to control the RF stage so that saturation of the earlier IF stages does not occur on very strong signals.

7.9 DOUBLE-CONVERSION RECEIVER

The front-end selectivity of any receiver must reject the first image frequency located at 2IF above the desired signal frequency, and for this to occur, the IF should be large. However, as the IF gets larger, so does its bandpass. Beyond the HF band (about 30 MHz), it becomes impossible to obtain the required bandpass with the good image rejection using ordinary circuits. Thus single-conversion superheterodyne receivers using only one IF are seldom used beyond 20 or 30 MHz.

The *double-conversion receiver* offers a way out of the dilemma, allowing the receiver to get good image rejection and narrow IF bandpass without compromise. Figure 7.7(a) shows the block diagram of a double-conversion receiver which might be used for the 150 MHz FM mobile band. A high first IF of 10.7 MHz is chosen, which allows sufficient selectivity to be obtained in the RF stage tuning to reject the image of the first IF at 171.4 MHz. However, with 15-kHz spacing between channels, several adjacent channels are passed to the first mixer. Variable tuning is seldom used, although more than one channel may be used by switching, so the first oscillator is usually a set of crystals selected by a switch to operate an oscillator in the 10-MHz region, followed by a series of harmonic multiplier stages

(a)

FIGURE 7.7. A double-conversion superheterodyne receiver: (a) Block schematic; (b) RF stage response; (c) 1st IF stage response; (d) 2nd IF stage response.

to obtain the desired oscillator signal in the 160-MHz region. The RF stage is fixed-tuned also, and usually is broad enough to pass several channels near the 150-MHz frequency, spaced 15 kHz apart. Figure 7.7(b) illustrates this RF-stage selectivity.

The first IF filter is a filter block designed with a bandpass of about 150 kHz (sufficient for FM broadcast signals) centered on 10.7 MHz. Usually the mixer stages will supply sufficient gain, and a separate amplifier is not required. The filters used are usually of the crystal-lattice type. Piezoelectric ceramic filters have also been developed which are somewhat cheaper than quartz crystals, but these do not provide as high Qs and have somewhat poorer selectivity characteristics. Figure 7.7(c) shows the selectivity of the first IF, which is sharp enough to eliminate the second image at 11.63 MHz but not sharp enough to eliminate the adjacent channels. Figure 7.7(d) shows the selectivity of the second IF filter centered on 465 kHz and 15 kHz wide, rejecting the adjacent channels at 480 kHz and 450 kHz.

Most of the communications in the VHF band above 30 MHz use FM, so the IF stages will be designed to saturate and provide amplitude limiting. An AGC signal is derived from the unlimited IF signal separately and used to control the gain of the IF and RF amplifiers.

7.10 HF COMMUNICATIONS RECEIVERS

Communications receivers for use in the HF bands from 2 to 30 MHz are usually multipurpose receivers, built for several modes of communications. These modes of communication include normal AM broadcast signals; SSB voice communications usually of the reduced or pilot-carrier type; interrupted carrier telegraph, including Morse, teletype, and digital data; and audio subcarrier telegraph (the subcarrier modulation may be interrupted tone, amplitude-modulated tone, FSK, or PSK, and there may be several channels on one voice carrier). These receivers are made continuously tunable over each of several frequency ranges covering the total spectrum from 1 to 30 MHz. Extra bands to cover the LF and MF bands from 100 kHz to 1.6 MHz may also be included.

Many different features may be included in a given communications receiver, and the block schematic of Figure 7.8 shows an arrangement which illustrates several of these. The circuit is basically a double-conversion superheterodyne receiver designed for reception of amplitude-modulated signals. The RF amplifier is double-tuned and designed to track the local oscillator. A multisection switch allows connection of one of four sets of coils and trimmers to a three-gang mechanical tuning capacitor, so that the range from 500 kHz to 30 MHz may be tuned in four overlapping ranges:

1. The MF broadcast range, from 500 to 1600 kMz.
2. 1.5 to 4.5 MHz, covering mostly aircraft and ship communications.

FIGURE 7.8. A general-purpose HF communications receiver.

3. 4.5 to 10 MHz covering general communication channels and two international broadcast bands.
4. 10 to 30 MHz, covering some international broadcast and general communications, on a sporadic basis depending on ionospheric conditions.

Bandspread is provided by a separate variable capacitor in parallel with the main oscillator tuning capacitor, which allows a calibrated small variation of tuning around the main-dial indicated frequency. It is usually arranged to allow tuning above and below the indicated frequency.

The first IF is chosen in this case to be 465 kHz. The bandpass on this first IF can be fairly broad, say ± 15 kHz. Most of the adjacent channel selectivity results in the second IF, which is here chosen to be 150 kHz. A fixed local oscillator at 615 kHz provides the down-conversion.

The second IF is fed directly to an ordinary AM detector and the AGC circuit. The AGC in this circuit serves several functions. On fading signals it performs its usual function of controlling the gain of the RF/IF amplifiers. The signal from the AGC detector drives a panel meter, which gives an indication of signal strength, calibrated in decibels. This signal-strength meter is useful in comparing the signal quality of received signals. The AGC signal also drives a muting or "squelch" circuit, which disconnects the audio output when signal strength falls below an adjustable threshold level, so disturbing noise during no-signal intervals is eliminated. A switch is provided to allow disabling of this circuit while tuning to different channels. Another switch allows disabling of the entire AGC circuit during reception of Morse telegraph.

A complete SSB detection circuit, including a carrier amplifier, switchable upper and lower sideband filters, and a balanced modulator, are provided. The sideband filters can be crystal, ceramic, or mechanical. Provision may also be made for ISB signals by including a local oscillator. Automatic frequency control may be used to stabilize the first oscillator when receiving reduced carrier SSB signals as well.

The reception of interrupted carrier telegraph signals poses a special problem. An ordinary detector will not put out an audible signal. This is corrected by including a beat-frequency oscillator (BFO) which can be tuned to any position within the passband of the second IF. If this BFO is tuned 1 kHz to one side of center frequency, and a telegraph signal is being received at center frequency, the two will mix and produce a 1-kHz modulation as long as the carrier is on. The result is demodulated to produce the resulting telegraph signals as bursts of 1-kHz tone which are audible. If an external relay is to be driven from the telegraph signal, either the tone version produced by beating, or the AGC signal, may be used to drive it.

Since received signals may be located within a few hundred hertz of each other in the spectrum, separation may be difficult. Sometimes a separate tunable notch filter which may be tuned to any position in the audio pass-band is used to "notch out" unwanted signals. Narrow-band IF filters are sometimes provided as well, which allow selection of passbands down to as narrow as 400 Hz.

When FSK telegraph is to be received, special telegraph channel filters are provided in the audio circuit. For FSK, "mark" and "space" frequencies combine with the BFO signal to produce mark and space tones. A separate filter is used to separate each of these tones and pass them on to a digital circuit, which reconstructs the telegraph signal in pulsed dc form. Since these filters are narrow-band, they can also be used to separate the beat frequency of an interrupted carrier signal from background noise.

Tuning calibration is sometimes a problem in multiband receivers, and a special "marker" oscillator is usually provided to facilitate the recalibration. The marker oscillator is usually a 100-kHz (or a 1-MHz) crystal oscillator which may be switched on when needed. It has a trimmer that allows a few-hertz variation of the marker frequency. The output signal drives a saturating amplifier to produce harmonics at 100-kHz intervals across the entire reception range. Dial-calibration adjustment is allowed either by another panel-mounted trimmer on the oscillator or by a mechanical offset device on the tuning scale. Calibration is carried out by first tuning the receiver to a frequency standard station (such as WWV on 10.0000 MHz) and zero beating the marker oscillator. Zero beating is achieved by simply adjusting the oscillator frequency until the audible beat-tone frequency drops to zero. This will be accurate within the low-frequency cutoff limit of the receiver audio circuits, usually about 100 Hz. Then the receiver is tuned to the portion of the dial in which calibration is desired. The bandspread trimmer is adjusted to zero, and the main dial is adjusted by using the BFO set to the center IF frequency and zero beating with the main tuning. Then the calibration adjustment is made to bring the scale calibration marks into line. The BFO and marker may then be turned off, and the dial will give a true indication as long as the bandspread tuner is kept at zero.

Many variations of this type of receiver have been produced, ranging in price from less than $100 for inexpensive kit models to several thousand dollars for the more sophisticated models. The advent of LSI, of course, will make a distinct improvement in the level of sophistication which can be obtained for a given price. Until recently, vacuum tubes provided the best characteristics for the point of view of noise, linearity, and spurious response, but they tended to be bulky. Entirely transistorized circuits are most commonly available now, and soon integrated-circuit versions should be available.

7.11 PROBLEMS

1. A receiver tunes the 3–30 MHz HF band in one range, using an IF of 40.525 MHz. Calculate the range of oscillator frequencies, the range of image frequencies, and the types of filters needed to make the receiver function properly.

2. A superheterodyne receiver is to tune the range from 4–10 MHz, with an IF of 1.8 MHz. A triple-gang capacitor with a maximum capacity per section of 325 pF is to be used. Find: (a) RF-circuit coil inductance; (b) RF-circuit frequency tuning ratio; (c) RF-circuit capacitance tuning ratio; (d) required minimum capacity per section; (e) oscillator frequency maximum and minimum and frequency ratio; (f) capacitance ratio for the oscillator.

3. (a) Calculate the image frequency range for the receiver of Problem 2. Do any fall in the receiver passband? (b) If the front-end circuits have combined effective Q of 50 at the top end of the band, calculate the image rejection ratio in decibels at that frequency.

4. Plot a spurious response chart for the receiver of Problem 2 for response numbers up to $m = n = 3$. Extend the chart to 2 × maximum frequency and ½ × minimum frequency and crosshatch the IF passband on the chart.

5. (a) Plot the response curve of C versus V_d for a tuning diode which has a $C_o = 510$ pF and a maximum voltage limit of 25 V (about 6 points). (b) If this diode is used to tune an LC oscillator with a coil of 100μ H and a trimmer capacitance of 40 pF, plot the oscillator frequency as a function of applied voltage. Is it linear? If not, suggest how the response might be linearized. (c) Replot f versus log V. Is it linear? (d) Replot log f versus log V. Is it linear? (See Section 10.5.)

6. Repeat Example 7.4 for the trimmer circuit of Figure 7.5(b).

7. Find the values of C_T and C_p required for the circuit of Figure 7.5(c), assuming the receiver of Example 7.1, a 350 pF per section tuning capacitor, and a tracking crossover frequency of 1000 KHz.*

*This is a more difficult problem.

Part Three
Modulation of Signals

Chapter 8
Amplitude Modulation

8.1 INTRODUCTION

To modulate means to regulate, or adjust, and specifically in the case of telecommunications it means to regulate some parameter of a high-frequency *carrier* wave by means of the lower-frequency information signal. The need for modulation first arose in the radio transmission of low frequency (e.g., audio-frequency) signals. It was found that for efficient radiation antenna dimensions had to be of the same order as the wavelength of the signal being radiated. As shown in Appendix B, Eq. (B.4), the frequency f and wavelength λ of an electromagnetic wave are related through the phase velocity v_p by

$$f\lambda = v_p \qquad\qquad (B.4)$$

Most low-frequency information signals have frequencies of the order of 1 kHz, and since electromagnetic waves in space travel at the speed of light the wavelength would be

$$\lambda = \frac{300 \times 10^6}{1000} \text{ m}$$

$$= 300 \text{ km (or about 188 miles)}$$

It is obviously impracticable to build antennas this size.

The problem is overcome by using the low-frequency signal to modulate a higher-frequency signal termed the *carrier wave*, which is then radiated. For example, if the high-frequency signal has a frequency equal to 100 MHz, the wavelength will be 3 m. The carrier wave is always sinusoidal (or cosinusoidal; both forms will be used here without further explanation), and the voltage-time variation may be represented by

$$e_c = E_{c_{\max}} \sin(\omega_c t + \Theta) \qquad (8.1)$$

The parameters that may be modulated are:

amplitude $E_{c_{\max}}$

frequency f_c (contained in $\omega_c = 2\pi f_c$)

phase angle Θ

Frequency and phase modulation both come under the general heading of angle modulation, which is covered in Chapter 10.

Modulation also led to the development of a form of transmission known as *frequency-division multiplexing*, which is discussed in Chapter 9.

Most of the important properties of amplitude modulation can be studied using the assumption that the modulating (low-frequency) signal is a sine or cosine wave (it having been shown in Chapters 2 and 3 that real basic signals are composed of series of sine/cosine waves). Unless otherwise stated, the modulating signal will be represented by

$$e_m = E_{m_{\max}} \sin 2\pi f_m t$$

or

$$= E_{m_{\max}} \sin \omega_m t \qquad (8.2)$$

8.2 AMPLITUDE MODULATION

Here the amplitude of the carrier voltage waveform is caused to vary in direct proportion to the modulating voltage, so that

$$e = (E_{c_{\max}} + e_m) \sin \omega_c t \qquad (8.3)$$

There are a number of ways by which amplitude modulation may be achieved, the most popular being by modulation of the voltage on the output electrode of an amplifying device. In large transmitters (e.g., kilo-

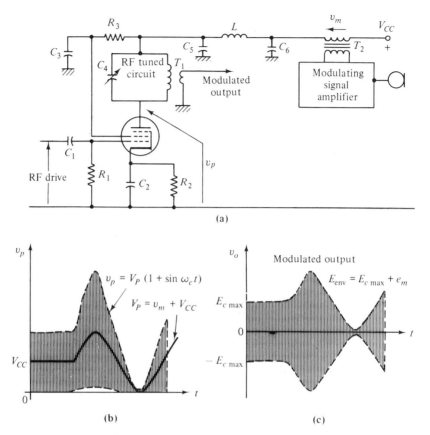

FIGURE 8.1.   Vacuum pentode plate modulator: (a) Circuit; (b) Plate voltage waveform showing the modulation envelope and the dc component; (c) Modulated output voltage waveform.

watt power) vacuum tubes are used and the modulating signal applied to the plate. Figure 8.1(a) shows the basic circuit for a pentode tube. Here the carrier input to the control grid biases the tubes into class C (Section 5.7) by means of the $R_1 C_1$ network; some additional bias for safety precautions is provided by the cathode bias network $R_2 C_2$. The modulating signal v_m is applied in series with the steady voltage V_{CC}, so that the effective "steady" plate voltage becomes

$$V_p = V_{CC} + v_m \qquad (8.4)$$

The radio-frequency drive into the grid of the class C amplifier is adjusted so that the radio-frequency plate voltage swings almost down to zero and up to $2\,V_p$, as shown in Figure 8.1(b); that is, the instantaneous plate voltage is

$$v_p = V_p\,(1 + \sin \omega_c t) \tag{8.5}$$

The steady component of plate voltage is prevented from reaching the antenna by the ac coupling, shown as mutual-inductive coupling in Figure 8.1(a). The modulated output wave has the form shown in Figure 8.1(c). The *envelope* of the modulated RF output is given by

$$E_{\text{env}} = E_{c_{\text{max}}} + e_m \tag{8.6}$$

where $E_{c_{\text{max}}}$ is proportional to V_{CC}, and e_m, the modulating component, to v_m.

The equation for the modulated output wave is then

$$e = E_{\text{env}}\,\sin \omega_c t \tag{8.7}$$

which in full is written as

$$e = (E_{c_{\text{max}}} + E_{m_{\text{max}}} \sin \omega_m t)\,\sin \omega_c t \tag{8.8}$$

A useful measure of the modulation is the *modulation index m*, defined as

$$m = \frac{E_{m_{\text{max}}}}{E_{c_{\text{max}}}} \tag{8.9}$$

In terms of m, Eq. (8.8) may be written as

$$e = E_{c_{\text{max}}}\,(1 + m \sin \omega_m t)\,\sin \omega_c t \tag{8.10}$$

Without loss of generality, the carrier amplitude may be assumed to be 1 V, so that Eq. (8.10) becomes

$$e = (1 + m \sin \omega_m t)\,\sin \omega_c t \tag{8.11}$$

Equation (8.11) is sketched in Figure 8.2 for three different values of m. It will be seen that, for m greater than unity, the inward peaks of the envelope are clipped. This condition must be avoided, as it results in distortion of the modulating signal; such distortion also produces a form of interference known as sideband splatter, described in the next section.

The smallest value of m is clearly zero (corresponding to $E_{.m_{max}} = 0$), so the practical limitations on m may be conveniently expressed by

$$0 \leq m \leq 1 \qquad\qquad (8.12)$$

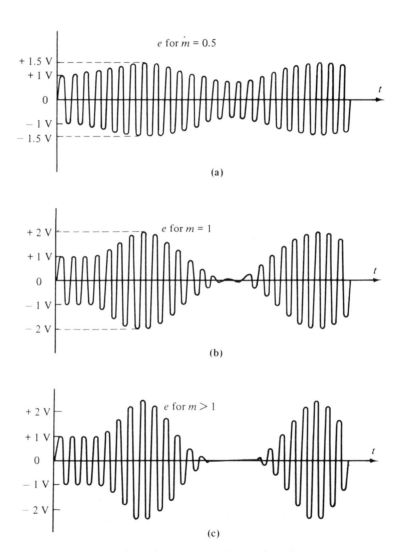

FIGURE 8.2.   Modulated output voltage waveform for various values of modulation index m: (a) For $m = 0.5$ (undermodulated); (b) For $m = 1.0$ (fully modulated); (c) For $m > 1.0$ (overmodulated).

8.2.1 Frequency Spectrum

The idea of a spectrum has already been introduced in Chapter 2, where it is seen that the spectrum shows the amplitude and frequency of the component sine and cosine waves making up a complex wave. The amplitude-modulated wave of Eq. (8.11) is complex, and therefore it also can be analyzed into sine and cosine components:

$$e = (1 + m \sin \omega_m t) \sin \omega_c t$$
$$= \sin \omega_c t + m \sin \omega_m t \sin \omega_c t$$
$$= \sin \omega_c t + \frac{m}{2}[\cos(\omega_c - \omega_m)t - \cos(\omega_c + \omega_m)t] \qquad (8.13)$$

which was arrived at making use of the trigonometric identity:

$$\cos(A \pm B) = \cos A \cos B \mp \sin A \sin B$$

Equation (8.13) consists of three separate components which may be considered to be three separate sinusoidal generators in series, as shown in Figure 8.3(a). The first term on the right-hand-side is clearly the carrier wave of amplitude 1 V and frequency f_c since $\omega_c = 2\pi f_c$. The second term is a cosine wave of amplitude ½ m, and frequency $f_c - f_m$, since $\omega_c - \omega_m = 2\pi(f_c - f_m)$. This component is known as the *lower side frequency*. The third term is also a cosine wave of amplitude ½ m, and frequency $f_c + f_m$. This is known as the *upper side frequency* component. The spectrum representing the amplitude wave is shown in Figure 8.3(b). It will be recalled that $E_{c_{max}}$ was set equal to 1 V. For other values of $E_{c_{max}}$, the heights of the spectrum arrows would be correspondingly scaled.

The frequency analysis expressed by Eq. (8.13) is of more than mathematical interest, and, in fact, one of the most important practical means of signal transmission, known as *single-sideband transmission*, is based on it (single-sideband methods are described in Chapter 9).

Example 8.1   A carrier wave of frequency 10 MHz and peak value 10 V is amplitude-modulated by a 5-kHz sine wave of amplitude 6 V. Determine the modulation index, and draw the spectrum.

Solution

$$m = \frac{6}{10}$$
$$= 0.6$$

The side frequencies are 10 ± 0.005 = 10.005 and 9.995 MHz. The

(a)

(b)

FIGURE 8.3. (a) Generator representation of a modulated wave; (b) Spectrum of a 100% modulated waveform; (c) Spectrum of a 10-MHz carrier modulated to 50% with a 5-kHz signal.

(c)

amplitude of each side frequency is $(m/2)E_{c_{max}}$ (note that this is the same as $\frac{1}{2}E_{m_{max}}$) which is 3 V. The spectrum is shown in Figure 8.3(c).

8.2.2 Average Power

Equation (8.13), expressed slightly differently, is

$$e = \sin \omega_c t + \frac{1}{2} m \cos \omega_L t - \frac{1}{2} m \cos \omega_U t$$

which, for brevity, may be written as

$$e = e_C + e_L - e_U \qquad (8.14)$$

where e_C = instantaneous carrier voltage
e_L = instantaneous lower side frequency voltage
e_U = instantaneous upper side frequency voltage

The instantaneous power developed by the modulated wave across a resistor R is

$$p = \frac{e^2}{R}$$

$$= \frac{(e_C + e_L - e_U)^2}{R}$$

$$= \frac{e_C^2}{R} + \frac{e_L^2}{R} + \frac{e_U^2}{R} + \frac{2}{R}(e_C e_L - e_L e_U - e_C e_U) \qquad (8.15)$$

The squared terms represent the instantaneous power from each of the component waves. The average power in a sine or cosine wave is $P_{av} = E^2/R$, where E is the rms voltage. The rms carrier voltage is $E_c = 0.707E_{c_{max}}$ and the average power associated with the first squared term on the right-hand side of Eq. (8.15)(the carrier term) may be written as

$$P_c = \frac{E_c^2}{R} \qquad (8.16)$$

The rms side frequency voltage is $E_s = 0.707(\tfrac{1}{2}m)E_{c_{max}} = \tfrac{1}{2}mE_c$, and therefore the average power in each side frequency component [corresponding to the instantaneous power terms, second and third on the right-hand side of Eq. (8.15)] is

$$P_{sf} = \frac{E_s^2}{R}$$

$$= \frac{m^2}{4}P_c \qquad (8.17)$$

Considering now the cross-product terms of Eq. (8.15) (within the parentheses), it is easily shown, in a manner similar to that of Eq. (8.13), that these cross-product terms may be expressed as the sum and difference of sine and cosine waves. This means that the instantaneous power represented by each cross-product term is also sinusoidal (or cosinusoidal), and therefore the mean, or average, value is zero. The total average power P_T in the modulated wave therefore consists of the sum of the separate component averages:

$$P_T = P_c + \frac{m^2}{4}P_c + \frac{m^2}{4}P_c \qquad (8.18)$$

$$= P_c \left(1 + \frac{m^2}{2} \right) \tag{8.19}$$

For 100% modulation, $m = 1$, the average power in either side frequency is, from Eq. (8.17),

$$P_{sf} = \frac{1}{4} P_c$$

Also, the total average power is, from Eq. (8.19),

$$P_T = 1.5 P_c$$

Therefore, the ratio of single side frequency power to total power is 1/6. Since the side frequency contains all the information (amplitude and frequency) of the modulating signal, it follows that only one side frequency need be transmitted, which results in a much more efficient use of transmitted power. In practice, of course, the modulating signal will be complex, so the power ratio of 1/6 will not necessarily apply; also a sideband as discussed in Section 8.2.4, rather than just a side frequency, will have to be transmitted. It is still generally true, however, that much more efficient use of transmitted power is made with single-sideband transmission.

8.2.3 Effective Voltage and Current

Let the *effective*, or rms, *voltage* of the modulated wave be E; then the total average power P_T can be expressed as

$$P_T = \frac{E^2}{R} \tag{8.20}$$

comparing this with Eq. (8.19),

$$\frac{E^2}{R} = P_c \left(1 + \frac{m^2}{2} \right)$$

$$= \frac{E_c^2}{R} \left(1 + \frac{m^2}{2} \right) \tag{8.21}$$

where E_c is the rms voltage of the unmodulated carrier. It follows from Eq. (8.21) that

$$E = E_c \sqrt{1 + \frac{m^2}{2}} \tag{8.22}$$

A similar argument can be applied to currents, resulting in

$$I = I_c \sqrt{1 + \frac{m^2}{2}} \tag{8.23}$$

where I is the rms current of the modulated carrier and I_c the rms current of the unmodulated carrier. Equation (8.23) is used as the basis for one method of measuring modulation index, by measuring antenna current, although the method is not very sensitive. Let the ratio of modulated to unmodulated rms currents be

$$I_r = \frac{I}{I_c}$$

Then in terms of I_r, Eq. (8.23) may be rearranged as

$$m = \sqrt{2(I_r^2 - 1)} \qquad (8.24)$$

By monitoring antenna current and setting the reading corresponding to I_c equal to unity, the ammeter may be calibrated directly in terms of m. It is essential that a true rms-reading ammeter be used.

Example 8.2

The rms antenna current of a radio transmitter is 10A when unmodulated, and it rises to 12 A when the carrier is sinusoidally modulated. Calculate the modulation index.

Solution

$$I_r = \frac{12}{10}$$

$$= 1.2$$

$$m = \sqrt{2(1.2^2 - 1)}$$

$$= 0.94$$

8.2.4 Modulating Signal for a Complex Wave

As shown in Chapter 2, suppose that the modulating signal is of the form

$$e_m = E_1 \sin \omega_m t + E_2 \sin 2\omega_m t + E_3 \sin 3\omega_m t + \cdots \qquad (8.25)$$

The modulated carrier wave will be given by Eq. (8.3):

$$e = (E_{c_{max}} + e_m) \sin \omega_c t$$

It follows that an expansion similar to that used to obtain Eq. (8.13) may be applied, resulting in a pair of side frequencies for each harmonic component of the modulating wave. A modulation index for each harmonic component may be defined:

$$m_1 = \frac{E_1}{E_{c_{max}}}$$

$$m_2 = \frac{E_2}{E_{c_{max}}} \qquad \text{etc.}$$

The spectrum is shown in Figure 8.4(a). It is seen from this that *sidebands* occur, consisting of the various upper and lower side frequencies.

Similar reasoning may be applied when the modulating signal consists of sine waves not necessarily harmonically related, e.g.:

$$e_m = E_1 \sin \omega_1 t + E_2 \sin \omega_2 t + E_3 \sin \omega_3 t$$

the spectrum then being as shown in Figure 8.4(b).

In general, the spectrum for the modulated wave is usually shown as in Figure 8.4(c), when the modulating signal consists of a band of frequencies such as speech or music. Modulating signal frequencies for AM broadcast signals in the MF band (550 to 1600 kHz) are limited to a maximum of 5 kHz, and station allocations are spaced 10 kHz apart, requiring a transmission bandwidth of 10 kHz.

An expression for the average power in a complex-modulated wave can be derived in exactly the same manner as Eq. (8.19), giving

$$P_T = P_c (1 + \tfrac{1}{2}(m_1^2 + m_2^2 + m_3^2 + \cdots)) \qquad (8.26)$$

It follows that the rms values for complex wave modulation are given by

$$E = E_c \sqrt{1 + \tfrac{1}{2}(m_1^2 + m_2^2 + m_3^2 + \cdots)} \qquad (8.27)$$

$$I = I_c \sqrt{I + \tfrac{1}{2}(m_1^2 + m_2^2 + m_3^2 + \cdots)} \qquad (8.28)$$

Measurement of rms voltage or current to determine modulation index will yield an effective value m_{eff}, where

$$P_T = P_c (1 + \tfrac{1}{2} m_{eff}^2) \qquad (8.29)$$

Comparison of Eqs. (8.26) and (8.29) gives

$$m_{eff} = \sqrt{m_1^2 + m_2^2 + m_3^2 + \cdots} \qquad (8.30)$$

It must be noted that in order to avoid overmodulation, the *modulation depth* must not exceed 100%, and this generally is more restrictive than the condition $m_{eff} \leq 1$. Modulation depth is defined as the ratio of peak down-

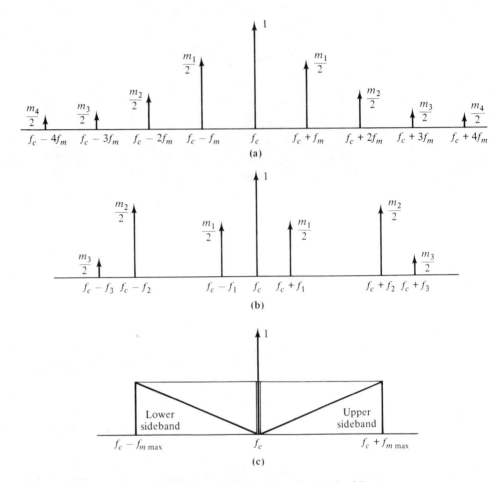

FIGURE 8.4.   Frequency spectrum of an AM carrier signal modulated with a signal containing several frequencies: (a) Spectrum containing harmonically related modulating frequencies; (b) Spectrum containing several unrelated modulating frequencies; (c) Modulation band representation for a complex modulating signal such as music or speech.

ward change in amplitude to carrier amplitude, expressed as a percentage. This is illustrated in Figure 8.5, the modulation depth being

$$\text{modulation depth} = \frac{E_m}{E_{c_{\max}}} \times 100\% \qquad (8.31)$$

Only for sinusoidal modulation does $E_m = E_{m_{\max}}$ and then

$$\text{modulation depth} = m \times 100\% \qquad (8.32)$$

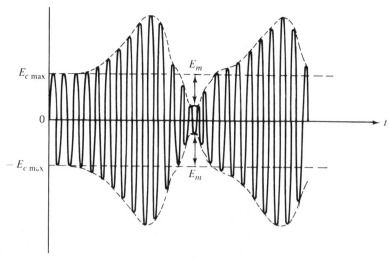

FIGURE 8.5.   Voltage waveform of an AM carrier modulated with a complex signal. The values of $E_{c\max}$ and E_m are extracted from an oscilloscope display to allow computation of an average modulation index for the signal.

8.2.5   Oscilloscope Display of Modulation

A pattern such as the one illustrated in Figure 8.5 may be obtained directly on an oscilloscope, and modulation depth measured directly from this. A better method is to apply the modulated wave to the vertical deflection circuit of the oscilloscope and the modulating signal to the horizontal deflection circuit. The resulting display will be as shown in Figure 8.6(c), where for simplicity a sinusoidal modulating voltage is assumed. Until point A on the modulating wave is reached, the display traces out a vertical line between A and A ' on the oscilloscope. As the modulating voltage moves on to B, the vertical display gradually increases in length until it reaches a maximum at B–B '. As the modulating voltage decreases to C, the display reduces in length, passing through A–A ' again, and reaching a minimum at C–C '.

Comparing Figure 8.6(c) with 8.6(b), it is seen that

$$L_1 = 2(E_{c\max} + E_{m\max})$$

$$L_2 = 2(E_{c\max} - E_{m\max})$$

$$\therefore \quad \frac{L_1}{L_2} = \frac{E_{c\max} + E_{m\max}}{E_{c\max} - E_{m\max}}$$

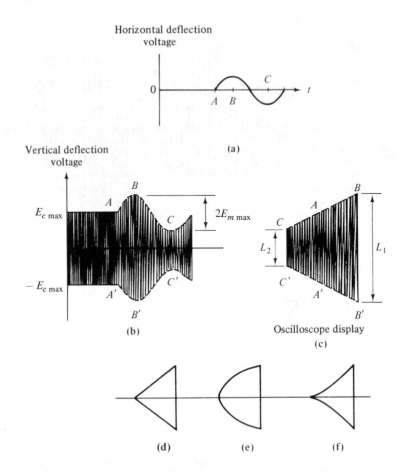

FIGURE 8.6. Trapezoidal display of modulation: (a) Sinusoidal modulating signal applied to the horizontal input; (b) Modulated carrier waveform with sinusoidal modulation signal applied directly to the vertical input of the oscilloscope; (c) Resulting trapezoidal display; (d) Pattern showing overmodulation; (e) and (f) Patterns showing envelope distortion.

$$= \frac{1 + m}{1 - m}$$

from which $$m = \frac{L_1 - L_2}{L_1 + L_2}$$ (8.33)

It will be seen that the trapezoidal pattern will be obtained on the oscilloscope for modulating voltages other than sinusoidal, since the horizontal deflection is synchronized with the peaks of the vertical deflection (the modulation envelope). If overmodulation occurs, the display will be as shown in Figure 8.6(d); the onset of this display is sharply pronounced, so it is a good indication of modulation conditions. Also, distortion in the modulation process shows up as distortion on the diagonal sides, as indicated in Figure 8.6(e) and (f).

8.2.6 Amplitude-Modulation Circuits

Because of historical precedent, double-sideband amplitude modulation is used in the medium-wave broadcast band (550 to 1600 kHz). The radio-frequency power may be of the order of 10 kW or greater, which at present requires the use of vacuum tubes: triodes, beam-power tetrodes, and pentodes are all used. Plate modulation is the most common, and the circuit for this has already been briefly discussed, Figure 8.1. The pentode tube of Figure 8.1 operates in class C, the bias being developed by components $R_1 C_1$ and $R_2 C_2$, as discussed in Section 5.7. The screen grid is supplied through the decoupling network $R_3 C_3$.

Tuned transformer T_1 provides the output coupling for the modulated signal. Components C_5, L, and C_6 make up an RF filter which prevents the radio frequency from entering the dc and audio-frequency lines. Modulation is applied through transformer T_2. For modulation to occur, the "steady" plate voltage must control the amplitude of the plate current. Since pentode plate current shows appreciable dependence on plate voltage only along the limit characteristic, OA, Figure 8.7(a), of the output characteristics, the plate voltage must shift the position of the load line on this limit line. For example, 100% upward modulation occurs when the load line shifts from $a–a'$ to $b–b'$, Figure 8.7(a). The plate current pulses for load lines $a–a'$ and $b–b'$ are shown in Figure 8.7(b). Current pulses for 100% square-wave modulation are sketched in Figure 8.7(c) and the corresponding instantaneous plate voltage in Figure 8.7(d). The RF variations of plate voltage are sinusoidal because the tuned circuit forming the plate load develops a voltage at its resonant frequency, this being the product of circuit dynamic impedance and first harmonic of the current pulses. The current maxima and voltage minima occur together, resulting in high plate efficiency of class C operation. It will be seen that for 100% modulation the plate voltage rises to $4 V_{CC}$ on the upward modulation cycle, and this must be taken into account when voltage ratings are being considered. AC coupling to the antenna results in a transmitted wave as shown in Figure 8.7(e).

The power in the side frequencies is supplied from the modulation source. This can be shown for sinusoidal modulation as follows. Let the modulating voltage be

$$v_m = V_{m_{max}} \sin \omega_m t \qquad (8.34)$$

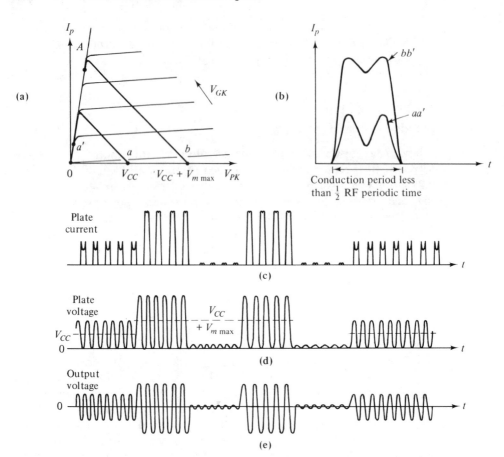

FIGURE 8.7. Pentode plate modulator circuit conditions, for two modulation levels: (a) Pentode plate characteristics showing the upward shift of load line with 100% modulation; (b) Plate current pulses; (c) Plate current waveform for square-wave modulation; (d) Plate voltage for square-wave modulation; (e) Output voltage waveform for square-wave modulation.

The "steady" plate voltage is

$$V_p = V_{CC} + V_{m_{max}} \sin \omega_m t \qquad (8.35)$$

For a correctly adjusted modulator, $E_{m_{max}}$ is proportional to $V_{m_{max}}$, and $E_{c_{max}}$ to V_{CC}, so the modulation index is

$$m = \frac{V_{m_{max}}}{V_{CC}} \qquad (8.36)$$

Therefore,

$$V_p = V_{CC}(1 + m \sin \omega_m t) \qquad (8.37)$$

The modulator sees an effective load resistance R_m, where

$$R_m = \frac{V_{CC}}{I_{dc}} \qquad (8.38)$$

where I_{dc} is the direct current to the plate.

The instantaneous power input to the plate is

$$p = \frac{V_p^2}{R_m}$$

and substituting from Eqs. (8.37) and (8.38) gives

$$p = V_{CC} I_{dc} (1 + m \sin \omega_m t)^2 \qquad (8.39)$$
$$= V_{CC} I_{dc} (1 + 2m \sin \omega_m t + m^2 \sin^2 \omega_m t)$$
$$= V_{CC} I_{dc} [1 + 2m \sin \omega_m t + m^2(\tfrac{1}{2} - \tfrac{1}{2} \cos 2\omega_m t)] \qquad (8.40)$$

The average input power, from Eq. (8.40), is, since the average of the sine and cosine terms is zero:

$$P_{av} = V_{CC} I_{dc} (1 + \tfrac{1}{2} m^2) \qquad (8.41)$$

Comparing Eq. (8.41) with Eq. (8.19), it is seen that the carrier component of power is supplied from the dc source and the side frequency power from the modulation source.

For smaller transmitters, transistors may be used, as shown in Figure 8.8. In this circuit, the transistor Q_3 stage is fully modulated, while diodes MSD6100 (dual package diodes) allow stage Q_2 to be modulated on the upward modulation swing; when the modulating voltage swings below 13.6V, the diode connected to the modulated supply ceases to conduct, thus cutting Q_2 off from the modulation while the other diode conducts, connecting Q_2 to the unmodulated 13.6-V supply. This means that the RF drive to Q_3 is increased at the same time as the collector voltage increases because of modulation, thus maintaining the high efficiency of the Q_3 output stage.

The tuned output stage for Q_3 is the series circuit of 470 pF and L_3, while the various radio-frequency chokes and capacitors in the collector line are for the purposes of filtering.

Since the collector output curves (I_C/V_C) are similar to the I_p/V_p curves for the pentode, the positioning of the load line follows the same principles as those for the pentode, and the conditions are similar to those described for the pentode circuit.

Modulation may also be applied to electrodes other than the output electrode, for example to the grid supply of a vacuum tube or the base supply of a transistor. Applications are discussed in Section 10.3.

FIGURE 8.8. A transistorized collector modulator circuit. Extracted from *Motorola Application Note AN507.* (Courtesy of Motorola, Inc.)

L_1 = 6T #26 wire wound on toroid (micro-metals T30-13) with $\frac{3}{32}$ spacing

L_2 = 2T #26 wire wound on toroid (see L_1) with $\frac{1}{8}$ spacing

L_3 = 2T #26 wire wound on toroid (see L_1) with $\frac{5}{16}$ spacing

L_4 = RF bead (one hole), $\frac{1}{8}$

L_5 = Ferrite Choke (Ferroxcube VK 200)

C_1 = 8 − 60 pF (Arco 404)

C_2 = 1.5-20 pF (Arco 402)

8.2.7   Demodulation

It is, of course, necessary to provide a circuit at the receiver which enables the information signal, the envelope, to be recovered from the modulated wave. The most common circuit in use is the envelope detector, which produces an output voltage proportional to the envelope of the input wave. The basic circuit is shown in Figure 8.9(a). The diode acts as a rectifier and can be considered an "on" switch when the input voltage is positive, allowing the capacitor C to charge up to the peak of the RF input. During the negative half of the RF cycle, the diode is "off," but the capacitor holds the positive charge previously received, so the output voltage remains at the peak positive value of RF. There will, in fact, be some discharge of C, producing an RF ripple on the output waveform, which must be filtered out. As the input voltage rises with the modulation cycle, the capacitor voltage has no difficulty in following this, but during the downward swing in modulation the capacitor may not discharge fast enough, unless a discharge path is provided; this is the function of resistor R in Figure 8.9(a). The time constant of the CR load has to be short enough to allow the output voltage to follow the modulation cycle, and yet long enough to maintain a relatively high output voltage. The constraints on the time constant are determined more precisely in the next section.

From Figure 8.9(a), it is seen that the diode voltage v_d is given by

$$v_d = e - v \qquad (8.42)$$

where e is the input voltage and v the output voltage. Figure 8.9(b) shows e, and Figure 8.9(c) shows v, both for sinusoidal modulation. By graphically subtracting v from e, the graph of Figure 8.9(d) is obtained, this showing v_d. It is interesting to see that the v_d is positive only for very short periods, as indicated by the peaks v_d +, and it is during these peaks that the capacitor is charged to make up for discharge losses. Also, the peak voltage across the diode is twice the output voltage, which can rise to $4E_{c_{\max}}$ at 100% sinusoidal modulation. This should be compared with the conditions at the plate of the pentode modulator described in the previous section.

Diagonal Peak Clipping.   This is a form of distortion which occurs when the time constant of the CR load circuit is too long, thus preventing the output voltage from following the modulation envelope. Figure 8.10(a) shows how the CR discharge curve may control the shape of the output voltage. At some time, t_A, the modulation envelope starts to decrease more rapidly than the capacitor discharges, so the output voltage follows the discharge law of the CR circuit until it once again meets up with the modulation envelope on the rise, at t_B. For sinusoidal modulation, the condition necessary for avoiding distortion of this type is found as follows. The diode,

(a)   (b)

(c)

(d)

FIGURE 8.9. The diode envelope detector: (a) The basic detector circuit; (b) The modulated input waveform; (c) The output voltage waveform; (d) The voltage across the diode.

Figure 8.10(a), appears to supply the RC load with a current I, the modulation component of which has a peak value, Figure 8.10(b):

$$|I_p| = \frac{m}{|Z_p|} \qquad (8.43)$$

where $|Z_p|$ is the modulus of $R \parallel C$, at modulating frequency; and a dc component

$$I_{dc} = \frac{1}{R} \qquad (8.44)$$

(recalling that $E_{c_{\max}} = 1$ V).

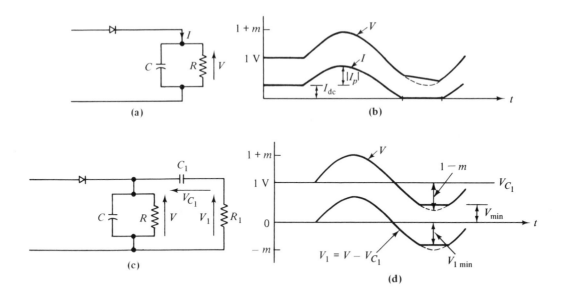

FIGURE 8.10. (a) Basic detector circuit; (b) Output waveform showing diagonal peak clipping; (c) Detector circuit showing the next stage input resistance; (d) Detector output voltage showing negative peak clipping.

If the envelope reduces faster than the capacitor discharges, the diode ceases to conduct (since the capacitor voltage biases it off), and the apparent supply current I goes to zero. During the period the current is zero, the load voltage follows the discharge law of the CR network resulting in the diagonally clipped peak as shown in Figure 8.10(b). Clearly, for the avoidance of diagonal peak clipping

$$I_{dc} \geq |I_p|$$

$$\therefore \quad \frac{1}{R} \geq \frac{m}{|Z_p|}$$

or
$$\frac{|Z_p|}{R} \geq m \qquad (8.45)$$

Negative peak clipping. This is similar to diagonal peak clipping, and results from the loading effect of the network following the diode load, C_1, R_1, Figure 8.10(c). C_1 is a dc blocking capacitor, and R_1 represents the input resistance of the following stage. C_1 is large ($\omega_m C_1 R_1 \gg 1$) so that the modulation component of voltage is passed unattenuated to R_1, and as a result, C_1 maintains a constant charge at the mean load voltage ($= 1\ V$). V, and hence V_1, follow the modulation envelope, maintaining the relationship $(V - V_1) = V_{C1}$ = constant. However, V cannot drop below the minimum level set by

$$V_{min} = V_{C_1} \cdot \frac{R}{R + R_1} = \frac{R}{R + R_1} \qquad \text{(for } V_{C_1} = 1\ V\text{)} \qquad (8.46)$$

This relationship is derived by applying Kirchhoff's voltage law to the loop formed by R_1, C_1, R. From Figure 8.10(d) it can be seen that the minimum level of V, which is $(1 - m)$, must be kept greater than V_{min} in order to avoid negative peak clipping:

$$(1 - m) \geq \frac{R}{R + R_1}$$

$$\therefore \quad \frac{R_1}{R + R_1} \geq m \qquad (8.47)$$

Eq. (8.47) can be rearranged as

$$\frac{R_p}{R} \geq m \qquad (8.48)$$

where $R_p = (R \cdot R_1)/(R + R_1)$. Equation (8.48) should be compared with Eq. (8.45).

8.3 AMPLITUDE-MODULATED TRANSMITTERS

The *amplitude-modulated (AM) transmitter* is basically the same as the keyed CW transmitter described in Section 17.13, except that the final power-amplifier stage is replaced by a modulator amplifier. Figure 8.11(a) shows the block diagram of a typical AM transmitter. The carrier source is a crystal-controlled oscillator at the carrier frequency or a submultiple of it. This is followed by a tuned buffer amplifier and a tuned driver, and if necessary frequency multiplication is provided in one or more of these stages.

The modulator circuit used is generally a class C power amplifier that is plate (or collector) modulated as described in Section 8.2.6. The audio signal is amplified by a chain of low-level audio amplifiers and a power amplifier. Since this amplifier is controlling the power being delivered to the final RF amplifier, it must have a power driving capability which is one-half the maximum power the plate supply must deliver to the RF amplifier under

(a)

(b)

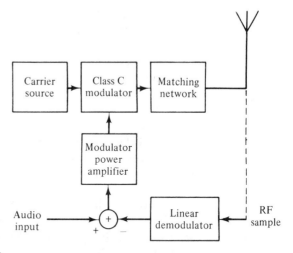

(c)

FIGURE 8.11. Amplitude-modulated transmitters: (a) Transmitter with a modulated class C final power amplifier; (b) Linear class B push-pull power amplifier used when modulation takes place in a low-level stage; (c) Negative feedback applied to linearize a class C modulator.

100% modulation conditions [see Eq. (8.41)]. A transformer-coupled class B push-pull amplifier is usually used for this purpose.

Low-power transmitters with output powers up to 1 kW or so may be transistorized, but as a rule the higher-power transmitters use vacuum tubes in the final amplifier stage, even though the low-level stages may be transistorized. In some cases where the reliability and high overall efficiency of the transistor is mandatory, higher powers can be obtained by using several lower-power transistorized amplifiers in parallel. The system is complicated, and usually the vacuum-tube version will do the same job at lower capital cost.

Sometimes the modulation function is done in one of the low-level stages. This allows low-power modulation and audio amplifiers, but it complicates the RF final amplifier. Class C amplifiers cannot be used to amplify an already modulated (AM) carrier, because the transfer function of the class C amplifier is not linear. The result of using a following class C amplifier would be an undesirable distortion of the modulation envelope that contains the signal. A linear power amplifier, such as the push-pull class B amplifier (section 5.7.3), must be used to overcome this problem (Figure 8.11(b)). Unfortunately, the efficiency of this type of amplifier is much lower than that of the comparable class C amplifier, resulting in more costly equipment. Larger tubes or transistors must be used which are capable of dissipating the additional heat generated.

The output of the final amplifier is passed through an impedance matching network which includes the plate tank circuit of the final amplifier. The Q of this circuit must be low enough so that all the sidebands of the signal are passed without amplitude/frequency distortion, but at the same time must present an appreciable attenuation at the second harmonic frequency. The band width required in most cases is a standard 3 dB at ± 5 kHz around the carrier. For amplitude-modulation broadcast transmitters, this response may be broadened so that the sidebands will be down less than 1 dB at 5 kHz where music programs are being broadcast and very low distortion levels are desired, or special sharp-cutoff filters may be used. Because of the high power levels present in the output, this is not usually an attractive solution.

Negative feedback is quite often used to obtain linear operation from a class C modulator system. The feedback is accomplished in the manner shown in Figure 8.11(c), where a sample of the RF signal sent to the antenna is extracted and demodulated to produce the feedback signal. The demodulator is designed to be as linear in its response as possible and to feed back an audio signal that is proportional to the modulation envelope. The negative feedback loop functions to reduce the distortion in the modulation.

8.3.1 AM Broadcast Transmitters

Most of the domestic AM broadcast services use the medium-wave band from 550 to 1600 kHz. International AM broadcast take place in several of the HF bands scattered from 1600 kHz up to about 15 MHz. The mode of

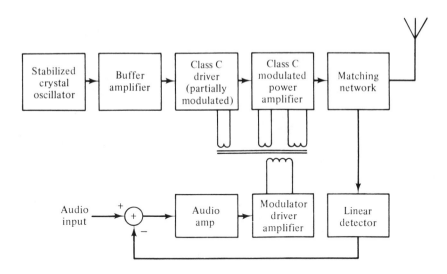

FIGURE 8.12.   An AM broadcast transmitter.

transmission in all cases is double-sideband full carrier, with an audio baseband range of 5 kHz. Station frequency assignments are spaced at 10 kHz intervals, and power outputs range from a few hundred watts for small local stations to as much as 100 kW in the MW band and even higher for international HF transmitters.

A main requirement of an AM broadcast transmitter is to produce, within the limits of the 5-kHz bandwidth available, the highest possible fidelity. The modulator circuits in the transmitter must produce a linear modulation function, and every trick available is used to accomplish this. A typical AM broadcast transmitter is shown in Figure 8.12. The crystal main oscillator is temperature-controlled to provide frequency stability. It is followed by a buffer amplifier, and then by tuned class C amplifiers which provide the necessary power gain to drive the final power amplifier. The modulator system is the "triple equilibrium" system, in which the main part of the modulation is performed by plate-modulating the final class C power amplifier. Secondary modulation of both the final grid and the plate of the driver stage is also included to compensate for bias shift in the final amplifier that is due to the nonlinear characteristic of the amplifier.

The final power amplifier is a push-pull parallel stage in which each side of the push-pull stage is comprised of several vacuum tubes operating in parallel, to obtain the power required. A further advantage of this system is that if one or more of the tubes in the system should fail, the remaining tubes will provide partial output until repairs can be made, thus making a more secure system. Power dissipation in these final tubes can be as high as 50 kW, in addition to several kilowatts of heater power. Water cooling systems are used to dissipate the large quantities of heat produced.

The modulator amplifier is an audio frequency push-pull parallel amplifier, which is transformer-coupled to the modulator. The audio pre-amplifier stage includes a difference amplifier and an envelope detector which demodulates a sample of the transmitter output and uses the signal to provide negative feedback. This feedback further linearizes the modulation characteristic of the system.

Antenna systems for AM transmitters are large, and usually must be located at some point remote from the studio operations. All the studio signal operations are performed at relatively low levels and transmitted to the main transmitter location either over telephone wire lines or a radio link such as a microwave system. Quite often the transmitters are unattended and are remotely controlled from the studio location. Service personnel make periodic visits to do routine maintenance.

8.4   AM RECEIVERS

The general principles of the superheterodyne receiver are described in Chapter 7, and specific operating details of the AM envelope detector in section 8.2.7. Most receivers in use today are assembled from discrete components, although there is a trend toward the use of integrated circuits for sub-sections in the receiver. Therefore, in this section, a very commonly encountered transistorized receiver will be described, followed by the description of two integrated circuit type receivers.

8.4.1.   Discrete Component AM Receiver

The circuit for a standard broadcast receiver using discrete components is shown in Figure 8.13. This is a superheterodyne receiver, transistor Q1 functioning as both a mixer and an oscillator in what is known as an autodyne mixer. The oscillator feedback is through mutual inductive coupling from collector to emitter, the base of Q1 being effectively grounded at oscillator frequency.

The AM signal is coupled into the base of Q1 via coil L1. Thus it is seen that Q1 operates in grounded base mode for the oscillator while simultaneously operating in grounded emitter mode for the signal input.

Tuned IF transformer T1 couples the IF output from Q1 to the first IF amplifier Q2. The output from Q2 is also tuned transformer coupled through T2 to the second IF amplifier Q3. The output from Q3, at IF, is tuned transformer coupled to the envelope detector D2 which has an RC load consisiting of a 0.01 μF in parallel with a 25 kΩ potentiometer. This potentiometer is the manual gain control, the output from which is fed to

GENERAL ELECTRIC CO.

Q1,Q3 2N2926 (RED) OR 2N2715 OR 2N3394
Q2,Q4 2N2926 (ORANGE) OR 2N2716 OR 2N3393
Q5,Q6 2N2714 (WITH HEAT SINK)
D1 IN60 (GERMANIUM)
D2,D3 IN4009 (SILICON)

RADIO INDUSTRIES, INC.

T1 - 13964 - R₁
T2,T3 - 13964
L1 16413
L2 16411
ΔC MODEL 42-2A

PERFORMANCE

NOMINAL SENSITIVITY	20 μv/m
RATED OUTPUT POWER	500 MW
BATTERY DRAIN	10 MA

OTHER COMPONENTS

T4 - 5K/2K CT
T5 - 250Ω CT/VC

*USE 1.0 pf WITH 2N2926 AND 2N3391 SERIES TRANSISTORS, 0.5 pf WITH 2N2715 SERIES.

FIGURE 8.13. A six transistor 9V receiver. (Courtesy General Electric Company)

BECAUSE OF THE SPECIAL NATURE OF THE MANY OF THE COMPONENTS USED IN THIS CIRCUIT, HOME CONSTRUCTION IS NOT RECOMMENDED.

the audio pre-amplifier Q4. The audio power output stage consists of the push-pull pair Q5, Q6.

Automatic gain control (AGC) is also obtained from the diode detector D2, the AGC filter network being the 15 kΩ resistor and 10μF capacitor, Figure 8.13. The AGC bias is fed to the Q2 base.

Diode D1 provides auxiliary AGC action. At low signal levels D1 is reverse biased, the circuit being arranged such that the collector of Q1 is more positive than the collector of Q2. As the signal level increases the normal AGC bias to Q2 reduces Q2 collector current, resulting in an increase in Q2 collector voltage. A point is reached where this forward biases D1, the conduction of D1 then damping the T1 primary and so reducing the mixer gain.

8.4.2 AM Receiver Using Integrated Circuit Sub-System

Figure 8.14 shows the details of the integrated sub-system and Figure 8.15 shows how this is connected as an AM receiver. The package itself, Figure 8.14(a), is a 14 pin dual-in-line package, measuring nominally 19 × 6.3 × 3.2 mm, and yet it contains six major circuit blocks, as shown in Figure 8.14(b). These blocks are integrated on one chip, the complete sub-system circuit being shown in Figure 8.14(c). The circuit action is better understood in relation to the AM receiver application shown in Figure 8.15. It will be immediately seen that certain bulky components, notably the tuned circuits, have to be added externally.

The AM signal input is fed via a tuned coupled circuit to pins 11 and 12 which are the RF inputs. Pin 11 is grounded at RF, while pin 12 is connected to the base of transistor Q2 (Figure 8.14(c)). Transistors Q2 and Q3 form a cascode amplifier (see section 5.3.2). The RF output at pin 13 is tuned circuit coupled to the mixer input, pin 1. The mixer transistors are Q6, Q7, connected as an emitter coupled pair with the base of Q7 being grounded for RF and IF signals. The local oscillator signal is generated by another emitter coupled pair Q4,Q5 (requiring an external tuned circuit at pin 2). The oscillator is seen to control the current to the mixer pair, Figure 8.14(c), and hence multiplicative mixing occurs between the AM input and the oscillator signals. An IF output is obtained from the mixer output, pin 14, which is tuned transformer coupled back into the integrated circuit at pin 7. This goes to the input of a cascode IF amplifier pair Q9,Q10, and the amplified IF output, at pin 6, is fed via a tuned transformer to an envelope detector.

The AGC in this case employs a diode system separate from the detector diode. The IF signal is coupled via the external 5 pF capacitor connected between pins 5 and 6 to the AGC diode D2 (see Fig. 8.14(c)). The rectifying action of D2 along with the filtering action of the externally connected capacitor at pin 10, Figure 8.15, produces an AGC bias which is fed through the coil between pins 11 and 12 (Figure 8.15) to the base of the RF amplifier

PIN CONFIGURATION

N PACKAGE

ORDER PART NO.
NE546N

(a)

BLOCK DIAGRAM

(b)

(c)

FIGURE 8.14. AM radio receiver sub-system available in integrated circuit form. (a) The package details, measuring nominally 19 × 6.3 × 3.2 mm. (b) Block diagram of the sub-system; (c) Equivalent schematic of the sub-system. "Permission to reprint granted by Signetics Corporation, a subsidiary of U.S. Philips Corp., 811 E. Arques Avenue, Sunnyvale, CA 94086."

AM RADIO (Capacitor Tuned)

VARIABLE CAPACITOR (Air Varicon)
ANT & RF   13pF ~ 190pF
OSC   12pF ~ 80pF

ANTENNA COIL
   10mm ϕ < 120mm Ferrite Antenna

RF COIL   OSC COIL

1–2   44 Turns
2–3   81 Turns
4–5   8 Turns

1–3   95 Turns

1st. IF COIL   2nd. IF COIL

FIGURE 8.15.   Details of an AM radio receiver utilizing the sub-system of Fig. 8.14. The receiver is for the standard broadcast band. "Permission to reprint granted by Signetics Corporation, a subsidiary of U.S. Philips Corp., 811 E. Arques Avenue, Sunnyvale, CA 94086."

Q2. Transistor Q1 along with associated circuitry provides the reference bias for the AGC operation, and diode D1 provides auxiliary AGC action for large signals through its damping action on the IF_2 transformer in a manner similar to that described for diode D1 in Figure 8.13.

Diode D7 and resistor R19 form the voltage regulator, and the diode chains D10, D9, D8, and D3, D4, D5, provide bias levels for Q3 and Q7 respectively. Transistor Q8 sets the bias level for Q9.

The active circuitry is easily integrated on a single chip, and because transistors are much more economical to fabricate than resistors and capacitors in integrated circuits the circuit design philosophy is to use transistors and diodes wherever possible for bias control.

8.4.3. AM Receiver Using a Phase Locked Loop (PLL)

This provides yet another approach to the use of integrated circuits in receivers. Figure 8.16(a) shows the basic circuit blocks in a phase locked loop (PLL). The input signal is compared in phase with a locally generated oscillation. The output of the phase detector contains a low frequency component which reduces to dc when both signals are of the same frequency. The low pass filter (LPF) selects this component which is then amplified and fed back to the oscillator. This bias alters the frequency of the oscillator in such a way as to reduce the output of the phase detector. Since the oscillator frequency is controlled by bias voltage it is termed a voltage controlled oscillator (VCO). In practice, the oscillator is a multivibrator type circuit producing a square wave output. For a sinusoidal input signal, the circuit, when properly adjusted, will lock the oscillator fundamental frequency to the input frequency and the dc output of the phase detector is then proportional to $V_i \cos \Theta_i$, where V_i is the amplitude of the input and Θ_i is the phase angle between input and oscillator fundamental. This dc bias automatically alters the frequency of the oscillator such that the bias itself reduces to zero, a condition which is met when the phase angle Θ_i is 90°.

When applied to detection of AM signals the VCO is locked exactly in frequency and phase to the carrier, and hence to compensate for the 90° phase difference which occurs within the PLL, the carrier is externally shifted by a further 90° as shown in Figure 8.16(b). It does not matter whether the total phase difference is zero or 180°, the fundamental component of the VCO output will be proportional to $\sin \omega_c t$ where ω_c is the angular frequency of the carrier.

Let the modulating signal be represented by m(t) and the AM signal therefore by $(1 + m(t)) \sin \omega_c t$. The output from the multiplier, Figure 8.16(b) is proportional to:

(a)

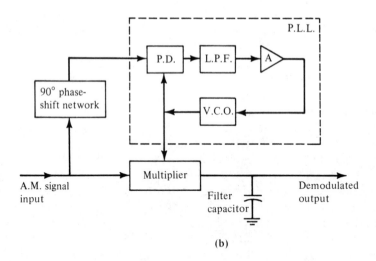

(b)

FIGURE 8.16. (a) The basic Phase Locked Loop (PLL). (b) AM Receiver utilizing the PLL.

$$(1 + m(t)) \cdot \sin \omega_c t \cdot \sin \omega_c t$$

$$= (1 + m(t))(\tfrac{1}{2} - \tfrac{1}{2} \cos 2 \omega_c t) \qquad (8.49)$$

The $\cos 2 \omega_c t$ term is filtered out and the modulating signal recovered from the term $\tfrac{1}{2} m(t)$. This type of detection is known as *synchronous detection*.

The circuit for a receiver using a commercially available PLL is shown in Figure 8.17(a), and the circuit for the PLL unit in Figure 8.17(b). For a complete description of the circuit the reader is referred to the Signetics Analog Data Manual. Briefly, Q11, 12, 13, 14 form the multivibrator for the VCO. Q10, 25, 22 amplify the feedback control signal from the PLL phase detector, acting through Q21, 23 to control the emitter currents of Q12, 13 and thus the charging current to the multivibrator timing capacitor C_o (connected to pins 2 and 3) to change the VCO frequency.

The PLL phase detector consists of Q6, 7, 8, 9 and Q17, 18. Q6, 9 and Q7, 8 are coupled through a resistor network to the VCO output Q12, 13. The AM signal (which may be the output of a conventional AM IF amplifier) is shifted by 90° by the network R_y, C_y and fed to the phase detector input on pin 13. Typical values of shifting components are $R_y = 3000$ ohms, $C_y = 135$ pF for standard broadcast reception. Bypass capacitor C_B from pin 12 completes the shifted signal return path. The output from the phase detector from Q7 drives the feedback amplifier Q10, 25, 22. Capacitor C_L connected between pins 14, 15 provides the low pass filtering of the control signal.

PHASE LOCKED AM RECEIVER

C_B = Bypass Capacitor
C_C = Coupling Capacitor

(a)

FIGURE 8.17.   (a) Phase locked AM receiver.

SCHEMATIC DIAGRAM OF 561N

FIGURE 8.17. (b) Schematic diagram of the integrated circuit block used in the receiver. "Permission to reprint granted by Signetics Corporation, a subsidiary of U.S. Philips Corp., 811 Arques Avenue, Sunnyvale, CA 94086."

Transistors Q1, 2, 3, 4 and Q 15, 16 form the multiplier circuit for the AM detector. This circuit operates in the same manner as the phase detector for the phase-locked loop. Q1,4 and Q2,3 are coupled to the VCO output (providing the synchronous carrier signal) and Q15,16 are differentially driven from the unshifted AM input signal at pin 4. The demodulated output from Q1,3 appears at pin 1, with C_x acting as a low pass filter to remove the RF components before the signal is passed to an audio amplifier.

It is worth noting that the action of the two multiplier circuits in this chip is identical to that of the balanced modulator circuit described in Section 9.3.2, which is also a multiplier. Also, with minor circuit connection changes, the same circuit can also be used to demodulate an FM signal, operating in the manner described in Section 10.6.1.

It should also be noted that no external tuned circuits are required with the PLL detector, as once the VCO locks onto the incoming carrier, selectivity is automatically achieved. In practice some RF selectivity will be provided ahead of the PLL detector to prevent the VCO locking onto large unwanted carriers.

8.5 PROBLEMS

1. Amplitude modulation is applied via the output electrode of a class C amplifier. The direct voltage to the electrode is 10V, and the peak sinusoidal modulating voltage is 4 V. Assuming ideal operating conditions for the class C stage, calculate the peak RF voltage at the output electrode.

2. A carrier of 10V peak and frequency 100 kHz is amplitude-modulated by a sine wave of 4 V peak and frequency 1000 Hz. Determine the modulation index for the wave, and sketch the spectrum.

3. The positive RF peaks of an AM voltage wave rise to a maximum value of 15 V and drop to a minimum value of 5 V. Determine the modulation index and the unmodulated carrier amplitude, assuming sinusoidal modulation.

4. An AM transmitter has an unmodulated power output of 1 kW. Plot the power output against modulation index, for sinusoidal modulation. Also plot power output against modulation index squared. Determine the increase in power when the modulation index is 0.5. Average powers are to be used in all cases.

5. The rms antenna current from an AM transmitter increases by 15% over the unmodulated value when sinusoidal modulation is applied. Determine the modulation index.

6. A complex modulating waveform consisting of a sine wave of amplitude 3 V and frequency 1000 Hz plus a cosine wave of amplitude 5 V and frequency 3000 Hz amplitude modulates a 500-kHz, 50-V peak, carrier voltage. Plot the spectrum of the modulated wave, and determine the average power when the modulated wave is fed into a 50-Ω load.

7. In a trapezoidal pattern displaying modulation, the length of the long vertical side is 5 cm, and of the short vertical side, 2 cm. Determine the modulation depth.

8. The dc power to a modulated class C amplifier is 500 W. Determine the power the modulator must supply for 100% sinusoidal modulation applied at the output electrode.

9. A diode detector load consists of a 0.01-μF capacitor in parallel with a 5-kΩ resistor. Determine the maximum depth of sinusoidal

modulation that the detector can handle without diagonal peak clipping when the modulating frequency is: (a) 1000 Hz; (b) 10,000 Hz.

10. Distinguish between *negative peak clipping* and *diagonal peak clipping* in an envelope detector. The output of a diode envelope detector is fed through a dc blocking capacitor to an amplifying stage, which has an input resistance of 10 kΩ. If the diode load resistor is 5 kΩ, determine the maximum depth of sinusoidal modulation the detector can handle without negative peak clipping.

Chapter 9
Single-Sideband Modulation

9.1 INTRODUCTION

Communications in the HF bands have become increasingly crowded in recent years, requiring closer spacing of signals in the spectrum. Single-sideband systems, which require only half the bandwidth of a normal AM signal and considerably less power, are used extensively in this portion of the spectrum as a result.

It was pointed out in Section 8.2.2 that all the modulation information necessary for signal transmission and recovery is present in each of the sidebands of an amplitude-modulated signal. It was also pointed out that at 100% sinusoidal modulation only 1/6 of the total power was present in one of the sidebands, while 2/3 of it is carrier signal, which contains no information. Thus, if the carrier and one of the sidebands can be eliminated from the signal before transmission, only half of the bandwidth is required for transmission (corresponding to the maximum modulating frequency to be transmitted), and only 1/6 of the total power need be transmitted for the same signal level. A comparison of the signal spectra of full AM signals (DSBFC) with double-sideband suppressed carrier (DSBSC) and with single-sideband suppressed carrier signals (SSBSC) using either sideband is shown in Figure 9.1. Note that in (c) and (d) only one sideband is present, and that it requires only one-half the bandwidth of either (a) or (b).

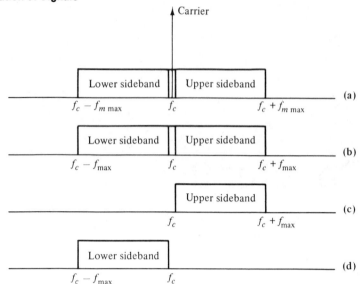

FIGURE 9.1. Amplitude-modulated signal spectra: (a) Double-sideband full carrier (DSBFC); (b) Double-sideband suppressed carrier (DSBSC); (c) Single-sideband suppressed carrier (SSBSC), using upper sideband (USB); (d) SSBSC using lower sideband (LSB)

9.2 SINGLE-SIDEBAND PRINCIPLES

Equation (8.13) shows that an ordinary sinusoidally modulated signal contains three components, at an upper side frequency, at a lower side frequency and at the carrier frequency. Further, this signal is the equivalent of the carrier sinusoid being multiplied by the modulation signal with a dc component added to it.

$$e_{am} = (1 + m \sin \omega_m t) \sin \omega_c t$$

$$= \sin \omega_c t + \frac{m}{2} \cos(\omega_c - \omega_m)t - \frac{m}{2} \cos(\omega_c + \omega_m)t \qquad (8.13)$$

The two side frequencies are due entirely to the product of the carrier and the modulation signal, while the carrier term is due only to the presence of the dc offset in the modulation signal. Therefore, if the modulation circuit can be balanced so that the dc term cancels, but the product term does not cancel, the output will contain only the two sideband terms, as shown in equation (9.1).

$$e_{bal\ mod} = m \sin \omega_m t \sin \omega_c t$$

$$= \frac{m}{2} \cos(\omega_c - \omega_m)t - \frac{m}{2} \cos(\omega_c + \omega_m)t \qquad (9.1)$$

Such a circuit is called a "balanced modulator," and several balanced modulator circuits are discussed in the next section.

The first method of generating an SSB signal is derived directly from the above. It consists of a balanced modulator which cancels the carrier, followed by a bandpass filter which eliminates the unwanted sideband. Either the upper or the lower sideband may be used, providing that the receiver can be adjusted to properly demodulate either one.

The "Phasing" method and the so called "Third Method" both rely on multiple phase shifting and differential cancellation to eliminate both the carrier and the unwanted sideband. All three methods are discussed in detail in Section 9.4.

Demodulation of a single-sideband signal can be achieved by multiplying it with a locally generated carrier voltage at the receiver. Detectors using this principle are known as "product detectors," and most balanced modulator circuits can also be used for this purpose since they rely on the process of multiplication for their operation. It is important that the carrier be as closely synchronized in frequency and phase with the original carrier as possible, as discussed further in Section 9.5. To demonstrate that the multiplying process demodulates the incoming single sideband, consider a lower side frequency $A_L \cos (\omega_c - \omega_m)t$, where the amplitude A_L is proportional to the amplitude of the modulating signal $E_{m_{\max}}$. Multiplying this by a carrier wave $\sin \omega_c t$ yields

$$A_L \cos (\omega_c - \omega_m)t \cdot \sin \omega_c t = \tfrac{1}{2}A_L \{ \sin[(\omega_c - \omega_m)t + \omega_c t] \quad (9.2)$$
$$- \sin[(\omega_c - \omega_m)t - \omega_c t] \}$$
$$= \tfrac{1}{2}A_L [\sin(2\omega_c - \omega_m)t - \sin(-\omega_m)t]$$
$$= \tfrac{1}{2}A_L [\sin(2\omega_c - \omega_m)t + \sin \omega_m t]$$

The second term on the right-hand side, $\tfrac{1}{2} A_L \sin \omega_m t$, is the required information signal. The circuit shown in Figure 9.3(a), with some modifications in the bias conditions, can be used as a product detector. The factor $\tfrac{1}{2}$ is not significant since the output voltage can easily be altered by the gain of the product detector as shown by Eq. (9.11). What is important is that the amplitude of the demodulated information signal is proportional to the amplitude of the received side frequency. The components around the carrier harmonics can easily be removed by low pass filtering.

9.3 THE BALANCED MODULATOR

The balanced modulator is the heart of all methods of single-sideband modulation and demodulation. Any circuit which can produce as one of the terms in its output the *product* of two separate input signals can be used as a balanced modulator. Three such circuits are discussed here.

9.3.1 An FET Balanced Modulator Circuit

This circuit is one of a class of circuits which use the non-linear characteristic of a semiconductor device to generate the product of two inputs. It is a form of bridge circuit in which the carrier portion of the signal is canceled in the push-pull output circuit shown in Figure 9.2. The field-effect transistors are used because they have a transfer characteristic which is nonlinear, so that the output contains a term which is the *product* of the input voltages. The transfer curve (I_d versus V_{gs}) of a field-effect transistor is almost parabolic, and may be approximated by

$$i_d = I_o + a v_{gs} + b v_{gs}^2 \qquad (9.3)$$

where i_o is the current for zero gate-source voltage, and a, b, ... are constants. Since the drain currents i_{d1} and i_{d2} flow in opposite directions in the primary winding of the output transformer, the effective primary current i_p is

$$
\begin{aligned}
i_p &= i_{d1} - i_{d2} \\
&= a(v_{gs\ 1} - v_{gs\ 2}) + b(v_{gs\ 1}^2 - v_{gs\ 2}^2) \\
&= a(v_{gs\ 1} - v_{gs\ 2}) + b(v_{gs\ 1} + v_{gs\ 2})(v_{gs\ 1} - v_{gs\ 2}) \qquad (9.4)
\end{aligned}
$$

Applying Kirchhoff's voltage law to the input loops of Figure 9.2 gives

$$
\begin{aligned}
v_{gs\ 1} &= \tfrac{1}{2} e_m + e_c \\
v_{gs\ 2} &= -\tfrac{1}{2} e_m + e_c
\end{aligned}
$$

FIGURE 9.2.   A balanced modulator circuit.

Substituting these in Eq. (9.4) gives

$$i_p = a(e_m) + b(2e_c)(e_m) \qquad (9.5)$$

The RF output transformer will reject the low-frequency (e_m) term, passing only the product term $2 b e_c e_m$. This term contains only the upper and lower sidebands; there is no carrier term as contained in Eq. (8.13). For example, for sinusoidal modulation, the product term contains $(\sin \omega_c t)(\sin \omega_m t)$, which can be expanded as

$$\sin \omega_c t \sin \omega_m t = \tfrac{1}{2}[\cos(\omega_c t - \omega_m t) - \cos(\omega_c t + \omega_m t)] \qquad (9.6)$$

The appropriate side frequency may be selected from this by means of a filter. The circuit requires matched transistors; that is, i_o, a, and b for each transistor are equal.

9.3.2 An Integrated Circuit Balanced Modulator

Balanced modulators are available in integrated circuit form, Figure 9.3 being the circuit for a commercially available unit. This is a very versatile unit which has many applications (see *Motorola Application Note AN531*). This circuit is one of a class of circuits which use switching to accomplish periodic signal polarity reversal, giving the effect of multiplying the signal by a square wave. An elementary analysis of the circuit when used as a balanced modulator with large carrier input follows. The carrier may be considered a switching voltage which alternately switches transistors Q_1, Q_4, and Q_2, Q_3 on and off, each pair being switched together. Figure 9.3(b) shows the circuit condition when the carrier has switched Q_2, Q_3 on (and Q_1, Q_4 off). Assuming base currents negligible in all cases, and summing the currents at junctions A and B gives

$$\text{At junction } A: \quad i_2 = i + i_e$$

$$\text{At junction } B: \quad i_1 = i - i_e$$

The output voltage v_o is

$$v_o = v_2 - v_1$$
$$= R(i_2 - i_1)$$
$$= R(2i_e) \qquad (9.7)$$

Applying Kirchhoff's voltage law to the loop containing e_m and R_e gives

$$e_m = V_{be} + v_e - V_{be}$$
$$= v_e$$

Therefore,
$$i_e = \frac{v_e}{R_e}$$
$$= \frac{e_m}{R_e} \qquad (9.8)$$

where e_m is the modulating voltage.

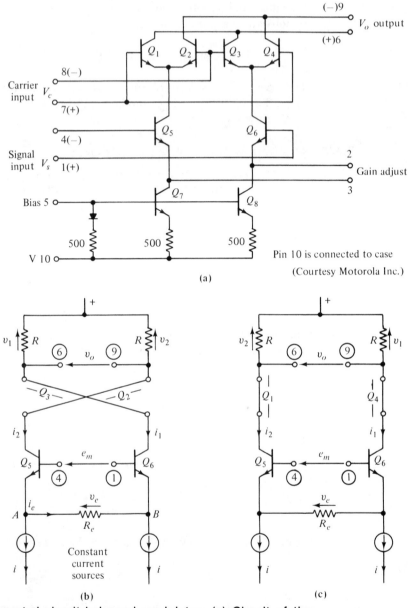

FIGURE 9.3. An integrated circuit balanced modulator: (a) Circuit of the Motorola MC1596 balanced modulator; (b) Equivalent circuit for the condition when negative carrier voltage has switched on transistors Q_2, Q_3; (c) Equivalent circuit for the condition when positive carrier voltage has switched on transistors Q_1, Q_4. Extracted from *Motorola Application Note AN531*. (Courtesy Motorola, Inc.)

Substituting Eq. (9.8) into Eq. (9.7),

$$v_o = \frac{2Re_m}{R_e} \tag{9.9}$$

When the carrier input changes polarity, transistors Q_1, Q_4 are switched on and Q_2, Q_3 off. The circuit is then as shown in Figure 9.3(c). The output voltage is now

$$v_o = v_1 - v_2$$
$$= -\frac{2Re_m}{R_e} \tag{9.10}$$

Thus the action of the carrier is to switch v_o, at the carrier frequency, between $\pm e_m 2R/R_e$, as shown by Eqs. (9.9) and (9.10). Representing the switching action by a square-wave function $p(t)$, at carrier frequency, Eqs. (9.9) and (9.10) can be combined to give

$$v_o = \frac{2R}{R_e} p(t) \cdot e_m \tag{9.11}$$

As shown in Chapter 2, a square wave can be analyzed into a sinusoidal series, and so ignoring the constant of proportionality, $p(t)$ can be expressed as

$$p(t) = \sin \omega_c t + 1/3 \sin 3\omega_c t + 1/5 \sin 5\omega_c t + ... \tag{9.12}$$

Therefore, from Eq. (9.11), on substituting Eq. (9.12), the output voltage is seen to contain a product term $e_m \sin \omega_c t$. For sinusoidal modulation this can be expanded as shown by Eq. (9.6), which shows that the output contains upper and lower side frequencies. The other components, which are side frequencies around the other harmonics of the carrier frequency [see Eq. (9.12)], are easily filtered out. The carrier itself and its harmonics do not appear in the output.

Transistors Q_1, Q_2, Q_3, and Q_4 could be switched by a low-level sinusoidal carrier such that the sidebands around the harmonics of the carrier do not appear in the output. This mode of operation has the advantage of requiring less filtering of the output, but the disadvantage is that the output level then depends on the carrier amplitude.

The advantages of the integrated-circuit type of balanced modulator are that the sections can be made more nearly identical (i.e., matched for characteristics) than is the case with discrete components; also, the circuit does not require the use of transformers.

9.3.3 The Double-Balanced Ring Modulator

A circuit known as the *double-balanced ring modulator*, which is widely used in carrier telephony, is shown in Figure 9.4(a). The name arises from the fact that the circuit is balanced for both carrier and modulating frequencies, and neither of these appear by themselves at the output; also, the diodes form a ring circuit *ABCD*. The operation is similar to that for the integrated-circuit balanced modulator described in the previous section. The carrier is large and acts as a switching signal, alternately providing conducting paths as shown in Figures 9.4(b) and (c), for the modulating signal. These are seen to be similar to the switching paths shown in Figure 9.3(b) and (c). The analysis of the circuit is similar, resulting in an output signal proportional to $p(t) \cdot e_m$, where $p(t)$ is a square-wave switching function at carrier frequency and e_m is the modulating signal.

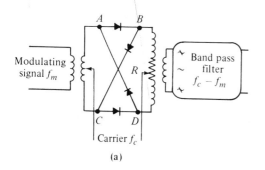

(a)   (b)

FIGURE 9.4. (a) The double-balanced ring modulator; (b) The conducting paths when diodes *AB* and *CD* are forward-biased; (c) The conducting paths when diodes *BC* and *DA* are forward-biased.

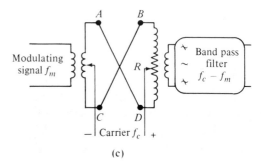

(c)

9.4 SSB GENERATION

9.4.1 The Balanced Modulator-Filter Method

The earliest form of SSB transmitter used a balanced modulator circuit to generate a DSBSC signal and then followed that with "sideband filters," narrow bandpass filters that only passed the desired sideband of frequencies. The system of Figure 9.5(a) shows such a transmitter which uses bandpass filters to eliminate the unwanted sideband. Initial modulation takes place at a low frequency such as 100 kHz because of the difficulty of obtaining bandpass filters with the necessary sharp characteristics at the transmitter frequency. A balanced modulator circuit performs this first modulation, which results in a signal that contains both sidebands but no carrier. Usually a single sideband pass filter is provided, and the operator may select the sideband which gives best results by switching in a different carrier crystal to move the carrier frequency to the other edge of the passband. A balanced mixer and crystal oscillator provide up-conversion to the final transmitter frequency, and a linear RF amplifier provides the output power amplification. Linear amplifiers must be used to prevent distortion of sideband and possible regeneration of the second sideband.

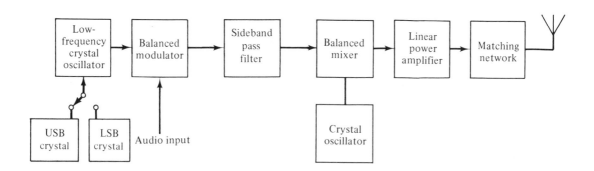

FIGURE 9.5.   Single-sideband suppressed carrier transmitter using bandpass filters to eliminate the unwanted sideband.

9.4.2   The Phasing Method

Figure 9.6 shows a different means of obtaining an SSBSC signal. This circuit does not have any filters and the primary modulation can be done at the final transmission frequency. It relies on phase shifting and cancellation to eliminate the carrier and the unwanted sideband. Expansion of the expression for a single lower side frequency, using the standard trigonometric identity, gives

$$\cos(\omega_c t - \omega_m t) = \tfrac{1}{2}(\cos \omega_c t \cos \omega_m t + \sin \omega_c t \sin \omega_m t) \quad (9.13)$$

The first term on the right-hand side is the product of the carrier and the modulating signal both phase-shifted by 90°, and the second term is the

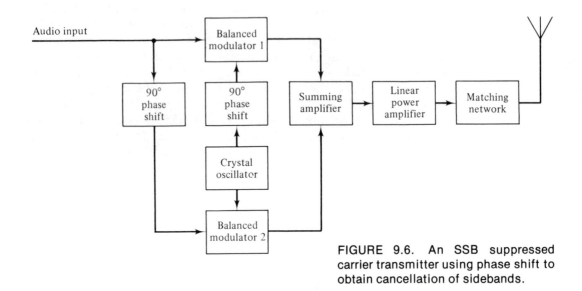

FIGURE 9.6. An SSB suppressed carrier transmitter using phase shift to obtain cancellation of sidebands.

product of the carrier and the modulating signal. The circuitry required to produce the phase shifts, multiplications, and addition, is relatively straightforward and is shown in block-diagram form in Figure 9.6. (The student should be able to show that with the arrangement of Figure 9.6, an upper side-frequency component $\sin(\omega_c + \omega_m)t$ is generated.)

The primary signal source is a crystal oscillator. Its signal drives one balanced modulator directly and the other through a circuit which shifts its phase so that it is 90° out of phase with the directly driven one. Both balanced modulators eliminate the carrier itself from the output signals. The audio signal is applied directly to the modulator with the shifted carrier, while the audio signal is shifted 90° before it is applied to the directly fed modulator. The first modulator puts out two sidebands, the upper sideband and the lower sideband, but each one is shifted in phase by +90°. The second modulator also puts out the upper and lower sidebands, but in this case the upper sideband is shifted by +90° while the lower is shifted −90°. The result is that the upper sidebands from both modulators are in phase with each other and add directly in the summing amplifier to produce the desired output sideband signal. The lower sidebands are shifted so that they are 180° out of phase with one another, and cancel when added. The remaining sideband is amplified by linear RF power amplifiers in the final stages before transmission. Switching to the lower sideband can be accomplished by replacing the carrier phase-shift network with one with a −90° phase shift.

While the system is more complex than that using filters, the individual circuits are not, and with careful adjustment of the modulators can provide better rejection of the unwanted sideband than can the filters. The elimination of the up-converter stage also reduces the possibility of distortion of the signal after modulation. It should be noted that the shifting network in the modulation input must provide the same amount of shift at all frequencies in the modulation sideband. Such circuits are possible to build but are complex and expensive. The "Third Method" eliminates the need for this wide-band shifting network.

9.4.3   The "Third Method"

The third method of accomplishing SSBSC modulation is called just that, the *third method*. It is attributed to D. K. Weaver, and was developed during the 1950s. It is similar to the phase-shifting method already presented in that it uses shifting and cancellation for its operation, but is different in that the audio signal is first modulated onto an audio subcarrier. The system is shown in Figure 9.7(c). The modulators 1 and 2 act to combine the audio signal with the audio subcarrier signal so that the output of modulator 1 contains the upper and lower sidebands, both shifted in phase by 90°, while the output of modulator 2 contains the unshifted upper and lower sidebands. The upper sidebands in both cases are removed by low-pass filters which cut off at the subcarrier frequency f_0. These signals are now presented to modulators 3 and 4, which are driven with the RF carrier fre-

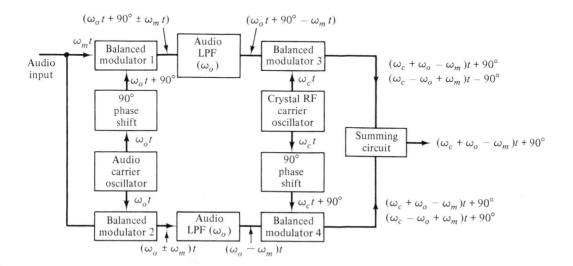

FIGURE 9.7.   The "third method" of generating an SSBSC signal.

quency and its 90° shifted version, respectively. The output from modulator 3 contains a sideband group $(f_c + f_o - f_m)$ shifted $+90°$ and a second sideband group $(f_c - f_o + f_m)$ shifted by $-90°$. The other modulator 4, puts out $(f_c + f_o - f_m)$ shifted by $+90°$, which is in phase with the first component of modulator 3 and adds directly to it, and also it puts out $(f_c - f_o + f_m)$ shifted by $+90°$, which is 180° out of phase with the corresponding component of modulator 3 and cancels it. The resulting output from the adder circuit is the component $(f_c + f_o - f_m)$ (the 90° phase shift can be ignored) which corresponds to the lower sideband of f_m on a carrier frequency of $(f_c + f_o)$. The other sideband and carrier have been suppressed.

If the carrier inputs to modulators 3 and 4 are interchanged, the output is the upper sideband on a carrier frequency of $(f_c - f_o)$. It should be noted that the audio subcarrier may be placed in the middle of the modulating frequency range. When this is done, the modulating frequency can be larger than f_o and half of the lower sideband from the modulators (1 and 2) is folded over in the range from 0 to f_o and mixed with the other half of the sideband. This is of no consequence since the final modulators (3 and 4) act in such a manner that the sideband frequencies created by them are totally on one side of the carrier $(f_c + f_o)$.

9.5 SSB RECEPTION

It was noted in Section 9.2 that if an SSB signal is multiplied with a syncronous carrier signal that the result will contain the original modulation signal. In practice, demodulation is accomplished using either product detectors or balanced modulator circuits in conjunction with sharp cutoff IF sideband filters to select the desired sideband from the received signals.

Since both the incoming signal and the local carrier signal must remain closely synchronized in frequency to avoid severe distortion, stability in both the final demodulating oscillator and either extreme stability or frequency tracking control (AFC) on the first oscillator must be provided. Crystal oscillators or frequency synthesizers are used to obtain this stability.

Very good adjacent channel selectivity must be provided since SSB signals are usually packed closely together in the frequency spectrum. Double conversion is nearly always used in SSB receivers. The second mixer oscillator is usually a crystal oscillator that also provides the primary frequency source for the final demodulator (through multipliers or dividers).

Several variations on single sideband are used in communications. First, either the upper sideband or the lower sideband may be used for the information channel, or in the case of independent sideband, both sidebands may be used, one for each of two channels. Next, a full carrier or a partially suppressed carrier may be transmitted, or the carrier may be fully suppressed.

Figure 9.8 shows the block diagram of a typical communications receiver designed for use with SSB reception in the HF range from 3 to 30 MHz. The circuitry is that of a standard double-conversion receiver down to the output of the second IF amplifier, except for the local oscillators. The first IF is at 2.2 MHz, with a bandwidth of 10 kHz, while the second IF is at 200 kHz, also with a 10-kHz bandwidth. The first local oscillator and RF amp are manually tuned, in two switched bands. The second local oscillator is a 2.0-MHz crystal oscillator. Its output is divided by 10 in a digital-counter circuit to provide the 200-kHz reference signal for the demodulator.

Two filters follow the second IF amplifier, one for each sideband with a bandpass of 2.7 kHz. The appropriate sideband is selected by a switch and this forms the other input to the detector, which is a product detector. The output of the detector is passed through a gated audio amplifier which turns off the output signal to keep down noise when the signal level drops below a minimum value (squelch). The amplified IF signal is rectified to provide the AGC voltage for the squelch circuit and the RF and IF amplifiers.

Manually variable receivers like this one are sometimes difficult to use. The demodulator oscillator is quite stable, but the first local oscillator must also be stable and variable. Any variation in this first oscillator will cause the SSB signal to move relative to the demodulation carrier and introduce a distortion effect, which is difficult to control. The availability of digital frequency synthesizers in integrated circuit form for reasonable prices which can be crystal controlled for stability has made it possible to build very good SSB receivers for very reasonable prices. One of the largest applications of this technique is in the multi-channel Citizens Band transceivers.

9.6 MODIFIED SSB SYSTEMS

9.6.1 Pilot Carrier SSB

The pilot carrier SSB system is arranged so that a low level carrier signal is transmitted with the single sideband, in its proper place in the spectrum, but at a much lower level than would be the case for DSBFC transmission. This pilot carrier is used at the receiver to synchronize the local oscillator used for the demodulator to the original carrier, thus greatly improving the demodulator operation.

Figure 9.9(a) and (b) show an SSB pilot carrier radio transmitter and receiver, and Figure 9.9(c) shows the frequency spectra of signals at various points within the system. The audio signal, which could be a telephone channel in the 0–4 kHz range (A), is fed to the balanced modulator to create upper and lower sidebands around the 100 kHz carrier position (B). An upper sideband filter passes the upper sideband between 100–104 kHz which then has a portion of the carrier added to it through an attenuator to

FIGURE 9.8. A single-sideband HF receiver.

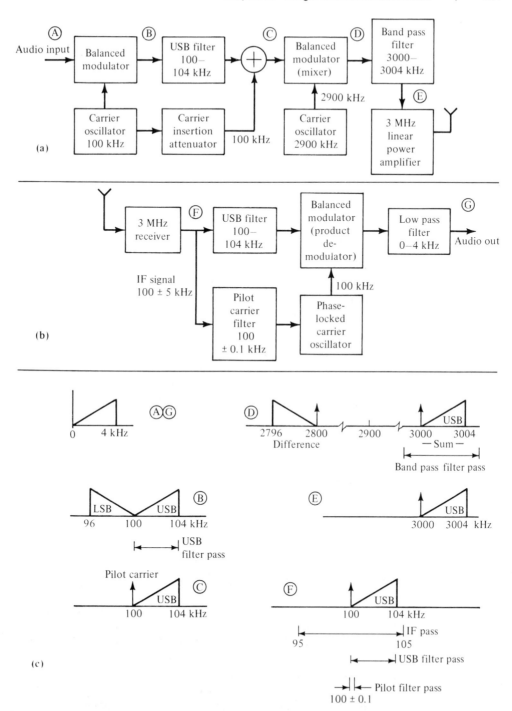

FIGURE 9.9.   SSB Pilot Carrier Radio System: (a) Transmitter; (b) Receiver;
(c) Signal spectra at various points in the system.

produce the signal (C). The reinserted carrier level is adjusted through the attenuator. This signal is now modulated on a 2900 kHz carrier by a second balanced modulator which acts as a mixer to produce an upper sideband with signals between 3000 and 3004 kHz and a lower sideband between 2800–2796 kHz (D). A bandpass filter passes the upper sideband and rejects the lower sideband to produce the signal (E), which is then amplified and transmitted.

At the receiver the 3 MHz signal is picked up, amplified and down-converted to the IF at 100 ±5 kHz, producing the pilot carrier at 100 kHz and the USB signal in the range 100–104 kHz. (F). This signal is passed through an upper sideband filter to the balanced modulator, and through a very narrow bandpass filter at 100 kHz and applied to the input of the phase-locked oscillator to produce the synchronized 100 kHz carrier for the demodulator. A final low pass filter removes the sum components of the demodulator, leaving the 0–4 kHz audio signal (G). Since the demodulator oscillator is locked to the pilot carrier, a small amount of drift in the circuits is automatically corrected for and stable demodulation occurs. The bias signal from the phase-locked oscillator can also be used to provide automatic frequency control (AFC) to the receiver tuning oscillator.

9.6.2   Independent Sideband (ISB)

For single sideband transmission, the carrier and one sideband are removed from the signal. It is possible to replace the removed sideband with another sideband of information created by modulating a different input signal on the same carrier, giving what is known as independent sideband (ISB) transmission. Both of the original signals have frequencies in the audio range, but in the transmitted signal each signal occupies a different group of frequencies in the spectrum. The process of distributing signals in the frequency spectrum so that they do not overlap is the process of frequency division multiplexing, or FDM. FDM is dealt with more fully in the next section.

Independent sideband modulation provides the basic mechanism for accomplishing frequency division multiplexing. Figure 9.10 shows the block diagram of an ISB transmitter which provides for four multiplexed radio-telephone channels on the same carrier. Each of the telephone channels is limited to frequencies in the 0.25–3 kHz range, somewhat less than what is usually provided for telephone channels, by low pass filters (A in Figure 9.10(b)). Channels 2 and 3 are applied to the inputs of two balanced modulators fed from a common 6.25 kHz carrier oscillator, creating lower sideband signals from 3.25–6 kHz and USB signals from 6.5–9.25 kHz on each output. Lower sideband filters with a bandpass of 6–3.25 kHz remove the upper sidebands, and the lower sidebands are then added to the signals from channels 1 and 4. The resulting two signals then have channels 1 and 2 frequency division multiplexed on one line and channels 3 and 4 frequency division multiplexed on the other line, as shown in the spectra (B). These

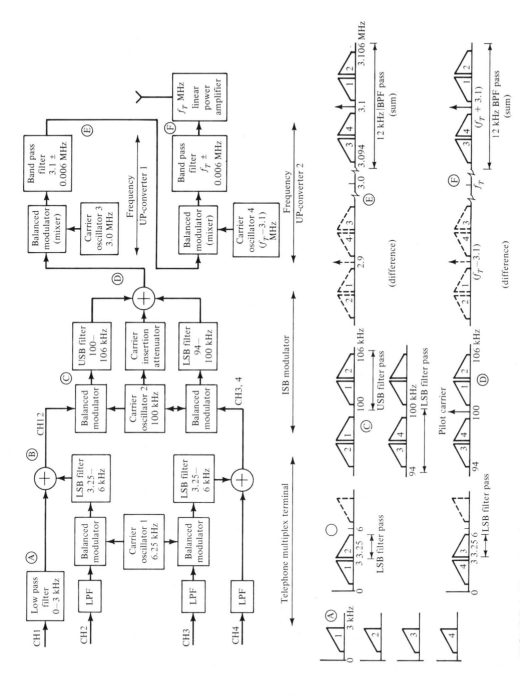

FIGURE 9.10. A 4-Channel ISB Radio-Telephone Transmitter: (a) Transmitter block diagram; (b) Signal spectra at various points.

293

two signals form the inputs to the ISB transmitter proper, and may be applied directly or connected over telephone lines of some length if the transmitter site is remote from the multiplex terminal.

In the ISB modulator section, the two signals 12 and 34 are applied to two balanced modulators which are also fed from a common 100 KHz carrier oscillator. The outputs are two signals, each of which contains upper and lower sidebands around the carrier frequency of 100 KHz, as shown in spectra (C). Channel 12 signal is passed through an USB filter with a passband of 100–106 KHz to remove its lower sideband, and channel 34 is passed through a LSB filter with a passband of 94–100 KHz to remove its upper sideband. The USB 12 and the LSB 34 and a small amount of 100 KHz pilot carrier (obtained through an attenuator from the carrier oscillator) are added to give the final signal (spectra (D). This signal has the four input channel signals spread out in frequency, two on either side of the 100 KHz carrier, with none overlapping the others.

The modulated 100 KHz signal could be transmitted directly on a high frequency cable link, or as in this case it can be raised to a higher radio frequency for atmospheric transmission. The remainder of the transmitter circuits provide two stages of frequency up-conversion, and power amplification to the antenna. Two stages of up-conversion are necessary because if only one is used for a frequency increase of more than about 10:1, the unwanted difference frequency components from the mixer will be too close to the wanted sum frequency components to be easily separated by filtering, especially if the final carrier frequency is more than a few MHz.

The first up-converter comprises a balanced modulator circuit used as a mixer, a 3 MHz carrier oscillator, and a bandpass sharp cutoff filter with a bandpass of $3.1 \pm .006$ MHz. This circuit produces the signal shown in spectra (E) which is the same as that of (D) except that it has been moved in frequency from a center of 100 KHz to a center of 3.1 MHz.

The final up-conversion works in exactly the same way, bringing the signal to its final center frequency f_T (spectra (F)). Again the sum frequency group is selected, but this time the difference frequencies are 6 MHz lower, making the final filtering operation very easy. A linear rf power amplifier tuned to the transmitting frequency f_T brings the signal up to the required antenna power level.

This circuit illustrates the use of ISB in three different areas. The first is to perform FDM at the low frequency levels required for direct cable transmission, which will be expanded on in the next section. The second is that of ISB modulation of a radio frequency carrier, and the third is its use in frequency conversion operations or mixing.

9.6.3 Frequency Division Multiplexing (FDM)

Frequency Division Multiplexing, as was noted in the previous section, is the process of combining several information channels by shifting their signals to different frequency groups within the frequency spectrum so that they can all be transmitted simultaneously on a common transmission facility. The process of frequency up-conversion and down-conversion makes this possible, and as noted in the previous section, SSBSC modulation is used extensively to accomplish these conversions.

Transmission of many signals by radiation in the radio frequency spectrum is the earliest form of FDM, and the techniques used in radio are also used in cable FDM systems. Single-sideband modulation is most often used because of its conservative use of the spectrum, although any of the radio modulation techniques may be used. Figure 9.11 shows how the various channel frequencies are assigned within the spectrum for a cable carrier system. These frequency assignments are set forth by the CCITT and international agreements so that systems using them in various countries are compatible.

Modulation is performed in several cascaded stages. First, every three telephone channels (4 KHz wide) are modulated to form 3-channel pre-groups. Four pre-groups are then combined to form a 12-channel group. Next, five groups are combined to form a super group of 60 channels, and then up to 16 supergroups are combined to give a 960-channel master group for transmission on the coaxial cable. The full master group requires a bandwidth of more than 4 MHz, since spaces are left between the super groups to make filter separation easier.

Radio microwave transmission systems provide also for two or more 6 MHz television channels, and a modified master group containing only 12 super groups (720 channels) requiring only 3 MHz bandwidth is often used. Two such modified master groups may be transmitted stacked in each of the 6 MHz television channel slots. A microwave system with a 12 MHz modulation capacity then could carry two television channels, or 2880 telephone channels.

The pregroup modulator provides three carrier oscillators with frequencies of 12, 16, and 20 KHz. Upper sideband modulation moves the first channel from the 0–4 KHz slot into the 12–16 KHz slot; the second channel goes into the 16–20 KHz slot and the third goes into the 20–24 KHz slot. The three signals are summed and passed on to one of the group modulators. A separate pre-group modulator set is required for every three channels, so that a 960 channel system would require 320 modulator sets. Each modulator set produces signals with the same frequency range of 12–24 KHz, as shown in Figure 9.11(a). All carriers are suppressed.

The group modulator provides 4 carrier oscillators with frequencies of 84, 96, 108, and 120 KHz. Four pre-group signals are combined with these frequencies to move them into four consecutive frequency slots, 60–72, 72–84, 84–96, and 96–108 KHz respectively. Lower sideband modulation is used, so that the frequencies within each channel are reversed in order. Note that the carrier associated with each slot is located 12 KHz above the upper edge of the slot, one slot away. Again all carrier frequencies are suppressed

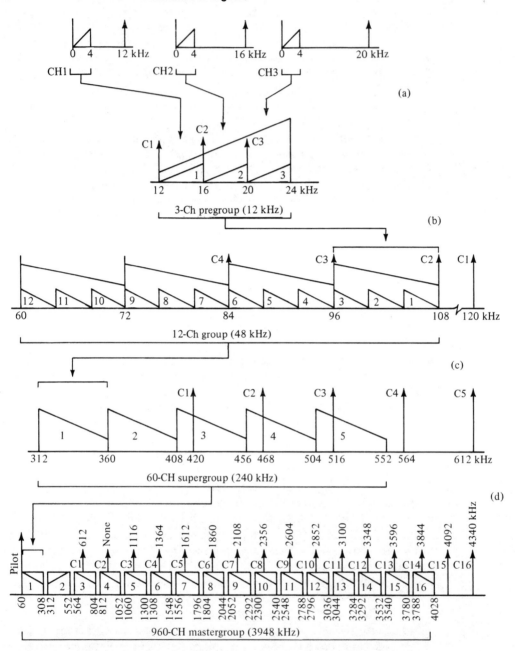

FIGURE 9.11. Cable Carrier System Frequency Allocations: (a) First modulation forms a 3-channel pregroup; (b) 3 pregroups form a 12-channel group (12 channels may also be directly modulated to form a group); (c) 5 groups form a 60-channel supergroup and; (d) 16 supergroups form a 960-channel mastergroup. (Courtesy Howard W. Sams & Co. Inc.)

in the modulation. The output signals from the modulators are combined and passed on to one of the supergroup modulators.

Each supergroup modulator provides carrier oscillators of 420, 468, 516, 564 and 612 KHz. These are combined again by lower sideband modulation with 5 group signals to move them from the 60–108 KHz slot to five consecutive slots, 312–360, 360–408, 408–456, 456–504, and 504–552 KHz. Again the order of frequencies within each group is reversed by the lower sideband modulation. The carriers are all suppressed, and the five signals are combined and passed on to a mastergroup modulator.

Each mastergroup modulator provides 16 carriers at frequencies of 612, none, 1116, 1364, 1612, 1860, 2108, 2356, 2604, 2852, 3100, 3348, 3596, 3844, 4092, and 4340 KHz. The second in the sequence is omitted because the second supergroup slot corresponds to the supergroup output frequencies and no conversion is necessary. Lower sideband modulation moves each of the other 15 supergroup signals into 240 KHz wide slots with 12 KHz spaces between them (to allow easier filtering), creating the final signal with frequencies from 60–4028 KHz (3968 KHz wide). All carriers are suppressed, but a 60 KHz pilot signal is transmitted to provide a synchronization signal for the demodulation oscillators. This final signal contains a maximum of 960 separate 4 KHz telephone channels. The actual maximum number used in a real system may be somewhat less than this because of the necessity to keep crosstalk and noise down and to provide spare channels in the case of faults occurring. Demodulation at the receiving end proceeds in the reverse order, going from mastergroup to supergroup to group to pregroup to channel in four separate demodulation steps.

9.7   COMPARISON OF SIGNAL-TO-NOISE RATIOS

As shown in Section 9.2 the amplitude of the output (information) signal is proportional to A_L, the received RF signal amplitude. A_L^2 is proportional to the power transmitted, P_T. The mean-square noise voltage, V_n^2, for a receiver bandwidth B, is proportional to kTB (see Chapter 4), and the output signal-to-noise power ratio will be, for the same constant of proportionality relating output voltage to input power for both signal and noise,

$$(\text{S/N})_{\text{SSB}} = \frac{A_L^2}{FV_n^2}$$

$$= \frac{P_T}{FkTB} \tag{9.14}$$

where F is the noise factor of the receiver.

For normal amplitude modulation, the detector output is $mE_{c_{\max}}$, so the output (information) signal power is proportional to $(mE_{c\max})^2$. $E_{c\max}^2$ is proportional to P_c, and, from Eq. (8.19);

$$P_c = \frac{P_T}{1 + \frac{m^2}{2}}$$

The noise bandwidth for double sidebands is $2B$; therefore, $V_n^2 \propto kT2B$, and the signal-to-noise power ratio is

$$(S/N)_{AM} = \frac{(mE_{c\max})^2}{FV_n^2}$$

$$= \frac{m^2 P_c}{FkT\,2B}$$

$$= \frac{m^2 P_T}{F(1 + \frac{m^2}{2})kT2B} \qquad (9.15)$$

Comparison of Eqs. (9.14) and (9.15) gives

$$\frac{(S/N)_{SSB}}{(S/N)_{AM}} = \frac{2(1 + \frac{m^2}{2})}{m^2} \qquad (9.16)$$

This assumes that the noise factor F is the same for both cases. For a modulation index, $m = 1$, Eq. (9.16) gives a ratio of 3:1, or single sideband shows an improvement of 4.77 dB over 100 % modulated AM.

The comparison just made is based on the assumption of equal average powers being transmitted in each case. Sometimes the comparison is based on peak power rating of the final amplifier stage of the transmitter. For 100 % sinusoidal amplitude modulation, the peak RF voltage is $4V_{CC}$, as shown in Figure 8.1(b), whereas for a single side frequency it will be $2V_{CC}$ (since the class C amplifier stage will be amplifying a single sinusoidal voltage and will be adjusted so that the peak-to-peak swing will be zero to $2V_{CC}$). Hence, for equal peak power ratings, the RF voltage for SSB can be doubled. This means that A_L at the receiver output can be twice the corresponding $E_{c\max}$, or the signal power output can be increased by a factor of four. The noise power for AM will still be twice that for SSB because of the double bandwidth, so the overall improvement in signal-to-noise power ratio for SSB over AM is 8:1, or 9 dB.

9.8   PROBLEMS

1.   Explain how the principle of operation of the balanced modulator of Figure 9.2 differs from that of Figure 9.3.

2. Draw the circuit for a single transistor multiplier stage and explain how it may be used to recover the information signal from a single-sideband transmission.

3. Use a phasor diagram to show that the output of the transmitter in Figure 9.7(c) contains only the upper-sideband component. What change is needed in the circuit if only the lower sideband is desired?

4. Show by means of trigonometric identities that the transmitter of Figure 9.6 generates an upper sideband signal.

5. The FET's in Figure 9.2 have a characteristic given by

$$i_d = IDSS \left(1 - \frac{V_{gs}}{V_P} \right)^2$$

where $IDSS = 10$ mA, $V_P = -0.8$ volts and the effective primary impedance of the transformer is 10 KOhms, at high frequencies. A 0.1 volt rms, 1 KHz modulating signal and a 0.5 volt peak carrier at 500 KHz are applied. Find the magnitudes and frequencies of each component appearing in the transformer primary voltage.

6. The modulator of Figure 9.3 is connected to an effective load resistance of 22 kΩ (on each side) and has a gain adjustment resistor of 1.2 kΩ. A square wave carrier of ± 1 volt peak at 2 MHz and a sinusoidal modulating signal of 0.5 volts rms at 4 KHz are applied. Find the magnitude and frequency of each component appearing in the output voltage V_o.

7. Sketch the block diagram of an SSB generator similar to Figure 9.6 which will generate a lower sideband signal. (Hint: see Equation 9.13)

8. (a) Show that shifting a sine function by $+90°$ turns it into a cosine function.

   (b) Show by means of the shifted angles in Figure 9.7 that interchanging the carrier inputs to Bal. Mods. 3 and 4 will cause the circuit to generate an upper sideband signal.

9. The 'Third Method' system of Figure 9.7 uses an audio carrier frequency of 2.5 KHz and a radio carrier frequency of 250 KHz. Two audio tones of 500 Hz and 4 KHz are modulated at once. (a) Sketch the spectrum of the output signal and calculate the frequency of each component present. (b) Also calculate the band-edge frequencies and the carrier location frequency and indicate these on the spectrum.

10. The receiver of Figure 9.8 receives an upper sideband signal carrying the original modulating frequencies of 500 Hz and 3 KHz. As the result of mis-tuning, the IF signal is 1 KHz lower than it should be. What audio frequencies are present in the receiver output?

11. The receiver of Figure 9.8 receives an upper sideband signal containing original modulating frequencies of 500 Hz and 2 KHz. However, the

receiver is switched to the lower sideband filter and is tuned 3 KHz low (so that the upper sideband appears in the lower sideband window of the filter). (a) What frequencies appear in the output and which of the original tones caused each? (b) What would this misadjustment do to a voice signal?

12. An AM transmitter with a total power output of 1000 watts is modulated by frequencies from 0 to 5 KHz at an average modulation index of 70%. This transmitter is replaced by a new SSB unit which puts out a total power of 2000 watts, with the same signal frequency range.

(a) What is the difference in S/N created for a given receiver?

(b) Is that change an improvement or a degradation?

(c) What portion of the change is due only to the change of modulation technique?

13. A frequency-division multiplex system is to provide six channels, three in each direction on a cable pair. An additional pair of channels at the bottom of the spectrum, including the base-band channel, is to be provided as a spare and for supervisory use. The channels are to each have a bandwidth of 4 kHz, and a pilot carrier is to be provided 500 Hz above the upper edge of each channel, with a pad band of 1.5 kHz between each pair of channels to allow easy filtering. Alternate channels are to transmit in alternate directions. Calculate the frequencies of the upper and lower edges of each band and the frequencies of each pilot carrier. Plot the spectrum response of the system, indicating the location of each of the channels and carriers. State the upper cutoff frequency necessary for the cable.

14. Calculate the maximum number of 4 kHz channels that can be frequency-division-multiplexed onto a 6 MHz television channel if 12.5% extra bandwidth must be allowed for each channel to prevent overlap, and the system is divided into groups of 12 channels with two additional channel spaces unused, one at either end of the group, and supergroups of five groups with one group extra space between supergroups, and further into master groups of 10 supergroups, with no extra zone between. State the number of groups, supergroups, and master groups which may be used, and the number of partial groups which could be included, to provide maximum usage. Compare the total to the maximum number of ideal 4-kHz channels.

Chapter 10
Angle Modulation

10.1 INTRODUCTION

In angle modulation, the information signal may be used to vary the carrier frequency, giving rise to *frequency modulation*, or it may be used to vary the angle of phase lead or lag, giving rise to *phase modulation*. Since both frequency and phase are parameters of the carrier angle, which is a function of time, the general term *angle modulation* covers both. Frequency and phase modulation have some very similar properties, but also some marked differences. The relationship between the two will be described in detail in this chapter.

Compared to amplitude modulation, frequency modulation has certain advantages. Mainly, the signal-to-noise ratio can be increased without increasing transmitted power (but at the expense of an increase in frequency bandwidth required); certain forms of interference at the receiver are more easily suppressed; and the modulation process can take place at a low-level power stage in the transmitter, thus avoiding the need for large amounts of modulating power.

10.2 FREQUENCY MODULATION

The modulating signal e_m, is used to vary the carrier frequency. For example, e_m may be used to alter the capacitance of the carrier frequency oscillator circuit (see Section 10.5.1). Let the change in carrier frequency be $k \cdot e_m$, where k is a constant known as the *frequency deviation constant*; the instantaneous carrier frequency is then

$$f_i = f_c + k \cdot e_m \qquad (10.1)$$

where f_c is the unmodulated carrier frequency.

For example, with e_m a sine wave,

$$e_m = E_{m\,\mathrm{max}} \sin \omega_m t \qquad (10.2)$$

The instantaneous carrier frequency becomes

$$f_i = f_c + k \cdot E_{m\,\mathrm{max}} \sin \omega_m t \qquad (10.3)$$

A sketch of f_i is shown in Figure 10.1(a). It is important to grasp that this is a frequency–time curve, not an amplitude–time curve. The amplitude–time curve for the frequency-modulated carrier is shown in Figure 10.1(b).

The factor $k \cdot E_{m\,\mathrm{max}}$ is seen to be the peak-frequency deviation and will be represented by Δf. Thus Eq. (10.3) becomes

$$f_i = f_c + \Delta f \cdot \sin \omega_m t \qquad (10.4)$$

In the more general case, e_m will be represented by $E_{m\,\mathrm{max}} \cdot m(t)$, where $m(t)$ is the modulating time function. Then

$$f_i = f_c + \Delta f \cdot m(t) \qquad (10.5)$$

For example, for sinusoidal modulation, $m(t) = \sin \omega_m t$ and Eq. (10.5) is equivalent to Eq. (10.4).

Example 10.1   Sketch the instantaneous frequency–time curve for a 100-MHz carrier wave, frequency-modulated by a 1-kHz square wave, the peak deviation being 90 kHz. The sketch is shown in Figure 10.1(c).

In order to get a quantitative understanding of frequency modulation it is first necessary to derive the equation for the modulated wave. The unmodulated carrier is a sine wave, as expressed in Eq. (8.1), for which, without loss of generality, $E_{c\,\mathrm{max}}$ may be set equal to unity:

(a)

(b)

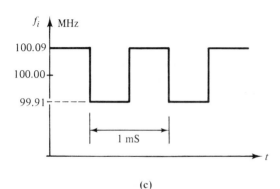

(c)

FIGURE 10.1. (a) Instantaneous frequency-time curve; (b) Carrier amplitude-time curve for a sinusoidally frequency-modulated carrier; (c) Instantaneous frequency-time curve for Example 10.1.

$$e_c = \sin(\omega_c t + \phi) \qquad (10.6)$$

where $\omega_c = 2\pi f_c$ = a constant angular frequency in rad/s, and ϕ is a constant phase angle in radians.

Equation (10.6) is a particular case of the more general expression:

$$e = \sin \Theta(t) \qquad (10.7)$$

The angular frequency of this general expression is the time rate of change of $\Theta(t)$, and only when the frequency is constant is the particular form in Eq. (10.6) valid. When the frequency is varied, as in frequency modulation, an instantaneous angular frequency may be defined as

$$\omega_i = 2\pi f_i = \frac{d\Theta(t)}{dt} \qquad (10.8)$$

or

$$\Theta(t) = \int \omega_i \cdot dt \qquad (10.9)$$

The instantaneous frequency f_i is related to the modulation by Eq. (10.5). For example, for constant (unmodulated) angular frequency ω_c

$$\Theta(t) = \int \omega_c \cdot dt$$
$$= \omega_c t + \phi \qquad (10.10)$$

where ϕ is the constant of integration. Equation (10.6) follows when Eq. (10.10) is substituted in Eq. (10.7).

For sinusoidal modulation, Eq. (10.4) is substituted in Eq. (10.9) to give

$$\Theta(t) = \int 2\pi(f_c + \Delta f \cdot \sin \omega_m t)dt$$
$$= \omega_c t - \frac{\Delta f}{f_m} \cdot \cos \omega_m t + \phi \qquad (10.11)$$

where $\omega_m = 2\pi f_m$.

The constant ϕ may be made equal to zero by appropriate choice of reference axis, and the equation for the sinusoidally frequency modulated wave obtained by substituting Eq. (10.11) in Eq. (10.7).

$$e = \sin\left(\omega_c t - \frac{\Delta f}{f_m} \cos \omega_m t\right) \qquad (10.12)$$

Note that Eq. (10.12) could not have been derived simply by substituting f_i for f_c in Eq. (10.6), the reason being that Eq. (10.6) is derived on the basis of *constant* frequency, and, of course, frequency modulation invalidates this.

The modulation index for frequency modulation is defined as

$$m_f = \frac{\Delta f}{f_m} \qquad (10.13)$$

The equation for the sinusoidally modulated carrier then becomes

$$e = \sin(\omega_c t - m_f \cos \omega_m t) \qquad (10.14)$$

Unlike amplitude modulation, the modulation index for frequency modulation can be greater than unity.

10.2.1 The Frequency Spectrum

The mathematical analysis of Eq. (10.14) leading to a frequency spectrum for a sinusoidally frequency modulated wave is much more difficult than the corresponding amplitude-modulation analysis (see, for example, Ben Zeines, *Electronic Communications Systems*, Prentice-Hall, Inc., Englewood Cliffs, N.J., 1970, Section 9.13), and only the results will be used here. The spectrum is found to consist of a carrier component, and side frequencies at harmonics of the modulating frequency, even though no harmonics are present in the original modulating tone. The amplitudes of the various spectral components are given by a mathematical function known as Bessel's Function of the First Kind, denoted here by $J_n(m_f)$; m_f is the modulation index defined in Eq. (10.13), and n is the order of side frequency. In mathematical notation, m_f is termed the argument, and n the order, of the Bessel Function. Bessel Functions are available in both graphical and tabular form as shown in Figure 10.2, and Table 10.1. $J_o(m_f)$ gives the amplitude of the carrier component.

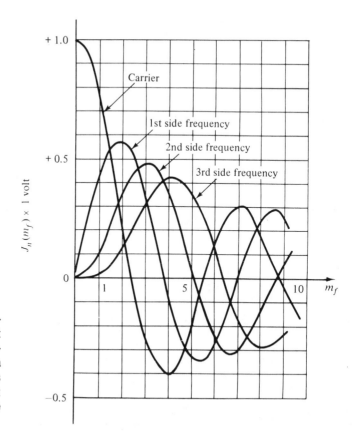

FIGURE 10.2. A plot of the magnitudes of the carrier and the first three side frequencies of a sinusoidally modulated FM wave with a carrier of one volt magnitude versus modulation index m_f. (This is a plot of the Bessel Functions of the wave.)

TABLE 10.1. Amplitudes of Spectrum Components for a Sinusoidally Frequency-Modulated Carrier of Unmodulated Amplitude IV (Amplitude Moduli Less than |0.01| not shown)

Modulation Index m_f	Carrier	Side Frequencies											
		1st	2nd	3rd	4th	5th	6th	7th	8th	9th	10th	11th	12th
0.25	0.98	0.12	0.01										
0.5	0.94	0.24	0.03										
1.0	0.77	0.44	0.11	0.02									
1.5	0.51	0.56	0.23	0.06	0.01								
2.0	0.22	0.58	0.35	0.13	0.03								
2.4	0	0.52	0.43	0.20	0.06								
3.0	−0.26	0.34	0.49	0.31	0.13	0.04	0.01						
4.0	−0.40	−0.07	0.36	0.43	0.28	0.13	0.05	0.02					
5.0	−0.18	−0.33	0.05	0.36	0.39	0.26	0.13	0.05	0.02	0.01			
5.5	0	−0.34	−0.12	0.26	0.40	0.32	0.19	0.09	0.03	0.01			
6.0	0.15	−0.28	−0.24	0.11	0.36	0.36	0.25	0.13	0.06	0.02	0.01		
7.0	0.30	0	−0.30	−0.17	0.16	0.35	0.34	0.23	0.13	0.06	0.02	0.01	
8.0	0.17	0.23	−0.11	−0.29	−0.10	0.19	0.34	0.32	0.22	0.13	0.06	0.03	0.01
8.65	0	0.27	0.06	−0.24	−0.23	0.03	0.26	0.34	0.28	0.18	0.10	0.05	0.02

As an example of the use of Table 10.1, it is seen that, for $m_f = 0.5$, the spectral components are

Carrier (f_c)	$J_o(0.5) = 0.94$
1st order side frequencies $(f_c \pm f_m)$	$J_1(0.5) = 0.24$
2nd order side frequencies $(f_c \pm 2f_m)$	$J_2(0.5) = 0.03$

The fact that the spectrum component at the carrier frequency decreases in amplitude does *not* mean that the carrier wave is amplitude modulated. The carrier wave is the sum of all the components in the spectrum, and these add up to give a constant amplitude carrier as shown in Figure 10.1(b). The distinction is that the modulated carrier is not a sine wave, whereas the spectum component at carrier frequency is. (All spectrum components are either sine or cosine waves.) It will be noted from Table 10.1 that amplitudes can be negative in some instances, but it is usually not necessary to show this on a spectrum graph, the modulus value only being shown. It will also be seen that for certain values of m_f (2.4, 5.5, 8.65, and higher values not shown), the carrier amplitude goes to zero. This serves to emphasize the point that it is the sinusoidal component of the spectrum, at carrier frequency, which goes to zero, *not* the modulated carrier, which is nonsinusoidal and which varies from positive to negative peak (1 V in this case) while the frequency varies.

The spectra for various values of m_f are shown in Figure 10.3(a), (b), and (c). In each case the spectral lines are spaced by f_m, and the bandwidth occupied by the spectrum is seen to be

$$B = 2 \cdot n \cdot f_m \qquad (10.15)$$

where n is the highest order of side frequency for which the amplitude is significant. From Table 10.1 it will be seen that where the order of side frequency is greater than $(m_f + 1)$, the amplitude is 5% or less of unmodulated carrier amplitude. Using this as a guide for bandwidth requirements, Eq. (10.15) can be written as

$$B = 2(m_f + 1)f_m \qquad (10.16)$$

or
$$B = 2(\Delta f + f_m) \qquad (10.17)$$

To illustrate the significance of this, three examples will be considered:

1. $\Delta f = 75$ kHz, $f_m = 0.1$ kHz:

$$B = 2(75 + 0.1)$$

$$= \mathbf{150\ kHz}$$

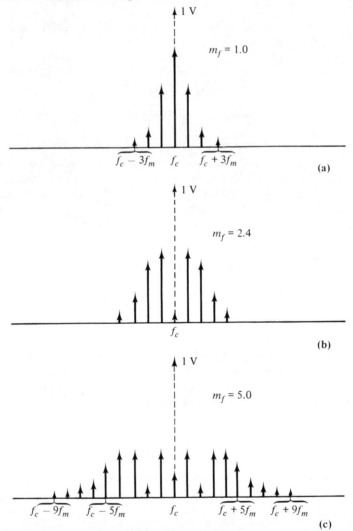

FIGURE 10.3. Spectra for sinusoidally modulated FM waves with various modulation indexes: (a) $m_f = 1.0$; (b) $m_f = 2.4$ (note missing carrier); (c) $m_f = 5.0$.

2. $\Delta f = 75$ kHz, $f_m = 1.0$ kHz:

$$B = 2(75 + 1)$$

$$= 152 \text{ kHz}$$

3. $\Delta f = 75$ kHz, $f_m = 10$ kHz:

$$B = 2(75 + 10)$$

$$= 170 \text{ kHz}$$

Thus, although the modulation frequency changes from 0.1 kHz to 10 kHz, or by a factor of 100:1, the bandwidth occupied by the spectrum alters very little, from 150 kHz to 170 kHz. These examples illustrate why frequency modulation is sometimes referred to as a constant-bandwidth system.

10.2.2   Average Power

The average power in a sinusoidally frequency-modulated wave remains constant at the unmodulated value. As modulation is applied, the power is redistributed over the various spectral components (and for this reason, the amplitude of the carrier component decreases as already shown). The corresponding mathematical condition is that the sum of the squares of the Bessel Functions, for a given m_f, is constant, since the average power in any spectral component is proportional to its amplitude squared. This is illustrated in the following example.

Example 10.2   A 15-W unmodulated carrier is frequently-modulated with a sinusoidal signal such that the peak frequency deviation is 6 kHz. The frequency of the modulating signal is 1 kHz. Calculate the average power output.

Solution   The total average power output P is 15 W modulated. To check that this is also the value obtained from the sum of the squares of the Bessel Functions,

$$m_f = \frac{6}{1}$$

$$= 6$$

The Bessel function values for $m_f = 6$ are read from Table 10.1 and

$$P_T = 15[0.15^2 + 2(0.28^2 + 0.24^2 + 0.11^2 + 0.36^2 + 0.36^2 + 0.25^2$$
$$+ 0.13^2 + 0.06^2 + 0.02^2 + 0.01^2)]$$
$$= 15(1.00)$$
$$= 15 \text{ W}$$

It follows that since the average power does not change with frequency modulation, the rms voltage, and current will also remain constant, at their respective unmodulated values.

10.2.3   Complex-Wave Modulation: Deviation Ratio

In the frequency-modulation process, intermodulation products are formed; that is, beat frequencies occur between the various side frequencies when the modulation signal is other than sinusoidal or cosinusoidal. It is a matter of experience, however, that the bandwidth requirements are determined by the maximum frequency deviation and maximum modulation frequency (harmonic) present in the complex modulating wave. The ratio of maximum deviation to maximum frequency component is termed the *deviation ratio*. Denoting this by M,

$$M = \frac{\Delta F}{F_m} \tag{10.18}$$

where ΔF is the maximum frequency deviation and F_m the highest frequency component in the modulating signal. The bandwidth is then given by Eq. (10.16) on substituting M for m_f, with the same limitations on accuracy. Thus

$$B_{\text{max}} = 2(M + 1)F_m \tag{10.19}$$

$$= 2(\Delta F + F_m)$$

This is known as *Carson's rule*.

Example 10.3   Canadian regulations state that for FM broadcast the maximum deviation allowed is 75 kHz and the maximum modulation frequency, 15 kHz. Calculate the maximum bandwidth requirements.

Solution   Using Eq. (10.19),

$$B_{\text{max}} = 2(75 + 15)$$

$$= 180 \text{ kHz}$$

Examination of Table 10.1 shows that side frequencies of 1% amplitude extend up to the ninth side frequency pair, so Carson's rule underestimates the bandwidth required. For M equal to 5 or greater, a better estimate is given by $B_{\text{max}} = 2(M + 4)F_m$. In this example, this would result in a maximum bandwidth requirement of 270 kHz. The economic constraints on commercial equipment limits the bandwidth capabilities of receivers to about 200 kHz.

10.2.4   Measurement of Modulation Index

The spectrum for a sinusoidally modulated wave can be measured directly on a spectrum analyzer and the carrier frequency deviation measured independently on a frequency deviation meter. For a given modulating frequency (e.g., 1 kHz) the amplitude of the modulating signal can be adjusted until the carrier component of the spectrum, as viewed on the spectrum analyzer, disappears. The modulation amplitudes for which this happens should be in the ratio (2.4):(5.5):(8.65), since the deviation should be proportional to modulating signal amplitude, and Table 10.1 shows that these are the values of m_f for which the carrier is zero. Measurement of the deviation enables m_f to be calculated, knowing f_m.

10.3 PHASE MODULATION

Phase modulation results when the phase angle ϕ of the carrier is made a function of the modulating signal. The unmodulated carrier is given by

$$e_c = \sin(\omega_c t + \phi_c) \qquad (10.20)$$

When phase modulated, ϕ_c is replaced by $\phi(t)$, where

$$\phi(t) = \phi_c + K \cdot e_m \qquad (10.21)$$

K is the *phase deviation constant* (analogous to k for frequency modulation) and e_m is the modulating signal, as before. Normally, ϕ_c, can be dropped from the equation since it is a constant that does not affect the modulation. Also, letting $e_m = E_{m_{max}} \cdot m(t)$, as before, Eq. (10.21) can be written as

$$\phi(t) = \Delta\phi \cdot m(t) \qquad (10.22)$$

where

$$\Delta\phi = K \cdot E_{m_{max}} \qquad (10.23)$$

$\Delta\phi$ is clearly the peak phase deviation.

Substituting Eq. (10.22) in Eq. (10.20) gives the expression for the phase-modulated wave:

$$e = \sin[\omega_c t + \Delta\phi \cdot m(t)] \qquad (10.24)$$

For sinusoidal modulation Eq. (10.24) becomes

$$e = \sin(\omega_c t + \Delta\phi \cdot \sin \omega_m t) \qquad (10.25)$$

And, in order to emphasize the similarity with sinusoidal frequency modulation, the peak phase deviation is termed the phase modulation index and the symbol m_p used. Equation (10.25) then becomes

$$e = \sin(\omega_c t + m_p \sin \omega_m t) \qquad (10.26)$$

Comparing Eq. (10.26) with Eq. (10.14), the similarity between phase modulation and frequency modulation for sinusoidal modulating signals will be evident, especially when it is remembered that the only difference between the sinusoidal and cosinusoidal modulating terms in the angles is one of a 90° phase difference which would not be readily apparent when the signals are demodulated.

10.3.1 Spectrum of a Sinusoidally Phase-Modulated Wave

It follows from the comparison of Eqs. (10.26) and (10.14) that for the same value of modulation index, the spectrum for the phase-modulated wave will be the same as the spectrum for the frequency-modulated wave. For example, for $m_p = 5.0$, the spectrum of Figure 10.3(c) applies.

10.4 EQUIVALENCE BETWEEN FM AND PM

The instantaneous angular frequency as defined in Eq. (10.8) is

$$\omega_i = \frac{d\Theta(t)}{dt} \tag{10.8}$$

For a phase-modulated wave, the phase modulation is expressed by Eq. (10.21) and

$$\Theta(t) = \omega_c t + \phi(t) \tag{10.27}$$

Therefore, applying Eq. (10.8), phase modulation has an equivalent angular frequency

$$\omega_{i_{eq}} = \omega_c + \frac{d\phi(t)}{dt} \tag{10.28}$$

Let $f_{eq}(t)$ represent the equivalent frequency modulation in Eq. (10.28); then

$$\omega_c + 2\pi f_{eq}(t) = \omega_c + \frac{d\phi(t)}{dt}$$

Therefore,
$$f_{eq}(t) = \frac{1}{2\pi}\frac{d\phi(t)}{dt} \tag{10.29}$$

The importance of Eq. (10.29) lies in the fact that all angle-modulation receivers interpret angle modulation always as frequency modulation (even the "phase discriminators" described in Section 10.5.3). This means that the demodulated signal output is proportional to the frequency deviation, actual or equivalent, of the received modulated signal. This is illustrated for the three separate waveforms of Figure 10.4, for the system shown in Figure 10.4(a). For the triangular modulation wave of Figure 10.4(b), the phase modulation is

$$\phi(t) = \quad at \quad \text{for } 0 < t < \tfrac{1}{2}T$$
$$= -at \quad \text{for } \tfrac{1}{2}T < t < T$$

where a is the modulus of the slope of the lines (assumed equal for positive and negative slopes). The term $\phi(t)$ has the same periodicity as $m(t)$. Applying Eq. (10.29),

$$f_{eq}(t) = \frac{1}{2\pi} \frac{d(at)}{dt}$$

$$= \frac{a}{2\pi} \quad \text{for } 0 < t < \tfrac{1}{2}T$$

$$= -\frac{a}{2\pi} \quad \text{for } \tfrac{1}{2}T < t < T$$

Thus $f_{eq}(t)$ is a square wave as shown, Figure 10.4(b), with $\Delta f_{eq} = a/2\pi$. The output voltage has the same waveshape as $f_{eq}(t)$.

For the square-wave modulating signal of Figure 10.4(a), the rate of change of $\phi(t)$ (the slope of the graph) is zero except at the points where the wave reverses sign when the rate of change is theoretically $\pm \infty$. Therefore, applying Eq. (10.29), $f_{eq}(t)$ will be zero except at the points of reversal, where it will be represented by impulses as shown, Figure 10.4(c). The output voltage waveform follows the $f_{eq}(t)$ waveform.

For the sinusoidal modulating signal, Figure 10.4(d),

$$\phi(t) = m_p \cdot \sin \omega_m t$$

Therefore,
$$f_{eq}(t) = \frac{\omega_m m_p}{2\pi} \cos \omega_m t$$

$$= f_m \cdot m_p \cdot \cos \omega_m t$$

The term $f_{eq}(t)$ is shown in Figure 10.4(d), and it will be seen that the maximum equivalent frequency deviation is

$$\Delta f_{eq} = f_m \cdot m_p \qquad (10.30)$$

The output voltage waveform follows the $f_{eq}(t)$ curve, and therefore the amplitude of the output voltage, which is proportional to Δf_{eq}, is pro-

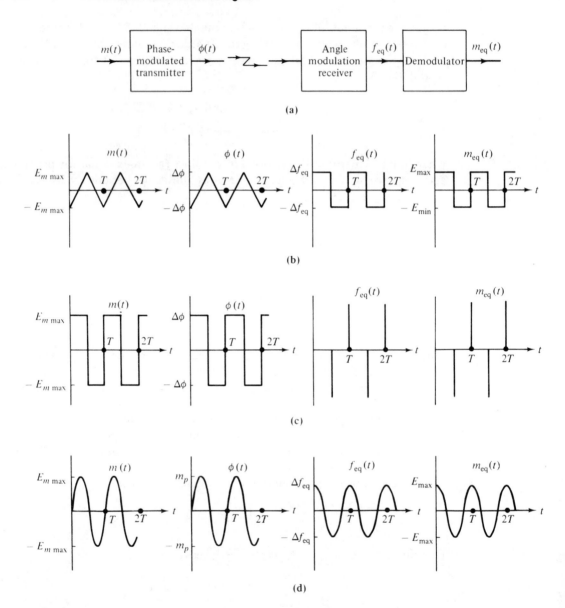

FIGURE 10.4. Phase modulation with various complex modulating signals:
(a) The angle-modulation system; $m(t)$ is the modulating input and $m_{eq}(t)$ is
the corresponding receiver output; (b) Triangular modulating wave resulting
in a square-wave output; (c) Square modulating wave resulting in an impulse output; (d) A sinusoidal modulation wave resulting in a cosinusoidal
output.

portional to $f_m \cdot m_p$. For a constant m_p, the output is proportional to the modulating frequency.

Example 10.4   A constant-amplitude 2-kHz sine wave is used to phase-modulate a carrier. At some later time, the frequency of the modulating signal is increased to 5 kHz. Explain what happens to the output signal from a receiver used to receive the modulated wave.

Solution   The frequency of the output voltage signal will increase from 2 to 5 kHz, and the amplitude will increase by a factor of 5/2, or 2.5 times.

The relationship expressed by Eq. (10.29) is used as the basis for obtaining frequency modulation from phase modulation. The theory is straightforward. Instead of making $\phi(t)$ proportional to $m(t)$, it is made proportional to the integral of $m(t)$, usually by means of a simple integrating network such as shown in Figure 10.5. Thus, applying Eq. (10.21) (and dropping the constant ϕ_c),

$$\phi(t) = K \cdot e_m$$

$$= \frac{K}{RC} \int m(t)\,dt$$

FIGURE 10.5.   Conversion of phase modulation to frequency modulation.

Applying Eq. (10.29),

$$f_{eq}(t) = \frac{1}{2\pi} \frac{K}{RC} \cdot m(t)$$

$$= k \cdot m(t) \tag{10.31}$$

where k is a constant equal to $K/2\pi RC$.

Equation (10.31) shows that the equivalent frequency modulation from the phase modulator and integrator is proportional to the original modulating signal, which is the desired condition.

10.5 ANGLE MODULATION CIRCUITS

In the analysis presented here, small signal conditions are assumed; it is also assumed that the modulation rate is sufficiently slow for *sinusoidal* analysis at the carrier frequency to be used.

10.5.1. The Varactor Diode

The *varactor diode* is a *pn* junction diode, the depletion capacitance of which varies with reverse bias, as shown in Figure 10.6(a). The name varactor comes from *var*iable re*actor*. For tuning applications the diode may be represented by the approximate equivalent circuit of the depletion capacitance C_d in series with a resistance R_s, which represents the resistance of the bulk *pn* regions, and the lead resistance.

Modulation voltage is applied as reverse bias, and the resulting variation in C_d is used to vary either the frequency or the phase of an LC-tuned circuit. For successful practical implementation, the oscillator voltage must produce negligible variation in C_d, and the oscillator frequency must be considerably higher than the modulating frequency. In effect, C_d varies slowly at the modulating frequency while carrying a small-signal capacitive current at oscillator frequency.

For an abrupt-type *pn* junction in silicon, semiconductor theory [see, for example, Motorola Application Note AN 178-A (1971)] gives the relationship between C_d and modulus of reverse bias $|V|$ as

$$C_d = \frac{C_0}{\left(1 + \frac{|V|}{\Phi}\right)^a} \qquad (10.32)$$

where C_0 is the capacitance at zero bias and Φ is the contact potential of the junction (volts), and the index a depends on the type of junction. For abrupt junctions, $a \cong 0.5$ and for silicon, $\Phi \cong 0.5$ V.

The frequency deviation constant k for the circuit of Figure 10.6(b) is given by

$$k = S_1 \cdot S_2 \qquad (10.33)$$

where S_1 is the slope of the varactor diode characteristic Figure 10.6(a) at the operating point determined by $|V_0|$, and S_2 is the slope of the frequency/diode capacitance curve also at the operating point, determined by C_{do}. The student should verify that the dimensions of k are Hz/V.

The slope S_1 is found by differentiating Eqn. (10.32), which for $a = 0.5$ and $\Phi = 0.5$ V gives:

$$S_1 = \frac{dC_d}{d|V|} = -\tfrac{1}{2}\frac{C_d}{1 + 2|V|} \qquad (10.34)$$

(a)

(b)

(c)

FIGURE 10.6. (a) Varactor diode characteristic; (b) Varactor diode used for frequency modulation; (c) Varactor diode used for phase modulation.

At the operating point $C_d = C_{do}$ and $|V| = |V_o|$ and therefore:

$$S_1 = -\tfrac{1}{2}\frac{C_{do}}{1 + 2|V_0|} \tag{10.35}$$

The frequency of the Colpitt's oscillator is given approximately by:

$$f = \frac{1}{2\pi\sqrt{L}}\sqrt{\frac{1}{C_d} + \frac{1}{C}} \tag{10.36}$$

Therefore,
$$S_2 = \frac{df}{dC_d} = -\tfrac{1}{2}\frac{f}{\left(1 + \frac{C_d}{C}\right)C_d} \tag{10.37}$$

(The differentiation of these expressions is left as a mathematical exercise for the student).

At the nominal operating frequency $f = f_o$ and $C_d = C_{do}$. Also, for the Colpitt's circuit, let $C_{do} = nC$, then:

$$S_2 = -\tfrac{1}{2}\frac{f_0}{(1 + n)C_{do}} \tag{10.38}$$

Combining Eqns. (10.33), (10.35) and (10.38) gives:

$$k = \frac{f_0}{4(1 + n)(1 + 2|V_0|)} \tag{10.39}$$

Example 10.5 Calculate the frequency-deviation constant for a Colpitts oscillator frequency modulated in accordance with Eq. (10.39), for which the unmodulated frequency is 50 MHz at a fixed bias of 15 volts, given that $n = 1$.

Solution
$$k = \frac{50 \times 10^6}{8(1 + 2 \times 15)}$$

$$= 202 \text{ Hz/mV}$$

The varactor diode may also be used as a phase modulator, one circuit being shown in Figure 10.6(c). The variation of the diode capacitance alters the phase angle of the tuned-circuit admittance, and hence the phase angle of the oscillator voltage developed across it. Let the oscillator feed the circuit with a constant current, *constant frequency*, signal; then the phase deviation constant K [see Eq. (10.21)] for the circuit found as follows. The total tuning capacity is

$$C_s = \frac{C \cdot C_d}{C + C_d} \qquad (10.40)$$

and at the operating point, let this be C_{s0}, determined by C_{d0}. The slope of the C_s/C_d curve at the operating point (as found by differentiation) is

$$S_s = -\left(\frac{C_{s0}}{C_{d0}}\right)^2 \qquad (10.41)$$

Next, the admittance of the tuned circuit is given by

$$Y = \frac{1}{R_D} + j\left(\omega C_s - \frac{1}{\omega L}\right) \qquad (10.42)$$

and therefore its phase angle is

$$\phi = \tan^{-1}\left[R_D\left(\omega C_s - \frac{1}{\omega L}\right)\right]$$

where R_D is as given by Eq. (1.72). For small angles, the angle is approximately equal to the tangent, and the slope of the ϕ/C_s curve at the operating point becomes

$$S_\phi = R_D \omega_0 \qquad (10.43)$$

Substituting for R_D from Eq. (1.73) gives

$$S_\phi = \frac{Q}{C_{s0}} \qquad (10.44)$$

The phase deviation constant K is then determined by

$$K = S_1 S_s S_\phi \qquad (10.45)$$

The student should verify that K has dimensions of rad/V.
Substituting from Eqs. (10.35), (10.41), and (10.43), and simplifying, gives

$$K = \frac{C_{d0} C_{s0} \cdot Q}{C_0^2} \qquad (10.46)$$

If, for the circuit, Fig. 10.6(c), $C = C_{d0}$, then this simplifies further to

$$K = \frac{1}{2}\left(\frac{C_{d0}}{C_0}\right)^2 Q$$

$$= \frac{Q}{2(1 + 2|V_0|)} \qquad (10.47)$$

Example 10.6 Calculate the phase deviation constant in accordance with Eq. (10.47) for $Q = 70$, and $|V_0| = 15$ volts.

Solution

$$K = \frac{70}{2(31)}$$

$$= 1.13 \text{ rad/v}$$

10.5.2 Transistor Angle Modulators

A transistor in which the g_m is a function of modulating voltage may be used for both frequency and phase modulation. The principle of operation is that the g_m varies in accordance with the slowly varying modulating signal, and the circuit, in turn, presents a reactance at *oscillator frequency* that varies with g_m and that influences the frequency or phase of the oscillator output. Bipolar transistors or FETs may be used, but for definiteness, FETs are shown in the circuits of Figure 10.7. For both circuits, circuit values are such that the oscillator output current I_o is approximately equal to the drain current I_d; that is, currents I_1 and I_2 are negligible at oscillator frequency. Hence

$$I_o \cong I_d = g_m V_{\text{in}} \qquad (10.48)$$

For the frequency modulation circuit, Figure 10.7(a),

$$V_{\text{in}} = V_o \frac{Z_2}{Z_1 + Z_2} \qquad (10.49)$$

The small-signal admittance presented to the oscillator can be found by combining Eqs. (10.48) and (10.49):

$$Y = \frac{I_o}{V_o}$$

$$= g_m \frac{Z_2}{Z_1 + Z_2} \qquad (10.50)$$

By making $Z_1 = 1/j\omega_o C$, $Z_2 = R$, and $|Z_1| \gg Z_2$, Eq. (10.50) reduces to

$$Y \cong jg_m \omega_o CR$$

This is equivalent to a capacitance C_{eq} across the oscillator output, where

$$C_{\text{eq}} = g_m CR \qquad (10.51)$$

Thus, the modulating voltage varies g_m, which varies C_{eq}, which, in turn, varies the oscillator frequency.

FIGURE 10.7. FET varactor circuits;
(a) Frequency modulation; (b) Phase
modulation.

For the phase modulation circuit of Figure 10.7(b), the oscillator output voltage, unmodulated, is V_o, and modulated, V_d; and it is required to find the phase relationship between V_d and V_o. From the circuit

$$I_o \cong (V_o - V_d) \cdot j\frac{\omega C}{2} \tag{10.52}$$

and

$$V_{in} \cong \tfrac{1}{2}(V_o + V_d) \tag{10.53}$$

(the approximations being valid to the extent that I_1 and I_2 can be neglected). Substituting Eq. (10.53) in Eq. (10.48) and equating to Eq. (10.52)

$$g_m\frac{(V_o + V_d)}{2} = (V_o - V_d) \cdot j\frac{\omega_o C}{2}$$

From which

$$V_d = -V_o \frac{(g_m - j\omega_o C)}{(g_m + j\omega_o C)} \qquad (10.54)$$

Since the modulus of the complex term in the numerator is equal to that in the denominator, it follows that the modulus of V_d is equal to that of V_o; that is,

$$|V_d| = |V_o| \qquad (10.55)$$

This means that the circuit does not introduce amplitude modulation, which is an advantage.

The phase of V_d with respect to V_o is equal to the phase angle of the complex fraction on the right-hand side of Eq. (10.54) and is

$$\phi = \tan^{-1} \frac{(2g_m\omega_o C)}{(\omega_o C)^2 - g_m^2} \qquad (10.56)$$

Thus the phase angle of the oscillator output voltage can be varied by varying the g_m of the transistor with the modulation voltage. By making $(\omega_o C)^2 \gg g_m^2$, then Eq. (10.56) reduces to

$$\phi \cong \tan^{-1}\left(\frac{2g_m}{\omega_o C}\right) \qquad (10.57)$$

By keeping the deviation ϕ less than about 0.1 rad, this reduces further to

$$\phi \cong \frac{2g_m}{\omega_o C} \qquad (10.58)$$

10.5.3 Basic Detection of FM Signals

In order to detect an FM signal, it is necessary to have a circuit whose output voltage varies *linearly* with the frequency of the input signal. The slope detector is a very basic form of such a circuit, although its linearity of response is not good. Figure 10.8(a) shows the basic arrangement. By tuning the circuit to receive the signal on the slope of the response curve, Figure 10.8(b), carrier amplitude V is caused to vary with frequency. The carrier is now both amplitude- and frequency-modulated, represented by $V \cdot \sin \Theta(t)$, and the modulation is recovered from the amplitude modulation by means of a normal envelope detector. However, the linear range on the voltage/frequency-transfer characteristic is limited.

Linearity can be improved by utilizing the arrangement of Figure 10.8(c), this circuit being known as the *Round-Travis detector*, or *balanced*

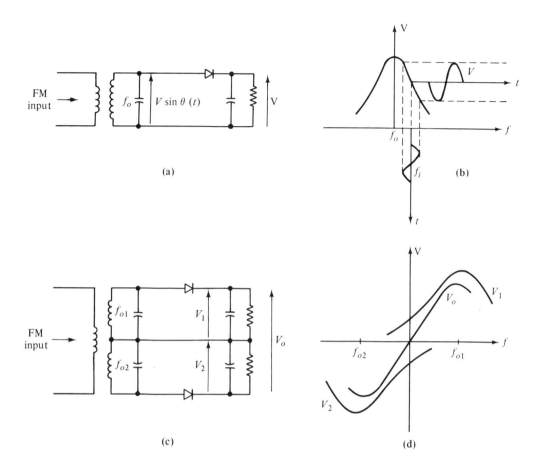

FIGURE 10.8. (a) FM slope detector; (b) Magnitude of tank circuit admittance plotted against frequency, showing output voltage constructions; (c) Balanced double-tuned slope (or Travis) detector; (d) Plot of tank circuit admittance magnitudes versus frequency, with constructions of output voltages and the S-shaped transfer function curve.

slope detector. One slope detector is tuned to f_{o1} above the incoming carrier frequency, and the other to f_{o2} below the carrier frequency, and the envelope detectors combined to give a differential output. This means that by showing the V_1 response as positive, the V_2 response can be shown negative on the same axes, and the output, which is $V_o = |V_1| + |V_2|$, will have an S shape when plotted against frequency, as shown in Figure 10.8(d). This S-curve is characteristic of FM detectors, and, of course, the linear range should be as large as possible. When the incoming signal is unmodulated, the output is balanced to zero; when the carrier deviates toward f_{o1}, $|V_1|$

increases while $|V_2|$ decreases, and the output goes positive; when it deviates toward f_{o2}, $|V_1|$ decreases while $|V_2|$ increases, and the output goes negative.

10.5.4 Foster-Seeley Discriminator

The Foster-Seeley discriminator recovers the modulating voltage from the frequency modulation by utilizing the phase-angle shift between primary and secondary voltages of a tuned transformer. The phase angle is a function of frequency, and by arranging for phasor-sum and phasor-difference components of primary and secondary voltages to be applied to two envelope detectors, the outputs of which are then combined, demodulation is achieved. Because the circuit relies on a phase-angle variation, it is also known as a *phase discriminator*, but it must not be thought that it detects phase modulation directly; it converts a frequency variation, real or equivalent, to a circuit phase-angle variation, which in turn is converted to an amplitude variation.

The basic circuit is shown in Figure 10.9(a). Capacitor C_c has negligible reactance at carrier frequency; therefore, the full primary voltage, approximately, appears across the radio-frequency choke (RFC), this having a high reactance at carrier frequency. The primary voltage is connected from the RFC to the center tap on the transformer secondary with the result that the radio-frequency voltage applied to diode D_1 is $V_1 + \frac{1}{2}V_2$, and to diode D_2, $V_1 - \frac{1}{2}V_2$. The phase relationship between V_1 and V_2 can be found using the steady-state analysis developed in Chapter 1, again bearing in mind that this gives only an approximate picture of how the circuit functions, since the applied signal is nonsinusoidal. The phase angle of V_2 with respect to V_1 is found to be

$$\Phi = (\tan^{-1}(yQ)) - \frac{\pi}{2} \qquad (10.59)$$

where yQ is defined in Eq. (1.54).

The current i_2, which is in phase with V_1, passes through C_2 to create the voltage drop V_2 with a lagging phase shift of $-\pi/2$, at resonance.

The phasor sum of $V_1 \pm \frac{1}{2}V_2$ is then as shown in Figure 10.9(b), (c), and (d) for three different conditions of carrier frequency. The envelope detector D_1 will produce an output voltage proportional to $|V_{D1}|$, and that of D_2, an output voltage proportional to $|V_{D2}|$. (For an explanation of the action of the envelope detector, see Section 8.2.7.) The output voltage is seen to be

$$V_o = V_{o1} - V_{o2}$$

$$= K(|V_{D1}| - |V_{D2}|) \qquad (10.60)$$

where K is a constant of the detector circuits.

To summarize, as the frequency increases, the phase shift decreases and $|V_{D1}|$ increases while $|V_{D2}|$ decreases; hence, V_0 will increase. When the

(a)

(b)

(c)

(d)

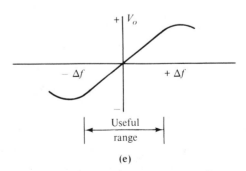

(e)

FIGURE 10.9. (a) Foster-Seeley discrimina-
tor; (b) Phasor sums of $V_1 \pm \frac{1}{2}V_2$ at resonance ($f = f_0$); (c) Phasor sums of $V_1 \pm$
$\frac{1}{2}V_2$ at $f > f_0$; (d) Phasor sums of $V_1 \pm \frac{1}{2}V_2$
at $f < f_0$; (e) Output voltage versus fre-
quency deviation.

frequency decreases, the phase shift increases and $|V_{D1}|$ decreases while $|V_{D2}|$ increases; therefore, V_o decreases. The curve of output voltage V_o against frequency deviation Δf is sketched in Figure 10.9(e). This S-curve is characteristic of discriminators, the curving at the extremes resulting from the secondary voltage becoming very small at frequencies well removed from resonance. Amplitude variations are reduced to negligible proportions by amplitude-limiting the signal before applying it to the discriminator. There are many practical variations of the circuit, and Figure 10.10 shows it being used with integrated circuits. In this application, amplifier block MFC6010 provides gain and amplifier block MC1355 provides gain limiting. It will be seen that the primary voltage is coupled into the secondary by means of a third winding (known as a tertiary winding) which is very closely

FIGURE 10.10. FM receiver unit utilizing integrated circuit amplifiers and a Foster-Seeley discriminator. (Courtesy Motorola, Inc.)

coupled to the primary. Also, the ground point is shifted so that the output may be taken with respect to ground, a much more practical arrangment.

10.5.5 Ratio Detector

A very simple change can be made to the Foster–Seeley discriminator, which improves the limiting action but at the expense of reducing the output. One of the diodes is reversed so that the two diodes conduct in series, Figure 10.11(a); the detector circuits then provide a damping action, which tends to maintain a constant secondary voltage, as will be shown.

Diodes D_1 and D_2 and associated loads RC form envelope detectors as before and the frequency-to-phase-to-amplitude chain of events occur as in the Foster–Seeley discriminator. Now, however, the polarity of voltage in the lower capacitor is reversed, so the sum voltage appears across the combined loads (rather than the difference voltage as in the Foster–Seeley). Hence, as V_{o1} increases, V_{o2} decreases and V_o' remains constant (and, of course, it remains constant as V_{o1} decreases and V_{o2} increases). Therefore, a large capacitor (in practice usually an electrolytic type) can be connected across the V_o' points without affecting the voltage except to improve the "constancy."

From the circuit of Figure 10.11(a), two equations can be written for the output voltage V_o,

$$V_o = \tfrac{1}{2} V_o' - V_{o2}$$

and
$$V_o = -\tfrac{1}{2} V_o' + V_{o1}$$

Adding,

$$2 V_o = V_{o1} - V_{o2}$$

Therefore,
$$V_o = \tfrac{1}{2}(V_{o1} - V_{o2}) \tag{10.61}$$

or
$$V_o = \tfrac{1}{2} K(| V_{D1}| - | V_{D2}|)$$

The output voltage is one-half that of the Foster–Seeley circuit.

Limiting action occurs as a result of variable damping on the secondary of the transformer. For example, if the input voltage amplitude ($V_{1\,max}$) were to suddenly increase, as would occur with a noise spike of voltage, the voltage V_o' could not follow immediately, since it is held constant by means of the large capacitor. The voltage across the diodes in series is $V_2 - V_o'$ and since V_2 will increase with V_1, the diodes conduct more heavily (i.e., more current flows). This results in heavier damping of the secondary (which is also reflected into the primary), which reduces the Q factor. This, in turn, tends to offset the increase in V_2 by reducing the gain of the limiting amplifier feeding the circuit.

FIGURE 10.11. (a) The ratio-detector circuit; (b) A high-quality FM receiver unit utilizing integrated circuit amplifiers and a ratio detector (Courtesy Motorola, Inc.).

If the input voltage should decrease suddenly, diode conduction is reduced and so is the damping. The gain of the limiting amplifier therefore increases, tending to offset the original decrease in voltage. The fact, too, that the diode load, as seen by the two diodes in series, has a long time-constant and therefore cannot respond to fast changes in voltage helps in the limiting process.

Of course, the limiting action will not be effective for slow changes in amplitude, as V_o' will gradually adjust to the new level determined by input voltage amplitude.

Figure 10.11(b) shows the circuit diagram of a high-quality FM stage utilizing a ratio detector in conjunction with integrated circuit amplifiers. Both amplifying blocks MC1355 provide limiting gain.

10.5.6   The Quadrature Detector

This type of FM detector also depends on the frequency/phase angle relationship of a tuned circuit but has the advantage that only one tuned circuit is required. As a result it is becoming increasingly popular in integrated FM strips.

Consider first the general principle. A sinusoidal current

$$i = I_m \sin \omega t \qquad (10.62)$$

flows in the circuit of Figure 10.12(a). The voltage across the inductor leads the current by 90°:

$$v_L = V_{L_{\max}} \cos \omega t \qquad (10.63)$$

FIGURE 10.12. (a) Circuit used to obtain phase shift in a quadrature detector. (b) Block schematic of the basic quadrature detector. (c) Block diagram of Signetics CA3089 FM IF system incorporating the quadrature detector. The system is available in a single 16-lead dual-in-line package. Externally required components are shown outside the main block. "Permission to reprint granted by Signetics Corporation, a subsidiary of U.S. Philips Corp., 811 E. Arques Avenue, Sunnyvale, CA 94086."

The voltage across the parallel tuned circuit will be in-phase with the current at resonance. At frequencies within a range of about $\pm 1\%$ of resonance the admittance phase angle of the circuit is, by Eqn. (1.68), assuming $\omega_o / \omega \cong 1$,

$$\Phi = \tan^{-1} yQ \qquad (10.64)$$

The impedance phase angle is $-\Phi$, and the voltage across the tuned circuit is

$$v_Z = V_{Z_{max}} \sin(\omega t - \Phi) \qquad (10.65)$$

The tuned circuit is externally damped (see Figure 10.12(c)) such that the damped Q-factor is of the order 15–20, and the variable y, as given by Eqn. (1.54) can be approximated as:

$$y = \frac{f}{f_o} - \frac{f_o}{f} \qquad (10.66)$$

$$\cong \frac{2\delta f}{f_o}$$

where $\delta f = f - f_o$ and f_o is the resonant frequency of the circuit.

Now consider these two voltages, v_L and v_Z applied as inputs to a multiplier, Figure 10.12(b). The output voltage is proportional to the product:

$$v_o \propto v_L \cdot v_Z$$
$$\propto \cos \omega t \cdot \sin(\omega t - \Phi) \qquad (10.67)$$

By means of trigonometric identities this can be expressed as:

$$v_o \propto \sin(2\omega t + \Phi) + \sin \Phi \qquad (10.68)$$

A low pass filter is used to select the $\sin \Phi$ component and reject the $\sin (2\omega t + \Phi)$ component.

For small angles, $\sin \Phi \approx \tan \Phi$, and as shown by Eq. (10.64), $\tan \Phi = yQ$. Therefore the output is proportional to y:

$$v_o \propto y$$
$$\propto \frac{2\delta f}{f_o} \qquad (10.69)$$

From Eq. (10.1) $\delta f = f_i - f_c = k \cdot e_m$ where e_m is the modulating signal. Hence $v_o \propto e_m$, or the output voltage is proportional to the original modulating signal. It will be observed here, as in previous FM analyses, the frequency modulation is assumed to be at a slow enough rate to allow *sinusoidal* analysis to be used.

Figure 10.12(c) shows in block diagram form a commercially available integrated circuit, Signetics CA3089 which incorporates the quadrature detector. The single chip also incorporates a three stage IF amplifier/limiter circuit with level detectors, an audio amplifier, and an automatic frequency control output. Automatic frequency control and limiting are discussed in Section 10.7 and 10.8.

10.6 NOISE IN FREQUENCY MODULATION

Noise voltages and currents at the input to the receiver clearly cannot directly frequency modulate the incoming carrier since its frequency is fixed at a distant transmitter, which may, in fact, be crystal-controlled. The noise, however, does produce both amplitude and phase modulation, and in a frequency-modulation receiver, the amplitude modulation is removed by limiters, while the phase modulation is detected as output noise.

The noise voltage at the limiter input may be represented by a phasor at the carrier frequency but which has a randomly varying amplitude E_n and a randomly varying phase Φ_n with respect to the carrier phasor E_c, as shown in Figure 13(a). The resultant phasor is E_r, and the tip of this, point A, will trace out a random path shown dotted. The random phase Φ_n results.

For the situation where $E_c \gg |E_n|$ most of the time (remembering that E_n varies randomly in time), the phase modulation is given approximately by

$$\Phi_n = \tan^{-1}\left(\frac{V_{nq}}{E_c}\right)$$

$$\cong \frac{V_{nq}}{E_c} \qquad (10.70)$$

where V_{nq} is the quadrature component of the noise phasor, Figure 10.13(a).

As shown in Section 10.4, for phase modulation the demodulated output voltage is proportional to the rate of change of the phase modulation [Eq. (10.29)], and this makes the spectrum density for the noise voltage proportional to frequency [rate of change is proportional to frequency]; the power-spectrum density for the noise output is, therefore, proportional to frequency squared. The spectrum densities are sketched in Figure 10.13(b). The noise voltage or power over a small bandwidth δf at frequency f_n is

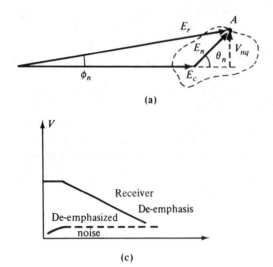

(a)

(b)

(c)

FIGURE 10.13. Noise in angle modulation circuits: (a) Phasor diagram for carrier voltage very much greater than noise; (b) Power and voltage spectrum density curves; (c) The effect of de-emphasis on noise; (d) Phasor diagram for carrier voltage comparable to noise voltage.

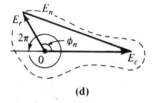

(d)

obtained by multiplying the respective spectrum density by δf; the average value over the total bandwidth B requires a summation (or integration).

A consequence of noise spectrum density increasing with frequency is that the signal-to-noise ratio is degraded at high audio frequencies which is unfortunate, as it is shown in Section 3.2 that good articulation efficiency of speech needs the high-frequency content. In practice, the situation is easily remedied by pre-emphasizing the high frequencies at the transmitter and using a de-emphasis filter in the receiver audio section which corrects for the pre-emphasis while leveling off the noise, as shown in Figure 10.13(c). Pre-emphasis and de-emphasis are discussed further in Sections 10.9.1 and 10.10.3.

From Eq. (10.62), the noise phase modulation is seen to be inversely proportional to E_c, and, therefore, the noise power will be inversely proportional to E_c^2, that is, to P_c, the unmodulated carrier power. Because of the spectrum density dependence on f_n^2, the average noise power obtained by integrating the spectrum-density curve will be proportional to f_n^3 and, therefore, to B^3 for a base-bandwidth B. Thus, the noise power is proportional to B^3/P_c. The signal power for sinusoidal modulation is proportional to $(\Delta f)^2$ where Δf is the peak signal deviation (it is assumed that the signal modulation does not interact with the noise modulation, this being nearly always the case). Hence, the power signal-to-noise ratio is proportional to $P_c(\Delta f)^2/B^3$, the detailed mathematical analysis giving

$$S/N_{FM} = \frac{3}{2kT} \cdot \frac{P_c(\Delta f)^2}{FB^3} \qquad (10.71)$$

where F is the receiver noise factor.

Comparing this to the signal-to-noise for a single sideband transmission, Eq. (9.14) (where the carrier power P_c is equal to the transmitted power P_T for the single sideband), it is seen that Eq. (10.71) can be rearranged as

$$S/N_{FM} = 1.5 \left(\frac{\Delta f}{B} \right)^2 \cdot S/N_{SSB} \qquad (10.72a)$$

Compared to a 100% amplitude-modulation transmission, the result, from Eq. (9.15), is

$$S/N_{FM} = 4.5 \left(\frac{\Delta f}{B} \right)^2 \cdot S/N_{AM} \qquad (10.72b)$$

From this, it is seen that the FM offers an improvement when $\Delta f/B$ exceeds about 0.5, but, of course, only at the expense of an increase in bandwidth. The ratio $\Delta f/B$ corresponds to m_f of Eq. (10.16) when the Δf is the peak deviation for sinusoidal modulation; thus, the increase in bandwidth required is given by Eq. (10.16) for a given increase in m_f. The value $m_f = 0.5$ is a convenient dividing line between what is termed "narrow-band" and "wideband" FM. (It must be kept in mind that Eq. (10.16) gives the RF bandwidth, which is that required by the modulated carrier, while B is the base-bandwidth, fixed by the highest audio frequency.)

The improvement factor contained in Eq. (10.72) only applies when the carrier is much greater than the noise, as shown by the phasor diagram of Fig. 10.13(a). This would be the situation, for example, well within the reception area of an FM broadcast transmission; the specified values for broadcast are $\Delta f_{max} = 75$ kHz, $B = 15$ kHz, and the signal-to-noise improvement, therefore, for a wideband FM broadcast system compared to an AM is about 20 dB, neglecting de-emphasis. There are other situations, however, for example, in mobile communications systems, where the received signal power may be very small, and the phasor diagram is as shown in Figure 10.13(d). Under these conditions, the noise phase-modulation can occasionally change abruptly by 2π radians, when the tip of the resultant phasor moves in a path to enclose the origin as shown. This gives rise to a "spike" of noise at the output (resulting from the high rate of change of noise phase) which has a high energy content and which rapidly degrades the signal-to-noise ratio. The level of input at which the spikes cause the signal-to-noise ratio to drop by 1 dB below the level given by Eq. (10.64) is termed the **FM** *threshold*. A number of special threshold detectors are available, one of which utilizes the phase-locked loop described in the following section.

10.6.1 The Phase-Locked Loop Discriminator

A phase-locked oscillator can be used to demodulate a frequency-modulated signal. The voltage-controlled oscillator (VCO) in Figure 10.14 oscillates at the center IF frequency when no signal is being received, or when the modulation on the received carrier is zero. Under the latter condition, the oscillator output is exactly the same as the received IF in frequency, and the phase comparator circuit puts out a zero signal. When the incoming frequency rises because of modulation to $f_{IF} + \Delta f$, the phase comparator output creates an output signal which drives the VCO frequency up until it again matches the IF, this time at $f_{IF} + \Delta f$. The signal appearing at the input to the VCO is the sum of a fixed dc bias plus the comparator output signal. Since the oscillator shifts to a higher frequency, and for this to be true the input to it must be larger than the bias value, there must be an output from the comparator when the oscillator is tracking. This means that the oscillator must be out of phase with the IF by an amount proportional to the deviation.

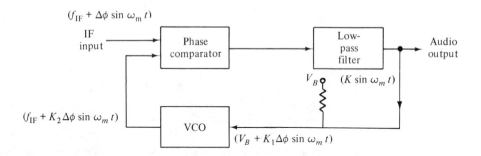

FIGURE 10.14. The phase-locked loop frequency discriminator.

Now if the modulation drives the received-signal frequency low, the oscillator will be forced to also move low in frequency, and the comparator output will adjust itself to the value necessary to produce this frequency. If the received signal frequency is varying in accordance with a modulation signal, the value of the voltage at the input to the VCO will vary about the bias value in accordance with the modulating signal. A coupling capacitor and a low-pass filter in the output lead remove the dc component and the carrier components from the bias voltage, leaving only the modulation signal.

10.7 AUTOMATIC FREQUENCY CONTROL

Automatic frequency control is used in FM receivers to "lock onto" the received signal and stabilize reception. The circuit is an application of negative feedback. A signal is derived that is proportional in amplitude to the average deviation of the received center frequency from the center of the receiver IF bandpass. This signal is used to vary the reactance of a tuning diode (voltage variable capacitor) in the oscillator tank circuit to shift its frequency enough to compensate for the deviation, and bring the signal back into the center of the IF bandpass.

Voltage-controlled oscillators (VCO's) are basically FM-modulator circuits. Earlier FM-modulator circuits such as the variable reactance tube modulator were quite complex, and their application in receivers for AFC was limited. The varactor diode became available in quantity and quality in the 1960's, and this made feasible the application of AFC to even the cheapest of FM receivers. The varactor diode is discussed in Section 10.5. Typical tuning varactors have ranges of tuning (f_{max}/f_{min}) of 2:1 up to 10:1, and maximum capacities of 10 pF (suitable for AFC circuits) to 500 pF (suitable for tuning directly AM broadcast receivers in the MF band).

The capacitance is maximum at zero bias, and decreases as voltage increases according to Eq. (10.32).

The circuit shown in Figure 10.15(a) uses a Foster-Seeley discriminator as the FM detector, although the circuit will work equally well with a slope detector or a ratio detector. The plot of output voltage versus frequency is shown in Figure 10.15(b). The voltage divider R_1, R_2 provides a quiescent bias level $-|V_o|$, which is applied to the varactor through R_4, R_5. If the average frequency drifts to $f_s + \Delta f$, the resultant bias goes more negative to $-|V_o + V_1|$, and the varactor capacitance decreases [see Figure 10.15(c)]. This lower capacitance causes the local oscillator to tune higher in frequency, and so "track" the received signal frequency. The oscillator frequency will rise until no further increase of bias is created, and the oscillator is said to have "locked onto" the received signal. Similarly, if the incoming signal is low in frequency, the resultant bias on the varactor will go less negative to $-|V_o - V_1|$, raising its capacitance and causing the oscillator to lower its frequency toward the signal. When no signal is being received, only the bias voltage will be applied to the varactor, and tuning will be dependent only on the tuning capacitor attached to the main dial.

Since the varactors may be controlled by varying the dc bias potential, the main tuning capacitor may also be replaced by a bias potentiometer feeding the varactor, thus eliminating a large mechanical device in the

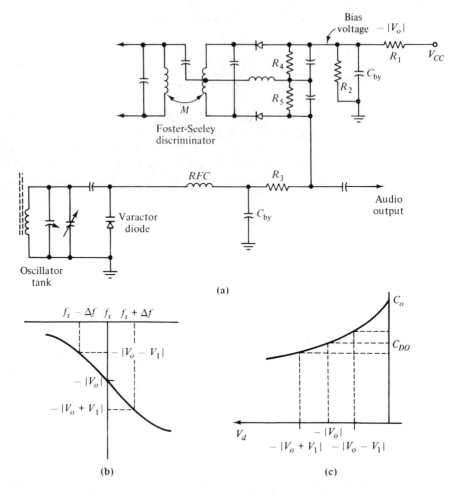

FIGURE 10.15. Automatic frequency control using a varactor diode: (a) Circuit; (b) Plot of bias output versus input frequency; (c) Plot of varactor diode capacitance versus applied voltage.

receiver. It is also useful in that it is readily adaptable to remote tuning, since no RF signals appear on the control leads.

10.8 AMPLITUDE LIMITERS

Amplitude limiters are amplifier circuits that are used to eliminate amplitude modulation and amplitude-modulated noise from received FM signals before detection.

FIGURE 10.16.   Amplitude limiter circuit: (a) Schematic; (b) Limiter response showing the expanded range of a double-stage limiter.

The limiter works in such a manner that limiting begins when the input signal becomes larger than that required to drive the amplifier from cutoff to saturation (i.e., across its active range). Figure 10.16(a) shows such an amplifier. It uses a bipolar transistor and double-tuned IF transformers, with the output transformer supplying the detector circuit. Resistors R_1, R_2, and R_E provide dc bias under zero signal conditions to maintain the transistor in the active region. R_{dc} acts to reduce the effective supply voltage and limit the saturation value of collector current to a low value, so that saturation will occur at a low-input-signal level.

For very low signal levels, the circuit acts as a normal class A amplifier. For larger signals, which drive the transistor into cutoff, the baseleak circuit formed by C_2 and R_2 charges up, driving the operating point toward cutoff. At the same time, the positive peaks drive the base current beyond the saturation point, and the collector-current waveform has both the positive and negative peaks clipped off to produce an approximately rectangular waveform. The fundamental of this rectangular current waveform drives the tuned circuit of the output transformer in the "flywheel" manner typical of the class C amplifier. The point at which the signal-input range exceeds the active range of the transistor forms the threshold of the limiter, beyond which limiting action takes place. Further increase of input signal does not significantly increase the collector-current magnitude, and its fundamental component remains almost constant. If a very large increase in input occurs, such as by a large noise pulse, the bias circuit will drive even further into cutoff, and the conduction angle of the amplifier will decrease. The limiter is said to have been "captured" by the noise. This effect puts an upper limit on the limiting range, and it means that if large noise pulses are received, they could cause the limiter to respond and reduce the desired input signal. The shape of the limiter response is indicated in Figure 10.16(b).

If the receiver is to respond to a very large range of input signals and noise signals, it may be necessary to increase the range of the limiter. This may be accomplished in two ways. First, for large-signal conditions, AGC may be provided so that the limiter is not driven beyond its limiting range. Second, a second stage of limiting may be provided. Two-stage limiting is much more effective and provides very good protection against large-amplitude noise pulses. Since there is more gain in the limiter circuits, the threshold at which limiting occurs is lower, and less preamplifier gain is required.

It was stated that most types of FM detectors require amplitude limiting in order to function properly. The ratio detector (see Section 10.5.5) is an exception to this, because it has a degree of inherent limiting built into it. In critical applications it is still necessary to provide additional limiting, but the ratio detector performs well enough otherwise.

10.9   FM BROADCAST RECEIVERS

FM commercial broadcasting in North America takes place in the VHF band between 88 and 108 MHz. Within this band, allotted frequencies are spaced 200 kHz apart and are allowed a maximum frequency deviation of ±75 kHz around the carrier frequency. Propagation at VHF frequencies is restricted to line of sight, and coverage is usually only for a radius of about 50 miles around the transmitter location. The programs broadcast on these channels in the past have been mostly music, since the basic modulating frequency bandwidth is 15 kHz, as opposed to the 5 kHz used on AM stations.

Figure 10.17(a) shows the block schematic of a typical FM broadcast receiver of the monaural or single-channel variety. It is a superheterodyne

FIGURE 10.17. (a) Block diagram of a typical FM monaural broadcast receiver; (b) IF amplifier band-pass characteristics; (c) Deemphasis network and transfer function.

circuit, with a tuned RF amplifier so that maximum signal sensitivity is typically between 1 to 10μV. The RF-stage-tuned circuits and the local oscillator are tuned by a three-ganged variable capacitor controlled from a panel knob. The oscillator frequency can be varied from 98.7 to 118.7 MHz, yielding an intermediate frequency (IF) of 10.7 MHz.

The IF amplifier section is comprised of several high-gain stages, of which one or more are amplitude limiters. The schematic shown here has one high-gain nonlimiting input stage, followed by one amplitude-limiting stage. All stages are tuned to give the desired bandpass characteristic, which is shown in Figure 10.17(c). This is centered on 10.7 MHz and has a 180-kHz bandwidth to pass the desired signal. Amplitude limiting is usually arranged to have an onset threshold of about 1 mV at the limiting-stage input, corresponding to the quieting level of input signal, which may be set at 10 μV or lower.

The FM detector may be any one of several types of FM detectors described in Section 10.5, and incorporating automatic frequency control as described in Section 10.7.

10.9.1 Deemphasis

It was shown in Section 10.6 that noise voltage output resulting from noise phase-modulation increased directly in proportion to frequency, or at 6 dB per octave. By introducing a filter, termed a *deemphasis network*, which attenuates at 6 dB per octave, the noise spectrum can be leveled off, thus improving the signal-to-noise ratio. A simple, but widely used deemphasis network, along with its transfer function, is shown in Figure 10.17(d). The transfer function is given by

$$H(\omega) = \frac{1}{1 + j\dfrac{\omega}{\omega_1}} \qquad (10.73)$$

where $\omega_1 = 1/CR$. The time-constant CR is standardized at 75 μs, and therefore, $f_1 = 2.1$ kHz. This should be compared with the preemphasis discussed in Section 10.10.3.

The reduction in average noise power is determined by the ratio of the area of the power output spectrum with and without deemphasis, and is found to be

$$\text{deemphasis improvement} = \frac{1}{3}\left(\frac{B}{f_1}\right)^2 \qquad (10.74)$$

where B is the audio bandwidth. For $f_1 = 2.1$ kHz and $B = 15$ kHz, the improvement is calculated to be 12.3 dB.

To compensate for deemphasis of the modulating signal, a matching preemphasis network must be used at the transmitter (see Section 10.3.3).

Deemphasis can also be used with other systems—for example, AM—but the improvement offered is not as great as with FM, and there are other difficulties which make its use in other systems not worthwhile.

10.9.2   FM Stereo

All new FM broadcast receivers are being built with provision for receiving stereo, or two-channel broadcasts. The left and right channel signals from the program material are combined to form two different signals, one of which is the left-plus-right signal and one of which is the left-minus-right signal. The (L–R) signal is double sideband suppressed carrier (DSBSC) modulated about a carrier frequency of 38 kHz, with the LSB in the 23–38 kHz slot and the USB in the 38–53 kHz slot. The (L + R) signal is placed directly in the 0–15 kHz slot and a pilot carrier at 19 kHz is added to synchronize the demodulator at the receiver. The composite signal spectrum is shown in Figure 10.18(b).

Figure 10.18(a) shows the block schematic of a stereo channel decoder circuit. The output from the FM detector is a composite audio signal containing the frequency-multiplexed (L + R) and (L − R) signals, and the 19-kHz pilot tone. This composite signal is applied through a muting switch to the input of the decode matrix. The muting switch is driven from a modified AGC signal so that the input signal must be nearly large enough to drive the limiting amplifier into saturation before any audio signal is produced. This has the effect of reducing or eliminating audio noise caused by low signals or during tuning between channels.

The composite audio signal is also applied to one input of a phase-error detector circuit, which is part of a phase-locked loop 38-kHz oscillator. The output drives the 38-kHz voltage-controlled oscillator, whose output provides the synchronous carrier for the demodulator. The oscillator output is also frequency-divided by 2 (in a counter circuit) and applied to the other input of the phase comparator to close the phase-locked loop. The phase error signal is also passed to a Schmitt Trigger circuit which drives an indicator lamp on the panel which lights when the error signal goes to zero, indicating the presence of a synchronizing input signal (the 19-kHz pilot tone).

The output from the 38-kHz oscillator and the filtered composite audio signals are applied to the balanced demodulator, whose output is the (L − R) channel. The (L + R) and (L − R) signals are passed through a matrix circuit which separates the L and R signals from each other. These are passed through deemphasis networks and low-pass filters to remove unwanted high-frequency components and then passed to the two channel audio amplifiers and speakers. On reception of a monaural signal, the pilot-tone indicator circuit goes off, indicating the absence of pilot tone, and closes the switch to disable the (L − R) input to the matrix. The (L + R) signal is passed through the matrix to both outputs. An ordinary monaural

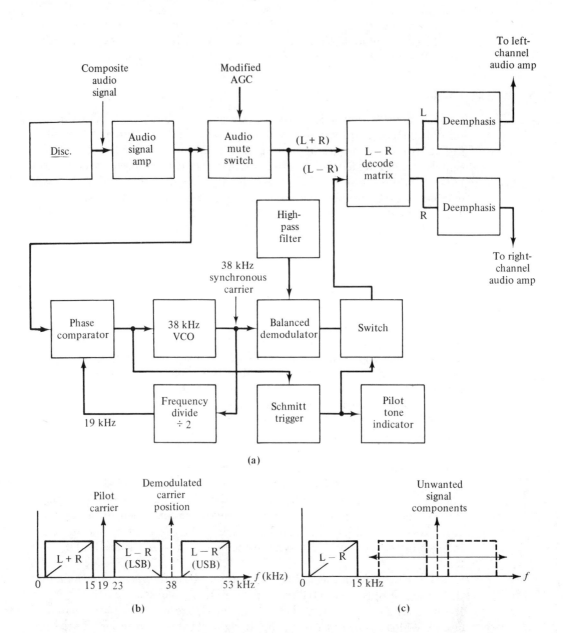

FIGURE 10.18. (a) Block diagram of an FM signal stero channel decoder system; (b) Spectrum of the composite audio signal from the FM detector; (c) Spectrum of the demodulated left minus right (L − R) signal after removal of higher frequencies.

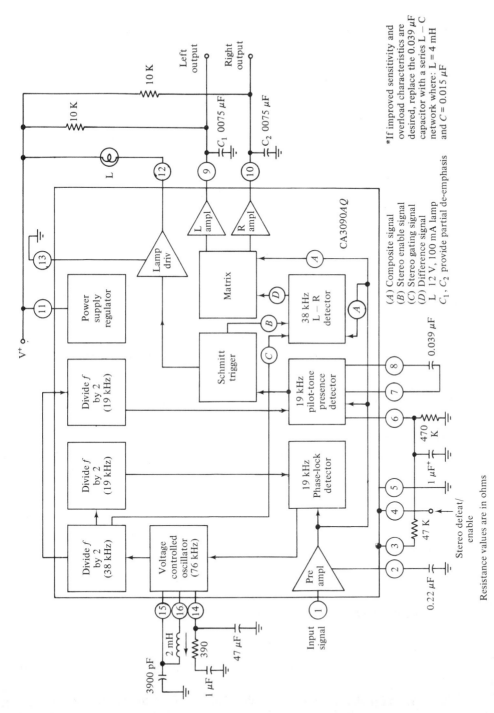

*If improved sensitivity and
overload characteristics are
desired, replace the 0.039 μF
capacitor with a series L – C
network where: L = 4 mH
and C = 0.015 μF

CA3090AQ

(A) Composite signal
(B) Stereo enable signal
(C) Stereo gating signal
(D) Difference signal
L 12 V, 100 mA lamp
C_1, C_2 provide partial de-emphasis

Resistance values are in ohms

FIGURE 10.19.   Functional block diagram of a typical stereo decoder IC
chip—the RCA CA3090AQ. The circuit is mounted in a 14-pin dual in-line
package (DIP). (Courtesy of RCA—Data File No. 684)

receiver tuned to a stereo signal would produce only the (L + R) signal, since all frequencies above 15 kHz are removed by filtering, and no demodulator circuitry is present. Thus the stereo signal is compatible with the monaural receivers.

Much of the circuitry for FM receivers is now available in integrated-circuit form. One of the first pieces of circuitry to be produced in IC's was the stereo decoder. Figure 10.19 shows a typical IC decoder chip, the RCA CA3090AQ. This chip contains all the circuits necessary to accomplish the functions of Figure 10.18(a) and comes with the chip mounted in a 14-pin DIP. Only a few external components are needed to make the circuit work. These include bias resistors and deemphasis capacitors on the output, reactive components (L and C) for the VCO and some bypass capacitors and bias resistors. The rest is built into the chip.

10.10 FM TRANSMITTERS

10.10.1 Direct FM

Direct frequency modulation, Figure 10.20(a), can be achieved by use of the circuits of Figure 10.6(b) or Figure 10.7(a). A conflict immediately arises between obtaining adequate frequency deviation while maintaining high frequency stability. Crystal oscillators can be directly frequency modulated since the crystal frequency can be "pulled" by a small amount, but to achieve usable final deviations, a high frequency multiplication factor is necessary, as described below. Even so, direct frequency modulation is only used for narrow band FM which employs relatively small deviations.

The distinction between frequency multiplication and up-conversion as obtained by mixing is important in the operation of FM systems. The general expression for a frequency-modulated carrier is given by Eq. (10.7). As shown in Section 5.7.1, a class C amplifier produces harmonics of the input signal and, provided the harmonic-tuned output circuit is sufficiently broadband to accept the sidebands, the nth harmonic of the input, Eq. (10.7), will be selected, giving as the output voltage

$$v_{out} = \sin(n\Theta(t)) \tag{10.75}$$

$\Theta(t)$ is given by Eq. (10.9), and therefore the output frequency is

$$\begin{aligned} f_{out} &= n \cdot f_i \\ &= n \cdot f_c + n \cdot \Delta f \cdot m(t) \end{aligned} \tag{10.76}$$

This shows that the deviation is multiplied by the harmonic number n.

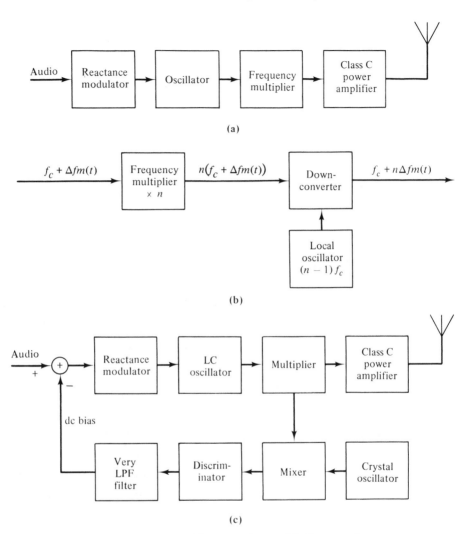

FIGURE 10.20.   (a) A directly modulated FM transmitter; (b) System for increasing the deviation of an FM signal; (c) Frequency stabilized reactance modulator.

When the signal is up-converted by mixing with an oscillator frequency f_o the final frequency is given by

$$f_{out} = f_o + f_i$$
$$= (f_o + f_c) + \Delta f \cdot m(t) \qquad (10.77)$$

The carrier frequency is raised to $f_o + f_c$ and the modulation is unaltered.

The foregoing theory is used in the scheme shown in Figure 10.20(b) to achieve an increase in the deviation without increasing of the carrier frequency. The input frequency f_i is multiplied up to nf_i. This is applied to a down-converter along with an oscillator frequency $f_o = (n - 1)f_c$, the resulting output frequency [f_i being given by Eq. (10.5)] being

$$f_{out} = nf_i - f_o$$
$$= f_c + n\,\Delta f \cdot m(t) \tag{10.78}$$

This shows that the carrier is converted back to its original frequency with the deviation multiplied by n times.

Where the main oscillator is only an LC oscillator, the direct-modulation scheme is not capable of meeting frequency stability regulations. Stability is improved in Figure 10.20(c) by an AFC circuit. A sample of the final output signal is mixed with the signal from a stable crystal oscillator. The IF produced contains the difference frequency between the carrier and the fixed oscillator. A discriminator circuit generates a voltage which is proportional to this difference frequency. It also contains the modulation signal, and a low-pass filter is used to remove this, leaving a varying dc level which is proportional to the difference between the carrier frequency and the oscillator. This voltage is added to the modulating audio signal and applied to the reactance modulator in a manner so as to correct any drift in the main oscillator frequency. The gain of the frequency feedback loop is determined by the frequency multiplication constant and by the modulator and discriminator gains. Care must be taken to be sure that the feedback loop is stable; otherwise, oscillations may occur at modulating frequencies.

Class C power amplifiers can be used for FM transmitters because any small variations in the amplitude of the FM signal are usually removed in the receiver circuits by limiting amplifiers. Further, they do not have any significant effect on the modulation itself, and interference from noise is greatly reduced. The result is that the FM transmitter is much more efficient than an equivalent AM transmitter.

10.10.2 Indirect FM

Phase modulation may be used to achieve frequency modulation by the indirect method, the theory being given in Section 10.4. It is only necessary to integrate the modulating signal prior to applying it to the phase modulator, the phase modulation being accomplished by either of the circuits of Figure 10.6(c) or Figure 10.7(b). The block diagram for such a transmitter is shown in Figure 10.21(a). This transmitter is widely used in VHF and UHF radio telephone equipment.

Another indirect method that is widely used is the Armstrong method, in which FM is achieved from a combination of DSB suppressed carrier and phase modulation. Figure 10.21(b) shows the block diagram of an Arm-

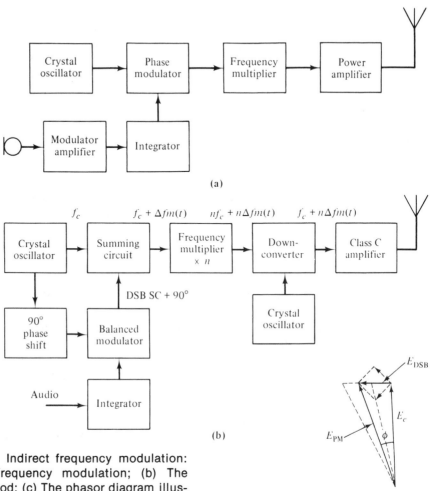

FIGURE 10.21.   Indirect frequency modulation: (a) Phase to frequency modulation; (b) The Armstrong method; (c) The phasor diagram illustrating the principle of the Armstrong method.

strong-modulated FM transmitter. The carrier source is a crystal oscillator with a frequency that is easy to handle in the modulators. Generally this will be quite low, say 100 kHz, because of the need to do several stages of frequency multiplication. A sample of the carrier is separated and shifted by 90° before application to a balanced modulator. The audio is passed through an integrator circuit before being applied to the modulator.

The output of the balanced modulator is reduced in amplitude so that it is very small compared to the oscillator output. This output is the phasor sum of the two sidebands, without any carrier and is displaced in phase by 90° from the oscillator output. When the sidebands are added to the oscillator output, phase modulation occurs. This can be seen from the phasor diagram of Figure 10.21(c). The sideband phasor sum leads the carrier by 90° and varies in amplitude. It is phasor-added to the carrier to produce the voltage E_{pm}. As the magnitude of the sidebands changes, so does the angle ϕ between E_{pm} and the carrier. This angle is given by

$$\phi = \tan^{-1}\left(\frac{E_{dsb}}{E_c}\right) \qquad (10.79)$$

However, if the angle ϕ can be kept less than about 10°, the tangent is approximately equal to the angle itself.

$$\tan\phi \cong \phi < 0.17 \text{ rad} \qquad (10.80)$$

Therefore, for small angular deviations less than 10°, an error of less than 1% in the modulation will occur and

$$\phi \cong \frac{E_{dsb}}{E_c} = \frac{KE_m}{\omega_m} \qquad (10.81)$$

This shows that the phase modulation ϕ is proportional to the double-sideband signal which, in turn, is proportional to the integrated modulation signal and, as shown previously, this produces the equivalent frequency modulation.

The wave at this point has a very small frequency deviation, and this must be increased before transmission. This is accomplished by passing the FM signal through a series of frequency multiplier amplifiers until the deviation is sufficiently large. The signal is then up- or down-converted to the final transmitting frequency and applied to drive a class C power amplifier.

Example 10.6   An Armstrong transmitter is to be used for transmission at 152 MHz in the VHF band, with a maximum deviation of 15 kHz at a minimum audio frequency of 100 Hz. The primary oscillator is to be a 100 kHz crystal oscillator, and the initial phase-modulation deviation is to be kept to less than 12°, to avoid audio distortion. Find the amount by which the frequency must be multiplied to give proper deviation and specify a combination of doublers and triplers which will give this. Also specify the mixer crystal and any multiplier stages needed.

Solution   Maximum Phase deviation of the modulator is

$$\Delta\Phi_{max} = 12° = 0.2096 \text{ rad} \equiv m_p$$

From Eq. (10.30) $\Delta f_{max} = \Delta\Phi_{max} f_{min} = 0.2094 \times 0.1 = 0.02094$ kHz

The frequency deviation increase required is

$$N = \frac{\Delta f_{\text{max allow}}}{\Delta f_{\text{max}}} = \frac{15 \text{ kHz}}{0.0209 \text{ kHz}} = 716.33 \text{ (use } 729 = 3^6)$$

The modulated waveform will be passed through a chain of six tripler stages, giving a final deviation of

$$0.02094 \times 729 = 15.265 \text{ kHz}$$

at a frequency of $0.1 \times 729 = 72.9$ MHz. The deviation is slightly high, but a slight attenuation of the audio signal will compensate for this. The mixer oscillator signal is

$$f_o = 152 - 72.9 = 79.1 \text{ MHz}$$

f_o is best obtained by using two tripler stages from a 8.7889 MHz crystal oscillator.

10.10.3 Preemphasis

Preemphasis of the modulating signal is necessary to compensate for the deemphasis introduced in the receiver to improve the signal-to-noise ratio (see Sections 10.6 and 10.9.1). A simple preemphasis network is shown in Figure 10.22 along with the modulus of the transfer function. Over the preemphasis range, $\omega_1 < \omega \ll \omega_2$

$$H(\omega) \cong \frac{R_2}{R_1 + R_2}\left(1 + j\frac{\omega}{\omega_1}\right) \qquad (10.82)$$

where $\omega_1 = (1/CR_1)$ and $f_1 = \omega_1/2\pi$ is standardized at 2.1 kHz. The frequency (ω_2) at which preemphasis levels off is chosen to be above the bandpass. It should be noted that phase modulation by itself provides the required preemphasis characteristic if the integrator is modified to be ineffective above the 2.1 kHz preemphasis cutoff frequency.

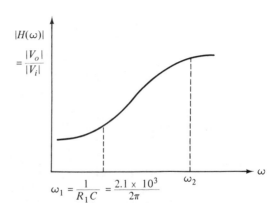

FIGURE 10.22. A preemphasis network and its transfer function.

$$\omega_1 = \frac{1}{R_1 C} = \frac{2.1 \times 10^3}{2\pi}$$

10.10.4   FM Broadcast

The prime requisite of FM broadcasting is excellent fidelity, since music provides the chief program material. Frequency modulation acts in several ways to improve this fidelity. First, since FM broadcasting takes place in the VHF band from 88 to 108 MHz, a much wider baseband can be used. The basic baseband width presently being used is 50 Hz to 15 kHz, with a maximum allowable deviation of ± 75 kHz. Channel spacing is 200 kHz and power outputs of as much as 100 kW are used.

Until recently single-channel monophonic FM broadcasts were common, but nearly all FM stations are now transmitting two-channel stereo programs. In the near future this may be further changed to provide four-channel stereo. Further, some FM stations are frequency-division-multiplexing an additional channel on their carrier for the purpose of providing background music for public buildings, a system licensed as a "subsidiary communications authorization," or SCA.

The transmitters used are typically of the Armstrong type discussed in Section 10.10.2. Initial deviations are kept small to limit modulation distortion, and many stages of frequency multiplication are used to bring the deviation up to that required at the output. Again, to provide the necessary power output, the output stage is a push-pull parallel class C amplifier. Water-cooled vacuum tubes are used in this stage.

The main differences between the FM systems already discussed and the broadcast system lies in the composition of the audio signal presented to the modulator. It is a composite signal carrying several signals, and these will be discussed.

First, if monophonic FM transmission is to be used, only one channel is needed, and the single audio channel is applied directly to the modulator input. It must be fully compensated to provide good fidelity in the band from 50 to 15,000 Hz.

Two-channel stereo is accomplished as follows. The two audio channels are not simply frequency-division-multiplexed before modulation. They are first mixed to provide two new signals one of which is a *balanced* monophonic signal. The first is the sum of the two input channels, and the second is the difference of the two. The sum channel is modulated directly in the baseband assignment between 50 and 15,000 Hz. The difference signal is DSBSC modulated in the 23–53 kHz slot about a carrier at 38 kHz. A pilot carrier at 19 kHz is also transmitted,. The sum signal in the audio portion of the band can be demodulated by a monophonic FM receiver to provide normal monophonic reception. A receiver with a stereo demodulator can also retrieve the difference signal and combine the two to produce the original L and R channel signals. Figure 10.23(a) shows the block diagram of the premodulation mixing circuits.

The L and R channels are summed and passed through a low-pass 15 kHz filter to form the monophonic portion of the baseband signal. The R

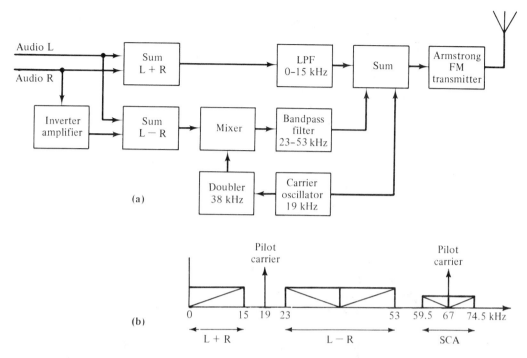

FIGURE 10.23. An FM stereo broadcast transmitter: (a) Block schematic;
(b) Baseband spectrum showing position of the auxiliary 7.5 kHz Channel.

channel is inverted and then added to the L signal to yield the difference
signal L − R. This signal is DSBSC modulated on the 38 kHz carrier by a
balanced modulator, and passed through a 23–53 kHz bandpass filter to
remove any unwanted signal components. The two channel bands and the
19-kHz pilot carrier are added together to produce the final baseband
signal, Figure 10.18(b). This final composite signal is presented to the
modulator input of the FM transmitter.

An additional channel is often modulated on the same carrier for
service to commercial operations, such as music to stores and public buildings. This channel is limited to a signal bandwidth of 7.5 kHz and is
multiplexed to lie in the range from 53 to 75 kHz with a pilot carrier at 67
kHz. The sideband frequencies are shown in Figure 10.23(b). This auxiliary
channel does not interfere in any way with the ordinary broadcast.

10.11 PROBLEMS

1. Sketch the instantaneous frequency-time curve and the amplitude–time curve corresponding to Figure 10.1 but with a sawtooth modulating wave.

2. In a frequency-modulating system, the frequency deviation constant is $k = 1$ kHz/V. A sinusoidal modulating signal of amplitude 15 V and frequency 3 kHz is applied. Calculate: (a) peak frequency deviation; (b) modulating index.

3. A carrier wave of amplitude 5 V and frequency 90 MHz is frequency-modulated by a sinusoidal voltage of amplitude 5 V and frequency 15 kHz. The frequency-deviation constant is 1 kHz/V. Sketch the spectrum of the modulated wave.

4. Explain why it is that in some circumstances the bandwidth required for a sinusoidally frequency modulated carrier is greater than twice the modulating frequency. Determine the bandwidth occupied by a sinusoidally frequency-modulated carrier for which the modulating index is 2.4.

5. The phase deviation constant in a phase-modulation system is $K = 0.01$ rad/V. Calculate the maximum phase deviation when a modulating signal of amplitude 10 V is applied.

6. Explain why, in an angle-modulation system, sinusoidal phase modulation gives rise to a receiver output which increases as the modulating frequency increases, even though the modulating signal amplitude remains constant.

7. Explain in detail the operation of the phase-modulator circuit of Figure 10.7(b). How could this circuit be modified to obtain frequency modulation?

8. Explain in detail the operation of the phase discriminator of Figure 10.11(b). Can this circuit detect direct phase modulation?

9. Sketch the graphs of: (a) equivalent frequency deviation; (b) average noise power output, for noise in a frequency-modulation receiver.

10. Explain how, in a frequency-modulation system, the signal-to-noise ratio can be improved without having to increase the transmitted power. How are other factors of the system affected?

11. It is required to transmit a complex modulating signal in which the highest-frequency component of the spectrum is 3 kHz. Compare the bandwidths required for AM, suppressed carrier single-sideband, and FM systems, given that the maximum frequency deviation in the latter system is 15 kHz. Also compare the signal-to-noise ratios when the modulating signal is a 1-kHz tone, the deviation in the FM system remaining at 15 kHz, the modulation index for the AM system being unity, and the signal-to-noise ratio for the SSB system being 30 dB.

12. Prove that frequency multiplication of an FM signal increases the deviation while frequency conversion does not increase the deviation.

13. An Armstrong FM modulation system uses a primary oscillator of 1 MHz, and maximum phase deviation for good linearity is limited to $10°$.

(a) Find the corresponding frequency deviation at the modulator output. (b) If the transmitted signal is to have a maximum frequency deviation of 30 kHz, at a carrier frequency of 120 MHz, specify the frequency-multiplication factor needed and suggest a chain of doublers and triplers to accomplish this. (c) For the chain you suggest, specify the local oscillator frequency needed for the final conversion operation.

14. Explain the method by which two-channel stereo signals are transmitted over an FM broadcast transmitter. Suggest a way in which four-channel stereo might be broadcast.

Chapter 11
Pulse Modulation

11.1 INTRODUCTION

Previous chapters have discussed the modulation of the amplitude, the frequency, or the phase of a sinusoidal carrier signal to transmit a low-frequency analog information signal, such as voice. This chapter will discuss several systems which modulate some characteristics of a continuous train of discrete pulses as a carrier instead of a sine wave.

Pulse modulation is an analog system even though *discrete* valued samples of continuous analog signal are used in the modulation process. These discrete samples can take on any value within the range of the continuous signal. This is one of the ways in which pulse transmission differs from digital transmission in which a discrete value can only be one of a finite set of numbers. Digital systems are described in chapter 17, but it should be borne in mind that digital systems also employ pulses so that many of the characteristics of the transmission channel described in the present chapter apply also to digital systems.

In the absence of noise and distortion it is possible to completely recover a continuous analog signal from its discrete samples, providing the samples are taken at greater than a certain minimum rate. This minimum rate (for

samples equispaced in time) is equal to twice the highest frequency contained in the continuous signal. For example, it is shown in chapter 3 that telephone speech may contain frequencies up to 3400 Hz. Assuming the highest frequency is 3400 Hz, then the telephone signal would have to be sampled at greater than 6800 samples per second. In practice, a sampling rate of 8000 Hz would be used. The minimum sampling rate is known as the *Nyquist Sampling Rate.*

Before describing specific methods of pulse modulation, some general properties of pulse transmission will be described.

11.2   PULSE TRANSMISSION

A perfect rectangular pulse is shown in Figure 11.1(a). It has a defined time duration or width t_w and a constant amplitude during that time period. A Fourier analysis of this pulse shows that it has a continuous frequency spectrum (see Figure 2.3(d)), of decreasing amplitudes. If such a pulse is passed through a low-pass filter, then all the frequencies above the filter cut-

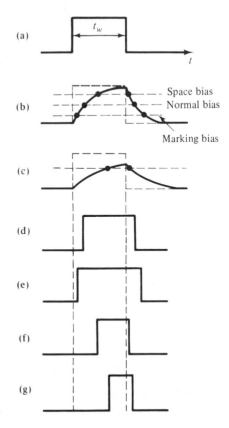

FIGURE 11.1.   Pulse transmission distortion: (a) A rectangular pulse; (b) A rectangular pulse which has not been severely distorted by bandwidth limitations; the intercepts for normal, marking, and spacing bias are shown; (c) A rectangular pulse distorted by transmission over a facility with too low a bandwidth; the threshold intercepts for normal bias are shown; (d) A reconstructed pulse with normal bias delayed but unchanged in length from (b); (e) A reconstructed pulse lengthened by marking bias; (f) A reconstructed pulse shortened by spacing bias; (g) A reconstructed pulse resulting because of reduced pulse amplitude with normal bias in (c).

off frequency will be eliminated, and the pulse at the output will be rounded off, as in Figure 11.1(b). This is discussed in more detail in Chapter 2. Since pulse-generating equipment is far from perfect, this is the type of pulse that will be produced in practice. It will still have a constant amplitude during the pulse, except for the lead and tail edges. If the rise and fall times of the edges are very much shorter than the pulse width t_w, we can treat the pulse as a perfect one, and ignore the rise and fall times.

If the transmission channel has a bandwidth that is too narrow or that introduces excessive phase distortion, the pulse will be smeared and reduced in amplitude as shown in Figure 11.1(c). If the distortion is too severe, it will be impossible to detect the pulse at the receiving end. Noise introduced during transmission may produce an unwanted pulse or cancel a wanted pulse, resulting in transmission error, as well as increasing the pulse distortion.

To reduce the effects of distortion, it is necessary to regenerate pulse signals at repeater stations or at the receiver. If the repeater or receiver is improperly adjusted, a further form of pulse distortion occurs. This is illustrated in Figure 11.1(b), (d), (e), and (f), and is termed *bias distortion*. The pulse of Figure 11.1(a) is transmitted and becomes distorted because of the bandwidth and phase characteristics of the cable. Receiver *bias* is the minimum level of pulse amplitude to which the receiver will respond. If the receiver is adjusted for normal bias [Figure 11.1(b)], then for equally spaced (square wave) pulses, the pulse area above the bias level will be equal to the area below for symmetrical pulses, and the regenerated pulse shown in Figure 11.1(d) will be delayed, but not lengthened or shortened. If the bias is set too low, then the pulse area above bias will be larger than that below, and the period of the regenerated pulse will be both lengthened and delayed, as shown in Figure 11.1(e). This is referred to as *marking bias distortion*. If the bias is set too high, then the pulse is both delayed and shortened, as shown in Figure 11.1(f). This is called *spacing bias distortion*. A similar type of distortion is produced when the received pulse is severely reduced in amplitude, but the bias is kept at the normal level. The result is that the pulse area above bias is smaller than that below, causing the same type of delay and shortening as spacing bias distortion, shown in Figure 11.1(g).

The effects of distortion can be minimized by proper receiver adjustment. This is done by sending over the transmission line a standard square-wave signal at the proper transmission speed. The speed and bias of the receiver are then adjusted until the receiver produces an undistorted signal from this transmission.

11.2.1 Intersymbol Crosstalk (Intersymbol Interference)

Unwanted signals such as noise and crosstalk can be added to the signal during transmission, which may mask the pulse so that it cannot be re-

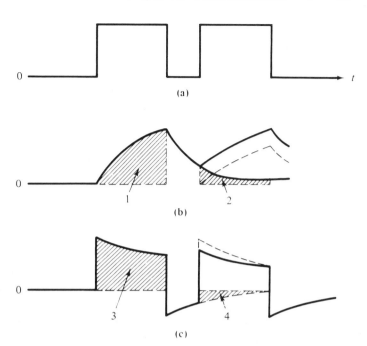

FIGURE 11.2. Intersymbol crosstalk: (a) Two adjacent pulses; (b) Upper frequency limitation causes energy from area 2 of the first pulse to be added to the second pulse, increasing its amplitude; (c) Lower frequency limitation causes energy from area 4 of the first pulse to be subtracted from the second pulse, decreasing its amplitude.

trieved. Figure 11.1(b) shows the typical shape of a pulse which has been passed through a bandwidth-limited channel. When a pulse is passed through a low-pass filter or limited channel, its corners are rounded off, its amplitude is reduced, and it is smeared by unequal time delays into the adjacent time slot. Figure 11.2(b) shows the result of increasingly lower filter cutoff frequency on the pulse shape. Note that the pulse "tail" endures long after the nominal pulse period and can interfere with a following pulse. This effect is known as *intersymbol crosstalk* or *intersymbol interference*. The following pulse has energy from the first pulse added to it. In a pulse amplitude-modulated system, this would cause serious distortion.

A similar form of intersymbol crosstalk results if the channel bandpass is low-frequency-limited as well, causing the top of the pulse to drop. When the pulse ends, the signal falls below the zero axis and may not return to zero before the next pulse appears. Energy is subtracted from the succeeding pulse, making it look lower than it is.

In a time-division-multiplexed pulse-amplitude-modulated system, this form of crosstalk can couple signal energy from one channel into another which may be of sufficient amplitude to be intelligible, hence the name "crosstalk."

11.3 PULSE AMPLITUDE MODULATION

Pulse amplitude modulation (PAM) results when a train of constant amplitude very short pulses $\delta(t)$ occuring at a fast pulse repetition rate, is caused to vary in amplitude with a slower modulating wave $m(t)$. The effect is that of multiplying the pulse train by the modulating signal. Figure 11.3(a), (b), and (c) shows a pulse train, a modulating sine wave, and the resulting PAM waveform. The envelope of the pulse heights corresponds to the modulating wave. If the original waveform is to be recovered, it is only necessary to pass the PAM waveform through a low-pass filter.

11.3.1 Instantaneous PAM Sampling

Instantaneous PAM sampling occurs if the pulses used in the modulator are infinitely short (i.e., they are impulses). The spectrum of the resulting train of pulses is shown, with one cycle of the pulses, in Figure 11.3(c). The tops of the pulses in the time-domain plot outline the waveform of the modulating sine wave. In the frequency spectrum, a pair of side frequencies is generated on either side of each harmonic of the sampling frequency, which now corresponds to the carrier frequency of amplitude modulation. For the case of instantaneous sampling, all side frequencies have exactly the same amplitude, which is proportional to the amplitude of the modulating wave. For complex modulating waveforms, the side frequencies are replaced by sidebands. The highest-frequency component of the complex waveform is limited to one-half of the sampling frequency f_s.

Since it is not possible to generate a true impulse, the real pulses used will have a finite length, and the resulting spectrum will be somewhat different from this ideal case.

11.3.2 Natural PAM Sampling

Natural PAM sampling occurs when finite-width pulses are used in the modulator, but the tops of the pulses are forced to follow the modulating waveform, as shown in Figure 11.3(d). The result again is a spectrum containing a pair of sidebands around each harmonic of the pulse-sampling frequency, and the modulating base-band itself. The sidebands around each harmonic are equal in amplitude, but the amplitude varies with the harmonic position in the spectrum according to the envelope $C(\omega)$, which is described by Eq. (11.1), and which is the spectrum of the train of pulses of finite width [see Eq. (2.6)].

$$C(\omega) = \frac{\sin(\omega\, t_w/2)}{\omega\, t_w/2} \qquad (11.1)$$

where ω = radian frequency,
t_w = pulse width

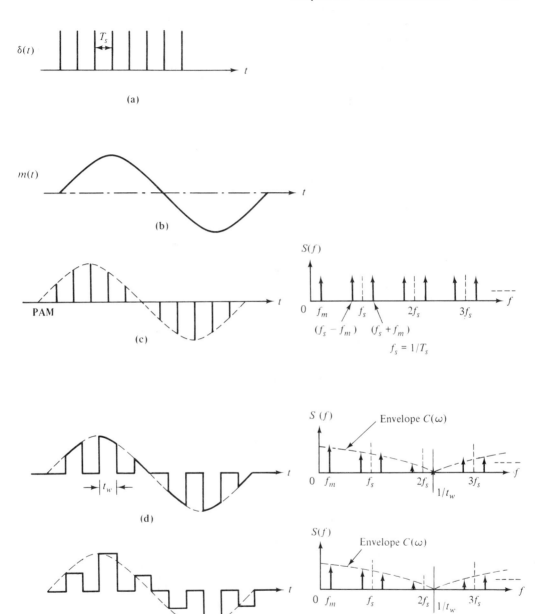

FIGURE 11.3.   Pulse amplitude modulation: (a) A train of equally spaced short constant-amplitude pulses; (b) A sine-wave signal; (c) A PAM signal resulting from multiplying (a) × (b); (d) Natural PAM sampling with its spectrum; (e) Flat-topped PAM sampling with its spectrum.

This function goes to zero first at a frequency $f = 1/t_w$. In both instantaneous and natural sampling, the base-band frequencies appear undistorted in the spectrum of the modulated wave, and may be recovered without distortion by simple low-pass filtering.

11.3.3 Flat-Topped PAM Sampling

Flat-topped sampling is a system quite often used because of the ease of generating the modulated wave. The waveform and spectrum for this case are shown in Figure 11.3(e). Finite-width pulses are used, but they have flat tops *after* modulation. Again, the spectrum shows the base band and all the harmonic sidebands present. However, this time the amplitudes of all the components are forced to conform to the envelope of $C(\omega)$ as defined by Eq. (11.1), including those in the base band. This causes a distortion of the base band that must be corrected by including a compensation network after the base band has been recovered by filtering.

PAM signals are very rarely used for transmission purposes directly. The reason for this lies in the fact that the modulating information is contained in the amplitude factor of the pulses, which can be easily distorted during transmission by noise, crosstalk, or other forms of distortion. They are used frequently as an intermediate step in other pulse-modulating methods, especially where time-division multiplexing is used.

11.4 TIME-DIVISION MULTIPLEXING

PAM waveforms can be generated which use a very small duty cycle so that if only one PAM wave were sent over a channel, much of the transmission time available would go unused. This time can be utilized by sandwiching the pulse trains of other PAM signals into the unused time intervals between pulses. Figure 11.4(a) shows how this would work for the *time-division multiplexing* (TDM) of five PAM signals, each with the same sampling rate. Only two of the five waves are shown for simplicity.

Figure 11.4(b) shows the block diagram of a TDM system which could be used to multiplex the five signals. A rotating switch called a commutator (realized with electronic switches) connects the output of each PAM channel modulator to the communication channel input in turn, dwelling on each contact only for the duration time of one pulse. The channel must have sufficient bandwidth to handle these pulses, which now occur at five times the sampling rate of one channel. The bandwidth required should be much greater than the system pulse repetition rate to make intersymbol crosstalk negligible. This includes a guard time between pulses as discussed below.

At the receiving end, another switch, rotating in synchronism with the sending commutator, decommutates the pulse trains and connects them to

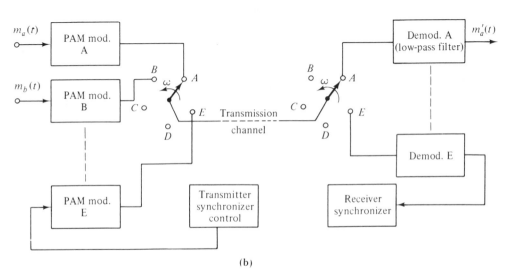

FIGURE 11.4. (a) A five-channel time-division-multiplexed (TDM) PAM signal; (b) A five-channel time-division-multiplexed system.

the appropriate demodulator circuits. Since it is possible for the receiver to get out of step with the transmitter, it is necessary to send synchronizing signals along with the information signals. One channel of the group is usually reserved for this purpose.

Because of the problem of intersymbol crosstalk, the pulses from the PAM modulators are made shorter than the allotted pulse-duration time, so that a "guard time" exists between each pair of pulses. This extra guard time means that the effective pulse width is about half of the pulse period.

The subject of multiplexing is dealt with also in Section 9.6.3.

11.5   PULSE-TIME MODULATION

Pulse-time modulation (PTM) is accomplished by four distinct methods as follows. The first three of these comprise a group known as *pulse-duration* or *width modulation* (PDM or PWM); the fourth is pulse-position modulation (PPM). Three variations of pulse-width modulation are possible, depending on whether the lead edge, the tail edge, or the center of the pulse is kept fixed in phase, as the pulse width is varied with the modulation. This form of modulation is also known as class D modulation. PPM, the fourth mode, is generated by changing the position of a fixed-length pulse within a fixed time slot. Figure 11.5(a)–(g) shows the results of each of these modes for two sample periods.

It should be noted that the same restrictions as to sampling rate, guard-time allowances, and time-division multiplexing apply to all forms of pulse-time modulation as apply to PAM signals. Added noise is not as much trouble, since PTM corresponds to FM and PM in form, and thus can run at fixed amplitude and be regenerated relatively easily to reduce noise. Figure 11.5(h) shows the form of the spectrum of a pulse-width-modulated signal for a sinusoidal modulating signal with a frequency near the upper edge of the base band, f_m. The spectrum is that of a frequency-modulated carrier, with the base band and many harmonics present. Since the sampling frequency is near the maximum base-band frequency ($(2$ to $10) \times f_m$), then if large deviations are allowed, the lower sidebands will appear in the base band and cause distortion. This can only be overcome by increasing the sampling frequency, or by keeping the deviation low (i.e., by keeping the pulse-width deviation to a small percentage of the pulse slot width). The same is true of the PPM signal.

11.5.1   Pulse-Width Modulation

Figure 11.6 shows a *pulse-width-modulation* (PWM) system. A PAM signal is generated first and may be multiplexed with other PAM signals. The PWM signal is generated from the PAM signal and transmitted. At the receiver, the PAM signal is regenerated, and then demodulated by low-pass filtering.

The modulating signal $m(t)$, (A), is applied to the input of a PAM modulating circuit, to generate the PAM signal (B). The same pulse train (C) which supplies the PAM modulator is used to gate on a ramp generator, to generate a train of ramp pulses (D) which all have equal slopes, amplitudes, and durations. These ramp pulses are added directly to the PAM pulses to produce the varying-height ramps of (E). The varying-height ramps gate a Schmitt trigger circuit to generate the varying-width rectangular pulses of the PWM wave (F). These PWM pulses can be transmitted directly or used as the input to a pulse-position modulator.

FIGURE 11.5. Pulse-time modulation (PTM) signals: (a) Carrier sampling pulses; (b) Modulating signal; (c) PAM signal; (d) PWM tail-edge modulated signal; (e) PWM lead-edge modulated signal; (f) PWM symmetrical signal; (g) PPM signal; (h) Spectrum of a PWM signal.

At the receiver, the received pulses (G) are put through a regenerating circuit to remove some of the noise and square up the pulses. These regenerated pulses (H) drive a reference pulse generator to produce a train of constant width/constant height pulses synchronized to the leading edge of the received pulses, but delayed by a fixed interval (I). The regenerated pulses also gate a ramp generator, which produces a constant-slope ramp for the duration of the pulse. At the end of the pulse, a sample-and-hold amplifier retains the final ramp voltage until it is reset at the end of the period, resulting in the ramp-and-pedestal waveform (J). The constant-

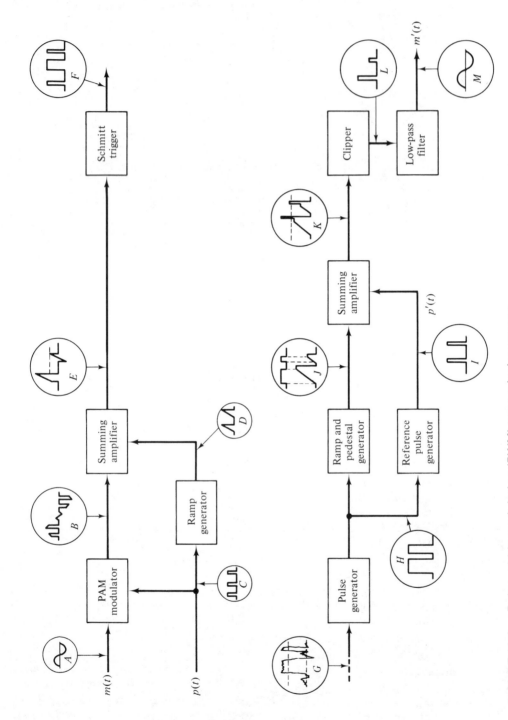

FIGURE 11.6. Pulse-width-modulation (PWM) transmission system.

amplitude pulses (I) are added to the pedestals to form (K), which is then clipped off at a threshold level to form the PAM signal of (L). The signal waveform $m'(t)$, (M), is recovered by low-pass filtering.

11.5.2   Pulse-Position Modulation

Pulse-position modulation (PPM) signals can be readily generated from the PWM signals by using the modulated edge of the PWM pulse to trigger a monostable multivibrator circuit which generates fixed width fixed amplitude pulses when triggered. At the receiver, a fixed-period reference pulse is generated from the incoming PPM waveform, and a flip-flop (bistable multivibrator) is set by the reference pulse and reset by the PPM pulse. The result is a rectangular width-modulated pulse at the output of the flip-flop.

11.6   PROBLEMS

1. What sampling rate would be appropriate for each of the following?

   (a) A telephone channel limited to 4 kHz bandwidth.
   (b) A music channel with a maximum signal frequency of 20 kHz.
   (c) A television video channel with a maximum bandwidth of 4.5 MHz.

2. Describe how spacing bias on a telegraph circuit can cause pulse shortening.

3. Describe how transmission distortion of a time division multiplexed signal can cause crosstalk between two adjacent channels.

4. Carefully plot the spectrum of a flat-top sampled PAM signal which has a 1 kHz sine modulating signal, a sampling frequency of 8 kHz and a pulse width of $31.25\,\mu$seconds, up to the 6th harmonic of the sampling frequency. Draw in with a dotted line the amplitude envelope curve.

5. Sketch a channel-interleaving scheme for time-division-multiplexing the following PAM channels: five 4-kHz telephone channels and one 20-kHz music channel. (b) Find the pulse repetition rate of the multiplexed signal. (c) Estimate the minimum system bandwidth required.

Part Four
Transmission and Radiation of Signals

Chapter 12
Transmission Lines and Cables

12.1 INTRODUCTION

Transmission of information as an electromagnetic signal always occurs as a *transverse electromagnetic* (TEM) wave, or as the combination of such waves as in a waveguide (see Chapter 13). The basic properties of the TEM wave are outlined in Appendix B, and propagation of these as radio waves is described in Chaper 14.

With transmission lines, the metallic conductors confine the TEM wave to the vicinity of the dielectric surrounding the conductors; as a result, some aspects of the transmission are best treated in terms of the *distributed circuit* parameters of the line, while others require the wave properties of the line to be taken into account. It must be clearly understood however that these are complementary views of the transmission; the voltages and currents on the line always accompany the TEM wave, and the particular viewpoint adopted usually depends on which properties are most easily measured.

Transmission lines may be *balanced* or *unbalanced* with respect to ground. The two basic types of transmission lines are the two-wire line which is usually operated in the balanced mode, Figure 12.1(a), and the coaxial line which is always operated in the unbalanced mode, Figure 12.1(b). The electromagnetic field configurations for each type are shown in

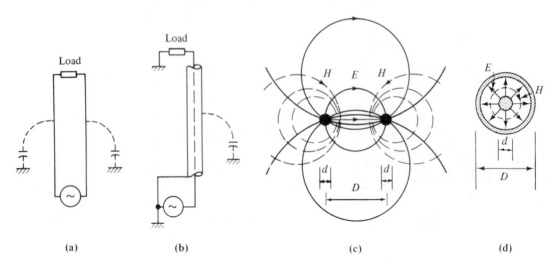

FIGURE 12.1. (a) A two-wire line; (b) A coaxial line; (c) Electromagnetic fields around a two-wire line; (d) Electromagnetic fields around a coaxial line.

Figure 12.1(c) and (d). In each case the direction of propagation of the TEM wave is into the page, and inspection shows that the E (electric) field is at right angles to the H (magnetic) field, and that both are at right angles to the direction of propagation, as required of a TEM wave.

With the coaxial line, the outer conductor forms a shield which confines the wave to the space between the conductors so that radiation from the line is negligible. However, the line is basically unbalanced since the external capacitance is between the outer conductor only and ground.

The two-wire line is normally operated in the balanced mode, the conductors being arranged so that they present equal capacitances to ground. (Of course, this may be a difficult condition to maintain in practice.) Radiation can occur from a two-wire line since the TEM wave can radiate out from the line as well as along it. The two-wire line is less expensive than the coaxial line, and is used for the majority of low-frequency telephone circuits. Care must be taken to maintain balance conditions, as described in Section 12.14. For high-frequency circuits (including multichannel telephony and radio feeders), the coaxial line is used to minimize radiation; and where balanced radio antennas have to be connected to coaxial lines, special transmission line transformers known as *baluns* (*bal*anced to *un*balanced) are employed.

12.2 PRIMARY LINE CONSTANTS

From the circuit point of view, a transmission line will have series resistance and inductance, which together go to make up the series impedance of the conducting wires, and shunt conductance and capacitance of the dielectric between the conductors, which go to make up the shunt admittance of the line. A small length δx of the line may therefore be represented approximately by the filter section, Figure 12.2, where, as part of the approximation, the values for both the *go* and *return* wires are included in the lumped components. The parameters R, L, G, and C shown in Figure 12.2 are known as the *primary line constants;* these are the series resistance R, ohms/meter; the series inductance L, henries/meter; the shunt conductance G, siemens/meter; and the shunt capacitance C, farads/meter. The primary constants take into account both the *go* and *return* lines. They are constant in that they do not vary with voltage and current; however, they are frequency-dependent to some extent. The series resistance R increases with frequency as a result of skin effect (see Section 1.10). The inductance L is almost independent of frequency for open lines but tends to decrease with increasing frequency for screened cables. The capacitance C is almost independent of frequency while the conductance G tends to increase with the frequency (i.e., the shunt resistance decreases) because of increasing dielectric loss with increase in frequency.

FIGURE 12.2.   Circuit approximations for a short length δx of transmission line.

No simple formulas can be given for the primary constants, covering all frequency ranges, but simplifications are possible for particular, well-defined operating ranges, e.g., low- or audio-frequencies, and high- or radio-frequencies. As will be shown in Section 12.4, the most practically useful characteristic of a line is the *characteristic impedance,* which at high frequencies is determined by the series inductance and shunt capacitance. These, as shown below, depend on line geometry, which therefore sets a limit on the range of characteristic impedance possible in practice.

For the two-wire line of Figure 12.1(c), with the conductors embedded in a medium of permittivity ϵ F/m and permeability μ H/m, and with the line dimensions in meters, the primary inductance and capacitance per unit length are given approximately by

2-wire line: $$L \cong \frac{\mu}{\pi}\ln\left(\frac{2D}{d}\right) \quad \text{H/m} \tag{12.1}$$

$$C \cong \frac{\pi \epsilon}{\ln\left(\frac{2D}{d}\right)} \quad \text{F/m} \tag{12.2}$$

For the coaxial line of Figure 12.1(d), with a dielectric of permittivity ϵ F/m and permeability μH/m, and again, with the line dimensions in meters, the approximate forms of the equations are

Coaxial line:
$$L \cong \frac{\mu}{2\pi} \cdot \ln(D/d) \quad \text{H/m} \tag{12.3}$$

$$C \cong \frac{2\pi \epsilon}{\ln(D/d)} \quad \text{F/m} \tag{12.4}$$

12.3 PHASE VELOCITY AND LINE WAVELENGTH

In Appendix B the phase velocity of a TEM wave is given by Eq. (B.11) as

$$v_p = \frac{1}{\sqrt{\mu \epsilon}} \tag{12.5}$$

For free space the values are $\mu = \mu_0 = 4\pi \times 10^{-7}$ H/m and $\epsilon = \epsilon_0 = 8.85 \times 10^{-12}$ F/m, giving $v_p = 3 \times 10^8$ m/s. This is the velocity of light, normally denoted by the letter c. For a transmission line the permeability may be assumed equal to the free-space value, but the permittivity may differ from the free-space value, depending on the dielectric used. The expression for permittivity is $\epsilon = \epsilon_r \epsilon_0$ where ϵ_r is the relative permittivity (or dielectric constant). Substituting this in Eq. (12.5) along with the free-space values gives

$$v_p = \frac{c}{\sqrt{\epsilon_r}} \tag{12.6}$$

Typically, ϵ_r may range from 1 to 5, and thus the phase velocity of the TEM wave on the line may be less than the free-space value.

The wavelength of the wave is given by Eq. (B.4) as

$$\lambda = \frac{v_p}{f} \tag{12.7}$$

Substituting Eq. (12.6) gives

$$\lambda = \frac{c}{f\sqrt{\epsilon_r}}$$

$$= \frac{\lambda_0}{\sqrt{\epsilon_r}} \tag{12.8}$$

where λ_0 is the free-space wavelength. The wavelength, as given by Eq. (12.8) is the value which must be used in transmission line calculations; for example, the phase shift coefficient, which is the phase shift per unit length, is given by

$$\beta = \frac{2\pi}{\lambda} \qquad (12.9)$$

where λ is as given by Eq. (12.8).

Another useful expression for the phase velocity can be obtained in terms of the inductance per unit length L, and capacitance per unit length C. From Eqs. (12.1) and (12.2) for the two-wire line, and Eqs. (12.3) and (12.4) for the coaxial line, it is seen that

$$LC = \mu\epsilon \qquad (12.10)$$

Hence, on substituting Eq. (12.10), in Eq. (12.5) the result is

$$v_p = \frac{1}{\sqrt{LC}} \qquad (12.11)$$

12.4   CHARACTERISTIC IMPEDANCE

Energy travels along a transmission line in the form of an electromagnetic wave, the wave set up by the signal source being known as the incident (or forward) wave. Only when the load impedance at the receiving end is a reflectionless match for the line, as discussed in Section 1.14, will all the energy be transferred to the load. If reflectionless matching is not achieved, energy will be reflected back along the line in the form of a reflected wave (and hence the name reflectionless matching). Because of the distributed nature of a transmission line, the question may be asked: Exactly to what impedance of the line must the load be matched? This can be answered by considering, first, a hypothetical line, infinite in length for which no reflection can occur, since the incident wave never reaches the end. The ratio of maximum voltage to maximum current at any point on such a line is found to be constant, i.e., independent of position. This ratio is known as the characteristic impedance Z_0. Now, if a finite length of line is terminated in a load impedance $Z_L = Z_0$, this will appear as an infinite line to the incident wave since at all points, including the load termination, the ratio of voltage to current will equal Z_0. Thus, the characteristic impedance of a transmission line is the ratio of voltage to current at any point along the line on which no reflected wave exists.

With a sinusoidal signal of angular frequency ω rad/sec, the characteristic impedance in terms of the primary constants is found to be

$$Z_0 = \sqrt{\frac{R + j\omega L}{G + j\omega C}} \quad \Omega \qquad (12.12)$$

At low frequencies, such that $R \gg \omega L$ and $G \gg \omega C$, the expression for Z_0 reduces to

$$Z_0 \cong \sqrt{\frac{R}{G}} \quad \Omega \qquad (12.13)$$

and at high frequencies, such that $R \ll \omega L$ and $G \ll \omega C$, to

$$Z_0 \cong \sqrt{\frac{L}{C}} \quad \Omega \qquad (12.14)$$

It will be observed that each limiting value is purely resistive (no j coefficient) and independent of frequency. Between these limits Z_0 is complex and frequency dependent, and it is found that for most practical lines it is capacitive. However, above a few tens of kilohertz for two-wire lines, and a few hundred kilohertz for coaxial lines, the high-frequency approximation for Z_0 is sufficiently accurate for most practical purposes, and this will be the expression used throughout this chapter.

Substituting Eq. (12.1) and (12.2) into Eq. (12.14) gives Z_0 in terms of line dimensions, permittivity, and permeability for the two-wire line as

$$Z_0 = \frac{1}{\pi}\sqrt{\frac{\mu}{\epsilon}} \cdot \ln\left(\frac{2D}{d}\right) \qquad (12.15)$$

And for the coaxial line from Eqs. (12.3) and (12.4), Eq. (12.14) gives

$$Z_0 = \frac{1}{2\pi}\sqrt{\frac{\mu}{\epsilon}} \cdot \ln\left(\frac{D}{d}\right) \qquad (12.16)$$

For the dielectrics encountered in practice, the permeability will be equal to that of free space, $\mu = \mu_0 = 4\pi \times 10^{-7}$ H/m; the permittivity will be given by $\epsilon = \epsilon_r \epsilon_0$, where $\epsilon_0 = 8.854 \times 10^{-12}$ F/m is the permittivity of free space and ϵ_r is the relative permittivity or dielectric constant. Substituting these into the impedance Eqs. (12.15) and (12.16) gives

2-wire line:
$$Z_0 = \frac{120}{\sqrt{\epsilon_r}} \cdot \ln\left(\frac{2D}{d}\right) \quad \Omega \qquad (12.17)$$

Coaxial:
$$Z_0 = \frac{60}{\sqrt{\epsilon_r}} \cdot \ln\left(\frac{D}{d}\right) \quad \Omega \qquad (12.18)$$

In each case, it will be seen that for a given dielectric constant, the characteristic impedance is determined by the ratio D/d [Figure 12.1(c) and (d)]. For dielectrics in common use, the dielectric constant will be within the range 1–5, and practical limitations on the ratio D/d for each type of line limit Z_0 to the range of about 40 to 150 ohms for coaxial, and 150 to 600 ohms for 2-wire.

12.5   THE PROPAGATION COEFFICIENT

The propagation coefficient γ determines the variation of current, or voltage, with distance x along a transmission line. The current (and voltage) distribution along a matched line is found to vary exponentially with distance, the equations being

$$I = I_s e^{-\gamma x} \tag{12.19}$$

$$V = V_s e^{-\gamma x} \tag{12.20}$$

where I_s is the magnitude of the current and V_s is the magnitude of the voltage of the input or sending end of the line.

Like the characteristic impedance, the propagation coefficient also depends on the primary constants and the angular velocity of the signal. It is given by

$$\gamma = \sqrt{(R + j\omega L)(G + j\omega C)} \tag{12.21}$$

This is also a complex quantity, and can be written as

$$\gamma = \alpha + j\beta \tag{12.22}$$

where α is known as the *attentuation coefficient* and determines how the voltage or current decreases with distance along the line, and β is known as the *phase-shift coefficient* and determines the phase angle of the voltage (or current) variation with distance. The phase-shift coefficient is the phase shift per unit length, and since a phase shift of 2π radians occurs over a distance of one wavelength, λ, then

$$\beta = \frac{2\pi}{\lambda} \tag{12.23}$$

To see how the propagation coefficient affects the current, consider the current equation:

$$I = I_s e^{-(\alpha + j\beta)x} \tag{12.24}$$

$$= I_s e^{-\alpha x}(e^{-j\beta x}) \tag{12.25}$$

FIGURE 12.3. (a) Current and (b) voltage phasor diagrams.

(a)

(b)

The last equation can be represented graphically as shown in Figure 12.3(a). The length of the phasor line represents $I_s e^{-\alpha x}$, and the angle of rotation from the reference line represents βx.

The attenuation is often expressed in terms of a unit known as the *neper*. The magnitude of the current (on the matched line) is

$$|I| = I_s e^{-\alpha x} \tag{12.26}$$

and the attenuation of the current, in nepers, is defined as

$$N = -\ln\left(\frac{|I|}{I_s}\right) \tag{12.27}$$

$$= -\ln(e^{-\alpha x})$$

$$= \alpha x \text{ nepers} \tag{12.28}$$

The attentuation coefficient α can therefore be alternatively expressed as the attenuation in nepers per unit length of line:

$$\alpha = \frac{N}{x} \tag{12.29}$$

Example 12.1 The input current in a matched line is 50 mA and the load current is 1 mA. The line is 1 km long. Calculate:

(a) The total attenuation in nepers.

(b) The attenuation coefficient.

Solution (a) $N = -\ln(1/50)$

$= 3.9$ nepers

(Note that by including a minus sign in the defining equation for the neper, the attenuation comes out a positive number.)

(b) $\alpha = \dfrac{3.9}{1000}$

$\qquad = 3.9 \text{ mN/m}$

The neper is a useful unit in theoretical work, but in practical work the decibel is more commonly used. In Appendix A, the relationship between the decibel value D and the neper value N of a given current ratio is shown to be

$$D = 8.686N \qquad\qquad (12.30)$$

Hence, for the transmission line where $N = \alpha x$,

$$D = 8.686\alpha x \qquad \text{decibels} \qquad (12.31)$$

Therefore, if the attenuation coefficient is *defined* in decibels per unit length, say $[\alpha]$, then

$$[\alpha] = 8.686\alpha \qquad \text{dB/m} \qquad (12.32)$$

Example 12.2   The attenuation coeffient of a line is 0.0006 N/m. Determine the attenuation coefficient in:

(a) dB/m

(b) dB/mile

Solution   (a) $[\alpha] = 8.686\alpha$

and since α numerically equals the attenuation in N/m,

$$[\alpha] = 8.686 \times 0.0006$$

$$= 0.00521 \qquad \text{dB/m}$$

(b) Since there are 1609 m in 1 mile, the attenuation coefficient in dB/mi is

$$0.00521 \times 1609 = 8.4 \text{ dB/mi}$$

For a matched line, $V = IZ_0$ at any point along the line, and for $Z_0 = Z_0 \angle -\Phi$ (assuming a leading phase angle), the voltage/distance phasor diagram will be similar to that for current, as shown in Figure 12.3(b). The length of the phasor is modified by Z_0, and the reference line for the voltage is displaced by $-\Phi$.

Both α and β are determined by the primary constants and the frequency, since

$$\gamma = \alpha + j\beta = \sqrt{(R + j\omega L)(G + j\omega C)} \qquad (12.33)$$

The square-root expression can be expanded by means of the binomial expansion, and an approximation sufficiently accurate for most practical purposes is to take the expansion to the third term. This results in the following expression for α:

$$\alpha \approx \frac{R}{2Z_0} + \frac{GZ_0}{2} \qquad (12.34)$$

where Z_0 in this particular case is $\sqrt{L/C}$ (i.e., the high-frequency limit to the characteristic impedance). In most practical lines G is very small, almost zero, so the further approximation is usually valid:

$$\alpha \approx \frac{R}{2Z_0} \qquad (12.35)$$

As an example, the primary constants for a coaxial cable at a frequency of 10 MHz were determined approximately as:

$$L = 234 \text{ nH/m}$$

$$C = 93.5 \text{ pF/m}$$

$$R = 0.568 \ \Omega/\text{m}$$

$$G = 0$$

Therefore, at a frequency of 10 MHz,

from (12.14), $\qquad Z_0 \cong \sqrt{\dfrac{234 \times 10^{-9}}{93.5 \times 10^{-12}}} = 50\Omega$

and (12.35), $\qquad \alpha = \dfrac{0.568}{2 \times 50} = 0.00568 \text{ N/m}$

The attenuation, in dB/m $[\alpha]$, is $0.00568 \times 8.686 = 0.0493$ dB/m. The major variation in R with frequency is due to skin effect, for which R is proportional to the square root of frequency.

The binomial expansion for γ results in the following expression for β:

$$\beta \cong \omega\sqrt{LC}\left[1 + \frac{1}{8}\left(\frac{R}{\omega L} - \frac{G}{\omega C}\right)^2\right] \qquad (12.36)$$

An interesting situation arises when

$$\frac{R}{\omega L} = \frac{G}{\omega C} \qquad (12.37)$$

The phase-shift coefficient is then seen to be equal to

$$\beta = \omega\sqrt{LC} \qquad (12.38)$$

This meets the condition, discussed in the following section, required for distortionless transmission (i.e., β proportional to ω). The condition for distortionless transmission is seen to be

$$\frac{R}{\omega L} = \frac{G}{\omega C}$$

and this can be rearranged as

$$\frac{R}{G} = \frac{L}{C} \qquad (12.39)$$

In any practical line R and G both will be as small as possible in order to keep losses at a minimum. The ratio L/C will not, in general, be equal to R/G and therefore, if distortionless transmission is desired, the ratio L/C will have to be altered to equal R/G. In all practical cases this is achieved by increasing L, a technique known as *loading*. One common form of loading is to add inductance coils in series with the line at regularly spaced intervals. However, it is not practical to load to achieve completely distortionless conditions, as it is found that this would require an inordinately large value of inductance. Furthermore, large inductance decreases phase velocity as shown by Eq. (12.11), which may introduce unacceptable delays on long distance telephone circuits. It is interesting to note that the introduction of pulse code modulation (see Section 17.12) on normal telephone lines requires the removal of the loading coils in order to increase the bandwidth of the lines.

12.6 PHASE AND GROUP VELOCITIES

The phase velocity of an electromagnetic wave has already been discussed briefly in Section 12.3. For wave motion generally, a simple relationship exists among frequency f, wavelength λ, and phase velocity v_p (see Appendix B):

$$\lambda f = v_p \qquad\qquad (12.40)$$

Since $\beta = 2\pi/\lambda$ and $\omega = 2\pi f$, multiplying the top and bottom of the left-hand side of Eq. (12.40) by 2π results in:

$$\frac{\omega}{\beta} = v_p \qquad\qquad (12.41)$$

It is seen therefore that while β is proportional to ω, the phase velocity will be constant (i.e., independent of frequency), and therefore all component waves making up a signal will be transmitted at the same velocity, v_p. This is the distortionless transmission condition referred to in the previous section.

The situation can occur where β is not proportional to ω, for example the general case, Eq. (12.36). Component sine waves of a signal will be transmitted with differing velocities, and the question then arises, at what velocity does the signal wave travel? An answer to this question can be obtained by considering two sinusoidal waves differing in frequency by amount $\delta\omega$. The combined wave will be as shown in Figure 12.4, where for clarity, the individual sine waves are assumed to have equal amplitudes, and

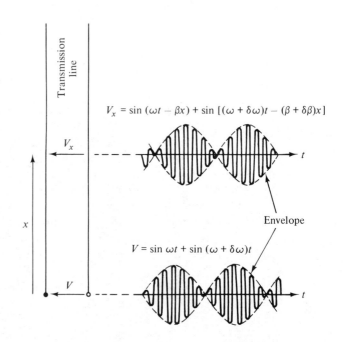

FIGURE 12.4. Wave group, used in determination of group velocity.

line attenuation is ignored. The composite signal is seen to consist of high-frequency waves (many zero crossings on the time axis) modulated by a low-frequency envelope. Detailed analysis shows that the envelope travels along the line with a velocity given by

$$v_g = \frac{\delta\omega}{\delta\beta} \qquad (12.42)$$

where the subscript g signifies *group velocity* [i.e., the velocity at which the group (of two sine waves) travels]. It is also the velocity at which the energy is propagated along the line.

In the limit the group velocity is given by the differential coefficient of ω with respect to β, and if β varies rapidly with ω, serious distortion will result.

The condition stated previously for distortionless transmission was that v_p be constant. A more general condition will now be stated, which is that for distortionless transmission, the β/ω graph should be a straight line, which may be expressed as

$$\beta = t_d\omega + \beta_0 \qquad (12.43)$$

where t_d is the slope of the line and is known as the *group delay time,* and β_0 is the intercept, which must be equal to $\pm n\pi$ for distortionless transmission. This graph is sketched in Figure 12.5 along with the line representing the simpler condition, $\beta = \omega/v_p$.

It will be seen that t_d is the reciprocal of the group velocity and therefore, in addition to the constraint that $\beta_0 = \pm n\pi$, v_g must be constant (for constant t_d) for distortionless transmission. This more general set of conditions covers situations where distortionless transmission is achieved even though the simpler condition ($\beta/\omega =$ Constant) is violated.

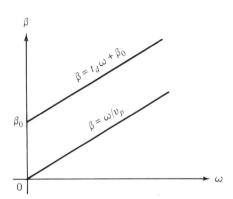

FIGURE 12.5. β/ω graph for distortionless transmission.

12.7 STANDING WAVES

When the load impedance does not match the line impedance, part of the energy in the incident wave is reflected at the load. This gives rise to a reflected wave traveling back along the line toward the source. If the source impedance does not match the line, a further reflection will take place, and in this way, multiple reflections can be set up at both load and source. The overall effect can be treated as the resultant of a single incident and a single reflected wave. These can be represented by rotating phasors in the manner of Figure 12.3, but with the reflected wave phasor rotating in the opposite direction to the incident wave phasor, Figure 12.6(a). This is because from a given point, an increase in x away from the source is also a decrease of amount x toward the point of reflection.

Clearly, at certain values of x, the phasors will be in opposition, giving rise to voltage minima, Figure 12.6(b), while at other values of x they will coincide, Figure 12.6(c), giving rise to voltage maxima. The voltage, as a function of distance x, is sketched in Figure 12.6(d), where it will be seen to go through a series of maxima and minima. This voltage pattern is stationary as regards position and is therefore referred to as the *voltage standing wave* (VSW). It is essential to grasp, however, that at any given point, the voltage is time-varying at the frequency of the input signal. Thus, at point x_1 corresponding to the first minimum, the voltage alternates sinusoidally as shown in Figure 12.6(e) between the peak values $\pm V_{1\min}$.

Another important feature of the voltage standing-wave pattern is that the distance between successive minima (and between successive maxima) is $\frac{1}{2}\lambda$. This is easily shown from the fact that when at a minimum, the phasors form a straight line, Figure 12.6(b). On moving from position x_1 to x_2 the phasors must rotate to interchange positions, (i.e., each phasor rotates by a phase angle of π radians). But each phasor also rotates by an angle given by $\beta(x_2 - x_1)$ where $\beta = 2\pi/\lambda$, the phase-shift coefficient. Therefore:

$$\frac{2\pi}{\lambda}(x_2 - x_1) = \pi \qquad (12.44)$$

$$\therefore (x_2 - x_1) = \frac{1}{2}\lambda \qquad (12.45)$$

In a similar way, it is easy to show that the distance between a minimum and the following maximum is $\frac{1}{4}\lambda$.

A current standing wave will also occur. For a purely resistive Z_0, the incident current wave will always be in-phase with the incident voltage wave, while the reflected current wave will always be anti-phase to the reflected voltage wave. This happens because either the electric or the magnetic field of the wave must reverse direction as shown in Figure B.1(b) of Appendix B. A consequence of the anti-phase relationship between re-

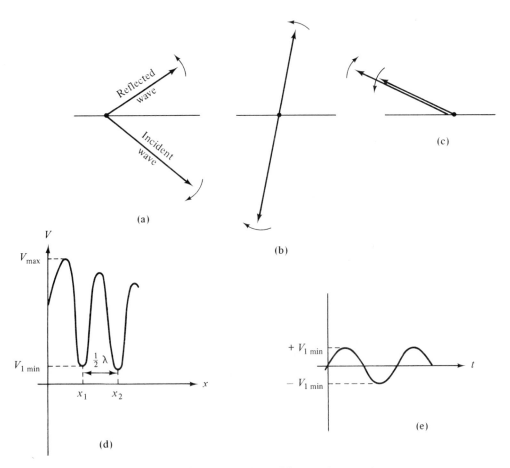

FIGURE 12.6.   (a), (b) and (c) Phasor representation of forward and reflected waves; (d) Voltage standing wave; (e) Voltage-time variation.

flected voltage and current is that the current maxima occur along with the voltage minima, and the current minima along with the voltage maxima, for the standing wave patterns (bearing in mind that these are the phasor sums of incident and reflected waves). As already mentioned, this condition only holds when Z_0 is purely resistive. It enters into the theory of slotted-line measurements discussed in Section 12.10.

12.8   LOSSLESS LINES AT RADIO FREQUENCIES

For many applications at radio frequencies, the losses in a transmission line are small enough to be ignored (for example, in short lengths of good-quality cable), and therefore the attenuation coefficient α can be set equal to zero. The propagation coefficient is then given by

$$\gamma = j\beta \tag{12.46}$$

It is often more convenient to measure distances from the load end, rather than from the sending end. Denoting this by ℓ, an equation for the incident voltage, similar in form to Eq. (12.20), may be written

$$V_i = V_I e^{j\beta\ell} \tag{12.47}$$

Here, V_i is the incident wave voltage at any distance ℓ from the load; V_I is the value at the load ($\ell = 0$), and which may be complex; and $j\beta$ replaces the γ of Eq. (12.20). A positive exponential is used in Eq. (12.47) compared to the negative exponential in Eq. (12.20) since ℓ is measured in the opposite direction to x.

A similar equation can be written for the reflected voltage wave:

$$V_r = V_R e^{-j\beta\ell} \tag{12.48}$$

Here, V_R is the value of the reflected voltage at the load (and may be complex), and, of course, a negative exponential is used since the reflected wave's phase changes in the opposite sense to that of the incident wave. At any point on the line

$$V = V_i + V_r \tag{12.49}$$

In particular, at the load ($\ell = 0$)

$$V_L = V_I + V_R \tag{12.50}$$

The equations for current are:

Incident wave:
$$I_i = \frac{V_i}{Z_0} \tag{12.51}$$

Reflected wave:
$$I_r = -\frac{V_r}{Z_0} \tag{12.52}$$

Note the minus sign for the reflected current wave, signifying the 180° phase change discussed in the previous section.

The resultant current at any point ℓ from the load is

$$I = I_i + I_r \tag{12.53}$$

$$= \frac{V_i - V_r}{Z_0} \tag{12.54}$$

In particular, the load current is

$$I_L = \frac{V_I - V_R}{Z_0} \qquad (12.55)$$

Normally it is not necessary to know V_I and V_R separately, the ratio V_R/V_I entering more into calculations. This ratio is termed the *voltage reflection coefficient*, Γ:

$$\Gamma = \frac{V_R}{V_I} \qquad (12.56)$$

Note that Γ is defined in terms of the incident and reflected waves *at the load*.

From Eqs. (12.50) and (12.55), the load impedance may be expressed as

$$Z_L = \frac{V_L}{I_L}$$

$$= \frac{V_I + V_R}{V_I - V_R} \cdot Z_0 \qquad (12.57)$$

From which

$$\Gamma = \frac{Z_L - Z_0}{Z_L + Z_0} \qquad (12.58)$$

The fact that the voltage reflection coefficient is determined solely by the load impedance and the characteristic impedance makes it an important practical parameter.

Three specific load conditions which occur frequently are (i) matched load; (ii) short-circuit load, and (iii) open-circuit load. For each of these, it is seen that:

(i) Matched load, $Z_L = Z_0$: $\Gamma = 0$
(ii) Short-circuit, $Z_L = 0$: $\Gamma = -1$
(iii) Open-circuit, $Z_L = \infty$: Here it is first necessary to rearrange the equation as:

$$\Gamma = \frac{1 - Z_0/Z_L}{1 + Z_0/Z_L} \qquad (12.59)$$

$$= 1 \qquad (\text{as } Z_L \text{ goes to infinity})$$

It is left as an exercise for the student to show that the corresponding load conditions for the three cases are:

$$(i) \quad V_L = V_I \text{ and } I_L = V_I/Z_0$$

$$(ii) \quad V_L = 0 \text{ and } I_L = 2V_I/Z_0$$

$$(iii) \quad V_L = 2V_I \text{ and } I_L = 0$$

12.9 VOLTAGE STANDING WAVE RATIO

The *voltage standing-wave ratio* (VSWR) is defined as

$$VSWR = \frac{V_{max}}{V_{min}} \qquad (12.60)$$

the quantities V_{max} and V_{min} being as shown in Figure 12.6. The line is assumed lossless so that the maxima all have the same value, V_{max}, and the minima all have the value, V_{min}.

As previously shown, Figure 12.6(c), a maximum occurs when the phasors are in phase:

$$V_{max} = |V_I| + |V_R| \qquad (12.61)$$

(Note: this is not the same as $|V_I + V_R|$, which is the modulus of the load voltage.)

$$= |V_I|(1 + |\Gamma|) \qquad (12.62)$$

A minimum occurs when the phasors are antiphase:

$$V_{min} = |V_I|(1 - |\Gamma|) \qquad (12.63)$$

Therefore,
$$VSWR = \frac{|V_I|(1 + |\Gamma|)}{|V_I|(1 - |\Gamma|)}$$

or
$$VSWR = \frac{(1 + |\Gamma|)}{(1 - |\Gamma|)} \qquad (12.64)$$

The VSWR can range in value from unity to infinity; that is,

$$1 \le VSWR \le \infty \qquad (12.65)$$

Ideally, the VSWR should equal 1, as this represents a matched condition, and practical adjustments on RF transmission lines are often aimed at minimizing the VSWR. Note that the VSWR is always a real number (i.e., it has no imaginary part).

The equation for VSWR can be rearranged to give

$$|\Gamma| = \frac{VSWR - 1}{VSWR + 1} \qquad (12.66)$$

12.10 SLOTTED-LINE MEASUREMENTS AT RADIO FREQUENCIES

Use is made of the voltage standing wave at high frequencies to determine unknown impedances which would otherwise be difficult to measure. In principle, the method requires only a determination of the VSWR and the distance of the first minimum from the load (the minimum rather than the maximum is chosen in practice because it is more sharply defined). The apparatus consists of a slotted section of coaxial line through which a probe can sample the electric field and hence the voltage standing wave. The output signal from the probe is often converted to a signal of lower frequency and then amplified and rectified to produce dc output proportional to the voltage standing-wave amplitude; alternatively, for simpler measurements, the probe output may be directly rectified and the dc read by a microammeter. The distance of the probe from the load can be read directly off a calibrated distance scale. There will always be specific corrections to make for a given apparatus, to allow for end effects, details of which should be included in the manufacturer's handbook. The theory of the measurement technique is as follows.

At distance l from the load, the impedance seen looking toward the load is

$$Z = \frac{V}{I} \tag{12.67}$$

which from Eqs. (12.49) and (12.54) is

$$Z = Z_0 \frac{V_i + V_r}{V_i - V_r} \tag{12.68}$$

$$= Z_0 \frac{1 + V_r/V_i}{1 - V_r/V_i} \tag{12.68a}$$

But from Eqs. (12.47) and (12.48) and from Eq. (12.56),

$$\frac{V_r}{V_i} = \frac{V_R\, e^{-j\beta l}}{V_I\, e^{+j\beta l}}$$

$$= \Gamma e^{-j2\beta l} \tag{12.69}$$

In particular, let the distance from load to first voltage minimum be $l_{\min}$ and let $2\beta l_{\min} = \Theta$; combining Eqs. (12.68) and (12.69) and substituting for Θ gives the impedance at the voltage minimum as

$$Z_{min} = Z_0 \frac{(1 + \Gamma e^{-j\theta})}{(1 - \Gamma e^{-j\theta})} \qquad (12.70)$$

The impedance at a voltage minimum will also be given by

$$Z_{min} = \frac{V_{min}}{I_{max}} \qquad (12.71)$$

since a current maximum coincides with a voltage minimum. Hence:

$$Z_{min} = \frac{|V_I|(1 - |\Gamma|)}{(1 + |\Gamma|)|V_I|/Z_0} \qquad (12.72)$$

$$= Z_0 \frac{1 - |\Gamma|}{1 + |\Gamma|} \qquad (12.73)$$

Therefore, on substituting from Eq. (12.64)

$$Z_{min} = \frac{Z_0}{\text{VSWR}} \qquad (12.74)$$

Equating the two expressions for Z_{min},

$$\frac{Z_0}{\text{VSWR}} = Z_0 \frac{1 + \Gamma e^{-j\theta}}{1 - \Gamma e^{-j\theta}} \qquad (12.75)$$

Therefore, $\qquad 1 - \Gamma e^{-j\theta} = \text{VSWR}(1 + \Gamma e^{-j\theta})$

which can be rearranged as

$$\frac{1 - \text{VSWR}}{1 + \text{VSWR}} = \Gamma e^{-j\theta} \qquad (12.76)$$

or $\qquad\qquad -|\Gamma| = \Gamma e^{-j\theta}$

or $\qquad\qquad \Gamma = -|\Gamma|e^{j\theta} \qquad (12.77)$

Z_L can be determined directly from Eq. (12.77) since

$$\Gamma = \frac{Z_L - Z_0}{Z_L + Z_0} \qquad (12.78)$$

(Note the need to distinguish carefully between Γ and $|\Gamma|$.)

$$\frac{Z_L - Z_0}{Z_L + Z_0} = -|\Gamma|e^{j\theta}$$

which can be rearranged as

$$Z_L = Z_0 \frac{1 - |\Gamma|e^{j\Theta}}{1 + |\Gamma|e^{j\Theta}} \qquad (12.79)$$

Example 12.3 Measurements on a 50-Ω slotted line gave a VSWR of 2.0 and a distance from load to first minimum of 0.2λ. Determine both the equivalent series and equivalent parallel circuits for Z_L.

Solution From Eq. (12.66),

$$|\Gamma| = \frac{\text{VSWR} - 1}{\text{VSWR} + 1} = \frac{2 - 1}{2 + 1}$$

$$= \frac{1}{3}$$

Also,

$$\Theta = 2\beta\ell_{min}$$

$$= 2 \times \frac{2\pi}{\lambda} \times 0.2\lambda$$

$$= 0.8\pi \text{ rad}$$

$$= 144°$$

But

$$e^{j\Theta} = \cos\Theta + j\sin\Theta \qquad \text{(Euler's identity)}$$

$$= -0.809 + j0.588$$

and

$$|\Gamma|e^{j\Theta} = \frac{-0.809 + j0.588}{3}$$

$$= -0.27 + j0.196$$

From Eq. (12.79),

$$Z_L = 50 \frac{1 - (-0.27 + j0.196)}{1 + (-0.27 + j0.196)}$$

$$= 50 \frac{1.27 - j0.196}{0.73 + j0.196} \qquad (12.80)$$

The series equivalent is $Z_L = R_s + jX_s$ and, therefore,

$$R_s + jX_s = 50 \frac{(1.27 - j0.196)(0.73 - j0.196)}{0.73^2 + 0.196^2}$$

$$= 77.8 - j34.3$$

from which

$$R_s = 77.8\,\Omega$$

$$|X_s| = 34.3\,\Omega \text{ (capacitive)}$$

The parallel equivalent is $Y_L = G + jB$, where $Y_L = 1/Z_L$, $G = 1/R_p$, and $B = 1/X_p$. Therefore, from Eq. (12.80),

$$G + jB = \frac{0.73 + j0.196}{50(1.27 - j0.196)}$$

$$= \frac{(0.73 + j0.196)(1.27 + j0.196)}{50(1.27^2 + 0.196^2)}$$

$$= 10.76 + j4.75 \text{ mS}$$

from which

$$R_p = \frac{1}{G}$$

$$= \frac{10^3}{10.76}$$

$$= \textbf{92.9 } \mathbf{\Omega}$$

and

$$\left| X_p \right| = \left| \frac{1}{B} \right|$$

$$= \frac{10^3}{4.75}$$

$$= \textbf{211 } \mathbf{\Omega} \textbf{ (capacitive)}$$

Note that R_p and X_p can be obtained by direct application of Eqs. (1.39) and (1.40).

12.11 TRANSMISSION LINES AS CIRCUIT ELEMENTS

From Eq. (12.56), $V_R = \Gamma V_I$, and substituting this, with Eqs. (12.47) and (12.48), in Eq. (12.68) gives

$$Z = Z_0 \frac{e^{j\beta l} + \Gamma e^{-j\beta l}}{e^{j\beta l} - \Gamma e^{-j\beta l}} \qquad (12.81)$$

Using the identities,

$$e^{\pm j\beta l} = \cos \beta l \pm j \sin \beta l$$

This can be written as

$$Z = Z_0 \frac{(1 + \Gamma) \cos \beta l + j(1 - \Gamma) \sin \beta l}{(1 - \Gamma) \cos \beta l + j(1 + \Gamma) \sin \beta l} \qquad [12.82]$$

(a)

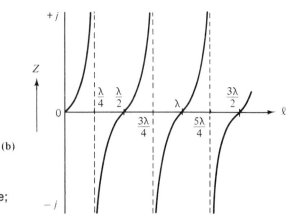

(b)

FIGURE 12.7.   (a) A short-circuited line;
(b) Reactance variation with line length.

Case (i): $Z_L = 0$ (a short circuit), Figure 12.7 (a)   With

$$Z_L = 0 \quad \Gamma = -1$$

$$Z = Z_0 \frac{0 + j2 \sin \beta l}{2 \cos \beta l + j0}$$

$$= jZ_0 \tan \beta l \tag{12.83}$$

The graph of Z/l is shown in Figure 12.7(b), where it is seen that for $0 \leqq l \leqq \lambda/4$ and $\lambda/2 \leqq l \leqq 3\lambda/4$, etc., Z is inductive $(+j)$. In practice, to obtain a variable inductive reactance, the short circuit on the line would be variable such that l could be varied between 0 and $1/4\lambda$. (The other possible ranges are usually avoided since the longer line lengths are practically undesirable.)

The equivalent inductance L_{eq} is obtained by equating

$$j\omega L_{eq} = jZ_0 \tan \beta l \qquad \left(0 \leqq l \leqq \frac{\lambda}{4} \right) \tag{12.84}$$

or
$$L_{eq} = \frac{Z_0}{\omega} \cdot \tan \beta l \tag{12.85}$$

Example 12.4   A 50-Ω short-circuited line is 0.1λ in length, at a frequency of 500 MHz. Calculate:

(a)   The equivalent inductive reactance

(b)   The equivalent inductance.

Solution
$$\beta l = 2\pi \times 0.1$$

$$= 36°$$

(a) $Z = j50 \times \tan 36°$

$= j50 \times 0.7265$

$= j36.33\,\Omega$

(b) $L_{eq} = \dfrac{36.33}{2\pi \times 500 \times 10^6} \times 10^9 \text{ nH}$

$= 11.6 \text{ nH}$

Because the inductive reactance is not directly proportional to frequency, but to $\tan \beta l$, L shows a frequency dependence. In the previous example, let the frequency be doubled; then

$$l = 0.2\lambda$$

$$= 72°$$

$$Z = j50 \times \tan 72°$$

$$= j153.9 \ \Omega(\text{i.e., well over four times the previous value})$$

$$L_{eq} = \dfrac{153.9}{2\pi \times 1000 \times 10^6} \times 10^9 \text{ nH}$$

$$= 24.5 \text{ nH}$$

From Figure 12.7(b) it is also seen that $\tfrac{1}{4}\lambda \le l \le \tfrac{1}{2}\lambda$ (or $\tfrac{3}{4}\lambda \le l \le \lambda$, etc.), the impedance appears capacitive, $(-j)$. The equivalent capacitive impedance is given by

$$-j\frac{1}{\omega C_{eq}} = -jZ_0 \tan \beta l \qquad (\tfrac{1}{4}\lambda \le l \le \tfrac{1}{2}\lambda) \qquad (12.86)$$

or

$$C_{eq} = \frac{1}{\omega Z_0 \tan \beta l} \qquad\qquad\qquad (12.87)$$

For example, let $l = 3\lambda/8$ at a frequency of 500 MHz; then

$$\beta l = 135°$$

$$Z = j50 \times \tan 135°$$

$$= -j50 \times \tan 45°$$

$$= -j50 \ \Omega$$

$$C_{eq} = \frac{10^{12}}{2\pi \times 500 \times 10^6 \times 50} \text{ pF}$$

$$= 6.4 \text{ pF}$$

(a)

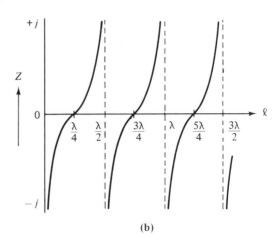

(b)

FIGURE 12.8. (a) An open-circuited line;
(b) Reactance variation with line length.

Case (ii): $Z_L = \infty$ *(an open circuit), Figure 12.8(a)*   In this case, $\Gamma = +1$, so Z becomes

$$Z = Z_0 \frac{2 \cos \beta l + j0}{0 + j2 \sin \beta l}$$

$$= -j Z_0 \cot \beta l \qquad (12.88)$$

The graph of Z/l is shown in Figure 12.8(b), where it will be seen that when $0 \leq l \leq \lambda/4$ the open-circuited line appears capacitive, and when $\lambda/4 \leq l \leq \lambda/2$, it appears inductive (with the pattern repeating at $\frac{1}{2}\lambda$ intervals). Although the open-circuit line finds some use, it is not as practically convenient as the short-circuit line. The short circuit provides a mechanical support for the end of the line, it is easily adjustable, and the length l is well defined. However, open circuit lines are readily fabricated in microstrip and stripline construction.

Case (iii): $l = \lambda/4$

$$\beta l = \frac{2\pi}{\lambda} \frac{\lambda}{4} = \frac{\pi}{2}$$

$$Z = Z_0 \frac{0 + j(1 - \Gamma)}{0 + j(1 + \Gamma)}$$

$$= Z_0 \frac{1 - \Gamma}{1 + \Gamma}$$

$$= Z_0 \frac{Z_0}{Z_L}$$

$$= \frac{Z_0^2}{Z_L} \qquad (12.89)$$

This important relationship shows that the impedance as seen at the input to the line, is Z_0^2/Z_L, and therefore a $\lambda/4$ section of line may be used to transform an impedance value from Z_L to Z_0^2/Z_L. For this reason, the $\lambda/4$ section is often known as a *quarter-wave transformer*.

Suppose, for example, it is required to match a 73-Ω antenna to a 600-Ω feeder line at a frequency of 150 MHz, the situation being as shown in Figure 12.9. In order to match the main feeder, the impedance Z_L' must equal 600 Ω. Therefore,

$$Z_L' = \frac{(Z_0')^2}{Z_L}$$

and

$$Z_0' = \sqrt{Z_L Z_L'}$$

$$= \sqrt{73 \times 600}$$

$$= 209 \ \Omega$$

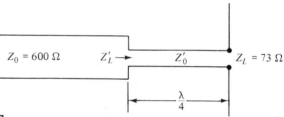

FIGURE 12.9. $\tfrac{1}{4}\lambda$ transformer matching.

With this arrangement there will be no standing waves on the main feeder line (600 Ω); that is, all of the power transmitted along the feeder will pass smoothly into the $\tfrac{1}{4}\lambda$ section. There will, of course, be a mismatch between the $\lambda/4$ section and the 73-Ω load, so a standing wave will occur on the $\lambda/4$ section; but, in practice, this can be tolerated because the matching section is considerably shorter than the main feeder. As can be easily verified, the reflection coefficient is -0.52 with, and -0.78 without, the $\lambda/4$ matching section.

Since the $\lambda/4$ section is a resonant element (i.e., it is only fully effective at the frequency which makes the length exactly $\lambda/4$), it is only useful over a narrow range of frequencies (e.g., voice-modulated radio waves). However, special broadbanding techniques are available.

Two cases of special interest arise when $Z_L = 0$ (short circuit) and $Z_L = \infty$ (open circuit). For the short-circuit load,

$$Z = \frac{Z_0^2}{0}$$

$$= \infty \qquad\qquad (12.90)$$

that is, the $\frac{1}{4}\lambda$ short-circuited section appears as a parallel resonant circuit (high impedance). In practice, line resistance will restrict Z to a finite, but high, value; the equivalent Q factor of the circuit will be high of the order of 3000.

For the open-circuit line,

$$Z = \frac{Z_0^2}{\infty}$$

$$= 0 \qquad (12.91)$$

that is, the open-circuit $\frac{1}{4}\lambda$ section appears as a series-resonant circuit (low impedance). Again, in practice, line resistance will result in Z being a small positive resistance, not zero.

12.12   SMITH CHART

The work involved in transmission-line calculations may be considerably reduced by using a special chart known as a *Smith chart* (devised by P.H. Smith in 1944). The theory behind the chart is too involved to be given here, but its use will be explained. Figure 12.10 shows a *normalized* chart; normalization simply means that the impedance values on the chart are given as a fraction of Z_0. Lowercase letters are used for normalized values, so the normalized impedance is written as

$$z = \frac{Z}{Z_0} \qquad (12.92)$$

Since Z may be written in the form

$$Z = R + jX$$

the normalized version becomes

$$z = r + jx \qquad (12.93)$$

where $r = R/Z_0$ and $x = X/Z_0$.

The chart can also be used for admittances which are normalized to $Y_0 (= 1/Z_0)$.

Considering the impedance components only for the moment, point A on Figure 12.10 represents a normalized impedance of

$$z = 4.0 + j3.0$$

determined by tracing along the circular arcs AA' and AA''. Note that the

IMPEDANCE OR ADMITTANCE COORDINATES

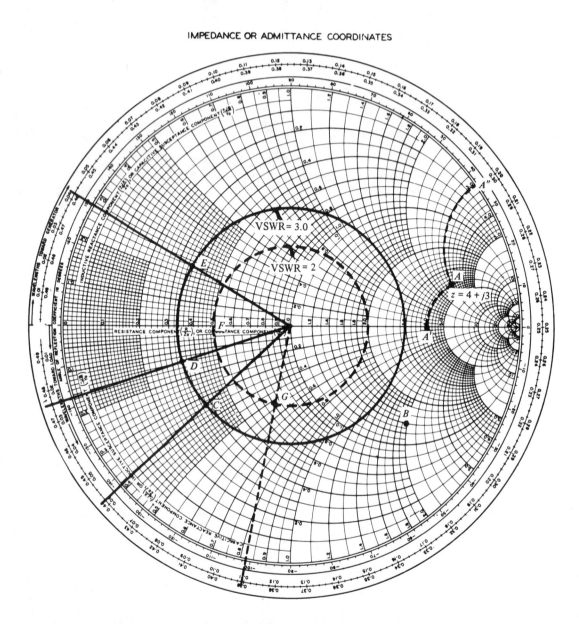

FIGURE 12.10. The Smith chart.

normalized impedance is dimensionless. If the chart is to be used with a 50-Ω line, the actual impedance represented by point A would be

$$Z = 50z$$

$$= (200 + j\,150)\,\Omega$$

As another example, point B represents

$$z = 1.4 - j\,2.0$$

A circle can be drawn centered on $r = 1$, and the chart axes are so arranged that the circle cuts the r (normalized resistance) axis at

$$r_{max} = \text{VSWR} \tag{12.94}$$

and

$$r_{min} = \frac{1}{\text{VSWR}} \tag{12.95}$$

For the example shown in Figure 12.10, it is seen that

$$r_{max} = 3.0$$

$$r_{min} = 0.33$$

Change of position along the transmission line is represented by rotation along the circle, the scale being calibrated on the outer rim of the chart, in wavelengths either toward generator or toward load. Suppose, for example, that point C, Figure 12.10, represents a load impedance of

$$z_L = 0.38 - j0.34$$

Moving *toward the generator* by a distance $(C - D)$; that is,

$$(0.475 - 0.441)\,\lambda$$

brings the impedance to point D, where

$$z = 0.34 - j0.14$$

The distance moved, in wavelengths, can be found on the outer scale.

Example 12.5   The load impedance represented by point C, Figure 12.10, is used to terminate a transmission line 0.1λ long. Find the input impedance of the terminated line.

Locate $z_L = 0.38 - j0.34$ on the chart as before. The radius from the center of the chart is extended through point C to cut the distance scale, and the scale reading is seen to be 0.441λ on the wavelengths-toward-generator scale. The wavelengths-toward-generator scale is used rather than wavelengths toward load since point C is the actual load point.

Movement toward the generator by 0.1λ moves the radius to the point

$$(0.441 + 0.1)\lambda = 0.541\lambda$$

It will be observed that the distance scale only goes as high as 0.5λ, so the new point is 0.041λ. The radius joining this point to the center of the circle cuts the circle at point E:

$$z = 0.35 + j0.24 \text{ (approx.)}$$

and this is the value of normalized impedance required. The new impedance is seen to be inductive, whereas the original load impedance was capacitive. This is due to the transforming property of the line, which is dependent on length.

The VSWR for a given load is very easily found using the chart, it only being necessary to construct a circle centered on $r = 1$ and passing through the impedance point in question. The circle cuts the r axis at the value $r_{max} = \text{VSWR}$.

The reverse procedure can be used to determine a load impedance from slotted-line measurements. In Section 12.10 it was shown that the impedance at a voltage minimum was purely resistive and given by

$$Z_{min} = \frac{Z_0}{\text{VSWR}} \qquad (12.96)$$

Normalizing this

$$z_{min} = \frac{1}{\text{VSWR}} \qquad (12.97)$$

This coincides with the point where the circle cuts the r axis at r_{min}. The distance from this point to z_L is the measured distance l_{min} which can be set off in wavelengths toward load and which therefore gives the load point on the chart.

Example 12.6 Measurements on a lossless 50-Ω slotted line resulted in a VSWR of 2.0 and a distance-to-first-voltage minimum of 0.11λ. Determine the load impedance.

Solution

Construct a circle centered on $r = 1$ and cutting the r axis at ½ (point F) and 2.0 (note that $|\Gamma|$ need not be known), Figure 12.10. From point F, rotate counterclockwise along the VSWR $= 2$ circle by 0.11λ to point G (as measured along the wavelengths-toward-load scale). The resulting normalized impedance z_L at point G is obtained as

$$z_L = 0.725 - j0.525$$

Therefore, $$Z_L = 36.25 - j26.25 \,\Omega$$

The Smith chart can be used to carry out all the calculations described in the previous sections, and many others besides; unfortunately, space does not permit a detailed description of these.

12.13   TIME-DOMAIN REFLECTOMETRY

The basic arrangement for a *time-domain reflectometry* (TDR) system is shown in Figure 12.11(a). The method utilizes direct measurement of the incident wave and the reflected wave as functions of time, hence the name "time-domain reflectometry." The incident wave is supplied by a step generator, the step voltage having a very fast rise time. The oscilloscope records the outgoing step, V_i , and, at a somewhat later time, the reflected voltage V_r. The time between V_i and V_r is a measure of the length of the cable.

The nature of the load shows up in the shape of the reflected wave. As shown in Section 12.8, for an open circuit, $\Gamma = 1$, and the incident wave is totally reflected at the load. Therefore, assuming a lossless line, the oscilloscope trace will be as shown in Figure 12.11(b). A short circuit results in a $\Gamma = -1$, so the incident step is totally reflected with a phase reversal, and therefore the oscilloscope trace is shown in Figure 12.11(c).

A purely resistive load of value $2Z_0$ results in a reflection coefficient of

$$\Gamma = \frac{2Z_0 - Z_0}{2Z_0 + Z_0} \qquad (12.98)$$

$$= \frac{1}{3}$$

That is, $$V_R = \frac{V_I}{3} \qquad (12.99)$$

The trace will be therefore as shown in Figure 12.11(d).

An example of a complex load is the parallel RC circuit shown in Figure 12.11(e). Initially, the capacitor behaves as a short circuit (assuming it is

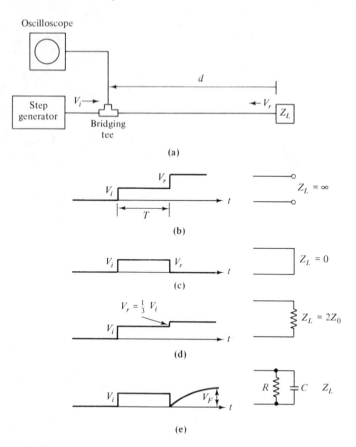

FIGURE 12.11. (a) A time-domain reflectometry system. Displays for: (b) Open-circuited termination; (c) Short circuit; (d) Resistive load $= 2Z_0$; (e) Parallel RC load.

initially uncharged). However, C will immediately start to charge up, the voltage following an exponential law. When C is fully charged it can be considered an open circuit, so the line is effectively terminated in R. The reflection coefficient for the final condition is, therefore,

$$\Gamma = \frac{R - Z_0}{R + Z_0} \tag{12.100}$$

and the final voltage V_F is

$$V_F = V_I + V_R$$
$$= V_I(1 + \Gamma)$$
$$= V_I \left(1 + \frac{R - Z_0}{R + Z_0} \right) \tag{12.101}$$

The oscilloscope trace is shown in Figure 12.11(e).

Knowing the elapsed time T between the incident and reflected voltages, and the phase velocity on the cable, the cable length between bridging tee and point of reflection can be found. Thus d, Figure 12.11(a) is given by

$$d = v_p \cdot \frac{T}{2} \qquad (12.102)$$

T is the "round-trip" time and therefore it is necessary to divide by 2, as shown.

This feature is particularly important in locating faults and sources of mismatch on a cable. These show up as reflections, the cable shown in Figure 12.12(a), for example, may result in a trace as shown in Figure 12.12(b). The phase velocity can be found by measuring T for a known length of cable. The various distances, Figure 12.12(a), then are

$$d_1 = v_p \frac{T_1}{2} \qquad (12.103)$$

$$d_2 = v_p \frac{T_2}{2} \qquad (12.104)$$

$$d_3 = v_p \frac{T_3}{2} \qquad (12.105)$$

TDR is a very versatile system of measurement for determining transmission-line properties, and fuller details will be found in the *Application Notes 62* and *67* issued by the Hewlett-Packard Company.

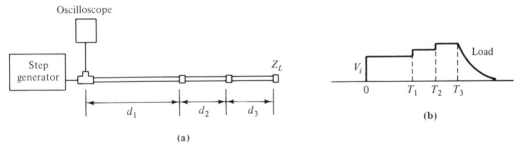

FIGURE 12.12. (a) TDR system used to determine discontinuities; (b) Display.

12.14 TELEPHONE LINES AND CABLES

The simplest type of line (apart from the single overhead wire with ground return) is the two-wire overhead line. The wire is usually made of cadmium copper, this providing better mechanical strength then hard-drawn copper. Bare wires are used where possible, but where insulation or protection is required, a polyvinyl chloride (PVC) covering is used.

Power lines (60 Hz) can induce interference in open-wire lines, but this can be eliminated by *transposing* the telephone wires. Figure 12.13(a) shows how interference may be picked up through both inductive and capacitive coupling. The induced interference voltage E_1 and E_2 act in opposition, but because they are not equal in magnitude, in general, the resultant interference voltage $E_1 - E_2$ will be other than zero. By transposing the wires as shown in Figure 12.13(b), the induced voltages in each wire can be equalized so that they cancel.

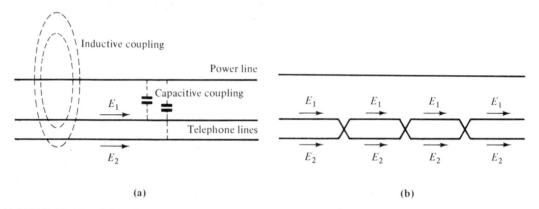

(a) (b)

FIGURE 12.13. (a) Induced interference; (b) Line transposition to eliminate interference.

Where open-wire lines are not feasible, the wires are formed into a multicore cable assembly which is usually carried underground in a ducting. For this type of cable the wires are annealed copper, which is flexible, and each wire is insulated with high-grade paper tape. A lead-alloy sheath is extruded over the wires to form the cable as shown in Figure 12.14(a).

For larger cable assemblies, for example those required between exchanges, the wires of a given pair are either twisted together in pairs to form a *twin cable*, Figure 12.14(b), or they may be twisted to form a *star quad*, Figure 12.14(c). These are then assembled in larger units either as a concentric assembly or in unit construction. The latter is favored for use in local distribution networks, as branching into smaller units is conveniently and tidily achieved.

For higher-frequency signals (e.g., multicarrier telephony or television), coaxial cables are normally employed, and the constructional features of a typical coaxial cable are shown in Figure 12.15(a). These, in turn, may form part of a composite cable assembly as shown in Figure 12.15(b).

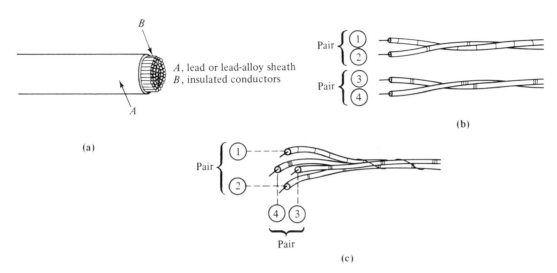

(a)

A, lead or lead-alloy sheath
B, insulated conductors

(b)

(c)

FIGURE 12.14.   (a) Lead-sheathed multicore cable; (b) Twin-cable assembly; (c) Star-quad cable assembly. (Courtesy BICC Telephone Cables Div.)

Inner copper conductor
0.047 inch (1.19 mm)
nominal diameter

Polythene tube dielectric

Serrated-edge
longitudinal
copper tape formed
as outer conductor

Two mild steel
tapes applied in
opposite directions
to provide screening
and mechanical stability

Two paper
tapes providing
insulation and pair
indentification

(a)

Four type 174 coaxial pairs

Five paper insulated pairs

Lapped paper tape

Lead sheath

Plastic protection

(b)

FIGURE 12.15.   (a) A coaxial cable; (b) A composite cable assembly. (Courtesy BICC Telephone Cables Div.)

12.15 RADIO-FREQUENCY LINES

For low-power applications, lines with solid dielectrics are normally used, such as the twin feeder, or the coaxial line. With high-power lines (such as would be used to feed radio-frequency power to antennas in the kilowatt range) the solid dielectric is omitted to keep losses at a minimum, and an open-type construction is used with well-spaced support insulators so that the main dielectric is air.

12.16 MICROSTRIP TRANSMISSION LINES

Microwave integrated and hybrid circuits require transmission-line elements both as circuit components and for interconnection purposes. The two types of transmission lines in use are the *microstrip* line and the *stripline* line, shown in Figure 12.16(a) and (b). The microstrip is obviously simpler to make, consisting of a ground plane which covers the underside of an insulating substrate, and a signal conductor on the top side. The stripline utilizes two ground planes, the signal conductor being embedded in the insulating substrate. The advantage of the stripline is that the signal conductor is better shielded and is surrounded by a uniform dielectric which leads to more uniform transmission properties.

FIGURE 12.16. (a) Microstrip and (b) stripline transmission lines.

12.17 PROBLEMS

1. Explain what is meant by the characteristic impedance of a transmission line. Explain why you would expect an infinitely long uniform line to have an input impedance equal to the characteristic impedance.

2. The primary constants (which may be assumed independent of frequency) for a transmission line are: $R = 0.5 \Omega/m$, $L = 250$ nH/m, $C = 100$ pF/m, and $G = 10^{-6}$ S/m. Plot the variation of $|Z_0|$ against frequency for this line.

3. For the transmission line in Problem 2, calculate the attenuation coefficient and the phase-shift coefficient at a frequency of 20 MHz.

4. The propagation coefficient γ for a transmission line is given by $\gamma = 0.0006 + j(\pi/10)$. The line is 32 m long and is correctly terminated to avoid reflections. Plot the phasor diagram showing the variation of current over the length of line (see, for example, Figure 12.3) but plot the phasor length in nepers, using one neper steps.

5. For the transmission line in Problem 4, determine the attentuation, in nepers, of 15 km of line.

6. Explain what is meant by the *group delay time* and why this should be constant for a transmission line. Given that $\beta = \omega\sqrt{LC}$, $L = 1\,\mu H/m$, and $C = 11.11$ pF/m, calculate: (a) group delay time: (b) group velocity.

7. Explain what is meant by the *voltage reflection coefficient* for a transmission line. The voltage reflection coefficient on a 50-Ω line is $0.7 \, \underline{/30°}$. Determine the load impedance terminating the line.

8. Explain how standing waves may be set up on a transmission line, and state the relationship between voltage and current standing waves for a line whose characteristic impedance is purely resistive.

9. Calculate the voltage standing-wave ratio for a lossless line of characteristic impedance 50 Ω when it is terminated in: (a) 100 Ω resistive; (b) $(30 - j50)$ Ω.

10. Sketch the variation of input impedance with length for a lossless transmission line terminated in a short circuit. A section of 50-Ω line, 0.15λ in length, is terminated in a short circuit. Determine the effective input reactance of the section, showing clearly whether it is inductive or capacitive.

11. A 600-Ω lossless line is terminated in a 5-pF capacitor. The line is operated at a frequency which makes it $\frac{1}{4}\lambda$ long. Determine the nature of the input impedance of the line, giving the equivalent inductance or capacitance value.

12. Measurements on a 50-Ω slotted line gave the following results: VSWR = 3.0; distance from load to first voltage minimum = 0.4λ. Determine, using a Smith chart, the value of load impedance.

13. An impedance $100 - j50$ Ω is used to terminate a 50-Ω lossless line. The line is 0.6λ long. Determine, using a Smith chart: (a) VSWR; (b) input impedance; (c) impedance at a voltage maximum.

14. In a time-domain reflectometer measurement on a terminated transmission line, the reflected voltage was found to be a vertical downward step, of magnitude one half the input step. If the line can be assumed lossless and has a characteristic impedance of 100Ω, determine the value of load impedance.

15. Sketch the form of trace expected on a TDR measuring set when applied to a line terminated in a series RL circuit.

16. A transmission line is made of two parallel copper # 18 AWG wires (1.024 mm diameter) spaced 10 mm apart, and embedded in a plastic spacer made of polyvinyl chloride (PVC). The wire has a resistance of 1.984 ohms/km and the insulation has a leakage conductivity of 2.5×10^{-10} Siemen/km. Find the primary line constants. For PVC, $\epsilon r = 3.3$.

17. Repeat Problem 16 for a coaxial line made of the same wire and insulating material, with a copper sheath of inside diameter of 2 cm. Assume the leakage to have the same value.

Chapter 13
Waveguides

13.1 INTRODUCTION

At frequencies higher than about 3000 MHz, transmission of electromagnetic waves along lines and cables becomes difficult, mainly because of the losses that occur both in the solid dielectric needed to support the conductors, and in the conductors themselves. It is possible to transmit an electromagnetic wave down a metallic tube, this being known as a *waveguide*. The commonest form of waveguide is rectangular in cross section, as shown in Figure 13.1(a). Induced currents in the walls of the waveguide give rise to power losses and to minimize these losses, the waveguide wall resistance is made as low as possible. Because of skin effect, the currents tend to concentrate near the inner surface of the guide walls, and these are sometimes specially plated to reduce resistance.

Apart from determination of losses, the walls of a waveguide may be considered to be perfect conductors. Two important boundary conditions result, which determine the mode of propagation of an electromagnetic wave along a guide. These are (1) electric fields must terminate normally on the conductor [i.e., the tangential component of electric field must be zero, Figure 13.1(b)]; (2) magnetic fields must lie entirely tangentially along the

FIGURE 13.1. (a) Rectangular waveguide; (b) Electric field boundary conditions; (c) Magnetic field boundary conditions.

wall surface [i.e., the normal component of magnetic field must be zero, Figure 13.1(c)]. Knowing these boundary conditions provides a simple way of visualizing how the various modes of waveguide transmission occur, and these will be discussed in the following sections.

Although the microwave frequency spectrum extends from about 300 MHz to 300 GHz (see Figure 14.13), transmission lines can be utilized for the lower part of the range. Above about 3000 MHz, waveguides become necessary.

13.2 RECTANGULAR WAVEGUIDES

The boundary conditions already referred to preclude the possibility of a waveguide supporting *transverse electromagnetic* (TEM) wave (see Appendix B) propagation, since the magnetic field is at right angles to the direction of propagation (along the axis of the waveguide) and therefore would have to terminate normally to the sidewalls, which cannot happen. One possible solution is for the magnetic field to form loops along the direction of propagation, as shown in Figure 13.2(a), these lying parallel to the top and bottom walls and tangentially to the sidewalls.

The variation of electric field as a function of distance along the direction of propagation is shown in Figure 13.2(b) and along the cross section in Figure 13.2(c). The propagation mode sketched in Figure 13.2 is known as a *transverse electric* (TE) *mode* because the electric field is entirely transverse to the direction of propagation. (It is also known as an *H mode*, signifying that part of the magnetic field lies along the direction of propagation.)

Subscripts are used to denote the number of half-cycles of variation which occur along the a and b sides. As shown in Figure 13.2, one half-cycle (i.e., one maximum) occurs along the a side and none along the b side; this mode is therefore referred to as the TE_{10} *mode*. The TE_{10} mode is the dominant mode in waveguide transmission, for, as will be shown, it supports the lowest-frequency waveguide mode.

FIGURE 13.2. (a) One possible field configuration for a waveguide; (b) Electric field amplitude along guide axis; (c) Electric field amplitude along guide width.

(a)

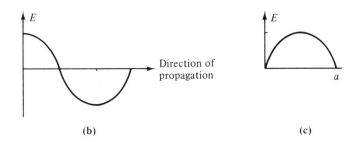

(b)   (c)

13.2.1 Properties of the TE_{10} Mode

Figure 13.3(a) shows how a TE_{10} wave may be formed as the resultant of two TEM waves crossing each other. At points of intersection shown, the individual waves add vectorially. At those points where the electric fields reinforce each other, shown by double crosses and double dots, the magnetic field is directed up and down; at the points where the electric fields cancel, shown by dots and crosses together, the magnetic field is directed left and right. Metallic walls may be placed along the L-R direction as shown in Figure 13.3(b) without violating the boundary conditions, as it will be seen that the electric field is zero, and the magnetic field tangential at these walls. Metallic top and bottom walls can be put in position as the electric field will terminate normally on these, and the magnetic field lies parallel to them.

The direction of the magnetic field loops alternates as shown in Figure 13.3(b), one loop occupying a distance of a half wavelength in the guide. This will be different from a half wavelength of the individual TEM waves and is shown as $\frac{1}{2}\lambda_g$, where λ_g is termed the guide wavelength.

The frequency of the TE wave will be the same as that of the TEM waves (i.e., it will have the same number of cycles in a second). Let v_p be the phase velocity of the TE wave; then, using the general relationship

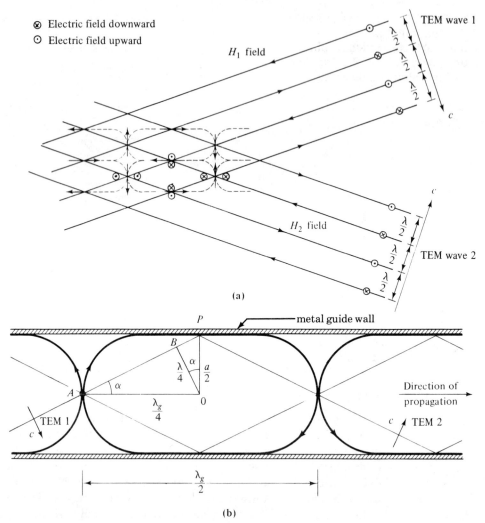

FIGURE 13.3. (a) Generating the waveguide mode from two TEM waves; (b) Geometry used in determining TE_{10} properties.

derived in Appendix B that $\lambda f = v_p$:

$$\text{TE wave:} \quad \lambda_g f = v_p \qquad (13.1)$$

$$\text{TEM wave:} \quad \lambda f = c \qquad (13.2)$$
$$\text{(in air)}$$

from which

$$v_p = c \frac{\lambda_g}{\lambda} \qquad (13.3)$$

From the geometry of Figure 13.3(b), it will be seen that:

$$\text{From right-angled triangle OBP}: \cos \alpha = \frac{\lambda}{2a} \tag{13.4}$$

$$\text{From right-angled triangle } ABO: \sin \alpha = \frac{\lambda}{\lambda_g} \tag{13.5}$$

and since $\qquad\qquad \sin^2 \alpha + \cos^2 \alpha = 1$

Therefore, $\qquad\qquad \left(\frac{\lambda}{\lambda_g}\right)^2 + \left(\frac{\lambda}{2a}\right)^2 = 1$

or $\qquad\qquad\qquad \frac{1}{\lambda_g^2} = \frac{1}{\lambda^2} - \frac{1}{(2a)^2} \tag{13.6}$

where λ_g is the guide wavelength of the TE$_{10}$ mode, λ the free-space wavelength of either TEM wave, and a the broad dimension of the guide.

From Eq. (13.6) it is seen that when $\lambda = 2a$, the guide wavelength becomes infinite; this corresponds to the individual TEM waves bouncing from side to side with no velocity component directed along the guide. Clearly, then, $\lambda = 2a$ represents the longest-wavelength TEM wave that can be induced into a guide, as a TE mode will not be generated for longer wavelengths. For shorter TEM wavelengths, Eq. (13.6) shows that the guide wavelength is real and positive so that TE-mode propagation takes place.

The term $2a$ is referred to as the cutoff wavelength of the TE$_{10}$ mode, λ_c, and, rewriting Eq. (13.6),

$$\frac{1}{\lambda_g^2} = \frac{1}{\lambda^2} - \frac{1}{\lambda_c^2} \tag{13.7}$$

From Eqs. (13.3) and (13.5) it is seen that

$$v_p = \frac{c}{\sin \alpha} \tag{13.8}$$

Since the sine of an angle is never greater than unity, v_p can never be less than c; it can, of course, be greater.

The individual waves have to travel a zigzag path and therefore the velocity component along the guide, which is the velocity at which the energy in the waves is conveyed, is less than c. From Figure 13.4 this component, known as the group velocity v_g, is seen to be

$$v_g = c \sin \alpha \tag{13.9}$$

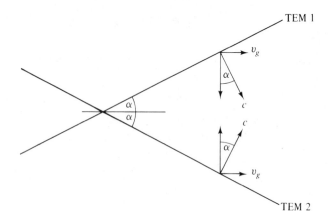

FIGURE 13.4. Group velocity as the horizontal components of c.

Combining Eqs. (13.8) and (13.9),

$$v_g \cdot v_p = c^2 \qquad (13.10)$$

Also, Eq. (13.9) can be rewritten in terms of wavelength, since these are the quantities that are normally known:

$$v_g = c \cdot \frac{\lambda}{\lambda_g} \qquad (13.11)$$

Unless otherwise stated, it is assumed that the waveguide dielectric is dry air, for which free-space permittivity and permeability apply.

Example 13.1 A rectangular waveguide has a broad wall dimension of 0.900 inch, and is fed by a 10-GHz carrier from a coaxial cable as shown in Figure 13.5. Determine if a TE_{10} wave will be propagated and, if so, its guide wavelength, phase, and group velocities.

Solution

$$a = 0.900 \text{ inch}$$
$$= 2.29 \text{ cm}$$

Therefore,

$$\lambda_c = 2 \times 2.29$$
$$= 4.58 \text{ cm}$$

$$\lambda = \frac{3 \times 10^8}{10^{10}}$$

$$= 3 \text{ cm}$$

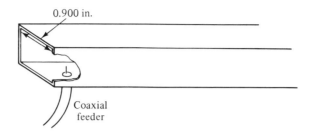

0.900 in.

Coaxial
feeder

FIGURE 13.5. Example 13.1.

(note that it is the free-space wavelength and not the wavelength along the coaxial cable which is used). Therefore, $\lambda_c > \lambda$ and a TE_{10} wave will propagate.

$$\frac{1}{\lambda_g^2} = \frac{1}{\lambda^2} - \frac{1}{\lambda_c^2}$$

Therefore,

$$\lambda_g = \frac{\lambda}{\sqrt{1 - (\lambda/\lambda_c)^2}}$$

$$= \frac{3}{\sqrt{1 - 0.042}}$$

$$= 3.97 \text{ cm}$$

$$v_p = c \times \frac{\lambda_g}{\lambda}$$

$$3 \times 10^8 \times 1.32$$

$$= 4.4 \times 10^8 \text{ m/s}$$

$$v_g = c \frac{\lambda}{\lambda_g}$$

$$= \frac{3 \times 10^8}{1.82}$$

$$= 2.27 \times 10^8 \text{ m/s}$$

The *wave impedance* is defined as the ratio of the transverse components of electric to magnetic fields. In synthesizing the TE_{10} mode the two TEM waves are of equal amplitude and in time phase; thus $E_1 = E_2 = E$ and $H_1 = H_2 = H$. The entire electric field E is transverse, along dimension b, while from Figure 13.3 it is easily ascertained that the transverse component of H lies along dimension a and is

$$H_a = H \sin \alpha \qquad (13.12)$$

Hence the wave impedance for the TE_{10} mode is

$$Z_w = \frac{E_b}{H_a}$$

$$= \frac{E}{H \sin \alpha} \qquad (13.13)$$

In Appendix B the wave impedance of a TEM wave in free space is shown to be (Eq. (B.10)).

$$Z_0 = \frac{E}{H}$$

$$= \sqrt{\frac{\mu_0}{\epsilon_0}} \qquad (13.14)$$

Thus substituting Eqs. (13.14) and (13.5) in Eq. (13.13) gives

$$Z_w = Z_0 \cdot \frac{\lambda_g}{\lambda} \qquad (13.15)$$

$$= 120\pi \cdot \frac{\lambda_g}{\lambda} \; \Omega \qquad (13.16)$$

when the numerical values for μ_0 and ϵ_0 are substituted.

The importance of the wave impedance concept is that it can be used in an analogous manner to the characteristic impedance of a transmission line, so that the theory of reflections, standing waves, and Smith charts developed in Chapter 12 can also be applied to waveguides.

13.2.2   Standing Waves

Consider a section of waveguide closed by a perfectly conducting sheet at the end. The boundary conditions require that the fields adjust so that the electric field is zero, and the magnetic field entirely tangential at the closure (i.e., the field patterns are similar to those at the walls of the guide). The resultant wave pattern can be accounted for in terms of the incident TE wave, and a reflected TE wave, the combination of which sets up a standing-wave pattern along the guide, similar to that described in Section 12.7 for transmission lines. It is important to realize that the resultant wave pattern is stationary in space and varies in time, whereas the traveling wave shown in Figure 13.3(b) is time-invariant but of course moves along the guide. Figure 13.6 emphasizes this point. On the left are shown the conditions in a short-circuited guide at time intervals of one fourth the periodic time of the wave, the reference time being chosen at a maximum field condition. The sequence on the right shows how a single traveling wave would vary over the same time intervals. (For clarity, only the magnetic field loops are shown.)

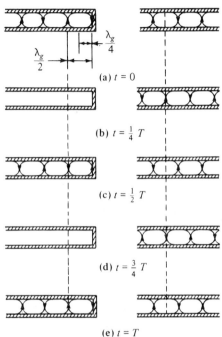

$\frac{\lambda_g}{4}$

$\frac{\lambda_g}{2}$

(a) $t = 0$

(b) $t = \frac{1}{4} T$

(c) $t = \frac{1}{2} T$

(d) $t = \frac{3}{4} T$

(e) $t = T$

FIGURE 13.6. Comparing standing waves (left) to traveling waves (right).

It will be observed that at $\frac{1}{4}\lambda_g$ from the closed end the transverse magnetic field is zero while the electric field is a maximum. Therefore, the wave impedance is infinite at this section across the guide. At the $\frac{1}{2}\lambda_g$ section, the electric field is zero while the transverse magnetic field component is maximum, so that the wave impedance is zero. Thus the quarter-wavelength and half-wavelength sections of guide have the same transforming properties as those of the transmission-line sections described in Section 12.11.

13.2.3 Waveguide Terminations

In order to terminate a waveguide without causing reflections, the terminating impedance must equal the wave impedance of the incident wave. Consider first a thin sheet of resistive material closing the end of the waveguide, Figure 13.7(a). Between the top and bottom of the guide, the sheet presents a resistance of path length b and cross-sectional area ta, where t is the thickness of the sheet; a and b are the guide dimensions defined previously. Only the sheet resistance between top and bottom need be considered, since the current direction is at right angles to the H-field at the sheet. Let ρ be the resistivity of the sheet material; then the terminating resistance is

$$R_T = \rho \frac{b}{ta} \tag{13.17}$$

(a)   (b)

FIGURE 13.7.   (a) Waveguide terminated with sheet resistance; (b) ¼λ_g section added to termination.

The *sheet resistivity* R_s is defined as

$$R_s = \frac{\rho}{t} \quad \Omega \text{ per square} \tag{13.18}$$

The units of the square do not matter. R_s will have the same value for a square inch, a square centimeter, and so on. What does matter is that the units of ρ and t should be consistent. If ρ is in Ω-m, then t must be in meters and R_s will be in ohms per square. IF ρ is in $\mu\Omega$-in, t must be in inches and R_s will be in $\mu\Omega$ per square.

Now, the current I in the sheet supports the tangential component of magnetic field H_T, where

$$H_T = \frac{I}{a} \tag{13.19}$$

Also, the voltage across the sheet gives rise to an electric-field component:

$$E_T = \frac{V}{b} \tag{13.20}$$

Therefore,

$$\frac{E_T}{H_T} = \frac{V \cdot a}{I \cdot b} \tag{13.21}$$

But $V/I = R_T = R_s \cdot b/a$, and substituting this in Eq. (13.21) gives

$$\frac{E_T}{H_T} = R_s \cdot \frac{b}{a} \cdot \frac{a}{b}$$

$$= R_s \qquad (13.22)$$

E_T and H_T will consist of three components: incident, reflected, and transmitted waves, shown in Figure 13.7(a) as W_i, W_r, and W_t, respectively. The transmitted wave can be eliminated by extending the guide $\frac{1}{4}\lambda_g$ beyond the termination sheet, as shown in Figure 13.7(b), and short-circuiting the end. The $\frac{1}{4}\lambda_g$ shorted section presents an infinite impedance; therefore, no wave can be transmitted into it. Next, the sheet resistivity R_s is made equal to the incident-wave impedance Z_w:

$$Z_w = R_s \qquad (13.23)$$

This ensures that $E_T/H_T = E_i/H_i = E/H$; that is, the incident wave is absorbed by the sheet just as though it were continuing down an infinitely long waveguide in which the wave impedance was Z_w (or R_s). Thus the reflected wave is eliminated.

The arrangement discussed illustrates two important principles, that of sheet resistivity and the idea of using a $\frac{1}{4}\lambda_g$ shorted section to isolate the load from external impedances. The arrangement is not satisfactory in practice, however, largely because it requires an adjustable short circuit on the $\frac{1}{4}\lambda_g$ section which is rather critical to adjust. More practical arrangements for terminating a guide are shown in Figure 13.8. The resistive strip is

(a)

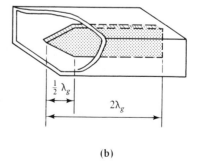

(b)

FIGURE 13.8. Practical waveguide terminations.

set in the plane of the maximum electric field, and the taper ensures a gradual change in electric field, which reduces reflections to a negligible level. Either form of taper shown in Figure 13.8 is satisfactory, and the dimensions shown are typical of those used in practice. A carbon-coated strip may be used, or for more stable operation, a glass strip covered with a thin film of metal which, in turn, has a thin dielectric coating for protection. Surface resistivities of the order of $500\,\Omega$ per square are typical.

13.2.4   Attenuators

An arrangement similar to that shown in Figure 13.8 can be used to provide attenuation in a waveguide. Two common methods are shown in Figure 13.9. In Figure 13.9(a), the thin resistive sheet can be moved from the sidewall, where it produces minimum attentuation, to the center of the guide, where it produces maximum attenuation. The mechanical drive for the sheet is often fitted with a micrometer control so that fine adjustment of attenuation can be made and accurately calibrated. The flap attenuator of Figure 13.9(b) is simple to construct, and, as shown in the next section, the slot position is such that radiation is minimized. However, some radiation does occur, and this type is not used for accurate work.

13.2.5   Currents in Walls

As already stated, the traveling-wave pattern is time-invariant, that is, the pattern appears to keep its shape as it moves down the guide. At any given cross section of the guide, however, the magnetic field (and the electric field) appears to vary in time as the loops of alternate polarity sweep by. This gives rise to induced currents in the walls of the guide, these currents being at right angles to the magnetic field. The currents for the TE_{10} mode are as shown in Figure 13.10(a). This pattern moves down the guide along with the field pattern at the phase velocity. It is emphasized that the pattern moves at the phase velocity, not the current (since that would imply electrons moving faster than the speed of light!). In effect, the current pattern builds up and decays as the TE wave sweeps by. An analogy can be drawn with a sea wave moving along a sea wall, creating a splash, Figure 13.10(b). The splash travels at the phase velocity (which is faster than the velocity at which the wave approaches the wall) and people standing at the edge of the sea wall will move back as the splash passes them, so the ripple in the line also moves at the phase velocity.

Knowing the current pattern is important, as it enables slots to be correctly positioned in the walls, to serve various purposes. Slots that do not noticeably interrupt the current flow are termed *nonradiating*, since they result in minimum disturbance of the internal fields, and therefore little electromagnetic energy leaks through them. The positions of two nonradiat-

(a)

(b)

FIGURE 13.9. Waveguide attenuators.

Magnetic
field

(a)

(b)

NR   R   R

NR   R

(c)

FIGURE 13.10. (a) Currents in walls for the TE_{10} mode; (b) Sea wave analogy illustrating phase velocity; (c) Nonradiating (NR) and radiating (R) slots.

ing slots are shown in Figure 13.10(c), these being labeled NR. It will be seen that a nonradiating slot can be placed along the center of the broad wall of the guide and use is made of this in the attenuator of Figure 13.9(b). Another application is the slotted waveguide, which enables standing waves to be measured, the technique being similar to that described in Section 12.10 for transmission lines.

Slots that do interrupt the current flow, such as those labeled R in Figure 13.10(c), are termed *radiating* slots. These produce maximum disturbance of the internal fields, which results in energy being radiated. Radiating slots form the basis of slot antennas.

13.2.6   Contacts and Joints

The properties of a short-circuited section can be used to provide an electrical short circuit without the necessity of providing a solid mechanical contact at the point of short circuit. This principle is incorporated into the design of some types of flanges used for coupling guide sections together and in the design of movable short-circuiting contacts. Two $\frac{1}{4}\lambda_g$ transformations take place, as shown in Figure 13.11(a). The top $\frac{1}{4}\lambda_g$ section transforms the solid short circuit at the top to an open circuit at the junction of the two $\frac{1}{4}\lambda_g$ sections. Here a mechanical joint occurs, but since this is a high impedance point the currents are small and the joint resistance is not important. The second $\frac{1}{4}\lambda_g$ section transforms the open circuit back to a short circuit at the entry point. Application of the principle to a coupling flange is illustrated in Figure 13.11(b) and to a movable short circuit in Figure 13.11(c). In the latter figure, a coaxial feeder is shown by way of example, the $\frac{1}{4}\lambda_g$ short-circuited section performing the same function as that shown in Figure 13.7(b).

13.2.7   Reactive Stubs

Equivalent reactive elements can be introduced into a waveguide in a variety of ways, a common method being to use an adjustable screw stub as shown in Figure 13.12. When the stub is only a short way in, as shown in Figure 13.12(a), it acts as a capacitor as it produces an increase in the electric flux density of the wave in the vicinity of the stub.

With the screw all the way in, such that it forms a post between the top and bottom of the guide, Figure 13.12(b), a path is provided for induced currents which set up a magnetic field; such a post therefore acts as an inductor. An equivalent series LC circuit is formed when the screw is sufficiently far in for both components to be significant but neither dominant, such as is shown in Figure 13.12(c). Screw stubs are used singly, and in groups of two and three, to provide matching devices between a waveguide and load.

(a)

(b)

(c)

FIGURE 13.11. Two ¼λ_g transforming sections in series; (b) A coupling flange utilizing (a); (c) A movable short-circuiting contact utilizing (a); the contact illustrated provides a ¼λ_g shorted section for the coaxial feeder.

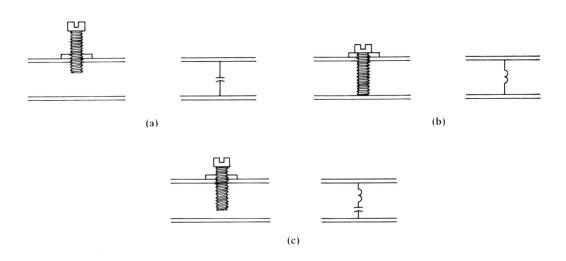

(a)

(b)

(c)

FIGURE 13.12. Reactive stubs: (a) Capacitive stub; (b) Inductive stub; (c) Series LC stub.

13.3 OTHER MODES

Higher modes can occur in waveguides, an example of the TE_{20} mode being sketched in Figure 13.13(a). *Transverse magnetic* (TM) *modes* can also occur, the TM_{11} mode being sketched in Figure 13.13(b). It can be shown that the cutoff wavelength for TE_{mn} and TM_{mn} modes in general is given by

$$\left(\frac{1}{\lambda_c}\right)^2 = \left(\frac{m}{2a}\right)^2 + \left(\frac{n}{2b}\right)^2 \tag{13.24}$$

where m and n are integers. Equation (13.24) is seen to reduce to $\lambda_c = 2a$ for $m = 1$ and $n = 0$, which is the condition already introduced in Eq. (13.7) for the TE_{10} mode.

The TM_{11} mode is the lowest TM mode that can occur as the boundary conditions exclude the TM_{10} mode. For transmission purposes only the TE_{10} mode is used, and the guide dimensions are chosen, in conjunction with the input frequency, to cut off all but the dominant mode (TE_{10}). For example, for a standard guide WR 90 the dimensions are:

Outside walls:	1.000×0.500 in
Wall thickness:	0.050 in

The inside wall dimensions are, therefore,

$$a = 2.286 \text{ cm}$$

$$b = 1.016 \text{ cm}$$

The cutoff wavelengths for some of the various modes are:

$$\text{TE}_{10}: \quad \lambda_c = 2a$$
$$= 4.572 \text{ cm}$$

$$\text{TE}_{20}: \quad \lambda_c = a$$
$$= 2.286 \text{ cm}$$

$$\text{TE}_{01}: \quad \lambda_c = 2b$$
$$= 2.032 \text{ cm}$$

$$\left.\begin{array}{c}\text{TE}_{11}\\\text{TM}_{11}\end{array}\right\} : \quad \left(\frac{1}{\lambda_c}\right)^2 = \left(\frac{1}{2a}\right)^2 + \left(\frac{1}{2b}\right)^2$$

Therefore, $\qquad\qquad\qquad \lambda_c = 1.857 \text{ cm}$

Tabulating these results:

Mode	λ_c (cm)	f_c (GHz)
TE$_{10}$	4.572	6.56
TE$_{20}$	2.286	13.1
TE$_{01}$	2.032	14.8
TE$_{11}$ TM$_{11}$	1.857	16.2

The recommended operating frequency range for the WR90 guide is 8.20 to 12.40 GHz, and it will be seen that only the TE$_{10}$ mode will be excited. Of course, if a higher frequency is fed into the guide, higher modes will be excited; for example, if a frequency of 15 GHz is used, the first three modes may exist simultaneously in the guide. For all these modes, including the circular mode described in the next paragraph, Eq. (13.7) applies.

Circular guides also support waveguide modes, the TE$_{11}$ circular mode being sketched in Figure 13.13(c). (The subscripts here denote circumferential and radial variations of the fields which are much more complex than the modes in the rectangular guide; only the TE$_{11}$ circular mode will be considered here.) The cutoff wavelength is related to the diameter of the

(a)

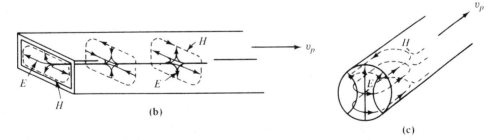

(b)

(c)

FIGURE 13.13. Other waveguide modes: (a) The TE$_{20}$ mode; (b) The TM$_{11}$ mode; (c) The TE$_{11}$ circular waveguide mode.

guide, the value derived from theory being

$$\lambda_c = 1.71d \qquad (13.25)$$

where d is the diameter of the circular guide.

Circular guides have special properties which enable them to be used for rotating joints, and the TE_{10} mode has the unusual characteristic of attenuation becoming less as the frequency is increased, which is attractive for transmissions at the higher microwave frequencies. However, the mechanical problems of making and maintaining precise dimensions in a circular guide are much more formidable than in a rectangular guide, and the latter finds greater use for transmission purposes.

13.4 PROBLEMS

1. Determine λ_c, λ_g, λ, v_p, and v_g for standard waveguide WR62 for which the outside dimensions are 0.702×0.391 inch, the wall thickness is 0.040 inch, when the exciting frequency is 10 GHz.

2. Determine the TE_{10} wave impedance for the WR62 guide of Problem 1.

3. Explain how standing waves can be produced in a waveguide. What is the spacing, in terms of wavelength, between successive minima along the standing-wave pattern?

4. By analogy with the transmission-line theory presented in Section 12.8, determine the reflection coefficient for the electric field of a TE_{10} wave of wave impedance 680 Ω terminated as shown in Figure 13.7(b), the sheet resistivity of the load being 500 Ω/square.

5. Also by analogy to the transmission theory presented in Section 12.9, determine the electric field standing-wave ratio for the guide conditions of Problem 4.

6. What is meant by sheet resistivity, and how does this differ from the resistivity of a material? What are the units for sheet resistivity?

7. Illustrate on a Smith chart the transformations that take place in the $\frac{1}{2}\lambda_g$ short-circuited section shown in Figure 13.11(a).

8. Explain the difference between radiating and nonradiating slots in a TE_{10} mode waveguide.

9. A standard waveguide, WR187, has the following dimensions: outside walls 2.000×1.000 inches, wall thickness 0.064 inch. Determine the highest frequency than can be transmitted if only the TE_{10} mode is permitted. What modes can exist in it if it is excited by a wave of frequency 6.00 GHz?

Chapter 14
Radio-Wave Propagation

14.1 INTRODUCTION

Radio communications use electromagnetic waves propagated through the earth's atmosphere or space to carry information over long distances without the use of wires. Radio waves with frequencies ranging from about 10 kHz in the VLF band to well above 300 GHz in the EHF band have been used for communications purposes, and more recently radiation in and near the visible range (near 1000 THz, or 10^{15} Hz) have also been used. Figure 14.16 shows the frequency-band designations in common use.

Some of the basic properties of a *transverse electromagnetic* (TEM) wave are described in Appendix B. Although the electric and magnetic fields exist simultaneously, in practice, antennas are designated to work through one or other of these fields. Antennas are described in Chapter 15. Basically, in order to launch an electromagnetic wave into space, electric charge has to be accelerated, which in practice means that the current in the radiator must change with time (e.g., be alternating). In this chapter, sinusoidal or cosinusoidal variations will be assumed unless stated otherwise.

14.2 PROPAGATION IN FREE SPACE

14.2.1 The Mode of Propagation

Consider first an average power P_T, assumed to be radiated equally in all directions (isotropically). This will spread out spherically as it travels away from the source, so that at distance d, the power density in the wave, which is the power per unit area of wavefront, will be

$$P_{Di} = \frac{P_T}{4\pi d^2} \qquad W/m^2 \qquad (14.1)$$

This follows since $4\pi d^2$ is the surface area of the sphere of radius d, centered on the source. P_{Di} stands for isotropic power density.

It is known that all practical antennas have directional characteristics; that is, they radiate more power in some directions at the expense of less in others. The directivity gain is the ratio of actual power density along the main axis of radiation of the antenna to that which would be produced by an isotropic antenna at the same distance fed with the same input power. Let G_T be the *maximum* directivity gain of the transmitting antenna; then the power density along the direction of maximum radiation will be

$$P_D = P_{Di} \times G_T$$

$$= \frac{P_T G_T}{4\pi d^2} \qquad (14.2)$$

A receiving antenna can be positioned so that it collects maximum power from the wave. When so positioned, let P_R be the power delivered by the antenna to the load (receiver) under matched conditions; then the antenna can be considered as having an effective area (or aperture) A_{eff}, where

$$P_R = P_D \cdot A_{eff}$$

$$= \frac{P_T G_T}{4\pi d^2} \cdot A_{eff} \qquad (14.3)$$

It can be shown that for any antenna, the ratio of maximum directivity gain to effective area is

$$\frac{A_{eff}}{G} = \frac{\lambda^2}{4\pi} \qquad (14.4)$$

Here, λ is the wavelength of the wave being radiated. Letting G_R be the maximum directivity gain of the receiving antenna, then, from Eqs. (14.3) and (14.4),

$$\frac{P_R}{P_T} = G_T G_R \left(\frac{\lambda}{4\pi d} \right)^2 \qquad (14.5)$$

This is the fundamental equation for free-space transmission. Usually it is expressed in terms of frequency f, in MHz, and distance d in kilometers. As shown in Appendix B, $\lambda f = c$, and on substituting this in Eq. (14.5) and doing the arithmetic, which is left as an exercise for the reader, the result obtained is

$$\frac{P_R}{P_T} = G_T G_R \frac{0.57 \times 10^{-3}}{(df)^2} \qquad (14.6)$$

By expressing the power ratios in decibels, Eq (14.6) can be written as

$$\left(\frac{P_R}{P_T}\right)_{dB} = (G_T)_{dB} + (G_R)_{dB} - (32.5 + 20\log_{10}d + 20\log_{10}f) \qquad (14.7)$$

The third term in parentheses on the right-hand side of Eq. (14.7) is the loss, in decibels, resulting from the spreading of the wave as it propagates outward from the source. It is known as the transmission path loss, L. Thus

$$L = (32.5 + 20\log_{10}d + 20\log_{10}f)_{dB} \qquad (14.8)$$

where d is in kilometers and f in megahertz.

Equation (14.7) then becomes

$$\left(\frac{P_R}{P_T}\right)_{dB} = (G_T)_{dB} + (G_R)_{dB} - (L)_{dB} \qquad (14.9)$$

Example 14.1   In a satellite communications system, free-space conditions may be assumed. The satellite is at a height of 36,000 km above earth, the frequency used in 4000 MHz, the transmitting antenna gain is 15 dB, and the receiveing antenna gain is 45 dB. Calculate:

(a)   The free-space transmission loss

(b)   The received power when the transmitted power is 200 W.

Solution   (a) $L = 32.5 + 20\log_{10}36,000 + 20\log_{10}4000$

$= 196$ dB

(b) $\left(\dfrac{P_R}{P_T}\right)_{dB} = 15 + 45 - 196$

$= -136$ dB

This is a power ratio of 0.25×10^{-13}, and since $P_T = 200$ W,

$$P_R = 200 \times 0.25 \times 10^{-13}$$

$$= 5 \times 10^{-12}\text{W} = 5\,\text{pW}$$

Frequently, it is required to know the electric field strength of the wave at the receiving antenna. In Appendix B, E is given by Eq. (B.12) in terms of power density P_D and wave impedance Z_0 as

$$E = \sqrt{Z_0 P_D} \qquad (14.10)$$

Also, Z_0 is given by Eq. (B.10) as

$$Z_0 = \sqrt{\frac{\mu}{\epsilon}} \qquad (14.11)$$

The free space values are as follows: $\mu = \mu_0 = 4\pi \times 10^{-7}$ H/m; $\epsilon = \epsilon_0 = 8.854 \times 10^{-12}$ F/m. Substituting these in Eq. (14.11) gives

$$Z_0 = 120\pi \text{ Ohms} \qquad (14.12)$$

The field strength may now be found by substituting Eqs. (14.2) and (14.12) in Eq. (14.10):

$$E = \frac{\sqrt{30 P_T G_T}}{d} \qquad \text{V/m} \qquad (14.13)$$

This is the fundamental equation which gives the field strength at the receiving antenna, for free-space propagation conditions. A receiving antenna has an effective length l_{eff} (analogous to effective area) such that the open circuit EMF of the antenna E_s, is given by

$$V_s = E l_{\text{eff}} \qquad (14.14)$$

Effective length is discussed in Section 15.13.

Example 14.2 Calculate the open-circuit voltage induced in a $\frac{1}{2}\lambda$ dipole when 10W at 150 MHz is radiated from another $\frac{1}{2}\lambda$ dipole, 50 km distant. The antennas are positioned for optimum transmission and reception.

Solution

$$\lambda = \frac{3 \times 10^8}{150 \times 10^6}$$

$$= 2 \text{ m}$$

For a $\frac{1}{2}\lambda$ dipole,

$$G_T = 1.64{:}1 \text{ [See Eq. (15.4)]}$$

$$l_{\text{eff}} = \frac{\lambda}{\pi} \text{ [See Eq. (15.12)]}$$

$$= \frac{2}{\pi}$$

Therefore, $\qquad V_s = \dfrac{\sqrt{30 \times 10 \times 1.64}}{50 \times 10^3} \cdot \dfrac{2}{\pi}$ $\qquad$ [Eq. (14.14a) and (14.13)]

$\qquad = 282 \, \mu V$

Equation (14.13) is sometimes expressed in terms of the field strength at unit distance, E_0. Thus, at $d = 1$ m:

$$E = E_0 = \frac{\sqrt{30 P_T G_T}}{1} \qquad V/m \qquad (14.15)$$

and therefore Eq. (14.13) can be written as

$$E = \frac{E_0}{d} \qquad V/m \qquad (14.16)$$

Note that both E and E_0 are in units of V/m, although Eq. (14.16) may tend to suggest that E was in units of (V/m)/m or V/m². Equation (14.16) really expresses a proportionality, and written in full it would be

$$E = E_0 \times \frac{1 \, (m)}{d \, (m)} \qquad V/m \qquad (14.17)$$

14.2.2 Microwave Systems

Microwave radio systems operating at frequencies above 1 GHz propagate mainly in a line-of-sight or free-space mode, whether they are on the ground, or satellite systems. Microwave radio systems have since the 1950s become the workhorses of long-distance telephone communications systems. These systems provide the needed transmission bandwidth and reliability to allow the transmission of many thousands of telephone channels as well as several television channels over the same route and using the same facilities. Carrier frequencies in the 3–12 GHz range are used. Since microwaves travel only on line-of-sight paths, it is necessary to provide repeater stations at about 50-km intervals. This makes the equipment costs for such a system very large, but this is more than made up for by the increased channel capacity. Transmitter output powers are low, (may be less than 1 watt), because highly directional high gain antennas are used.

Figure 14.1(a) shows the equipment needed to provide one channel of a microwave system. It consists of two terminal stations and one or more repeater stations. At the sending terminal, the inputs comprising several hundred telephone channels and/or a television channel are frequency multiplexed within the base-band bandpass of 6 MHz. The base-band frequency modulates a 70-MHz IF signal, which is then up-converted to the

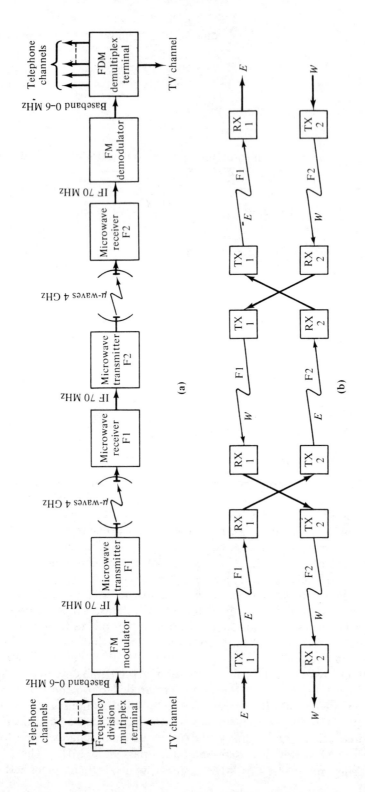

FIGURE 14.1. A microwave relay system: (a) A one-way channel showing the equipment used on the route; (b) A two-way channel pair showing frequency interchanges at intermediate repeater stations.

microwave output frequency f_1 within the 4-GHz band. This signal is amplified and fed through a directional antenna toward a repeater station some 50 km distant. At the repeater station, the signal at f_1 is received on one antenna pointed toward the originating station, down-converted to the IF, amplified, and up-converted to a new frequency f_2 for retransmission toward the receiving terminal station. When the signal is passed through a chain of several repeaters, alternate links in the chain use alternate frequencies so that retransmitted energy at a repeater station does not feed back into its own receiver.

With two frequencies in use, alternating at each repeater, two channels, one in each direction, can be provided, as illustrated in Figure 14.1(b). In some microwave systems several two-way channel pairs are provided, and a more complex system of frequency switching is used at the repeater stations.

At the receiving terminal station, the signal is down-converted to the IF, and then demodulated to recover the base-band signal. This base-band signal is then demultiplexed to recover the individual telephone or television channel signals.

Terminal stations use two antennas, one for receiving and one for transmitting. The system may have several transmitters and receivers, but they all use the same antennas. Repeater stations are provided with two antennas pointing in each direction, for a total of four. Repeater station sites are chosen at high points such as on hilltops or tall buildings, and sturdy towers provide additional elevation to maximize the distance between stations.

One-way single-channel microwave systems using portable terminal and repeater stations are frequently used for remote television pickup of special events and for other temporary installations such as the testing of new microwave routes. This equipment is often mounted in mobile vans outfitted with telescopic towers that can be quickly erected.

14.2.3   Satellite Communications

Any satellite in orbit around the earth may be used as a repeater station in a microwave system. The repeater station may be passive, reflecting signals from a ground transmitter, or, more likely, it will be powered by either solar energy or a nuclear power plant and will function in a manner similar to a ground-based repeater.

Synchronous satellites are favored over the asynchronous ones because of the antenna-tracking problems involved with satellites that are continually changing their position relative to the earth's surface. Anik III, the third in a series of commercial synchronous communications satellites, was launched in May 1975 to provide nearly complete coverage of the earth's surface. A synchronous satellite rotates about the earth's axis at the same speed as does the earth, completing one cycle every 24 hours and in the same direction as the earth's rotation. It is held at an almost constant altitude above the earth's surface of about 36,000 km, just over the equator. Under these conditions, the satellite remains in a stationary position relative to the earth's surface, and can be used full-time as a repeater station. Three such satellites located at 120° intervals around the earth's circumference provide complete coverage of the earth's surface, except for the extreme polar regions, as illustrated in Figure 14.2(a).

The transmitting and receiving equipment on a satellite repeater station is similar to that in a ground station, except that it is designed to minimize power drain and miniaturized to reduce weight. The station may carry as many as 12 separate transmitter-receiver pairs, to provide several simultaneous channels. All of these transmit and receive using the same antenna, so the frequency assignments are widely spaced. The antenna is a wide-angle broad-band antenna to provide full coverage.

Transmitter power outputs are limited to a few hundred watts, and since the antenna has a relatively low gain, most of the system gain must be provided through high-powered ground transmitters and high-gain ground antennas.

The round-trip distance for a satellite relay is of the order 70,000 km, resulting in a considerable amount of transmission delay. This means that

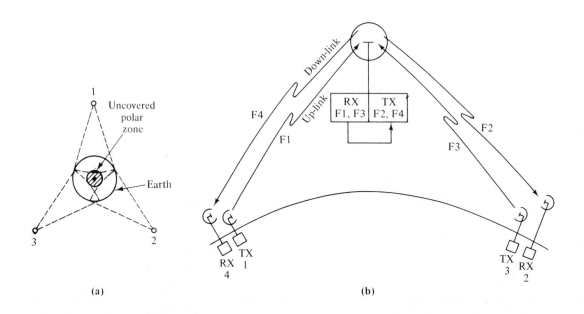

(a)

(b)

FIGURE 14.2. A communications satellite system: (a) Earth coverage provided by three equatorial synchronous orbit satellite repeater stations, as viewed over the polar zone; (b) A relay satellite system.

echo suppressors must be included in two-way telephone circuits to reduce the delayed echo to reasonable levels.

Ground-station transmitters are not limited in power output, and several kilowatts of power can be used. The type of antenna used for radio telescopes is frequently used for ground terminal stations. For remote locations, smaller ground stations which are not as expensive, but which do not perform as well because of reduced noise immunity, can be provided. The antennas used for these stations may be 3 to 5 m in diameter and light enough to be transported easily. Mobile units using smaller dishes mounted on vans can be used for temporary installations such as might be used at remote construction sites.

14.3   TROPOSPHERIC PROPAGATION

14.3.1   The Mode of Propagation

The troposphere is the region of the earth's atmosphere immediately adjacent to the earth's surface and extending upward for some tens of kilometers (i.e., the region in which we normally live and travel, including high-flying jet planes). In this region, the free-space conditions are modified by (1) the surface of the earth, and (2) the earth's atmosphere.

Considering first the effect of the earth's surface, a much-simplified model has been developed which successfully describes the propagation over a wide range of practical circumstances and is illustrated in Figure 14.3(a). In this simplified picture the earth is assumed to be flat, and the space wave reaching the receiver has two components: the direct wave, which follows a ray path s_d, and a ground reflected wave, which follows a ray path s_i. The reflected wave travels a greater distance than the direct wave, and although this has negligible effect on the amplitude, it does introduce a phase difference which is highly significant. Let Δs be the path difference; then, since a phase angle of 2π radians corresponds to a path length of one wavelength (λ), the phase angle corresponding to Δs is

$$\phi_s = \frac{2\pi}{\lambda} \Delta s \qquad (14.18)$$

(Note that $2\pi/\lambda$ is simply the phase-shift coefficient introduced in Eq. (12.23)).

The problem now is to find Δs, and this can be solved from the geometry of Figure 14.3(b); h_T is the height of the transmitting antenna above ground, h_R of the receiving antenna, and d is the distance along the flat earth between the two. From triangle FBD, Figure 14.3(b),

$$s_i^2 = (h_T + h_R)^2 + d^2$$

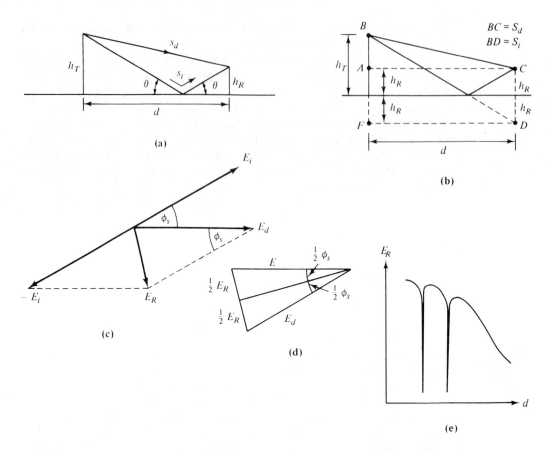

FIGURE 14.3. (a) Simplified model for tropospheric propagation ray paths; (b) Geometry used to determine phase difference; (c) The field strength phasor diagram at the receiver; (d) Geometry used to find the resultant field strength; (e) Sketch of field strength modulus versus distance, Eq. (14.23).

From triangle ABC

$$s_d^2 = (h_T - h_R)^2 + d^2$$

Therefore,

$$s_i^2 - s_d^2 = (h_T + h_R)^2 - (h_T - h_R)^2$$

$$= 4 h_T h_R \tag{14.19}$$

Also, applying the formula for the difference of two squares yields

$$s_i^2 - s_d^2 = (s_i + s_d)(s_i - s_d)$$

$$= (s_i + s_d) \Delta s$$

For most practical purposes, $s_i \cong s_d \cong d$. Therefore,

$$s_i^2 - s_d^2 \cong (2d)\, \Delta s \qquad (14.20)$$

Equating Eqs. (14.19) and (14.20), the result is

$$2d\, \Delta s = 4h_T h_R$$

Therefore,
$$\Delta s = \frac{2h_T h_R}{d} \qquad (14.21)$$

Substituting this in Eq. (14.18), gives

$$\phi_s = \frac{4\pi h_T h_R}{\lambda d} \qquad (14.22)$$

This is not the only phase change which takes place. Reflection at the earth's surface also affects the amplitude and phase of the reflected wave relative to the direct wave. The nature of the reflection depends in a complicated way on the constitution of the reflection surface, the angle of incidence of the wave, and whether the wave is horizontally or vertically polarized (meaning whether the electric field of the wave is horizontal or vertical, respectively, with respect to the earth's surface). For a wide range of conditions it is found that the amplitude change is negligible, and the phase change is 180°. In effect, the reflection coefficient [analogous to that given by Eq. (12.56)] is -1, or the reflected wave is in antiphase to the direct wave; these two waves would cancel each other if it were not for the additional phase shift ϕ_s. The phasor diagram is shown in Figure 14.3(c). Assuming that the amplitude of the reflected wave E_i equals that of the direct wave E_d, the resultant amplitude E_R is found from Figure 14.3(d):

$$\sin\left(\frac{\phi_s}{2}\right) = \frac{\frac{1}{2}E_R}{E_d}$$

$$E_R = 2E_d \sin\left(\frac{\phi_s}{2}\right) \qquad (14.23)$$

Equation (14.16) gives E_d as

$$E_d = \frac{E_0}{d}$$

and, substituting Eqs. (14.16) and (14.22) in Eq. (14.23) results in

$$E_R = \frac{2E_0}{d} \sin\left(\frac{2\pi h_T h_R}{\lambda d}\right) \qquad (14.24)$$

The variation of E_R with d is sketched in Figure 14.3(e). The sharp dips toward zero occur where the sine term goes to zero. When d is large, such that the angle within the brackets of Eq. (14.23) is small (less than about 0.5 rad), the following approximate form may be used:

$$E_R \cong \frac{2E_0}{d} \left(\frac{2\pi\, h_T h_R}{\lambda d} \right)$$

or
$$E_R = E_0 \frac{4\pi h_T h_R}{\lambda d^2} \qquad (14.25)$$

Example 14.3   In a VHF mobile radio system, the base station transmits 100 W at 150 MHz, and the antenna is 20 m above ground. The transmitting antenna is a $\frac{1}{2}\lambda$ dipole for which the gain is 1.64. Calculate the field strength at a receiving antenna of height 2 m, at a distance of 40 km.

Solution

$$\lambda = \frac{300 \times 10^6}{150 \times 10^6}$$

$$= 2\ \text{m}$$

$$E_0 = \sqrt{30 \times 100 \times 1.64} \qquad \text{[Eq. (14.15)]}$$

$$= 70\ \text{v/m}$$

The angle $2\pi\, h_T h_R / \lambda\, d$ is very much less than 0.5 rad, as an approximate calculation will show. Therefore, Eq. (14.25) can be used.

$$E_R = \frac{70 \times 4 \times \pi \times 20 \times 2}{2 \times (40 \times 10^3)^2}$$

$$= 11\ \mu\ \text{V/m}$$

Equation (14.25) shows the importance of antenna heights. For example, doubling the height of the base-station antenna in the previous example will double the field strength at the receiving point. Note also that the field strength is proportional to E_0, which, in turn, is proportional to the square root of the transmitted power. Doubling the power results in only a $\sqrt{2}$ increase in field strength.

Equation (14.24) and (14.25) also apply when a transmission takes place from the h_R antenna and is received at the h_T antenna, it only being necessary to change E_0 to the new value determined by the gain of the antenna at h_R and the power transmitted from there.

As the distance d increases, it becomes necessary to take into account the curvature of the earth. Reflection from the curved surface reduces both the amplitude of the reflected wave and the phase difference. These two effects tend to offset each other, so that the resultant amplitude does not vary rapidly as a result of these effects.

14.3.2 Radio Horizon

Earth curvature has a more important effect in that it presents a horizon that limits the range of transmission. This range is greater than the optical range because the effect of the earth's atmosphere is to cause a bending of the radio wave, which carries it beyond the optical horizon. Figure 14.4(a) shows a typical radio-wave ray path, and Figure 14.4(b) shows how the path can be considered straight by assigning a greater radius

(a)

(b)

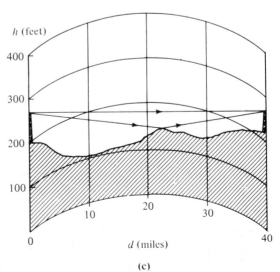

FIGURE 14.4. (a) Curvature of ray path resulting from change of the refractive index of air; (b) Equivalent straight-line ray path for fictitious earth's radius a'; (c) Example of a countour map of radio path planning.

(c)

to the earth than it actually has. For standard atmospheric conditions the increase in radius has been worked out at $\frac{4}{3}$, so that

$$a' = \frac{4}{3}a \qquad (14.26)$$

where a is the actual earth's radius and a' the fictitious radius which accounts for refraction. From Figure 14.4(b),

$$(a')^2 + d_1^2 = (a' + h_T)^2$$

Therefore, $\qquad\qquad d_1^2 = 2a'h_T + h_T^2 \qquad (14.27)$

But since $a' \gg h_T$

$$d_1^2 \approx 2a'h_T \qquad (14.28)$$

Similarly, $\qquad\qquad d_2^2 \approx 2a'h_R \qquad (14.29)$

The maximum radio range d_{max} is

$$d_{max} \approx d_1 + d_2$$
$$= \sqrt{2a'h_T} + \sqrt{2a'h_R} \qquad (14.30)$$

Substituting in the numerical values, $a' = \frac{4}{3} \times 3960$ miles, and expressing h_T and h_R in feet results in the useful expression

$$d_{max} \text{ (miles)} = \sqrt{2h_T \text{ (feet)}} + \sqrt{2h_R \text{ (feet)}} \qquad (14.31)$$

Alternatively, in metric units,

$$d_{max} \text{ (km)} = \sqrt{17h_T \text{ (m)}} + \sqrt{17h_R \text{ (m)}} \qquad (14.32)$$

Example 14.4 Calculate the maximum range for a tropospheric transmission for which the antenna heights are 100 ft and 60 ft.

Solution $\qquad\qquad\qquad d_{max} \text{ (miles)} = \sqrt{200} + \sqrt{120}$
$$= 25.1 \text{ miles}$$

The phenomenon of *diffraction* will extend the range in practice somewhat beyond the radio horizon.

14.3.3 Contour Maps

All the results derived so far are applicable only for smooth earth conditions (e.g., transmission over water or over reasonably flat land). Where the earth contour is rugged, a profile map is drawn to enable proposed transmission paths to be studied. Special graph paper is available for this purpose, in which the abscissa lines are curved to allow for the fictitious radius a', and the graphs can be scaled for d in miles and heights in feet (or d in km and h in meters). Figure 14.4(c) shows an example of a profile map.

Additional problems arise in built-up areas, where buildings and structures can cause multiple reflections and shielding, which are particularly troublesome with mobile radio equipment. The only satisfactory solution is to conduct field trials to determine an acceptable site for the base station.

14.3.4   Super- and Subrefractions

Irregularities in the earth's atmosphere also affect tropospheric transmissions. A condition known as *superrefraction* occurs when the refractive index of the air decreases with height much more rapidly than normal so that the bending of the radio wave is much more pronounced than that shown in Figure 14.4(a). The radio wave may then be reflected back from the earth to follow a path as sketched in Figure 14.5(a). In this way, the radio range is considerably increased. Unfortunately, the effect is not sufficiently reliable for it to be utilized for commercial communications systems, but it does account for some of the abnormally long-distance interference which has been observed at VHF.

(a)   (b)   (c)

FIGURE 14.5.   (a) Superrefraction;   (b) Subrefraction;   (c) Tropospheric scatter propagation.

An increase of temperature with height (known as temperature inversion) gives rise to superrefraction, as does an increase of humidity with height. It is most noticeable when both these effects occur together. The region in which superrefraction occurs is termed a *duct*, and these can be formed both at the earth's surface and in elevated strata, as sketched in Figure 14.5(a).

It is also possible for the opposite effects to occur, giving rise to *subrefraction*, which reduces signal strength by bending the rays away from the receiving point, Figure 14.5(b).

Inhomogeneities in the atmosphere can give rise to a scattering of radio signals, and by using highly directional high gain antennas, and large transmitted power, reliable communication links well beyond the radio horizon can be established, Figure 14.5(c). The method is referred to as *tropospheric scatter propagation;* ranges up to 400 miles, in the frequency band 40 to 4000 MHz, have been achieved.

14.3.5   Attenuation in the Atmosphere

The space wave is affected by atmospheric conditions but only seriously at frequencies in the microwave region, above about 10 GHz. Heavy rain such as occurs in the tropics results in serious attenuation of electromagnetic waves at frequencies above about 10 GHz, while moderate rain, cloud, and fog will seriously attenuate electromagnetic waves at frequencies above about 30 GHz. Hail has little effect except at extra-high-frequencies (e.g., above about 100 GHz) and the effect of snow is negligible at all frequencies.

The gas molecules in the air can result in attenuation of electromagnetic waves. Vibrational resonances in the water vapor molecule (H_2O) result in absorption peaks at wavelengths of 1.35 cm and 1.7 mm. The oxygen molecule (O_2) exhibits similar absorption peaks at 5 mm and 2.5 mm. Clearly, frequencies at which these resonances occur must be avoided in space-wave transmissions.

14.3.6   VHF/UHF Radio Systems

Propagation in the VHF and UHF bands between 30 MHz and 3 GHz takes place in the tropospheric mode.

The major use of two-way radio communications in the VHF and UHF bands (see Figure 14.16) is communications between a fixed base station and several mobile units, located on vehicles, ships, or aircraft in the frequency band 30–470 MHz. Typical applications are in control-tower-to-aircraft communication at airports, fire departments, ship control within harbors, police departments, armed-forces field operations, pipeline and transmission line maintenance, highway maintenance, taxicab and delivery vehicle dispatch, and personnel paging systems. Since these systems operate in frequencies above 30 MHz, their range of operation is limited to within the line-of-sight horizon of the base station (see Section 14.3.2) or that much further again if a repeater station is used. Large obstacles such as hills or tall buildings in an urban zone create shadows and odd reflection patterns which make complete coverage of the zone from a single base station difficult. For this reason, and to increase the horizon somewhat, it is usual practice to locate the base-station antenna on top of a high hill or building to gain additional height.

A limited number of channel assignments is available within the spectrum, mostly within the bands 148 and 174 MHz and 450 to 470 MHz. FM operation is preferred, and the maximum permissible channel spacing for this service has been progressively reduced from 120 KHz to the 15 kHz presently allowed, so that more channels can be assigned. Because of the narrow bandwidths used, the transmitters and receivers must be very stable, and must maintain their operating frequency within ±5 parts per million. Crystal control is a must if this type of stability is to be realized.

Dispatch systems for automobiles are usually required to cover as much area as possible, and omnidirectional vertically polarized antennas are usually used to accomplish this, both at the base station and in the mobile units. In some applications, such as pipeline and highway maintenance systems, the field of operations is strung out in a line over many miles, and for these systems vertically polarized multielement Yagi antennas aimed along the path are frequently used. This provides little coverage off the sides, but does provide better coverage along the line up to the horizon. The antennas used on the vehicles are nearly always short ground-whip antennas mounted on top of the vehicle. The longer whips used for the 50-MHz VHF band are not as popular.

Transmitter power in both the mobile units and the base-station units is usually limited to about 150 W, mainly because of the limited power available from the vehicle system. For automobiles, 13 to 15 V is available; for aircraft 28 V and 48 V are popular; and in railway locomotives 48 V is usual. The base stations are usually operated directly from the 110 V 60-Hz power mains, although for some applications back-up battery power is also provided in case of power failures.

The transceivers are designed to alternately transmit and receive on the same frequency. For aircraft and ship control use, and such systems as police and fire operation, the units may be designed to operate on one of several channels, with manual switching between channels provided. Each mobile unit is provided with a control head which is usually separate from the main chassis, conveniently located near the operator. The control head provides a power on/off switch, audio volume control, muting threshold control, and a handset containing a microphone, a telephone receiver, and a push-to-talk switch. The base station may be self-contained and directly connected to an antenna near the operator's location, but usually the base-station transceiver unit is located with the antenna at a convenient high point and the operator is provided with a remote-control console. Connection between the base station and the control console is made by means of a pair of wires if the distance is short, or a leased telephone line if the distance is considerable. A typical dispatch system is shown in Figure 14.6(a).

Often it is found that it is impossible to cover the desired area from the single base-station location. In this case one or more additional base stations can be established. These may be connected back to the operator's console over wire lines and operated independently of each other by the operator. Alternatively, a radio repeater link can be established. This requires the use of a second frequency for the link between the main base station and the repeater station. Figure 14.6(b) shows an arrangement that might be used.

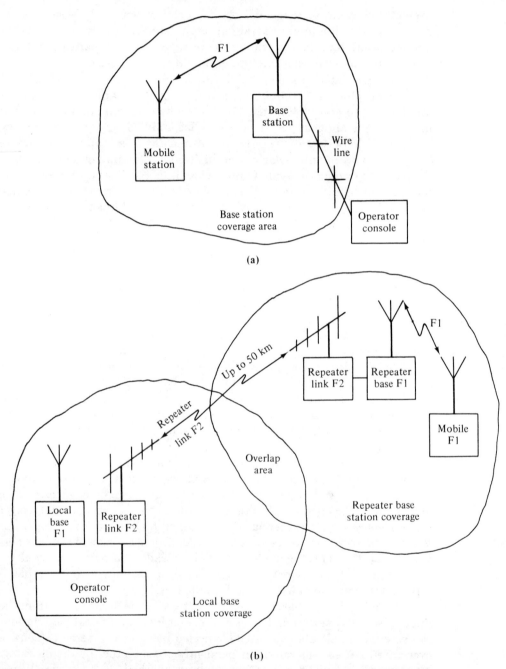

FIGURE 14.6. (a) A simple mobile dispatch system; (b) A dispatch system with a repeater station to extend coverage area.

Under normal operation the base operator can communicate over the local base station on Frequency 1 with any mobile unit within coverage area 1. When it is necessary to reach a vehicle in coverage area 2, he may turn off the local-area base station and turn on the repeater link on Frequency 2. Now when the base operator transmits, he transmits on F2 toward the repeater. The repeater receives from control on F2 and retransmits on F1 to the extended-coverage area. When a mobile unit in the extended area transmits, it is received at the repeater on F1 and retransmitted on F2 toward the base station.

When a system with several fixed stations is being operated in a repeater mode, the base operator must continuously monitor all the incoming signals from all the repeaters. If a mobile unit should be in an overlap area between two repeater stations, he may "key" both repeaters, causing interference at the control console. The operator must be able to purposely disable all but one repeater during a conversation. This can be accomplished by sending a coded tone signal to turn off the desired repeater stations, and then turn them back on when the conversation is complete. The detection characteristics of FM are such that a receiver located in the presence of two co-channel (same frequency) transmissions (such as f_1 base and f_1 repeater in Figure 14.6(b)) will suppress the weaker signal. This is known as the *capture effect*.

14.4   IONOSPHERIC PROPAGATION

14.4.1   Ionospheric Layers

The upper reaches of the earth's atmosphere are ionized (i.e., electrons are detached from atmospheric gas atoms), mainly as a result of receiving ultraviolet radiation from the sun, although other sources, such as cosmic rays, also contribute.

A state is reached where the free electron density is maintained almost constant, the ionization rate being balanced by the recombination rate of electrons with positive ions. Clearly, the electron density will vary between day and night conditions, and will also show a variation between winter and summer, as the ionization rate is dependent on solar radiation.

Various peaks are observed in electron density corresponding to the heights at which various gases settle in the upper atmosphere. The layers follow a meteorological classification, being known as the *C layer, D layer, E layer,* and *F_1 and F_2 layers.* Figure 14.7(a) shows some recently published results for typical electron-density distribution with height. It will be seen that for nighttime conditions, only the F_2 layer remains. This is because in the lower layers, collision processes in the denser gas atmosphere cause a more rapid recombination rate compared to the less-dense F_2 region.

Figure 14.7(a) also shows the main ionizing radiations, and along the top of the graph is shown the *plasma frequency* f_N, an important parameter in radio communications via the ionosphere.

14.4.2 Plasma Frequency and Critical Frequency

When an electromagnetic wave enters an ionized region at vertical incidence, as shown in Figure 14.7(b), the electric field acts as a force on the charged particles (electrons and ions), resulting in charge movement and hence current flow. Although a positive ion will carry the same magnitude of charge as an electron, it is more than 1000 times as massive and, therefore, its velocity will be correspondingly smaller and the ionic contribution to the current can be neglected.

The electron cloud will oscillate in the electric field of the wave, but with a phase retardation of 90° (for a sinusoidal wave) because of the electron mass inertia. This motion of the electron cloud produces a space current; in addition, the electric field has its own capacitive displacement current which leads the field by 90°. The space current is therefore in phase opposition to the displacement current, and it appears to reduce the relative permittivity (dielectric constant) of the ionized medium, which is then given by

$$\epsilon_r = \left(1 - \frac{Nq_e^2}{\epsilon_o m\omega^2}\right) \qquad (14.33)$$

where N = Electron density, m^{-3}
   m = Electron rest mass = 9.11×10^{-31} kg
   q_e = Electron charge magnitude = 1.6×10^{-19} C
   ω = Angular frequency of wave, rad/sec
   ϵ_o = Permittivity of free space = 8.854×10^{-12} F/m

The angular velocity of the wave can have a value that makes ϵ_r equal to zero, and this is termed the *plasma angular velocity*, ω_N. From Eq. (14.33), ω_N is seen to be

$$\omega_N^2 = \frac{Nq_e^2}{m\,\epsilon_o} \qquad (14.34)$$

or

$$f_N^2 = \frac{Nq_e^2}{(2\pi)^2 m\,\epsilon_o} \qquad (14.35)$$

Putting in the numerical values for the constants gives

$$f_N = 9\sqrt{N} \qquad (14.36)$$

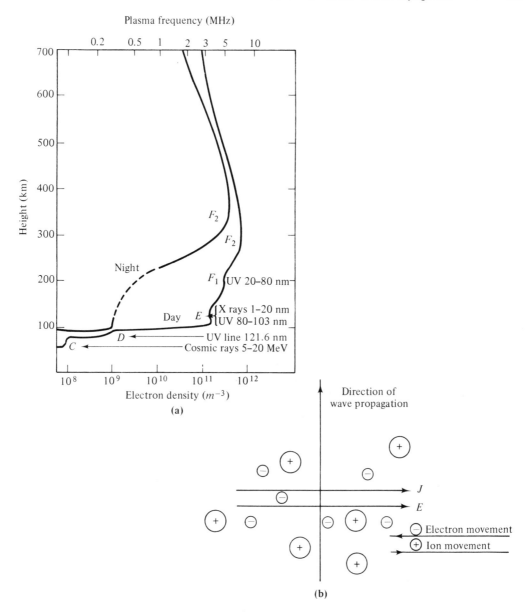

FIGURE 14.7.   (a) Typical electron density distributions for summer noon and midnight conditions at mid-latitudes, and the principal ionizing radiations at each level—plasma frequency f_N (Hz) is related to electron density (m^{-3}) by $f_N = 9\sqrt{N}$; the plasma frequency at the peak of a layer is called the critical frequency (f_0) (Reprinted by permission of the IERE); (b) Electric field E and electric current density J vectors in an ionospheric layer.

Equation (14.33) can now be rewritten as

$$\epsilon_r = 1 - \frac{f_N^2}{f^2} \tag{14.37}$$

The significance of f_N is that when a wave of this frequency reaches a region of electron density N as given by Eq. (14.36), the relative permittivity, as given by Eq. (14.37), is seen to be zero. This, in turn, means that the total displacement current density is zero, and hence the *effective* electric field is zero. This can be accounted for in terms of a reflected wave which exactly cancels the incident wave at the point of reflection. Of course, it should be possible to receive this reflected wave, which is exactly what happens in short-wave radio communications via the ionosphere.

The highest frequency wave that will be reflected from a given layer will be determined by the maximum electron density of that layer, and will be given by

$$f_0 = 9\sqrt{N_{\max}} \tag{14.38}$$

Here f_0 is known as the *critical frequency*.

14.4.3 Phase and Group Velocities

An interesting point arises in connection with the velocities associated with the wave. The phase velocity has already been shown [Eq. (12.6)] to be

$$v_p = \frac{c}{\sqrt{\epsilon_r}} \tag{14.39}$$

Hence, in the ionosphere, when the wave reaches a height such that ϵ_r is zero, v_p becomes infinite! Now, as stated in Section 12.6, the energy in a wave travels at the group velocity v_g, and it can be shown that for an ionized layer

$$v_p v_g = c^2 \tag{14.40}$$

(This was shown to hold for the special case of a waveguide, Eq. (13.10)). The wavefront in the ionosphere is a step function that will propagate energy at the group velocity, and hence, from Eq. (14.40), when the phase velocity is infinite, the group velocity is zero, so that the energy ceases to be propagated upward.

14.4.4 Secant Law and Maximum Usable Frequency

When a wave enters an ionized layer at an oblique angle of incidence i, it follows a curved ray path, Figure 14.8(a). The phase velocity v_p at any

(a)

(b)

FIGURE 14.8.   (a) Curved path of a wave in
the ionosphere entering at oblique incidence;
(b) Ray paths for fixed angle of incidence and
varying frequencies; (c) Ray paths for fixed
frequencies and varying angles of incidence.

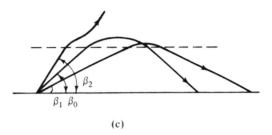

(c)

given height can be determined by application of Snell's law of refraction for
optics, the details of which will be omitted here. The result is that

$$\frac{\sin i}{c} = \frac{\sin r}{v_p} \qquad (14.41)$$

Here, r is the angle of refraction at the height where v_p occurs, as shown in
Figure 14.8(a).

At the apex of the path, $r = 90°$, and therefore

$$v_p = \frac{c}{\sin i} \qquad (14.42)$$

It will be seen that as the angle of incidence i approaches zero, the phase
velocity approaches infinity, in agreement with the results in the previous
section.

As already shown,

$$v_p = \frac{c}{\sqrt{\epsilon_r}}$$

It follows, therefore, that

$$\sqrt{\epsilon_r} = \sin i$$

Substituting Eq. (14.37) for ϵ_r,

$$\left(1 - \frac{f_N^2}{f^2}\right) = \sin^2 i$$

from which the reader should be able to derive that

$$f = f_N \sec i \qquad (14.43)$$

This is known as the *secant law*. The highest frequency that can be used will be determined by N_{max} and hence f_0; this is known as the *maximum usable frequency* (MUF):

$$MUF = f_0 \sec i \qquad (14.44)$$

It is possible for the wave to travel a considerable distance in the horizontal direction in the layer, as shown by the dotted ray path in Figure 14.8(a), but irregularities in the ionized layer will eventually deflect the wave.

Figure 14.8(b) shows what happens when the angle of incidence is kept fixed and the frequency varied. At frequencies lower that the MUF, the wave is reflected from a lower point in the layer. At higher frequencies than MUF, refraction is insufficient to return the wave to earth and it escapes through the layer (it may, of course, be reflected from a more dense layer higher up).

Figure 14.8(c) shows what happens when the frequency is held constant while the angle of incidence is varied. Since in practice it would be the angle of elevation of the antenna beam (sometimes referred to as the takeoff angle) that would be varied, this is shown. The critical angle of elevation is shown as β_0, and at this angle, f becomes the MUF. At angles less than critical, the wave is reflected from a lower region than N_{max}, and at angles greater than critical, the wave escapes.

In the discussion so far, the curvature of the earth, and the ionosphere have been ignored. This introduces little error where the ground distance between transmitter and receiver is less than about 1000 km. Beyond this, a correction factor has to be introduced in order to apply the secant law and the MUF equation.

14.4.5 Optimum Working Frequency

The frequency normally used for ionospheric transmissions is known as the *optimum working frequency* (OWF) and is chosen to be about 15 % less than the MUF. It is desirable to use as high a frequency as possible, as the attenuation of the wave as it passes through the lower ionospheric layers is inversely proportional to the square of the frequency. This arises because as the electrons collide with the gas molecules, they lose kinetic energy which they gained from the passing wave. (Electrons that do not collide return the energy periodically through reradiation in correct phase.) The kinetic energy of an electron of mass m is $\frac{1}{2}mv^2$, where v is the velocity. The velocity will be proportional to the time which the electric field acts in any given direction, and this will be proportional to the periodic time of the wave. But the periodic time is equal to $1/f$ (Eq. (B.3)) where f is the frequency. Therefore, the kinetic energy lost is proportional to $(1/f^2)$.

The argument then is to use the highest possible frequency, which of course is the MUF. Irregularities in the ionosphere may, however, result in a MUF wave being occasionally deflected upward to escape through the layer. Practical experience has shown that frequencies about 15% lower than the MUF should be used.

14.4.6   Virtual Height

A wave traveling in a curved path has a horizontal component of group velocity v_h, given by [see Figure 14.9(a)]

$$v_h = v_g \sin r \qquad (14.45)$$

From Eq. (14.40),

$$v_g = \frac{c^2}{v_p}$$

Therefore,

$$v_h = c^2 \frac{\sin r}{v_p}$$

Substituting for $(\sin r)/v_p$ from Eq. (14.41),

$$v_h = c^2 \frac{\sin i}{c}$$

$$= c \sin i \qquad (14.46)$$

This shows that the horizontal component of group velocity is constant, independent of height in the ionized layer. Therefore, the time t required for the wavefront to reach the highest point in the path will be

$$t = \frac{AC}{v_h} \qquad (14.47)$$

where AC is the horizontal distance from point of entry to the vertical dropped from the highest point, Figure 14.9(a).

FIGURE 14.9. (a) Determination of virtual height; (b) Determination of path distance.

Substituting from Eq. (14.46) for v_h, Eq. (14.47) becomes

$$t = \frac{AC}{c \sin i}$$

But from Figure 14.9(a), $AC = AB \sin i$, and therefore

$$t = \frac{AB}{c} \qquad (14.48)$$

Thus the wave can be considered to have traveled distance AB at constant velocity c, in time t. The virtual height h of a layer is then OB, Figure 14.9(a), which is the height the wave appears to be reflected from had it been traveling at constant velocity c. The virtual height has the great advantage of being easily measured, and it is very useful in transmission-path calculations.

For flat-earth assumptions, and assuming that the ionospheric conditions are symmetrical for the incident and reflected waves, the transmission-path distance TR, Figure 14.9(a), is

$$TR = \frac{2h}{\tan \beta} \qquad (14.49)$$

Where the curvature of the earth is taken into account, the transmission-

path distance can be determined from geometry of Figure 14.9(b).

$$\frac{\sin i}{a} = \frac{\sin (180 - \alpha)}{a + h}$$

$$= \frac{\sin \alpha}{a + h} \qquad (14.50)$$

Also, $$180 - \alpha = 180 - (i + \Theta)$$

Therefore, $$i = \alpha - \Theta$$

Substituting Eq. (14.51) in Eq. (14.50),

$$\frac{\sin (\alpha - \Theta)}{a} = \frac{\sin \alpha}{a + h}$$

Therefore, $$\Theta = \alpha - \sin^{-1}\left(\frac{a}{a + h} \cdot \sin \alpha\right) \qquad (14.52)$$

In terms of the angle of elevation, Eq. (14.52) becomes

$$\Theta = (90 - \beta) - \sin^{-1}\left(\frac{a}{a + h} \cdot \cos \beta\right) \qquad (14.53)$$

Also, from Figure 14.6(b), the arc length

$$\frac{d}{2} = a \cdot \Theta \qquad (14.54)$$

where the angle Θ is in radians. Substituting for Θ from Eq. (14.53) and using radian measure for all angles,

$$d = 2a\left[\left(\frac{\pi}{2} - \beta\right) - \sin^{-1}\left(\frac{a}{a + h} \cdot \cos \beta\right)\right] \qquad (14.55)$$

Example 14.5 Calculate the transmission path distance for an ionospheric transmission that utilizes a layer of virtual height 200 km, the angle of elevation of the antenna beam being 20°.

Solution Flat-earth approximation, Eq. (14.49),

$$d = \frac{2 \times 200}{\tan 20°}$$

$$= 1100 \text{ km}$$

Using Eq. (14.55) gives

$$d = 2 \times 6370 \left[(1.57 - 0.349) - \sin^{-1} \left(-\frac{6370}{6570} \cdot \cos 20° \right) \right]$$

$$= 966 \text{ km}$$

Measurement of virtual height is usually carried out by means of an instrument known as an *ionosonde*. The basic method is to transmit vertically upward a pulse-modulated radio wave, the pulse duration being about $150\mu s$. The reflected signal is received close to the transmission point, and the time T required for the round trip is measured. The virtual height is then

$$h = \frac{cT}{2} \qquad \text{where } c = \text{speed of light} \qquad (14.56)$$

The ionosonde will have facilities for sweeping over the radio-frequency range; typically, it will sweep from 1 MHz to 20 MHz in 3 minutes. It will also have facilities for the automatic plotting of virtual height against frequency, the resultant graph being known as an *ionogram*, Figure 14.10. It will be seen that two critical frequencies, $f_0 F_2$ and $f_x F_2$ are shown, and this is explained in the next section.

14.4.7 Effects of Earth's Magnetic Field

When a charged particle is displaced in a magnetic field it experiences a force that causes it to move in a curved path. The magnetic field of the earth exerts such a force on the electrons in an ionized layer which are displaced by the electric field of a radio wave. (There is also the magnetic field of the radio wave, but the force exerted by it is negligible in this situation.) In general, the electron paths will be helixes, as sketched in Figure 14.11(a). At one particular wave frequency, known as *the gyrofrequency*, where the periodic time of the wave is equal to the time required for one complete revolution about the magnetic field axis, the electron path becomes a very wide single loop, Figure 14.11(b). The gyrofrequency can be shown to be equal to

$$f_g = \frac{q_e}{2\pi m} \cdot B \qquad (14.57)$$

where q_e is the charge, m the mass of the electron, and B the magnetic field strength. Substituting values for q_e and m, and using an average value of 0.5×10^{-4} T for the earth's magnetic field results in a gyrofrequency of 1.4 MHz.

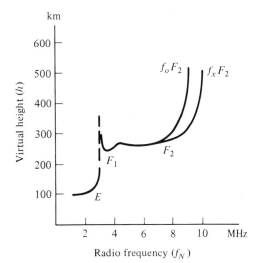

FIGURE 14.10.   Sketch of an ionogram.

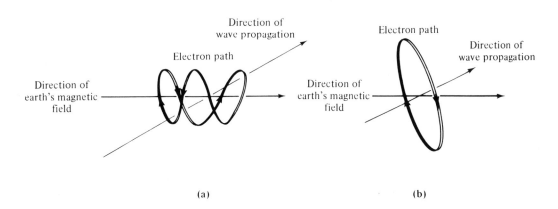

(a)   (b)

FIGURE 14.11.   (a) Helical path of an electron moving in the earth's magnetic field; (b) Electron path at gyrofrequency.

The significance of the gyrofrequency is that because of the wide path followed by the electrons, the number of collisions between electrons and molecules in the D layer is increased, resulting in increased attenuation in the reflected wave at frequencies in the vicinity of f_g. Thus most of the medium-wave broadcast band suffers high attenuation of the reflected-wave component during the day when the D layer is present.

Another effect of the earth's magnetic field is that the relative permitivity of the ionized layer develops two components. The details are complicated and will not be shown here, but the result is that two critical frequencies occur for an ionized layer. In practice this only shows up for the F_2 layer, the two critical frequencies being known as the critical frequency for the ordinary ray, denoted by $f_0 F_2$, and the critical frequency for the extra-ordinary ray, $f_x F_2$. These are shown in Figure 14.10.

14.4.8 Service Range

The service range of a transmission of a given frequency is determined by the critical ray at the nearest point and the glancing ray at the farthest point, as shown in Figure 14.12(a). Rays from the transmitting antenna at angles greater than the critical angle of elevation (or what is equivalent at angles of incidence less than the critical value) will escape, creating a skip distance in which no signal is received.

The maximum possible range is reached when the critical ray coincides with the glancing ray, Figure 14.12(b) (i.e., when the glancing ray is returned from the greatest virtual height h_m). The geometry of Figure 14.12(b) is similar to that of Figure 14.9(b) with β equal to zero and h being replaced by h_m. The angle Θ is

$$\Theta = \cos^{-1}\left(\frac{a}{a + h_m}\right)$$

and, from Eq. (14.54),

$$d = 2a\Theta$$

$$= 2a \cos^{-1}\left(\frac{a}{a + h_m}\right) \tag{14.58}$$

Equation (14.58) gives the maximum possible distance for a "single hop," that is, one reflection involving the ionosphere. The range can be increased by using multiple hops, in which the wave is reflected from the earth after the first hop, to be reflected from the ionosphere once again farther on.

Of course, the ionospheric conditions at the point of reflection must be used in calculations to determine the transmission path. With multiple hop transmissions the situation becomes more complicated, since two or more points must be taken into consideration. This is particularly so for paths following lines of latitude, since conditions may change from day to night over the path.

Irregularities in the ionosphere have been used successfully for *scatter propagation* similar to that which occurs in the troposphere. With ionospheric scatter, distances of the order of 1000 miles are achieved at frequencies in the low end of the VHF band (i.e., between about 20 and 60 MHz). Fading effects are more troublesome in ionospheric scatter systems

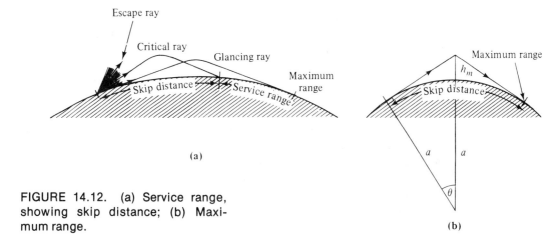

FIGURE 14.12. (a) Service range, showing skip distance; (b) Maximum range.

compared to tropospheric scatter systems, which tend to limit *ionoscatter* propagation to narrow-band (e.g., 3 kHz) signals.

14.4.9   Ionospheric Irregularities and Disturbances. Fading

In previous sections, a very simple model of the ionosphere was assumed in which electron densities varied smoothly and uniformly, and changes resulting from diurnal and seasonal variations were assumed to be predictable. Calculations of MUF, virtual height, and so on, based on this model provide only an estimate for average conditions. In practice, the ionosphere exhibits irregularities in electron densities in the various layers, the extent of these irregularities ranging from less than 100 m to many hundreds of kilometers. It is known that some irregularities travel through the ionosphere with a horizontal component of velocity ranging from a few meters per second to greater than 1 km/s. These are known as *traveling ionospheric disturbances* (TID's) and they can seriously affect the accuracy of high-frequency direction finders.

Many of the causes of ionospheric disturbances are not well understood, some of the factors being large-scale gravity waves in the atmosphere, electric currents and plasma instabilities in the ionosphere, and, in particular, solar activity. It has been observed that severe attenuation, or complete loss of radio signals, accompanies solar flares. Intense X radiation from the flares increases the ionization of the D layer, resulting in increased absorption, as described in Section 14.4.5. The fade-outs occur very suddenly and are known as *sudden ionospheric distubances* (SID's). They are also known as *Dellinger fade-outs* and *Mogel–Dellinger* fade-outs, having been reported by Mogel in Germany in 1930 and by Dellinger in the United States in 1937.

Protons are also discharged from the sun during solar flares. These affect the outer reaches of the earth's magnetic field about 30 hours after a flare has been observed, and they give rise to what is termed a *magnetic storm*. These storms adversely affect radio communications, particularly at high latitudes (near the magnetic poles). Magnetic storms not connected with solar flares but associated with sunspots have been recorded; yet others have been observed apparently not connected with solar flares or sunspots but which have a periodicity of recurrence of about 27 days, the rotational period of the sun. These appear to originate in well-defined regions of the sun (labeled M regions) and, in fact, are more noticeable at sunspot minima. They rise much more gradually than those associated with sunspots or solar flares, and although they are weaker, they persist much longer, sometimes up to about 10 days. Weak sporadic magnetic storms apparently not directly related to solar activity have also been observed.

Another form of ionospheric disturbance which can seriously affect radio communications is known as *sporadic E*. Thin, highly ionized layers occur in the E layer from time to time; the extent, position, and timing of these are all irregular, hence the term "sporadic E layer." Because of its high electron density, sporadic E can often take over a transmission normally beamed on the F layer; VHF reflections have also been observed from sporadic E, resulting in interference in the VHF television channels (e.g., the "freak" reception of distant stations which sometimes occurs).

Fluctuations in electron densities occur continuously in the ionosphere, giving rise to fluctuating phase differences in the various ray paths of a signal. Since the waves following these ray paths combine as phasors at the receiver, fluctuations in the received signal strength will be observed, this being known as *interference fading*. Another form of fading, known as *polarization fading*, occurs where the ordinary and extraordinary rays combine phasorally; the ordinary and extraordinary waves are always perpendicularly polarized with reference to each other, and because of the random variations in amplitude and phase of each, when they combine, the net polarization also varies in a random manner. The receiving antenna will of course be arranged for reception of a fixed polarization (e.g., vertically polarized).

With modulated signals, fading can affect a very narrow range of the frequency spectrum independently of other parts of the spectrum, and this gives rise to what is termed *selective fading*. It comes about essentially because the ray paths in the ionosphere will be different for different frequencies and they will not necessarily all experience a distubance in a given region. Selective fading limits ionospheric transmissions to narrow-band signals (e.g., 3-kHz bandwidth).

14.4.10 Summary of Layers

In spite of the difficulties and uncertainties inherent in ionospheric transmissions, it does provide an inexpensive and relatively quick means for setting up medium- to long-distance radio communications. Of course, it has been superseded on many circuits by satellite systems or submarine cables, both of which provide much better service, but at increased cost.

Methods are being developed for predicting ionospheric conditions which may be utilized in the planning of radio circuits. Equipment is also being developed that will automatically select optimum frequency for transmission in an effort to combat fading.

The main features of the various layers are summarized here, values having been obtained from Figure 14.7(a). Frequencies, heights, and so on, will of course, vary considerably, as already discussed, and the values are presented simply to give an order-of-magnitude comparison for the various layers.

C and D layers   Virtual height, 60 to 80 km. Reflect low and very low frequencies (see Section 14.6) but for HF communications, the D layer, in particular, introduces attenuation.

E layer   Virtual height ~110 km. Critical frequency, ~4 MHz. Maximum single-hop range, ~2350 km.

F_1 *layer*   Virtual height, ~180 km. Critical frequency, ~5 MHz. Maximum single-hop range, ~3000 km.

F_2 *layer*   Virtual height, ~300 km daytime, ~350 km nighttime. Critical frequency, ~8 MHz daytime, ~6 MHz nighttime. Maximum single-hop range, ~3840 km daytime, ~4130 km nighttime.

14.4.11   HF Radio Systems

High-frequency radio systems using the bands from 1.6 to 30 MHz have been popular since the early days of radio in applications where relatively long distances must be covered at a low cost and under relatively light traffic conditions. Recent advances in satellite communications have usurped many of the traditional applications, but communications by satellite tend to be costly in terms of equipment, and HF radio will continue to be used for many applications.

The typical HF radio system is a two-point system with a transmitter and a receiver located at each end of the link. The transmitter and receiver used is usually a general-purpose communications set, although for some fixed applications single-frequency units can be used. Transceiver units are popular for temporary systems where one of the terminal points may be frequently moved to different locations.

The mode of transmission most often used for HF systems is single-sideband either with or without pilot carrier operated in the simplex mode. Independent sideband suppressed carrier transmission is useful where full duplex operation is desired with only one frequency assignment available.

Separate transmitting and receiving antennas separated by some distance are required to prevent overloading of the local receiver by its associated transmitter. Dipoles are favored because they give some directional gain while being structurally simple. Fixed telephone stations may use more-complex arrays, such as broadsides, to provide greater directivity. Transmitter powers ranging from a few watts to several kilowatts are commonly used.

The main advantages of HF systems lie in their ability to provide communication over great distances at relatively low cost. This makes them ideal for communications between remote settlements or camps where the density of calls is low. HF systems do have several severe disadvantages which have resulted in a search for other means of communications, mainly because of the overall unreliability of the systems resulting from variable propagation conditions (see Section 14.4.9). The problem of variable propagation conditions can partially be overcome by using frequency diversity, where a given system is provided with several frequency assignments spanning the HF band of frequencies, so that the operator may choose the channel that gives the best results at any given time. However, this gives no protection against the total blackouts which periodically occur because of magnetic storms and other solar-induced phenomena.

Skip is also a problem. If HF stations are located closely enough together to use ground-wave propagation, distant stations frequently interfere through sky-wave propagation. Fading and distortion because of the changing ionospheric conditions cause annoying interference, especially in the longer circuits. Sometimes space diversity can be used to ease the problem, but since the diversity stations must be separated by several wavelengths, this becomes very expensive. In regions above the arctic circle, auroral phenomena frequently make HF communications impossible by disturbing the necessary ionospheric layers. HF systems in equatorial regions are much more reliable.

Perhaps the most limiting disadvantage of the HF system is the fact that the bandwidth allowed for a channel is very narrow, only sufficient for one voice channel. This means that for every voice circuit a separate pair of radio circuits is required. Further, since transmission is unreliable, the use of HF in public telephone systems is limited. In the past HF radio was used extensively for overseas telephone communications. Recent advances in cable telephony and in satellite communications has just about eliminated this application except for some remote areas. It is still being used extensively in the South Pacific area.

Probably the major application and the one which will continue for many years is that of marine communications. Ships at sea are out of range of all land stations except HF stations, and it is unlikely that satellites will be used extensively in marine applications for some time because of the cost of terminal equipment.

14.5 SURFACE WAVE

14.5.1 The Mode of Propagation

A radio wave propagating close to the surface of the earth will follow the curvature of the earth as a result of the phenomenon of *diffraction*. This is the same phenomenon which causes sound waves, for example, to travel around an obstacle. Diffraction effects depend on the wavelength in relation to the size of the obstacle, and are greater the longer the wavelength. In the case of radio waves, the "obstacle" around which the wave must travel is the earth itself, and the surface wave is of importance at frequencies below about 2 MHz.

The conductivity and permittivity of the surface play an important part in the propagation of the surface wave, as the wave will induce both displacement and conduction currents in the surface. These currents may penetrate to depths of from about 1 m at the highest frequency to tens of meters at the lowest, so the actual conditions on top of the surface are relatively unimportant.

The energy lost in the surface comes from the radio wave, which is therefore attenuated as it passes over the surface. The attenuation increases with increase in frequency, which is another factor which limits the usefulness of the surface wave to frequencies below about 2 MHz.

The surface wave in practice is always vertically polarized, as the conductivity of the ground would effectively short-circuit any horizontal electric field component.

The electric field strength as given by Eq. (14.13) can be modified to take into account the various factors affecting propagation, by introducing an attenuating factor A, such that

$$E = \frac{A\sqrt{30 P_T G_T}}{d} \quad \text{V/m} \qquad (14.59)$$

It is normal practice to evaluate E for standard conditions of 1 kW radiated from a short unipole antenna, which has a power gain of 3. Equation (14.59) then becomes

$$E = 300 \frac{A}{d} \quad \text{V/m} \qquad (14.60)$$

Graphs are available which present the factor A as a function of distance for various values of permittivity, conductivity, and frequency. At large distances (e.g., $d \geq 100\lambda$) the factor A becomes inversely proportional to distance, and the field strength plotted against distance is shown in Figure 14.13(a) for a frequency of 500 kHz.

The change of refractive index with height of the atmosphere also

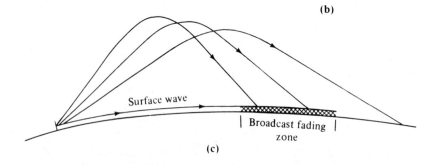

FIGURE 14.13. (a) Example of variation of surface-wave field strength with distance; (b) The ground wave; (c) Broadcast fading zone.

causes diffraction of the surface wave, which can be allowed for by adopting an earth's radius of $\frac{4}{3}$ times the actual radius, a. The main low-frequency diffraction is then determined for an obstacle of radius $4a/3$.

14.5.2 Ground Wave

At low frequencies, such that the height of the transmitting antenna above ground, in terms of wavelength, is small, the direct wave and the ground reflected wave (both of which go to make up the space wave, see Section 14.3) effectively cancel each other, leaving only the surface wave. At higher frequencies the height of the antenna may be such that the space wave is comparable in magnitude with the surface wave, the resultant wave being the phasor sum. The resultant wave is termed the *ground wave* (not to be confused with surface wave alone), the situation being as shown in Figure 14.13(b). Normally, the ground-wave field strength is greater than that of the surface wave alone, and this is taken into account by introducing a multiplying factor in Equation (14.60), known as *height-gain* factor. The height-gain factor depends on the physical heights of the transmitting and receiving antennas and also on the factors that are used in the determination of the attenuation factor A. Like A, the height-gain factor is available in graphical form for a wide range of practical conditions.

14.5.3 Broadcast Fading Zone

The medium-wave (550 to 1600 kHz) broadcast service normally utilizes the surface wave. Some energy will, however, be transmitted into the ionosphere, where during daytime conditions it is almost completely absorbed in the D layer.

During nighttime conditions, an appreciable portion of the ionospheric wave is returned to earth, which extends the service area of the station well beyond that covered by the surface wave. There will also be a zone in which both the surface wave and the ionospheric wave are of the same order of magnitude and the resultant signal strength is the phasor sum of the two. Unfortunately, fluctuations in the ionosphere produce fluctuations in the phase of the reflected wave relative to the surface wave, resulting in severe fading of the combined wave. The area in which this occurs is known as the *broadcast fading zone* and is shown in Figure 14.13(c).

14.6 LOW-FREQUENCY PROPAGATION AND VERY-LOW-FREQUENCY PROPAGATION

At frequencies below about 300 kHz it is convenient to consider propagation in two bands: 3 to 30 kHz, this being termed the very-low-frequency (VLF) band, and 30 to 300 kHz, this being the low-frequency (LF) band. It is an interesting point that the transatlantic radio links engineered by Marconi were at these low frequencies in the year 1901.

At frequencies in these bands, propagation is by means of surface waves up to distances of about 1000 km; beyond this, the sky wave plays an increasingly important part. This is propagated by means of multiple hops between ionosphere and earth. In the LF part of the band, theoretical treatment based on multiple hops of a TEM wave gives satisfactory results, while in the VLF band, the propagation is best considered to take place as a TM waveguide mode (see Chapter 13), the earth and the ionosphere forming the walls of a spherical waveguide.

Because of the low carrier frequencies and consequent narrow bandwidths available, communications channels are limited to slow data rates. There are broadcast services of standard frequencies and time transmitted from various countries. The main characteristic of these low and very low frequencies is that they provide highly reliable radio links. Of course, the antenna structures have to be very large, and they are unfortunately inherently inefficient.

Radio navigational systems make extensive use of the low and very low frequency bands. The highly stable phase characteristics of the propagation means that the phase delay in a wave as a function of distance is accurately known in advance, and this can be measured by receiving equipment on the ship, aircraft, and so on, to determine position. The most common method is to use two or more transmissions to generate a pattern of *lines of position*, which can then be superimposed upon a map. Referring to Figure 14.14(a), the signals received at position X, as given by Eq. (B.1), will be:

$$\text{From transmitter } A: \quad A \sin (\omega_a t - \beta_a |s_1|) \quad\quad (14.61)$$

$$\text{From transmitter } B: \quad B \sin (\omega_b t - \beta_b |s_2|) \quad\quad (14.62)$$

By making ω_a and ω_b multiples of a common generating frequency ω_0 to which both are synchronized, it becomes possible to compare the phase of the two signals. The phase angles are $\beta_a |s_1|$ and $\beta_b |s_2|$, where the phase-shift coefficients β are as defined by Eq. (12.23). Let $\omega_a = 2\pi a f_0$ and $\omega_b = 2\pi b f_0$; then, by putting both signals through frequency dividers, at the receiver, as shown in Figure 14.14(b) and comparing phases, a measure of $|s_1| - |s_2|$ is obtained. The phase of the signals after frequency division will be

$$\text{phase of signal } A = \frac{\beta_a |s_1|}{a} \quad\quad (14.63)$$

$$\text{phase of signal } B = \frac{\beta_b |s_2|}{b} \qu\quad (14.64)$$

Now, $\beta_a = 2\pi/\lambda_a$ and $\lambda_a = \lambda_0/a$, so the phase angles of signals A and B, after frequency division, becomes

$$\text{phase of signal } A = \frac{2\pi}{\lambda_0} |s_1| \qu\quad (14.65)$$

$$\text{phase of signal } B = \frac{2\pi}{\lambda_0} |s_2| \qu\quad (14.66)$$

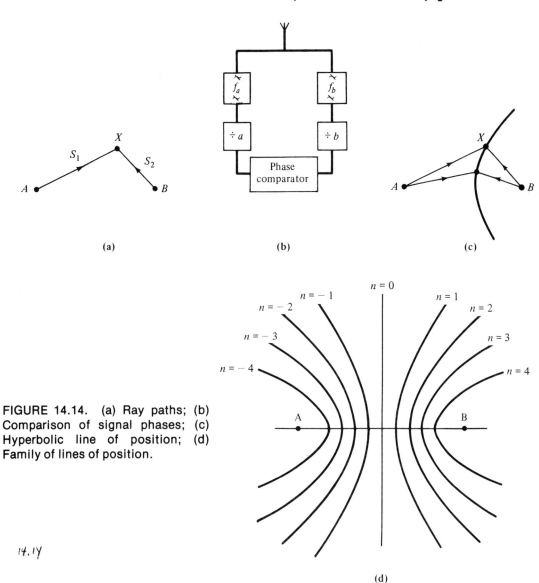

FIGURE 14.14. (a) Ray paths; (b) Comparison of signal phases; (c) Hyperbolic line of position; (d) Family of lines of position.

14.14

Therefore, the phase difference Δ is

$$\Delta = \frac{2\pi}{\lambda_0}\left(|s_1| - |s_2|\right) \qquad (14.67)$$

In effect, the phase difference goes through a series of maxima and minima with change in distance, just like that which occurs for standing waves on transmission lines (see Section 12.7). The two signals will be in phase when $\Delta = n2\pi$, where n is an integer. It follows, therefore, that

$$|s_1| - |s_2| = n\lambda_0 \qquad (14.68)$$

For a given value of n, $|s_1| - |s_2|$ is a constant (since λ_0 is also fixed). Now, this is a property of a hyperbola, Figure 14.14(c), so that for a given value of n, a hyperbolic curve can be drawn along which $|s_1| - |s_2|$ is constant, and hence along which the signals are in phase. A whole family of curves can be constructed, one curve for each value of n, as shown in Figure 14.14(d), these being the lines of position. The space between lines of position are known as *lanes*.

Along the base line joining A and B, the spacing is narrowest. Let L be the width of a lane on the base line. Then, on moving from line n to $n + 1$ along the base line, the total change in the path difference will be $2L$, since $|s_1|$ increases by L and $|s_2|$ decreases by L. In terms of wavelength the change will be $(n + 1)\lambda_0 - n\lambda_0 = \lambda_0$. Hence

$$2L = \lambda_0$$
$$L = \frac{1}{2}\lambda_0 \qquad (14.69)$$

This applies for the phase-comparison system shown in Figure 14.14(b). In other systems the frequencies may be multiplied up to their lowest common multiple of f_0, or the carrier may first be divided down to f_0 and then multiplied up to the slave frequency to which it is being compared. The term *master* is used to denote the transmitter to which the others are synchronized, while the others are known as *slaves*. In the *Decca navigational system*, the master is at $6f_0$, the red slave at $8f_0$, the green slave at $9f_0$, and the purple slave at $5f_0$. (The colors refer to the color of the grids superimposed on the navigation map.) By using more than one slave, two or more families of hyperbolas are made to intersect, enabling a position to be pinpointed as in Figure 14.15(a). The receiving equipment has to be able to integrate the phase change measured, in effect, to count the number of lines of position crossed as well as to indicate the position within a lane.

The Decca System works very well with surface-wave coverage, but phase variations resulting from the ionosphere reduce its accuracy where the sky wave has to be used. A worldwide radio-navigational system named *Omega*, being developed by the U.S. Navy, operates in the VLF band. In this band, phase variations resulting from ionospheric changes are tolerable. Eight stations are involved, labeled A, B, ..., H, and some of these are presently in operation, for example, A in Norway, B in Trinidad, and D in New York. The schedule of transmissions for the Omega system is shown in Figure 14.15(b).

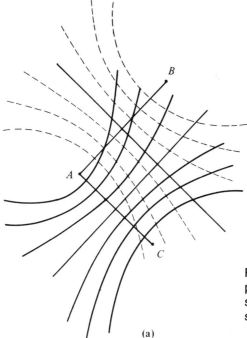

(a)

FIGURE 14.15.   (a) Intersecting lines of position; (b) Chart showing the transmission schedule for the *Omega* navigational system.

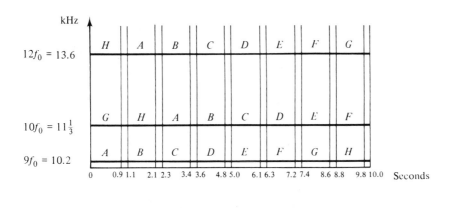

(b)

14.7   SUMMARY OF RADIO-WAVE PROPAGATION

The chart in Figure 14.16 summarizes the classification of the various radio bands in terms of frequency and wavelength. It should be realized, of course, that sharp boundaries do not exist between the bands.

FIGURE 14.16.   Classification by frequency of the various radio bands.

14.8   PROBLEMS

1. Part of a microwave link can be approximated by free-space conditions. The antenna gains are each 40 dB, the frequency is 10 GHz, and the path length is 80 km. Calculate: (a) transmission path loss; (b) received power for a transmitted power of 10 W.

2. A VHF radio link is set up between a shore station and an island in a lake 10 miles offshore. The antenna site on the island is atop a 100-ft cliff. Calculate the minimum height of the shore-station antenna if the minimum acceptable signal strength at either station is 10 μV/m. The frequency is 150 MHz and the transmit power is 1 W from a ½ λ dipole from each station.

3. Derive Eq. (14.32).

4. Explain the significance of the plasma frequency in connection with ionospheric radio communications. How is the critical frequency for an ionized layer related to the plasma frequency?

5. A radio communications link is to be established via the ionosphere, the maximum virtual height of the layer being 100 km at the midpoint of the path, and the critical frequency 2 MHz. The distance between stations is 600 km. Determine suitable values for the optimum working frequency and the angle of elevation for the antenna main beam.

6. Explain what is meant by the gyro frequency and why frequencies in the region of the gyro frequency are not suitable for ionospheric transmissions.

7. Calculate the maximum range obtainable in a single-hop transmission utilizing the F_2 layer for which h_{max} is 400 km. The earth's radius may be taken as 6370 km.

8. Discuss briefly the factors that give rise to fading in ionospheric radio transmissions.

9. Explain the difference between the surface wave and the ground wave for radio transmissions in the frequency range 300 kHz to 2 MHz.

10. Given that the free-space velocity of light, c, is 299792.5 km/s and the ratio of phase velocity in the atmosphere to the free space values, v_p/c is 0.9974, calculate the wavelength of the generating frequency f_0 in the Omega navigation system.

11. List the advantages and disadvantages of HF radiotelephone circuits.

12. Why are VHF systems popular for dispatch work?

13. Why can a radio repeater station not retransmit on the same frequency on which it receives?

14. What feature of the microwave relay system makes it attractive for providing telephone trunk circuits? How many repeater stations would be required on a 6000-km route?

15. Calculate the round trip or echo delay on a satellite circuit using a synchronous satellite that is located 37,000 km from station A and 40,000 km from station B. Assume that radio waves transmit at the velocity of light.

16. Calculate the one-way path loss on link A of the satellite circuit in Problem 15. If the ground-station transmitter puts out 10 kW of signal, the antenna system on the ground station has a net gain of 65 dB, and the satellite antenna has a net gain of 10 dB, calculate the power input to the satellite receiver.

Chapter 15
Antennas

15.1 INTRODUCTION

In a radio system, an electromagnetic wave travels from the transmitter to the receiver through space, and antennas (or aerials) are required at both ends for the purpose of coupling the transmitter and the receiver to the space link. Many of the important characteristics of a given antenna are identical for both transmitting and receiving functions, and the same antenna is often used for both.

Antennas, whether used for transmitting or receiving, fall into one of two categories: *resonant antennas*, which can be developed from a transmission line section on which standing waves exist; and *nonresonant antennas*, which can be developed from a matched transmission line carrying an incident traveling wave. (Standing waves and traveling waves on transmission lines are discussed in Chapter 12.)

The types of structures used for antennas are many and varied, ranging from a simple length of wire suspended above the ground to the curtain arrays used for very low frequency (VLF) broadcasting, from the insignificant-looking lens antenna on a traffic policeman's radar apparatus, to the huge parabolic dish antennas of the astronomer's radio telescope. Several of these will be discussed in detail in this chapter.

15.2   PRINCIPLES OF RADIATION

An electric current in a wire is always surrounded by a magnetic field. When the current is alternating, the free electric charges in the wire are accelerated which gives rise to an alternating electromagnetic field which travels away from the wire in the form of an electromagnetic wave. (An analogy may be made by considering a semi-rigid sheet being moved at constant velocity which results in a steady air displacement. If the sheet is vibrated, which in effect imparts acceleration to some areas of it, a sound wave will be generated which travels through the air away from the sheet.)

The total field originating from an alternating current in a wire is complicated, consisting of (i) an electric field component which lags the current by 90°, and which decreases in amplitude as the cube of the distance; (ii) an electromagnetic field (i.e., a combined electric and magnetic field) which is in phase with the current, and which decreases in amplitude as the square of the distance; and (iii) an electromagnetic field which leads the current by 90° and which decreases in amplitude directly as the distance increases. Only the latter electromagnetic field reaches the receiver in a normal radio communications system, where it appears to the receiving antenna as a plane transverse electromagnetic (TEM) wave. The basic properties of a TEM wave are discussed in Appendix B.

15.3   ISOTROPIC RADIATOR

The isotropic, or point-source, radiator is one that radiates electromagnetic waves equally well in all directions. Such a radiator cannot be physically produced, but the concept is useful because it provides a theoretical standard to which other antennas may be compared.

The power density in the radiated wave from an isotropic radiator is given by Eq. (14.1), and the electric field strength from this hypothetical radiator is given by Eq. (14.13) with the gain G_T set equal to unity, since by definition, it radiates equally in all directions. In Section 15.5, the concept of the antenna polar diagram is introduced; for the isotropic radiator, the polar diagram would be circular in all planes.

15.4   THE ELEMENTARY DOUBLET (OR HERTZIAN DIPOLE)

This is also a hypothetical radiating element consisting of a length of wire very much shorter than a wavelength, carrying a uniform alternating current (that is, the current has the same magnitude at all points along the wire).

It is hypothetical in the sense that it is not possible to have an isolated wire carrying a uniform current, but a practical approximation to this can be made by having a short, center-fed length of wire terminated in capacitive spheres as shown in Figure 15.1(a).

(a)

(b)

FIGURE 15.1. The elementary doublet: (a) Antenna structure; (b) Polar diagram of field strength in the horizontal plane containing the wire axis.

The Hertzian dipole is often used in preference to the isotropic radiator as a standard or reference antenna, as it is easier to visualize a real antenna being made up of a series of such dipoles, or elementary doublets, and the theoretical analysis from this approach yields very useful practical results. The magnitude of the field strength E, at distance r, from an elementary doublet of length L_e, carrying a current of amplitude I, is given by

$$E = \frac{60\pi L_e I}{\lambda r} \cdot \sin \theta \qquad (15.1)$$

where θ is the angle between the wire axis and the direction line from the doublet to the point of reception, and λ is the wavelength of radiation. Maximum radiation is seen to occur along a line normal to the wire axis where $\sin \theta = 1$, $\theta = 90°$, and radiation is zero along the line of the dipole, since θ is zero and therefore $\sin \theta$ is zero.

The maximum radiation is seen to be

$$E_{max} = \frac{60\pi L_e I}{\lambda r} \qquad (15.2)$$

By normalizing the field strength to the maximum value, an expression for the relative field strength as a function of angle θ is obtained, this enabling the field-strength polar diagram in the meridian plane to be plotted as described in the following section. For the doublet, the field-strength polar diagram function, from Eqs. (15.1) and (15.2) is simply sin θ, and this results in the double circle polar diagram shown in Figure 15.1(b).

15.5 POLAR DIAGRAM

All practical antennas radiate better in some directions than they do in other directions; that is, they have the property of directivity. The profile of radiation must be looked at in three dimensions, and the polar diagram is an aid to providing a two-dimensional representation of this three-dimensional pattern.

For many antennas (although not all) there will be one plane in which the field strength at some distance r from the antenna will be constant for all angular directions from the antenna within that plane. This is called the *equatorial plane*. Any plane at right angles to the equatorial is called a *meridian plane*. This is illustrated in Figure 15.2.

The polar plot is generated by plotting a locus of the radius vectors of field strength in one plane (i.e., the field strength for all points which are the same distance of at least several wavelengths from the antenna). Two plots

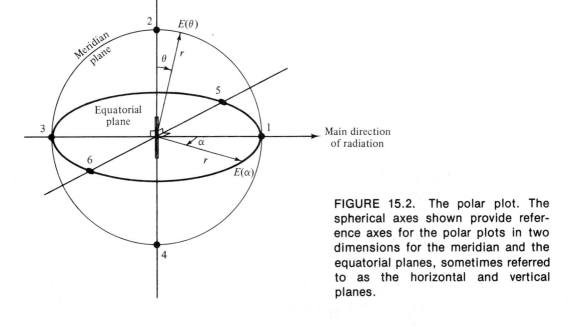

FIGURE 15.2. The polar plot. The spherical axes shown provide reference axes for the polar plots in two dimensions for the meridian and the equatorial planes, sometimes referred to as the horizontal and vertical planes.

are necessary to define the field strength for all directions in the case of the dipole, the meridian and the equatorial. If field strength is measured at a distance r from the doublet in a plane perpendicular to the wire axis for all angles of rotation around the origin (the antenna), it is found that the field strength is constant. The resulting plot is a circle centered on the origin. This is chosen as the equatorial plane.

Any plane perpendicular to the equatorial plane which contains the wire axis can be chosen as the meridian plane. When the field strength at the same constant distance r is plotted in this plane as a function of the angle of rotation Θ, the figure-of-eight plot of Figure 15.1(b) results, with the maximum axis coinciding with the equatorial plane.

The three-dimensional plot of the field-strength pattern could be generated for the doublet by rotating the meridian plot of Figure 15.1(b) around the $\Theta = 0$ axis, which would generate a toroid, or doughnut-shaped, solid figure.

The maximum value of field strength in the plot is usually taken as unity, and the resulting plot then gives the relative field strength as referred to this maximum value. It must be emphasized that the field-strength measurements or calculations must be made for a distance r which is at least several wavelengths from the antenna. If this condition is met, the polar plot of relative field strength will be practically independent of the distance r. Some polar plots show a dependency on the distance r because of interference produced by ground reflections from nearby objects. Usually the polar plot is given for the antenna as if it were in free space with no ground plane or nearby objects present.

15.6 ANTENNA POWER GAIN OR DIRECTIVITY

The *directive power gain* of an antenna is defined as the ratio of the total power input required to a reference antenna to the total power input required to the subject antenna to produce the same electric field intensity at the same distance along their lines of maximum radiation. The gain is usually expressed in decibels.

Two important results derived from theory are

Gain of the Hertzian dipole
relative to isotropic radiator　　$= 1.5{:}1$　(power ratio)

　　　　　　　　　　　　　　　　$= 1.76 \, \text{dB}$　　　　　　　　　(15.3)

Gain of $\tfrac{1}{2}\lambda$ dipole relative
to isotropic radiator　　　　　$= 1.64{:}1$　　(power ratio)

　　　　　　　　　　　　　　　　$= 2.15 \, \text{dB}$　　　　　　　　　(15.4)

The $\tfrac{1}{2}\lambda$ dipole is discussed in detail in Section 15.9.

It must be emphasized that directivity only refers to the comparison of power radiated along the line of maximum radiation for each antenna in question. It should not be confused with the comparison of power densities in different directions from the same antenna, such as the front-to-back ratio for a beam antenna.

The direct measurement of antenna gain is made by first measuring the power necessary in the antenna being measured to produce a reference level of field strength at a reference distance, and then finding the power necessary to produce the same level of field strength from a reference antenna such as a half-wave dipole. The gain over the half-wave dipole is measured directly and then multiplied by the theoretical gain of the dipole over the isotropic source to give the effective gain of the antenna over the isotropic source.

15.7 BEAMWIDTH AND POLARIZATION

Beamwidth is a measure of the directiveness of an antenna. When the polar plot of radiation in the meridian plane is derived or measured, it is seen that most of the energy from the antenna is radiated along certain "lobes" in the pattern. The beamwidth is a quantitative measure of the width of these lobes or beams, and is defined as the angular displacement between the two points of the major lobe of radiation at which the power received at a distant point is one half of that received on the axis of the lobe at the same distance. This may also be derived in terms of the field strength, and corresponds to the points where the field strength is 0.707 of the maximum. Figure 15.1(b) illustrates the beamwidth of a doublet antenna. In other words, the beamwidth is defined by the 3 dB vectors on either side of the maximum. For the Hertzian dipole, Figure 15.1(b), the *half*-beamwidth $\frac{1}{2}\beta$ is the complement of the angle Θ', i.e., $\frac{1}{2}\beta + \Theta' = 90°$. Thus the beamwidth is defined by sin $\Theta = 0.707$, which gives $\Theta' = 45°$ and a beamwidth $\beta = 90°$.

Practically, the beamwidth of an antenna is derived graphically from the generated polar plot of field strength in the meridian plane. It should be noted that certain types of antennas have lobes in the equatorial plane also, which may have beamwidths different from those in the meridian plane. A complete description of the antenna will contain a description of beamwidth in both planes.

Polarization of an antenna refers to the plane in which the electric field vector of the antenna is launched from the antenna. For doublets, this will be the meridian plane, which contains the length of the radiator wire. An antenna is said to be horizontally polarized if the electric field lies in a plane horizontal to the earth's surface. This is accomplished for the doublet by placing the doublet parallel to the earth and at some distance above it. Vertical polarization occurs when the radiator is placed vertically above the earth and the electric field is launched in the vertical plane. In some types of antennas the electric field is continuously changing its polarization by rotating around the line of transmission. In this case the antenna is said to be circularly polarized. Horizontal polarization is generally preferred because it does not pick up as much man-made interference, which is mostly vertically polarized. Low-frequency antennas are usually vertically polarized because the vertical is the most convenient structure for large antennas and because of the effect of ground losses (see Section 14.5).

15.8 RADIATION RESISTANCE

Radiation resistance is that value of resistance which if it replaced the radiation mechanism of an antenna, would dissipate exactly the same amount of power that the antenna radiated. This resistance is a fictitious but useful quantity which greatly simplifies the calculation of antenna efficiency.

Since any real wire carrying a current will also dissipate power because of its metallic resistance, antennas also exhibit I^2R losses. The total power delivered to the antenna from the feed cable is then the sum of losses dissipated in the antenna and the power radiated:

$$P_{in} = P_d + P_{rad} \tag{15.5}$$

If this power summation is now stated in terms of the driving current flowing in the antenna at its feed point,

$$I^2R_{in} = I^2R_d + I^2R_{rad} \tag{15.6}$$

and $$R_{in} = R_d + R_{rad}$$

From this expression it is seen that the resistance seen looking into the antenna terminals is the sum of the dissipation loss resistance R_d and the radiation resistance, R_{rad} . The efficiency of the antenna may now be stated as

$$\eta = \frac{R_{rad}}{R_{rad} + R_d} \times 100\% \tag{15.7}$$

It should be noted that the dissipation resistance of the antenna R_d is a combination of several things, representing loss in the wire radiator itself, and losses due to currents induced in nearby structures and in the earth itself. The gain of the antenna as defined in section 15.6 takes this efficiency into account.

Evaluation of the radiation resistance is difficult and follows from the integration to obtain the total radiated power in the calculation of antenna gain. Practically, this involves measuring the field strength contours of the antenna using the polar plots, and then estimating the total radiated power from these quantities.

At lower frequencies, efficiencies of 75 to 90 % can be easily achieved, with values approaching 100 % at higher frequencies. Radiation resistance values from a few ohms to several hundred ohms can be obtained, depending on the antenna structure and the choice of feed point.

15.9   HALF-WAVE DIPOLE

The *half-wave dipole* is a resonant antenna, the total length of which is nominally ½λ at the carrier frequency. Standing waves of voltage and current exist along the antenna, a good approximation to the distribution being obtained by assuming the antenna to be an opened-out ¼ λ section of an open-circuited transmission line. As shown in Section 12.7, the spacing between a standing wave maximum and minimum is ¼λ, and since the current must be zero at the open circuit, it will be a maximum ¼λ in from the end, while the voltage is a maximum at the end, going to a minimum at the ¼λ point. Figure 15.3(a) shows how the magnitude of voltage and current vary as a function of distance from the end, while Figure 15.3(b) shows the line opened out to form the ½λ dipole, along with the voltage and current distributions which are assumed unchanged. Because a 180° phase shift also occurs along the ¼λ section (½π radians for the incident wave, and ½π radians for the reflected wave in the opposite direction), it is convenient to show the voltage and current as in Figure 15.3(b). The voltage is assumed to go through zero at the feed point (in fact, it must remain at a small finite value), and the arrows inside the current curve indicate the change in polarity of current. Of course, the voltage must be finite at the feed point, and the amplitude distribution cannot be identical to that of the transmission line section since the geometry of the antenna is different; however, results based on these assumptions agree very well with the measured results. The ½λ dipole may then be considered as consisting of a large number of Hertzian dipoles connected in series, the current in each being determined by the current distribution shown in Figure 15.3(b). This alters the polar diagram from that of the Hertzian dipole, and for comparison, the field strength polar diagrams for both the Hertzian dipole and the ½λ dipole are sketched in Figure 15.3(c). These are the polar diagrams in the meridian plane; the corresponding equatorial plane diagrams are circles with radius equal to the maximum value in each case.

In Figure 12.8 is shown the impedance of an open-circuited transmission line as a function of length. This diagram may be used to obtain an idea

FIGURE 15.3. The half-wave dipole: (a) Current and voltage standing waves on an open-circuit line; (b) Current and voltage standing waves on a ½λ dipole; (c) Radiation of ½λ dipole compare to that of a Hertzian dipole.

of how the impedance of a ½λ dipole varies with frequency, remembering that the ½λ dipole corresponds to a ¼λ line length. At $l = \frac{1}{4}\lambda$, the impedance is seen to be zero, but this was for a lossless line; the antenna has losses, represented by the radiation resistance (plus conductor resistance which is usually negligible). At lower frequencies the fixed length l is less than ¼λ and the impedance is seen to be capacitive, while at higher frequencies the length l is greater than ¼λ and the impedance is seen to be inductive. Thus, at a frequency which makes the antenna length ½λ (or line length ¼λ), the impedance is purely resistive equal to the radiation resistance, and by choosing a line which has a characteristic impedance equal to the radiation resistance, there will be no standing waves on the *feeder section* of the line, as shown in Figure 15.3(b).

The physical length of the antenna wire is not a half-wavelength of the wave transmitted in free space, but a half-wavelength on a transmission line. The velocity of propagation of the waves on this line is slower than in space, and as a result the physical length of wire necessary to properly tune the antenna is less than a free-space wavelength by about 5%. This is true for frequencies below about 30 MHz.

Transmitted waves are rarely single-frequency waves but are modulated. All modulated waves are made up of a carrier and a number of side-band frequencies spread out on either side. Since the half-wave dipole (or any other tuned antenna) is resonant at only one frequency, and behaves like a frequency-dependent reactance at other frequencies, the sideband frequencies will be distorted somewhat. For narrow-band transmissions this distortion is not significant, but at higher bandwidths it can cause trouble. The characteristics can be improved slightly by spoiling the effective Q of the antenna by making the radiating conductors large in diameter. This has the effect of increasing the capacitance and lowering the inductance, and thus lowering the Q of the antenna. The result is a wider-frequency deviation between the 3-dB cutoff frequency points, or a wider bandwidth.

The radiation resistance of the half-wave dipole is about 73 Ω, which is very convenient for matching with 75-Ω coaxial cables. The radiation pattern in the meridian plane is similar to that for the elementary doublet, but, as shown in Figure 15.3(c), it is more pointed in the direction of the lobe. The beamwidth of the ½λ dipole is 78°. This pattern is valid only if the antenna is mounted sufficiently high above the ground (several wavelengths) so that ground reflections do not alter the pattern. The directive gain resulting is 1.64 over the isotropic antenna.

Resonance in the dipole is not limited to the half-wave frequency but occurs also at all integer multiples of the half-wave frequency. The current distributions are different for each case, and the result is a different radiation pattern for each resonant frequency. This is illustrated in Figure 15.4 for the cases of the effective length being 1, 2, 3, and 4 times the half-wavelength. It is seen from the drawings that the number of lobes on each side of the radiator is equal to the multiple of half-wavelengths used. The lobes are the result of waves from the different node sections causing multiple cancellations. Again these patterns are the ones that would result if the antenna were mounted free in space, away from reflections. It must also be noted that the current node occurs at different positions on the antenna length, and if a resonant feed point is to be maintained, it must be located at one of the current nodes that occur; that is, it must be located at ¼λ, ¾λ, $^5/_4$λ, ...away from either end of the radiator.

With the increase in the number of lobes, the lobes nearest the antenna axis will always be larger than the others. These are the major lobes, and they get progressively closer to the axis with increasing numbers of lobes.

15.10 VERTICAL ANTENNAS

15.10.1 Ground Reflections

The ground will act as an almost-perfect reflecting plane for any antenna placed near its surface, and an apparent mirror image of the

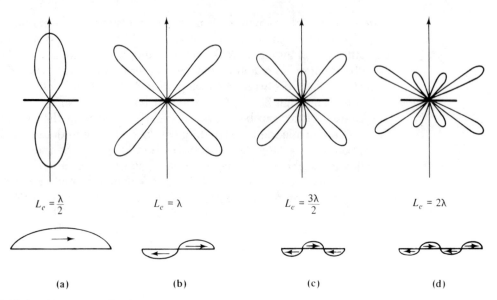

$$L_c = \frac{\lambda}{2} \qquad\qquad L_c = \lambda \qquad\qquad L_c = \frac{3\lambda}{2} \qquad\qquad L_c = 2\lambda$$

(a)   (b)   (c)   (d)

FIGURE 15.4.   Resonant dipole radiation patterns with their current distributions: (a) For $L_e = 1 \times \lambda/2$; (b) For $L_e = 2 \times \lambda/2$; (c) For $L_e = 3 \times \lambda/2$; (d) For $L_e = 4 \times \lambda/2$.

antenna will appear to be located immediately beneath the surface below the antenna. This is illustrated by Figure 15.5, which shows a distant observer receiving a direct wave from a point on the antenna, and a reflected wave which appears to come from the corresponding point on the image antenna.

Because of the interaction between the direct and reflected waves, the radiation polar pattern is drastically modified and appears to be the vector sum of radiation from two separate antennas, the real one and the image. The amount of interaction is dependent on how far above the ground the antenna is placed. If the effective height is several wavelengths, then practically no interaction will occur, and the antenna may be considered to be mounted in free space. For heights up to a few wavelengths, the reflections must be considered, and the antenna and its image act as a phased array of two antennas.

The image antenna is an exact mirror image of the real antenna and the apparent currents within it are at each point the same as those within the real antenna, except for reversed polarity. This is true whether the antenna is grounded or not grounded, horizontally or vertically polarized.

15.10.2   Grounded Vertical Antennas

Most of the medium-frequency (MF) broadcast antennas fall into this category, as do the VHF mobile-whip antennas. This type of antenna,

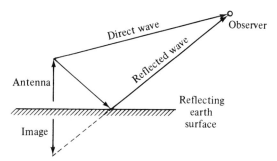

FIGURE 15.5.   A vertical antenna and its reflected image.

known as the *Marconi antenna*, is made up of a vertical mast, pole, or rod which forms the main radiating conductor. It may be free-standing, or supported by insulated guy wires, and is placed in a location where good electrical ground is available. Good locations for MF antennas include marshy fields and seacoast flats. If poor soil conditions exist, an artificial ground plane may be created by burying a mat of heavy conductors extending radially from the mast for up to at least a quarter-wavelength and preferably at least half a wavelength from the mast. The ends of the buried radials are usually connected together and deep grounding stakes driven at their extremities. The base of the mast is electrically insulated from ground, and the feed line from the transmitter is connected between the mast base and the ground. (In some special cases the feed point may be located at a current node farther up the mast.)

Since high-power transmitters may generate potentials of several hundred kilovolts on the antenna structure, high-quality insulators are a must. At lower frequencies special plastics such as polystyrene and Teflon are used.

The grounded vertical antenna combines with its image to act in exactly the same manner as a doublet or dipole, with the radiator vertical to the ground surface. Figure 15.6 shows grounded verticals of various lengths with the current distributions on the antenna and its image and the resulting radiation pattern in the vertical plane. The radiation pattern in the horizontal plane is circular. For vertical radiators of $\frac{1}{4}\lambda$ or less in effective height, the current distributions on the combined antenna–image structure is identical to a doublet or dipole of twice the length of the radiator, and produces a radiation pattern that is the same. However, half of the radiation pattern "appears" to lie below the ground surface, and in fact does not exist. All the power from the radiator is contained in that portion of the pattern which is above the surface. The $\frac{1}{4}\lambda$ vertical acts similarly to the half-wave dipole. The current distribution and radiation pattern are shown in Figure 15.6(a). The structure behaves like two antennas being fed in parallel, the radiation resistance is reduced to half that of the dipole, or about 36.5 Ω.

Figure 15.6(b) shows the current distributions and pattern for a $\frac{1}{2}\lambda$ vertical radiator. The structure no longer behaves like a combined dipole,

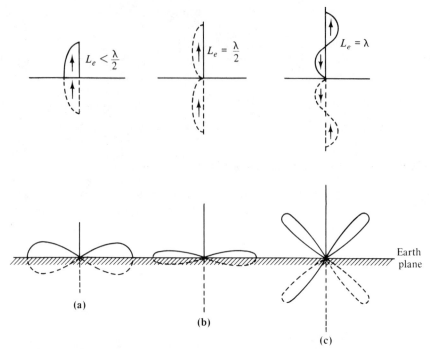

FIGURE 15.6. Grounded vertical radiators. Current distributions and vertical radiations patterns are shown for effective lengths of: (a) Less than $\lambda/2$; (b) $\lambda/2$; (c) λ.

but more like an array of two separate antennas of the same length fed 180° out of phase with each other. Each half is a $\frac{1}{2}\lambda$ antenna, and they are aligned so that their radiation patterns are in phase along the ground surface. This makes the antenna appear to have the same pattern shape as the $\frac{1}{2}\lambda$ dipole, but with an additional gain of 3 dB.

When the length of the radiator is increased above $\frac{1}{2}\lambda$, side lobes begin to appear, and the main lobe lifts off the ground. Figure 15.6(c) shows the result for the 1λ radiator. This is identical in shape to the pattern for the 1λ dipole shown in Figure 15.4(b), except that the bottom half of the pattern has been folded over and added to the top half. It is obvious from this that if a vertical is to radiate along the surface of the ground, it must not be higher than $\frac{1}{2}\lambda$, or too much power will be radiated into the sky. If sky waves are to be used, a longer radiator must be used to get the main lobe off the ground.

The $\frac{1}{4}\lambda$ verticals are favored because they may be fed directly with a cable at the low impedance current node which occurs at the base of the mast. At low frequencies it is often not physically feasible to build a mast which is a full $\frac{1}{4}\lambda$ in height, so a form of "top-hat" loading is employed to make the radiator look longer than it physically is. A horizontal wire is

connected to the top of the mast to make up the missing length. This may be a simple wire, as in the inverted L and T antennas, or it may be in the form of a disk. The length of the horizontal or the disk radius is adjusted so that the current node occurs at the base of the mast, and from the feed point the antenna appears to be a ¼λ tuned vertical. The current density in the horizontal portion is low and does not radiate nearly as much power as does the vertical portion, with the result that little change occurs in the radiation pattern. Some minor lobes in the upward direction do occur, but the major lobe is caused to lie closer to the ground because of more even current distribution within the vertical mast. This type of antenna is sometimes referred to as a *unipole antenna*, because only one radiating element is fed.

Grounded verticals are frequently used at VHF for mobile service because of their simple structure. In this case the radiator length varies from a few feet down to a few inches, and a real earth ground cannot be used. For fixed antennas a series of radial ground-plane rods are frequently used, while for the mobile antennas, the flat metal top of the vehicle is used to provide the ground plane. Figure 15.7 illustrates these grounds.

(b)

FIGURE 15.7. Whip antennas: (a) VHF vertical with simulated ground plane; (b) UHF mobile whip mounted on car top.

15.11 FOLDED ELEMENTS

The antennas discussed so far all use single-conductor radiators. However, if each conductor is twinned with a second conductor, insulated from it but closely parallel to it, and connected together at the voltage node points, then a similar current pattern will be induced in the second conductor. The radiation pattern will be exactly the same as for the single-conductor antenna, but the radiation resistance will be different. The radiation resistance will be just four times that produced by the single radiator. Thus a folded vertical antenna as shown in Figure 15.8(a) will have a radiation resistance four times that of the single vertical (4×36.5), or 146Ω. The folded dipole shown in Figure 15.8(b) has a radiation resistance of 4×73, or 292Ω.

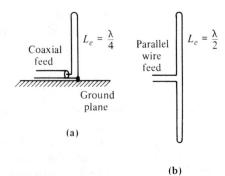

FIGURE 15.8. Folded dipoles: (a) Folded quarter-wave vertical; (b) Folded half-wave dipole.

The folded dipole antenna is favored as the driving element of VHF dipole arrays because it can be made with self-supporting tubing very inexpensively and provides a higher terminal impedance, which tends to offset the reduction of impedance resulting from the loading of the parasitic elements. Since the center of the second conductor is at a current node, it may be electrically connected to a grounded support rod without affecting the characteristics, making a very sturdy mechanical structure.

15.12   RECIPROCITY THEOREM FOR RECEIVING ANTENNAS

Any antenna that is used for transmitting may be used also for receiving. Its action as a receiving antenna will yield reciprocal results to those of a transmitting antenna, and these reciprocal relations are formalized in the *Rayleigh–Carson reciprocity theorem*. Some of the important consequences of this theorem, which are stated here without proof, are

1.   The directive gain of an antenna is exactly the same whether it is being used to transmit or to receive. This means that a polar diagram for an antenna derived under receive conditions for a given antenna will be identical to the one derived under transmit conditions. As a result, if identical antennas are used in a transmission link, and both are aligned to give maximum signal, the net dB antenna gain in the system will be exactly twice that of one of the antennas alone.

2.   The Thévenin equivalent circuit of the receiving antenna will be an induced EMF V_s in series with a terminal load resistance, and an antenna resistance which is identical to the radiation resistance that would occur if the antenna were being used to transmit (ignoring antenna losses).

3.   The antenna has the same effective length whether it is used for transmitting or receiving.

15.13 EFFECTIVE LENGTH

The effective length ℓ_{eff} of an antenna has different meanings for transmit and receive conditions, but as stated above, the same value applies for a given antenna for either condition.

Consider, first, a receiving dipole. For maximum induced signal, the dipole must lie parallel to the electric field of the wave, when the induced EMF is

$$V_s = E\ell_{\text{eff}} \qquad (15.8)$$

where E is the electric field strength of the wave at the receiving antenna and ℓ_{eff} is the effective length of the antenna under receiving conditions. The effective length is used in Example 14.2.

If the dipole is inclined at an angle Ψ to E, the induced EMF is reduced by a factor $\cos \Psi$; secondly, if the dipole is inclined at an angle Θ to the wavefront, the EMF is reduced further by a factor $\cos \Theta$. Under these conditions the effective length of the dipole becomes

$$\ell'_{\text{eff}} = \ell_{\text{eff}} \cos \Psi \cos \Theta \qquad (16.9)$$

Normally the antenna would be aligned experimentally for maximum induced signal, in which case $\cos \Psi = \cos \Theta = 1$; proper alignment is critical for good performance.

When used to transmit, the effective length of the antenna is determined as follows. The radiated field is proportional to the product of physical antenna length and average current, i.e., to the area under the current-length curve. Let I_o be the current at the input terminals to the antenna; then the effective length is defined as the length which, if it carried a uniform current I_o, would result in the same radiated field; i.e., the rectangular area $I_o \ell_{\text{eff}}$ is equal to the actual area under the current-length curve. As a specific example, for the ½ λ dipole, the current distribution is as shown in Figure 15.3(c), and from the transmission line theory, this is found to be cosinusoidal with a maximum value I_o. The average current is $(2I_o)/\pi$ and the area under the curve is

$$\text{Area} = \text{Average current} \times \text{Length}$$

$$= \frac{2I_o}{\pi} \cdot \frac{\lambda}{2} \qquad (15.10)$$

Hence

$$I_o \ell_{\text{eff}} = \frac{2I_o}{\pi} \cdot \frac{\lambda}{2} \qquad (15.11)$$

or

$$\ell_{\text{eff}} = \frac{\lambda}{\pi} \qquad (15.12)$$

For low and medium frequency antennas which are mounted vertically from the earth's surface, the effective length is usually referred to as the *effective height* h_{eff}. This is directly related to the physical height. Effective height must not be confused with the physical heights h_T and h_R introduced in Section 14.3. For example, a ½λ dipole may be mounted at some mast height h above the ground, but its effective length is *always* λ/π, as given by Eq. (15.12).

15.14 EFFECTIVE AREA (OR APERTURE) OF A RECEIVING ANTENNA

The effective area A_{eff} of a receiving antenna is defined by Eq. (14.3), and as stated for Eq. (14.4), the ratio of effective area to gain (relative to isotropic) is the same for all antennas, and is

$$\frac{A_{\text{eff}}}{G} = \frac{\lambda^2}{4\pi} \tag{15.13}$$

For a ½λ dipole, $G = 1.64$, and therefore

$$A_{\text{eff}} \ (\text{½λ dipole}) = 0.13\lambda^2 \tag{15.14}$$

For any antenna, the effective area can be expressed in terms of effective length. From the maximum power transfer theorem (Section 1.14), the received power P_R under matched conditions is

$$P_R = \frac{V_s^2}{4R_{\text{rad}}} \tag{15.15}$$

$$= \frac{(E \ell_{\text{eff}})^2}{4R_{\text{rad}}} \tag{15.16}$$

But from Eq. (B.12), $E^2 = P_D Z_0$, and from Eq. (14.12), $Z_0 = (120\pi)\,\Omega$. Also from Eq. (14.3), $P_R = P_D A_{\text{eff}}$, and substituting these in Eq. (15.15) gives

$$A_{\text{eff}} = \frac{30\pi \ell^2_{\text{eff}}}{R_{\text{rad}}} \tag{15.17}$$

Although the concept of an effective area may be difficult to associate with a wire antenna such as a ½λ dipole, the antenna does cast an "electromagnetic shadow," as a result of re-radiation from the induced currents. For microwave antennas employing parabolic reflectors, it can be shown that the effective area is approximated by the physical area of the reflector aperture.

15.15 LOOP AND FERRITE-ROD RECEIVING ANTENNAS

15.15.1 Loop Antenna

The *loop antenna* is made up of one or more turns of wire on a frame, which may be rectanglular or circular, and is very much smaller than one wavelength across. This antenna is popular for two reasons: (1) it is relatively compact, lending itself to use with portable receivers; and (2) it is quite directive, lending itself to use with direction-finding equipment.

A loop antenna is shown in Figure 15.9(a), with its radiation pattern. The radiation pattern is the doughnut shape of the doublet antenna, except

(a)　　　　　　　　　　(b)

(c)

FIGURE 15.9. Loop antennas: (a) Square-loop antenna with its radiation pattern; (b) Ferrite-rod antenna; (c) Equivalent circuit for the ferrite-rod antenna.

that the plane of the doughnut corresponds to the plane of the loop, so that the loop will radiate equally well in all directions within its own plane. A distinct null of response occurs along the axis of the loop, and it is this null which is used in direction finding. The physical shape of the loop does not drastically affect the radiation pattern except when the length and width of the loop are unequal, which yields a squashed doughnut shape.

Loop antennas made of several turns of wire around a rectangular frame were popular for earlier model broadcast receivers, with the loop being mounted in the back of the cabinet. Recently, these have been almost entirely replaced by the smaller ferrite-rod antenna.

When the loop is aligned for maximum signal strength, the magnetic flux linkages are BAN where B is the rms magnetic flux density in Teslas, A is the physical loop area in m^2, and N is the number of turns in the loop. The induced EMF is given by Faraday's law as the rate of change of flux linkages, which for a wave of angular frequency ω gives

$$V_s = \omega BAN \qquad (15.18)$$

When the loop is tuned by means of an external capacitor to the received frequency, the voltage at the capacitor terminal is magnified by the circuit Q to give

$$V_{max} = V_s Q = \omega BANQ \qquad (15.19)$$

Since the loop is usually much smaller than the received wavelength, the size of the induced voltage may be quite small. It can be increased by increasing any one of the factors in Eq. (15.19). The Q is determined by the desired selectivity; the area must be kept small; increasing the number of turns increases the coil inductance and changes the Q, and even changing the flux density B affects the Q. However, changing the flux density by using a magnetic core can be achieved with a minimal change of Q using ferrite cores. This alternative is now in widespread use.

15.15.2 Ferrite-Rod Antenna

The *ferrite-rod antenna* is made by winding a coil of wire on a ferrite rod similar to the one illustrated in Figure 15.9(b). Ferrites are materials that exhibit the properties of ferrimagnetism. The material exhibits a high relative permeability in the same manner as magnetic metals do, but unlike the ferromagnetic metals they also have a high bulk resistivity. This means that at high frequencies, eddy currents induced within the material are practically nonexistent and high-Q coils can be made. Typical values for μ are around 100 and for resistivity 10,000 Ω-cm. A high length-to-diameter ratio for the rod gives a high permeability, which is desirable.

The size of coil is a compromise of several factors. If the coil is too long compared to the rod length, the change of permeability with temperature will cause a noticeable change in the inductance. If it is too short, the Q will be low. Positioning the coil on the core is critical as well, since the effective permeability is a function of position on the rod, ranging from maximum at the center to a minimum at either end. The coil is usually placed near the quarter-point, allowing adjustment in either direction to trim the coil inductance. When more than one coil is mounted on the same rod, they must be placed at opposite ends to minimize interaction between them.

The coil of wire on the ferrite rod is basically a modified loop antenna, so the induced maximum EMF appearing at its terminals is given by

$$V_s = \omega BAN \cdot F \cdot \mu_r \qquad (15.20)$$

where F = modifying factor accounting for coil length, ranging from unity for short coils to about 0.7 for one that extends the full length of the rod

μ_r = effective relative permeability of the rod, as measured for the actual coil position

A = rod cross-sectional area.

An expression for the effective length of a ferrite rod antenna can be derived by combining Eqs. (B.4), (B.8), (15.8), and (15.20) to give

$$\ell_{\text{eff}} = \frac{2\pi ANF\mu_r}{\lambda} \qquad (15.21)$$

Since the voltage appearing at the terminals is of more importance in a receiving antenna, the factor $Q\ell_{\text{eff}}$ is often given as a figure of merit for rod antennas. The directional properties of the ferrite-rod antenna are similar to those of the loop antenna, although the null may not be quite so pronounced.

15.16 NONRESONANT ANTENNAS

15.16.1 Long-Wire Antenna

The *long-wire antenna* is just that, a wire several wavelengths in length that is suspended at some height above the earth. The wire is driven at one end and has a resistive termination at the remote end, which is matched to the characteristic impedance of the line at that end. This forms a transmission line with a ground return, and a matched termination. When an alternating current wave is transmitted down this line toward the terminated end, about half of the energy is radiated into space. Since there is no reflection at the far end, no return wave exists, and no standing waves appear on the wire, regardless of its length-to-wavelength ratio. Of the energy not radiated, a small amount is dissipated in the wire, and the remainder is dissipated in the terminating resistance.

The long wire is illustrated in Figure 15.10(a), with its horizontal radiation pattern. The radiation pattern shown would be true for any direction at right angles to the wire if the wire were mounted in free space. Usually it is a fraction of a wavelength above the ground, and ground reflections cause most of the energy to be radiated upward so that the vertical pattern would be a single lobe of twice the strength of the horizontal lobes.

This antenna is not often used because it is not very efficient, has a comparatively low gain, and takes up a lot of space. Also, matching the

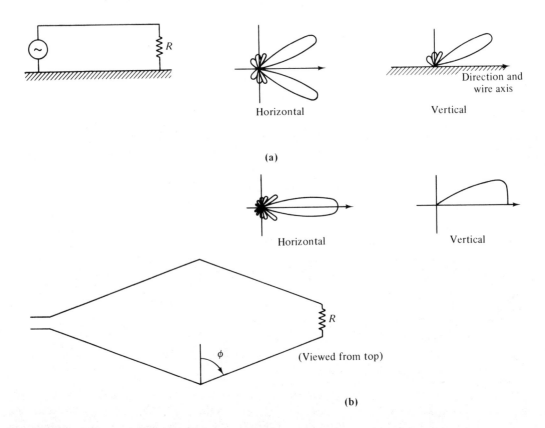

FIGURE 15.10. Nonresonant antennas: (a) The long-wire antenna, with its radiation patterns in the horizontal and vertical planes along the wire axis; (b) The rhombic antenna, with its radiation patterns in the horizontal and vertical planes along the rhombic major axis.

transmitter to the line can be a problem. However, since no standing waves exist, the antenna has no resonances, and as long as the length of the wire lies in the range 2λ to 10λ, its characteristics remain relatively constant for all frequencies in that range. It is thus used as a broadband antenna for low-cost point-to-point communications, especially in the HF band from 3 to 30 MHz. The upward tilt of the pattern lends itself to skywave propagation in this band.

15.16.2   Rhombic Antenna

The *rhombic antenna* takes its name from its diamond-shaped layout. It is an array of four interconnected long-wire antennas, laid out in the manner shown in Figure 15.10(b). Each of the four legs has the same length and lies in the range 2λ to 10λ. The transmission line feeds one end and transmits an unreflected current wave down each side toward the resistive termination at the far end. The lengths of the sides and the angle ϕ are interrelated and must be carefully chosen so that the side lobes cancel properly, leaving only a single main lobe lying along the main axis of the rhombus. Again, ground reflections cause the lobe to be tilted upward into the sky, and the amount of tilt is a function of the length of the legs.

The resistive termination is chosen so that no reflections occur, and the antenna is untuned, just as long wire is. Its frequency range is broad, almost 10 to 1, allowing a single structure to be used over most of the HF bands. It is highly directional and, if the tilt is chosen properly, is ideal for point-to-point skywave propagation.

The feed-point impedance falls in the range 600 to 800 Ω, allowing direct feed with an open-wire parallel line, and the terminating resistor is in the same range. The angle ϕ falls between 40° and 75° and the leg length between 2λ and 10λ. The resulting directive gain obtained with the rhombic ranges from 15 to 60. The physical structure is relatively simple and inexpensive and usually takes the form of four poles placed at the apexes of the rhombus and wires supported on tension insulators for the radiators. The feed line is a parallel line and can be any length within reason, although it is usual practice to place the transmitter house near the feed end of the rhombus. For example, a 2λ rhombic for 3 MHz would have diagonals of about 320 m long by about 250 m wide. This antenna is not practical in an urban environment.

15.17   DRIVEN ARRAYS

15.17.1   Broadside Array

The *broadside array* is a system of several identical antennas all laid out parallel to each other, each driven from the same source in phase with one another. Dipoles may be arrayed side by side as shown in Figure 15.11(a), with the spacing between them typically $\lambda/2$ to form a broadside array. Spacing is not critical, but the $\lambda/2$ value is convenient as the feeder may be crossed as shown in Figure 15.11(a) to maintain in-phase currents in the elements.

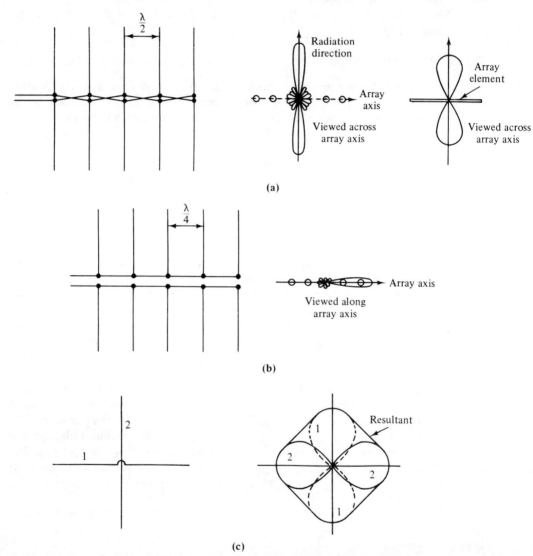

FIGURE 15.11.   Driven arrays: (a) Broadside array with radiation patterns seen from across and along the axis of the array; (b) End fire array with its radiation pattern seen across the axis of the array; (c) The turnstile antenna, showing its radiation pattern as the sum of two dipole patterns at right angles to each other.

At a point in the equatorial plane that is distant from the antenna but along a line perpendicular to the plane of the array, radiation from each of the elements will have traveled approximately the same distance and will arrive in phase so that the radiation from all elements add along that line.

At a distant point along the line of the array axis, since the elements are spaced by $\lambda/2$, the radiation from adjacent elements will arrive out of phase, and complete cancellation will occur along this axis. In a plane normal to the array axis, the polar diagram will be that of a single element of the array, while in the plane containing the array, little radiation occurs since radiation is zero from the ends of the dipoles and from the end of the array. The resulting radiation pattern has two main lobes perpendicular to the plane of the array. Small secondary lobes will be present in other directions, but these will be much smaller than the main lobe. Polarization is in the direction of the radiator axes. This pattern is illustrated in Figure 15.11(a).

Quite often the broadside array is used in conjunction with a second array of reflectors, which is made the same size and mounted a half-wavelength behind the main array. The back lobe is now reflected forward and adds directly to the forward lobe, improving its gain and directivity, and making the structure unidirectional. The reflectors may be driven, or they may be parasitic reflectors.

A variation of this array, known as *Collinear*, is formed when a number of dipoles driven in phase are spaced in line along the same axis. This array radiates equally well in all directions within the plane normal to the axis but produces very little radiation off this plane and none along the array axis. The radiation pattern is similar to the broadside pattern of Figure 15.11(a).

15.17.2 End Fire Array

The *end fire array* has a physical layout similar to the broadside array, but in this case the antennas are spaced and phased so that radiation from the back antenna arrives at each succeeding antenna just in time to be in phase with the radiation from it. A convenient arrangment is to space the elements $\lambda/4$ along the feeder as shown in Figure 15.11(b). All of the radiation is then directed along the axis of the array in the forward direction. The radiation pattern is a single beam aimed along the axis of the array from back to front. The spacing is not critical except that for a given spacing, each antenna must be fed with the proper phase lag so that the radiation adds along the axis. Longer radiators provide narrower beam widths. Polarization is in the radiator axes, so if the array is placed horizontal to the ground, the pattern will be horizontally polarized.

Both the broadside and the end fire arrays may be used for any frequency band. Because of their physical size, they are usually limited to the HF bands and higher, but have been used in the LF bands for point-to-point communications. Overseas broadcasting stations in the MF and HF bands frequently use them as well, for repeated broadcasting to the same distant area.

15.17.3 Turnstile Antenna

Figure 15.11(c) shows a simple *turnstile antenna*. It consists of two half-wave dipoles placed at right angles to each other and fed 90° out of phase with each other. This results in the two dipole patterns combining in the manner shown in Figure 15.11(c), producing an almost circular pattern in the plane of the turnstile. The pattern also has the feature that it is polarized in that same plane, so that if it were mounted in the horizontal plane, the antenna would radiate horizontally polarized waves about equally well in all directions along the ground. Several of these turnstiles may be stacked along a vertical axis and phased so as to improve the radiation directivity along the ground (i.e., in the plane of polarization). This type of antenna is frequently used for television broadcasting in the VHF-UHF bands.

15.18 PARASITIC ARRAYS

15.18.1 Parasitic Reflectors

Parasitic elements are secondary antennas which are placed in close proximity to the main or driven antenna. These parasitic elements are not directly fed, but have currents induced in them from the main element (or from the received wave in the case of a receiving antenna). These secondary antennas are tuned so as to cause a lagging or leading phase shift in energy which is reradiated from them and this changes the radiation pattern of the main antenna, as shown in Figure 15.12(a) and (b).

The reflector element is placed behind the driven dipole and is made about 5% longer than the driven ($\lambda/2$) dipole so that it is inductive. Spacing is adjusted until maximum radiation occurs along the normal in front of the dipole (array axis) as shown in Figure 15.12(a). Optimum spacing, which is found by experiment, is usually about 0.15λ.

15.18.2 Parasitic Directors

The director element, which is placed in front of the driven dipole, is made about 5% shorter than the dipole so that it is capacitive. It is spaced to provide maximum radiation in the forward direction, and optimum spacing is again found experimentally to be about 0.15λ. The pattern is shown in Figure 15.12(b).

15.18.3 Yagi-Uda Array

The *Yagi-Uda* (or simply the *Yagi*) *antenna* is a parasitic array comprising a driven half-wave dipole antenna which is usually a folded dipole, a

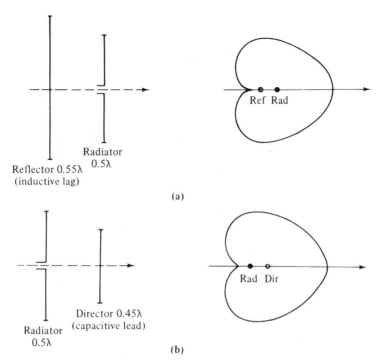

FIGURE 15.12. The effects of parasitic elements on the radiation pattern of a dipole: (a) Reflector; (b) Director.

single parasitic reflector, and one or more (up to 13) director elements with each director cut to act as if the previous one were the driven element, so that the whole structure tapers in the direction of propagation. The structure is illustrated in Figure 15.13. All the elements are electrically fastened to the conducting, grounded central support rod. This has no effect on the currents since the support point in the center of each element is at a current node.

Only one reflector need be used since the addition of a second or third reflector adds practically nothing to the directivity of the structure. The directive gain is improved considerably by the addition of more directors to give directive gains from about 7 dB for a three-element Yagi to about 15 dB for a five-element Yagi. The pattern consists of one main lobe lying in the forward direction along the axis of the array, with several very minor lobes in other directions. Polarization is in the direction of the element axes.

A folded dipole is often used as the driven element to raise the antenna terminal impedance. The parasitic elements are quite closely coupled to the driven element and result in lowering of the effective radiation resistance. The four-times multiplication of the folded dipole brings the impedance level back up to reasonable levels. A Yagi with a folded dipole would have a terminal reistance of 200 to 300 Ω.

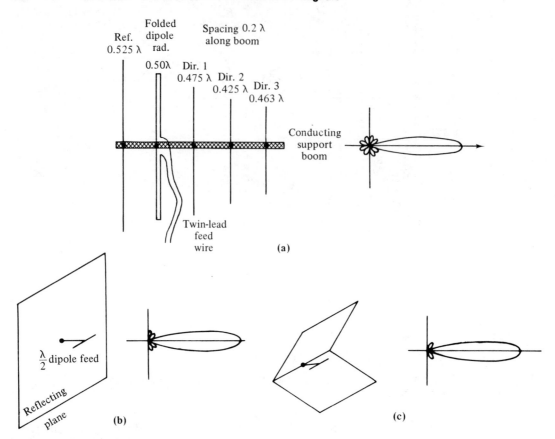

FIGURE 15.13. (a) A five-element Yagi-Uda array; the structure of the antenna is shown with its dimensions and the radiation pattern along its major axis. (b) A plane reflector with a dipole feed. (c) A corner reflector with a dipole feed.

This type of antenna would be very bulky at low frequencies but is used most often in the VHF range. Radio amateurs have built Yagis for the 20-m band, but the structure is large and cumbersome. Its high directional gain makes it ideal for point-to-point fixed-frequency communications networks, either at terminal or at repeater stations. They have also been used for base stations on mobile communications systems where the working area is strung out along a line, such as railroads, highways, or pipelines.

15.18.4 Plane Reflector Arrays

At UHF it is common practice to use a *plane reflecting surface,* either a flat surface or a corner of two surfaces, in place of the single reflector element of the Yagi. The reflecting surface must be at least one wavelength across in each direction, and can be much larger. It may be a solid metal surface, or it may be wire mesh or a network of interconnected metal rods.

Somewhat sharper directivity is obtained with the corner reflector, shown in Figure 15.13(b), but only in the plane across the fold.

The plane reflector is arranged so that the driven dipole (or directional antenna of any type) is mounted a quarter-wavelength ahead of the reflector surface. A mirror image of the driven antenna occurs a ¼-wavelength behind the surface, and appears to radiate a wave which arrives at the driven antenna in phase with the driving antenna radiation, but delayed one period. The resulting radiation pattern appears to be the vector sum of the radiation from two in-phase antennas, one of which is the image.

15.19 VHF–UHF ANTENNAS

15.19.1 Discone Omni

The *discone antenna* is designed to radiate an omnidirectional pattern in the horizontal plane, with vertical polarization. It is a broadband antenna with usable characteristics over a frequency range of nearly 10:1. It is usually designed to be fed directly from a 50-Ω coaxial line and is mounted directly on the end of that line. The discone is illustrated in Figure 15.14(a).

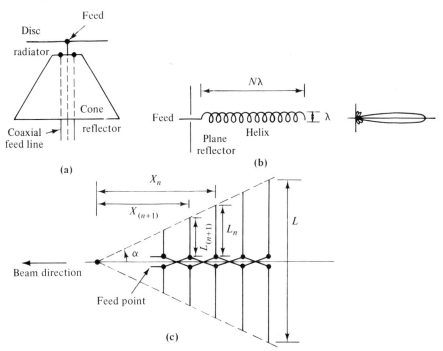

FIGURE 15.14.   VHF-UHF antennas: (a) Discone omnidirectional antenna; (b) End fire helix antenna; (c) Log periodic dipole array.

This type of antenna is ideal for base-station operation for urban mobile communication systems, since it gives a good omnidirectional pattern, is physically very compact and rugged, and is quite inexpensive to construct. Its directional gain along the horizontal plane is comparable to that of the dipole antenna.

15.19.2 Helical Antenna

The radiator element of a *helical antenna* is basically a coil of wire. If the helix diameter is much less than one wavelength, its length less than one wavelength, and it is center-fed, the whole structure will behave very much like a compact dipole antenna and radiates in the "normal" mode. Since the current wave must propagate along the helix conductor, its actual velocity along the axis will be much less than free-space velocity. That velocity will be determined by the diameter and pitch of the helix coil, and the half-wave resonant length of the helix will physically be very much less than the free-space half-wavelength. For most combinations of helix, the polarization is elliptical. This type of antenna is sometimes used in locations where it is not possible to mount a full-sized dipole, such as in urban areas, or on rooftops.

If the helix diameter is made approximately one wavelength, and the helix made several wavelengths long and end-fed, the helix radiates in an end fire mode, producing a narrow beam of circularly polarized waves. The 3-dB beam width obtainable with single helixes is on the order of 15° to 30°. When used in this mode, the radiator is usually end-fed and a plane reflector is placed behind the feed end. The result is a highly directional antenna which is physically compact and which can be easily mounted on a movable table for tracking moving sources. Arrays of end fire helixes are often used for tracking satellites. These structures are much less expensive than the large parabolas used for radio astronomy and have been very popular with amateur satellite trackers. The end fire helix is illustrated in Figure 15.14(b).

15.19.3 Log Periodic Antenna

The *log periodic antenna* is basically an array of dipoles, fed with alternating phase, lined up along the axis of radiation. The structure is illustrated in Figure 15.14(c). The element lengths and their spacing all conform to a ratio, which is given as

$$\tau = \frac{L_{(n+1)}}{L_n} = \frac{X_{(n+1)}}{X_n}$$

(15.22)

Also, the angle of divergence is given as

$$\alpha = \tan^{-1}\left(\frac{L_n}{X_n}\right)$$

(15.23)

The open-end length L must be larger than $\frac{1}{2}\lambda$ if high efficiency (90%) is to be obtained.

This antenna has the unique feature that its impedance is a periodic function of the logarithm of the frequency, and hence its name. The antenna characteristics are broadband, and it has the directional characteristics of a dipole array. This type of antenna is often used for mobile-base-station operations, where many channels must be handled over a single antenna system with good directive characteristics.

15.20 MICROWAVE ANTENNAS

15.20.1 Horns

Radio waves can be radiated directly from the end of a waveguide in the same way as from the end of an open transmission line. The end of the waveguide represents an abrupt transition from the characteristic impedance of the waveguide into that of free space and the radiation resulting is neither efficient nor very directive. This state of affairs can be improved considerably by flaring out the end of the waveguide to form a hornlike structure. A gradual transition can thus take place as the wave passes from the mouth of the horn.

Narrow-mouthed horns with long flare sections produce sharper beams than the shallow, wide-mouthed ones. Also, the wider-mouthed horns tend to produce a wavefront with a distinct curvature, which is undesirable. The ideal would be for the waves to leave the horn with a completely planar wavefront, and to accomplish this a focusing mechanism may be used with the horn such as a curved reflector or a lens.

Three types of horns are shown in Figure 15.15. The first is the sectoral horn, which is flared in only one plane, Figure 15.15(a); the second is the pyramidal horn, which is flared in both planes, Figure 15.15(b). Both of these are used with rectangular waveguides. The third is conical, Figure 15.15(c), and is used with a circular waveguide to produce a circularly polarized beam. Horn-type antennas do not provide very high directivity but are of simple, rugged construction. This maked them ideal as primary feed antennas for parabolic reflectors and lenses.

The choice of horn dimensions is dependent on the desired beam angle and directive gain and involves specification of the ratio of flare length to wavelength L/λ and flare angle ϕ.

15.20.2 Parabolic Reflectors

The *parabolic reflector* is a dish-shaped metal reflector which is formed so that the cross section made by a plane along the focal axis is a parabolic curve. The surface of this reflector is a paraboloid, which can be produced by rotating the parabolic cross section around its focal axis. The cross section

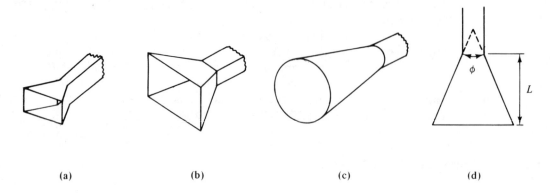

(a)   (b)   (c)   (d)

FIGURE 15.15.   Microwave horn antennas: (a) Sectoral horn; (b) Pyramidal horn; (c) Conical horn; (d) Horn flare dimensions.

of such a reflector is shown in Figure 15.16. The parabolic curve has the feature that the distance from the focal point F to the parabolic curve A and back to a plane perpendicular to the axis CD at B is a constant no matter at what angle the line FA leaves the focal axis, so

$$FA + AB = FA' + A'B' = FA'' + A''B'' = \text{constant} \quad (15.24)$$

The value of the constant controls the size and shape of the parabola and can be different for different antennas.

If an isotropic radiator is placed at the focal point, waves leaving the focal point in phase must all travel the same distance to arrive at the mouth plane CD. The result is a planar wavefront which radiates in only one direction along the focal axis, producing a narrow beam along the focal axis.

To get maximum efficiency and narrowest beam width, any radiation in the forward direction from the source which does not fall on the parabolic reflector must be rereflected back toward the reflector. Ideally, the source antenna should be one that will "illuminate" the reflector surface evenly over its entire area, but not radiate any energy outside that surface. Usually the primary radiators are dipoles and horns. The horn antennas come closest to meeting the requirement for even illumination.

Since neither the horn nor the dipole provide perfectly even illumination of the parabola surface, and the dipole radiates in the forward direction as well, the beam is not as directive as it should be. Side lobes, usually very small, are present, and the main beam is wider that it should be. Further degradation of the characteristic results because of the need to mount the feed antenna structure directly in the line of radiation from the reflector.

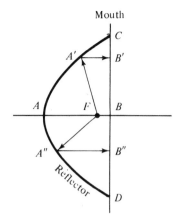

FIGURE 15.16. The parabolic reflector antenna
in cross section.

Fringing around this antenna and its supports cause further side lobes to be produced, as well as a significant reduction in the total area available for receiving. Some of the more important characteristics of parabolic reflector antennas follow.

The parabolic reflector is entirely analogous to its optical counterpart, and it, too, has an aperture number given by

$$\text{aperture} = \frac{\text{focal length}}{\text{mouth diameter}} = \frac{FA}{CD} \qquad (15.25)$$

The gain relative to a $\lambda/2$ dipole of a parabolic reflector with aperture diameter D and assumed to be uniformly illuminated is

$$G = 6\left(\frac{D}{\lambda}\right)^2 \qquad (15.26)$$

The effective aperture under these conditions is equal to the physical aperture. Most usually, with nonuniform illumination, the gain is less and the effective aperture is reduced to about 0.65 times the physical aperture. The beamwidth of the antenna is described in terms of the 3-dB beam angle, given by

$$\phi'_{3\,dB} = \frac{70\lambda}{D} \qquad (15.27)$$

$$\phi_{null} = 2\phi_{3\,dB} \qquad (15.28)$$

Example 15.1   Find the gain, beamwidth, and capture area for a parabolic antenna with a 6-m-diameter dish and dipole feed at a frequency of 10 GHz.

Solution

$$\lambda \; = \frac{c}{f} = \frac{300 \times 10^{6}}{10 \times 10^{9}} = 0.03 \text{ m} = 3 \text{ cm}$$

$$A \; = \frac{\pi D^2}{4} = \frac{3.14 \times 6^2}{4} = 28.26 \text{ m}^2$$

$$A_{\text{eff}} \; = 0.65A = 18.4 \text{ m}^2$$

$$G \; = \frac{4\pi}{\lambda^2} A_{\text{eff}} = 257{,}000 \; (54.1 \text{ dB})$$

$$\phi_{3\text{ dB}} \; = \frac{70\lambda}{D} = \frac{70 \times 0.03}{6} = 0.35°$$

$$\phi_{\text{null}} \; = 2 \,_{3\text{ dB}} = 2 \times 0.35 = 0.70°$$

15.20.3 Variations on the Parabolic Reflector

The *parabolic reflector* is a favorite antenna for fixed point-to-point microwave communications systems. It is relatively simple in construction, and unless large in size, quite inexpensive. Huge steerable parabolic dishes have been built for use with the radio telescopes, up to 200 ft in diameter, and mounted on a movable turret which allows rotation in both the horizontal and vertical directions to allow the tracking of moving targets such as satellites and radio stars.

Antennas used for radioastronomy must utilize all their area for reception to get the highest efficiency and the lowest noise figure. Special feed systems are used so that the feed antenna is reduced in size or physically located out of the path of the incoming radiation. Two types of feed are shown in Figure 15.17. The first of these uses a dipole antenna, which normally radiates outside the parabola as well as onto it, but has a spherical reflector placed directly in front of the dipole to prevent direct radiation. The forward radiation is reflected back at the parabola and is added to the main portion of the radiation. Some tuning is necessary since the reflector position is different for different frequencies.

The second method is known as the *Cassegrain feed system*, Figure 15.17(b). The horn feed antenna, the paraboloid reflector, and the hyperboloid subreflector have a common axis of symmetry as shown, and the virtual focal point of the hyperboloid is coincident with the focal point of the paraboloid. Radiation reflected off the subreflector illuminates the main reflector approximately uniformly, and equally important, "spill-over" at the edges is low. This is of particular advantage in low-noise receiving systems where large spill-over results in high noise levels.

Two types of modified horns also use parabolic surfaces. The first of these is the *Cass horn*, Figure 15.17(c). Incoming radiation is reflected from a large lower parabolic section which has a rectangular sectional front and forms the bottom of the horn, up to a smaller parabolic surface which forms the top of the horn, and then to a horn antenna located at the focal point of

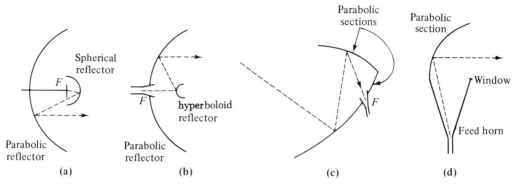

FIGURE 15.17. Methods of feeding microwave antennas: (a) Parabolic reflector fed from a dipole and a small spherical reflector; (b) Parabola fed from a horn and a small hyperboloid reflector, called the Cassegrain feed; (c) Cass horn; (d) hog horn.

the combined parabolas. This horn has the advantage that incoming radiation is not blocked by the feed structure, but it is much more complex to build.

The second horn is the *hog horn*, Figure 15.17(d). This is basically a large horn antenna with a parabolic reflector mounted directly in front of it and oriented to radiate at right angles to the axis of the horn. It is often used for microwave communication links, such as the Bell TD-2 system, because it is compact and simple in construction while giving the high directivity of the parabola and also high efficiency. It also has the advantage that it may be rotated at the neck on a sliding joint, allowing steering of the beam without undue manipulation.

15.20.4 Dielectric Lens Antennas

Electromagnetic radiation is refracted when it passes through the surface separating a zone of lower dielectric constant from one of higher dielectric constant in exactly the same manner that light is refracted. The angles of incidence and refraction are related by the modified version of Snell's law, which states that [referring to Figure 15.18(a)]

$$\frac{\sin \phi_r}{\sin \phi_i} = \sqrt{\frac{\epsilon_{ri}}{\epsilon_{rr}}} = \frac{1}{n} \qquad (15.29)$$

for waves entering the region of high dielectric constant, where n is the refractive index of the material. The refractive property is reciprocal, and the same relationships pertain when the radiation passes from the higher dielectric medium into the lower dielectric medium, except that the subscripts *i* and *r* are interchanged.

The material used for the lens is usually one of the high-dielectric plastics, such as polystyrene or Teflon.

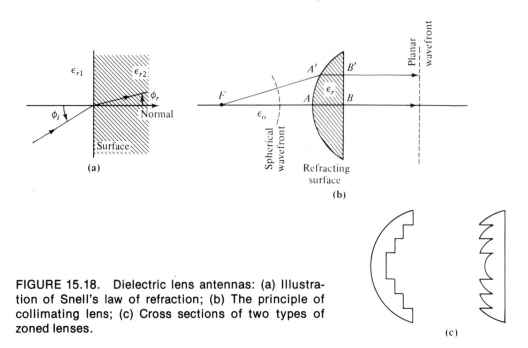

FIGURE 15.18. Dielectric lens antennas: (a) Illustration of Snell's law of refraction; (b) The principle of collimating lens; (c) Cross sections of two types of zoned lenses.

Figure 15.18(b) illustrates the principle of the collimating lens, which is used to make a diverging beam of radiation into one traveling in only one direction with a planar wavefront. The lens in this case is a convex one. Radiation along the axis of the lens passes through both surfaces at right angles, so no refraction takes place. Radiation at an angle from the axis is incident at the curved interface at an angle other than normal and is refracted toward the normal as it passes into the lens, at A'. The curvature of the lens is such that the rays after refraction are all parallel to the axis.

Radiation at the angle along FA' takes slightly longer to reach the refracting surface, and arrives with a slight time lag compared to that along the axis FA. However, the velocity of propagation within the dielectric is slower than that in air, and a compensating delay occurs in the radiation along the axis AB as compared to that along $A'B'$, and all the radiation arrives at the flat interface BB' in phase. The result is a planar wavefront leaving the lens.

Many types of lens systems can be used for the collimating or paralleling function. Two of these are shown in Figure 15.18(c). These are *zoned lenses*, which are basically the same in function as the convex lens illustrated in Figure 16.18(b). However, the zoned structure allows a large reduction in the volume of dielectric material which must be used to make the lens, with a corresponding saving in cost and weight. This saving is made at slight sacrifice of directivity.

Again, ideally, the lens should be fed with even illumination over its entire surface to achieve maximum efficiency and gain. The horn antenna is the most popular method of feed, and most closely approximates the even-illumination requirement. For the higher microwave frequencies, the lens makes a very compact, highly directive narrow-beam antenna which is popular for applications such as portable communication links and mobile radar systems of the type used for vehicle-speed monitoring.

15.20.5 Slot Antennas

When a slot in a large metallic plane is coupled to an R.F. source it behaves like a dipole antenna mounted over a reflecting surface. Figure 15.19(a) shows a rectangular slot in a large plane. It is coupled to a line or feed waveguide in such a manner that the E field lies along the short axis of the slot, as indicated. At microwave frequencies, the slot may be energized as described in Section 13.2.5. At lower frequencies, a transmission line may be connected directly across the slot as shown in Fig. 15.19(a).

The behavior of this *slot antenna* can be shown to be equivalent to complementary antenna in which the slot is replaced by a sheet dipole with a reflector behind it in free space, as shown in Figure 15.19(b). The dimensions of the slot are usually such that the long axis is approximately a half-wavelength at the operating frequency. The resulting radiation pattern is similar to that for the dipole with a reflector.

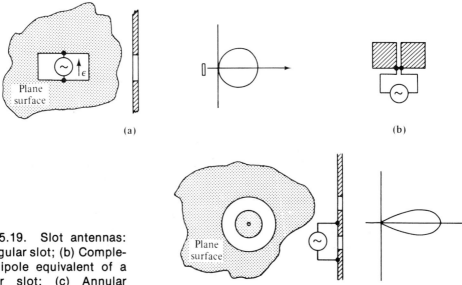

(a)

(b)

(c)

FIGURE 15.19. Slot antennas: (a) Rectangular slot; (b) Complementary dipole equivalent of a rectangular slot; (c) Annular slot.

The feed impedance of the slot can be calculated by first calculating the impedance for the complementary dipole. The actual slot impedance is related to the dipole impedance by the complementary characteristic, which states that

$$Z_r \times Z_c = \left(\frac{Z_{0\ space}}{2} \right)^2 = (60\pi)^2 \qquad (15.30)$$

where Z_r is the radiation impedance of the slot and Z_c the radiation impedance of the complementary (dipole) antenna. The shape of the slot does not have to be rectangular but can be any convenient shape. Rectangular and circular (annular) slots are favored because they are easy to make and relatively easy to analyze. Figure 15.19(c) shows an annular slot, which produces a narrow beam of radiation.

Arrays of slots are ideal for use in aircraft. The slots can be formed directly in the metal skin of the aircraft, and then windowed with a dielectric material such as polystyrene. The smooth surface produced does not interfere with the streamlining of the aircraft. Phasing the feed to the slots allows production of a beam which may be swept through a wide angle without physically moving the structure, thus allowing its use for mobile radar systems.

A variation of the slot antenna is the *notch antenna,* where an appropriately shaped notch is cut out of the edge of a large metal surface and connected to an R.F. source. Again, the chief use is on aircraft, where the notches can be made in the edges of the wing surfaces, and filled with dielectric material to make them aerodynamically smooth.

15.21 PROBLEMS

1. An isotropic antenna radiates energy equally in all directions. The total power delivered to the radiator is 100,000 W. Calculate the power density and electric field intensity at distances of: (a) 100 m; (b) 1 km) (c) 100 km; (d) 1000 km. Plot the power density against distance on log-log paper.

2. An elementary doublet has an electrical length of 0.0625λ and carries an RF current of 2.5 A rms. Calculate the field intensity at a point located 40 km from the doublet and at an angle of $25°$ from the main lobe of radiation.

3. Plot the normalized radiation pattern for a dipole antenna, using Eqn. (15.1) on a polar graph, for $0 < \Theta < 360°$. Calculate values for each $10°$ displacement of Θ.

4. A directional antenna has an effective radiated power of 1.1 kW

when it is fed with a terminal input power of 90 W. The radiation resistance is found to be 74 Ω at resonance and the measured antenna current is 1.088 A rms. Find: (a) antenna efficiency; (b) terminal resistance; (c) antenna power loss; (d) antenna directive gain, in dB, over an isotropic radiator.

5. Calculate the 3-dB beam width of the doublet antenna in Problem 3.

6. Calculate the effective length of an antenna which has a directive gain over an isotropic antenna of 17 dB and a radiation resistance of 350 Ω at a frequency of 144 MHz.

7. Calculate the current induced in the terminals of a vertical receiving antenna if it has a gain of 6 dB over isotropic antenna, a terminal impedance of 35 Ω, a load impedance of 35 Ω, and is in an electric field with an intensity of 10μ V/m, at a frequency of 7 MHz.

8. Calculate the capture area of the antenna in Problem 7.

9. A loop antenna is made by winding 10 turns of wire on a 1-m² frame. It is located in a magnetic field of 0.015 μ Teslas, at 10 MHz and oriented for maximum signal strength. Find: (a) induced EMF in the antenna; (b) terminal voltage if the antenna is tuned to resonance at 10 MHz, with a total resistance of 65 Ω in series with a 25-pF capacitor.

10. A direction finder using a loop antenna is used to locate an illegal transmitter. The operator goes to location A, where he receives a good signal. He mounts his receiver so that the antenna faces due north and then rotates the antenna from 0° north clockwise through 48° to obtain a null. He moves the direction finder to a new location B, which he determines is exactly 2550 m due east of A, and obtains a new bearing by rotating the antenna 15° counterclockwise from 0° north. Compute the distance from point A and from point B to the transmitter.

11. Calculate the effective length of a ferrite-rod receiving antenna which has 120 turns wound on a 1.40-cm-diameter ferrite rod which has a relative permeability of 160. Assume the length factor to be 0.75 and the frequency to be 1 MHz.

12. Calculate the lengths of the elements and spacing for a five-element Yagi antenna for Channel 4 television (66 to 72 MHz). The effective length factor is to be 5%, and each element is to be 95% of the previous one in length.

13. Calculate the element lengths for a 10-element log-periodic array if the smallest element is not less than 10% of the largest element, the angle of divergence $\alpha = 15°$, and the longest element is cut for a frequency of 50 MHz.

14. (a) Specify the diameter of parabolic reflector necessary if it is to provide a gain of 75 dB at a frequency of 15 GHz. The area factor in the feed is 0.65. (b) Calculate the capture area of the antenna and its 3-dB beam-width.

Part Five
Communications Systems

Chapter 16
Telephone Systems

16.1 WIRE TELEPHONY

16.1.1 Telephone Circuits

The word *telephone* is derived from the Greek words *tele*, meaning far, and *phone*, meaning sound. In today's context, *telephony* involves the conversion of the sound signals into an audio-frequency electrical signal which can then be transmitted over an electrical transmission system and then reconverted to sound pressure signals at the receiver end. The electrical signals may be transmitted by radio or by wire, and a system may well use both means to establish any given circuit. The wire telephone system was the earliest of such systems and still forms the backbone of modern communications.

Telephone systems may be categorized by the mode of transmission used. The simplest is a single one-way voice system which connects a single transmitter in one location to a single receiver in another location. Such one-way systems are rare, and most systems provide two-way communications in one of the following two ways.

The *simplex* system allows transmission in only one direction at a time but provides communication in either direction alternately on a push-to-talk basis. The operator at the end originating the transmission closes a switch to turn on the transmitter and turn off the receiver, so that he or she may talk toward the far-end receiver. As long as the receiving operator does not close his transmit switch, he will receive the signals from the far end. If both should attempt to transmit at the same time, the message will be lost and must be repeated. Simplex operation is most often used with radio systems, where transmission in both directions must take place on the same frequency.

Duplex systems allow simultaneous transmission in both directions. This may be accomplished by simply providing two separate circuits, one for each direction, but this is not economical because of duplication of facilities. Duplex in most telephone systems means simultaneous transmission over the same pair of wires without the need for switching. Since most telephone systems today use full duplex operation, this mode will be described in detail.

A telephone system must satisfy the following requirements. It must be able to transmit voice signals in both directions. It must provide a means of signaling from each terminal toward the other. This signal originally only summoned the person at the far receiver, but this rapidly was changed to the process of signaling a central operator who connected the desired line and then signaled the far-end receiver. The same signal channel is used in automatic telephone systems to operate automatic line-switching apparatus at the central location, so that an intermediate operator is not needed.

A simple two-point telephone circuit uses a single pair of wires (or one wire with ground return) and two telephone sets of the self-contained type used on manually operated rural multiparty lines. Each set is self-contained and does not use any central office equipment. The telephone set is similar to that used in the subscriber loop circuit of Figure 16.1, except that the dial pulsing unit is left out, and a battery and a source of ac such as a hand-cranked alternator for signaling are included. With all of the handsets hung on the hook switches, the signaling circuit is complete, and turning the alternator crank at one set will cause the bells at all other sets to ring. Several sets may be included on one line in the multiparty configuration. When the handsets are picked up, the battery in each set is connected to the carbon transmitter and the conversation may proceed. Only the ac component of the voice is transmitted on the line.

Telephone systems that require switching at a central location to connect the calling party line to the called party line operate on a "loop" basis. The telephone "subscriber's loop" consists of a pair of wires between the subscriber's location and the telephone switching center, a telephone terminal set, and a circuit at the switching location to supply battery current, signaling current, and a means of connecting to the switching machine.

Figure 16.1 shows a typical subscriber's loop circuit which might be used with a step-by-step or cross-bar switching office. Signaling inward is

FIGURE 16.1. A telephone subscriber's loop circuit.

done by dc switching, while signaling outward is an ac source to ring the subscriber's bell. The subscriber's terminal consists of a handset containing a carbon transmitter and an earphone receiver. This is connected to the line through an autotransformer (induction coil) which provides the necessary impedance matching between the line and the handset. The impedance ratios are adjusted so that the "sidetone" or signal feedback from the local transmitter into the local receiver is adjusted to an acceptable level, while still providing a good match to the line itself. If sidetone is extremely objectionable, a special transformer is included which cancels out part of the sidetone while not interfering with normal operation. A signal bell is connected across the line through the hook-switch contact.

Current to operate the transmitter is supplied from the central office battery over the loop pair. This current also passes through the pulsing contact B in the dial pulsing unit, which interrupts current to transmit the coded information to select the proper "address" in the automatic switching machine. Contact A closes to short-circuit the receiver while dialing is in progress so that the dialer is not subjected to the clicks of the pulse train. It releases as the dial returns to its rest position.

The loop circuit at the central office location contains a bridging transformer which allows separation of the voice signal from dc signaling current. The direct current is supplied from the common central office battery through the coils of the sensitive E relay, which relays the dial pulses and the fact that the hook switch is open (busy), and two ballast resistors which are used to compensate for different loop resistances and provide about the same value of loop current regardless of loop length. A second M relay operates on a demand signal from the switching machine to connect the ac bell-ringing supply to the line. Signaling operation is now described.

On originating a call, the subscriber picks up the handset, which closes the hook switch to connect the handset to the line and disconnect the bells. This action closes the dc path in the loop, and the flow of direct current from the central battery picks up the E relay. The E-relay contacts send a signal to the switching machine, indicating that the line is busy, and also disengage the M or ringing relay. The talking circuit is now energized. A slow-operating relay also operates to "hold" the busy condition during dialing. Operating the dial sends several trains of 1 to 10 pulses at a rate of about 10 pulses per second through the E relay to select the proper switch combination in the switching machine. If the called line indicates a busy condition, a special busy tone is sent back. If it is not busy, the M relay of the called loop is energized and a special ringing tone is sent back to the originator's receiver to indicate that signaling is proceeding.

When the demand signal from the switching machine energizes the M relay to the called loop, its contacts connect the ac ringing source to the line. This signal is an ac supply of several hundred volts at 20 Hz frequency which is interrupted for about 1 out of every 2 s, and which rings the bell at the called station. When the called party lifts his receiver, his hook switch closes the dc path in the called loop, operates the E relay, and disconnects the M relay and ringing source. The conversation can then proceed.

Loop lengths are primarily limited by the dc resistance in the loop. If the dc loop resistance becomes greater than about 1200 Ω, dc signaling becomes unreliable. Depending on the type of cable used for the loop pair, this value of resistance allows loops from as little as 3 miles using 26 AWG copper to as much as 28 miles using 16 AWG copper. Open wire lines using heavy-gauge copper-clad steel conductors are frequently used for long rural loops.

A further limitation is placed on the loop length by the attenuation factor of the cable. Loops with losses in excess of 10 dB total are not acceptable, and repeater amplifiers must be included in the loop to make up for these losses. Table 16.1 shows typical exchange cable characteristics. Uncompensated or unloaded cable exhibits an increasing attenuation factor as frequency increases. It is necessary in long loops to correct this. The correction or compensation is known as *loading* and consists of placing series

TABLE 16.1.   Characteristics of Cables Used for Customer Loops in Telephone Exchanges

Cable Awg Gauge No.	Loop Resistance (Ω/Loop-Mile) Round Trip	Attenuation Factor (dB/Mile)		Length for 1200Ω Loop Resistance (Miles)	Total 1200Ω Loop Loss (dB)	
		Unloaded	M88 Loading*		Unloaded	Loaded
26	431	2.67	—	2.8	7.5	—
24	271	2.15	1.31	4.5	9.7	5.9
22	170	1.80	0.92	7.1	12.8	6.5
19	85	1.12	0.44	14.1	15.8	6.2
16	42.4	0.76	0.24	28	21.3	6.7

*M88 loading: 88-mH loading coils placed at 9000-ft intervals.
Source: *IT & T Reference Data for Radio Engineers*, 5th ed., Howard W. Sams & Co., Inc., Indianapolis, Ind., 1969.

inductances at intervals along the cable. These inductances act with the cable capacity to create a distributed filter with a cutoff frequency of about 3.5 kHz and a flat attentuation function over the frequency range from 300 to 3000 Hz. The attenuation factor tends to be lower than in the case of the unloaded cable, as indicated in Table 16.1. The total loop attentuation for unloaded cable cut for 1200-Ω dc resistance rises as the physical length increases (lower gauge number or larger-diameter wire), while that for the loaded cable works out about the same in each case at about 6 dB.

Touch-tone signaling has become popular in the last 10 years and will probably completely replace the familiar dial signaling in the next few years. Touch-tone signaling uses a two-of-seven code to represent the 10 decimal digits and two other symbols. Each of the seven states is designated by the presence of a separate tone, each of which falls in the voice-frequency band. The dial unit on the telephone terminal set is replaced by a touch pad or keyboard with 12 pushbutton switches. When one of the switches is depressed, two of the seven tone generators are energized, and the two tones are sent out audibly in the voice channel. Tone-recognition equipment at the switching center decodes the dial information and sets up the switches. The E relay is still present, but it is only used to provide indication of whether or not the loop is busy. Table 16.2 lists the tones used in the North American telephone system for tone signaling. The actual frequencies used have been carefully selected to minimize duplication by the normal voice signals.

16.1.2   Transmission Bridges

The term *transmission bridge* applies specifically to the circuit used at the central office end of the loop to separate the voice path from the signal-

TABLE 16.2. Touch-Tone Dial Signaling Frequency Assignments

Low Group (HZ)	Code Designation*		
697	1	2	3
770	4	5	6
852	7	8	9
941	Spare	0	Spare
	1209	1336	1477 (HZ) High Group

*Each code consists of one tone from the high group and one from the low group of frequencies.

Source: *IT & T Reference Data for Radio Engineers*, 5th ed., Howard W. Sams & Co., Inc., Indianapolis, Ind., 1969.

ing path and pass it on to another loop. This circuit must isolate the voice signals from the dc signaling circuit and from the central battery supply, and pass these signals into the switching network for cross-connection to another loop.

Figure 16.2(a) shows a simple bridge circuit. The loops are operated in an unbalanced (one-side-grounded) mode, and the dc from the battery is injected through the coil of a relay and an inductor or choke coil. The choke provides the large impedance necessary to prevent voice signals from entering the signal and battery circuit. Capacitors are used to couple the voice signals into the switching network, while keeping direct currents in the loop. Such systems are not often used because of transmission and noise problems created by the unbalanced transmission mode, even though the switching system is simpler because it only has to switch one wire.

The unbalance problems are not present in the Stoneman bridge shown in Figure 16.2(b). In this circuit, each loop has two inductors, one for each side of the loop line. No connection is made to earth or ground, so noise due to ground currents is reduced. The inductors have large reactance, and most of the voice currents are passed through the blocking capacitors to the switching network. The switching network in this case must switch two wires instead of one so that the entire circuit, including both loops, may be operated in a balanced mode. Ballast resistors are included in the battery leads to compensate for various loop lengths (loop resistances). The signaling relays shown are simple two-coil relays which operate when current flows. In practice, special multicoil "polarized" relays of the type used in wire telegraph loops are used. These relays operate in a differential mode and provide much more sensitivity than ordinary relays. They also provide a bias adjustment which allows compensation for any pulse distortion due to the limited frequency response of the loop cables.

Figure 16.2(c) shows a variation of the Stoneman bridge. The only difference between this circuit and that of Figure 16.2(b) is that transformer

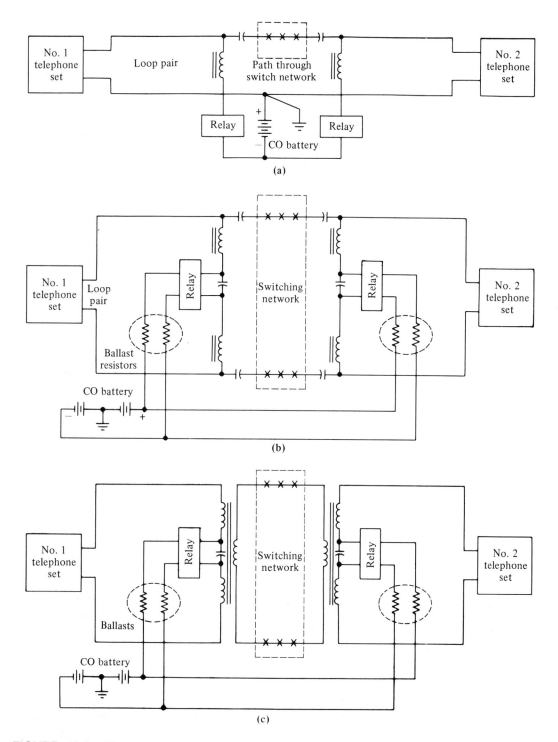

FIGURE 16.2. Transmission bridges: (a) Simple bridge; (b) Stoneman bridge; (c) Transformer bridge.

coupling is used to connect the loop into the switched network. Transformer coupling reduces the insertion loss of the coupling and also eliminates frequency distortion due to reactance. As well, the transformer allows impedance matching between the loop and the switching system, which may be operating at a different characteristic impedance than that of the loop circuit. Typically, the characteristic impedance of loop circuits is about 900 Ω while that of interoffice trunk circuits is 600 Ω.

16.1.3   The Four-Wire Terminating Set

The *four-wire terminating set* shown in Figure 16.3(a) is used to provide 2-wire to 4-wire connection, as required by repeater stations. This circuit uses two separate transformers, each with four identical windings. The two-wire line is connected to the two A windings connected in series aiding. The passive termination is connected to the two B windings connected in series opposing. The transmit pair of the four-wire line is connected to the C, D, windings of one transformer in series aiding, and the receive pair to the C, D windings of the other transformer. The passive termination is built out to have an impedance identical to that of the two-wire line.

Figure 16.3(b) shows the equivalent circuit for currents applied from the two-wire line. Currents in windings A induce identical EMF's in windings B in both transformers. But these windings are connected series opposing, so that the EMF's cancel and no current flows in the passive termination. Currents are induced in the C, D windings of both transformers. Those in the output port are transmitted on one side of the four-wire line, but those applied to the input port are blocked because of unilateral amplifiers in the input line. Half of the power sent in is sent out the output pair, so that the set creates a 3-dB *insertion loss* in the line.

When current is applied to the input port, as in Figure 16.3(c), equal currents are induced in the A, B windings. These currents flow from the A windings down the two-wire line and the B windings into the passive termination, and are returned through the A, B windings of the other transformer. But these windings are connected series opposing, so that no current is generated in the output port. In practice, a small amount (typically less than -50 dB) of the signal applied to the input port leaks through to the output port, this being termed the *feedthrough loss.* Again, the input power is split two ways, causing a 3-dB insertion loss.

16.1.4   Two-Wire Repeaters

Repeaters are amplifiers which are inserted in transmission lines at intervals to amplify the signal and compensate for transmission loss on the cable. On two-wire transmission lines, transmission takes place in both directions, and the amplifier must also be bilateral. "Negative impedance

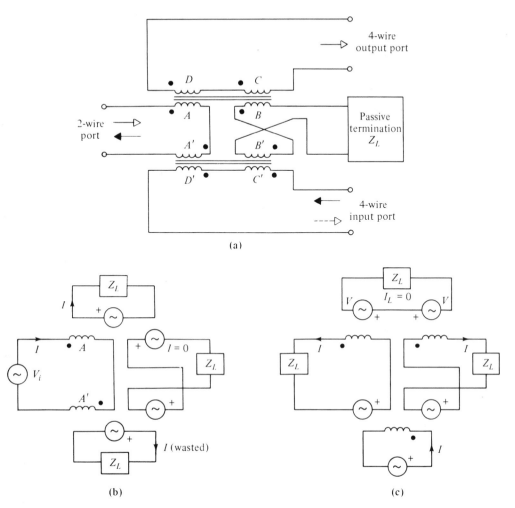

FIGURE 16.3. The four-wire terminating set: (a) Circuit; (b) Equivalent circuit showing the currents and EMF's due to a two-wire signal; (c) Equivalent circuit showing the currents and the EMF's due to a received four-wire signal; the input may be applied to either of the four-wire ports.

amplifiers" employing a principle similar to the negative resistance oscillators described in Section 6.8 are used, which have become available in the last 20 years. Negative impedance amplifiers are two-terminal bilateral devices. Before this, only unidirectional amplifiers were available, and it was necessary to split the two-way transmission into two separate paths before unilateral amplifiers could be applied.

Special terminal sets like the 4-wire terminating set of Section 16.1.3 are required to divide the two-way path into 2 one-way paths or to convert from two-wire to four-wire transmission.

Figure 16.4(a) shows the typical arrangement of a two-wire repeating amplifier. Two unilateral amplifiers provide the necessary gain to overcome the insertion losses of the terminating sets and the transmission losses over a section of the line. Two terminating sets split the two-wire circuit into two one-way circuits containing the amplifiers, connected back to back. If ordinary transformers were used to accomplish this split, there would be a loop-transmission path around the two transformers and the two amplifiers with a net loss of only 6 dB. Any amplifiers would have to have a gain of less than this if oscillations were to be avoided. The terminating set prevents signals from the output of an amplifier from reaching the other amplifier around this short loop, and the gain of the amplifiers can be made much higher. The total gain is limited by the degree of matching on the lines necessary to reduce reflected waves which can cause oscillations. For the repeater to be stable, it is necessary for the net repeater loop-gain including the two amplifier gains, and the hybrid feedthrough losses, to be less than unity. For the system to be stable, it is also necessary for the net line loop-gain, including the two amplifier gains, the terminating set insertion losses, and the reflection losses of the two cables, to be less than unity. Here, *reflection loss* is the ratio (in dB) of the reflected power to the transmitted power at the transmitting point on a cable and includes both return losses at reflection points and line attenuations.

Example 16.1 (a) If the repeater of Figure 16.1(a) uses hybrid transformers with a direct feed-through loss of −50dB, and the lines are matched so that reflections are negligible, calculate the maximum gain in each direction if they are to be equal and if a gain margin against singing (oscillation) of 12 dB is to be provided.
(b) If the line reflection loss measured on the west line were −20dB and that on the east line were −40dB, find the maximum gain in each direction for a 12-dB singing margin.

Solution (a) The net loss around the loop is twice the feed-through loss of the hybrids used:

$$\text{Net loss} = -50 \times 2 = -100 \text{ dB}$$

The net allowed loop gain if stability is to be maintained:

$$\text{gain} = -\text{loss} - \text{margin} = 100 - 12 = 88 \text{ dB}$$

The net repeater amplifier gain is one half of the net loop gain, or **44 dB.**

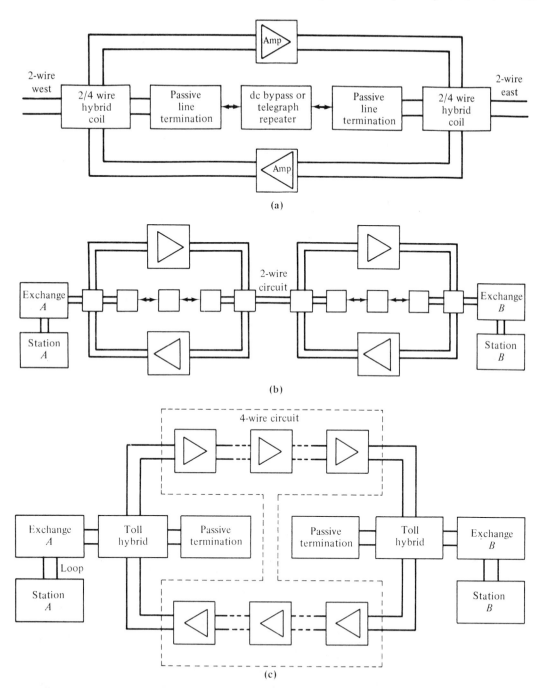

FIGURE 16.4. (a) A two-wire repeater station; (b) A two-wire circuit with 2 two-wire repeaters incorporated; (c) A four-wire toll trunk circuit.

(b) The net loop loss is twice the insertion loss of the hybrid (since the signal passes through each hybrid twice, once going and once on return) times two again because there are two transformers, plus the two reflection losses of the lines:

$$\text{net loss} = (-3\,\text{dB} \times 2 \times 2) + (-20) + (-40) = -72\,\text{dB}$$

$$\text{allowed net loop gain} = 72 - 12 = 60\,\text{dB}$$

$$\text{Maximum repeater amplifier gain} = 60 \div 2 = 30\,\text{dB}$$

Figure 16.4(b) shows a two-wire circuit incorporating 2 two-wire repeater stations.

Negative resistance amplifiers may also be used for loop gain. The use of such repeaters is dependent on how well the lines can be matched to prevent reflections from occurring, because the amplifier is simply connected in parallel with the two-wire line, and there is no local feedback loop. The only way oscillations can occur is if the total inserted gain of the negative resistance amplifier is greater than the sum of the two reflection losses on the lines. The better the lines are matched, the higher these reflection losses are, and the more the allowed gain. Since there is no break in the line itself, no dc bypass circuit is needed, and only a blocking capacitor to the amplifier need be provided. Transformer coupling can also be used, to insert the negative resistance in series with the line. The Bell System E6 exchange loop repeater is a good example of this. It is a transistorized amplifier which operates directly from the dc talk battery current in the line, and allows the reduction of losses on long loops. Separate signaling repeaters may also be required to regenerate the dc loop signals on very long loops.

16.1.5   Four-Wire Transmission

Two-wire circuits are difficult to balance accurately, and the maximum gain that can be included in repeaters is limited. For this reason, long distance and interoffice trunk circuits are nearly always done on a four-wire basis, with two wires providing the transmission path in one direction and the other two providing the transmission path in the other direction. When carrier circuits are used, four-wire or two-path transmission must be used because the carrier amplifiers along the route only allow transmission in one direction. Figure 16.4(c) shows the typical arrangement of equipment along the path of a long-distance circuit. The customer's loop at each end is switched on a two-wire basis into a toll (long-distance) switching center. A four-wire terminating set located at the toll center converts the circuit to the two-path transmission mode. The long-distance facilities between this center and the far toll center are all four-wire and may include cable circuits, repeaters, cable carrier circuits, and radio circuits. At the far toll center the transmission is converted back to two-wire before being connected to the far customer's loop.

16.2   PUBLIC TELEPHONE NETWORK

16.2.1   The System

The basic purpose of the public telepone system is to provide two-way voice communication between any pair of subscribers within the system. A wide variety of subsidiary services have been added to the list in recent years, such as communication with subscribers in other systems, telegraph, teletypewriter and facsimile service, computer communications, conference calls, and private network service. The basic components of this system are a network of cable and radio channels linking many centers, switching devices at each center to allow interconnection, and local subscriber stations.

The basic component of the system is the exchange switching machine, or "office." This is a switching system that allows interconnection directly of up to 10,000 subscriber stations located mostly within a radius of about 10 km of the office, each of which is assigned a separate four-digit number. The office also provides facilities for connection through exchange interoffice trunk circuits to several other nearby exchanges, or into toll connecting trunks to a nearby toll or long-distance switching center. Early telephone switching offices were manually operated by operators who physically made the connections necessary to complete a call by means of plug leads on a switchboard. Manual switchboards are still used to serve private company systems with a few hundred lines, but nearly all public system switching is now done automatically.

In the 1950's the Bell System introduced the concept of continent-wide automatic toll switching, or *direct distance dialing* (DDD). Before this time all long-distance connections were done by means of manual switching by long-distance operators. Each exchange could automatically switch the connections between a subscriber and the nearest toll office, but then the toll operator had to manually complete the call to the far end. This often involved switching by several operators at intermediate centers along the route of the call. With DDD, the connections at the toll center between the toll connecting trunks and the intertoll long-distance trunk circuits are made automatically, and billing information is automatically recorded by a computer. Backup manual facilities are maintained on a limited basis in case of difficulty or for the establishment of special service calls such as person-to-person calls and conference calls.

For the purpose of making long-distance calling more efficient with respect to the use of toll-trunk circuit facilities, a hierarchy of toll offices was established. Figure 16.5 illustrates the interconnections possible within the DDD system. A specific location was chosen within each major population center for the establishment of the local toll-connecting offices. These toll-connecting offices might serve anywhere from 10 to 100 exchange offices, depending on the local population density. Toll-connecting trunk circuits link each exchange office to the toll-connecting office. Within each exchange

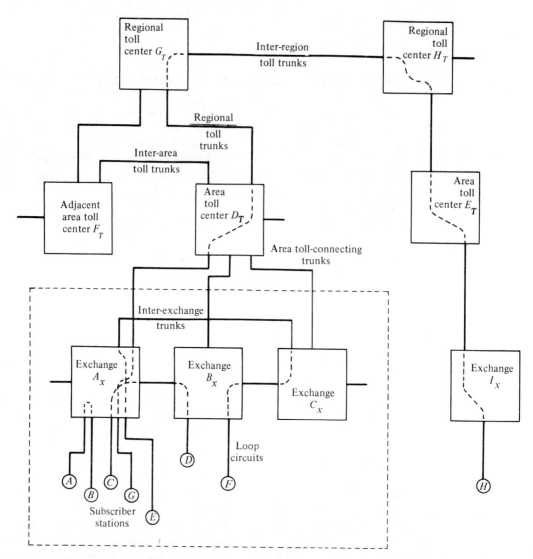

FIGURE 16.5. A public telephone system.

calls are made mostly on a flat-rate basis, so that call-connection recording is not required, such as A to B in Figure 16.5. Exchange interoffice trunk circuits allow flat-rate calls to be made to other nearby exchange locations within a designated flat-rate calling area such as C to D in Figure 16.5. Again, no record is kept of the calls.

Any call that requires a specific charge must be routed through the nearest toll office, where the record of the call is made. At the toll-connecting level, three levels of long distance calls are possible. First, the call may be to a second exchange which is served by the same toll center, in which case a direct connection between two toll-connecting trunks is made. Second, the call may be to an exchange served by a nearby toll center, in which case the call may be routed over a direct toll trunk between the two centers. Third, the call may be between centers in two different regions, separated by a considerable distance. Each region is served by a regional toll switching center, and any calls between regions are routed through these centers. The facilities linking these regionals centers are mostly heavy-route microwave relay systems, or the satellite relay system.

A limited number of trunk circuits is provided between any two nearby switching machines, be they exchange or toll. The number provided is based on long-range forecasts of area population growth and future demand for service, done on a statistical basis to provide a certain maximum probability of not being able to complete a call during maximum "busy hours." Calls between each pair of exchanges within the system are assigned first-, second-, and third-choice routes if they are available, and the switching machine automatically selects these in sequence before indicating a "trunk-busy" condition. An example of this is provided by C to D and E to F in Figure 16.5. C was able to establish a direct trunk connection to D through offices A_x and B_x, a first-choice selection. When E tried to make a call to F, between the same two offices, all the A_x to B_x trunks were busy, and the alternate route through office C_x was chosen. In a similar manner, toll calls within a region may be made on first choice over direct trunks, and on second choice through one or more intermediate toll offices, or through the regional toll office.

The automatic switching machines for each exchange are designated by a three-number address code. Any local call within an area must be established by means of seven address digits, three prefix numbers for the office address, and four for the particular subscriber's station being called. The digit "1" is reserved as an access code within each exchange to make connection to a toll-connecting trunk circuit. A second three-digit code immediately after the "1" addresses the toll area in which the destination subscriber is located. This is followed by the seven-digit number which completes the call in the destination area.

16.2.2 Step-by-Step Switching

The heart of the automatic telephone system is the switching machine. The first of these systems used step-by-step switching by means of the *Strowger stepping switch*, whose basic mechanism is illustrated in Figure 16.6(a). The switch is constructed with a single pair of contacts attached to an arm at the end of the shaft. These contacts can make with any of 100 pairs of contacts in a stator assembly laid out in 10 rows of 10 sets of contacts

(a)

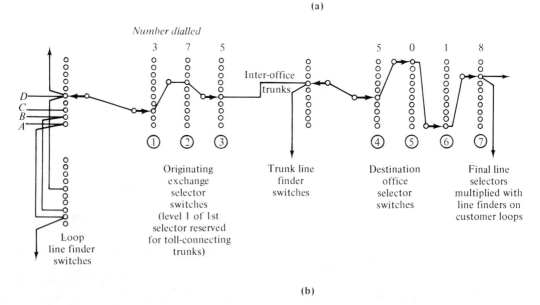

(b)

FIGURE 16.6. Dial step-by-step switching: (a) The stepping switch; (b) Connections for a call made through a step-by-step switching machine.

in a semicylindrical array around the shaft axis. A rachet and pawl operated by a magnet allows the armature to be stepped up one level of contacts for each of 10 pulses received, from a rest position below the bottom row of contacts, and to one side of the array. A second rachet and pawl allows the armature to be stepped along any previously selected row, one step for each received pulse. Variation of the switch allows the armature to step continuously along each horizontal row until it reaches an unoccupied set of contacts in the row, or until it reaches the end of the row and drops out completely to the rest position.

Within a step-by-step office, these switches are used for two different purposes, line finding and line selecting. Figure 16.6(b) shows the typical chain of switching which takes place in making an exchange call with step-by-step equipment. Each subscriber station is equipped with a dial pulsing unit which sends out trains of 1 to 10 pulses representing the 10 decimal digits by interrupting the loop dc current. These pulses are relayed to the switching train to activate the switches completing the call. Each subscriber loop is connected to one pair of points on each of several *line-finder* switches. The number of line finders to which each line is connected is chosen to minimize the possibility of finding all the line finders within the group busy. When a subscriber attempts to make a call, he engages the hook switch at his set by lifting his receiver. This closes the loop circuit, and a relay energizes one of the line-finder switches in the group which is not already engaged with another call. The line finder then automatically steps up until it finds the level on which the demanding subscriber is located, and then across until it connects to that point. As long as loop current is maintained, the line finder will remain in that position. When the loop is broken for a period exceeding the dial pulse period (about half a second), it drops out and returns to the idle position.

Each line finder has its armature connected directly to the armature of the first-group selector switch, which is now ready to receive the dial pulses for the first digit of the number being called. Each level of the selector corresponds to the digits 1 through 0. If the first number dialed is a 3, the first selector will step up three levels as the three dial pulses are received. When loop current is maintained for a period longer than the dial pulse, the switch automatically steps along the third row until it finds an unoccupied point. Each point in the third row may be connected to the armature of a selector switch in the second group, level 3 subgroup. Each of these second-group selectors is connected to several first-group selectors in corresponding points, so that each subscriber has access to several group 2–3 selectors, and so several different subscribers may use each selector at different times. Again the number of selectors in the group is chosen to minimize uncompleted calls.

If the second digit dialed is a 7, the second-group selector steps up the seventh level and searches for a free group 3–7 selector, as the pulses are received. Dialing the third digit operates this switch to step up to the appropriate level and search for a free point. The points on one row of one group of these final selectors are connected back into the local office, while all the others are connected to interoffice trunks so that connections can be made to them.

The far ends of the trunk circuits appear on the banks of line-finder switches which operate in the same manner as the subscriber line-finder switches. Two succeeding stages of group selector switches follow and respond to the first two of the last four digits in the number being called. The outputs of these switches are connected to the wipers of several multipled final selector switches. These final switches are arranged to step both up and across according to the last two digits. The point arrived at is connected to corresponding points of each of the other multipled final selectors, and to several initial line finders, and to the loop circuit of the called subscriber. If the line is already busy, the final selector will drop out and send back a busy-tone signal. If it is free, it will send ringing current out to ring the bells, and when the subscriber answers, it will disconnect ringing tone and hold the chain of switches until the calling subscriber breaks the loop.

The step-by-step office contains many hundreds of mechanical switches, each with moving parts and wiping contacts. As a result, maintenance on this type of system is costly and difficult. The switching of currents in magnetic circuits also generates a high level of impulse-type switching noise within the system, which, while tolerable in voice communications, is completely unacceptable in data communications. As a result, very few new step-by-step offices are being installed. The immediate successor of the step-by-step office is the cross-bar switching office, which is discussed in the next section.

16.2.3   Cross-Bar Switching

The *cross-bar switching system* derives its name from the switching device used, the cross-bar switch. Figure 16.7(a) shows the mechanical layout of a 200-point cross-bar switch unit. This unit is laid out in 10 horizontal rows and 20 vertical columns, with a set of four contacts located at each of the 200 cross-points. Each cross-point contact set can be actuated by energizing one horizontal magnet and one vertical magnet, first causing a horizontal bar to rotate and then a vertical holding bar to rotate. There are only 5 horizontal bars, each of which can rotate in two directions so that each bar can control cross-point switches in one of two rows at any one time. There are 20 vertical holding bars which rotate in only one direction, so that only 20 simultaneous independent paths can be held through the switch.

Figure 16.7(b) and (c) shows one of the cross-points in more detail. Each horizontal bar carries 20 selecting fingers or wires, which in the idle state lie in the gap between two sets of cross-point contacts (Fig. 16.7(b)). When one of the horizontal magnets is energized, the horizontal selecting bar rotates, causing all 20 selecting fingers to move over on top of the contact sets on one side. Now when one of the vertical holding magnets is energized, its vertical holding bar pushes down on the selecting spring at the desired cross-point and closes the four contact sets under it through the push rod. When the horizontal selecting bar is released, all springs except the held

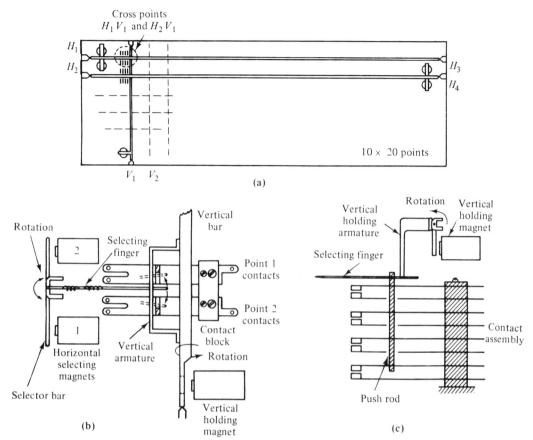

FIGURE 16.7. (a) Illustration of the structure of a cross-bar switch unit; the horizontal selecting bars and the vertical holding bars are shown with their activation magnets; (b) Two contact assemblies showing the action of the selection wire; (c) Contact assembly showing the holding armature action.

spring move back into the idle position. The operated spring remains trapped under the vertical holding armature to hold the contacts down until the vertical holding magnet is released. Each of the 200-point cross-bar switch units is capable of making and holding a total of 20 independent contact closures at one time. Switch units are used in pairs, and several pairs are multipled within a frame to provide the required fan-out of the connections in the switching system.

Figure 16.8 shows the major pieces of equipment in a typical cross-bar exchange office and the path of a call established through it. The line link, district link, office link, line connecting link, and incoming trunk line are crossbar switch banks used to establish signal paths through the machine. The sender link is a crossbar switch used to connect the district junctor to a

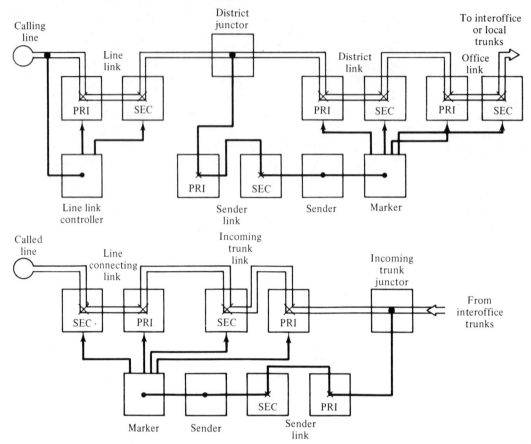

FIGURE 16.8.   Exchange cross-bar switching system; the route of a local
call is shown.

sender during call establishment. The district junctor, sender, marker, and
line link controller are each special purpose computers made of electromechanical relay circuits that control the action of the various switches as
described below. An incoming subscriber's loop is connected to several
vertical points within one or more cross-bar switches so that it has access to
several horizontals. When the calling station loop is energized, a relay
network searches for and engages an idle line-link controller. This, in turn,
controls the action of the line-link cross-bar switches. It searches to find a
primary cross-point to engage on the incoming line, and a secondary
cross-point to engage an idle district junctor unit. Once these have been
found, the two cross-bar switchpoints necessary to complete the connection
are closed and holding control is passed to the district junctor unit. At this
point the line-link controller disconnects. The district junctor unit searches
for an idle sender unit and operates the two switches in the sender link to
connect the junctor to the sender. The sender, in turn, connects itself to an

idle marker unit. Now the district junctor provides a dial tone, indicating it is ready to receive dial pulses.

The first three digits of the number being dialed are passed directly to the marker unit, which decodes and stores them as the address of the office in which the called station is located. It then searches for and makes cross-point connections in the district link and office link frames necessary to connect the district junctor through to an idle trunk circuit out to the destination office. At this point, the marker and sender have completed their part of the job, and the marker, sender, and sender link are all released, leaving the district junctor to hold the connections in the district and office link switches. At the far end of the trunk circuit, which may terminate in a remote office or in the originating office itself, an incoming trunk junctor circuit similar to the district junctor takes over control. It engages a new sender and marker unit, and waits for the final four digits of the number. These are received, decoded, and stored, and the called line is searched for. A path between the incoming trunk junctor and the called line is searched for through the incoming link switches and the line-link switches and, if the line is not already engaged, makes the connection. At this point the marker and sender are dropped, leaving control to the incoming trunk junctor. If the line is already busy, the connection is dropped and a busy tone transmitted back to the originating station. If it is free, the connections are held and ringing current sent out to the called station. Operating the hook switch in the called loop to close the dc path cuts off the ringing current and the conversation can proceed. Control is maintained by the calling party's loop current, and the connection is not dropped until the calling party hangs up. When it does, the two junctor circuits release all the cross-bar switch points in the circuit, which now become available to establish other connections.

The number of units of each type provided in an office depend on the statistical probability that a call cannot be completed because all the units are busy. The line link must provide at least one vertical on its primary for each line in the office, and each is multiplied over several verticals. The number of other switch units in the district and office links and the incoming links is considerably smaller and depends on the expected maximum traffic. The sender and marker units are important, but since they do their job in a very short period of time, only a few are needed in a given office. Generally, for a 10,000-line office, only six markers are necessary. Only two junctor circuits are necessary for each call in process at a given time. One or two hundred of these would be sufficient to operate the office.

16.2.4 Electronic Switching

In the 1950s electronic switching systems were developed for use in telephone exchanges. The earliest of these simply replaced the cross-bar switch with its electronic equivalent, and replaced the wire spring relays used in the sender, marker, and link control units with electronic circuits. Of course, such an approach is not the most efficient way to realize such a system, and an alternative was found in the general-purpose time-shared computer. Future electronic switching systems will use such digital computers to realize most of the functions involved in such switching.

Figure 16.9 illustrates how a digital computer may be used for message switching in a telephone system. Each subscriber loop and interoffice trunk circuit terminates on an electronic cross-point switch which performs the same function as the line link in a cross-bar system. The switch points are provided by using such devices as light-coupled silicon-controlled rectifiers. A unit providing 200 cross-points as in the cross-bar unit can be mounted on a single printed circuit card, and occupy a smaller volume than does the mechanical version.

In attempting to make a call, loop A energizes the link control circuit, which searches for a free computer terminal circuit and closes the link points to connect it. A junctor circuit separates the control signals and supplies the loop currents. The loop control circuit receives the dialed or pulsed number, which is the address of the distant terminal, and enters it in the address register. The proper command number is entered into the control register to tell the computer to complete the connection. Once the terminal circuit has been engaged, the computer periodically samples the address and control registers, and when the command is picked up, it acts to find a second free terminal in the group which can access the destination loop. The control and address numbers are entered into the second unit registers, and the loop control circuit picks up the free link circuit to connect the called loop. Busy or ring-down signals are sent, and once the distant party answers, the two loop control circuits hold the connections until such time as either loop is broken. terminating the call. The voice signals are separated by four-wire hybrid terminating transformers, with transmitted signals being encoded by the analog-to-digital (A/D) converter into a number which the computer can handle, and the numbers transferred from the far terminal being converted back to an analog signal by the digital-to-analog (D/A) converter. The computer periodically connects to each busy terminal in turn, picks up the number from the A/D converter along with the two addresses of the terminal points and the command status, and transfers the data to the proper D/A converter. Each register is sampled at least 8000 times per second so that no frequency distortion of the 4 kHz audio signals occurs. In a 10,000-line office, several hundred terminal units may be provided, but at any one time only a few of these would be in use. The number provided would depend on the maximum busy-period call rate, so that the chance of having an uncompleted call is minimized.

This is only one of several possible equipment arrangements, and new versions of the electronic office are being developed continually by several companies as new technology becomes available. The availability of single-chip micro-computers opens up a whole new field of possibilities for such switching centers. The British Post Office (BPO) has recently revealed its plans to modernize its entire telephone system by the early 1900s. The heart

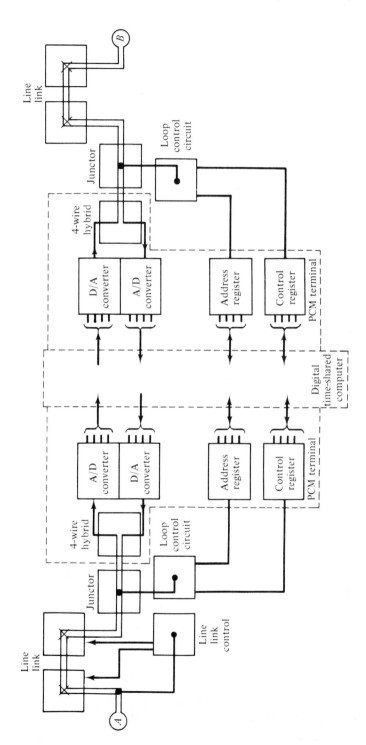

FIGURE 16.9. An electronic telephone exchange switching system.

of this modernization is a flexible computer-based digital switching system, which is illustrated in Figure 16.10. Analog telephone circuits are pulse-code modulated and time division multiplexed onto high-speed data transmission lines (at 2 Mbits/second) before being connected to the switching system. Switching is done in both a spatial mode and a time mode within the switching network. All of these switches will be electronic in nature.

A multiprocessor unit controls the action of the switching network. Within this network are several microcomputor units such as the Intel 8080 series or the General Instruments 1650. These microcomputers are each assigned a specific task within the system such as the Maintenance Control Subsystem (MCS), the Call Processing Subsystem (CPS), and the Digital Switching Subsystem (DSS). All of these microcomputers share a large common memory system, and one of the microcomputers acts as the Operating System (OS) to provide the central control in passing instructions to the other microcomputers and taking care of the housekeeping chores.

The PCM encoding circuits (CODEC) and multiplexers may be adjacent to the switching unit, but are more likely to take the form of line concentrator units in the neighborhood centers surrounding the switching office. Most of the interconnecting transmission will be at 2 Mbits/second, either on coaxial cables or on optic fiber cables.

System flexibility is maintained by using similar equipment subsystems and operating programs, whether the switching unit is to be used as a large central office or as a small PBX.

16.2.5   Trunk Circuits

Trunk circuits are transmission circuits interconnecting two different switching centers. These centers may be two adjacent exchanges, or they may be separated by a considerable distance and the connection will involve one or more toll (long-distance) circuits.

Exchange interoffice circuits are merely extensions of the loop circuits connected at either end. They must provide a two-way voice channel, which can be done on either a two- or four-wire basis, and they must provide a two-way telegraph channel for supervisory control signals such as dial information and busy signals. Although two-wire circuits operating in the same manner as loops may be used, they are not favored for interoffice connections. Carrier systems are more commonly used so that fewer cable pairs between offices may be used. The transmission objective on such an interoffice trunk circuit is that the total transmission loss between the points where the two loops are connected should approach 0 dB. Each loop is allowed a 3- to 5-dB loss maximum so that the net connection loss measured at 1000 Hz is no more than 6 to 10 dB.

Toll connecting and intertoll trunks are always designed on a four-wire basis. Ideally, the total transmission loss from end to end of any toll connection should be 0 dB. However, since each end is terminated in a two-wire

Unwrapped. BPO's telephone switching and signaling system, dubbed System X, uses a modular approach to ensure compatibility and interchangeability. Circles in multiprocessor indicate software; hexagons indicate software handlers.

FIGURE 16.10. BPO's telephone switching and signaling system, dubbed System X, uses a modular approach to ensure compatibility and interchangeability. Circles in multiprocessor indicate software; hexagons indicate software handlers. Reprinted from Electronics, May 24, 1979; Copyright © McGraw-Hill, Inc., 1979 all rights reserved.

SIS — SIGNALING INTERWORKING SUBSYSTEM
TS16 — TIME-SLOT SIXTEEN (COMMON-CHANNEL SIGNALING)
DLT — DIGITAL LINE TERMINATION
MF — MULTIFREQUENCY SIGNALING
MTS — MESSAGE-TRANSMISSION SUBSYSTEM
DMA — DIRECT MEMORY ACCESS

MCS — MAINTENANCE-CONTROL SUBSYSTEM
MSS — MANAGEMENT-STATISTICS SUBSYSTEM
OCS — OVERLOAD-CONTROL SUBSYSTEM
OS — OPERATING SYSTEM
CPS — CALL-PROCESSING SUBSYSTEM
DSS — DIGITAL-SWITCHING SUBSYSTEM

system which does reflect energy, it is possible to get energy reflected from the far end returning on the return channel to the source. This can result in one of two things happening. If the loss is too low and the phase is right, oscillations or singing may occur. More likely there will be sufficient loss in the loops to prevent singing, but there will be an echo. Since the velocity of propagation over long circuits is finite, it is possible to have return delays in excess of about 45 ms, with levels that make the echo intolerable to the user. The echo on circuits with shorter delays can also be unacceptable if the return level is too high. Toll-trunk circuits are designed on the *via net loss* (VNL) *principle*, so each circuit has a minimum amount of return loss built into it to keep the echo within acceptable levels. The VNL required for a toll circuit is calculated from the equation

$$\text{VNL} = \frac{0.2L}{V} + 0.4 \text{ dB} \qquad (16.1)$$

where V = velocity of propagation on the facility, km/ms
   L = circuit length kilometers
   0.2 = No. of dB loss that must be inserted for each millisecond of transmission delay, to maintain acceptable echo levels
   $\dfrac{0.2}{V}$ = VNLF (via net loss factor) for a given facility, dB/km of length

   Tables of VNLF's for various facilities are available. (See "Reference Data for Radio Engineers," 1972, Howard W. Sams.)
   If the total VNL of a given trunk circuit exceeds about 2.5 dB, devices called *echo suppressors* are inserted in the channel. These are voice-operated relays which sense the high level of a near-end talker on the outgoing channel and inserts a high loss in the return channel, as long as the speech continues. It disconnects in about 100 ms after speech ceases, so that the far end party can start talking. A second circuit on the return channel does the same for transmission in the other direction. Because the velocity of propagation varies widely depending on the type of transmission facilities, spacing of echo suppressors may vary from a few hundred kilometers on cable circuits to a thousand kilometers on microwave circuits.
   Noise on trunk circuits must also be kept to acceptable levels. Noise on long circuits must be kept below 44 dBrn and those on short and medium-length circuits must be kept below 38 dBrn. The reference level for the noise measurements is derived from an arbitrary minimum level of output from a white-noise source which has first been passed through a weighted filter network with a frequency response similar to a standard telelphone circuit. In terms of the Western Electric 3A telephone set (C message weighting, or the 500-type telephone receiver), 0 dBrn of noise corresponds to −90 dBm

(ref. 1 mW) of 1000-Hz pure tone, or to -88 dBm of white noise equivalent to thermal noise) in the frequency passband of 0 to 3 kHz. Special noise-measuring sets are used in practice which contain a white-noise source, a weighting filter, a calibrated attenuator, and a meter for measuring and comparing the channel noise to the reference-source noise. The abbreviation dBrn simply means decibels relative to reference noise level.

16.2.6 Private Telephone Networks

Many companies and institutions use private telephone networks to facilitate communication among their own members. These systems can be anything from two or three handsets on a single loop to an international network involving several centers, each with hundreds of stations. Private networks may be operated on a fully manual basis with all control and switching performed by operators, they may be fully automatic switching systems similar to the public telephone network, or, as is more probable, they can be a combination of both manual and automatic operations.

The small manually operated system with several telephone stations near a single switchboard is known as a *private branch exchange* (PBX). Internal switching is performed by the company telephone operator, who often doubles as the office receptionist. One or more dial trunk circuits connect the PBX to a nearby public exchange office where they terminate on loop circuits corresponding to the number assigned to the company. Usually this is a single number, with access to several trunk circuits and a special switch which searches to find an idle trunk circuit.

The small automatic system is known as a *private automatic branch exchange* (PABX). This system is usually set up so that calls between stations within the system are done on an automatic switching basis by equipment similar to that used in the dial exchange office of the public system. One or more dial trunks connect the switching system with a nearby public exchange and may be arranged for automatic dial-out operation with manual answering or may be completely handled by the operator. An operator is usually provided with a manual switchboard to allow handling of ouside calls and also special-service internal calls.

Large companies may have several PBX's or PABX's at different locations many kilometers apart. Communication between these PBX's may be done by means of long-distance calls over the public network, but if the volume of traffic is high, the company can get preferred rates by renting the use of private trunk circuits or tie lines between the various PBX's, reserved only for their use. Some large companies may even install their own transmission facilities over considerable distances.

Although a company may purchase, install, and maintain its own private telephone system, it has generally been more convenient to rent such systems from the public telephone companies. All the station and switching equipment then remains the property of the public company, but its use is reserved specifically for one customer. The service provided under these conditions must be at least as good as that provided by the public system, and in some instances must meet even higher requirements because of special services, such as computer interconnections.

16.3 PROBLEMS

1. Calculate the dc-loop resistance of a telephone subscriber's loop comprised of 5.6 km of AWG22 cable and a further 10 km of 19 AWG cable. If M88 loading is used, calculate the overall signal attenuation at 1000 Hz.

2. Explain the purpose of the induction coil in a telephone station set.

3. Explain the term "full duplex" as applied to telephony.

4. Explain the principle of operation of the transformer-type transmission bridge shown in Figure 16.2(c).

5. A repeater circuit similar to that of Figure 16.4(a) is to be included in a two-wire trunk circuit. The maximum return loss on the east circuit is −40 dB and that on the west circuit is −55 dB. The two hybrid coils each have a feed-through loss of −50 dB and a transmission loss of 3 dB in either direction. If a 10-dB gain margin against singing is to be provided, calculate the maximum loop gain in the two amplifiers and the net gain of the repeater under these conditions between the two two-wire ports.

6. Explain with the aid of equivalent circuits the operation of the 4-wire terminating set.

7. Explain the function of a line-finder switch in a step-by-step switching system. Explain the function of a line-selector switch.

8. What is the main advantage of the cross-bar switching system over the step-by-step system? What advantage does the electronic system have over the cross bar?

9. Calculate the via net loss of a trunk circuit which involves 2000 km of microwave relay circuits with an average velocity of propagation of 299×10^6 m/s. How long would this circuit have to be before an echo suppressor must be included?

10. Explain the term "dBrn" as used in connection with telephone-circuit noise measurement. Give the definition of 0 dBrn in reference to a pure tone of 1000 Hz.

11. Find the via net loss required for a 5000 km cable circuit on which the average propagation velocity is 80% of the speed of light. Does the circuit require an echo suppressor?

12. For the satellite circuit of Problem 14.15, find the circuit Via Net Loss. Is an echo suppressor necessary?

Chapter 17
Digital
Communications

17.1 INTRODUCTION

When a finite set of discrete values is used to represent information, the resulting signal is known as a *digital signal.* This differs from pulse modulation, described in Chapter 11, where although discrete values of the information signal were used these could take on *any value* within the range of the continuous signal.

Digital data may arise in one of two ways. It may be sampled data from a continuous signal, as in pulse modulation but with the sample quantized to the nearest value within the finite set of numbers. The second possibility is that the data may originate in digital form, for example a sequence of numbers giving the quantities of parts in a stockroom.

In the decimal system any one of the numbers from 0 to 9 inclusive, is a digit. In the binary system, only two digits, 0 and 1, are used. The majority of digital electronic equipment utilizes the binary number system because of the ease with which the 0 to 1 states can be generated and manipulated. A binary digit is sometimes referred to as a *binit,* but more usually it is known as a *bit.* There is a distinction between these two abbreviated forms which can be important in certain circumstances. The *bit* is a measure of information content, and in a binary message where the O's and 1's are *equiprobable*, one binary digit (binit) contains one bit of information, by definition. However, if the 0's and 1's do not occur with equal probability, a binit (which is still either one of the binary digits) will contain more or less than one bit of information. The distinction is not always observed simply because in many cases the equiprobable condition applies (or is assumed) and *bit* has become a synonym for binit. Following popular usage, the term *bit* will be used here.

17.2 BIT TRANSMISSION

Regardless of the origin of the data, a binary digital signal will consist of a sequence of bits which must be represented by a voltage or current waveform. Figure 17.1(a) shows the sequence 01000111011 as it would originate from a teletypewriter sending the character **G** in ASCII (American Standard Code for Information Interchange). Figure 17.1(b) shows the waveform that results for *unipolar synchronous transmission* in which 1 bits are sent as positive voltage pulses ($+V$), and 0 bits as zero voltage. In ASCII, the first 0 bit is used for *start synchronization*, the following seven digits contain the character being transmitted. (see Figure 17.8 for ASCII listing), the eight bit is for a form of error detection, and the last two 1 bits are for *stop synchronization*. Coding and error detection are described in more detail in section 17.10. For the moment, the point being made is that the digital message appears as a pulse type waveform.

Unipolar transmission is wasteful of power in that a dc component is transmitted (approximately $V/2$) which does not add to the information content of the signal. This dc component can be eliminated by using *polar transmission* in which the 1 bits are sent as a $+V$ pulses and the 0 bits as $-V$ pulses, The polar synchronous waveform for the sequence **01000111011** is shown in Figure 17.1(c).

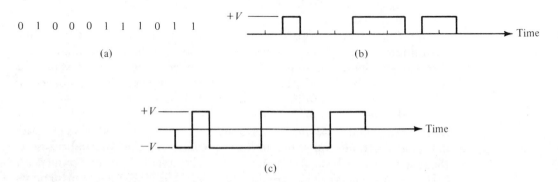

FIGURE 17.1. Binary digital sequence: (a) In digital form; (b) As a unipolar synchronous wave; (c) As a polar synchronous wave.

The most important parameters in digital transmission are *signalling rate* and *error probability*, and these are discussed next.

17.3 SIGNALLING RATE

Signalling rate is measured in bits/sec. The maximum signalling rate will be limited by the frequency bandwidth of the transmission channel. Nyquist showed that for an ideal low-pass channel (one that has a frequency response as shown in Figure 17.2(a)), the signalling rate r cannot exceed 2B bits/s, where B is the bandwidth of the channel. This can be seen by considering the periodic binary sequence *...0101010101...* as shown in Figure 17.2(b), applied as input to the ideal low-pass channel. The waveform in this case is seen to be a periodic square wave, which represents the fastest possible signalling rate. The *lowest* harmonic component in such a wave (see Figure 2.1(c) and (d)) is:

$$f_{min} = \frac{1}{T_o} = \frac{1}{2T_p} \qquad (17.1)$$

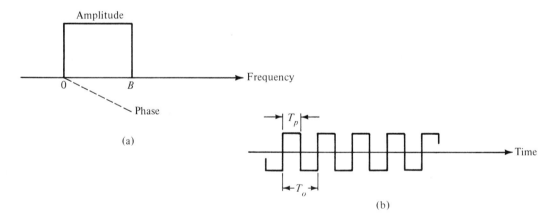

FIGURE 17.2.   (a) Characteristics of an ideal LPF. (b) A periodic binary digital waveform.

Since this is the lowest frequency component, if this is greater than B, the channel bandwidth, the signal will not be transmitted. From Figure 17.2(b) it is seen that T_p is the duration of one bit. But signalling rate is:

$$r = \frac{1}{T_p} \qquad \text{bits/s} \qquad (17.2)$$

Substituting for r in Eq. (17.1) gives:

$$f_{min} = \frac{r}{2} \qquad (17.3)$$

As already stated, f_{min} cannot be greater than B for transmission, therefore the signal will not be transmitted for $r > 2B$.

For $r < 2B$ the signal will be transmitted although in a distorted form, since the higher order harmonics in the wave will be removed by the filtering action of the channel. However, this does not matter for binary transmission since all that is required is that the positive and negative peaks of the wave be distinguished; these can be used to regenerate a square wave using the appropriate digital hardware. This illustrates one of the strong points of binary digital transmission.

For $r = 2B$ the maximum signalling rate is achieved, but this condition can be met only if a special pulse shape is used, the details of which are too advanced to be included here.

To give some idea of the range of values encountered in practice, manually operated teletypewriters generate data at a rate of the order of 100 bits/s, while at the higher end, for a pulse-code modulated color video signal, the rate is of the order of 100 Mbits/s (megabits/s).

17.4   ERROR PROBABILITY

Errors can occur in a digital message as a result of noise. As described in chapter 4, there are many sources of noise, some fundamental, some a result of improperly designed equipment. In binary digital systems it is possible for a pulse in one part of the system to induce a pulse in other parts, giving rise to an error. Even where all precautions are taken to minimize unwanted coupling, thermal noise (see Section 4.2) will be a limiting factor.

For baseband polar synchronous transmission in the presence of thermal noise, the probability of error depends on the probability that the noise voltage plus signal will cross a "decision level" of zero volts. This means that when a 0 bit $(-V)$, is being transmitted an error will occur if the noise drives the voltage positive, and for a 1 bit $(+V)$ transmission, if the noise drives the voltage negative. This is illustrated for the 01000111011 bit sequence in Figure 17.3(a). Note that zero volts is termed a decision level because the system is designated so that any positive voltage received is interpreted by the receiver as a 1 bit, and any negative voltage as a 0 bit.

The probability of error is a function of the ratio of signal amplitude $|V|$ to the r.m.s. noise voltage V_n. Figure 17.3(b) shows in graphical form the probability of error versus the ratio $|V|/V_n$. Acceptable error limits depend on application. For example, telemetry data such as temperature

(a)

FIGURE 17.3.   (a) Errors in a binary signal resulting from noise; (b) Graph of error probability vs. signal to noise ratio for polar baseband transmission.

(b)

and pressure measurements which in analog form may be measured to an accuracy of 10%, would probably be satisfactory in digital form with an error probability of 10^{-2}. Other data, such as fault monitoring on power transmission lines may require an error probability of 10^{-6} or less.

Knowing the error probability, the average number of errors in a message m bits long may be calculated from:

$$\text{Avg. No. of Errors} = m \times \text{Error Probability} \qquad (17.4)$$

For m ≫ 1 and (error probability) ≪ 1, the *standard deviation* of the error distribution is approximately equal to the square root of the mean (for the Poisson probability distribution assumed for this situation). Thus:

$$\text{Std. Dev.} = \sqrt{\text{Avg. No. of Errors}} \qquad (17.5)$$

There is about a 95.5% probability that the number of errors will not be more than Mean + 2(Std. Dev.) nor less than Mean − 2(Std. Dev.).

Example 17.1 A digital message is 10^7 bits long and the error probability has been calculated as 10^{-5}. Calculate the average number of errors and the likely range in the number of errors.

Solution

$$\text{Avg. No. of Errors} = 10^7 \times 10^{-5}$$
$$= 100$$
$$\text{Std. Dev.} = \sqrt{100} = 10$$
$$\text{Range} = \text{mean} \pm 2 \times \text{Std. Dev.}$$
$$= 100 \pm 20$$

Thus, one can expect anywhere from 80 to 120 errors.

17.5. DIGITAL FILTERING

As shown in Chapter 2, an analog signal may be filtered such that the output time function is some modified version of the input time function. In effect, the filter removes, or attenuates, certain frequencies relative to the others in the spectrum. For example, Figure 2.10 shows how a low pass filter (LPF) can convert a square wave to a triangular wave.

Digital filters can be made to *simulate* analog filters. Additionally, new filter forms can be realized digitally, not possible in the analog counterpart. Special purpose digital hardware may be used to construct a digital filter, or alternatively the digital input information may be processed in a general-purpose computer to produce the output required. Thus a wide range of very powerful tools is available for digital signal processing generally. It should also be noted that it is possible to simulate a digital filter by means of analog components.

As an example, Figure 17.4(a) shows a LPF in an analog system to which a continuous signal, a step function, is applied. The corresponding output is the well known charging curve for a capacitor. Figure 17.4(b) shows a similar filter in digital form. This is known as a *recursive* filter because the output depends on the previous output sample, which is seen to

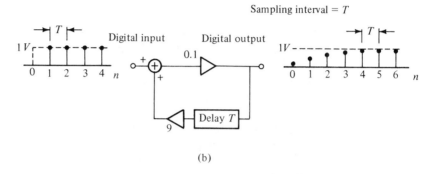

(b)

FIGURE 17.4.   (a) An analog LPF with a step voltage input, and the corresponding output. (b) The simulation of (a) in digital form.

be fed back to the input. The detailed design of digital filters is too advanced to be included here, but the filter performance can be described. It may be noted that the gain factors depend on the ratio of T/τ, where T is the sampling interval for the digital filter, and τ is the time-constant for the analog filter. The value in use here is $T/\tau = 0.105$.

An input sample x_n has *added* to it the previous output sample *multiplied* by a factor 9, i.e., $9y_{n-1}$ is fed back to the input. This is achieved by having a delay of one sampling period (T) in the feedback line, followed by a gain of 9. The feedback sample is *added* to the input sample and the combination *multiplied* by a factor of 0.1. To illustrate, consider the sample at $n = 4$. $x_4 = 1$, and $y_4 = 0.344$ (this value was obtained by detailed calculation not included here). The next output value, with $X_5 = 1$, is obtained by:

$$y_5 = 0.1(x_5 + 9y_4) \qquad (17.6)$$

$$= 0.41$$

In general, the digital filter shown represents the recursive relationship:

$$y_n = 0.1(x_n + 9y_{n-1}) \qquad (17.7)$$

From the previous example it will be seen that digital filtering consists of a number of operations: multiplication by constants, summation and delay. These can all be carried out in binary digital arithmetic. Note however that the digital filtering action can be described in terms of decimal digits, and it would also be possible to build an analog system using amplifiers and a delay line to simulate the digital filter!

17.6   PULSE-CODE MODULATION

Pulse code modulation (PCM) is used to convert analog signals into binary digital form. As already mentioned, the pulse modulation techniques described in Chapter 11 are analog methods. They suffer from transmission distortion and noise to an appreciable extent, and are therefore not used that often for direct transmission, but more often as intermediate steps in the generation of *pulse-code modulation* (PCM). In the PCM system, groups of pulses or codes are transmitted which represent binary numbers corresponding to modulating voltage levels. Recovery of the transmitted information does not depend on the height, width, or energy content of the individual pulses, but only on their presence or absence. Since it is relatively easy to recover pulses under these conditions, even in the presence of large amounts of noise and distortion, PCM systems tend to be very immune to interference and noise. Regeneration of the pulses on route is also relatively easy, resulting in a system that produces excellent results for long-distance communication.

17.6.1   Quantization

The first step in the PCM system is to *quantize* the modulating signal. The modulating signal can assume an infinite number of different levels between the two limit values which define the *range* of the signal. In PCM, a coded number is transmitted for each level sampled in the modulating signal. If the exact number corresponding to the exact voltage were to be transmitted for every sample, an infinitely large number of different code symbols would be needed. Quantization has the effect of reducing this infinite number of levels to a relatively small number which can be coded without difficulty.

In the quantization process, the total range of the modulating signal is divided up into a number of small subranges. The number will depend on the nature of the modulating signal and will be from as few as 8 to as many as 128 levels. A number that is an integer power of 2 is usually chosen because of the ease of generating binary codes. A new signal is generated by producing, for each sample, a voltage level corresponding to the midpoint level of the subrange in which the sample falls. Thus, if a range of 0 to 4 V were divided into four 1-V subranges, and the signal were sampled when it was 2.8 V, the quantizer would put out a voltage of 2.5 V and hold that level until the next sampling time; 2.5 V corresponds to the midpoint of the third range. The result is a stepped waveform which follows the contour of the original modulating signal, with each step synchronized to the sampling period. Figure 17.5 illustrates the quantization process.

FIGURE 17.5. Quantization of a signal. $m(t)$ is the signal to be quantized. $m_q(t)$ is the quantized result. The difference of $m(t) - m_q(t)$ is the quantization error.

17.6.2 Quantization Noise

The quantized *staircase* waveform is an approximation to the original waveform. The difference between the two waveforms amounts to "noise" added to the signal by the quantizing circuit. The mean square quantization noise voltage has a value of

$$E_{nq}^2 = \frac{S^2}{12} \qquad (17.8)$$

where S is the voltage of each step, or the subrange voltage span. As a result, the number of quantization levels must be kept high in order to keep the quantization noise below some acceptable limit, given by the power signal-to-noise ratio, which is the ratio of average signal power to average noise power. For a sinusoidal signal which occupies the full range, the mean square signal voltage is

$$E_s^2 = \tfrac{1}{2}\, E_{peak}^2 = \tfrac{1}{2}\left(\frac{MS}{2}\right)^2 = \frac{(MS)^2}{8} \qquad (17.9)$$

where M is the number of steps and S is step height voltage. The signal-to-noise ratio is now given by

$$\frac{\text{Signal}}{\text{Noise}} = \frac{E_s^2}{E_{nq}^2} = \frac{(MS)^2}{8} \times \frac{12}{S^2} = \frac{3}{2}M^2 \qquad (17.10)$$

Example 17.2   In a PCM system the signal-to-noise (quantization noise) ratio is to be held to a minimum of 40 dB (a power ratio of 10000). Determine the number of levels needed.

Solution   From equation (17.10),

$$M = \sqrt{\frac{2}{3}\frac{\text{Signal}}{\text{Noise}}} = \sqrt{\frac{2}{3} \cdot 10000} = 81.7$$

The number of binary bits required is found from Eq. (17.11) as

$$I = \text{Log}_2(81.7) = 6.35$$

The next higher integer (7) would be used, giving an actual value of $M = 128$ and an actual signal-to-noise ratio of $1.5 \times 128^2 = 24{,}576$ (49.9 dB).

17.6.3   Companding

The signal-to-noise ratio derived above was related to a maximum amplitude signal, one with a peak-to-peak voltage equal to the full signal range. In practice, the signal may be many times smaller than this, as much as 30 dB less. Since the noise level is dependent on the step size, which is a constant, then with small signals a much lower signal-to-noise ratio will result. The process of *companding* is used to overcome this degradation of the *S/N* ratio. Companding is a compound process of volume compression before transmission combined with volume expansion after transmission. Companding itself does not produce any distortion in the recovered signal, but it does reduce the level of quantization noise during low-signal-level periods. The compressor amplifier amplifies low-level signals more than it does high-level signals, thus compressing the input voltage range into a smaller span. The steps transmitted have equal amplitudes, but are equivalent to using smaller steps in the low-level signals and larger steps in the high-level signals. The result is lower-amplitude quantization noise during the low-level periods.

17.6.4   PCM Encoding

The encoding process generates a binary code number corresponding to the quantization level number to be transmitted for each sampling interval. Any one of the codes mentioned in the following sections (such as the ASCII, or biquinary) may be used as long as it provides a sufficient number of different symbols to represent all the levels to be transmitted. Ordinary binary coding is most often used, where the binary number corresponding to the decimal number of the level in question is transmitted. This binary number will contain a train of "1" and "0" pulses with a total of $\log_2 N$ pulses in each number (N is the number of levels in the full range). This system is very economical to realize, because it corresponds exactly to the process of analog-to-digital (A/D) conversion. Microcircuits containing complete converters are available at very low cost.

17.6.5 PCM System

The block diagram of a PCM system is shown in Figure 17.6. The modulating signal $m(t)$ is applied to the input of the volume compressor unit. A sampling circuit generates a PAM signal from the compressed signal, which is then multiplexed with signals from other input channels. An analog-to-digital converter performs the two function of quantization and encoding, producing a binary-coded number for each channel-sampling period. A commutator circuit transmits the code bits in serial fashion.

At the receiver, a two-level quantizing circuit reshapes the incoming pulses and eliminates most of the transmission noise. A distributor circuit decommutates the pulses, and passes the bits in parallel groups to a digital-to-analog (D/A) converter for decoding. Another distributor demultiplexes

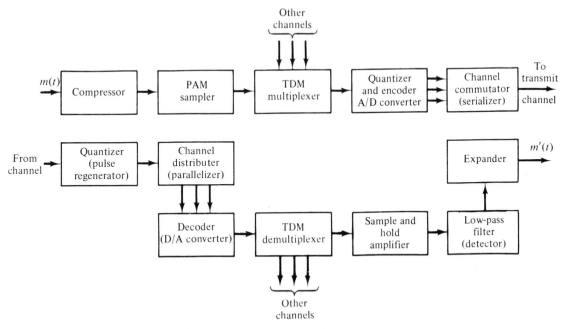

FIGURE 17.6. Pulse-code modulation (PCM) transmission system.

the several PAM signals and routes them to the proper output channels. Each channel has a sample-and-hold amplifier which maintains the pulse level for the duration of the sampling period, recreating the staircase waveform approximation of the compressed signal. A low-pass filter may be used to reduce the quantization noise, and finally an expander circuit removes the amplitude distortion which was intentionally introduced in the compression of the signal, to yield the output signal $m'(t)$.

17.7   DELTA MODULATION

Delta modulation (DM) is a process of modulation where a train of fixed-width pulses is transmitted, whose polarity indicates whether the demodulator output should rise or fall at each pulse. The output is caused to rise or fall by a fixed step height at each pulse. Figure 17.7(a) shows the block diagram of a DM system.

The modulating signal $m(t)$ is applied to the noninverting input of a high-gain differential comparator. A reconstructed version of this signal $m'(t)$ is applied to the inverting input. The differential comparator will be in saturation, either positive or negative, depending on the polarity of the *difference* voltage between the input signals. Thus the output will be ± 1, ignoring the ambiguous range in the middle.

The modulator receives a train of unipolar pulses $p_i(t)$ recurring at the desired sampling rate, and either transmits them directly for a $+1$ input or inverts their polarity for a -1 input. This signal is transmitted as the output signal $p_0(t)$ and also is passed to a local integrating circuit. This integrator causes $m'(t)$ to rise or fall by a fixed step height for each $+$ or $-$ pulse applied to its input. The height of the pulse can be adjusted by changing the gain factor of the integrator. An increase will cause the step waveform to have a higher maximum rate of rise R_{max}.

At the receiver, a regenerator reshapes the received signal and removes most of the noise. The signal is then fed to another integrator, which reconstructs $m'(t)$, the step waveform. This is then passed through a low-pass filter to remove the quantization noise, leaving a replica $m''(t)$ of the original signal.

17.7.1.   Slope Overload

The integrator will not be able to follow a signal with a very fast rate of rise. Figure 17.7(b) shows how the pulse train and the reconstructed step waveform follow a slowly rising or falling input. Figure 17.7(c) shows the case where the input is rising at the same rate as the staircase (i.e., it is rising at its maximum rate). At this rate, the output signal $p_o(t)$ will be only

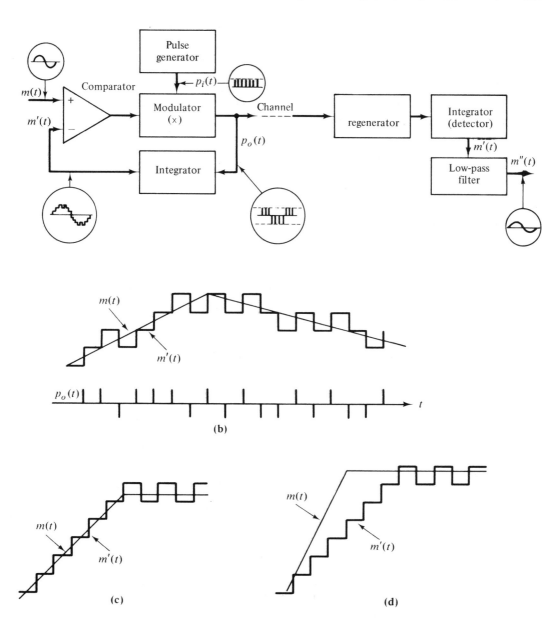

FIGURE 17.7.   (a) A delta modulation (DM) transmission system; (b) Input, output, and regenerated signal for input slope less than R_{max}; (c) Input and regenerated signal for slope equal to R_{max}; (d) Input and regenerated signal slope greater than R_{max}. R_{max} is the maximum rate of rise of the step waveform.

positive pulses. When the signal levels off, the step waveform will alternate above and below it, or "hunt." The output will be alternating positive and negative pulses. Figure 17.7(d) shows the case where the input is rising faster than the step waveform. The step waveform will continue to rise constantly at its maximum rate, until it catches up, but in the meantime, it will be less than the input, causing an error in the demodulated signal. This condition is known as *slope overload.*

17.7.2   Adaptive Delta Modulation

To counteract slope overload, a variation called *adaptive delta modulation* has been developed. This system works in exactly the same manner as ordinary DM, except that a variable-gain amplifier is included in the input to the integrator. The gain of this amplifier is controlled by the average rate of pulses, either positive or negative, being transmitted. Thus, if more positive pulses are transmitted than negative pulses, the gain will increase. Also, if more negative pulses are transmitted than positive pulses, the gain will increase. The gain will be lowest when the number of positive and negative pulses are equal, or at constant input signal level. The effect of this is to cause the step height to be larger for faster-rising signals, so the step waveform can follow faster waveforms than the ordinary DM system.

Finally, comparing DM and PCM systems, DM requires a higher sampling rate and larger bandwidth than PCM to yield comparable fidelity, but DM requires much simpler and less costly hardware than PCM.

17.8   CODING

17.8.1   Information Content—The Bit

Information theory was developed by Shannon and others to provide a means of quantitatively measuring the rate and efficiency of information flow. According to this theory, the most basic piece of information possible is the choice of one of two equiprobable events. The answer is the familiar true or false, or, in the case of binary signals, one or zero. This basic unit of information is called the *binary digit*, or *bit*, and is the basis of the binary number system. In a communication system, the basic bit of information may be conveyed as the presence or absence of signal during a specified time period (i.e., by a pulse). The PCM system is a case in point. Each pulse carries one bit of information. Several of these bits must be combined to extract enough data to reconstruct the signal level again.

If we consider a system of N equiprobable events (such as the N quantization levels in the PCM system), and we wish to specify *one* of those equiprobable events so that it cannot be confused with any other of that set of events, a certain minimum amount of information has to be provided.

The number of bits required to define 1 out of N events in the binary system is

$$I = \log_2 N \qquad (17.11)$$

Since a fraction of a bit is an impossible situation, the next higher integer number of bits must be used for the message, which specifies the 1-out-of-N event.

Coding can be done in higher-base-number systems as well, although these cannot be so readily transmitted as the binary codes. Suppose that each pulse in a train of pulses can be amplitude-modulated to 10 levels. Then each pulse can carry the information to choose 1 out of 10 equiprobable events. Trains of pulses of this nature would allow coding in terms of ordinary decimal numbers. Each unit is a *decimal* dig*it*, or *dit*, and to encode a single event out of N events would require

$$I = (\log_{10} N) \text{ dits of information} \qquad (17.12)$$

One dit is equivalent to $\log_2 10$, or 3.32 bits, but 4 (the next higher integer) bits must be used to represent it.

17.8.2 Code Efficiency

Code efficiency is defined as the ratio of the exact number of bits necessary to define 1-of-N events divided by the total number of bits that are used to transmit information.

Example 17.3 In the BCD code, 4 bits of information are transmitted in each *character* or message to define a single event. The total number of events out of which each is chosen is $N = 10$. However, 4 bits can allow the choice of 1 out of 16 events. The efficiency is calculated as

$$\text{code efficiency} = \frac{\log_2 N}{B} \qquad \text{where } B = \text{bits used} \qquad (17.13)$$

$$= \frac{\log_2 10}{\log_2 16}$$

$$= \frac{3.32}{4.00} = 0.83$$

17.8.3 Telegraph Speed

Several types of binary codes, notably the international Morse code and the 5-bit Baudot teletype code, use unequal length pulses in their coding. A special measure of message transmission speed was developed to describe this situation. The baud is defined as the inverse of the period of the shortest information unit used in the code transmission, which corresponds to 1 bit. The *baud* is thus the maximum information rate of the code transmission:

$$\text{telegraphic speed} = \frac{1}{T_{p\min}} \quad \text{baud} \qquad (17.14)$$

where $T_{p\min}$ is the duration of the shortest information unit. This measure is used primarily in connection with teletypewriter codes.

In transmitting English text, the average word length has been found to be six characters, including the space separating it from the next word. The speed of transmission on a teletype or telegraph channel is quite often referred to in terms of words per minute (wpm). This can be readily converted to a baud rate if the character structure of the code is known.

Example 17.4   Suppose that a teletypewriter circuit uses the ASCII code and transmits at a speed of 100 wpm. Each character contains 11 bits, all of equal length. Eight bits carry message information, one is used for start synchronization and two are used for stop synchronization. The code has an efficiency of 8/11, or 0.727. The baud rate is the same as the bit rate and is calculated as

$$\text{speed} = \frac{100 \text{ wpm}}{60 \text{ s/min}} \times 6 \text{ char/word} \times 11 \text{ bits/char}$$

$$= \textbf{110.0 baud (bits/s)}$$

The period of each bit is $1/110.0 = $ **9.1 ms.**

17.8.4   Parallel Transmission

In a given code, each character of the code is represented by I bits of information. In the teletype codes this information is usually transmitted in the bit-serial mode, with extra bits added for synchronization. Message transmission may be speeded up if a separate transmission channel is provided for each bit of the code character, and the message sent out in bit-parallel (character-serial) mode with synchronization characters included after a block of characters has been transmitted. For the same bandwidth of channel, information may now be transmitted at I times the speed, but this increase of speed is at the expense of providing the additional parallel channels, i.e., at the expense of increased total bandwidth.

17.9   CODES

One of the earliest binary codes was the code developed by Samuel Morse for use on his telegraph system. This system used alternate on and off periods of current on the telegraph wire to code the information. The current caused the armature of a solenoid coil much like a relay to rise if current was on, and fall when current was off. Each time the armature rose or fell, an audible click was produced. Two different lengths of pulses were used, and various combinations of up to six long and short pulses made up each character. The code was deciphered aurally by the operator, and a good telegrapher could read the code at speeds up to 150 wpm. The Canadian National Railways in Canada discontinued the last of their Morse telegraph circuits in 1970.

A variation of Morse's code was adopted for use by radio-telegraphers which is still being used by radio amateur operators all over the world. This code uses combinations of long and short bursts of tone to define each character. The code may be transmitted by turning on and off a radio transmitter to produce the dots and dashes. The character symbols have been modified and many new ones added from Morse's original. A partial listing of the code is shown in Figure 17.8(a).

The advent of the teletypewriter machine produced the need for codes with a fixed character length and structure. The earliest of these, developed in the early 1900s, was the Baudot code. The character structure of this code is shown in Figure 17.9(a) Each character contains five equal-length bits of information, a start bit and a longer stop synchronizing pulse of 1.5-bit units, making a total of 7.5 bits per character. The coding allows a basic block of $2^5 = 32$ characters, but two of these characters are used as uppercase shift and lowercase shift. In uppercase, the same block of 30 characters have different meanings than they do in the lowercase. Thus a code containing 60 useful characters is generated. The machines will remain in uppercase until a lowercase shift is received. The listing for one variation of this code, the CCITT-2 code, is shown in Figure 17.8(b). Most of the teletypewriters using this code operate at a speed of 60 wpm.

The ASCII code has recently been developed to provide a standard code for transmitting data between computers and for teletypewriters. The structure of this code is shown in Figure 17.9(b), and a partial listing is shown in Figure 17.8(d). It uses 11 equal-length bits per character: one start, two stop, and eight information bits. The eighth bit is usually reserved for parity, leaving a total character complement of $2^7 = 128$. This allows plenty of room in the code for all the common alphanumerics and punctuations, as well as a number of special functions. Only about 80 of the characters available are used in the eight-level teletypewriter machine coding, although the meaning of each character may vary considerably depending on the use the machine is put to. It should be noted from Figure 17.8(d) that the 10 decimal digits are assigned within one block of characters so that the last four bits of the character form the binary equivalent of the digit, resulting in very easy decoding of numerical data for computer entry.

Ordinary binary coding is quite often used for the interchange of

(a) International Morse code

Character	Symbol
A	·—
B	—···
C	—·—·
D	—··
E	·
F	··—·
G	——·
H	····
I	··
J	·———
K	—·—
L	·—··
M	——
N	—·
O	———
P	·——·
Q	——·—
R	·—·
S	···
T	—
U	··—
V	···—
W	·——
X	—··—
Y	—·——
Z	——··
.	·—·—·—
,	——··——
?	··——··
EOM	·—·—·
EOT	···—·—
ERROR	······
Ø	————
1	·————
2	··———
3	···——
4	····—
5	·····
6	—····
7	——···
8	———··
9	————·

(b) CCITT-2 and (c) ARQ teleprinter codes

Character			Bit position 12345	Bit position 1234567
1	A	—	11000	0011010
2	B	?	10011	0011001
3	C	:	01110	1001100
4	D	WRU	10010	0011100
5	E	3	10000	0111000
6	F	%	10110	0010011
7	G	@	01011	1100001
8	H	£	00101	1010010
9	I	8	01100	1110000
10	J	BELL	11010	0100011
11	K	(	11110	0001011
12	L	)	01001	1100010
13	M	.	00111	1010001
14	N	,	00110	1010100
15	O	9	00011	1000110
16	P	Ø	01101	1001010
17	Q	1	11101	0001101
18	R	4	01010	1100100
19	S	'	10100	0101010
20	T	5	00001	1000101
21	U	7	11100	0110010
22	V	=	01111	1001001
23	W	2	11001	0100101
24	X	/	10111	0010110
25	Y	6	10101	0010101
26	Z	+	10001	0110001
27	CARR. RETURN		00010	1000011
28	LINE FEED		01000	1011000
29	FIGS. SHIFT		11011	0100110
30	LETT. SHIFT		11111	0001110
31	SPACE		00100	1101000
32	BLANK		00000	0000111

(b)   (c)

(d) US-ASCII teleprinter code

Bit position: 8   76   54321

76=01	76=10	8 76	54321
SPACE	@		00000
!	A		00001
"	B		00010
#	C		00011
$	D		00100
%	E		00101
&	F		00110
'	G		00111
(	H		01000
)	I		01001
*	J		01010
+	K	PARITY	01011
,	L		01100
—	M		01101
.	N		01110
/	O		01111
0	P		10000
1	Q	or 1	10001
2	R		10010
3	S		10011
4	T		10100
5	U		10101
6	V		10110
7	W		10111
8	X		11000
9	Y		11001
:	Z		11010
;	[		11011
<	\		11100
=	]		11101
>	Λ		11110
?	—		11111

76 = 00 group-control codes
76 = 11 group-lower case alpha and special marks

(d)

FIGURE 17.8. Partial listings of some commonly used codes: (a) International Morse code; (b) CCITT-2 teleprinter code; (c) ARQ teleprinter code; (d) US-ASCII teleprinter code. (Courtesy Howard W. Sams and Company, Inc.)

number data between computers, especially on high-speed links. Such data are usually transmitted in blocks of characters, each block containing some form of error detection and correction mechanism. Numerical data are also quite often transmitted in the form of *binary coded decimal* (BCD). This code uses four-bit binary characters to represent the 10 decimal digits; each

FIGURE 17.9.   (a) Character structure of the five-level teletype code; (b) Character structure of the eight-level teletype code; (c) Some binary numeric codes.

one is the direct binary equivalent of the digit it represents. The code is shown in Figure 17.9(c) and is known as a binary-weighted code. Several different weighted and unweighted codes are derived by choosing a different group of 10 characters out of the 16 available with four-bit coding.

17.10   ERROR DETECTION AND CORRECTION CODES

17.10.1   Parity

The simplest form of error detection is *parity*. Single parity is established as follows; first, the information is coded in the normal manner using one of the standard binary codes. Each character is then examined to determine whether it contains an even or an odd number of 1 bits. If even parity is to be established, a 1 bit is added to each odd character, and a 0 bit is added to each even character. The result is that all the characters now contain an even number of 1 bits. After transmission, each character is examined to see if it still contains an even number of 1 bits. If it does not, the presence of an error is indicated. If it does the parity bit is removed and the data passed to the user. This form of parity will only detect errors if an odd number of bits were disturbed. An even number of errors within the same character will compensate for each other and go undetected. The total error security for this type of detection is quite low.

Multiple forms of parity provide a more secure system. In this case, a group of several characters are combined to form a block of information. Within a block, each character forms a row, and each character has simple parity applied to it. In addition, each column in the block may have parity established for it by adding a parity word to the end of the block. Now if a single error occurs within the block, a parity error will be indicated for the word in which the error occurs, and also for the column in which it occurs. The intersection of the row and column is the location of the faulted bit, and *correction* can be achieved by merely inverting that bit. The system will also detect multiple errors, but if these occur in more than one word, or in more than one row of the block, correction cannot be accomplished. The coordinates for two errors will intersect at four locations, and unless a third parity (such as spiral) is added, there is no way to distinguish which of the four locations are in error. In that event retransmission is requested.

17.10.2   Redundant Codes

A highly redundant code with natural built-in parity was developed in the 1940s for radio telegraphy. This is the ARQ code. Each character contains seven bits, of which only three are 1 bits, which gives the code its error-detection capability. There are 35 symbols of this type out of the 128 symbols possible with 7 bits, and only 32 of these are used. They are designated on the same basis as the CCITT-2 teletype code. The efficiency of the code is only 5/9.5 as compared to 5/7.5 for the CCITT-2, but this is more than compensated for by the increased security against errors. The ARQ code is listed in Figure 17.8(c).

Another code which is similar to the ARQ code is the bi-quinary code. This is used for transmitted numerical data. It is also a 7-bit code, of which only two 1 bits are transmitted in each character. The bits are weighted from left to right as 50-43210, so the character 1000100 represents the decimal digit 7. The efficiency is 3.32/7, but it is very unlikely that an error would go undetected. This code is listed in Figure 17.9(c).

The Gray code is an unweighted reflected binary code which is often used for transmitting telemetry data. It has the advantage that in progressing up or down throught the code, in counting, adjacent characters differ by only one bit. Telemetry data are usually slowly varying so that the same character may be transmitted for several successive sampling periods before a change occurs. When that change does occur, it will be to the next higher or the next lower count. If a greater change is received, the character may be rejected, or an error indicated. Such a scheme also eliminates the ambiguity that occurs between two characters. Thus, if the sequence 8 8 8 4 7 7 7 ... were received, the receiver could correctly interpret that the 4 was a spurious signal, and that a transition from the 8 to the 7 level occurred at the time that the 4 was encoded. The Gray code for the 10 decimal digits is shown in Figure 17.9(c). Its similarity to the binary number sequence should be noted.

17.10.3 Hamming Codes

A somewhat different form of error detecting and correcting coding is developed by adding three or more check bits to each character, usually less than the number of bits in the original coding. These check bits are chosen so that the expanded characters used differ from each other by at least three bits. The number of bits difference is known as the *Hamming distance* and a code of this type is known as a *Hamming code*. Obviously, many variations can be derived.

All the preceding codes treat the data on a block basis. The data are divided up into blocks of bits of predetermined length, and the error-detecting redundancy applied to each block independently of the other. With a Hamming code, a continuous form of error checking is applied to form a convolution code. In this case, m code bits are derived by a logical combination of n successive bits of the original bit stream. The original code is shifted through a shift register serially, and at each shifting the combinational circuit produces a group of m bits of the coded stream. Thus the information for each input bit is contained in mn of the coded bits, and the likelihood of errors disturbing all the mn bits is very low. At the receiving end, another shifting and combinational operation decodes the original bit stream. A coding system of this type would be ideal for application to a PCM system or to any process that produces a continuous stream of code bits.

17.11 DIGITAL CARRIER SYSTEMS

Slow-speed data systems such as teletypewriters are usually modulated on a tone carrier, which is then frequency-multiplexed into a slot in a voice channel.

17.11.1 Frequency-Shift Keying

Two-tone frequency-shift keying is commonly used. In this system, two tones within the voice channel, which can be separated easily with bandpass filters, are assigned as carriers. One tone is transmitted for the 1 bit, and the other for a 0 bit. Two bandpass filters, rectifiers, and a differential amplifier demodulate the signal. Figure 17.10(a) shows a possible FSK system. Teletype carrier systems used on the telephone system divide the 4-kHz voice band up into as many as 20 channels, with a channel separation of about 120 Hz for 60 wpm, or as few as six 170-Hz channels for 100-wpm eight-level teletypes.

Radio-telegraph systems quite often frequency-modulate the RF carrier directly, transmitting the nominal carrier frequency for the 0-bit condition and transmitting a frequency about 70 Hz lower for the 1 bit. Alternatively, the two-tone FSK system can be either amplitude-modulated or frequency-modulated onto the RF carrier.

17.11.2 Phase-shift Keying

Phase-shift keying is also used. For simple phase-shift keying, the unshifted carrier $V\cos\omega_o t$ is transmitted to indicate a 1 condition and the carrier shifted by 180° or π radians $(V\cos\omega_o t + \pi) = -V\cos\omega_o t)$ is transmitted to indicate a 0 condition. The modulating circuitry is quite simple for this, since it is only necessary to provide two switches and an inverter. Figure 17.10(b) shows a possible phase-shift keyer arrangement. Demodulation is accomplished by subtracting the received carrier from a derived synchronous reference carrier of constant phase.

17.11.3 Differential Phase Shift Keying

Phase shift keying requires a local oscillator at the receiver which is accurately synchronized in phase with the unmodulated transmitted carrier, and in practice this can be difficult to achieve. Differential phase shift keying (DPSK) overcomes the difficulty by utilizing the phase shift between successive bits, hence the name *differential* PSK. The phase of the first message bit has to be compared to a reference bit which may be arbitrarily chosen as 0 or 1. Figure 17.11(a) shows a 0 reference bit. If the compared bits do not differ, this is encoded as a 1, or zero phase shift of carrier. If they do differ, this is encoded as a 0, or π radians shift of carrier. Figure 17.11(a) shows the sequence of events for the message 01100. Comparing the first message bit with the reference they are seen to be the same, so this is encoded as a 1, and transmitted as zero phase shift. (Note that the first transmitted bit is the reference bit, a 0 in this case.) The second message bit is compared with the second encoded bit, both are seen to be 1, so this information is also encoded as a 1, and the carrier phase shift remains at zero. Continuing in this way, the third message bit is seen to be the same as the third encoded bit, so again this is encoded as a 1, or zero phase shift of carrier. The fourth message bit is compared with the fourth encoded bit. They are seen to be different, so this is encoded as a 0, and the carrier phase shift is π radians. The last message bit is compared with the fifth encoded

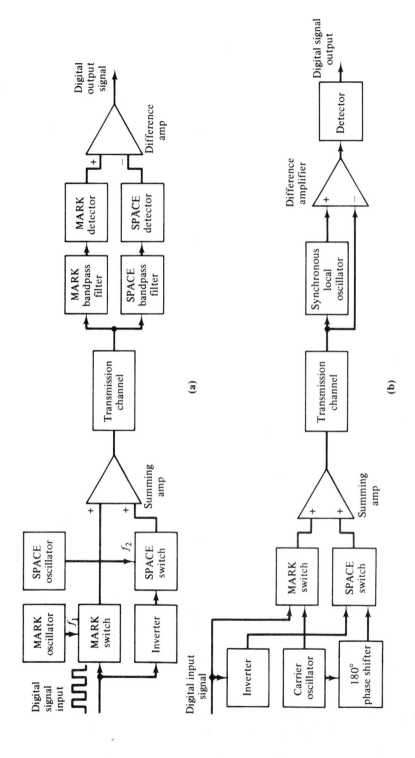

FIGURE 17.10. (a) FSK (frequency-shift keying) digital transmission system; (b) PSK (phase-shift keying) digital transmission system.

bit; they are the same, so this is encoded as a **1**, or again, a carrier phase shift of zero. Figure 17.11(b) shows how encoding might be achieved by digital hardware.

At the receiver, the signal is multiplied by a delayed version of itself, the delay being equal to one bit duration. This is shown schematically in Figure 17.11(c). If the delayed signal is in phase with the direct signal, the output

(a)

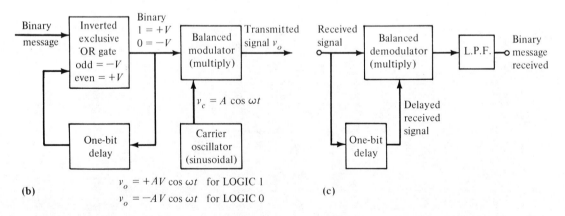

$$v_o = +AV \cos \omega t \quad \text{for LOGIC 1}$$
$$v_o = -AV \cos \omega t \quad \text{for LOGIC 0}$$

(b)

(c)

FIGURE 17.11. Differential Phase Shift Keying. (a) Encoding and decoding a message sequence; (b) An encoding arrangement; (c) The receiver.

following the low pass filter will have a positive dc component, and will be decoded as a 1. If the two signals differ in phase by π radians, the dc output will be negative, and interpreted as a binary 0. This sequence of events at the receiver is illustrated also in Figure 17.11(a).

17.12   TELEPRINTERS AND TELEGRAPH CIRCUITS

17.12.1   Teleprinters

Teleprinters were originally designed for the transmission and reception of printed text, including both letters and numbers. They were a logical extension of the ordinary typewriter, and the early models were simply modified typewriters. The basic operation of a teleprinter unit can be followed from Figure 17.12(a). This shows the various functional blocks involved in a teleprinter circuit connecting two keyboard-send-receive (KSR) units, which are used for direct communication between two operators. Each KSR consists of a keyboard with one key for each pair of symbols to be transmitted. A "shift-up" character in the five-level teletypewriter system shifts the printer up into the second group in the same manner as the uppercase shift on a typewriter, where it remains until a "shift-down" character is received. Each code character is used for two different symbols. In eight-level systems a shift key and another control key allow the generation of four different characters by each of the other keys, and the printer simply prints the corresponding symbol.

The keyboard and the printer are both mechanical. Both units are driven from a common motor through a set of shafts. Depression of a key on the keyboard sets a series of mechanical latches in the encoding section and releases the transmission clutch. The transmitter shaft makes a single revolution, during which a set of cams causes a contact to open and close according to the selected code. This contact breaks the current in the electrical transmission loop whenever a 0 is transmitted, and makes the current whenever a 1 is transmitted. This transmitter is called a *commutator* and serves the function of time-division multiplexing of the bits of information that make up each character.

The current pulses are transmitted over telegraph circuits to the distant station where a relay in the receiver section reconstructs the pulses and passes them to an electromagnet which controls the receiver operation. When this electromagnet is deenergized, it trips the printer clutch in the machine, which then makes one revolution. During this revolution a series of cams set or leave unset a series of mechanical latches in the decoder unit, depending on whether or not the receive magnet is energized. Once the code has been interpreted by setting the latches, a final cam operates the printer to strike the selected character.

(a)

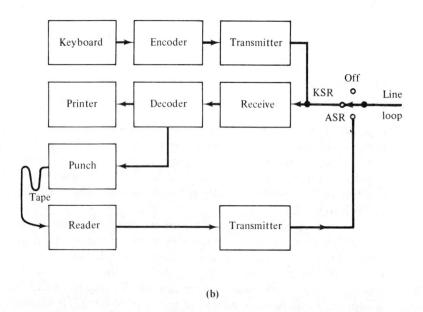

(b)

FIGURE 17.12. (a) Teletypewriter keyboard-send-receive (KSR) circuit; (b) Automatic send-receive (ASR) station.

The receive unit and printer at the sending location also monitors the line and prints the character as it is transmitted. Some machines are arranged so that the mechanical functions of the transmitter and receiver are combined, and the printer is operated directly from the keyboard by mechanical linkages. The keyboard must be locked out while the receiver is receiving a character from the line in order to prevent interruption errors. Special send-only machines are arranged in this manner but have the receiver-decoder functions omitted. These are known as *keyboard-send*-only (KSO) *machines*. *Receive-only* (RO) *machines* contain only the receiver-decoder-printer mechanisms and are often used for monitoring purposes.

Paper-tape punches and readers are also available, either as separate units or as integral parts of send-receive machines. Figure 17.12(b) shows the equipment features of an *automatic send-receive*, or ASR, *station*. It is comprised of a keyboard with its encoder and transmitter, and a printer with its receiver and decoder, which can be connected and used as a KSR unit on-line, or it can be used off-line on a local loop for tape preparation as a keyboard with a local printer. The tape punch is attached to and operates as part of the printer unit but can be disabled by a panel switch. Operated off-line, the station can be used to prepare a punched-tape message which can later be sent on-line by a paper tape reader with its own encoder and transmitter. The reader may also be used off-line to feed the punch so that duplicate tapes may be prepared, or so that the taped message may be typed for reading locally. This type of machine is particularly useful in applications on busy telegraph circuits where the manual operation of a keyboard at speeds less than continuous maximum would be wasteful of transmission capacity. A tape is prepared of the message off-line at the operator's leisure, and then transmitted at maximum speed when the telegraph circuit becomes available.

All the preceding machines have printers which produce a single copy of text, with up to five carbon copies, using fanfold or roll paper. A special form of the receive-only machine is frequently used in stock-exchange applications, in which the message is printed out on a narrow paper tape. This machine is called a *ticker*, because of the ticking noise the early machines made. It is enclosed in a soundproofed enclosure to reduce annoyance in quiet office surroundings. Similar machines are sometimes used in commercial telegraph offices, where an incoming message is typed on ticker tape and then cut up into sections and glued to a standard telegram form. It is doubtful that such practices will survive for long with computers available that can automatically format a message on a form using a standard printer.

Teletypewriter machines are used at continuous speeds in the range from 60 wpm to about 200 wpm, corresponding to bit rates of 45 Baud for 60-wpm five-level, and 220 Baud for 200-wpm eight-level machines. Several telegraph channels of this nature may be frequency-division-multiplexed onto a single voice channel.

High-speed paper-tape readers and punches are also available which operate at speeds up to 2000 wpm eight-level. These machines need a channel bandwidth of at least 1100 Hz, and only two or three channels may be carried on a single voice channel. They are useful in speeding up service on heavy-traffic circuits or for use with computer terminals. Transmission is always at the maximum rate, so line utilization is maintained at a high level.

Special versions of the keyboard, printer, tape punch, and tape reader are available which transmit and receive data in bit-parallel form. These machines require an eight-channel parallel transmission facility and are typically used in computer terminal applications.

Special very high-speed page-printing units have been developed for use as computer terminals. These may be classed as teleprinters, and could be used in the same manner if broadband communications circuits are available. These machines feature printing on a line-at-a-time basis rather than a character at a time, usually print only a single copy on fanfold or roll paper, and can print at speeds up to 100 lines per minute, with as many as 200 characters per line. A small control computer with facilities for storing two or more lines of data at a time is needed with such a machine to control its formatting and operation. Data are transmitted to it and operated on in blocks which are usually one line in length. Transmission bandwidths for such applications are in the megahertz region, and long distance use is not common, except on intercomputer links. Such machines are usually used as the hard-copy output machines associated with local computer systems.

17.12.2 Telegraph and Teletype Transmission

Telegraph and teletype circuits operate by interrupting or reversing the polarity of a direct current in a pair of wires, in pulse fashion. The current level used is between 20 and 200 mA and is provided by batteries usually located at a central switching office. Local batteries located at the terminal machine are sometimes used to aid the central battery to guarantee enough current in long loop circuits. The loop circuits are usually telephone subscriber loop pairs especially assigned for the telegraph circuit, although in some cases the telegraph circuit may be multiplexed on a voice circuit which does not use dc signaling.

The polar relay has two opposing windings and a double magnetic circuit which is arranged so that if the difference between the currents in the two coils is positive, it will operate in one direction; and if the difference is negative, it will operate in the other direction. It is extremely sensitive, and a very small difference is sufficient to cause it to operate.

The polar relay is used to square up pulses in telegraph circuits and to provide an adjustable threshold. Polar relays located at intervals along a long telegraph line sense pulses from the sending end and apply fresh battery current to send on toward the receiver. The result is to square up pulses that have been skewed by the line, and to correct for bias distortion, but it will not correct timing distortion once it has been introduced by characteristic distortion or by a misadjusted circuit.

Figure 17.13(a) shows a simplified half-duplex (alternate transmission in either direction similar to simplex mode) teletype circuit. This circuit operates on unipolar current pulses in both the loop and the line, with the presence of current being a mark, or 1, condition and the absence of current being a space, or zero. When the circuit is idle, mark current flows in both loops and in the trunk circuit. Mark current for the sending station loop is provided by two batteries, one positively connected to one side of the loop pair and one negatively connected through the contacts of the receiver relay and the coil of the sending relay. This battery also supplies bias current for the sending relay, at one half of the line current level. The net flux generated by the two coils is such as to hold the sending relay in its mark position.

When the sending contact of the teletype machine opens, signaling a zero or space bit, the line current is interrupted, and the net flux in the sending relay coils reverses polarity so that the relay operates to the space position. This provides battery of the opposite polarity to the loop, which opposed by the battery of that same polarity at the far end, and the loop current drops to zero. The bias current is reversed, so that the receive relay remains in the mark position. Transmission toward the teletype machine proceeds in a similar manner. A third break relay (which is not shown) is included to prevent false operation if the trunk circuit should attempt to send into the loop when the loop is open-circuited, by forcing the trunk circuit current to remain marking.

Half-duplex circuits of this nature may be quite long and can span several exchange offices. If they are long, it may be necessary to include a regenerative-type repeater circuit somewhere in the middle of the circuit. The repeater is either a mechanical device similar to the receiver and transmitter of a teletype machine, or it may be an electronic circuit. This circuit acts to receive and interpret a distorted signal from one side, reconstruct it so that the transitions from mark to space and space to mark all occur at the proper time intervals, and retransmit it on the other side with fresh battery.

DC trunk circuits of great length are not used. Instead, the teletype signals are received at the local exchange office and applied to a *modem* or data terminal set, which modulates the pulses onto a tone carrier which can be transmitted over an ordinary telephone circuit. The modulation method may be one of several types, but is frequently FSK. The *modem* (derived from *mo*dulator–*dem*odulator) also contains narrow bandpass filters to separate the desired carrier signals from others which may be on the same voice circuit, or from interference from supervisory signals. A single voice channel can accommodate as many as twenty 60-wpm five-level teletype channels or twelve 100-wpm eight-level channels, with FSK modulation.

Figure 17.13(b) illustrates a carrier teletype circuit. The loops at either

(a)

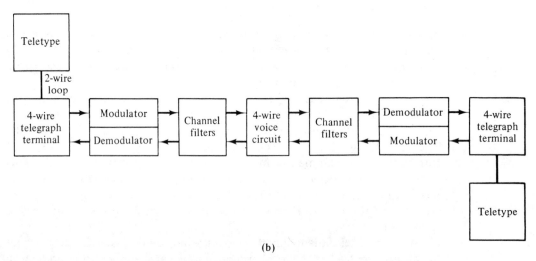

(b)

FIGURE 17.13. (a) Simplified half-duplex telegraph circuit; the circuit operates on unipolar or neutral pulses; (b) A carrier telegraph circuit; a teletypewriter system uses a tone carrier telegraph circuit superimposed on a telephone voice circuit.

end are arranged in the same manner as those of the dc circuit previously discussed. Relay terminal circuits separate the east- and west-bound signals. Outgoing signals are applied to the modulator input of the data modem circuit, and incoming signals are picked off the demodulator output. The outputs from the modems are connected to the voice trunk circuit through channel bandpass filters.

Quite often the data modem is included directly at the teletype machine. This has the advantage that the signal may be placed directly on an ordinary telephone loop circuit without the necessity of modifying any line equipment. Dial switching networks similar to the telephone switching networks have been developed by several companies. In some of these, special interoffice trunk circuits have been constructed and assigned just for teletype service, but some telephone companies use the same switching network for both telephone and teletype service. The terminal machines for such service include a data modem, dial-pulse generator, monitor handset, and calling and answering circuits, as well as the teleprinter machinery. The TWX service offered by Bell System companies and AT&T in North America operate such a service using the telephone network, while several railway companies and Western Union Telegraph operate a system called Telex.

Slow-speed data with rates less than about 200 bauds can be transmitted over standard telegraph circuits such as the ones discussed in the previous section. Higher-speed data transmission needs special facilities. Data transmission with rates up to about 2000 bauds can be transmitted on tone carriers over standard telephone channels. Rates up to about 4000 bauds can be accommodated on compensated broad-band voice circuits of the type used to feed radio network signals, while higher rates require special circuits.

Modified telephone carrier systems with special broad-band data channels can be set up to accommodate data rates up to about 500,000 baud. Terminal loops for such systems require the use of coaxial cables, to provide the necessary bandwidth, and require special installations. Higher bandwidths yet can be provided over television channels on the radio systems. If such facilities are leased from telephone companies, the circuit is reserved specifically for the one user or customer. Most facilities of this type are used to interconnect computer systems and tend to be very costly.

In some cases of large systems interconnecting many computers, it may be more economical for the companies involved to construct their own microwave relay system. The costs of such a system are very high, and unless the system is very large and has a heavy volume of traffic it would not be economical.

Standard data modems using a variety of modes of transmission and modulation have been developed. All of these have been designed so that the terminal connections and mode of operation overall are the same for all the various types of data sets. Thus any data user with a standard data interface circuit can connect to a standard circuit and communicate with any other data user with similar terminal equipment. Interconnection of various types of equipment becomes a simple matter.

17.13 RADIO-TELEGRAPH TRANSMITTERS

Figure 17.14(a) shows the block diagram of an interrupted continuous wave (ICW) transmitter. Such transmitters are rarely used these days, except for emergency communications and by radio amateurs and the military. These communications are for the most part concentrated in the HF band from 1.6 MHz up to 30 MHz, although some are used in the LF band below 0.5 MHz. Most modern telegraph communications use an audio-tone subcarrier which is then modulated on a continuous RF carrier by one of the standard voice-modulation techniques. However, many sections of the ICW transmitter are common to all types of transmitters and these are briefly described here.

The circuit in Figure 17.14(a) shows that the first and main component of the CW telegraph transmitter is a stable oscillator circuit at the assigned frequency. The oscillator is nearly always followed by a buffer amplifier, which is a tuned class A amplifier. This amplifier is used to prevent variations of load in subsequent amplifiers because of tuning from affecting the frequency of the main oscillator circuit. It also acts to provide any impedance transformation that may be required. All the tuned circuits in the CW transmitter are constructed with as high Q as possible, consistent with circuit stability, to provide as much rejection of harmonics as possible.

The buffer amplifier is followed by one or more tuned class C amplifiers which amplify the signal to the level necessary to drive the final amplifier. The final amplifier may have an output of several kilowatts or more, and the drive power may well be several hundred watts. Thus the driver amplifier itself is really a power amplifier. If the frequency to be radiated is above about 15 MHz, it is unlikely that the crystal oscillator will be tuned to the final output frequency. The oscillator itself may be tuned to the second harmonic so that the crystal operates in an "overtone" mode, or one of the driver amplifier stages may be used to double or triple the frequency to the final output frequency value.

The final power amplifier is a class C amplifier with self-bias. Provision is made to measure the signal-induced bias current in the input circuit and the direct current supplied to the output circuit. A "keying" circuit is also provided. This allows the current in the final amplifier to be interrupted, either by a relay contact directly in the current lead, or, as is more likely for high-power transmitters, by biasing the final amplifier into cutoff. In either case, a filter circuit is provided so that the cutoff does not occur suddenly but over many cycles of the carrier. A typical keying time constant would be

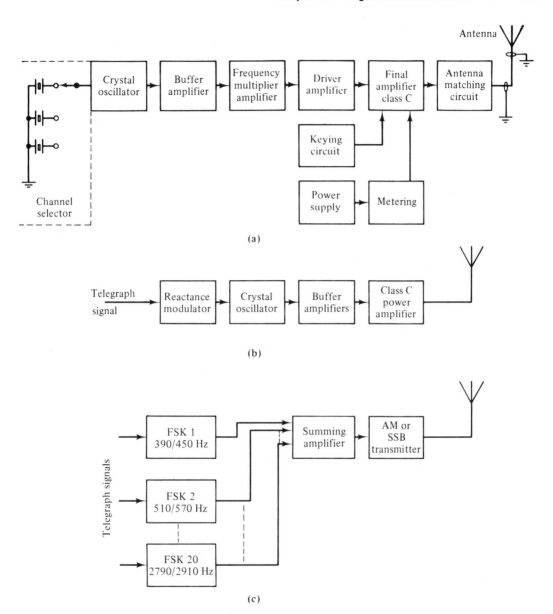

FIGURE 17.14.   (a) ICW telegraph transmitter; (b) Frequency-shift-keyed transmitter; (c) Audio signal transmitter with several telegraph channels frequency-division-multiplexed in the voice channel.

about 1 ms. This allows the carrier to decay and rise slowly enough so that the sideband frequencies do not spread into adjacent channels where they would give rise to interference heard as clicks or thumps.

Earlier stages of the transmitter might be keyed, but since the output stage relies on a continuous drive signal for most of its bias, heavy amounts of dc current would be drawn during the "key-up" intervals. Thus the output stage is nearly always keyed.

On-off keying is not the most satisfactory method of transmitting radio telegraph as it may be difficult to detect the off-period when background noise is high. Alternative methods are frequency shift keying (FSK) of the carrier and two-tone modulation. For the frequency shift keying of the RF carrier, a reactance modulator can be provided in which the variable reactance shifts the main crystal oscillator by a small amount. The amount of shift necessary for 60-wpm teletype signals would be about 60 Hz, and a channel bandwidth of about 150 Hz is sufficient to accommodate any sidebands created. Such a transmitter is shown in Figure 17.14(b). The comments made about keying transients apply equally well here. In order to keep sideband generation to a minimum, the pulse-rise time is limited so that it is perhaps 1/10 of the total pulse length. Higher-speed telegraph systems require more bandwidth, with 100-wpm signals requiring about 170 Hz bandwidth, and 2000-wpm signals needing the full 4-kHz audio channel bandwidth.

Commercial transmission systems more commonly use an audio subcarrier system for transmission. Figure 17.14(c) shows a possible arrangement for such a transmitter. This system uses an ordinary voice-type transmitter, which may be full-AM, SSB, FM, or PM modulated. Up to 20 telegraph channels at 60 wpm can be provided on a single voice channel by frequency-division multiplexing. Figure 17.14(c) shows 3 of the 20 internationally assigned telegraph channels, showing the "mark" and "space" frequencies used for the audio subcarriers which are frequency-shift-keyed (FSK). Each telegraph channel is modulated on its own subcarrier, and the subcarriers are then summed to produce the audio input for the transmitter modulator.

17.14 PROBLEMS

1. The PAM signal of Problem 11.5 is to be transmitted by PCM. (a) Find the number of coding bits required for each sample if the signal-to-quantization-noise ratio is to be at least 30 dB in all channels. (b) Find the minimum channel bandwidth required to transmit the PCM system signal.

2. Describe how a delta-modulation system works, and explain what is meant by slope overload.

3. Explain how adaptive delta modulation improves the system's tolerance to slope overload.

4. A basic 8-bit teletype code is transmitted bit-serially with a 2-bit stop pulse and a 1-bit start pulse delineating each character. The code uses a complement of 165 characters. (a) Find the code efficiency of the basic 8-bit code. (b) Find the overall code efficiency for the 165-character code.

5. A teletype circuit uses the Baudot code and transmits at 200 words/minute. (a) Find the Baud rate of the transmission. (b) Find the minimum channel bandwidth required.

6. A block of teletype code contains the following message. "The rate is $2.58." (a) List the ASCII coding for the block in a column with even parity. (b) Generate the parity character for longitudinal odd-block parity for this list.

7. (a) Explain the terms FSK, PSK, and DPSK. (b) Give the advantages and disadvantages of each for transmitting binary information.

8. Draw the block diagram of an ICW telegraph transmitter and explain the purpose of each block.

9. A PCM system uses 12 bits to encode each sample and handles telephone signals with a volume range of 40 dB (difference between the largest and smallest signals). (a) What is the signal-to-quantization noise ratio for maximum sinusoidal signal level? (b) What is the signal-to-noise level for the smallest signal level? (c) If a compander were used which provided a 10 dB compression of the volume range, what would be the new signal-to-noise ratio in (b)?

10. How many bits would have to be used in the system of problem 9(a) to give an overall improvement in the signal-to-noise ratio of 10 dB?

Chapter 18
Facsimile and Television

18.1 INTRODUCTION

In addition to basic signals consisting of speech, music, or telegraph codes, a telecommunications system is often required to transmit signals of a visual nature. *Facsimile* means an *exact reproduction*, and in facsimile transmission an exact reproduction of a document or picture is provided at the receiving end. *Television* means *visually at a distance*, and a television system is used to reproduce any scene at the receiving end. It differs from facsimile in that the scene may be "live" (i.e., include movement).

In television transmission, compared with facsimile transmission, the information is transmitted at a much faster rate. As a result, the television transmission requires a much larger bandwidth, and special wideband circuits are required. The small bandwidth required for facsimile makes it suitable for transmission over normal telephone lines.

18.2 FACSIMILE TRANSMISSION

Some of the uses of facsimile telegraphy are:

1. Transmission of photographs (e.g., for the press).

2. Transmission of documents, weather maps, and so on.
3. Transmission of language texts for which the teleprinter is not suitable (e.g., Chinese). Facsimile also has the advantage that many of the other language difficulties of international operation do not arise.

18.2.1 Facsimile Sender

The message to be scanned may take one of three forms:

1. A single page, which may be a photograph, which is usually wrapped around a cylindrical drum in the sender to permit scanning to take place.
2. Narrow continuous tape.
3. Continuous-sheet paper, which may be thought of as broad tape.

Two methods of scanning are in general use:

1. Optical scanning, in which a light spot traverses the message.
2. Resistance scanning, in which the characters of the message offer varying resistance, and these are brought into circuit by means of a stylus touching and moving over them.

The first method is the most common, and is invariably used for picture transmission. Two such methods will be described.

Cylindrical scanning.   In this method, the message is first fixed around the drum by means of clips. The drum is then simultaneously rotated about its axis, and traverses along it under a fixed scanning spot. The light reflected from the scanning area is focused onto a photocell, the electrical output of which represents the signal. The layout of this system is shown in Figure 18.1. The chopper disk found in older equipment converts the signal into a modulated wave, the carrier frequency being determined by the speed of the disk. The modulated signal is easier to amplify than a direct signal from the photocell. In newer equipment, solid state amplifiers capable of amplifying the photocell output directly are used, eliminating the need for the "chopper."

In the method shown in Figure 18.1, a comparatively large area of the message is illuminated, and a mask with small aperture forms the spot which illuminates the photocell. An alternative method is to focus a very small scanning spot onto the message, thus eliminating the need for the mask and aperture. However, the first method has the advantage of avoiding distortion caused by mechanical irregularities of the drum, and is the most common.

In the usual scanning arrangement, the spot follows a spiraled path around the drum. An alternative but less common arrangement is to scan in a

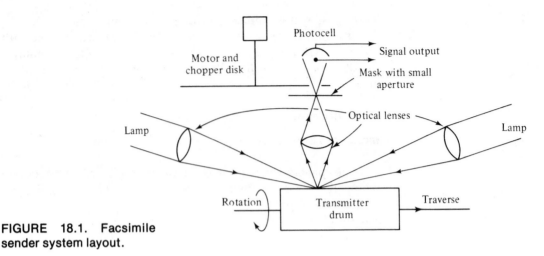

FIGURE   18.1.   Facsimile
sender system layout.

series of closed rings, the spot moving from one ring to the next as the fixing
clips pass under it. It is also possible to keep the drum fixed and to move the
scanning spot instead, but this again is not common. Typical scanning
values are traversing speed, 1/100 inch per second; speed of rotation, 60
revolutions/minute (rpm). This means that there will be 100 scanning lines
on each 1-inch width of picture. European systems work to four lines per
millimeter as typical.

Tape Scanning.   In this system the message is taken directly off a
printed tape. The scanning beam is arranged to travel across the tape at
right angles to the direction of tape travel. One method of achieving this is
shown in Figure 18.2. The light beam will leave the hexagonal prism
parallel to the incident beam, but its position will be deflected as the prism
rotates. The spot thus travels across the tape as shown and starts a new scan
each time a new face of the prism intercepts the incident beam.

The scanning of wide tape has been carried out in practice, but the
difficulties encountered have limited its application.

The Scanning Spot.   The shape of the scanning spot is important as it
determines the waveshape of the signal output. Its effect on waveshape is
discussed more fully in a later section, but it may be mentioned here that a
rectangular-shaped spot is preferred. This is arranged so that there is no
overlap or gap at the sides, as shown in Figure 18.3(a). Less frequently a
trapezoidal spot is used as shown in Figure 18.3(b), and this is arranged such
that average length of the top and bottom sides (the unequal sides) is equal
to the scanning width, or scanning pitch P. This means that although the
corners of the spot overlap on successive scans, the average illumination over
the area of overlap is equal to the average illumination over the rest of the

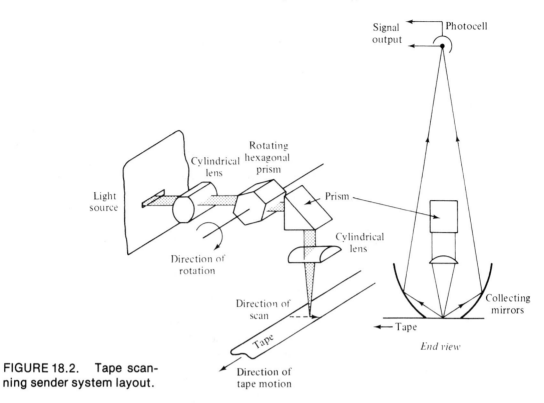

FIGURE 18.2. Tape scanning sender system layout.

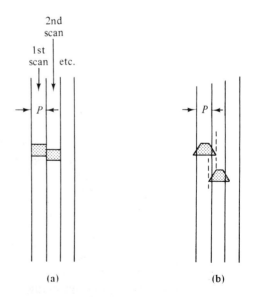

FIGURE 18.3. Scanning spot shapes:
(a) Rectangular; (c) Trapezoidal.

spot area. It must be remembered that the spot is extremely small, and at any given instant can be considered as covering an area of constant illumination on the message. It is the changes in average illumination that convey the picture information.

18.2.2 Facsimile Receiver

The mechanical aspects of scanning in the receiver are similar to those in the sender, and very often identical equipment is used at both ends. Scanning in the receiver must of course produce an optical output from the electrical input signal, the reverse of what happens in the transmitter. This aspect of the receiver is discussed later.

In order for the received signal to have the correct relationship to the transmitted signal, it is necessary for the signals to be synchronized, to be phased correctly, and to have the same height/breadth ratio.

Synchronization. Where the message is documentary (e.g., a written message), it is sufficient to use synchronous motors for both sender and receiver, and operate off frequency-controlled supply mains. Where picture transmission is involved, a synchronizing signal must be sent, and this by international agreement has a frequency of 1020 Hz. The sender speed bears a known relationship to this, and the receiver speed is adjusted by means of a stroboscope to correspond to the relationship. An accuracy of about 1 in 10^5 can be obtained this way. For example, if the sender speed is 60 rpm, the receiver speed can be expected to remain within $\pm$ 0.0006 rpm of the sender speed.

With carrier transmission (i.e., when the signal is modulated onto a carrier as, for example, in frequency multiplexing), it is necessary to send the carrier along with the sideband transmitted (this is usually the upper sideband). The carrier being present enables the *exact* 1020-Hz synchronizing signal to be recovered. This is an added requirement of facsimile transmission, as with normal telegraph signals it is not necessary to send the carrier, a local oscillator at the receiver being adequate for recovery of the signal. The effect of a constant-speed error is shown in Figure 18.4(b).

Phase. Correct phasing is necessary to ensure that the image of the clips holding the paper to the drum does not intersect the transmitted picture. Phasing adjustment need only be made once for each picture transmitted and is carried out as follows. The operator at the receiver first adjusts the speed to the correct value by means of the synchronizing signal and then sets the drum in the correct start position. This is held in position by means of a switch. At the sender, a pulsed signal is sent to indicate the start of the transmission (this may be the 1020 Hz pulsed momentarily), and the pulse releases the switch holding the receiver drum. The effect of incorrect phasing is shown in Figure 18.4(c).

(a)

(b)

(c)

FIGURE 18.4.   The effects of constant-speed error and incorrect phasing.

Index of Cooperation.   The ratio height/breadth must be the same for
both the transmitted and received pictures, and this in turn depends on the
scanning pitch and the diameters of the drums used in the sender and the
receiver.

Referring to Figure 18.5, let

$$D = \text{diameter of sending drum}$$
$$d = \text{diameter of receiving drum}$$
$$P = \text{scanning pitch of sender}$$
$$p = \text{scanning pitch of receiver}$$
$$n = \text{number of lines scanned}$$

The breadth of the transmitted picture is nP, and the breadth of the
received picture is np. The height of the transmitted picture is proportional
to D, and that of the received picture, to d (same constant of proportionality). Hence for the correct height/breadth ratio to be maintained.

$$\frac{D}{nP} = \frac{d}{np} \quad \text{or} \quad \frac{D}{P} = \frac{d}{p} \tag{18.1}$$

Thus the ratio of diameter to scanning pitch is a constant of the sender and
the receiver. In Europe, the Comité Consultatif International Telegraph-
ique et Telephonique (CCITT) defines this ratio as the Index of Cooperation
(IOC). In the USA, the IEEE defines the IOC as the product of Stroke
Length times Scan Density. For the drum scanner, the Stroke Length is πD,

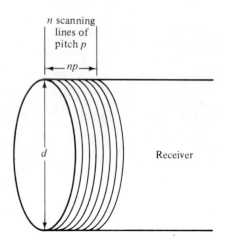

FIGURE 18.5. Facsimile sender and receiver pitch of scan.

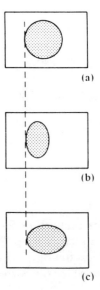

FIGURE 18.6. The effect of different indexes of cooperation.

and the Scan Density is the Lines per Unit Length $= 1/P$, so that for the Drum Scanner:

$$IOC \text{ (IEEE)} = \frac{\pi D}{P} \qquad (18.2)$$

$$IOC \text{ (CCITT)} = \frac{D}{P}$$

Example The drum diameter of a facsimile machine is 70.4 mm, and the scanning pitch is 0.2 mm. Calculate the index of cooperation.

Solution From Eq. (18.1): $\text{IOC (IEEE)} = \dfrac{\pi \times 70.4}{0.2} = 1106$

$$\text{IOC (CCITT)} = \dfrac{70.4}{0.2} = 352$$

When the electrical signal is received, it must be converted to an optical image, and this may be achieved either through photographic reception or through direct recording reception.

Photographic Reception. In this method the received signal is used to control the intensity of a light beam, which in turn scans the photographic material. Figure 18.7 shows the essential features of the Duddell mirror

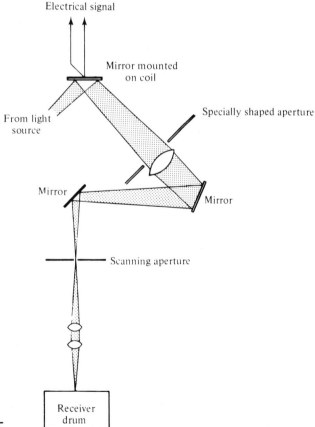

FIGURE 18.7. Photographic facsimile receiver system.

oscillograph, which may be used for this. A small coil of fine wire is suspended in a strong magnetic field. Mounted on the coil is a very small mirror, the dimensions of which are about 0.03 inch × 0.06 inch. The loop and the mirror, which form the movement of the system, offer negligible inertia. The demodulated signal (i.e., the basic signal representing the message from the sender) is passed through the loop and causes it to deflect, the angle turned through being proportional to the signal current. A beam of light focused onto the mirror is reflected through the various apertures and lens shown in Figure 18.7 onto the photographic paper, or film, on the drum. It can then be arranged that maximum deflection of the mirror corresponds to maximum light through the aperture, if photographic paper is to be used (providing positives) and therefore lesser degrees of deflection put lesser amounts of light onto the photographic paper. Alternatively, if film is to be used to produce negatives, minimum deflection of the mirror can be arranged to give maximum light through the aperture.

Another method widely used employs the *crater lamp*. This is a lamp which contains neon, argon, or helium, and which glows when the voltage is applied across its terminals. The intensity of the glow is approximately proportional to the applied voltage. The signal voltage is applied to the lamp, and the light from this is focused onto the photographic paper on the drum. This method is not capable of responding to the full tonal range of some pictures, which may be as high as 30 dB (i.e., the differences between maximum light area and maximum dark area on the picture may be 30 dB), which is a voltage ratio of about 32:1. The maximum range of the lamp is about 15 dB, but this is found to be adequate for most purposes.

Positives or negatives may be made from the methods described. Positives are usually made since these can be processed and finished much faster, and speed is usually the important factor. Negatives have some advantages. More than one copy can be made of the original; they are more sensitive, and can therefore be produced with lower lamp power; they allow for retouching and thus the quality of the final picture can be improved.

Direct Recording Reception. In one form of this method, a highly absorbent, chemically treated paper is used, in which the electrolyte held by the paper dissociates when a voltage is applied across it. The signal voltage is applied to the paper via a metal stylus, and one of the dissociation products reacts with the stylus to from a metallic salt. This, in turn, reacts with a color chemical in the paper which produces a mark on the paper. The intensity of the mark depends on the amount of dissociation, which in turn depends on the signal voltage. A steel stylus is often used, as this produces a very intense black coloration.

The paper used is damp and must be kept in sealed containers. It has a lifetime of about 1 month after opening. It is reasonably cheap, but the tonal range is much less than that obtained with photographic methods. It is usually found to be adequate for low-grade work.

A second form employs a resistance paper known commercially as *Teledeltos paper*. This consists of a metallized backing on which is deposited a substance similar to carbon black, and on top of this a very thin layer of insulation. A stylus exerts a steady pressure on the paper, and when the signal voltage is applied, burning occurs, which causes blackening of the paper. The tonal range is similar to the previous method, but definition is not so good and the paper is fairly expensive.

18.2.3   Transmission of Facsimile Telegraph Signals

The bandwidth requirements may be found by a similar method to that used for telegraph signals. The worst condition will be assumed, that in which alternate black and white squares occur, each square being the width of the scanning pitch. This also assumes therefore that the vertical resolution need be no better than the horizontal resolution [see Figure 18.8(a)]. The

FIGURE 18.8.   (a) A one-line scan with equal horizontal and vertical resolution; (b) Signal produced by slit scanning; (c) Signal produced by square scanning; (d) Signal produced by rectangular scanning, midway between (b) and (c).

ideal output wave would be produced using a scanning *slit*, as shown in Figure 18.8(b). However, the available output from a slit is very small, and a compromise must be reached between output and desired waveform. A *square* scanning spot would produce a triangular waveform, as shown in Figure 18.8(c), and this would give maximum output. The triangular waveform is not the best, and the compromise is reached using a rectangular scanning spot, shown in Figure 18.8(b), in which the height is about 0.8 times the width.

As before, let

$$D = \text{diameter of drum}$$
$$P = \text{scanning pitch}$$
$$n = \text{revolutions per second (rps)}$$

The number of squares along one circumference of the drum is

$$\frac{\pi D}{P}$$

and therefore this is also the number of squares scanned in one revolution. The number of squares scanned in 1 s is

$$\frac{\pi D \cdot n}{P} \qquad (18.3)$$

Every two squares form one cycle of output, and therefore the output frequency is

$$f = \frac{\pi D \cdot n}{2P} \qquad \text{hertz} \qquad (18.4)$$

This only gives the fundamental frequency of the trapezoidal waveform shown in Figure 18.8(d). The actual wave will also contain higher harmonics, but in practice it is usually found that only the fundamental need be transmitted, bearing in mind that the extreme picture conditions postulated will seldom be encountered. Typical values are

$$D = 66 \text{ mm} \qquad P = 0.1875 \text{ mm (or 3/16 mm)} \qquad n = 1.0 \text{ rps}$$

Then $$f = 553 \text{ Hz}$$

The bandwidth is determined by the range of frequencies to be transmitted in an actual signal. The equation for f gives the highest frequency, and as the lowest frequency is very close to zero, the bandwidth is approximately f Hz.

Example 18.2 If the drum in the facsimile machine of Example 18.1 rotates at 120 rpm, find the theoretical bandwidth required for transmission of the signal.

Solution

From Eq. (18.4),

$$f = \frac{\pi}{2} \times \frac{D}{p} \times n \qquad \text{where } n = \text{speed, rps}$$

$$= \frac{\pi}{2} \times 352 \times 2$$

$$= 1106 \text{ Hz}$$

This is also the bandwidth required.

Line Transmission. The basic signal, as obtained from the information scanned, is not suitable for direct transmission, because it is difficult to amplify the low frequencies involved. Modulation (AM or FM) is therefore employed. This also allows frequency division multiplexing to be used, and two channels can be fitted in the normal 300- to 3400-Hz telephone channel. The carrier frequencies agreed upon internationally for AM are 1300 Hz and 1900 Hz. All forms of distortion and interference must be kept at a very low level, and a signal-to-noise ratio of at least 35 dB is recommended operating practice. Echo signals must also be avoided, and because of echo signals, long lines are not suitable for phototelegraphy (as distinct from documentary). The gain stability of amplifiers must also be high. Level changes and impulsive type noise affect AM worse than FM and the latter method, known as sub-carrier FM (SCFM) is preferred. However, it must be limited to narrow band FM.

Radio Transmission. The main difficulty with radio transmission is the fading which can occur over the radio path, and which can completely destroy the picture information. Although special methods are in use to compensate for fading in normal telegraph and telephone radio services (e.g., diversity systems and automatic gain control systems), these are not satisfactory for picture telegraphy. As a result, SCFM is used over some part of the transmission path as this is less affected by amplitude fading. A simplified block diagram is shown in Figure 18.9(a). The frequency spectra of the various sections in the transmission chain are shown in Figure 18.9(b). Any fading over the radio path, provided that it is not frequency selective, will not affect the FM.

Example 18.3

If the signal in Example 18.2 is used to frequency-modulate a subcarrier, and only the first pair of sidebands need be taken into account, calculate the bandwidth of the SCFM system.

Solution

$$\text{Bandwidth} = 1106 \times 2 \text{ Hz} = \mathbf{2212 \text{ Hz}}$$

In Fig. 18.9 the sender/receiver equipment is shown as producing AM, as would occur for example in older equipment utilizing a chopper disk (Fig. 18.1). In this case, AM/FM and FM/AM converters are required as shown. The radio carrier is shown AM although FM may be used also.

As quoted previously, a typical traversing speed in facsimile is 1/100 inch per second. Therefore, to transmit a picture 6 inches long requires a scanning time of 10 minutes. In television systems discussed in Section 18.3 electronic scanning is employed which enables all sections of the transmitted

(a)

(b)

FIGURE 18.9.   (a) Subcarrier frequency modulation system for transmitting facsimile signals; (b) Frequency spectrums of signals at various points in the system.

picture to appear almost simultaneously at the receiver. This, however, requires a very wide bandwidth, and although television has been used for the transmission of documentary information, its real development has been for broadcasting (entertainment, news, etc.) to the general public.

Incorporation of modern electronic techniques in facsimile equipment was initially rather slow with the result that equipment of older design is still to be found in service. However, recent advances include the use of specially designed cathode-ray tubes for electron beam scanning, and use of lasers as light sources. A good account of the history and developments will be found in *Electronic Delivery of Documents and Graphics* by Daniel M. Costigan, published by Van Nostrand Reinhold Co. (1978).

18.3   TELEVISION

Watching television is North America's favorite pastime, so the manufacture of television receiver sets forms a large portion of today's electronics industry. The systems used for television have been thoroughly standardized, so sets vary little from one manufacturer to another. The system presently used in North America is common to all North American countries, Japan, Korea, the Netherlands, and a few others. The system common to most European countries differs from the American system mainly in the use of different scanning rates.

The standard frequency assignments for the television channels used in North America are shown in Table 18.1. Channels 2 through 13 are in the VHF band and are the most generally used. Channels 14 through 83 occupy the UHF band and are being used more often as the number of transmitters increases. Earlier receiver sets were built with only a VHF tuner, but all new sets are now required to have a UHF tuner built in. Each channel provides a 6-MHz bandwidth, which is sufficient to transmit the 4.2 MHz of video bandwidth with an additional MHz for the vestigial sideband.

Most television broadcasting is now done in color, and although black and white sets may still be obtained, these are usually used for special applications such as security monitoring systems. The color system and all color receivers are made to be compatible with black and white transmissions.

18.3.1   Television Camera

The TV camera tube is the device which converts the optical image of the program material into an electrical signal which can be transmitted over cable or by radio to a receiver, where the original image can be reconstructed from the received signals. Several types of tubes using different principles of operation are available, and two of these will be discussed here, the Image Orthicon tube and the Vidicon tube. Both of these tubes were developed at RCA Ltd, in the late 1940s.

The *Image Orthicon tube* is illustrated in Figure 18.10. Its action may be explained as follows. The tube consists of an electron-beam gun in one

TABLE 18.1.   Television Channel Frequency Assignments*

Channel Number	Band (Megahertz)	Channel Number	Band (Megahertz)	Channel Number	Band (Megahertz)
2	54–60	29	560–566	57	728–734
3	60–66	30	566–572	58	734–740
4	66–72	31	572–578	59	740–746
5	76–82	32	578–584	60	746–752
6	82–88	33	584–590	61	752–758
7	174–180	34	590–596	62	758–764
8	180–186	35	596–602	63	764–770
9	186–192	36	602–608	64	770–776
10	192–198	37	608–614	65	776–782
11	198–204	38	614–620	66	782–788
12	204–210	39	620–626	67	788–794
13	210–216	40	626–632	68	794–800
14	470–476	41	632–638	69	800–806
15	476–482	42	638–644	70	806–812
16	482–488	43	644–650	71	812–818
17	488–494	44	650–656	72	818–824
18	494–500	45	656–662	73	824–830
19	500–506	46	662–668	74	830–836
20	506–512	47	668–674	75	836–842
21	512–518	48	674–680	76	842–848
22	518–524	49	680–686	77	848–854
23	524–530	50	686–692	78	854–860
24	530–536	51	692–698	79	860–866
25	536–542	52	698–704	80	866–872
26	542–548	53	704–710	81	872–878
27	548–554	54	710–716	82	878–884
28	554–560	55	716–722	83	884–890
		56	722–728		

*Courtesy of Howard W. Sams and Co., Inc.

FIGURE 18.10. The structure and operation of the Image Orthicon camera tube. (Courtesy RCA).

end which emits an electron beam for scanning the target at the other end. Focusing coils mounted around the neck of the tube sharpen the beam so that it has a very narrow cross section when it reaches the target. Deflection coils also mounted around the neck of the tube cause the beam to be offset from its central axis by a controlled amount so that its point of impact on the surface of the target may be positioned anywhere on the target surface.

In the image section of the tube, the end of the tube is an optical glass plate, the inside surface of which is coated with a photoemissive material. The image to be converted is focused through an optical lens system onto the glass plate and the photoemissive layer. Where light strikes the layer, it emits electrons from its surface in proportion to the light intensity. These electrons are accelerated away toward the target by a positively charged screen placed behind the photoemissive layer, so that an electron image of the photo image is transferred toward the target.

The target is a thin layer of semiconducting material which emits several secondary electrons for every accelerated electron that strikes it. The semiconductor material is charged up as it loses the secondary electrons, and since it has a high resistivity, a charge pattern is created on its surface with the most positive areas corresponding to the lightest regions of the photoimage. The dislodged secondary electrons are collected by a screen or collector mesh through which the original image electrons passed to reach the target and are returned to the photoemissive cathode through an external circuit.

On the scanning side of the target, the electron beam is caused to move from left to right in lines across the target, repeating the lines down the face of the target until the whole target has been scanned. To reach the target, the beam must pass through a repelling or decelerating grid with a negative charge on it, so that the average beam velocity at the target is near zero. Some of the beam electrons will be captured by the positive image charges on the target while the rest will be turned and accelerated back toward the gun end of the tube by the decelerator grid potential. The larger the positive charge on the target at the point of impact of the beam, the smaller the return beam magnitude. Thus a lighter image causes a reduction in the beam current which returns. The returning beam current is collected and passed through a multiple-stage electron multiplier. This is a series of anodes at progressively higher potentials, each one coated with a material that emits secondary electrons in large numbers when struck by high-energy electrons. Thus the returned beam current is multiplied several hundred times before being passed through a load resistor to develop the video signal voltage.

The Orthicon tube is a very sensitive one which can be used under normal to low lighting conditions, and which responds to light over most of the visible spectrum. This makes it ideal for live television use, and it is widely used for both studio and remote camera applications.

The *Vidicon tube* is much simpler and cheaper to build than the Orthicon, but it is far less sensitive than is the Orthicon because it does not have the built-in electron multiplier stages. This tube finds its greatest application in studios for converting the images from moving picture and still slide projectors, where high light intensity levels are easily maintained. The structure of a Vidicon tube is illustrated in Figure 18.11.

The Vidicon tube works on the photoconductive principle. The tube is provided with an electron-beam gun in one end, and focusing and deflection coils on its neck in much the same manner as the Orthicon. The electrons in the beam are not accelerated to very high velocities and a decelerating screen slows them almost to a stop before impact, so that they do not cause any secondary emission. The target is a layer of photoconductive material on the beam side of an optically transparent conducting film on the inside of the glass window. This conducting film acts as the beam-signal pickup connection. When the beam scans across the target, it charges up the surface

FIGURE 18.11. The structure and operation of the Vidicon camera tube. (Courtesy RCA).

of the target with a uniformly large negative charge. Since the photo material normally has a very low conductivity, this charge will remain on the surface for some time after the beam has passed.

The light image is focused through a lens, the window, and the transparent metal film onto the photoconductive layer, and the conductivity of the layer increases in proportion to the light intensity. This increase in conductivity allows the negative charge to leak off in the more conductive regions, but it is held in the less conductive regions, so that a charge image is created on the target. When the electron beam scans the charge image, the area under the beam is recharged to its negative level, and a current flows in the signal lead which is proportional in magnitude to the amount of decrease of negative charge on the target, or to the intensity of the light that struck the scanned point. The beam current flows through the charged target and its conductive backplate, and through an external load resistor to generate the video signal voltage, as shown in Figure 18.12.

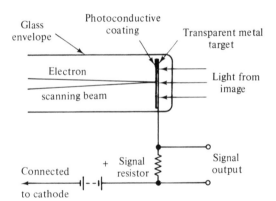

FIGURE 18.12. The structure of the photoconductive camera tube.

The video signal voltage, along with the synchronizing signals to control the receiver scanning functions, is transmitted. At the receiver, this signal controls the electron beam in a cathode-ray tube in such a way as to reproduce the image on a fluorescent screen (this is discussed below). The scanning at the receiver must be tied, or synchronized, with that at the transmitter. The scanning process is very fast, and this, along with the *persistence of vision* of the viewer, makes it appear that all parts of the picture are being reproduced simultaneously.

18.3.2   Cathode-Ray Tube

The *cathode-ray tube* in the receiver performs the opposite function to the camera tube in the transmitter. It converts the electrical signal into an optical image. Figure 18.13 shows in outline the action of the cathode-ray

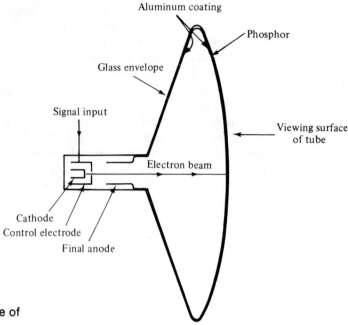

FIGURE 18.13.   The structure of
the cathode-ray picture tube.

tube, where for the moment the deflecting and focusing arrangements are
omitted. The electrical signal, which represents the picture, is applied to the
control electrode, which functions in a manner similar to that of the control
grid in a tube. The signal causes the potential of the control electrode to
vary about a mean level, and as this goes more negative, it reduces the
intensity of the electron beam with a resulting reduction in the brightness of
the spot formed on the fluorescent screen. Likewise, as it goes less negative,
it increases the brightness of the spot on the screen. The fluorescent screen is
made out of a *phosphor*, which is a material that emits light when bom-
barded with an electron beam. In modern tubes, the back of the phosphor is
coated with a very thin film of aluminum, and this coating is continued
down the inside walls of the tube and connected to the final anode. The
purpose of the coating is to increase the brightness of the screen (for a given
intensity of electron beam) and to ensure that the brightness is even (i.e., no
dark patches occur). The coating, being at final anode potential, prevents
electrons from the beam accumulating on the screen, which otherwise
would tend to repel the incident beam of electrons, thus reducing brightness. Furthermore, if electrons were allowed to accumulate, they would do
so unevenly over the surface of the screen, thus producing dark patches. The
aluminum coating improves brightness in another way, in that it *reflects*
light forward onto the viewing side, light that would otherwise be lost inside

the tube. Some of the electron-beam energy is lost in penetrating the aluminum coating, but since this is kept very thin, the energy lost is more than offset by the gain in brightness.

In both the transmitter camera tube and the receiver picture tube, the electron beam must be made to *scan* the screen. The beam usually starts at the top left-hand corner of the screen and moves across to the right in an almost horizontal line. There has to be a small downward deflection of the beam as each line is traversed so that the complete picture is eventually scanned. When the beam reaches the right-hand side, it is very quickly deflected back to the left-hand side again (this being known as the line *flyback*), where it starts a new line. The flyback is initiated by a *line synchronizing signal* called the *horizontal sync pulse.* This is a special pulse signal introduced at the transmitter which ensures that the receiver flyback occurs at the same time as the transmitter flyback.

When the scanning beam reaches the bottom right-hand corner of the picture, it must be returned to the top left-hand corner again, to repeat the whole scanning procedure. Thus a second synchronizing signal must be transmitted at this time to ensure that the receiver recommences complete scanning at the same time as the transmitter. This is the *field synchronizing signal,* called the *vertical sync pulse.*

The deflection of the beam for scanning may be achieved either electrically or magnetically, but magnetic deflection permits a shorter tube to be used, which is an important advantage in television. Hence magnetic deflection is the most common. It is known that a magnetic field exerts a force on electrons in a beam in just the same way as it does on electrons in a conductor (e.g., in the armature winding of a motor). Figure 18.14(a) illustrates this. In the television tube, the magnetic field must build up steadily so that the spot formed by the beam is deflected at a constant velocity and traces out a line. This is achieved by utilizing an electromagnetic field rather than a permanent magnet field. The current to the coils can then be controlled in the desired manner, with the synchronizing pulse causing the beam to return to the start of the next line. Figure 18.14(b) and (c) shows two methods of achieving magnetic deflection. In practice, the coils of Figure 18.14(b) are saddle-shaped so that they fit closely around the neck of the tube. For practical reasons, it is found best to use the saddle-shaped coils for line deflection, and the toroidal-shaped coil of Figure 18.14(c) for field deflection.

As well as being deflected for scanning, the electron beam must be *focused* in order to form a sharp spot on the screen. Again, focusing may be achieved either magnetically or electrically. Magnetic focusing is usually employed in camera tubes, and either type will be found in receiver picture tubes. Figure 18.15(a) shows how a long coil may be used for focusing, and this is the type used in camera tubes. The coil produces a magnetic field which is directed mainly along the axis of the tube (and hence known as an

Magnetic field directed into paper

Electron beam

Deflection

(a)

Direction of
magnetic field

Electron beam
deflection

Deflecting
current

Electron beam

(b)

Direction of electron beam
deflection

Magnetic field

Deflecting
current

(c)

FIGURE 18.14. Electromagnetic deflection of an electron beam.

axial field). Electrons that tend to diverge from the beam are deflected by the magnetic field and the electron paths become helixes. It is found that the electron paths meet at fixed points along the tube axis as shown in Figure 18.15(a), and it is only a matter of adjusting the focusing current so that one of these points falls on the target surface. The beam is then focused.

A short magnetic field may also be used, and may be obtained either by means of a short coil or a permanent magnet. Either system can be used in television receivers. Figure 18.15(b) illustrates the principle of short magnetic focusing, where for clarity only one divergent electron path is shown. As the electrons enter the magnetic field along this path, they first meet the component of magnetic field directed inward (or *radial component*). This causes the electrons to be deflected to the right. As they move farther into the field, they encounter the axial component, which results in a downward shift to the particular path shown. As the electrons emerge from the other side of the field, the radial component there is directed outward,

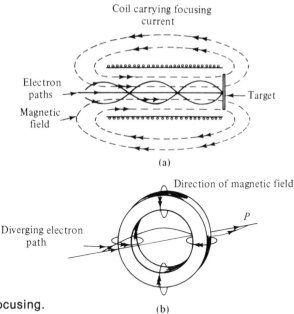

FIGURE 18.15.   Electromagnetic beam focusing.

which results in the electrons being deflected to the left. The result is that the electron path meets the axis at some point P, and it can be shown that all divergent paths meet at this point. Thus the strength of the magnetic field is chosen such that point P falls on the screen.

Electric focusing is now becoming widely used in television receiver tubes. Figure 18.16 illustrates the principle. An electric field is set up between cylindrical electrodes, one of which is the final anode in the tube. By definition, an electric field is a region in which electric charges experience a force, and by convention, the direction of the force is that along which a positive charge would be moved. Thus the lines of force are directed from the high positive potential electrode to the zero potential electrode. Since the electrons in the beam are negative charges, they will tend to be deflected in the direction opposite to the field. If the beam is divergent on entering the field, it will be convergent on leaving it, and thus forms a focal point. The electrodes are shaped as shown in Figure 18.16 in order to prevent voltage breakdown, as a high potential exists between them.

18.3.3   Interlacing and Picture Scan Repetition Rate

One complete scanning of the target area will allow reproduction of one complete picture at the receiver of a television system. A large amount of information must be transmitted during this period, and if the picture is repeated at a high rate, then the bandwidth required for transmission will

FIGURE 18.16. Electrostatic beam focusing.

become excessive, as is shown in Section 18.3.6. In television, if the picture scan rate is made too low, moving scenes will develop a stop-and-go jerky movement in the same manner that slow-motion moving pictures do. Further, the phosphors used in the receiver picture tubes have a relatively low persistence, and allow the picture to fade out between scans, and the scanning will produce a "flicker" at the picture rate. The picture rate must be sufficiently high so that the normal persistence of the viewer's eyes will override the flicker and merge the picture series into smooth motion. This minimum picture rate has been found to be about 35 to 50 pictures per second.

It has also been found that in television systems, if the scanning rate is near, but not exactly equal to, the supply frequency, voltage pickup from the ac power circuits modulate the scanning circuit amplifiers and cause annoying distortion and jitter in the picture. This interference can be minimized by making the picture scanning rate a multiple of the supply frequency. In the American system, the picture or frame scan rate is 30 Hz, which is a submultiple of the supply frequency of 60 Hz.

The 30-Hz picture repetition rate is too low, and if scanning were done in a straightforward sequential manner, the flicker produced because of picture fading between scans would become objectionable. For this reason, the scanning of each picture frame is divided into two separate *fields*, and the entire area scanned twice during a picture period. A total of 525 lines is included in each picture, so that during the first field, 262½ lines are scanned, and during the second field, the remaining 262½ lines are scanned.

At the end of the first 262½ lines, a vertical retrace occurs, and the second scan begins at the top center of the picture, as shown in Figure 18.17. As a result, the second field scan lines fall midway between the positions of

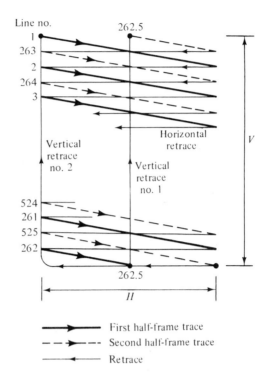

FIGURE 18.17. Television frame scan interlacing pattern.

the first field lines, so that the two fields merge to form a complete scan frame. The effective flicker rate is now 60 Hz, well above the threshold, and the frame, or picture repetition rate of 30 per second is low enough to minimize video signal frequencies. European supplies are generally operated at 50 Hz, and the picture rate for this system is 25 per second, with a field rate of 50 per second.

Two vertical retraces take place during each complete picture frame period, and for each of these a synchronizing pulse (the vertical sync pulse) is produced in the master camera control unit, which is used to initiate the vertical retracing of both the camera and the receiver scanning beams, so that the two remain in synchronization with each other. The vertical sync frequency equal to the field frequency, is:

$$f_v = 2P \qquad \text{pulses/second} \qquad (18.5)$$

where P is the frame, or picture repetition rate in pictures/second. The vertical sync pulse is superimposed on top of a longer "blanking" pulse, which is used to turn off the electron beam of the receiver CRT during the retrace period so that the retrace lines cannot be seen. The structure of the combined vertical sync and blanking pulses is shown in Figure 18.19(d), from which it can be seen that about 20 lines of video information are lost during each vertical retrace period, or about 40 lines out of each complete frame.

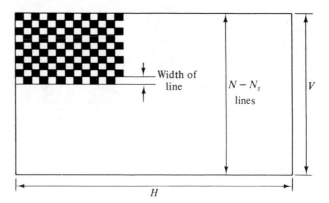

FIGURE 18.18. Checkerboard pattern of alternating black and white minimum elements which yields maximum video signal frequency.

18.3.4 Picture Definition

Picture definition is determined by the size of the smallest element in a picture. Let N represent the total number of lines in a frame, and let N_s represent the number suppressed during frame synchronization. The number of *active lines* (i.e., actually presented to the viewer) is then $N - N_s$. If V (Fig. 18.18) represents the vertical dimension on the viewer's picture, the active lines will just fill this and the line width will be:

$$W = \frac{V}{(N - N_s)} \tag{18.6}$$

For the same definition in the horizontal direction, H in Fig. 18.18, the number of elements will be:

$$N_{\text{hor}} = \frac{H}{W}$$

$$= \frac{H}{V} \cdot (N - N_s)$$

$$= a \cdot (N - N_s) \tag{18.7}$$

where $a = H/V$ is known as the *Aspect Ratio*.

Example 18.4   In the American TV system, $a = 4/3$, $N = 525$, $N_s = 40$. Calculate the number of active lines, and the number of smallest horizontal elements.

Solution   No. of Active Lines $= 525 - 40$

$$= 485$$

and from Eq. (18.7) $N_{hor} = \dfrac{4}{3} \times 485$

$$= 647$$

18.3.5 Horizontal Sync. Frequency

Since two fields go to make up one frame the total number of lines in a field is $N/2$. The field repetition frequency as given by Eq. (18.5) is $f_v = 2P$, and therefore the number of lines generated per second is $(N/2) \times (2P) = NP$. Since a synchronizing pulse must be sent at the end of each line, the horizontal (or line) synchronization frequency is:

$$f_H = NP \quad \text{Pulses per second.} \tag{18.8}$$

The time available for one electrical line scan (i.e., including the *line* synchronization time) is:

$$T_H = 1/f_H \tag{18.9}$$

Example 18.5
In the American TV system $N = 525$ and $P = 30$ frames/sec. Calculate the horizontal sync. frequency and the total line time.

Solution
From Eq. (18.8) $f_H = 525 \times 30$

$$= 15{,}750 \text{ Pulses/sec.}$$

From Eq. (18.9) $T_H = \dfrac{1}{15750}$

$$= 63.5 \,\mu\text{s}$$

The sync-pulse generating circuits in the camera use a very stable oscillator to generate a primary timing pulse train with a frequency of twice the horizontal sync frequency (31,500 pulses per second in the American system). This pulse train is then frequency-divided by 2 using digital circuits to produce the horizontal-sync-pulse train and it is also divided by 525 to produce the vertical-sync-pulse train.

18.3.6 Video Bandwidth

This is estimated on the basis that two successive smallest elements of the pattern shown in Fig. 18.18 go to generate one cycle of video output. The time available for the beam to scan the horizontal elements N_{hor}, as given by Eq. (18.7) will be T_H less the line suppression time required for line

FIGURE 18.19. Television signal characteristics: (a) Signal spectrum within the 6-MHz channel assignment; (b) Video IF bandpass characteristic; (c) Horizontal sync pulse structure; (d) Vertical sync pulse structure.

synchronization. Let the line suppression period be represented by T_s , then the highest video frequency is:

$$f = \frac{N_{hor}}{2} \cdot \frac{1}{T_H - T_s}$$

$$= \frac{a(N - N_s)}{2(T_H - T_s)} \qquad (18.10)$$

Experiments have shown that a reduction in resolution by a factor of 0.7 (known as the Kell factor) can be tolerated, and so the highest video frequency is standardized at:

$$f = \frac{0.7\,a\,(N - N_s)}{2(T_H - T_s)}$$

$$= 0.35\,a\frac{(N - N_s)}{(T_H - T_s)} \qquad (18.11)$$

The lowest frequency in the video signal will be near zero, therefore Eq. (18.11) also gives the video bandwidth required.

Example 18.6   Given that $T_s = 10\,\mu s$ in the American TV system and the other values are as given in two previous examples, calculate the video bandwidth required.

Solution   From Eq. (18.11) $f = 0.35 \times \dfrac{4}{3} \times \dfrac{(525 - 40)}{(63.5 - 10) \times 10^{-6}}$

$$= 4.23\,\text{MHz}$$

18.4   THE TELEVISION SIGNAL

The television signal as transmitted is a complex one. Four separate components are included in the signal, the sound, the picture brightness or luminance scan information, synchronization information for both vertical and horizontal scans, and color chrominance information. The video information is transmitted as an amplitude-modulated vestigial (partially suppressed) sideband carrier located 1.25 MHz from the lower edge of the channel band. All of the 4.2-MHz wide upper sideband and 1 MHz of the lower sideband are transmitted along with the carrier, with the remainder of the lower sideband being removed. Figure 18.19(a) shows the transmitted video spectrum with the sound and chrominance carriers indicated. The sideband envelope for the composite video information is shown as well.

In the North American TV system, the sound carrier is located 4.50 MHz above the video carrier and is frequency-modulated, requiring a bandwidth of about 200 kHz centered around the carrier. This is well outside the video band, and can easily be removed with filtering. The chrominance information is carried by a special two-phase phase-modulated suppressed carrier signal which is amplitude-modulated on the video carrier, effectively providing two additional channels on which to transmit the color information without increasing the video bandwidth required. Only the sidebands are transmitted. The main video signal becomes the Y or luminance signal, and the two chrominance channels are the I and Q channels. The Q signal requires a sideband width of $\pm$ 0.5 MHz, and the I signal a lower sideband of 1.5 MHz and a vestigial upper sideband of 0.6 MHz around the 3.58-MHz subcarrier.

Synchronizing information is carried on the video carrier during retrace periods between lines, and between frames. The picture is scanned horizontally 15 750 times per second and vertically 60 times per second in two interlaced frames. Thus a horizontal retrace occurs every 63.5 μs and vertical retrace every 16-2/3 ms. During the horizontal retrace, for which 0.165 of a horizontal period is allowed, the video signal is raised to the black level, to blank out the retrace. A synchronizing pulse 0.075 T_H wide (where T_H is the horizontal scanning period) is provided to trigger the horizontal oscillator of the receiver, and a burst of 8 or more cycles of 3.58-MHz chroma carrier is provided to synchronize the color demodulator circuits. The shape of the video signal as a function of time during a horizontal sync pulse is shown in Figure 18.19(c).

Vertical retrace takes longer, and a period of from 14 to 21 line periods is blanked out to provide this time. The synchronizing is accomplished by changing the shape of the horizontal sync pulses. As shown in Figure 18.19(d), 6 regular-sized horizontal sync pulses are provided at twice the rate for equalization, followed by the vertical sync pulse, which is three horizontal periods long and serrated every half-period by a negative-going sync pulse for horizontal stabilization, and then followed by another 6 equalizing pulses. The video signal remains blanked for another 4 to 12 periods to allow sufficient time for vertical retrace to be completed.

18.5 TELEVISION RECEIVERS

Figure 18.20 shows the block diagram of a typical black-and-white television receiver. Starting from the antenna, which is usually of the "rabbit-ear" type, but can be a multielement Yagi or a cable-system transmission line, the first section is the tuner assembly. The input signal is coupled into the RF-amplifier stage, which is a tuned class A stage, and then to a mixer-oscillator circuit. For the UHF channels a diode mixer is used with a separate oscillator circuit operating in the frequency-doubling mode. The second harmonic is used to provide the local oscillator signal to the mixer. Tuning is accomplished by means of a turret switch, which places a different set of coils and capacitors in the circuit for each channel. Means are provided for adjusting the oscillator frequency for each channel internally, as well as a vernier trimmer for fine tuning, which can be controlled from the front panel.

The IF used for all receivers and all channels has been standardized to lie in the band 41 to 47 MHz, and since the sidebands are flipped over in conversion (for oscillator frequency above signal frequency), the video carrier appears at 45.75 MHz and the sound carrier at 41.25 MHz. The bandpass of the video amplifier strip is designed to pass all of these frequencies, with some sloping because of the vestigial sideband. The typical shape of this bandpass is shown in Figure 18.19(b). The bandpass characteristics and gain are realized in the IF amplifier string, which can be three to five stages of stagger-tuned amplifiers. AGC is applied to two or more of the IF stages and to the RF-tuner stage. Video detection is accomplished by simple envelope detection at the end of the IF string.

The detected video signal is fed to the input of the audio string, where tuned circuits isolate the audio carrier, which is now at 4.5 MHz. The audio IF amplifier stages are designed to pass and limit a band of frequencies about 200 kHz wide around the 4.5-MHz center frequency. The audio detection circuit is usually a ratio detector but may be any of the FM detector circuits mentioned in Section 10.5. The detector is followed by the audio amplifier stages, which feed the speaker.

The detected video signal is also passed to the video amplifier, which raises the level of the video signal, removes the sound carrier, and provides the dc bias level for the picture tube cathode. The video signal applied to the picture tube cathode varies the beam intensity and thus the light intensity produced at the screen.

The detected video signal is also passed to the synchronization circuits, where the video portion is removed by clipping to leave only the sync pulses. The clipped sync pulses are amplified and passed on to trigger the horizontal sweep oscillator. The ramp voltage produced by the oscillator is amplified to drive the horizontal output transformer and the horizontal deflection coil. The large flyback pulse is rectified to provide the high voltage (10 to 20 kV) for the picture tube target and also provides the gating signal to control the AGC circuit.

The color-television receiver is complicated by the necessity to decode

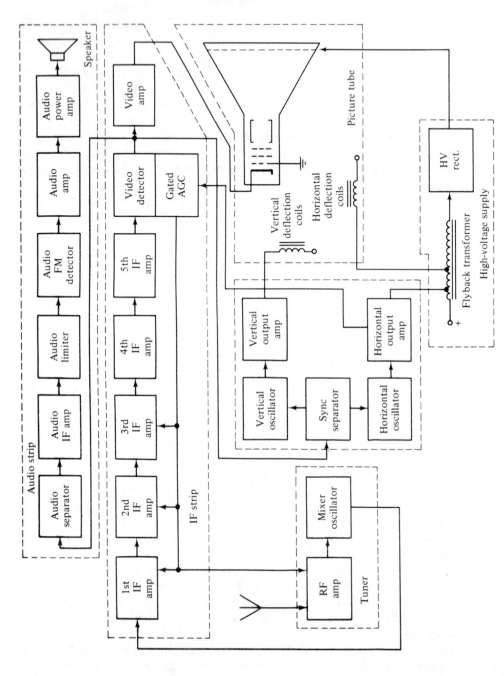

FIGURE 18.20. Black-and-white television receiver block diagram.

the color signals from the carrier before application to the picture tube. The circuitry included by the tuner, the IF strip, the deflection circuits, and the audio strip have exactly the same functions and specifications regardless of whether the set is black and white or color. The video amplifier has different characteristics, the picture tube used has three separate electron-beam guns, and the additional circuits to decode the color information and to control the convergence of the three electron beams are the differences. Figure 18.21 shows the segments of circuitry which differ from those in a black-and-white set.

The detected video signal is passed through the video preamp, which raises the level to compensate for the following four-way split. This amplifier has a 4.2-MHz bandwidth, with a "trap" (filter) to remove the sound carrier at 4.5 MHz. The video signal is passed to the synchronization separator and deflection circuits, which function in exactly the same manner as those of a black-and-white set. It is also passed through a delay line, which compensates for the delays in the chroma demodulator circuits to the Y video amplifier. This amplifier has the full 4.2-MHz bandwidth and provides the video signal during black-and-white reception periods.

The video signal also passes to the chroma amplifier, which has a bandpass of +0.6, −1.5 MHz around the 3.58-MHz carrier frequency, and thence to the I and Q signal demodulators. The video signal is also passed to a special circuit which responds to the short bursts of 3.58-MHz carrier present with each horizontal sync pulse. The output from this burst pickoff circuit provides a gate signal which turns off the chroma amplifier during black-and-white transmission when no bursts are present (color killer circuit which prevents random color blooming during black-and-white reception), and also provides the phase synchronization signal for the 3.58-MHz local carrier oscillator for the demodulator. This oscillator is a crystal-controlled voltage-modulated oscillator which is part of a phase-locked loop. Each burst of transmitted carrier causes the phase of the oscillator to shift enough to correct for frequency drift which occurs during the horizontal sweep time period.

The I and Q demodulators decode the two chroma signals from the chroma carrier and present them, along with the Y signal, to the inputs of the color matrix. The signals are added in weighted proportions according to the equations

$$
\begin{aligned}
R &= +0.62Q &&+0.95I &&+Y \\
G &= -0.64Q &&-0.28I &&+Y \\
B &= +1.73Q &&-1.11I &&+Y
\end{aligned}
\qquad (18.12)
$$

to be compatible with the transmit conditions, Eq. (18.13).

FIGURE 18.21. Color-television receiver block diagram. The diagram shows those parts of the receiver that differ from those of a black-and-white set.

The color matrix combines the *I*, *Q*, and *Y* signals to give the three primary color signals, *R*, *G*, and *B* (red, green, and blue), each of which controls a separate electron beam in the picture tube. Special convergence controls steer the electron beams so that they only illuminate the desired phosphors on the screen, which are laid out either in parallel strips or in an alternating dot matrix, and thus recreate the color image.

The picture tube power supplies are complicated by the need for carefully regulated voltages to keep the three beams converged on the correct spots on the screen. The high-voltage target supply of 20 kV must be regulated. It is derived in the same manner as for black-and-white sets but has a shunt regulator circuit to maintain a constant voltage. This tube is carefully shielded to prevent the radiation of X rays that may be produced because of the high voltages. A separate rectifier provides the voltage to the focusing anode, and the voltage for the convergence anode is provided by a voltage divider from the target supply.

The design of all television sets is undergoing a major evolutionary step. The ready availability of large-scale integrated circuits in quantity has made it practical to make nearly all of the television set in integrated-circuit form. Sets have been built for several years now using discrete semiconductors for all sections except the picture tube and high-voltage sections. Now whole sections of the receiver are available as integrated circuits. For instance, a single microcircuit is available with all the chroma demodulator and color matrix circuits in one package. Whole IF strips are available as a chip, and whole audio IF strips as well. All the low-level circuits can be built on one small board, which is dwarfed in comparison to the picture tube. The next step is the picture tube itself. A semiconductor light-emitting-diode display has already been produced on an experimental basis by the Japanese, which will produce a coarse color picture. Within a few years such solid-state displays should be on the market, and television sets that are only a few centimeters thick will be available which can be hung on the wall like a picture.

18.6 TELEVISION TRANSMITTERS

18.6.1 Black-and-White Television

The details of the signal structure of a black-and-white television receiver were presented in Section 18.5. The channel is 6 MHz wide, with the video carrier located 1.25 MHz from the bottom edge and the sound carrier 0.25 MHz below the upper edge. The sound is FM, while the video is AM vestigial sideband. Most of the present televisions use the 12 VHF channels, but increasing use is being made of the many UHF channels that have been reserved.

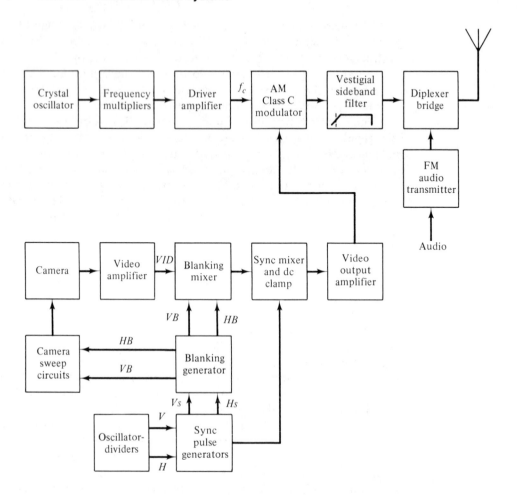

FIGURE 18.22. A black-and-white television transmitter.

The typical layout of a black-and-white TV transmitter is shown in Figure 18.22. The sound carrier transmitter is typical of those discussed in Section 10.10, probably using an Armstrong modulator system. The video carrier is generated from a crystal oscillator followed by frequency-multiplier stages up to the final carrier frequency and class C power driver and amplifier stages. The power output to the antenna typically is 50 or 100 kW, so the driver power output may be as high as 1 kW. Amplitude modulation is accomplished from the composite video signal by a plate-modulated class C amplifier. Feedback may be incorporated to reduce modulation distortion. The output from the power amplifier is passed through a filter to suppress the lower sideband and a portion of the carrier, and then to a diplexer bridge. This diplexer bridge has the function of preventing the video transmitter from loading the sound transmitter, and vice versa, so that all the power from both transmitters is passed through the antenna. It takes the form of a bridge circuit like that shown in Figure 18.23. The antenna is made up of two phased sections driven from separate drive points, each presenting the same radiation resistance at its input. The two inductances L are equal in value and made of shorted sections of line. The video modulated carrier is fed through a balun transformer T to points Y of the bridge, while the audio modulated carrier is fed to the points X and G of the bridge. The voltage between points X and G due to the voltage applied to points Y is zero as long as the two inductances are equal and the two antenna impedances are equal. Similarly, voltage between points Y due to that applied to points X-G is zero. Voltage from the video transmitter is applied across the two antenna sections in series and that from the audio transmitter is applied in parallel. The two antenna sections are oriented in space quadrature to obtain circular pattern generation, so that cancellation does not take place in radiation. The turnstile antenna may be used for this (see Sect. 15.17.3.).

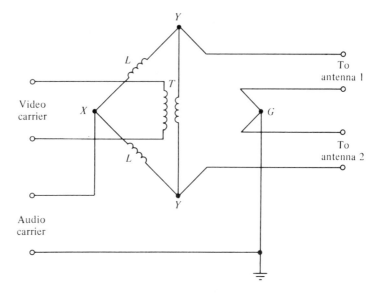

FIGURE 18.23. A diplexer bridge—used for mixing the outputs of two transmitters that use the same antenna system.

18.6.2   Color Television

The RF portion of a color TV transmitter is identical to that of a black-and-white TV transmitter. The only differences occur in the way in which the composite video signal is made up, since it must also carry information about color. Figure 18.24 shows the block diagram of such a transmitter. The video signal is generated by a special color camera. This camera is comprised of three separate image tubes of the same type used in black-and-white systems. The color image is optically separated into three components and converted to red, green, and blue signals by the three image tubes. The three signals, R, G, and B, are combined in the color matrix circuits to produce the luminance signal Y and the two chrominance signals I and Q according to the following equations:

$$Y = + 0.30R + 0.59G + 0.11B$$

$$I = + 0.60R - 0.28G - 0.32B$$

$$Q = + 0.21R - 0.52G + 0.31B \qquad (18.13)$$

The luminance or Y signal contains all the information required to reconstruct a black-and-white picture from the signal. It is passed through a low-pass filter to limit its output to a bandwidth of 4.1 MHz. The I signal is limited further, with a bandwidth of 1.5 MHz and the Q signal even further, with 0.5-MHz bandwidth. This limiting is used to reduce interference between the three signals when receiving with a black-and-white set.

A 3.58-MHz crystal oscillator generates the subcarrier for carrying the chroma signals. System reference phase is specified as zero degrees, and the transmitted carrier burst for synchronization lags reference phase by 180°. The Q-signal carrier leads reference by 33° and the I-signal carrier leads the Q-signal carrier by 90° giving a quadrature relationship between the two. These phase relations are shown in the phasor diagram in Fig. 18.24. In the block diagram the color burst is taken directly from the output of the carrier oscillator. The oscillator output is also passed through a 147° phase delay to give the Q-carrier signal and this is in turn given a 90° phase lead (or a 270° phase delay) to give the I-carrier signal. The two modulators are balanced modulators and create double-sideband suppressed carrier signals around the 3.58-MHz frequency. A color burst gate allows a short burst of the 3.58-MHz carrier to be transmitted during each horizontal blanking period to allow synchronization of a carrier reinsertion oscillator at each receiver, so that the chroma signals can be demodulated.

The same 3.58-MHz oscillator feeds a divider chain which generates the 15,750-Hz and 60-Hz (approximately) signals from which the horizontal and vertical sync and blanking pulses are generated. These signals are used

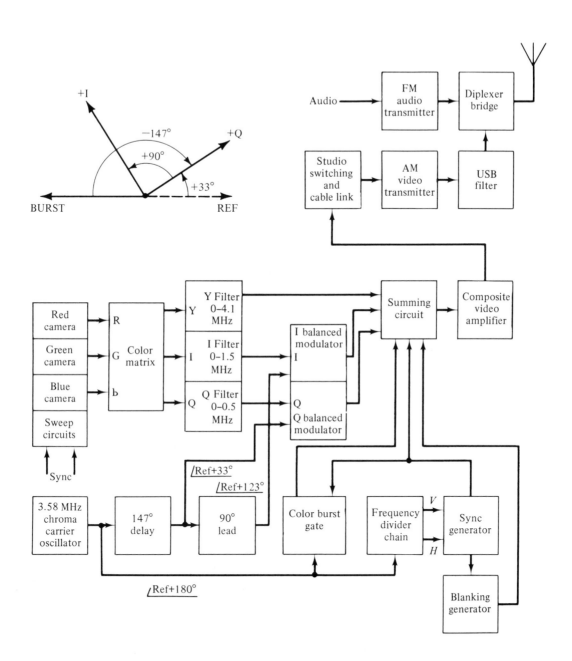

FIGURE 18.24.   An NTSC color-television transmitting system.

to control the three-color camera systems and are also transmittéd to synchronize the receivers.

An adder circuit combines the Y signal, the modulated I and Q signals, the color burst, and the sync and blanking pulses to form the composite video signal. This is then amplified and applied to the video modulator input, by a high-power broadband video amplifier. The structure of the composite video signal is shown in Figure 18.19(b).

18.7   PROBLEMS

1. Discuss and compare television and facsimile telegraphy as methods of transmitting documentary information such as photographs.

2. Discuss one form of facsimile transmitter, and explain in detail how the scanning spot is obtained. Explain also how the basic signal may be modulated during the scanning process.

3. Explain what is meant by synchronization and why this is necessary in picture transmission. Show, with the aid of a sketch, the form of distortion that would occur in a facsimile link if the receiver speed is greater than the transmitter speed.

4. Explain what is meant by index of cooperation and why this is important in facsimile telegraphy. Show also how it affects the bandwidth of the signal. If the index of cooperation of a facsimile transmitter is 352, what must be the index of cooperation of the corresponding receiver?

5. The index of cooperation of a facsimile machine is 352, and its speed of rotation is 60 rpm. The scanning pitch is 5/16 mm. Determine the theoretical bandwidth required.

6. Explain what is meant by subcarrier frequency modulation. A facsimile signal is transmitted on a SCFM system, the carrier frequency being 1800 Hz. The SCFM signal then amplitude-modulates an RF carrier. Assuming that only the first-order sidebands need to be considered in each modulation process, estimate the bandwidth required at RF if the highest frequency in the basic signal is 550 Hz.

7. FCC specifications for a facsimile drum scanner are: Line Length 18.85 in., Scan Density, 96 Lines per Inch (LPI). Determine the Index of Cooperation as defined both by the IEEE and the CCITT. For a scan speed of 90 Lines per Minute (LPM) determine the bandwidth required.

8. Explain the purpose of the aluminum coating used on the inside of cathode-ray tubes for television. Why is this coating held at final anode potential?

9. Explain how scanning may be achieved in a television system. What is the purpose of the synchronizing signals? In the U.S. 525-line, twin-interlace system, how many field synchronizing signals occur during one frame?

10. Describe and compare magnetic and electric methods of focusing an electron beam in a cathode-ray tube.

11. In the British television system, the number of lines is 625, the number of pictures transmitted per second is 25, and the aspect ratio is 4/3. The number of lines suppressed during the field blanking period is 48, and twin interlace is used. Line blanking period is 16% of line duration. Calculate the video bandwidth.

12. Outline the differences between a black-and-white television signal and a color signal. Use a sketch of the waveforms to illustrate, and explain the reason for each component. Also sketch the signal frequency spectra.

Appendix A
Logarithmic Units

A.1 THE DECIBEL

Two powers P_1 and P_2 differ by D decibels where

$$D = 10 \log_{10} \left(\frac{P_1}{P_2} \right) \qquad (A.1)$$

A positive number of decibels indicates that P_1 is greater than P_2; a negative number, that P_1 is less than P_2. For example, 50 W is greater than 10 W by $D = 10 \log_{10} (50/10) = 7$ decibels (dB), whereas 10 W is less than 50 W by $D = 10 \log_{10} (10/50 = -7$ dB. The decibel is one-tenth of a larger unit, the bel, defined as $\log_{10} (P_1/P_2)$; in practice, the bel is inconveniently large and the decibel is the preferred unit.

Although the decibel is based on power ratios, it can also be used to express voltage and current ratios. Let the power P_1 be developed in a resistor R_1 across which the voltage is V_1 and the current through which is I_1; let the corresponding quantities for P_2 be R_2, V_2, and I_2. Then,

$$D = 10 \log_{10} \left(\frac{V_1^2/R_1}{V_2^2/R_2} \right)$$

$$= 20 \log_{10} \left(\frac{V_1}{V_2} \right) + 10 \log_{10} \left(\frac{R_2}{R_1} \right) \tag{A.2}$$

By similar reasoning, it is easily shown that D can be expressed as

$$D = 20 \log_{10} \left(\frac{I_1}{I_2} \right) + 10 \log_{10} \left(\frac{R_1}{R_2} \right) \tag{A.3}$$

Therefore, it can be seen that a knowledge of the resistance values is needed, in addition to voltage or current, in order to determine the decibel value. Because of the widespread use of the decibel, its meaning has been extended to cover voltage and current ratios. By definition, two voltages, V_1 and V_2, differ by D_v decibels where

$$D_v = 20 \log_{10} \left(\frac{V_1}{V_2} \right) \tag{A.4}$$

Similarly, two currents, I_1 and I_2, differ by D_i decibels where

$$D_i = 20 \log_{10} \left(\frac{I_1}{I_2} \right) \tag{A.5}$$

As already shown, D_i and D_v can only be related to D when the ratio R_1/R_2 is known.

It is meaningless to state absolute values of voltage, current, or power, in decibels. The decibel represents a ratio, and therefore a reference level must also be stated if absolute values are required. For example, the statement "a power of 20 dB" is meaningless, but "20 dB relative to 1 W" means 100 W. Very often the reference level is understood implicitly, a common example of this being where noise levels are quoted in decibels, the reference level being the threshold of hearing (see Fig. 3.5). Another common example in telecommunications engineering is the selectivity curve of a tuned circuit, where the resonance value is used as reference (see Fig. 1.20).

Sometimes the reference level is indicated in abbreviated form, the best example of this being the dBm, meaning "decibels relative to 1 milliwatt." Other examples are dBμV and dBV, these being decibels relative to 1 microvolt and 1 volt, respectively.

A.2 THE NEPER

The neper is a logarithmic unit originally introduced to express the attenuation of current along a transmission line, using natural (or naperian, hence the name "neper") logarithms rather than common logarithms. Two currents, I_1 and I_2, differ by N nepers where

$$N = \ln\left(\frac{I_1}{I_2}\right) \qquad \left(= \log_e\left(\frac{I_1}{I_2}\right)\right) \tag{A.6}$$

The relationship between decibels and Nepers is easily established. Equation (A.5) gives

$$D_i = 20 \log_{10}\left(\frac{I_1}{I_2}\right)$$

and on changing the logarithmic base

$$D_i = (20 \log_{10} e)\left(\ln\frac{I_1}{I_2}\right)$$

$$= 8.686\,N \tag{A.7}$$

__Example A.1__ Express (a) 3 nepers in decibels; (b) 3 decibels in nepers

__Solution__ (a) $D = 8.686 \times 3$

$$= 26.06 \text{ dB}$$

(b) $N = \dfrac{3}{8.686}$

$$= 0.345 \text{ N}$$

A.3 LOGARITHMICS SCALES

By graduating graph axes in lengths proportional to the logarithms of numbers rather than to the numbers themselves, a much wider range of values can be accommodated on a given scale. Scales based on common logarithms are usually employed. Figure A.1 illustrates graph paper that has one axis graduated logarithmically and the other, linearly. This is known as "semilog" graph paper, and because the logarithmic scale pattern repeats itself four times, it is referred to as "four-cycle." The logarithmic scale of Figure A.1 can accommodate values ranging over four orders of magnitude (e.g., 1 to 10^4, 10 to 10^5, 0.01 to 10^2, etc.). It will be apparent that a zero origin cannot be shown on a logarithmic scale, and care must be taken when interpreting graphs plotted on logarithmic scales. Also, the slope of the graph must be carefully interpreted, as it involves the logarithms of numbers. Figure A.1 shows the decibel equations (D, D_i, and D_v) plotted

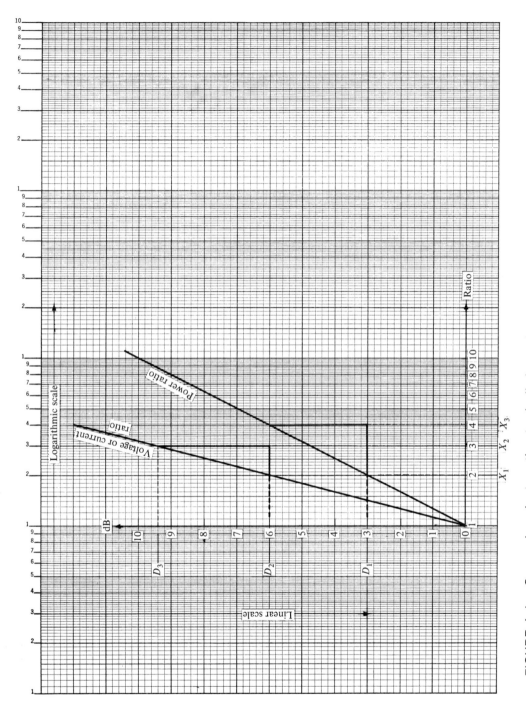

FIGURE A.1. Conversion chart—ratios to decibels—using semilog graph paper.

against a ratio scale, which is logarithmic. The slope of the *voltage or current ratio line* should be 20, and this is obtained from

$$\text{slope} = \frac{D_3 - D_2}{\log_{10}X_2 - \log_{10}X_1} \qquad \left(\text{not}\frac{D_3 - D_2}{X_2 - X_1}\right) \qquad (A.8)$$

$$= \frac{9.5 - 6}{0.4771 - 0.3010}$$

$$= 20$$

Similarly, the slope of the *power ratio line* is

$$\text{slope} = \frac{D_2 - D_1}{\log_{10}X_3 - \log_{10}X_1} \qquad \left(\text{not}\frac{D_2 - D_1}{X_3 - X_1}\right)$$

$$= 10$$

Appendix B:
The Transverse Electromagnetic Wave

Electromagnetic energy is propagated through space and is guided along transmission lines in the form of a *transverse electromagnetic wave* (TEM wave). For this type of wave, the electric field E (V/m), the magnetic field H (A/m), and the direction of propagation x, along which the wave travels with phase velocity v_p (m/s), are mutually at right-angles, as shown in Figure B.1(a). If the TEM wave is reversed in direction, then either the E or the H field [as shown in Figure B.1(b)] must reverse. This is similar to the condition required when reversing direction of rotation of a dc generator while maintaining same polarity of induced EMF.

To illustrate some of the basic properties of the TEM wave, a sinusoidal variation will be assumed; the field equations then are

$$e = E_{max} \sin(\omega t - \beta x) \qquad V/m \qquad (B.1)$$

$$h = H_{max} \sin(\omega t - \beta x) \qquad A/m \qquad (B.2)$$

where $\omega = 2\pi f = 2\pi/T$, and $\beta = 2\pi/\lambda$. The periodic time T and the wavelength λ are shown in Figure B.1(c) and (d).

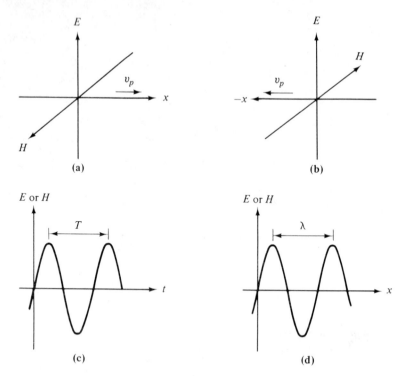

FIGURE B.1.   Transverse electromagnetic (TEM) waves.

Clearly, since one cycle occurs in T seconds, then the number of cycles in one second, which is the frequency f in Hertz, is

$$f = 1/T \qquad (B.3)$$

Also, since the wave generates f cycles in one second and covers a distance v_p meters in one second, the wavelength λ, which is the distance spanned by one cycle, is

$$\lambda = \frac{v_p}{f}$$

or

$$\lambda f = v_p \qquad (B.4)$$

In the following equations, rms values, indicated by E, H, B, and D, will be used for simplicity.

The electric field E will be accompanied by an electric flux density D C/m² given by

$$D = \epsilon E \qquad (B.5)$$

The magnetic field H will be accompanied by a magnetic flux density B Teslas, given by

$$B = \mu H \qquad (B.6)$$

Here, ϵ is the absolute permittivity and μ the absolute permeability of the medium in which the wave travels.

Two further experimental facts are as follows: (1) an electric field density D moving at velocity v_p will induce a magnetic field H given by

$$H = D \cdot v_p \qquad (B.7)$$

and (2) a magnetic field density B moving at velocity v_p will induce an electric field E given by

$$E = B \cdot v_p \qquad (B.8)$$

The vector directions in each case are as shown in Figure B.1(a). The fact that each type of field, when moving, generates the other in the proper direction gives rise to a self-sustaining electromagnetic wave, once the initial disturbance of either type of field is made.

The relationships in Eqs. (B.7) and (B.8) may not be familiar, but a common application of the latter is in the electromechanical generation of an EMF by rotating armature conductors to cut a magnetic field at right angles.

From the four field equations (B.5), (B.6), (B.7), and (B.8), the following important relationships are easily obtained:

Wave impedance

$$Z_o = \frac{E}{H} \qquad \Omega \qquad (B.9)$$

$$= \sqrt{\frac{\mu}{\epsilon}} \qquad (B.10)$$

[This should be compared with Eqs. (12.15) and (12.16).]

Phase velocity

$$v_p = \frac{1}{\sqrt{\mu\epsilon}} \qquad \text{m/s} \qquad (B.11)$$

Average power density in wave

$$P_D = E \cdot H \qquad \text{W/m}^2 \qquad\qquad (B.12)$$

$$= \frac{E^2}{Z_0}$$

$$= H^2 \cdot Z_0$$

(These relationships should be compared with the circuit equations relating V, I, R, and power P.)

Index

Current equivalent source, 3
Cylindrical scan, 573

Decca navigation, 464
Decibels, 612
Decilogs, 122
De-emphasis, 332, 340
Deflection:
  electrostatic, 591
  magnetic, 591
Delta modulation, 548
Demodulation, 259
Detector:
  AM, 259
  FM, 322
Deviation ratio, 309
Diagonal peak clipping, 259
Differentiator, 70
Diffraction, 459
Digital:
  filter, 542
  signal, 537
  system, 557
Diplexer, 607
Dipole:
  folded, 481, 493
  half-wave, 475
  Hertzian, 469
Direct distance dialing, 521
Directivity, 426
Director, 492
Discone, 495
Discriminator:
  Foster-Seeley, 324
Distortion:
  amplitude, 69
  bias, 356, 564
  crossover, 181
  harmonic, 87, 175, 181, 206
  phase, 67
  sound, 87
Distributor, 547
Double conversion, 232
Double spotting, 221

Doublet, 469
Duplex, 457, 510, 565
Dynamic impedance, 141, 183

Echo suppressors, 433, 534
Electronic switchboard, 529
End-fire array, 491
Envelope detector, 259
Equatorial plane, 471
Error detection, 555
Error probability, 539

Facsimile, 572, 576
Fading, 456, 461
Feedback, positive, 192
Field strength, 470
Filter:
  bandpass, 52, 73
  ceramic, 57
  complex transfer function, 57
  crystal, 51
  digital, 542
  electromechanical, 56
  high-pass, 49, 70
  LC, 49
  lattice, 55
  low-pass, 49, 73
  m-derived, 51
Fletcher-Munson curves, 84
Flicker noise, 115
Flyback, 591
Focusing:
  electric, 593
  magnetic, 591
Folded dipole, 481, 493
Foster-Seeley discriminator, 324
Fourier series, 63, 177
Frequency:
  compensation, 170
  conversion, 158
  critical, 444
  division multiplexing, 294
  gyro, 452